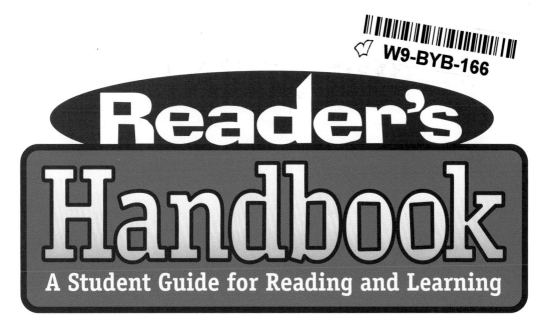

Reader's Handbook

A Student Guide for Reading and Learning

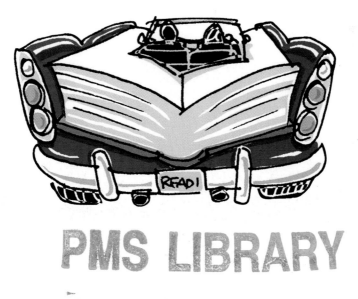

Great Source Education Group
a Houghton Mifflin Company
Wilmington, Massachusetts

www.greatsource.com

AUTHORS

Jim Burke
Author

Burlingame High School, Burlingame, California
Jim Burke, author of *Reading Reminders: Tools, Tips, and Techniques* and *The English Teacher's Companion,* has taught high school English for 13 years. His most recent books, *Tools for Thought* and *Illuminating Texts: How to Teach Students to Read the World,* further explore reading and those strategies that can help all students succeed in high school. He was the recipient of the California Reading Association's Hall of Fame Award in 2001 and the Conference on English Leadership's Exemplary English Leadership Award in 2000. He currently serves on the National Board of Professional Teaching Standards for English Language Arts.

Ron Klemp
Contributing Author

Los Angeles Unified School District, Los Angeles, California
Ron Klemp is the Coordinator of Reading for the Los Angeles Unified School District. He has taught Reading, English, and Social Studies and was a middle school Dean of Discipline. He is also a coordinator/facilitator at the Secondary Practitioner Center, a professional development program in the Los Angeles Unified School District. He has been teaching at California State University, Cal Lutheran University, and National University.

Wendell Schwartz
Contributing Author

Adlai Stevenson High School, Lincolnshire, Illinois
Wendell Schwartz has been a teacher of English for 36 years. For the last 24 years he also has served as the Director of Communication Arts at Adlai Stevenson High School. He has taught gifted middle school students for the last 12 years, as well as teaching graduate-level courses for National Louis University in Evanston, Illinois.

Editorial: Developed by Nieman Inc. with Phil LaLeike

Design: Ronan Design: Christine Ronan, Sean O'Neill, Maria Mariottini and Victoria Mullins

Illustrations: Mike McConnell

Printed in the United States of America
International Standard Book Number: 0-669-49008-3 (hardcover)
1 2 3 4 5 6 7 8 9—RRDC—08 07 06 05 04 03 02

International Standard Book Number: 0-669-49006-7 (softcover)
1 2 3 4 5 6 7 8 9—RRDC—08 07 06 05 04 03 02

PMS LIBRARY
Contents

3 Reading Know-how......44

Reading Textbooks......70

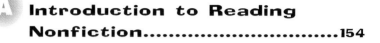

5 Reading Nonfiction......152

6 Reading Fiction......264

7 Reading Poetry......386

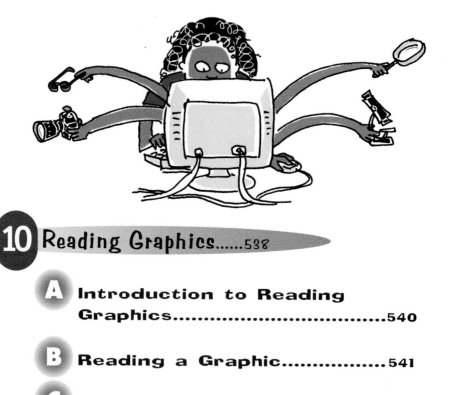

Reader's Almanac......690

C Reading Tools..............................738

D Word Parts: Prefixes, Suffixes, and Roots..............758

Acknowledgments......766

How to Use This Book

You might think it's strange to begin a book by telling how to use it, but reading is complex and often confusing. How you read anything depends on your purpose and the kind of material it is. You read novels straight through, letting the plot pull you along. You might skim an article, looking for the main point. This book, however, you will read in pieces, using it to answer your questions. You might search its pages to learn how to read a poem, for example. Or, you might look for information on ways to understand word problems in math.

Researchers have found that the most common type of learning in the workplace is what they call "Hey Bob!" learning. You call out, "Hey, Bob! Can you show me how to create a spreadsheet?" Bob says, "Sure," and then shows you how to do it step by step, making certain you understand

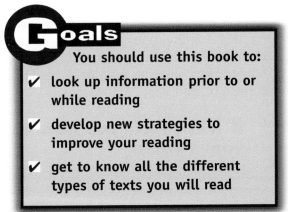

Goals

You should use this book to:

✔ **look up information prior to or while reading**

✔ **develop new strategies to improve your reading**

✔ **get to know all the different types of texts you will read**

as he goes along. That's how we hope you will use this book. We want this book to be your "Bob."

Everyone needs a good guide. No one would assume you know how to drive just because you turned sixteen. If you don't learn how and when to do certain things while driving, you crash. Think of this book as a guide to keep you from crashing at school, at work, at home, online, and out in the world.

Like all good guidebooks, this one has a few simple but important goals.

1 It will show you how to become a better reader.

People who are good at things always make it look easy. Good readers are no different. They use strategies that you, too, can use to help you read well. Throughout this book you will learn to do what good readers do when they read: ask questions, make connections to their own experiences, and listen to the thoughts that help them hear and see what they read.

2 It will introduce tools, tips, and strategies to help you read better and be more successful in school.

Remember the first time you logged on to the Internet? You didn't quite know what was what or how it worked. But soon you were a pro and had developed strategies that helped you use the Internet better and faster. This book will help you take better notes using different strategies and various graphic organizers. You will also learn how to ask good questions and when to ask them. You will learn not only how to skim through long passages but also how to read below the surface to find deeper meanings.

3 It will teach you how to monitor your reading.

Good readers constantly evaluate their understanding, asking questions while they read and after they finish. They ask, "What does this mean?" "Do I know what the author is referring to? Am I finding the information I need to get from this article? If not, am I asking the right questions?" Good readers also evaluate other aspects of their reading. They determine early on how to read the text, whether they should read it fast or slow, for surface details, or for deep insights into the subject. This book will help you evaluate what you read.

4 It will improve your ability to write and talk about reading.

Whether on tests or in the classroom, you often have to write or talk about a story or poem. Perhaps you find it difficult to know how to begin, what to say, or which questions to ask. This handbook will show you not only how to read a text but also how to write and talk about it. That will help you better participate in class discussions and probably improve your scores on essays and tests.

5 It will provide you with a quick reference guide.

You often need additional information to help you understand or prepare for what you read. In this handbook, you can learn how paragraphs are organized, how to learn new words, how to understand graphs and charts, and how to evaluate websites. Keep this book handy, and refer to it often.

6 It will introduce various kinds of readings.

You don't read everything the same way. This book includes a wide range of readings—from an essay to an editorial, from a speech to a sonnet. You will see how your purpose changes with different kinds of readings, as do the strategies and tools you use. One of the harder things to do as a reader is to use the right strategy and right reading tools for each type of reading you do. This handbook will guide you in making the right choices.

You might wonder, "How do I use this handbook?" Here are a few suggestions:

1 Friendly Guide

Think of this handbook as a resource for help with anything you don't understand. Are you having trouble with your history textbook? Look up "Reading History," and you'll find tips to help you understand and remember that material. Are you puzzled by the language in a Shakespeare play? Find "Focus on Shakespeare," and you'll see ways to "translate" Shakespeare's language into words you understand.

2 Personal Tutor

Whenever you need it, you can get individual, personal instruction right here in the handbook. Think of it as a personal tutor always ready with a lesson on what you need to know about reading. Here you'll find lots of tools, strategy ideas, and suggestions. Tips on taking notes, outlining, understanding analogies, or evaluating reference sources may be just what you need at some point in your school year. Use the table of contents or index at the back of the handbook to help you find what you need. Look up "graphic organizers" or "reading strategies," for example, and you'll find a wealth of material. And that's just a start.

3 Desk Reference

When you come across a term, strategy, or tool you don't know, you'll find help here in the handbook. Elements sections define and give examples of such terms as *metaphor, soliloquy,* and *protagonist.* The Reader's Almanac at the back of the handbook contains examples of all the strategies and tools. You don't have to try them all, but look them over to see which ones work best for you.

4 Complete Support for Different Kinds of Readings

This handbook focuses on the many kinds of reading you have to do every day. Tips and tools for reading in the workplace, on tests, when reading graphics and websites, and doing library or Internet research are all included in this one handy volume. So, when you have to read a new kind of material, look it up!

Book Organization

In this handbook, you'll see four different kinds of lessons.

1 Reading Lessons

These lessons show you how to follow a step-by-step reading process to read different kinds of materials— from textbooks and websites to novels and poems.

Each reading lesson includes several key features:

- list of **goals** that tell what the lesson is about
- **preview checklist** that tells you what to look for in a particular type of reading
- one **reading** and another **rereading strategy** to help you find the information you want
- several **reading tools** to help you keep track of information
- information on **how the text is organized**
- **summing up** box that highlights what you should remember

Focus Lessons

These lessons are brief close-ups of a single subject. They take a closer, more detailed look at one kind of reading or a specific element, such as setting, plot, or theme.

Focus on Plot ▣

Focus on Plot

In his book *On Writing*, Stephen King says that he tends to depend on "situation rather than story." He goes on to explain: "I want to put a group of characters (perhaps a pair; perhaps just one) in some sort of predicament and then watch them work their way free. . . . The situation comes first. The characters . . . come next." How these characters respond to their predicament is the plot. The **plot** is what happens.

Most plots move in *chronological order*. This is also called a *linear* design because a plot moves from point A to point B. Some writers believe there are only two basic plots: a stranger came to town, or a person went on a journey. The plot then describes what happened when the stranger came to town or the person went on a journey. The other elements—theme, characters, setting, point of view—all influence the plot and the story's meaning.

Goals

Here you'll learn how to:
✔ follow the events of a plot
✔ identify the story's subplots and how these relate to the main plot
✔ consider how plot contributes to a story's theme

Before Reading

Before you ever begin reading, it helps to know the parts of a plot. When you know these parts, you know how stories work. Whether you realize it or not, you are probably pretty familiar with the structure of a story.

313

Each focus lesson starts with a list of **goals.** Most include several **helpful tips, reading strategies,** or **reading tools** to try. Each lesson concludes with a brief **summary.**

3

Elements Mini-lessons

These mini-lessons explain all of the key terms related to a particular type of writing.

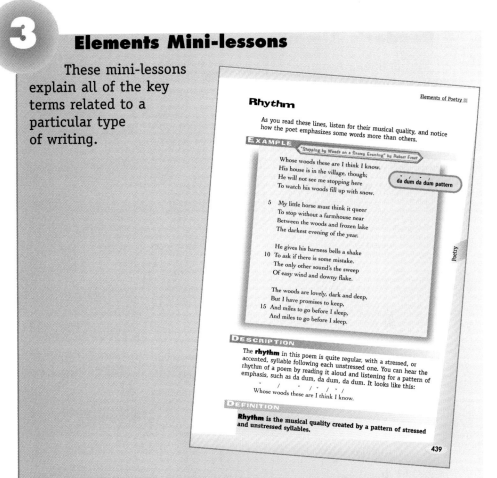

Each elements mini-lesson starts with an **example** of the term. Then, you'll find a **description** and a short **definition** of what the term means.

4 Reader's Almanac

The Reader's Almanac contains four kinds of information for easy reference: a section on doing research, descriptions of reading strategies, examples of reading tools, and lists of word parts.

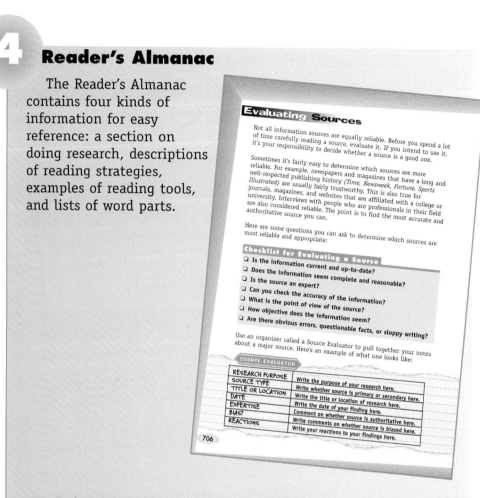

Evaluating Sources

Not all information sources are equally reliable. Before you spend a lot of time carefully reading a source, evaluate it. If you intend to use it, it's your responsibility to decide whether a source is a good one.

Sometimes it's fairly easy to determine which sources are more reliable. For example, newspapers and magazines that have a long and well-respected publishing history (*Time, Newsweek, Fortune, Sports Illustrated*) are usually fairly trustworthy. This is also true for journals, magazines, and websites that are affiliated with a college or university. Interviews with people who are professionals in their field are also considered reliable. The point is to find the most accurate and authoritative source you can.

Here are some questions you can ask to determine which sources are most reliable and appropriate:

Checklist for Evaluating a Source

☐ Is the information current and up-to-date?
☐ Does the information seem complete and reasonable?
☐ Is the source an expert?
☐ Can you check the accuracy of the information?
☐ What is the point of view of the source?
☐ How objective does the information seem?
☐ Are there obvious errors, questionable facts, or sloppy writing?

Use an organizer called a Source Evaluator to pull together your notes about a major source. Here's an example of what one looks like:

SOURCE EVALUATOR

RESEARCH PURPOSE	Write the purpose of your research here.
SOURCE TYPE	Write whether source is primary or secondary here.
TITLE OR LOCATION	Write the title or location of research here.
DATE	Write the date of your finding here.
EXPERTISE	Comment on whether source is authoritative here.
BIAS?	Write comments on whether source is biased here.
REACTIONS	Write your reactions to your findings here.

706

■ **Doing Research** provides an overview of how to find useful material, keep track of information, and document sources.

In addition to Doing Research, the Reader's Almanac includes three more parts:

■ **Strategy Handbook** describes each of the 12 main strategies used in this handbook.

■ **Reading Tools** describes and gives examples of 38 reading tools used in this handbook.

■ **Word Parts** lists Greek and Latin roots, prefixes, and suffixes.

Reader's Almanac, continued

- ■ The **Strategy Handbook** explains in detail each of the 12 reading strategies used in the handbook.
- ■ The **Reading Tools** section describes and gives examples of 38 tools used throughout the lessons.
- ■ The **Word Parts** section lists common prefixes, suffixes, and Greek and Latin roots.

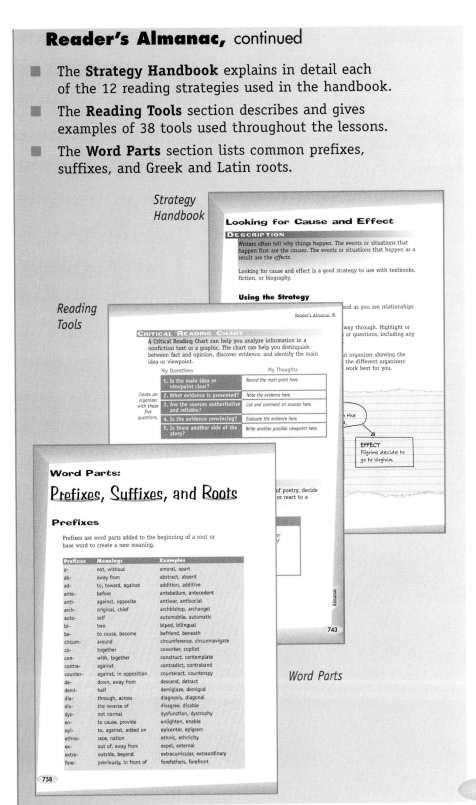

Strategy Handbook

Looking for Cause and Effect

DESCRIPTION

Writers often tell why things happen. The events or situations that happen first are the *causes*. The events or situations that happen as a result are the *effects*.

Looking for cause and effect is a good strategy to use with textbooks, fiction, or biography.

Using the Strategy

...and as you see relationships

Reading Tools

Reader's Almanac ■

CRITICAL READING CHART

A Critical Reading Chart can help you analyze information in a nonfiction text or a graphic. The chart can help you distinguish between fact and opinion, discover evidence, and identify the main idea or viewpoint.

...way through. Highlight or ...or questions, including any

...n organizer showing the ...the different organizers ...work best for you.

	My Questions	My Thoughts
Create an organizer with these five questions.	1. Is the main idea or viewpoint clear?	Record the main point here.
	2. What evidence is presented?	Note the evidence here.
	3. Are the sources authoritative and reliable?	List and comment on sources here.
	4. Is the evidence convincing?	Evaluate the evidence here.
	5. Is there another side of the story?	Write another possible viewpoint here.

EFFECT
Pilgrims decide to go to Virginia.

Word Parts:

Prefixes, Suffixes, and Roots

of poetry, decide or react to a

Prefixes

Prefixes are word parts added to the beginning of a root or base word to create a new meaning.

Prefixes	Meanings	Examples
a-	not, without	amoral, apart
ab-	away from	abstract, absent
ad-	to, toward, against	addition, additive
ante-	before	antebellum, antecedent
anti-	against, opposite	antiwar, antisocial
arch-	original, chief	archbishop, archangel
auto-	self	automobile, automatic
bi-	two	biped, bilingual
be-	to cause, become	befriend, beneath
circum-	around	circumference, circumnavigate
co-	together	coworker, copilot
con-	with, together	construct, contemplate
contra-	against	contradict, contraband
counter-	against, in opposition	counteract, counterspy
de-	down, away from	descend, detract
demi-	half	demiglaze, demigod
dia-	through, across	diagnosis, diagonal
dis-	the reverse of	disagree, disable
dys-	not normal	dysfunction, dystrophy
en-	to cause, provide	enlighten, enable
epi-	to, against, added on	epicenter, epigram
ethno-	race, nation	ethnic, ethnicity
ex-	out of, away from	expel, external
extra-	outside, beyond	extracurricular, extraordinary
fore-	previously, in front of	forefathers, forefront

Word Parts

Almanac

743

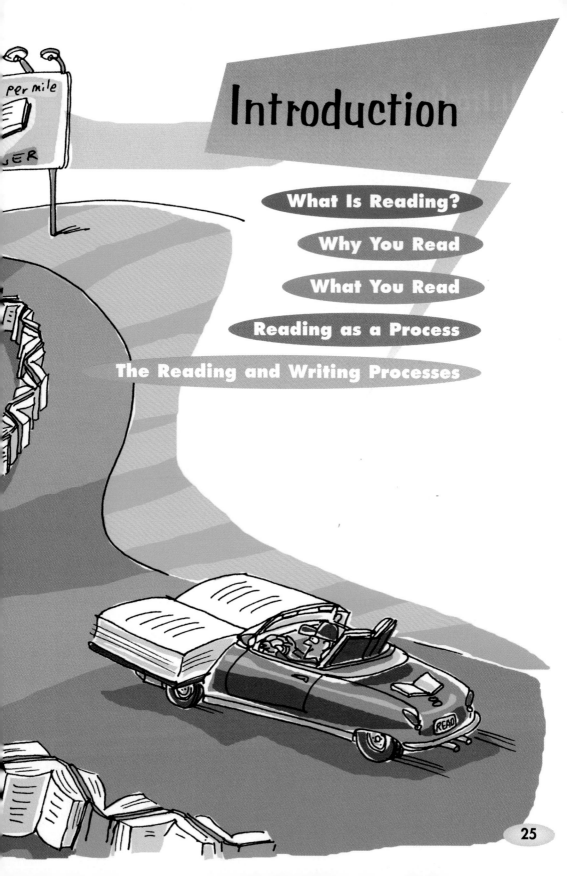

Introduction

Introduction

As you start, think about what reading is. You've been reading for years, but how would you describe reading?

What Is Reading?

> *I cannot open a book without learning something.*
> *—Chinese proverb*

Reading is what happens in your head, in your heart, and, if you're reading something really good, in your gut. Reading is both an experience and an activity, a skill and an ability. It is also a complex process that you must continually improve because you are always coming across new texts.

Reading requires tools. Think of those cluttered tool belts you see hanging off the hips of telephone repair workers. This might strike you as a strange way to picture reading, but think about it. When you read, your "tool belt" is equipped with strategies, skills, and knowledge to help you better understand what you read. Some tools help you organize your thoughts. Other tools make new information familiar by connecting it to your own knowledge and experience. When you don't understand what you read, you need to know which tool will help you understand the text.

Reading is a set of habits and abilities. You develop these skills over time, through experience, practice, and help from your teachers. You learn to pay attention to clues on the page as you "make meaning" from different pieces of information. The detective Sherlock Holmes was probably a great reader: no clue ever got past him!

Reading is thinking. Every serious reader understands that reading is thinking. To read is to take time to think about something—an idea, an issue, a question—that matters to you. To read is to enter into a conversation with interesting, important people about ideas and issues.

Reading is power. When you read, you gain not only intellectual strength but important knowledge about the world. This strength and knowledge prepare you to be successful, and they also allow you to be an independent thinker. Such power, thanks to your reader's tool belt, will always serve you well at home and at work, in the present and the future.

Why You Read

We read to succeed. We read to learn and to understand. We also read, as the author C. S. Lewis wrote, "to know we are not alone." Why you read often depends on what you read. You *hang out* with the newspaper or a favorite magazine, reading these to keep up, relax, and learn. You *study* textbooks, trying to gain knowledge and gather information. You *use* manuals to search for solutions to problems or learn how to use, for example, a computer. At work, you *consult* many different types of materials, all of which help you in different ways to do your job.

Keeping the above examples in mind, you can organize reading into a few distinct categories.

1 **Academic Reading** This is the kind of reading you do at school: textbooks, maps, poetry, novels, math problems, and scientific procedures. Your teacher usually determines why you read these.

2 **Personal Reading** Personal reading might include websites or magazines you read to learn about the latest styles or your favorite bands. It might include inspirational books or self-help books you think will help you overcome some troubles or better understand yourself. It may be manuals for computer programs you want to learn or cars you want to fix. This is the reading you choose to do for your own enjoyment or personal growth.

3 **Workplace Reading** At work you might have policies or manuals you must read as part of your job. Mostly, however, workplace reading is what you will do when you graduate. Such reading includes memos, emails, reports, documents, or professional journals.

4 **Functional Reading** A fourth category includes the informational reading you do every day. Examples are schedules, labels, directions, and rules. This type of reading is important since you are reading in order to make a decision about where to go, what to eat, how to get someplace, or how to use something.

Reading well for school is essential, but these students have some other good reasons to read.

"Reading transports me to another world. I can pick up my book and not worry about school, family, or what people think. All I care about is what is going to happen next. It's a way to get away without going anywhere."
—Jessica Batchelor

"If you want to have a good job, you better know how to read well."
—Michael Daciuk

"Reading allows me to know people I cannot meet from places I cannot visit."
—Maricela Vega

"I read so I can make my own movies in my head."
—Tony Arteaga

Why not write down your own reasons for reading?

PMS LIBRARY

What You Read

Shakespeare wrote, "All the world's a stage,/And all the men and women merely players." These days it often feels as if all the world is a text and we are readers trying to make sense of it. Ads, for example, appear everywhere, even on gas pumps, buses, and elevators. We read people's facial expressions and clothing, trying to determine their mood, attitude, or status.

Reading Tastes

People have very different tastes in reading. Some like novels, but not all novels. They might like only mysteries or fantasy, romance or suspense novels. Others prefer magazines. Many like to read facts or information about products, procedures, people, or places. Some people read the dictionary. Others enjoy reading encyclopedias and other reference books. Still others look for inspiration and guidance from self-help books or a sacred book such as the Bible.

Technology and Reading

Technology has changed what we read. Students read secret, coded messages on their pagers or cell phones. Letters are once again very popular, thanks to email and Instant Messages. People throughout the country "read" audio books while driving to work, enjoying anything from Shakespeare to best-selling novelists. And, sooner rather than later, your textbook may not be paper but plastic, and the pages will probably contain images that move and buttons that will allow you to read your textbook through your ears *and* your eyes. You will probably also be able to take notes on that digital textbook which, by the way, may look and weigh the same as a clipboard.

Though you read many different types of texts, this handbook will focus on the texts that are most crucial to your success in school and in life.

Reading as a Process

Reading begins before you ever look at the first word, and it continues after you read the last sentence. After all, the process of building a house does not begin with the first nail hammered in. The process begins before, with all the planning and preparation. Before you ever start reading, you bring certain things to the act of reading: expectations, values, experience, knowledge, and more. These factors determine your purpose and attitude toward whatever you read. Sometimes, you might realize that you do not know anything about a subject—that is, you have no background knowledge or prior experience in a particular area. Then, you might need to do some work to prepare yourself to read.

In short, you bring yourself to the process. You know this is true, because as soon as you start reading you say, "Hey, that reminds me of that experiment we did last year in science," or "I don't see how this relates to me." In other words, you interact with what you read throughout the process, asking questions and making connections to help you understand what you read. Your particular reading process is personal. There are, however, certain common features found in the process all readers follow. The reading process falls into three stages: Before, During, and After.

Before Reading

You're an effective reader when you . . .	You're an ineffective reader when you . . .
determine what you already know and need to learn.	begin reading without asking yourself what you know or need to learn.
read the directions.	ignore or barely look at the directions.
establish a purpose for the reading and know what you are supposed to understand or do after you finish reading.	do not establish a purpose or, because you did not read the directions, establish an incorrect purpose.

You're an effective reader when you . . .

gather any tools or materials you might need (pen, pencil, paper, highlighter) and determine how best to use them.

• • • • • • • • • • •

have a quiet environment in which to read.

• • • • • • • • • • •

identify the type of text or genre.

• • • • • • • • • • •

make predictions about the content and its meaning.

You're an ineffective reader when you . . .

lack the tools or materials that would help you be an active reader.

• • • • • • • • • • •

try to read in an environment filled with distractions.

• • • • • • • • • • •

treat most texts equally, reading a poem the same way you would an essay.

• • • • • • • • • • •

make no effort to predict what the text might be about.

During Reading

continually check what you read against the predictions you made, revising your understanding as necessary.

• • • • • • • • • • •

use all your senses to help you see, hear, and imagine what you read.

• • • • • • • • • • •

check your understanding as you read.

• • • • • • • • • • •

make connections between what you are reading and your own experiences.

read without asking questions, wondering, or responding to what you read.

• • • • • • • • • • •

do not read with your senses and thus have trouble seeing, hearing, and understanding what you read.

• • • • • • • • • • •

pay no attention to whether you understand what you read.

• • • • • • • • • • •

do not make any connections.

You're an **effective** reader when you . . .	You're an **ineffective** reader when you . . .
pace yourself, recognizing the importance of stamina in reading longer texts.	*plunge ahead until you get tired or frustrated and then give up.*
make inferences or read "between the lines."	*read at the surface or literal level and do not ask questions that would lead to deeper reading of the text.*
know which questions to ask and which strategies to use while reading. You are an active reader.	*do not ask questions or read strategically. You are a passive reader.*
use subject-area knowledge and vocabulary to read.	*do not pay attention to new words or concepts that will help you read the text successfully.*

After Reading

check for understanding, asking such questions as, "Do I understand what I read?" and "Did I achieve my reading goal?"	*do not check for understanding or consult others if you did not understand the text.*
return to the text or consult others who can help you better understand and remember what you read.	*make no effort to remember what you read. When you finish, the reading act is finished.*

This might be a new way of thinking about reading for you, so let's compare reading to a related process that is more familiar, the writing process.

The Reading and Writing Processes

No one sits down and expects to write a perfect paper in one sitting. Neither should readers assume they can run their eyes over a page and understand everything they read. Reading and writing are both processes made up of several steps.

Writer Anne Lamott, in her book *Bird by Bird: Some Instructions on Writing and Life,* says the writing process gives her a place to begin, a way to get herself going. "Almost all good writing begins with terrible first efforts. You need to start somewhere. Start by getting something—anything—down on paper. A friend of mine says that the first draft is the down draft—you just get it down. The second draft is the up draft—you fix it up."

When you read, you are creating a "first draft" of your understanding. Looking at reading as a process allows you to relax and know that you can "fix up" your understanding later on. This does not mean you have to reread everything. Your first reading of a book might leave you thinking the narrator is young or old, mean or brilliant. Only later on, as you continue to read and "fix up" your impressions, do you realize you were wrong. Such realizations show that you are an active reader, one who is always checking your current understanding against previous interpretations.

Writing Process	Reading Process
Prewriting	**Prereading**
Decide on a topic.	*Establish your purpose.*
Establish a purpose.	*Preview the reading.*
Determine appropriate genre.	*Predict what the reading will be about.*
Gather ideas.	*Determine the genre in order to plan how the material needs to be read.*

Writing Process	Reading Process

Drafting

Write your way into the topic.

Don't expect to "get it right" yet.

Identify problems and interesting connections.

Revising

Think about your initial purpose.

Evaluate your current draft.

Use questions, further research, and new connections to go more deeply into your subject.

Editing and Proofreading

Identify errors in wording and style.

Correct these errors, consulting other people or reference books if necessary.

Clean up any remaining errors or inconsistencies in the text.

Reading

Read actively, keeping your purpose in mind.

Make predictions and mark and highlight as you read.

Understand how the text is organized.

Connect what you're reading to your own experiences, ideas, and prior knowledge.

Looking Back

Think about your initial purpose.

Evaluate what you do and don't understand.

Use various strategies to go more deeply into the meaning of the text.

Rereading

Identify and determine the source of any remaining confusion.

Fix these misunderstandings by reading parts again.

Writing Process	Reading Process
Publishing and Presenting	**Remembering**
Prepare a final draft to present to your teacher.	*Discuss your ideas about the text with others.*
Publish for appropriate audience at school or in the community.	*Summarize your ideas about or reactions to it.*
Present your writing to an audience by reading, performing, or discussing.	

Looking at both reading and writing as processes makes you realize how many decisions you must make along the way. You must decide not only why you are reading, but what is important as you read. You must decide whether you should read quickly or patiently. You must decide whether to read for the basic facts or for deeper meanings that might require more time and attention. You must also decide when you have achieved a "good enough" reading or whether you should go back and reread some parts.

The Reading
Process

- Before Reading
- During Reading
- After Reading

The Reading Process

The description of a reading process here will help you become a better reader of all types of materials. Remember, this is one process, not *the* process. Reading is a personal process through which you make meaning using your own experiences, knowledge, and abilities.

Before Reading

Imagine you are doing a report on World War I as part of your world history class. Or maybe your English class is reading *All Quiet on the Western Front*, a novel that takes place during World War I. The first steps in the process take place before you ever begin to read.

A. Set a Purpose

B. Preview

C. Plan

A Set a Purpose

Your teachers often determine your reading purpose. They might ask you, for example, to read through a chapter to find examples of a certain theme or to determine the validity of an author's argument. If your assignment is to do a report on World War I, your purpose in reading is to gather essential background information on the war. To help you clarify your purpose and evaluate information, you might come up with the following questions:

Who? *Where?* *How?* *What?* *When?* *Why?*

This purpose will help you to read better because you can evaluate any details according to whether they answer any of these questions. You now have a destination and are almost ready to take off.

B Preview

Previewing a reading assignment with a quick skim-through tells you what to expect. A preview of a reading gives you important information about vocabulary, organization, and content. You might notice, for example, some subheadings. You also notice that some words are in boldface or italic type. If you're reading a poem, you may note that some lines rhyme. A preview may also tell you that a text will not answer your questions and that you should not spend valuable time reading it.

You know you have previewed a reading effectively if you can answer the following questions:

What is it about?

What else do I know about this subject?

How is it organized?

Chances are, unless you are a history buff, you don't know too much about World War I. But think about what you do know. You might, for instance, have some idea about when or where it happened or know what started it. Thinking about what you know about a topic is a useful place to begin.

C Plan

Rock climbers spend days, sometimes even weeks or months, studying the rocks they want to climb. They check their "tool belt" of strategies for the ones that will meet the demands of each particular climb. Sometimes they will even try out a strategy on a part of the rock just to see whether the strategy works.

Strategies lead to success in rock climbing and in reading. For some reading assignments, note-taking may be a good strategy. Timelines, which help you keep track of events as you read, are good tools to use with some readings. Since one of the questions you have to answer is *why*, you might want to make a Cause-Effect Organizer, showing how one event led to another.

This handbook explains many strategies: using graphic organizers, paraphrasing, visualizing and thinking aloud, outlining, and skimming, just to name a few.

During Reading

The middle part of the reading process is what happens when you are actually reading.

D. Read with a Purpose

E. Connect

D Read with a Purpose

Read actively and interact with the text. Some of these interactions—asking questions, for example—might take place in your head. Other interactions make your thinking visible. Taking notes, having a discussion, and using graphic organizers help make you a more active reader.

When you set out to go somewhere, you pay attention to the signs and check your map to make sure you are headed in the right direction. Sometimes friends will give you directions that end with a note like this: "If you see the donut shop on the corner, you know you've gone too far." Keep a close eye on your progress as you read. If what you are reading makes no sense, stop and turn around. Revisit your original purpose. Ask yourself regularly, "Now why am I reading this again?" or "What am I looking for in this article?"

Sometimes your purpose changes. Sometimes you read for multiple purposes. State tests, for example, ask you to read a story or an article for several different purposes. You might have to read the same passage up to three times, each time with a different purpose.

Check your understanding as you read. You know how sometimes you are at the movies with a friend, and halfway through the movie your friend leans over and asks, "The guy in the blue shirt is the undercover agent, right?" She is doing what good readers do. They make predictions and clarify what they've learned, then check to see whether their predictions and understanding are correct. If new information comes in that does not support those initial predictions, then good readers adjust their predictions accordingly.

E Connect

Try to tie what you read to your life or to what you already know. You may do this automatically at times. Say you read a biography of a once-famous tennis star. As you read, you realize that she's the same person your mother used to talk about. You've made a connection that can help you enjoy and understand what you read.

Ask yourself some questions like these to help you connect:

How do I feel after reading this? Why?

Do I agree with the author's point of view?

How does this affect me?

Have I read anything else by this author?

After Reading

Think of this last stage in the process as what happens once your eyes read the last sentence.

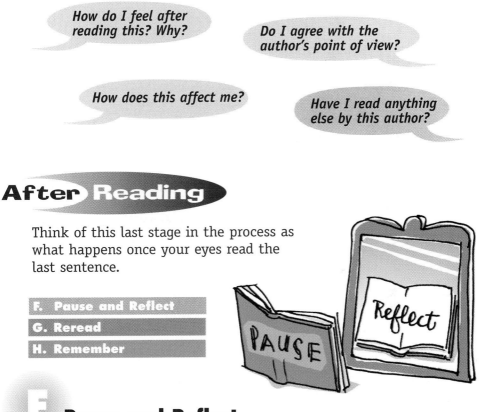

F. Pause and Reflect

G. Reread

H. Remember

F Pause and Reflect

When you get to the end of whatever you are reading, take a moment to think about what you have read. Have you understood what you just read? Have you achieved your stated purpose? If there are important gaps in your understanding, identify what puzzles you. If you can't figure these things out on your own, then work with your teacher or a classmate to "fix up" your understanding.

G Reread

As a natural part of reading, you reread. Not every kind of text requires rereading, but many do. You will often reread parts of a novel or play that were a little hazy the first time through. Textbooks often get clearer the second time you read them.

Rereading helps you experience a selection again in a new way. You now know a lot more, so when you start to reread you have a better base of knowledge to start from. Rereading makes some of the confusing parts seem clearer.

Use another reading strategy when you reread. To find the information you need, you might have to outline or do close reading the second time through a selection. Another reading strategy helps uncover more—and different—information related to your reading purpose.

H Remember

Some people have remarkable memories. Ask them who won the World Series in 1948, the dates of the Russian Revolution, or Harry Houdini's real name, and they come right up with the information. How do they do it, and how can you develop this amazing talent?

The key to remembering is to make the information your own. Do something. Make a summary, write a review, start a conversation. Some people even make up rhymes to help them remember important dates or names. With a little practice, you, too, can ace those tests.

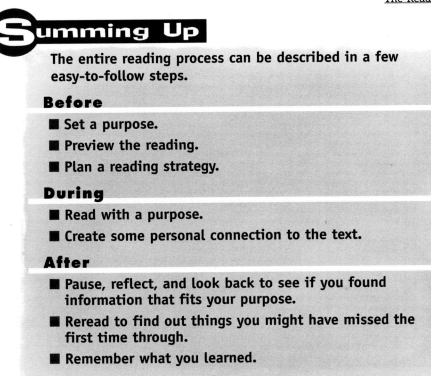

Summing Up

The entire reading process can be described in a few easy-to-follow steps.

Before

- Set a purpose.
- Preview the reading.
- Plan a reading strategy.

During

- Read with a purpose.
- Create some personal connection to the text.

After

- Pause, reflect, and look back to see if you found information that fits your purpose.
- Reread to find out things you might have missed the first time through.
- Remember what you learned.

Do I Always Have to Use the Reading Process?

By now you may be thinking, "What ever happened to just sitting down and reading for fun?" Your question highlights the differences among the various types of reading. Reading for pleasure allows you to read as much as you like, at whatever pace you prefer. You don't have to follow any particular process. However, for academic reading and some workplace reading, you will need a reading process to help you get the information you need.

Reading Know-how

- Essential Reading Skills
- Reading Actively
- Reading Paragraphs
- Kinds of Paragraphs
- Ways of Organizing Paragraphs

Reading Know-how

Learning to read well means building from the ground floor up, as you would a house. Start by creating a strong reading foundation. Then, add reading skills bit by bit, and watch your reading ability grow.

Essential Reading Skills

Every day you make inferences, draw conclusions, compare and contrast, and evaluate. For example, you make inferences about what people mean based on their tone of voice. You draw conclusions about what to wear to school after hearing the weather report. You compare and contrast movies and books, and you evaluate a new computer game. These skills are the same ones you need to use when reading. They are the most important part of your reading foundation.

Making Inferences

When you make an inference, you make a reasonable guess about meaning. Making inferences means reading "between the lines" to discover the author's meaning.

MAKING INFERENCES

What I learned
+ What I already know

= My inference

For example, if an author describes a character as *red-faced,* you can make the inference that the character is embarrassed. If a poem contains the words *gloomy, tear-streaked,* and *heavy-hearted,* you can infer that someone is sad. You don't know these things for certain, of course, but they are reasonable guesses—inferences—that make a lot of sense. Making inferences as you read helps you understand a writer's meaning.

Drawing Conclusions

People draw conclusions all the time, so it makes sense that readers are expected to draw conclusions as well. Drawing conclusions means gathering bits of information and then deciding what that information means.

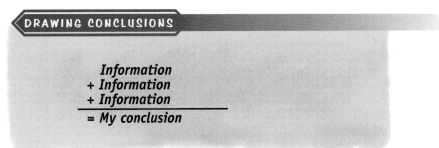

DRAWING CONCLUSIONS

Information
+ Information
+ Information
──────────────
= My conclusion

For example, suppose you read that the mayor has urged that people drive less, plant trees, and recycle. You could probably conclude that the mayor is worried about the environment and maybe even air quality.

Drawing conclusions is a reading fundamental. Use charts or other graphic organizers to keep track of the information you find and the conclusions you draw.

DRAWING CONCLUSIONS

MAYOR'S STATEMENTS	CONCLUSION
1. drive less	Mayor is worried
2. plant trees	about the environment
3. recycle	and air quality.

Comparing and Contrasting

Suppose you read two reviews of a movie. You note that both reviewers give the film a thumbs-up. You've compared the two reviews and decided that they basically agree. However, you also notice that one reviewer thinks the special effects are the best part of the movie. The other reviewer thinks the effects add nothing to the plot and could have been eliminated. You have contrasted the two reviews to identify their differences.

Seeing how things are alike and different helps you gather vital information and draw important conclusions. For example, you might compare and contrast two books by the same author or two characters or settings in a single book or play.

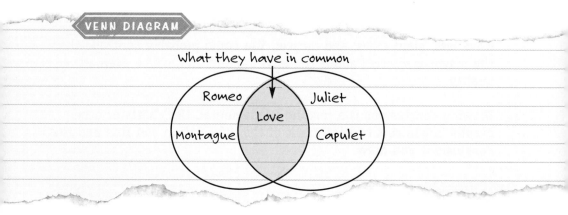

Evaluating

To evaluate is to make a value judgment. You'll use the skill of evaluating with all types of reading. For example, when you read an editorial, you evaluate the quality of the writer's argument. When you read a novel, you evaluate a character's actions and judge whether or not the actions are reasonable. Evaluating is a skill—just like making inferences, drawing conclusions, and comparing and contrasting—that active readers use each time they pick up a text and read.

Reading Actively

Did you know that there are two kinds of readers: active readers and passive readers? Passive readers let a writer's words wash over them without giving much thought to what the words mean. As a result, passive readers can find themselves drowning in a sea of words.

Active readers, on the other hand, take control of what they're reading—from the very first page. They think about what a writer has to say, and at the same time they think about their own responses to the reading. Active reading means asking questions, agreeing and disagreeing, and applying what you've learned from reading to your own life. An active reader interacts with the writer.

How can you be an active reader? Here are some tips. →

One of the most important things you'll learn in this handbook is that active readers know and use strategies and tools that can help them get *more* out of a selection. Active readers keep track of their during-reading thoughts, reactions, ideas, and questions.

ACTIVE READING

✔ Always read with a pencil or pen in hand.
✔ Make notes about everything you think is interesting or important, confusing or puzzling.
✔ Keep your thinking cap on. Don't expect the writer to do your thinking for you.

If you can, mark the text itself. If you can't write in your book, use sticky notes or jot down your thoughts in a notebook or reading journal. It's best to write down your thoughts as they occur to you. This habit makes reading more interactive.

The example on the next page shows six common ways that you—as an active reader—might mark up, or annotate, a passage.

from *The Bonesetter's Daughter* by Amy Tan

1. Mark

2. Question

What does this mean?

3. Clarify

She doesn't want to breathe smoke.

4. React

Precious Auntie does everything for narrator.

5. Visualize

6. Predict

The story will probably explain why she can't talk.

I was sleepy, still lying on the brick k'ang bed I shared with Precious Auntie. The flue to our little room was furthest from the stove in the common room, and the bricks beneath me had long turned cold. I felt my shoulder being shaken. When I opened my eyes, Precious Auntie began to write on a scrap of paper, then showed me what she had written. "I can't see," I complained. "It's too dark."

She huffed, set the paper on the low cupboard, and motioned that I should get up. She lighted the teapot brazier, and tied a scarf over her nose and mouth when it started to smoke. She poured face-washing water into the teapot's chamber, and when it was cooked, she started our day. She scrubbed my face and ears. She parted my hair and combed my bangs. She wet down any strands that stuck out like spider legs. Then she gathered the long part of my hair into two bundles and braided them. She banded the top with red ribbon, the bottom with green. I wagged my head so that my braids swung like the happy ears of palace dogs. And Precious Auntie sniffed the air as if she, too, were a dog wondering, What's that good smell? That sniff was how she said my nickname, Doggie. That was how she talked.

You may have your own ways of marking up a passage. Even so, take a look at these suggestions. They model for you six ways you get *more* from a text.

Ways of Reading Actively

Here are six ways of reading actively.

WAYS OF READING ACTIVELY

① Mark or Highlight *The most common way to mark a text is by highlighting with a marker or pen. Highlighting helps you mark important words, phrases, and sentences. Your highlighting and marking will also help you later, when you are studying for a test or rereading for a discussion or writing assignment. If you can't mark in a book, write on sticky notes and attach them to the page.*

② Ask Questions *Active readers ask lots of questions. Questions that occur to you—such as "What does this mean? Why is the writer talking about this?"—can help you think more critically about a text.*

③ Clarify *A lot is happening when you read. You're taking in information and responding to it at the same time. Keep track of what you've learned by making notes that clarify ideas and details. For example, jot down a sequence of events or list important details.*

④ React and Connect *Listen to your own thoughts, feelings, and reactions as you read. Think about how the writing makes you feel and what it reminds you of in your own life. Compare and contrast the author's ideas or a character's experiences to your own.*

⑤ Visualize *Visualize the people, places, and actions an author describes. Visualizing helps you "see" and remember the author's most important ideas. Get into the habit of making quick sketches in your reading journal or in the margins of your books. Use sensory details to help you visualize.*

⑥ Predict *Active readers constantly ask themselves: "How will things turn out? What will happen next?" Write your predictions as you make your way through a text.*

Finding a Place to Read

Reading actively means reading with full concentration. Finding a good spot to read can strengthen your concentration. Of course, you can read anywhere—on the bus, in the car, at the beach, or at the kitchen table. But you'll find you can get *more* from your reading if you find a place that is comfortable, quiet, and well lighted. Here's a checklist of what to look for in a good reading spot.

A GOOD READING PLACE HAS

✔ good light
✔ peace and quiet
✔ a comfortable chair
✔ a pen, pencil, or highlighter
✔ paper or a reading notebook or sticky notes nearby

Making Time for Reading

Making time for reading is just as important as finding the right place. As a high school student, ideally, you should be reading about 20–30 minutes a day. This doesn't include the time you spend studying. But how can you add extra time for reading if your schedule is full already? Create a daily schedule that includes time for reading. If you have a busy day, try dividing the reading period into two time slots: 10–15 minutes in the morning and 10–15 minutes before you go to bed.

Reading Paragraphs

Essays, stories, and articles consist of a series of paragraphs. One paragraph builds on another to convey a writer's thoughts and ideas. While each paragraph has its own main idea, all the paragraphs relate to each other and ultimately to the subject of the reading. Your job is to find the **main idea** in each paragraph and its relationship to the subject as a whole. To understand a paragraph, take two steps.

1. Find the subject.

2. Find the main idea.

In most works, one or two key paragraphs contain the meaning of the work as a whole. In an essay or an article, they are very likely to be the first or last paragraphs. Analyze these key paragraphs closely.

Finding the Subject

Your first step is to find the subject of the paragraph. You can find the subject by looking at

■ the title of a whole work

■ a heading or subheading

■ the first sentence of the paragraph

■ any key words or repeated words or names

■ the last sentence of the paragraph

Read the paragraph on the next page from a guidebook. Can you spot the subject of the paragraph?

The Battle of Gettysburg *(Heading)*

(Subheading) JULY 1–3, 1863

(First sentence) On July 1, Southern General Henry Heth took his division into Gettysburg to retrieve a reported store of shoes for his men. Just west of town he met with a Northern brigade. For two hours these forces fought and throughout the day, more and more Union and Confederate divisions joined the fight until Union troops retreated from Gettysburg to rally on Cemetery and Culp's Hills. Neither side had planned to fight at Gettysburg, but this unintended meeting had sparked one of the decisive battles of the war.

(Key words and names) *(Repeated word)* *(Last sentence)*

1 Look at the heading and subheading.

Your first clue about the subject of the paragraph may be in the heading and subheading. This heading tells you that the paragraph is about a battle at Gettysburg. The subheading tells you when the battle occurred.

2 Look at the first sentence.

The first sentence of the paragraph provides some additional information. It tells you that a Southern general went to Gettysburg on July 1. You can expect to find out what happened after that.

3 Look at key or repeated words or names.

Notice the words that are highlighted in the paragraph. The words *Southern, Northern, Union,* and *Confederate* are clues that the battle took place during the Civil War.

DETAILS

- *First sentence tells why a Southern general went to Gettysburg.*
- *Second sentence tells that he met a Northern brigade.*
- *Third sentence tells that more divisions on both sides joined the battle and that Union troops retreated.*
- *Last sentence tells that this meeting set off a major battle.*

The subject of the paragraph is how the Battle of Gettysburg started.

Finding the Main Idea

Once you discover the subject of the paragraph, you need to determine the main idea. Remember that the main idea is what the author says about the subject.

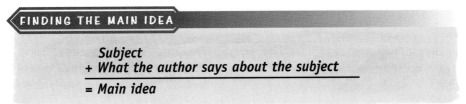

FINDING THE MAIN IDEA

Subject
+ What the author says about the subject
= Main idea

Finding the Main Idea in the First Sentence

In some types of writing, the author comes right out and tells you the main idea in the first sentence. If this is the case, the paragraph has what is called a *stated main idea*. Many paragraphs in textbooks have a stated main idea in the first sentence.

Finding the Main Idea in the Last Sentence

Sometimes authors place the main idea in the last sentence, as in the following paragraph.

from "Florida Flashbacks" by Gary Paterson

Details

① As the canoe sliced through the black water, an alligator slipped from its perch atop a submerged log and disappeared beneath the surface. Off to the right, a green ② heron stalked its prey from the shore as slivers of sunshine shone through the canopy of ③ Spanish moss and cypress. This was a glimpse of what Florida was—before the rise of Mickey, Miami, and millions of tourists.

Main idea

Here the author puts the main idea in the final sentence. The previous sentences give details about the way much of Florida used to look. These details build up to the paragraph's main idea.

Here's how one reader used an organizer to separate the main idea from the details.

Subject: Florida		
Detail #1: alligator	Detail #2: heron	Detail #3: Spanish moss and cypress
Main idea: This is a glimpse of what Florida used to be like.		

Finding an Implied Main Idea

It would make things easy if writers always stated the main idea, but they don't. Sometimes a paragraph will have what is called an *implied main idea*. In such paragraphs, the writer expects you to *infer* the paragraph's most important idea, using those clues scattered throughout the paragraph. Look at this example from a history textbook.

from *Land of Promise*

Heading

Labor Struggles for Reform

First sentence

Imagine that you were a coal miner in Schuylkill County, Pennsylvania. Poverty probably forced you to quit school as a boy and join your father in the deep pits of the anthracite mines nearby. Here you lived your life in darkness, for you rose before the sun each morning and spent your day in the blackness beneath the earth. You earned little for your labor, because there was no minimum wage and no recognized voice to represent the interests of

Four details

the miners. Although you lived with the threat of gas explosions, cave-ins, and death, your employers took no responsibility for working conditions in mines. In the Gilded Age, labor unions struggled to improve your life and the lives of other miners.

Last sentence

Were you able to find clues about the main idea?

Heading
The heading gives you a clue about the subject, labor reform.

First Sentence
The first sentence asks you to imagine that you were a coal miner in Pennsylvania. Understanding what being a coal miner was like requires information from the rest of the paragraph.

Details
The rest of the paragraph gives examples of what it was like to be a coal miner. Poverty forced miners to go to work at a young age, the work was dangerous, and miners were underpaid for the long hours they worked.

These details all point to the fact that labor reform was badly needed. You need to add together all the information about the coal miners' lives to see why reform was needed.

Last Sentence
This sentence states that labor unions tried to improve the lives of miners. That is, they tried to reform working conditions. Use an organizer like this one to help you come up with the main idea.

MAIN IDEA ORGANIZER

Subject: the life of a coal miner

Detail #1	Detail #2	Detail #3	Detail #4
You had to quit school as a boy.	You worked long days in darkness.	You earned little money.	Although the work was dangerous, your employer was not responsible for working conditions.

Main Idea: Because of working conditions in coal mines, labor reform was badly needed.

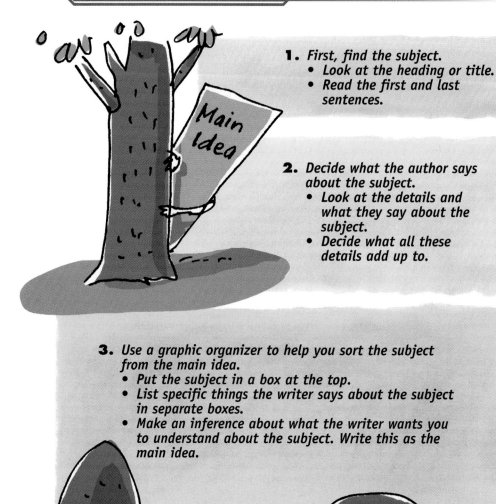

1. First, find the subject.
- Look at the heading or title.
- Read the first and last sentences.

2. Decide what the author says about the subject.
- Look at the details and what they say about the subject.
- Decide what all these details add up to.

3. Use a graphic organizer to help you sort the subject from the main idea.
- Put the subject in a box at the top.
- List specific things the writer says about the subject in separate boxes.
- Make an inference about what the writer wants you to understand about the subject. Write this as the main idea.

Kinds of Paragraphs

If you know how something is built, you can take it apart and put it back together again. You know it inside and out. For the same reason, you need to understand how different types of paragraphs are organized. This knowledge will help you understand and analyze how writers communicate their ideas.

Writers use four types of paragraphs: *narrative, descriptive, expository,* and *persuasive.*

KINDS OF PARAGRAPHS

Narrative Paragraphs

- *A narrative paragraph tells a story.*
- *It has a clear progression from beginning to middle to end.*

Expository Paragraphs

- *An expository paragraph presents facts, gives directions, defines terms, and so on.*
- *The purpose of an expository paragraph is to offer information or explain something.*

Descriptive Paragraphs

- *A descriptive paragraph presents a single, clear picture (description) of a person, place, thing, or idea.*
- *Descriptive paragraphs often contain imagery and sensory language.*

Persuasive Paragraphs

- *A persuasive paragraph presents information to support or prove a point.*
- *The writer of a persuasive paragraph expresses an opinion and tries to convince the reader that the opinion is correct or valid.*

Most paragraphs are organized around a single, unifying idea. The writer chooses how to order the details in a paragraph. It's up to you, the reader, to follow the ways the details in paragraphs have been organized. With this understanding, you can:

1. know which details are important and which are not

2. figure out the author's purpose

3. remember what you've read

Ways of Organizing Paragraphs

One clue to understanding paragraphs is to see how they are organized. Good writers establish a clear order most of the time, but not always. There's no single set of rules for how a paragraph should be written, so writers often organize their paragraphs to suit their needs in a given situation. Good readers look for patterns in the arrangement of details. Here are the eight most common ways of organizing the details in a paragraph.

ORGANIZING PARAGRAPHS

Time Order
- Details are arranged in the order in which they happen.
- This organization is used for narrating personal experiences, describing steps in a process, or explaining events.

Geographic Order
- Details are arranged in geographic, or spatial order (left to right, right to left, top to bottom, and so on).
- This organization is often used in descriptive paragraphs.

Order of Importance
- Details are arranged in order of importance: least important to most important, or most important to least important.
- This organization is often used in descriptive and persuasive paragraphs.

Comparison-Contrast Order
- Details are arranged to show similarities and differences between two or more subjects.
- This organization is used in all types of paragraphs.

Cause-Effect Order
- Details are arranged to show connections between a result and the events that preceded it. It is also known as "problem-solution" order.
- This organization is used in all types of paragraphs.

Classification Order
- Details are placed into categories or groups.
- This organization is often used in descriptive and expository paragraphs.

Listing Order
- Details are arranged in a simple list.
- This organization is often used in descriptive and expository paragraphs.

Mixed Order
- Some details are arranged one way, and other details are arranged in another way.
- This organization is used in all types of paragraphs.

Time Order

For an example of time order, read Mark Twain's description of being on a stagecoach with several companions. Note how the highlighted words offer clues to the organization.

from *Roughing It* by Mark Twain

1 As the sun went down and the evening chill came on, we made preparation for bed. We stirred up the hard leather letter-sacks, and the knotty canvas bags of printed matter (knotty and uneven because of projecting ends and corners of magazines, boxes, and books). We stirred them up and redisposed them in such a way as to make our bed as level as possible. And we *did* improve it, too, though after all our work it had an upheaved and billowy look about it, like a little piece of a stormy sea. Next we hunted up our boots from odd nooks among the mail-bags where they had settled, and put them on. Then we got down our coats, vests, pantaloons and heavy woolen shirts from the arm-loops where they had been swinging all day, and clothed ourselves in them. . . . Then we smoked a final pipe, and swapped a final yarn, after which, we put the pipes, tobacco, and bag of coin in snug holes and caves among the mail-bags, and then fastened down the coach curtains all around, and made the place as "dark as the inside of a cow," as the conductor phrased it in his picturesque way. It was certainly as dark as any place could be—nothing was even dimly visible in it. And finally, we rolled ourselves up like silk-worms, each person in his own blanket, and sank peacefully to sleep.

> Series of events

Use Sequence Notes to help you keep track of events.

SEQUENCE NOTES

> Continue listing times and events.

• preparation for bed   • hunted up boots   • put on clothes

Geographic Order

Some paragraphs move in an organized way from one location to another. The writer opens with a description of one place and then moves smoothly around a room or from one place to another. The purpose of this type of paragraph is to establish what is happening where.

I went out onto the sidewalk and walked down toward the Boulevard St. Michel, passed the tables of the Rotonde, still crowded, looked across the street at the Dome, its tables running out to the edge of the pavement. Someone waved at me from a table, I did not see who it was and went on. I wanted to get home. The Boulevard Montparnasse was deserted. Lavigne's was closed tight, and they were stacking the tables outside the Closerie des Lilas. I passed Ney's statue standing among the new-leaved chestnut-trees in the arc-light. There was a faded purple wreath leaning against the base. I stopped and read the inscription: from the Bonapartist Groups, some date; I forget. He looked very fine, Marshal Ney in his top-boots, gesturing with his sword among the green new horse-chestnut leaves. My flat was just across the street, a little way down the Boulevard St. Michel.

Geographic order

You can draw a map to help you keep track of geographic details.

MAP

Order of Importance

When the details of a paragraph are organized by order of importance, a writer begins with the most important idea and moves to the least important idea. Or, a writer can begin with examples and build up to the larger idea.

Most Important to Least Important

This paragraph from a National Park Service brochure starts with the most important idea and offers details that support it.

First Battle of Bull Run

On a warm July day in 1861, two great armies of a divided nation clashed for the first time on the fields overlooking Bull Run. Their ranks were filled with enthusiastic young volunteers in colorful new uniforms, gathered together from every part of the country. Confident that their foes would run at the first shot, the raw recruits were thankful that they would not miss the only battle of what surely would be a short war. But any thought of colorful pageantry was suddenly lost in the smoke, din, dirt, and death of battle. Soldiers on both sides were stunned by the violence and destruction they encountered. At day's end, nearly 900 young men lay lifeless on the fields of Mathews Hill, Henry Hill, and Chinn Ridge.

Most important idea

Four details

MAIN IDEA ORGANIZER

Main idea: Two armies fought for the first time near Bull Run.

Detail 1:	Detail 2:	Detail 3:	Detail 4:
armies filled with volunteers	recruits glad to participate	soldiers "stunned" by horror of war	nearly 900 dead

Least Important to Most Important

Here, in another paragraph from the same brochure, the writer begins instead with the least important details and builds toward the most important idea, which appears in the final sentence.

First Battle of Bull Run

Three details

Most important idea

On the morning of July 21, McDowell sent his attack columns in a long march north toward Sudley Springs Ford. This route took the Federals around the Confederate left. To distract the Southerners, McDowell ordered a diversionary attack where the Warrenton Turnpike crossed Bull Run at the Stone Bridge. At 5:30 A.M., the deep-throated roar of a 30-pounder Parrott rifle shattered the morning calm and signaled the start of the battle.

Note how this paragraph begins with a series of details that lead toward the most important idea—the start of the battle.

MAIN IDEA ORGANIZER

Detail 1: McDowell sent attack columns "toward Sudley Springs Ford."	**Detail 2:** Route took "the Federals around the Confederate left."	**Detail 3:** McDowell ordered "diversionary attack."
Main idea: The Battle of Bull Run began.		

Comparison-Contrast Order

When a paragraph is organized to compare and contrast, the writer shows how two or more things are alike or different. In this paragraph, the writer compares the Second Battle of Bull Run to the first battle.

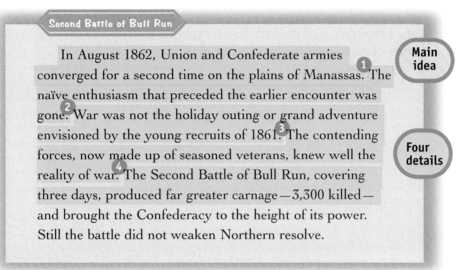

Second Battle of Bull Run

In August 1862, Union and Confederate armies converged for a second time on the plains of Manassas. The naïve enthusiasm that preceded the earlier encounter was gone. War was not the holiday outing or grand adventure envisioned by the young recruits of 1861. The contending forces, now made up of seasoned veterans, knew well the reality of war. The Second Battle of Bull Run, covering three days, produced far greater carnage — 3,300 killed — and brought the Confederacy to the height of its power. Still the battle did not weaken Northern resolve.

Main idea

Four details

Use a Venn Diagram to keep track of important details in a comparison-contrast paragraph.

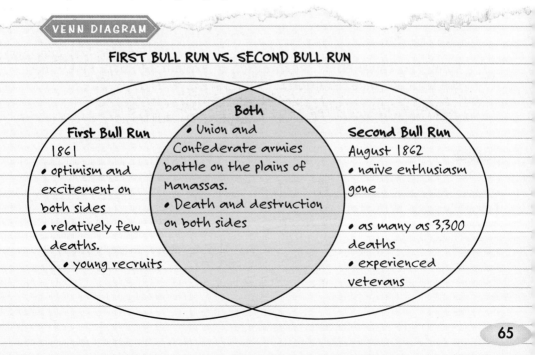

VENN DIAGRAM

FIRST BULL RUN VS. SECOND BULL RUN

Both

First Bull Run
1861
• optimism and excitement on both sides
• relatively few deaths.
• young recruits

• Union and Confederate armies battle on the plains of Manassas.
• Death and destruction on both sides

Second Bull Run
August 1862
• naïve enthusiasm gone
• as many as 3,300 deaths
• experienced veterans

Cause-Effect Order

In a cause-effect paragraph, the writer establishes a logical relationship between a cause or causes and one or more effects. Sometimes a writer explains the effect first and then offers information about the causes. Other times, the writer begins with the causes and then explains the effects.

Note here how Judith Ortiz Cofer explains the effects a terrible case of the chicken pox had on her as a child.

from "The Story of My Body" by Judith Ortiz Cofer

Cause

Effects

I started out life as a pretty baby and learned to be a pretty girl from a pretty mother. Then at ten years of age I suffered one of the worst cases of chicken pox I have ever heard of. My entire body, including the inside of my ears and in between my toes, was covered with pustules which in a fit of panic at my appearance I scratched off my face, leaving permanent scars. A cruel school nurse told me I would always have them—tiny cuts that looked as if a mad cat had plunged its claws deep into my skin. I grew my hair long and hid behind it for the first years of my adolescence. This was when I learned to be invisible.

Cofer uses cause-effect organization to explain her main idea—how she learned to be "invisible."

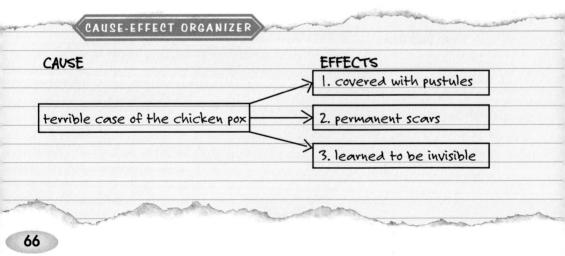

CAUSE-EFFECT ORGANIZER

CAUSE

EFFECTS

1. covered with pustules

terrible case of the chicken pox

2. permanent scars

3. learned to be invisible

Classification Order

Writers use classification order to explain a term or concept. They put things into categories to explain an idea. Often a writer describes each category by mentioning its special characteristics. Here a writer explains how society was organized under feudalism.

> from "Feudal Society" in *Human Heritage*
>
> Under feudalism, the people of Western Europe were divided into groups. One group was the clergy, or religious leaders. Their duty was to teach Christianity and to help the poor and sick. A second group was the nobles. Their duty was to govern, enforce laws, and protect the people. The third group included the peasants and townspeople. Their duty was to support the clergy and nobles by farming the land and providing services.

Three categories

Sometimes a paragraph about different groups or types can be hard to keep straight as you read. Classification Notes can help you remember the details in a paragraph that classifies things.

CLASSIFICATION NOTES

CLERGY	NOBLES	PEASANTS AND TOWNSPEOPLE
• teach Christianity • help poor and sick	• govern • enforce laws • protect people	• support clergy and nobles by farming and services

Listing Order

Some paragraphs are simply lists of details in no particular order. Here a writer lists the details of Viking houses.

from "Viking Houses" in *Human Heritage*

   Most Vikings lived in villages scattered all through the country. Their houses were made of logs or boards. The roofs, which were made of sod-covered wood, slanted deeply to shed the heavy winter snows. Carved dragons decorated the roofs at either end. Each house had a small porch at its front that was held up by carved pillars.

You can keep track of the details simply by making a list. A Web is another convenient way to organize details.

LIST

VIKING HOUSES
- made of logs or boards
- roofs were sod-covered
- carved dragons on roof
- small porch and carved pillars

WEB

dragons at ends of roof

made of logs or boards

small front porch

VIKING HOUSES

sod-covered wooden roofs

carved pillars

slanted roof to shed snow

Mixed Order

Sometimes a single paragraph is organized in more than one way. For example, this paragraph mixes, or combines, comparison-contrast and cause-effect order. How would you state the main idea?

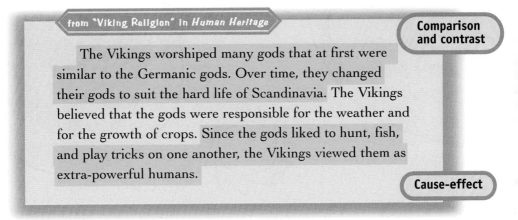

from "Viking Religion" in *Human Heritage*

Comparison and contrast

The Vikings worshiped many gods that at first were similar to the Germanic gods. Over time, they changed their gods to suit the hard life of Scandinavia. The Vikings believed that the gods were responsible for the weather and for the growth of crops. Since the gods liked to hunt, fish, and play tricks on one another, the Vikings viewed them as extra-powerful humans.

Cause-effect

When you read a paragraph that uses several methods of organization, you can identify those methods in the margin or on sticky notes to help you follow the main idea. If you said that the main idea of the paragraph above is that the Vikings' concept of their gods changed to suit the Viking environment, you would be correct.

Not all paragraphs fit into one neat category. But knowing the way paragraphs are organized helps you unpack their meaning.

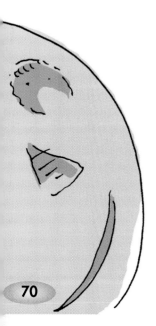

Reading
Textbooks

Introduction to Reading Textbooks

Textbooks are one of the tools of the trade for students. If you know how to use them, you can learn a lot.

Have you noticed that textbooks have some of the same standard parts? They generally start with a table of contents. They are organized into units and chapters. They have headings, different typefaces, and photos and illustrations. They often have a glossary or index in the back.

Obviously, textbooks vary in content, depending on the subject matter. Each type of textbook follows a slightly different organization, and each one uses its own special language. In this chapter, you'll find terms, concepts, and definitions that relate to history, science, math, and foreign language. The more you understand what's in your textbooks, the more you'll learn.

Reading History

History textbooks contain a lot of information: names, dates, charts, graphs, maps, photographs, and all kinds of special features about people and events. How are you going to read and remember all that material? The task is not as hard as you might think. What you need is a plan for understanding and remembering.

Goals

Here you'll learn how to:

✔ read **history**
✔ use the strategy of **note-taking**
✔ see **the way history textbooks are often organized**

Before Reading

To get the most out of what you read, think about your assignment before you even start to read. Set a purpose, do a quick preview, and plan how to make efficient use of your reading time.

A Set a Purpose

One way to set a purpose for reading history is to place yourself in the role of an investigative reporter. A reporter asks the questions *who, what, when, where, why*, and *how*. Ask yourself these same questions about the text you are getting ready to read called "The Rise of Islam."

Setting a Purpose

- **Who** started Islam?
- **What** is Islam?
- **When** did Islam begin?
- **Where** is Islam important or practiced?
- **Why** is Islam important?
- **How** did Islam spread?

B Preview

Take a quick look over the next few pages from a world history textbook. Look for these things as you preview "The Rise of Islam":

Preview Checklist

✔ the title, the list of terms and names, and the introductory information near the title

✔ the first and last paragraphs

✔ the headings

✔ any names, dates, words, or terms set in bold type or that are repeated

✔ any bulleted lists

✔ any photos, maps, or pictures and their captions

The reason for previewing is to get an idea of what to expect before you begin to read. Now preview "The Rise of Islam" on pages 75–79. As you do, think about what you already know about the subject.

Textbooks

PREVIEW
Title

1 The Rise of Islam

TERMS & NAMES
- Allah
- Muhammad
- Islam
- Muslim
- Hijrah
- Qur'an
- mosque
- hajj
- Sunna
- shariah

PREVIEW
Terms and names

PREVIEW
Introductory information

MAIN IDEA

Muhammad unified the Arabic people both politically and through the religion of Islam.

WHY IT MATTERS NOW

As the world's fastest growing major religion, Islam has a strong impact on the lives of millions today.

SETTING THE STAGE The cultures of the Arabian Peninsula were in constant contact with each other for centuries. Southwest Asia (often referred to as the Middle East) was a bridge between Africa, Asia, and Europe, where goods were traded and new ideas were shared. One set of shared ideas would become a powerful force for change in the world—the religion of Islam.

PREVIEW
Headings

PREVIEW
First paragraph

Deserts, Towns, and Travelers

The Arabian Peninsula is a crossroads of three continents— Africa, Europe, and Asia. At its longest and widest points, the peninsula is about 1,200 miles from north to south and 1,300 miles from east to west. Only a tiny strip of fertile land in south Arabia and Oman and a few oases can support agriculture. The remainder of the land is desert, which in the past was inhabited by nomadic Arab herders.

Vocabulary
oases: places in the desert made fertile by the presence of water.

Desert and Town Life On this desert, the nomads, called Bedouins (BEHD-oo-ihnz), were organized into tribes and groups called clans. These clans provided security and support for a life made difficult by the extreme conditions of the desert. The tribesmen took pride in their ability to adapt to the desert conditions and to defend themselves against raids by other clans seeking water, grazing territory, livestock, or food supplies. Because of the desert nomads' fighting ability, they eventually became the core of armies who would build a huge empire in the 600s and 700s. The Bedouin ideals of courage and loyalty to family, along with their warrior skills, would become part of the Islamic way of life.

The areas with more fertile soil and the larger oases had enough water to support farming communities. By the early 600s, many Arabs had chosen to settle in an oasis or in a market town. A few generations earlier, the town dwellers had themselves been nomads. They, however, left the Bedouin life behind for life in settled areas. Larger towns near the western coast of Arabia became market towns for local, regional, and long-distance trade goods.

Crossroads of Trade and Ideas By the early 600s, trade routes connected Arabia to the major ocean and land trade routes. Trade routes through Arabia ran from the extreme south of the peninsula to the Byzantine and Sassanid empires to the north. Merchants from these two empires moved along the caravan routes, trading for goods from the Silk Roads of the east. They transported spices and incense from Yemen and other products to the west. They also carried information and ideas from the world outside Arabia. By the early 600s, cities such as Petra and Palmyra had

Petra, one of the early Arab trading cities, was literally a rock city. Buildings were carved out of the red sandstone cliffs. The name Petra means "rock" in Greek.

The Muslim World

PREVIEW
Photo and caption

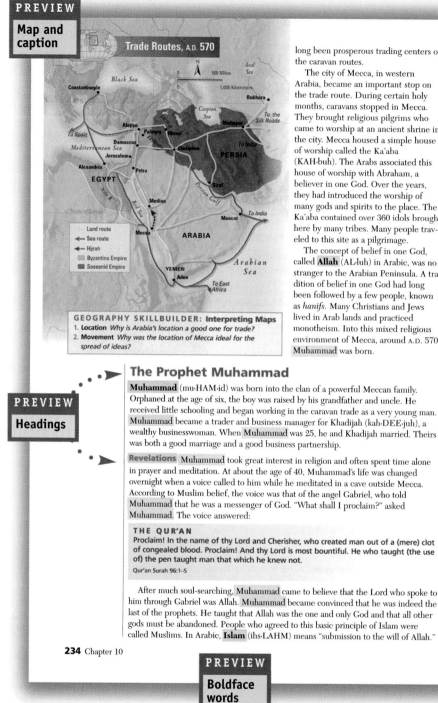

Trade Routes, A.D. 570

GEOGRAPHY SKILLBUILDER: **Interpreting Maps**
1. **Location** Why is Arabia's location a good one for trade?
2. **Movement** Why was the location of Mecca ideal for the spread of ideas?

long been prosperous trading centers on the caravan routes.

The city of Mecca, in western Arabia, became an important stop on the trade route. During certain holy months, caravans stopped in Mecca. They brought religious pilgrims who came to worship at an ancient shrine in the city. Mecca housed a simple house of worship called the Ka'aba (KAH·buh). The Arabs associated this house of worship with Abraham, a believer in one God. Over the years, they had introduced the worship of many gods and spirits to the place. The Ka'aba contained over 360 idols brought here by many tribes. Many people traveled to this site as a pilgrimage.

The concept of belief in one God, called **Allah** (AL·luh) in Arabic, was no stranger to the Arabian Peninsula. A tradition of belief in one God had long been followed by a few people, known as *hanifs*. Many Christians and Jews lived in Arab lands and practiced monotheism. Into this mixed religious environment of Mecca, around A.D. 570, Muhammad was born.

THINK THROUGH HISTORY
A. Summarizing
What religious traditions were in practice in the Arabian Peninsula?

The Prophet Muhammad

Muhammad (mu·HAM·id) was born into the clan of a powerful Meccan family. Orphaned at the age of six, the boy was raised by his grandfather and uncle. He received little schooling and began working in the caravan trade as a very young man. Muhammad became a trader and business manager for Khadijah (kah·DEE·juh), a wealthy businesswoman. When Muhammad was 25, he and Khadijah married. Theirs was both a good marriage and a good business partnership.

Revelations Muhammad took great interest in religion and often spent time alone in prayer and meditation. At about the age of 40, Muhammad's life was changed overnight when a voice called to him while he meditated in a cave outside Mecca. According to Muslim belief, the voice was that of the angel Gabriel, who told Muhammad that he was a messenger of God. "What shall I proclaim?" asked Muhammad. The voice answered:

THE QUR'AN
Proclaim! In the name of thy Lord and Cherisher, who created man out of a (mere) clot of congealed blood. Proclaim! And thy Lord is most bountiful. He who taught (the use of) the pen taught man that which he knew not.
Qur'an Surah 96:1–5

After much soul-searching, Muhammad came to believe that the Lord who spoke to him through Gabriel was Allah. Muhammad became convinced that he was indeed the last of the prophets. He taught that Allah was the one and only God and that all other gods must be abandoned. People who agreed to this basic principle of Islam were called Muslims. In Arabic, **Islam** (ihs·LAHM) means "submission to the will of Allah."

Background
Muhammad is often referred to as The Prophet.

234 Chapter 10

PREVIEW

Boldface words

PREVIEW

Headings

NOTE

Time order

NOTE

Geographic order

Muslim (MOOZ·lim) means "one who has submitted." Muhammad's wife, Khadijah, and several close friends and relatives were his first followers.

By 613, Muhammad had begun to preach publicly in Mecca. At first, he had little success. Many Meccans believed his revolutionary ideas would lead to neglect of the traditional Arab gods. They feared that Mecca would lose its position as a pilgrimage center if people accepted Muhammad's monotheistic beliefs. Some of his followers were even beaten up or stoned in the streets.

The Hijrah Facing such hostility, Muhammad decided to leave Mecca. In 622, following a small band of supporters he sent ahead, Muhammad resettled in the town of Yathrib, over 200 miles to the north of Mecca. This migration became known as the **Hijrah** (hih·JEE·ruh). The Hijrah to Yathrib marked a turning point for Muhammad. He attracted many devoted followers. Later, Yathrib was renamed Medina, meaning "city of the Prophet."

In Medina, Muhammad displayed impressive leadership skills. He fashioned an agreement that joined his own people with the Arabs and Jews of Medina as a single community. These groups accepted Muhammad as a political leader. As a religious leader, he drew many more converts who found the message and the Messenger appealing. Finally, Muhammad also became a military leader in the hostilities between Mecca and Medina.

Returning to Mecca Many of the region's Bedouin tribes converted to Islam and joined Muhammad and his followers. During the years that the Muslims and the Meccans battled against each other, Mecca's power as a city declined. In 630, the Prophet and 10,000 of his followers marched to the outskirts of Mecca. Facing sure defeat, Mecca's leaders surrendered. The Prophet entered the city in triumph.

When he entered the city, Muhammad went to the Ka'aba and declared, "Truth has come and falsehood has vanished." Then he destroyed the idols in the Ka'aba and had the call to prayer made from the roof of the Ka'aba.

Most Meccans pledged their loyalty to Muhammad, and many converted to Islam. By doing so, they joined the *umma*, or Muslim religious community. Muhammad died two years later, at about the age of 62. However, he had taken great strides toward unifying the entire Arabian Peninsula under Islam.

THINK THROUGH HISTORY
B. Summarizing Identify four major events in the life of Muhammad.

SPOTLIGHT ON

The Dome of the Rock

The Dome of the Rock, located in Jerusalem, is the earliest surviving Islamic monument. It was completed in 691. It is situated on Mount Moriah, the site of a Jewish temple destroyed by Romans in A.D. 66.

The rock on the site is the spot from which Muslims say Muhammad ascended to heaven to learn of Allah's will. With Allah's blessing, Muhammad returned to earth to bring God's message to all people. Jews identify the same rock as the site where Abraham was prepared to sacrifice his son Isaac.

The dome itself is wooden and about 60 feet in diameter. The supporting structure includes mosaic designs, columns, and many windows.

PREVIEW

Photo and caption

Beliefs and Practices of Islam

The main teaching of Islam is that there is only one God, Allah. All other beliefs and practices follow from this teaching. Islam teaches that there is good and evil, and that each individual is responsible for the actions of his or her life. The holy book of the Muslims, the **Qur'an** (KUR·an), states, "And if any one earns sin, he earns it against his own soul" (Surah 4:111). Muslims believe that each person will stand before Allah on a final judgment day and enter either heaven or hell.

Artists decorating the Qur'an do it as a holy act. The design is geometric and often repeats to show the infinite quality of Allah. Muslims use abstract designs because they are not permitted to picture Muhammad or the angels.

The Five Pillars To be a Muslim, all believers have to carry out five duties. These duties demonstrate a Muslim's submission to the will of God. These duties are known as the Five Pillars of Islam.

- **Faith** To become a Muslim, a person has to testify to the following statement of faith: "There is no God but Allah, and Muhammad is the Messenger of Allah." This simple statement is heard again and again in Islamic rituals and in Muslim daily life.
- **Prayer** Five times a day, Muslims face toward Mecca to pray. They may assemble at a **mosque** (mahsk), an Islamic house of worship. Or they may pray wherever they find themselves. The duty of praying serves to bring Muslims closer to God.
- **Alms** Muhammad taught that all Muslims have a responsibility to support the less fortunate. Muslims meet that social responsibility by giving alms, or money for the poor, through a special religious tax.
- **Fasting** During the Islamic holy month of Ramadan, Muslims fast. They eat and drink nothing between dawn and sunset. A simple meal is eaten at the end of the day. The duty of fasting reminds Muslims that they have "greater needs than bread."
- **Pilgrimage** All Muslims perform the **hajj** (haj), or pilgrimage to Mecca, at least once in a lifetime. In the past, this involved a grueling journey across deserts, mountains, and seas. Today, many pilgrims arrive by airplane. During the pilgrimage events in Mecca, pilgrims wear identical garments so that all stand as equals before God.

This tenth-century Turkish prayer rug has a traditional design. The design has an arch at one end. The arch must point to Mecca while the prayers are taking place.

A Way of Life Muslims do not separate their personal life from their religious life. Carrying out the Five Pillars of Islam ensures that Muslims live their religion while serving in their community. Along with the Five Pillars, there are other customs, morals, and laws for Islamic society that affect Muslims' daily lives. Believers are forbidden to eat pork or to drink wine or other intoxicating beverages. Friday afternoons are set aside for communal worship and prayer. Muslims who are able to do so gather at a mosque to worship. Unlike many other religions, Islam has no priests or central religious authority. Every Muslim is expected to worship God directly. Islam does, however, have a scholar class called the *ulama*, who are concerned with learning and law. The ulama includes religious teachers who study the words and deeds of Muhammad and apply them to everyday life.

Sources of Authority The original source of authority for Muslims is Allah. According to Islamic belief, Allah expressed his will through the Angel Gabriel, who

PREVIEW

Repeated word

PREVIEW

Boldface words

PREVIEW

Heading

PREVIEW

Last paragraph

THINK THROUGH HISTORY
C. Summarizing
What are the sources of authority for Muslims?

Background
Arab Muslims consider themselves descended from Abraham's son Ismail.

revealed it to Muhammad as the Qur'an. While Muhammad lived, his followers listened to his prayers and teachings and memorized and recited the Revelations. Soon after the Prophet's death, it was suggested that the revelations of Muhammad be collected in a book. This book is the Qur'an.

The Qur'an is written in Arabic, and Muslims consider only the Arabic version to be the true word of God. Only Arabic can be used in worship. Wherever Muslims carried the Qur'an, Arabic became the language of worshipers and scholars. Thus, the Arabic language spread widely as Muslim control expanded into different lands.

Muslims believe that Muhammad's mission as a prophet was to receive the Qur'an and to demonstrate how to apply it in life. To them, the **Sunna** (SOON-uh), or Muhammad's example, is the best model for proper living. The guidance of the Qur'an and Sunna was assembled in a practical form to aid Muslims in applying the will of Allah to their daily lives. This body of law is known as **shariah** (shah-REE-ah). This system of law regulates the family life, moral conduct, and business and community life of Muslims. It does not separate religious matters from criminal or civil matters, but brings all aspects of life together. Because shariah applies to all who follow the teachings of the Prophet, it brings a sense of unity to all Muslims.

Links to Judaism and Christianity To Muslims, Allah is the same God that is worshiped in Christianity and Judaism. However, Muslims view Jesus as a prophet, not the Son of God. The Qur'an is regarded as the word of God as revealed to Muhammad, in the same way that Jews and Christians believe the Torah and the Gospels were revealed to Moses and the New Testament writers. Muslims believe that the Qur'an perfects the earlier revelations from God. To them, it is the final book, and Muhammad was the final prophet. All three religions believe in heaven and hell and a day of judgment. The Muslims trace their ancestry to Abraham, as do the Jews and Christians.

•• The bonds among the three monotheistic religions were reflected in the way the Muslims treated Christians and Jews. Both Christians and Jews were known as "people of the book," because each religion had a holy book with teachings similar to those of the Qur'an. Shariah law required Muslim leaders to extend religious tolerance to Christians and Jews. A huge Muslim empire, as you will learn in Section 2, grew to include people of many different cultures and religions. •••

PREVIEW

Photo and caption

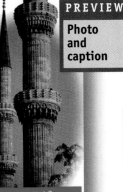

Daily *Life*

Muslim Prayer

Five times a day—dawn, noon, mid-afternoon, sunset, and evening—Muslims face toward Mecca to pray. Worshipers are called to prayer by a *muezzin*. The call to prayer sometimes is given from a *minaret* tower like those pictured above. In large cities, muezzins call worshipers to prayer using public address systems and even the radio.

Because they believe that standing before Allah places them on holy ground, Muslims perform a ritual cleansing before praying so that they will not contaminate the holy ground. They also remove their shoes.

Muslims may pray at a mosque, called a *masjid* in Arabic, meaning "place of kneeling to God." This term refers to the movements of prayer, which involve both the body and the mind in worship.

C Plan

Now stop and think about what you learned in your preview. From reading headings, the bulleted list, boldface words, and the first and last paragraphs, you might have learned the following facts:

- Arabia was a crossroads of trade and ideas.
- Muhammad was a prophet.
- Islam is a way of life for its believers.
- Islam has five pillars, or duties, that its followers must carry out.
- The Qur'an is the most important, sacred Islamic text.

You have already learned a great deal simply by previewing the material. Your next step is to make a plan to meet your purpose for reading. One of the best strategies to gather historical information is note-taking. Here you will learn about two types of note-taking: 5 W's and H Organizer and Key Word or Topic Notes.

NOTE-TAKING

✔ 5 W's and H Organizer
✔ Key Word or Topic Notes

Reading Strategy: Note-taking

The 5 W's and H Organizer answers the questions *who, what, where, when, why,* and *how*. You can use it, or Key Word or Topic Notes.

5 W'S AND H ORGANIZER

The Rise of Islam

WHO	WHAT	WHEN	WHERE	WHY	HOW

KEY WORD OR TOPIC NOTES

KEY WORDS OR TOPICS	COMPLETE NOTES

You can also use Key Word or Topic Notes when you read textbooks and when you listen to lectures. Key Word or Topic Notes, sometimes called Cornell notes, focus on key points. Here are the first two steps to follow:

Step One: Get Ready

1. *Use a loose-leaf notebook and 8 1/2 x 11 paper. Write the date at the top of the page so if your notes get out of order, you can easily organize them again.*
2. *Use one side of the page only. This way, you can add extra information on the back later, as you learn more.*
3. *Draw a vertical line about 2 inches from the left side of the paper. This forms your "key word" column. It will be filled in with key words and phrases later. The 6-inch column on the right is where you will record your notes.*

Step Two: Take Notes While Reading the Text

1. *Record short notes. Put key words in the left hand column. Write longer, detailed notes about the key words on the right.*
2. *Use bullets and abbreviations if you wish.*
3. *Write clearly and legibly so you can read your notes later.*

Note-taking helps you read actively and stay focused on the material. You can add to the 5 W's and H Organizer or Key Word Notes easily as you read and reread and as you listen to teacher presentations on the material. With Key Word Notes, you can add information on the back of the paper. The important thing is to use the note-taking method that works best for you.

During Reading

Now you're ready to read the chapter with a clear purpose and plan in mind.

D Read with a Purpose

Keep your purpose questions in mind as you read. Who started Islam? What is Islam? When did it begin? Where is it practiced? Why is it important? How did it spread? A 5 W's and H Organizer can help you keep track of basic information about a subject.

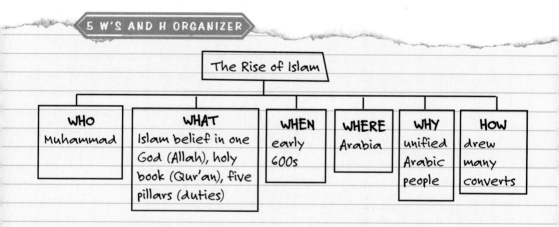

5 W'S AND H ORGANIZER

The Rise of Islam

WHO	WHAT	WHEN	WHERE	WHY	HOW
Muhammad	Islam belief in one God (Allah), holy book (Qur'an), five pillars (duties)	early 600s	Arabia	unified Arabic people	drew many converts

KEY WORD OR TOPIC NOTES

KEY WORDS OR TOPICS	COMPLETE NOTES
Arabian Peninsula	• a crossroads of Africa, Europe, and Asia • mostly desert • Bedouins lived there.
Muhammad	• born about A.D. 570 in Mecca. • greatly interested in religion • while meditating, a voice called to him • Voice said he was a prophet. • began to preach about Allah, the one God

How History Textbooks Are Organized

Because history is a narrative of what has happened in the past, history book authors often write in *chronological,* or

1. Chronological Order

2. Geographical Order

time, order. That is, they tell what happened first, what happened next, and what happened after that. They might also be organized in *geographical,* or *location, order.* That is, they discuss the events in one area before going on to tell of events in another area.

Look at this example from a world history textbook. Note the names, dates, and locations. Notice how the dates follow chronological order and how the writing moves clearly from one town to another. The highlighting calls your attention to signal words that help you understand how the passage is organized. If you can't highlight in your book, use sticky notes to write down names, dates, and locations.

Textbooks

---

from "The Rise of Islam"

Muslim (MOOZ-lim) means "one who has submitted." Muhammad's wife, Khadijah, and several close friends and relatives were his first followers.

By 613, Muhammad had begun to preach publicly in Mecca. At first, he had little success. Many Meccans believed his revolutionary ideas would lead to neglect of the traditional Arab gods. They feared that Mecca would lose its position as a pilgrimage center if people accepted Muhammad's monotheistic beliefs. Some of his followers were even beaten up or stoned in the streets.

The Hijrah Facing such hostility, Muhammad decided to leave Mecca. In 622, following a small band of supporters he sent ahead, Muhammad resettled in the town of Yathrib, over 200 miles to the north of Mecca. This migration became known as the **Hijrah** (hih-JEE-ruh). The Hijrah to Yathrib marked a turning point for Muhammad. He attracted many devoted followers. Later, Yathrib was renamed Medina, meaning "city of the Prophet."

In Medina, Muhammad displayed impressive leadership skills. He fashioned an agreement that joined his own people with the Arabs and Jews of Medina as a single community. These groups accepted Muhammad as a political leader. As a religious leader, he drew many more converts who found the message and the Messenger appealing. Finally, Muhammad also became a military leader in the hostilities between Mecca and Medina.

Returning to Mecca Many of the region's Bedouin tribes converted to Islam and joined Muhammad and his followers. During the years that the Muslims and the Meccans battled against each other, Mecca's power as a city declined. In 630, the Prophet and 10,000 of his followers marched to the outskirts of Mecca. Facing sure defeat, Mecca's leaders surrendered. The Prophet entered the city in triumph.

NOTE
Chronological order

NOTE
Geographic order

E Connect

You have to read actively in order to really understand. You can't just glance at the words, turn the pages, and expect the information to sink in. Take notes or create graphic organizers to nail down the information in a form that you can easily study and review.

Try to connect in a personal way with your reading. Ask yourself, "What do I think of this?" "Have I ever felt the way this person feels?" "Have I had similar experiences?" Your answers to these questions can help you understand people and events.

Note how one reader responded to this part of "The Rise of Islam."

Muslim (MOOZ·lim) means "one who has submitted." Muhammad's wife, Khadijah, and several close friends and relatives were his first followers.

By 613, Muhammad had begun to preach publicly in Mecca. At first, he had little success. Many Meccans believed his revolutionary ideas would lead to neglect of the traditional Arab gods. They feared that Mecca would lose its position as a pilgrimage center if people accepted Muhammad's monotheistic beliefs. Some of his followers were even beaten up or stoned in the streets.

How could they do this? This isn't right!

After Reading

After you read a chapter, ask yourself whether you can recall some of the important facts. If you are like most people, you will not be sure that you have absorbed everything in the chapter. Be honest with yourself. Would you feel comfortable taking a test on the chapter at this point?

If you have taken Key Word or Topic Notes, now is the time to follow the third step.

Step Three: After-text Study
1. *Read your notes. Underline or box words with main ideas.*
2. *Write key words or phrases in the lefthand column.*
3. *Cover the right side of your paper. Recall and say aloud the facts you can remember in your own words.*
4. *Uncover your notes and check what you recited.*
5. *Review the notes before the exam.*

F Pause and Reflect

As soon as you've finished a chapter, stop for a moment to reflect. Then, ask yourself these questions:

Looking Back

- Did I meet the reading purpose I set in the beginning?
- Do I know the answers to the 5 W's and H?
- Do I know enough details to be able to discuss the ideas in the chapter intelligently?
- Does anything confuse me?

G Reread

Now is the time to go back over the material, looking for details you need to expand your notes or make certain concepts clearer. Maybe you're not sure of what is expected of a Muslim in his or her daily life. Perhaps you aren't clear about the origins of the ideas in Islam. Rereading the material can help make you confident that you truly understand the subject.

Rereading Strategy: Using Graphic Organizers

Using a graphic organizer can help you group information in a visual way. Using a Web is an easy way to group details around key topics. Here is a Web one reader created after rereading the passage on Islam.

Textbooks

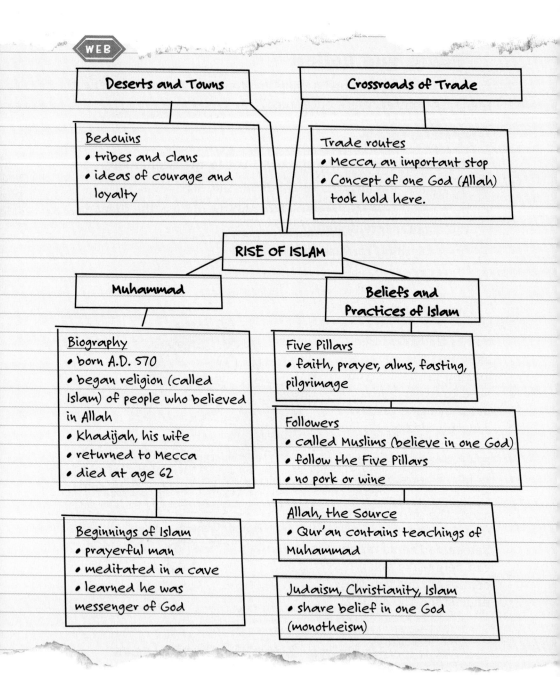

Deserts and Towns

Bedouins
- tribes and clans
- ideas of courage and loyalty

Crossroads of Trade

Trade routes
- Mecca, an important stop
- Concept of one God (Allah) took hold here.

RISE OF ISLAM

Muhammad

Beliefs and Practices of Islam

Biography
- born A.D. 570
- began religion (called Islam) of people who believed in Allah
- Khadijah, his wife
- returned to Mecca
- died at age 62

Five Pillars
- faith, prayer, alms, fasting, pilgrimage

Followers
- called Muslims (believe in one God)
- follow the Five Pillars
- no pork or wine

Beginnings of Islam
- prayerful man
- meditated in a cave
- learned he was messenger of God

Allah, the Source
- Qur'an contains teachings of Muhammad

Judaism, Christianity, Islam
- share belief in one God (monotheism)

Rereading the text and adding to your notes is another effective way to reinforce your learning. If you make rereading a habit, you will find that you will retain a much larger percentage of what you read. You also will be better able to discuss the material or write about it on a test.

H Remember

Sometimes, even if you have taken good notes and reread carefully, you won't remember all of the material in a given chapter. Here are two suggestions to help you remember what you read.

1. Do Some Research
Was there something in your reading that you'd like to know more about? Log on to the Internet for more information. After reading about Islam, you might find out about the city of Mecca today or some facts about the Dome of the Rock, both good topics for an oral or written report connected with the topic of Islam.

2. Conduct an Interview
With a partner, conduct an interview based on the material you have read. One of you can take the role of someone who was there at the time. The other can be a reporter who is interested in the facts.

Textbooks

Summing Up

To understand and remember what you read in history textbooks, use the reading process. Preview the chapter and set a purpose for your reading. Then choose a reading strategy, such as **note-taking.** You can use several tools such as:

■ 5 W's and H Organizer

■ Key Word or Topic Notes

■ Web

As you read, pay attention to the organization of the material. Is it organized in **chronological,** or **time, order?** Is it organized in **geographical,** or **location, order?** After reading, use a rereading strategy, such as **using graphic organizers.**

Reading Science

A science textbook can seem very intimidating at first. As you glance through it, you see new and difficult words that you might not be able to pronounce, let alone understand. But if you have trouble reading science texts, maybe you need a plan and some effective strategies.

Here you'll read "Biology in Your World" from a high school textbook. Apply the strategies you learn here to your own science textbook.

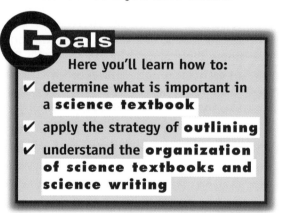

Goals

Here you'll learn how to:

✔ determine what is important in a **science textbook**

✔ apply the strategy of **outlining**

✔ understand the **organization of science textbooks and science writing**

Before Reading

Say that you've just been assigned "Biology in Your World." Should you just begin reading the first paragraph? Definitely not! The first thing you should do is think about what you already know about the subject. Make predictions about what might be in the chapter, and form a plan for finding out more information.

A Set a Purpose

One way to set a purpose is to turn the title or the or the main heading of the chapter into a question. For example, you might ask, "What is the role of biology in the world?" Then, you read to find out the answer.

Another good idea is to check the first page of the chapter to see if it includes a list of objectives or goals. If it does, you can use this information to set your purpose for reading. You can also set your purpose based on a subheading or on key terms listed on the first page.

Textbooks

Setting a Purpose

■ **What are some real-world problems that biology can help solve?**

B Preview

Once you've determined your purpose, the next thing to do is preview this part of the chapter. The reason for the preview is to get an idea of what to expect before you begin to read.

When you preview, you glance over each page, paying special attention to the following items:

Preview Checklist

✔ the title
✔ the first and last paragraphs of the chapter
✔ the headings
✔ any words set in bold type or repeated
✔ any boxed material
✔ any photos, charts, or pictures and their captions
✔ the list of objectives and any review questions

Now that you know what to look for, preview "Biology in Your World."

Section 1-2   # Biology in Your World

Objectives

- **Evaluate** the role biologists play in saving our tropical forests. (p. 10)
- **Describe** the role biologists play in trying to increase and improve our food supply. (p. 11)
- **Describe** efforts to combat three diseases that are the subject of current scientific research. (pp. 12–13)

Key Terms
HIV
cancer
cystic fibrosis

internetconnect

SCiLINKS.
NSTA

TOPIC: Population growth
GO TO: www.scilinks.org
KEYWORD: HX010

Biology Can Help Solve Today's Real-World Problems

You are unlikely to read a newspaper or magazine today without noticing issues involving biology. We learn that biologists are working to save our tropical rain forests, to find a cure for AIDS, and to develop genetic engineering techniques that can help cure certain diseases. In this textbook you will encounter many areas in which biologists are actively working to solve some of today's problems. Like the students in **Figure 1-9,** you too can contribute to this effort.

Living in harmony with our environment

In 1999, the world's human population passed 6 billion people. The growing human population has begun to seriously harm other creatures that share the planet. For example, some people have had to clear rain-forest land in order to have space to live and to grow crops. Since the world's tropical forests are home to one-half of the world's species of plants and animals, the impact of this destruction on the diversity of plants and animals has been catastrophic.

The world's tropical forests are being destroyed at the rate of more than an acre per second. At this rate, all of the rain forests will be gone in less than 30 years! With them will be lost more than a million species, the greatest extinction event since the disappearance of the dinosaurs 65 million years ago. Extinction is forever—future generations will never see any of these animals or plants alive again. Who knows what potential medicines and foods we are discarding? Like burning a library without reading the books, extinction caused by humans is a tragedy beyond measure. Biologists are studying the plants and animals in the rain forests in order to better understand how we can maintain a balance between people's growing need for land and the need to protect these plants and animals.

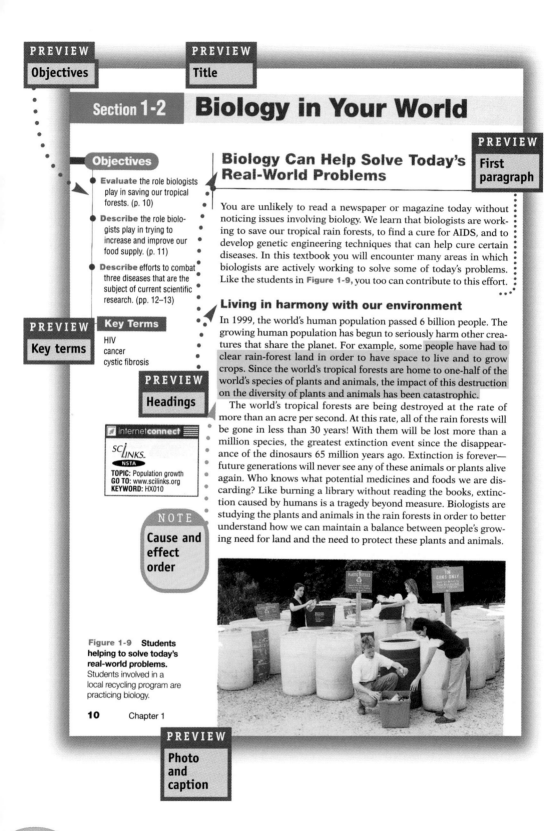

Figure 1-9   Students helping to solve today's real-world problems. Students involved in a local recycling program are practicing biology.

10   Chapter 1

PREVIEW

Heading

Textbooks

Photo and caption

Feeding a growing population

As the population continues to grow, the demand for food is going to strain our ability to feed all the people. Biologists are vigorously seeking new crops that grow more efficiently in tropical soils and crops that grow without intensive use of fertilizers and insecticides (chemicals used to kill insects).

Genetic engineers are transplanting beneficial plant genes into other plants to create crops that are more resistant to insects and microorganisms. Although there is some apprehension about this technology, it is hoped that genetically engineered crops, such as the crops shown in **Figure 1-10,** will both reduce the need for insecticides and increase crop yields. For example, some genetically engineered plants are now resistant to frost damage because of new genes inserted into the plants. Other genetically engineered crops made resistant to insects allow farmers to decrease or avoid the use of chemical pesticides. Clearly the efforts of biologists will have an enormous impact on the world's future.

Figure 1-10 Genetically engineered crops. Crops such as barley have had their genetic material altered in an effort to help the crops resist attack by viruses.

NOTE

Problem and solution order

MATH LAB

Evaluating the effectiveness of insecticides

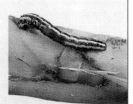

Background

Insecticides are chemicals used to kill insects, some of which may harm valuable crops. Sometimes insects can become resistant to the insecticides—that is, the insects are not affected by the chemicals and instead survive.

Analysis

1. **Describe** how the number of insects resistant to insecticides has changed over time.

2. **Calculate** the number of years that passed between data points *A* and *B*.

3. **Calculate** the number of years that passed between data points *B* and *C*.

4. **Determine** approximately how many insect species were resistant to insecticides at points *A*, *B*, and *C*.

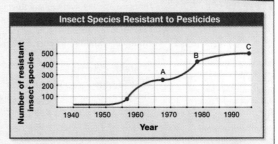

5. **Determine** whether the increase in the number of insecticide-resistant species was greater between points *A–B* or points *B–C*.

6. **Predict** the effect the numbers in the table might have on farmers who use insecticides.

Boxed material

PREVIEW

Heading

PREVIEW

Boldface
words

Biology Can Help Fight Diseases

PREVIEW

Photo
and
caption

One of the most direct ways in which progress in biology affects our lives is in medicine, where scientific advances are improving health and health care every day. New technologies have enabled biologists to combat disease in ways scarcely imagined only a few years ago. Among the many diseases that you will study in this text, consider the following.

Figure 1-11 AIDS counseling

How many? AIDS is now the leading cause of death among American males between the ages of 24 and 44.

AIDS

Since 1981, when this disease was first recognized, over 50 million people worldwide have been infected with HIV (human immunodeficiency virus). **HIV** is a virus that destroys the immune system, causing acquired immune deficiency syndrome, or AIDS.

People with AIDS are not able to defend themselves from infection, so they can die of diseases that are not normally fatal. Most of the people infected with HIV are expected to develop AIDS. Fourteen million people have already died of AIDS, and about 2 million more die each year. As the number of people with HIV infection and AIDS grows, there is intense research to find a way to help those already suffering from AIDS and to halt the spread of the disease, as shown in Figure 1-11.

PREVIEW

Headings

Cancer

Cancer is a growth disorder of cells that occurs when cells divide uncontrollably within the body. Although the number of people with cancer is increasing, scientists studying this disease have found that many cancer deaths are preventable. Your diet and the chemicals that you are exposed to can affect whether or not you get a particular form of cancer. For example, research indicates that most lung cancers are caused by the use of tobacco. Eliminating cigarette smoking would prevent many lung cancers.

biobit

Can trees cure cancer?

In the early 1990s, the bark of the Pacific yew tree was found to contain an anti-cancer chemical called taxol. Today taxol is obtained from different sources and is used to treat different types of cancer, including ovarian and breast cancers.

Cystic fibrosis

Cystic fibrosis is a fatal disorder in which abnormally thick mucus builds up in many organs, including the lungs. The accumulation of mucus causes difficulty in breathing. Cystic fibrosis is caused by a defective gene.

In cystic fibrosis patients, the gene for making a protein that helps pump chloride ions into and out of cells has the wrong instructions. Because the protein is not made correctly, the cells cannot pump chloride ions into and out of cells. This eventually results in chloride ions building up within cells. Like sponges, these cells soak up the surrounding water, turning the fluid around the outside of the cells into thick mucus.

PREVIEW

Repeated
term

PREVIEW

Heading

PREVIEW

Repeated term

PREVIEW

Boxed material

Textbooks

Since 1990, biologists have been attempting to transfer a healthy version of the gene into cystic fibrosis patients. They are hopeful that the healthy gene will enable the body's cells to efficiently pump chloride ions.

The replacement of a defective gene with a normal gene is called gene therapy. Other serious genetic disorders, such as muscular dystrophy, are also good candidates for gene therapy. Transferring normally functioning genes into affected individuals offers the first real hope of curing genetic disorders. The difficulty lies in introducing the normal cells into the correct cells and inserting them into the cells' DNA. These efforts continue, and progress is being reported in solving both of these problems. Although still experimental, the future of gene therapy looks very bright.

Biologists actively work to solve world problems

It is clear that biology must play a major role if we are to improve the quality of life for ourselves and for future generations. Addressing problems like the growing human population, increasing damage to the environment, and life-threatening diseases requires a thorough understanding of biological systems.

As you proceed through this text, you will encounter biologists in many settings, as laboratory and field researchers, as technicians performing analyses, as animal keepers in zoos, and as doctors in hospitals. Many careers are open to biologists, who can make important contributions to improving the future. Even if you do not become a biologist, a knowledge of biology will help you to make informed decisions as a citizen in shaping our future world.

Exploring Further

Biologists at Work

The word *biologist* often calls to mind an image of a person wearing a white coat in a windowless laboratory filled with strange chemicals. While many biologists do work in laboratories, some biologists work in other environments, such as outer space, swamps, forests, deserts, jungles, oceans, volcanoes, and computer labs.

Biologists also differ in the tools they use. For example, a biologist involved in deep-sea research might use a submarine with sophisticated cameras, and a biologist who tracks animals to study their behavior might use radio transmitters.

What do biologists do?
Regardless of the environment in which they work or the tools they use, all biologists study the origin, development, structure, function, geographic distribution, and other basic aspects of living organisms. For example, botanists study the growth, structure, and classification of plants. Ecologists study the relationships between organisms and their environment, including their relationships with other organisms. Marine biologists specialize in the study of organisms that inhabit the sea.

Biologists apply their knowledge in many ways: by drawing scientific illustrations, by guiding visitors through national parks, by working in greenhouses, by treating people who are ill. Yet others do research to advance the fields of medicine, agriculture, and industry. Biologists are at work all around us.

Ecologist

PREVIEW

Photo and caption

Review   *SECTION 1-2*

1. **Relate** two ways that the growing human population is disturbing the Earth's resources.

2. **Evaluate** why saving tropical forests is such an important issue.

3. **Apply** genetic engineering to the development of new crops.

4. **Describe** why mucus builds up in cystic fibrosis patients.

Critical Thinking

5. **SKILL Evaluating Viewpoints** Your teacher believes that a knowledge of biology is essential in the battle against diseases. Do you agree or disagree? Explain.

PREVIEW

Review questions

Biology and You   **13**

C Plan

Now stop and think about what you learned in your preview. From reading headings and boldface words, looking at photos and reading the captions, and reading the first and last paragraphs, you may have a list that includes these facts:

- Biology can solve today's real-world problems.
- Knowledge of biology can help us improve our environment.
- Biologists can help develop stronger food crops.
- Insecticides can lead to insecticide-resistant species.
- Biology can help fight diseases.
- Many different careers are open to biologists.

Now you have a broad idea of what this reading is about. Your next step is to find a strategy that will help you meet your reading purpose.

Reading Strategy: Outlining

One excellent strategy to use when reading a science textbook is **outlining.** You can do a Topic Outline or a Sentence Outline. You can use an informal or formal method. An informal Outline might use simple indentations and bullets to show how ideas relate to one another. A formal Outline might look like this:

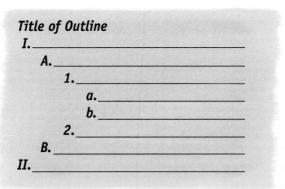

Title of Outline
I. _____
   A. _____
     1. _____
       a. _____
       b. _____
     2. _____
   B. _____
II. _____

In a formal Outline, main topics are numbered with Roman numerals. The first sublevel uses capital letters, the second uses Arabic numerals, and the third uses lowercase letters.

During Reading

Now that you have a reading purpose and strategy, go back and read this section of the chapter.

D Read with a Purpose

Remember when you previewed the headings? The headings can help you create an effective Outline. An Outline helps you understand the organization of a text. You can start your Outline with just the headings, and later you can go back and fill in the sublevels as you read the paragraphs. Here is how one reader started an Outline. Notice that the headings match the headings on the textbook pages.

OUTLINE

Biology in Your World
I.   Biology Can Help Solve Today's Real-World Problems
     A. Living in harmony with our environment
         1.
         2.
     B. Feeding a growing population
         1.
         2.
II. Biology Can Help Fight Diseases
     A. AIDS
         1.
         2.
     B. Cancer
         1.
         2.

Leave space for other additions to your Outline. You'll fill it in later as you read.

If you follow this example, you will have a clear record of the key points of the chapter.

How Science Textbooks Are Organized

Scientists try to explain how and why things happen. To do this, they might ask questions about cause and effect, such as "What causes cystic fibrosis?" They might ask classification

1. **Cause and Effect**
2. **Classification**
3. **Problem and Solution**

questions, such as, "What do different biologists do?" Or they might pose a problem-solution question, such as, "How can we prevent lung cancer?" You can use graphic organizers like these to connect different ideas. Refer to the notes that identify these types of organization in the sample reading.

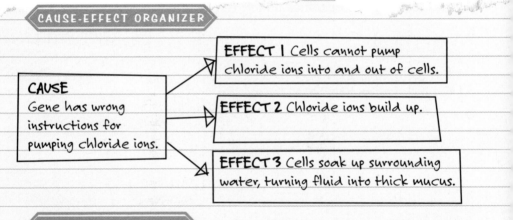

CAUSE-EFFECT ORGANIZER

EFFECT 1 Cells cannot pump chloride ions into and out of cells.

CAUSE
Gene has wrong instructions for pumping chloride ions.

EFFECT 2 Chloride ions build up.

EFFECT 3 Cells soak up surrounding water, turning fluid into thick mucus.

CLASSIFICATION NOTES

BOTANISTS	ECOLOGISTS	MARINE BIOLOGISTS
study plants	study relationships between organisms and their environment	study organisms in the sea

PROBLEM-SOLUTION ORGANIZER

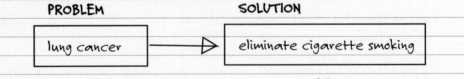

PROBLEM

lung cancer

SOLUTION

eliminate cigarette smoking

When you read science textbooks, you will notice that these patterns are used over and over. If you use graphic organizers like the ones above, you will understand connections among different ideas.

E Connect

Can you see any connection between the subject matter and your own life? Should you care about genetically altered barley?

As you read, make notes about things that you do care about. It might surprise you to see how many connections you can make to the text. Maybe you remember seeing a television news story about why some people are worried about genetically altered corn. Here is how one reader connected to a part of "Biology in Your World."

biobit

• **Can trees cure cancer?**

In the early 1990s, the bark of the Pacific yew tree was found to contain an anti-cancer chemical called taxol. Today taxol is obtained from different sources and is used to treat different types of cancer, including ovarian and breast cancers.

When Aunt Carol was sick, I remember that she was using taxol. What would have happened if taxol hadn't been available?

Textbooks

After Reading

As soon as you finish a chapter, try to recall what you have learned using the headings in your Outline as a guideline.

F Pause and Reflect

Do you think you understand everything that was discussed? The answer, most likely, is *no*. Not many students absorb all the information on a first reading. In fact, hardly anyone does. Before you continue, ask yourself these questions:

PAUSE Reflect

Looking Back

■ **Did I accomplish the reading purpose I set in the beginning?**

■ **Do I know what the main topics in the chapter are?**

■ **Do I understand how the material is organized?**

■ **Would I feel comfortable taking a test on this material now?**

G Reread

How will you remember everything you've read? Maybe all you have to do is review your Outline or ask the teacher a question to clarify some of the material. But you might benefit from rereading at least part of the chapter.

Rereading Strategy: Note-taking

Note-taking on Study Cards can help you learn and remember important ideas and key terms. You can also use Study Cards in study groups and when you are studying for a quiz or test. Put your notes on an index card as shown below. On one side, write the key word or term. On the other side, write the definition or explanation.

> STUDY CARDS
>
> gene therapy
>
> the replacement of defective genes with normal genes inserted into the cells' DNA

Using Study Cards with note-taking will help you gather a lot of details and terms as you reread.

H Remember

Try one of these activities to help you remember what you read in a science textbook.

1. Research

Do some research to find out the latest developments in genetically engineered food, and give a report on your findings.

2. Create a Practice Test

You can prepare for a test by writing your own practice test. Exchange practice tests with a partner, and take each other's tests as a way of preparing for the real test. Return to your Outline or Study Card notes to generate practice test questions.

PRACTICE TEST FOR "BIOLOGY IN YOUR WORLD"

Textbooks

1. The leading cause of death among American males between the
   ages of 24 and 44 is
   a. genetically altered food   c. AIDS
   b. cystic fibrosis   d. accidents
2. Cystic fibrosis is caused by
   a. poor diet   c. the HIV virus
   b. a defective gene   d. thick mucus

Answers: 1. c. 2. b.

Summing Up

When you read a science textbook, follow the reading process and use the strategy of **outlining.** You can use the headings in the chapter to start your Outline, filling in details as you read. You can use these tools:

- ■ Outline
- ■ Cause-Effect Organizer
- ■ Classification Notes
- ■ Problem-Solution Organizer
- ■ Study Cards

Remember to look for the **organization** of science textbooks: **cause-effect, classification,** or **problem-solution.** Use the rereading strategy of **note-taking** to help you make sure you have identified and understood all the important information in the chapter.

Reading Math

You're probably well aware that a math book is quite different from your other textbooks. It's full of special signs and symbols, and the writing is straightforward and to the point. Reading in math is, in a way, like looking for a road sign. If you miss it, you'll be off in the wrong direction.

In fact, when you read math, you'd better go slowly because every word counts. Every symbol, every example, and every diagram is important. To be good at math, you have to be a careful reader.

Goals

Here you'll learn how to:

✔ read about **math** and understand **concepts and operations**

✔ use the strategy of **visualizing and thinking aloud**

✔ understand **how math books are organized**

Before Reading

In math books, one concept often builds on another. If you don't understand the material in chapter one, by the time you get to chapter three, you'll be lost. The instruction in a math text is concentrated, so you have to focus on it without distraction. Make sure that you're fresh, alert, and comfortable when you sit down to study math.

A Set a Purpose

Suppose you have been assigned a lesson in your math text. Set a purpose before you begin reading. One way to do this is to turn the lesson or section title into a question. For example, a section titled "Numbers and Number Operations" might lead to the following purpose-setting questions:

Setting a Purpose

■ **What are number operations?**

■ **What do I need to know about numbers and number operations?**

Turn briefly to the next page, and note the goals in the upper left corner of the page. You can turn these statements into questions (How do I represent numbers and number operations?), and use these as your purpose for reading instead.

B Preview

Now that you have a purpose, you can go ahead and preview the chapter. This way you'll know what to expect when you actually read the material. As you preview, watch for the following things:

Preview Checklist

✔ the title
✔ any listed goals
✔ the introductory paragraph
✔ the headings, boldface words, color, and highlighted items
✔ the models, diagrams, and examples
✔ the boxed items
✔ the review questions

For practice, preview a lesson from an algebra textbook. How many items on the Preview Checklist can you find?

Textbooks

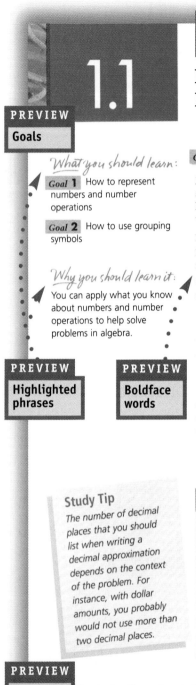

PREVIEW

Title

Numbers and Number Operations

PREVIEW

Introductory paragraph

PREVIEW

Goals

What you should learn:

◀ **Goal 1** How to represent numbers and number operations

Goal 2 How to use grouping symbols

Why you should learn it:

You can apply what you know about numbers and number operations to help solve problems in algebra.

Goal 1 **Numbers and Number Operations**

Much of what you will learn in algebra is based on numerical skills that you already have. For instance, you already know how to add, subtract, multiply, and divide numbers, and you will continue to use these skills in algebra.

Different kinds of numbers have different names. For example, the numbers 0, 1, 2, 3, and 4 are **whole numbers,** and the numbers $\frac{1}{2}, \frac{2}{3},$ and $\frac{5}{4}$ are **fractions.** What you call a number sometimes depends on the way it is written. For example, the number $\frac{1}{2}$ can be written in three forms.

Fraction: $\frac{1}{2}$ Decimal: 0.5   Percent: 50%

The decimal form of some numbers contains too many digits to write. For instance,

$\frac{3}{7} = 0.4285714285 \ldots$

(The three dots mean that the number has more digits than are shown.) You can *approximate* this number to different degrees of accuracy. For instance, rounded to two decimal places, you could write $\frac{3}{7} \approx 0.43$. The symbol $\approx$ means *is approximately equal to.*

PREVIEW

Highlighted phrases

PREVIEW

Boldface words

Study Tip

The number of decimal places that you should list when writing a decimal approximation depends on the context of the problem. For instance, with dollar amounts, you probably would not use more than two decimal places.

LESSON INVESTIGATION

■ **Investigating Fractions and Decimals**

Partner Activity The decimal form of a fraction must either have a finite number of digits or an infinite number of digits. Decide the decimal form of each of the following fractions.

a. $\frac{3}{8}$ **b.** $\frac{1}{3}$ **c.** $\frac{5}{6}$ **d.** $\frac{5}{16}$ **e.** $\frac{4}{7}$ **f.** $\frac{2}{9}$

If the decimal has an infinite number of digits, must the digits occur in a repeating pattern? Give examples with your answer.

PREVIEW

Boxed item in color

There are four basic operations that can be performed with numbers: **addition, subtraction, multiplication,** and **division.**

PREVIEW

Boldface words

Example 1 *Four Basic Number Operations*

a. *Addition:* The **sum** of 12 and 7 is 19.

$$12 + 7 = 19$$

b. *Subtraction:* The **difference** of 15 and 8 is 7.

$$15 - 8 = 7$$ *The difference of a and b is a − b.*

c. *Multiplication:* The **product** of 3 and 6 is 18.

$$3 \cdot 6 = 18, \quad 3(6) = 18, \quad (3)6 = 18, \quad (3)(6) = 18$$

In algebra, we usually do not use the multiplication symbol × because it is easily confused with the letter *x*, which is used for another purpose.

d. *Division:* The **quotient** of 24 and 6 is 4.

$$24 \div 6 = 4, \quad \frac{24}{6} = 4$$ *The quotient of a and b is $\frac{a}{b}$.* ■

You can perform each of the operations shown in Example 1 in your head. We call this **mental math.** For more complicated problems, you may want to use a calculator.

PREVIEW

Examples

Real Life
Building Costs

Example 2 *Building a Basketball Court*

A basketball court is 46 feet wide and 84 feet long. The court has a border that is 10 feet wide. The cost of a hardwood floor is $9 per square foot. How much will it cost to put a new floor on both the court and its border?

Solution To find the cost of the floor, multiply the cost per square foot times the area (in square feet). Recall that the area of a rectangle is found by multiplying its length times its width.

Verbal Model	Total cost	=	Cost per square foot	·	Area (in square feet)

Labels
Cost per square foot = 9   ($ per square ft)
Area = Length · Width   (square ft)
Length = 10 + 84 + 10 = 104   (ft)
Width = 10 + 46 + 10 = 66   (ft)

Equation   Total cost = (9)(104)(66) = 61,776   ($)

Thus, it would cost $61,776 to put a new floor on the basket-ball court and its border. ■

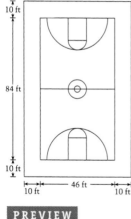

10 ft

84 ft

10 ft

10 ft   46 ft   10 ft

PREVIEW

Diagram

1.1 ▪ *Numbers and Number Operations*   **3**

Textbooks

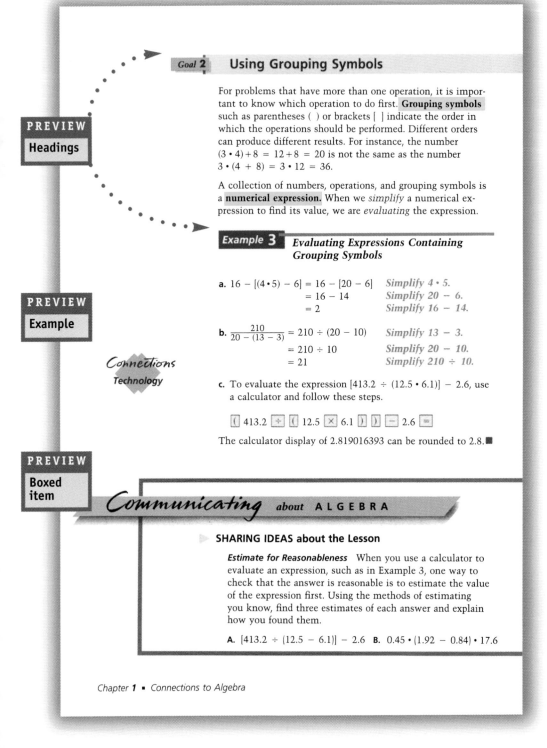

Goal 2   Using Grouping Symbols

For problems that have more than one operation, it is important to know which operation to do first. **Grouping symbols** such as parentheses ( ) or brackets [ ] indicate the order in which the operations should be performed. Different orders can produce different results. For instance, the number $(3 \cdot 4) + 8 = 12 + 8 = 20$ is not the same as the number $3 \cdot (4 + 8) = 3 \cdot 12 = 36$.

A collection of numbers, operations, and grouping symbols is a **numerical expression.** When we *simplify* a numerical expression to find its value, we are *evaluating* the expression.

Example 3   *Evaluating Expressions Containing Grouping Symbols*

a. $16 - [(4 \cdot 5) - 6] = 16 - [20 - 6]$ *Simplify 4 • 5.*
$= 16 - 14$ *Simplify 20 − 6.*
$= 2$ *Simplify 16 − 14.*

b. $\dfrac{210}{20 - (13 - 3)} = 210 \div (20 - 10)$ *Simplify 13 − 3.*
$= 210 \div 10$ *Simplify 20 − 10.*
$= 21$ *Simplify 210 ÷ 10.*

Connections
Technology

c. To evaluate the expression $[413.2 \div (12.5 \cdot 6.1)] - 2.6$, use a calculator and follow these steps.

[(413.2 ÷ [(12.5 × 6.1)])] − 2.6 =

The calculator display of 2.819016393 can be rounded to 2.8. ∎

Communicating about ALGEBRA

▷ **SHARING IDEAS about the Lesson**

Estimate for Reasonableness   When you use a calculator to evaluate an expression, such as in Example 3, one way to check that the answer is reasonable is to estimate the value of the expression first. Using the methods of estimating you know, find three estimates of each answer and explain how you found them.

A. $[413.2 \div (12.5 - 6.1)] - 2.6$ **B.** $0.45 \cdot (1.92 - 0.84) \cdot 17.6$

Plan

Take a minute now to think about what information the preview gave you. You probably learned a lot:

■ Numbers can be written as fractions, decimals, and percents.

■ The four basic number operations are addition, subtraction, multiplication, and division.

■ The results of the four basic number operations are called sum, difference, product, and quotient.

■ Grouping symbols are sometimes used in math expressions.

At this point, you have some idea of what is in the chapter. Now you need to find a reading strategy to help you get the most out of the chapter.

Reading Strategy: Visualizing and Thinking Aloud

One of the most useful strategies in math is **visualizing and thinking aloud.** The reason visualizing is so useful is that it helps you take an abstract idea (the math problem) and turn it into a concrete image. You can visualize mentally, or you can make a drawing to help you. As you draw, talk to yourself about what you're doing. By thinking aloud, you reinforce your mental processes.

Visualize

In the pages you previewed, Example 2 includes a diagram. Suppose it did not have the diagram. If you had only the word problem itself, you would probably want to draw the diagram on your own. The diagram helps you see what you are being asked to figure out.

On the next page is another example. You may need to visualize this problem before you can figure it out. You can do this in your head, or you can draw a diagram.

A garden area is 5 meters wide and 6 meters long. A gravel walkway that is 2 meters wide surrounds the garden. How much will it cost to put a fence around the outside of the walk if the fencing sells for $18 per meter?

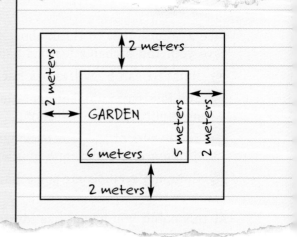

Once you figure out the perimeter of the gravel walkway, you can multiply by $18 to solve the problem.

Think Aloud

When you use words to explain what a diagram or equation means, you're thinking aloud. For example, here's how one reader wrote down her thoughts about the garden problem:

THINK ALOUD

1. I have to figure out how much it costs to put a fence around a garden. The garden is 5 meters wide and 6 meters long.
2. That means there are 2 sides of the garden 5 meters long and 2 sides 6 meters long.
3. The garden is surrounded by a walkway 2 meters wide. By adding the sides, I know that the distance around the garden without the walkway is 22 meters.
4. The walkway adds another 2 meters to each side. That's 8 more meters. So I need to add 22 and 8. That's 30 meters around.
5. $30 \cdot \$18 = \$540$ The answer must be $540. I better check.

Thinking aloud lets you do three things:

 Put the steps into words you understand.

 Listen to yourself say those words.

 Work toward a solution, one step at a time.

During Reading

Now that you have a reading purpose and strategy, go back to pages 102–104 and read the text carefully.

D Read with a Purpose

As you read, keep your purpose questions in mind: "What are number operations?" and "What do I need to know about numbers and number operations?" Consider the numerical expression in Example 3a on page 104:

$$16 - [(4 \cdot 5) - 6]$$

If you have read the instruction under the heading Goal 2, Using Grouping Symbols, you know that the operations within parentheses and brackets must be performed first. For easy problems, you can often do these operations using mental math. Thus, $4 \cdot 5$ becomes 20 in your mind, and once you subtract 6 from this, you know that the bracketed numbers represent 14. It is now easy to subtract 14 from 16 to evaluate the expression.

You may want to draw a diagram of the bracketed operations to help you visualize the problem. Thus, $[(4 \cdot 5) - 6]$ might be drawn as:

VISUALIZING

Sometimes, with an easy problem, you won't need to make a drawing. But if you ever get stuck, visualizing a problem may help you solve it.

How Math Textbooks Are Organized

Math texts are organized by chapters, with each chapter covering a major topic. Often, the chapters are further divided into sections that might be numbered with decimals: 1.1, 1.2, 1.3, and so on. Each decimal indicates a new subheading in the chapter.

Usually, a math chapter begins with an opening explanation, which is followed by sample problems. These problems may include graphs and diagrams to make the explanations clearer. These elements are followed by exercises.

ORGANIZATION

1. *opening explanation*
2. *sample problems*
3. *graphs and diagrams*
4. *exercises*

Notice these four parts in the sample math pages. As you read a math chapter, start with the explanation and then carefully study the sample problems and the graphs and diagrams, if any. Place a piece of paper over the answer section to make sure you're following the explanation. If you find that you have difficulty with the sample exercises, go back to the opening explanation and reread it carefully. You need to fully understand the samples before you can proceed to the practice exercises.

E Connect

You may think that math has no connection with real life, but you couldn't be more wrong. You use *addition* and *decimals* when you figure out how much money you'll need for a new jacket or outfit. You use *fractions* and *division* when you split a few pizzas among a group of friends. Can you think of other examples of how you use math in your daily life? Make it a habit to turn abstract problems into real-life ones. Here's an example.

REAL-LIFE PROBLEM

ABSTRACT PROBLEM	REAL-LIFE PROBLEM
$(3 \bullet 4) + 8$	Suppose 3 different groups of 4 people each arrived at a party. Then 8 people came individually. How many people would be at the party?

Textbooks

After you make a connection like this and "translate" the problem into something meaningful to you, solve it. (The answer is 20.)

After Reading

When you finish reading a math lesson, try to recall the key ideas of the lesson.

F Pause and Reflect

Think back to your reading purpose. Ask yourself what you've learned about numbers and number operations.

Looking Back

■ Do I understand the key vocabulary?

■ Can I explain how to use grouping symbols?

■ Are the sample problems clear to me?

■ Would I do well on a test that covered this material?

G Reread

It is probably safe to say that you can't answer *yes* to all these questions. At this point, you should go back to the pages with the examples, exercises, or terms that are still not clear to you.

With difficult material, **note-taking** is an excellent rereading strategy. Go back over the chapter, taking Key Word Notes. For example, you may have forgotten what the word *quotient* means. Draw a vertical line down the middle of a sheet of notebook paper. Write the heading "Key Words" over the first column. Write "Examples" over the second column. Instead of using the examples that are in the book, write your own. This will help you think through the material and set it firmly in your mind.

KEY WORD NOTES

NUMBERS AND NUMBER OPERATIONS

Key Words	Examples
whole numbers	7, 8, 9
fractions	$1/3$, $5/8$, $7/9$
decimals	0.3, 0.8, 3.7
percent	25%, 42%, 100%
sum	$10 + 3 = 13$
difference	$48 - 7 = 41$
product	$11 \cdot 5 = 55$
quotient	$48 \div 6 = 8$
grouping symbols	$(6 \cdot 7), (18 - 3)$
numerical expression	$(5 \cdot 3) - (9 - 4) + [(2 + 7) \div 3]$

H Remember

You will probably get regular homework assignments in your math class. Be sure that you do each one. If you get behind in math, it's difficult to catch up again. Here are two suggestions to help you remember what you've learned.

1. Form a Study Group

Get together with a few friends and talk about what you're learning in math. Help one another learn difficult concepts by discussing them and by comparing notes taken in class. Turn abstract problems into word problems based on real-life situations.

2. Create Practice Tests

Put yourself in the teacher's place, and make up a test. Decide what questions would be important. Go over your test with a partner, and then go over your partner's test. This is a very effective way of preparing for the real test.

PRACTICE TEST

Numbers and Number Operations

1. What are three ways to write the number 1/4?

2. Write the decimal form of 2/3 rounded to two decimal places.

3. What are the four basic number operations?

4. Evaluate the following numerical expressions.
   a. 48 – (32 + 6)
   b. 74 + [(3 • 4) – 2]
   c. 20 – [(20 + 6) – 9]

Answers: 1. 1/4, .25, 25% **2.** .66
3. add, subtract, multiply, divide
4. a. 10 **b.** 84 **c.** 3

Textbooks

Summing Up

When you read a math lesson, use the strategy of **visualizing and thinking aloud.** To help visualize a problem, try these tools:

- ▪ Sketch or Diagram
- ▪ Think Aloud
- ▪ Key Word Notes

As you read, remember to look for the typical **organization of a math chapter** into four parts. Then, after reading, use the rereading strategy of **note-taking.**

111

Focus on Foreign Language

You will find some special challenges in a foreign language textbook. For one thing, the text is in English *and* a foreign language. For another, you are not only expected to memorize foreign words, you have to learn how to pronounce and write them as well. But don't let this subject rattle you. You probably know more about reading foreign language texts than you think.

Goals

Here you'll learn how to:

✔ **read and understand foreign language textbooks**

✔ **remember new vocabulary and grammar rules**

Before Reading

Chapters in foreign language textbooks usually include these elements:

■ new vocabulary and grammar rules

■ assignments in speaking and writing

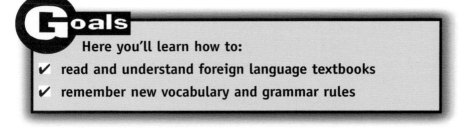

Previewing the chapter will help you get an idea of what you'll be covering. Here you'll read part of a Spanish textbook. As you preview, look for these items:

Preview Checklist

✔ the title and headings
✔ the objectives
✔ any photos and captions
✔ any key terms and ideas in boldface or repeated

PREVIEW
Title

PREVIEW
Objectives

PREVIEW
Photo and captions

¡A describir!

VOCABULARIO Y GRAMÁTICA

OBJECTIVES
• Describe people and places

Cuidad de Nueva York Look at the pictures and read about these teenagers in New York City.

Ⓐ ¿Cómo son los jóvenes? ¿Qué tienen?

Carlos

Linda

Panza, el perro

Raúl

Sofía

Carlos es alto, de pelo castaño. Tiene un suéter verde.

Linda es baja y delgada. Tiene pelo rubio y largo. Su suéter es amarillo y su falda es de muchos colores.

Raúl tiene una camisa anaranjada y jeans. Es muy guapo.

Sofía tiene pelo corto. Usa un vestido azul y una bolsa morada.

Panza, el perro, no es delgado. Es gordo. También es feo.

6 seis
Etapa preliminar

113

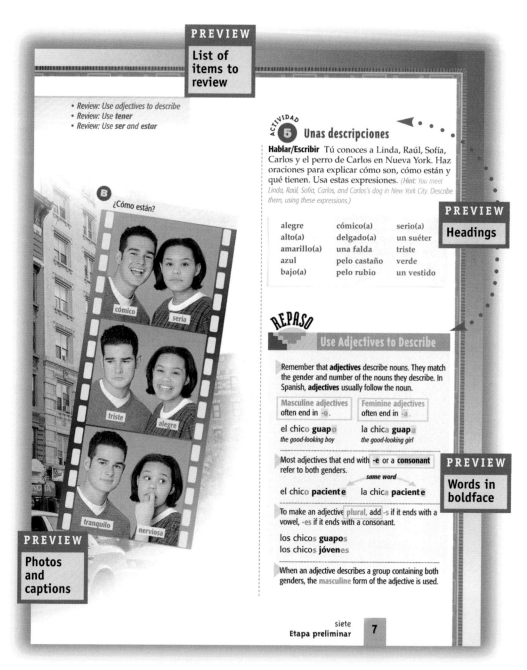

PREVIEW

List of items to review

- Review: Use adjectives to describe
- Review: Use **tener**
- Review: Use **ser** and **estar**

B

¿Cómo están?

cómico   seria

triste   alegre

tranquilo   nerviosa

PREVIEW

Photos and captions

ACTIVIDAD

5 Unas descripciones

Hablar/Escribir Tú conoces a Linda, Raúl, Sofía, Carlos y el perro de Carlos en Nueva York. Haz oraciones para explicar cómo son, cómo están y qué tienen. Usa estas expresiones. *(Hint: You meet Linda, Raúl, Sofía, Carlos, and Carlos's dog in New York City. Describe them, using these expressions.)*

PREVIEW

Headings

alegre	cómico(a)	serio(a)
alto(a)	delgado(a)	un suéter
amarillo(a)	una falda	triste
azul	pelo castaño	verde
bajo(a)	pelo rubio	un vestido

REPASO

Use Adjectives to Describe

Remember that **adjectives** describe nouns. They match the gender and number of the nouns they describe. In Spanish, **adjectives** usually follow the noun.

Masculine adjectives often end in -o .	Feminine adjectives often end in -a .
el chico **guap**o	la chica **guap**a
the good-looking boy	*the good-looking girl*

Most adjectives that end with **-e** or a **consonant** refer to both genders.

same word

el chico **pacient**e   la chica **pacient**e

PREVIEW

Words in boldface

To make an adjective plural, add -s if it ends with a vowel, -es if it ends with a consonant.

los chicos **guapo**s
los chicos **jóven**es

When an adjective describes a group containing both genders, the masculine form of the adjective is used.

siete **7**
Etapa preliminar

You probably learned a great deal from your preview.

- adjectives that describe males end in *o*
- adjectives that describe females end in *a*
- adjectives that end with *e* or a consonant refer to both genders

Since the objective on the first page of the Spanish lesson is to describe people and places, one way to organize words is by making a Web.

114

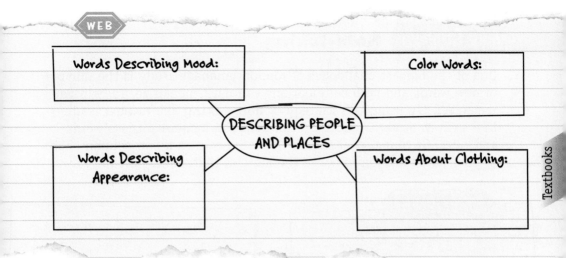

WEB

| Words Describing Mood: | Color Words: |

DESCRIBING PEOPLE AND PLACES

| Words Describing Appearance: | Words About Clothing: |

Textbooks

A Web is useful when you know you will be studying one big idea or new vocabulary. You can cluster words, rules, or other information about the topic, keeping similar things together. Try not to be concerned with the number of boxes you make at this point. You can add more as you read the chapter, or you can leave some blank.

Sometimes, you might find that a Web doesn't help you, particularly if you're concentrating on learning verbs. When this happens, choose another tool.

Reading Strategy: **Note-taking**

One of the biggest challenges of foreign language study is the number of new words and verb conjugations you must memorize. To help you remember, try using the strategy of **note-taking** and using a reading tool such as Study Cards. They can help you memorize these words and rules. Of course, you can write these notes in a two-column chart in your notebook, too. Choose the method that works best for you.

STUDY CARDS

yellow

amarillo(a)

to have = tener

tengo   tenemos
tienes tenéis
tiene   tienen

During Reading

With a reading plan and a strategy, you are ready to begin reading the chapter. As you do so, jot down notes in your Web. Remember that these notes are for your own use. They do not have to be perfect. You can always come back later, when you are rereading, and add or rearrange details.

What follows is a Web one reader made based on the Spanish lesson shown earlier. Use this as an example of how you would fill out a Web based on your own foreign language textbook.

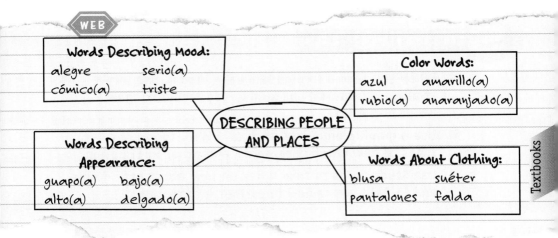

WEB

Words Describing Mood:
alegre   serio(a)
cómico(a)   triste

Color Words:
azul   amarillo(a)
rubio(a)   anaranjado(a)

Words Describing Appearance:
guapo(a)   bajo(a)
alto(a)   delgado(a)

DESCRIBING PEOPLE AND PLACES

Words About Clothing:
blusa   suéter
pantalones falda

Textbooks

After Reading

Take time to reflect after you read a foreign language lesson. Figure out what you need to go over again, and then do some rereading. Rereading is a normal part of reading foreign language textbooks. For instance, you may want to review the sections on idioms.

No matter what foreign language you're studying, one of the biggest challenges is learning idioms. An *idiom* is an expression that cannot be understood by the individual meanings of the words. English idioms, such as "slip of the tongue," or "under the weather" are usually clear to English speakers. Idioms in a foreign language are hard for English speakers to remember. Again, use Study Cards, one for each idiom. Write the idiom on the front of the card and its meaning on the back.

REVIEW TIPS

1. Look at your notes or organizers.
Do your notes make sense to you? Are they clear? If not, go back to the chapter and add any information that will clarify your notes or organizers.

3. Play a game.
With a partner, write all the new words you learned in the chapter on small pieces of paper. Take turns picking a word and using it in a sentence.

2. Make up a practice test.
One of the best ways to study is to make up a test. This is a good partner activity. You can answer each other's questions. Here are a few examples of the types of questions you might make up:

- How would you say "the good-looking boy" in Spanish?
- What does *pelo rojo* mean?
- What is the third-person singular form of the verb *tener*?

- When you read a foreign language lesson, use the strategy of note-taking to help you memorize new words and rules.

- Use a graphic organizer, such as a Web, to group rules, types of new vocabulary words, and other information.

- Use Study Cards to take notes on new words and idioms and to help you review important information.

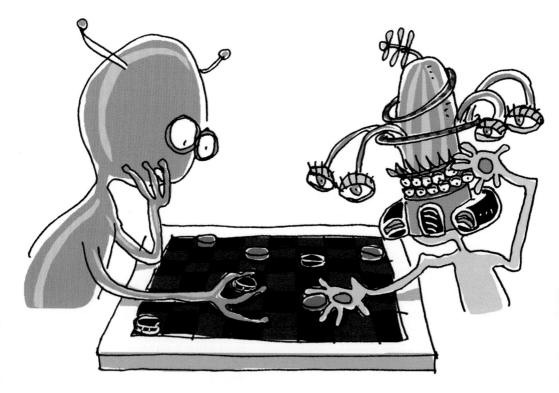

Focus on Science Concepts

Science textbooks are filled with concepts. A concept in science is another word for a general idea. For example, "gases such as carbon dioxide cause the earth's atmosphere to trap solar radiation" is a major concept in science. Understanding science concepts can be much easier if you learn a few helpful tools.

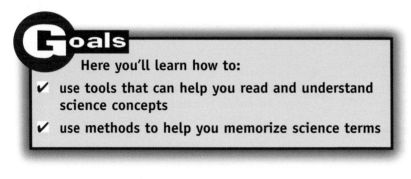

Goals

Here you'll learn how to:

✔ **use tools that can help you read and understand science concepts**

✔ **use methods to help you memorize science terms**

Before Reading

Many science concepts you'll read about involve two things:

▪ vocabulary you'll want to remember

▪ a process or series of steps to read about or to follow

Previewing material will give you a basic idea of what you'll be studying. Here you'll read the beginning of a chapter about the scientific process. As you read, look for these things:

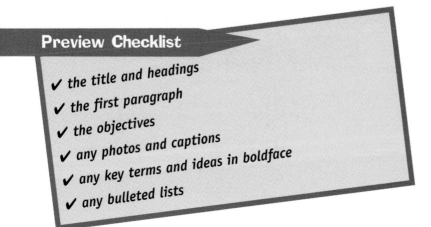

Preview Checklist

✔ the title and headings

✔ the first paragraph

✔ the objectives

✔ any photos and captions

✔ any key terms and ideas in boldface

✔ any bulleted lists

PREVIEW
Title

PREVIEW
Headings

Section 1-3

The Scientific Process

PREVIEW
First
paragraph

Objectives

- **Describe** the stages common to scientific investigations. (pp. 14–20)
- **Distinguish** between forming a hypothesis and making a prediction. (p. 16)
- **Differentiate** a control group from an experimental group and an independent variable from a dependent variable. (p. 17)
- **Define** the word *theory* as used by a scientist. (p. 19)

PREVIEW
Objectives

Key Terms

observation
hypothesis
prediction
pH
experiment
control group
independent variable
dependent variable
theory

PREVIEW
Key terms

Science Is Based on Careful Observation

Recognizing the properties of living organisms and knowing why biology is important in your world are good first steps in your exploration of biology. All scientists, including biologists, have a certain way of investigating the world. Studying an actual scientific investigation is an exciting way to learn how science is done. Our story begins many years ago with two biologists, David Bradford and John Harte, but the story continues to develop even today.

Shared observations help to solve scientific puzzles

In the summer of 1988, Bradford reflected on the silence that surrounded him. He had spent the summer looking for a small frog in the many lakes of the Sequoia & Kings Canyon National Parks. The frog had lived in the parks' lakes for as long as anyone had kept records. In the last count of the frog's populations, the frogs had been everywhere. Now, for some reason, they had disappeared from 98 percent of the lakes.

Observation is the act of noting or perceiving objects or events using the senses. As Bradford reported his observations to other biologists, he found that local populations of amphibians (frogs, toads, and salamanders) elsewhere were also disappearing. Amphibians have been around for 370 million years. The disappearance of amphibians from their natural homes sounded an alarm among biologists that something was seriously damaging the environment. Amphibians are particularly sensitive to their environment; their moist skin absorbs chemicals from water.

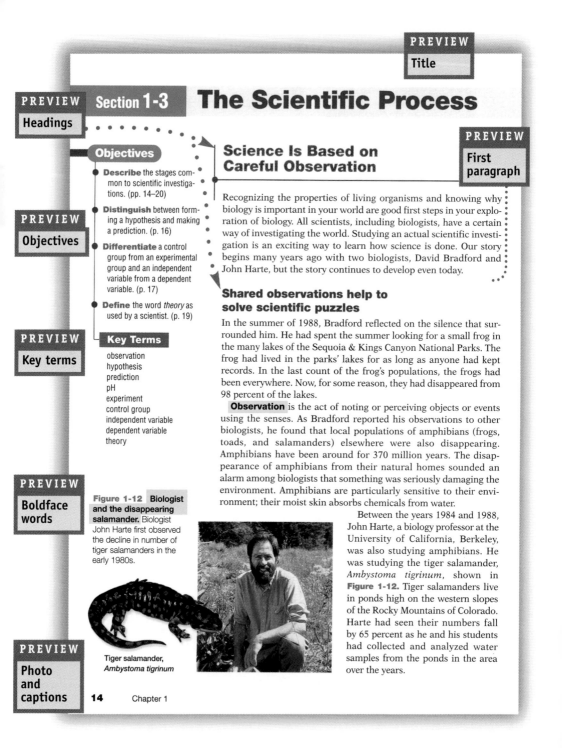

Figure 1-12 Biologist and the disappearing salamander. Biologist John Harte first observed the decline in number of tiger salamanders in the early 1980s.

Tiger salamander, *Ambystoma tigrinum*

Between the years 1984 and 1988, John Harte, a biology professor at the University of California, Berkeley, was also studying amphibians. He was studying the tiger salamander, *Ambystoma tigrinum*, shown in **Figure 1-12.** Tiger salamanders live in ponds high on the western slopes of the Rocky Mountains of Colorado. Harte had seen their numbers fall by 65 percent as he and his students had collected and analyzed water samples from the ponds in the area over the years.

PREVIEW
Boldface
words

PREVIEW
Photo
and
captions

14   Chapter 1

PREVIEW

Headings

Several Stages Are Common to Scientific Investigations

Harte wanted to discover the facts surrounding the disappearance of the salamanders. Like other scientists, Harte began a scientific investigation that combined knowledge, imagination, and intuition to get a sense of what might be true. Even though scientists might expect certain results, they do not form conclusions until they have enough evidence to support them.

Although there is no single "scientific method," all scientific investigations can be said to have common stages: collecting observations, asking questions, forming hypotheses and making predictions, confirming predictions (with controlled experiments when appropriate), and drawing conclusions. These stages are summarized in **Figure 1-13.**

internet**connect**

SC*LINKS.*
NSTA

TOPIC: Biology careers
GO TO: www.scilinks.org
KEYWORD: HX015

Textbooks

Collecting observations

The heart of scientific investigation is careful observation. Harte had studied the Colorado salamander population for years. He had learned what they eat, how they behave, when they reproduce, and the conditions they thrive in. His students had helped him collect water samples from the ponds, as shown in Figure 1-13. Frequent visits to the ponds helped him realize the salamander population was decreasing in number. Keeping careful records of the lakes' conditions helped him find an explanation.

PREVIEW

Headings

Asking questions

Observations of the natural world often raise questions. Harte questioned why the number of salamanders was dropping. He talked to other scientists, carefully observed the organisms and environment in the Rocky Mountains of Colorado, and read scientific reports. He answered many of his questions through his observations, but some key questions remained unanswered.

In the natural world, the moisture that falls as rain and snow are neither acidic nor basic. In the Rocky Mountains of Colorado, however, the moisture is high in sulfuric acid from power plants that burn high-sulfur coal. This acidic moisture, called acid rain, is released into mountain ponds each spring when the snow melts,

PREVIEW

Boldface words

Figure 1-13 Testing the acidity of water. Asa Bradman, a student of John Harte, helps in Harte's scientific investigation by collecting water samples from a Colorado pond.

Scientific Process

- Collecting observations
- Asking questions
- Forming hypotheses and making predictions
- Confirming predictions (with experiments when needed)
- Drawing conclusions

PREVIEW

Photo and caption

PREVIEW

Bulleted list

Biology and You **15**

causing the water in the ponds to become more acidic in late May. Most of the mountains' annual moisture falls as snow. Harte thought acid rain was important in the puzzle of the declining salamander population, but he needed evidence.

From your quick preview, you have already learned a lot:

- The scientific process follows five steps or stages.
- Careful observation is important in the scientific process.
- Key terms include *observation, hypothesis,* and *prediction.*

It's important to remember what you are studying. One good way to remember science concepts is to use the strategy of outlining.

Reading Strategy: Outlining

Outlining helps you recall the information in a chapter. Start your Outline by borrowing the headings provided in the book. Add details from the text as you go along.

OUTLINE

THE SCIENTIFIC PROCESS
I.   Science Is Based on Careful Observation
     A.
     B.
II. Several Stages Are Common to Scientific Investigations
     A.
     B.

During Reading

Armed with a reading plan and a way to organize information, you are now ready to read the chapter. As you read, jot down notes in your Outline. You can use these notes later, when you review.

THE SCIENTIFIC PROCESS

I. Science Is Based on Careful Observation
   A. David Bradford noticed that amphibians were disappearing.
   B. John Harte noticed that the number of tiger salamanders was declining.

II. Several Stages Are Common to Scientific Investigations
   A. Collecting observations is first stage.
   B. Asking questions is second stage.

Textbooks

As you make your Outline, don't try to write down everything. Look for the main idea of the paragraph or paragraphs under each head or subhead in the text. Then write what you think that main idea is in your Outline.

You may want to use a Flow Chart to include information based on the science book lesson. Use this as another example of how you can take notes based on your own science book.

FLOW CHART

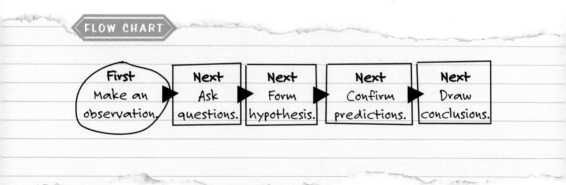

A Flow Chart shows processes or a sequence of steps. You can add specific examples to your Flow Chart as you read the chapter.

After Reading

When you're finished reading a chapter, think about what you've read. Then, go back and review. Do you understand the stages of scientific investigation and why they are important? Reread all the headings and ask yourself whether you could discuss each heading thoroughly. If you couldn't, then reread the material under that heading. You can also follow these tips to improve your understanding of the information.

REVIEW TIPS

1. Review your Flow Chart and Outline.
Is your Flow Chart clear? Does your Outline make the chapter easier to understand and remember? If not, review the chapter and add information to your Flow Chart and Outline as necessary.

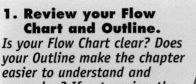

2. Have a conversation.
Talking about the material is an excellent way to test yourself. If you can explain the ideas to a partner, you have good command of them. If not, your partner can help fill in the blanks. If both of you are having trouble, a conversation will certainly point out where you need help.

Summing Up

- Science textbooks usually include a number of key terms and one or more processes.
- An Outline can help you review the main ideas of a science chapter.
- A graphic organizer, such as a Flow Chart, can also help you learn important information.

Focus on Study Questions

Study questions often appear at the end of textbook chapters. You have probably answered many of these questions.

Goals

Here you'll learn how to:

✔ follow a four-step plan when answering study questions

✔ recognize and understand key words in questions

Before Reading

Before you can answer a study question, you should have a plan. This four-step plan will help you answer any question you might come across.

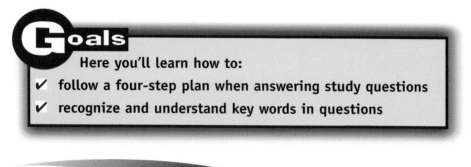

FOUR-STEP PLAN FOR STUDY QUESTIONS

Step 1: Read
Start by reading the question two or more times to make sure you know exactly what is being asked.

Step 2: Plan
Think of a way you can arrive at the answer.

Step 3: Write
Write your answer, following the strategy you chose.

Step 4: Reread and Edit
Reread the question and your answer, making sure it is clear and that it answers the question. Make any corrections that are necessary.

A good way to make sure you understand a question is visualizing and thinking aloud. Visualizing means making a picture in your mind. Thinking aloud means talking through a problem.

Visualizing and Thinking Aloud

Visualizing and thinking aloud lets you focus on how to answer a question correctly. Here's the question: How are three of the seven major themes of biology related to the life of an owl? Visualize how your answer will look.

THINK ALOUD

I know that the word <u>relate</u> has a special meaning. I have to show what three themes of biology have to do with the life of an owl. So I know that I don't have to discuss all seven major themes. Merely listing three of the themes wouldn't be enough. I have to explain three of the themes, <u>but</u> I also have to show their relation to the life of an owl.

During Reading

Some study questions are not worded as questions. They merely direct you to do something. See the chart below for a list of some key words you might come across.

KEY WORDS IN QUESTIONS

analyze *break down something into parts to examine its nature*
compare and contrast *examine in order to discover similarities and differences*
describe *tell what something looks like or give a detailed account of something*
determine *find out exactly*
draw conclusions *use facts and inferences to come to a judgment or decision*

estimate *judge or determine generally but carefully; calculate approximately*
evaluate *judge or determine the worth or value of something*
explain *make clear, plain, or understandable*
find *get by searching or making an effort*
hypothesize *assume or suppose that an unproved thing is true*
identify *name*

infer *conclude or decide from something known or assumed*
interpret *explain the meaning of*
predict *say what might happen in the future*
relate *show how one idea is connected to another*
summarize *make a brief statement or account of the main points*
synthesize *combine analysis of one thing with knowledge of another thing*

As you read a question, you should underline, highlight, or make note of the key word or words.

After Reading

Here's how one reader marked up, answered, and then corrected the answer to a question about Eliza, one of the main characters in George Bernard Shaw's play *Pygmalion*.

EXAMPLE

(Explain) how Eliza is <u>representative</u> of the beginning of the <u>women's movement</u> at the <u>start</u> of the <u>twentieth century</u>.

⊗

support
herself ⊗

characteristics

campaigned

Eliza has become independent. She has earned her living as a flower girl and plans to continue ~~to earn her living.~~ She is outspoken and not afraid of what people think of her. All these ~~charactistics~~ characteristics are typical of many women at the start of the twentieth century. These women challenged the ~~typical~~ roles of women, (traditional) though they were often made fun of for their views. They went out to work and publicly ~~campagned~~ campaigned for the right to vote. Some of them even went on hunger strikes to impress the public with their determination.

Sometimes, even after a careful reading of a question, you're still not sure what to do. If it is a study question, and not a test question, you're in luck because you can get some help.

1. Ask a partner for help.

Talk over the question with a study partner. Get your partner's ideas about what the question is asking.

2. Review.

Since study questions often focus on big ideas, go back and review chapter and section introductions. Then, reread the material under any heads labeled "preview," 'summary," or "review." Textbook writers often state these big ideas at the beginning or end of a chapter. You just have to know where to look for them.

Summing Up

■ Use a four-step plan for working with study questions: read, plan, write, and reread and edit.

■ Thinking aloud can help you determine what the study question means.

■ Get help from a partner if you still don't understand the question.

Focus on Word Problems

In a way, word problems are more challenging than math problems that include just numbers or diagrams. That's because you have to set up the problem yourself before you can solve it. But word problems are not as difficult to interpret as you may think.

Goals

Here you'll learn how to:

✔ use a four-step plan to solve word problems

✔ visualize what the problem asks for

Before Reading

The trick to solving word problems is to read the question very carefully. Sometimes word problems have extra information in them—information that you won't need to solve the problem. Sometimes every word is important, so read carefully.

You can follow the same basic four-step plan described in "Focus on Questions" for even the most complicated word problems:

FOUR-STEP PLAN FOR WORD PROBLEMS

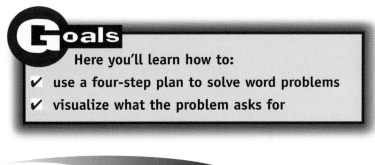

Step 1: Read
The first step is to read the problem several times. Be sure it makes sense to you.

Step 2: Plan
Determine a strategy that will be useful in getting the answer.

Step 3: Solve
Use your strategy to solve the problem. If your strategy does not work, try something else.

Step 4: Check
The last step is to check your work. Is your answer reasonable?

Understanding Word Problems

Do a preliminary reading of the problem. Do not make any notes at this stage. As you read the problem for the first time, think about these questions:

What is the topic?

What is given? What information do I know?

What is the "unknown factor"? What am I supposed to find?

Making Notes

Read the problem a second time. As you read, make notes. If you can, use a highlighter, or you can make notes on a separate sheet of paper. Here's an example.

EXAMPLE	NOTES
Sally wants to paint the walls in her room. The room is 15 feet by 12 feet, and the walls are 9 feet high. Each gallon of the paint she wants to buy covers 400 square feet and costs $24.95. This paint is also sold by the quart at $9.99. How much paint should Sally buy?	**TOPIC:** paint **GIVEN:** size of room, amount of coverage for each gallon **TO FIND:** amount of paint needed

After reading the problem, choose a strategy that will help you solve it. One of the best strategies to use with word problems is to visualize, or make a mental picture of, the problem as you think through it.

Reading Strategy: Visualizing and Thinking Aloud

Visualizing means making a picture in your mind and drawing what you "see." **Thinking aloud** means talking through a problem, either mentally or aloud. This is a useful strategy when there are no diagrams in your textbook. Use the information in the problem to draw a picture of the problem.

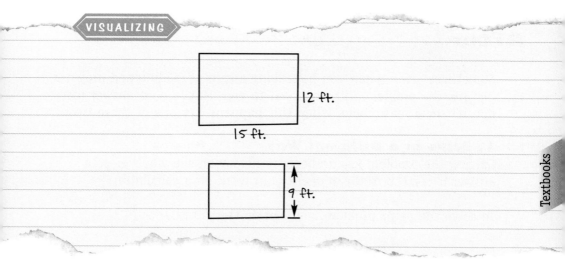

Textbooks

A drawing like this can help you see the relationship between the pieces of the problem. It can help you figure out how to write an equation when it's time to solve the problem.

During Reading

After you've read the problem and decided on a plan, you can begin to solve it. With your notes and your drawing, write an equation that will help you solve the problem. Thinking aloud can help.

THINK ALOUD

Two walls are 15 feet wide and 9 feet high. Two walls are 12 feet wide and 9 feet high. I need to find the area of each wall and then add the areas of all four walls to find the total number of square feet that have to be painted. So,

$(15 \cdot 9) + (15 \cdot 9) + (12 \cdot 9) + (12 \cdot 9) = $ area of all four walls

After I figure out the area, I need to determine how much paint is needed. If one gallon covers 400 square feet, then one quart (1/4 of a gallon) will cover 100 square feet (1/4 of 400). By working the equation, I find out that the area of all four walls is 486 square feet, so one gallon and one quart would be enough paint. The information about the price of the paint is just extra data that I don't need to solve the problem.

131

After Reading

Sometimes, even when you have done a careful reading and drawn a picture, the problem still isn't clear to you. Maybe your answer just doesn't seem reasonable. When this happens, try one of these tips:

1. Solve in a Different Way

Solving the problem in another way helps you see whether your answer is correct. You can check your work on a calculator.

To solve the paint problem, you can do this:

> Multiply 15 and 9 and 2 (270)
> Multiply 12 and 9 and 2 (216)
> Add 270 and 216 (486)

If one gallon covers 400 square feet, then you still have to cover 86 square feet. Since one-fourth of a gallon is a quart, divide 400 by 4 to get 100. One-fourth of a gallon, or one quart, will cover 86 square feet.

2. Estimate, Using Simpler Numbers

Sometimes, it's a good idea to round off numbers so you can estimate the answer. Then work the problem. If the answer is somewhat close to the estimate, then you know it's probably right.

EXAMPLE

Darla earns $5.75 per hour for baby-sitting. She wants to buy a new dresser for her room. The dresser costs $420. How many hours will Darla have to baby-sit before she can get the dresser?

Suppose you're not sure about how to solve this problem. You might round off the $5.75 to $6.00. It's easier to divide $420 by $6. You can easily see that it will take Darla at least 70 hours of baby-sitting to earn enough for the dresser. In fact, she will have to work a little more than 73 hours.

3. Work Backward

If you're given the answer ahead of time, this method works. You can work backward to figure out the steps that lead up to the answer.

> **EXAMPLE**
>
> Tom got to the library at 5:45. It took him 30 minutes to get from his house to the store, he spent 25 minutes at the store, and then it took him 15 minutes to get from the store to the library. What time did he leave the house?

You can solve this problem in several ways: you can add up the minutes (30 + 25 + 15 = 70), convert them to hour and minutes (70 minutes = 1 hour, 10 minutes), and subtract that number from 5:45 (5:45 - 1:10 = 4:35). Or you can work backward.

THINK ALOUD

If I work backward, starting at 5:45 and subtracting 30 minutes, that puts me at 5:15. Then I subtract 25 minutes from 5:15. That puts me at 4:50. Finally, I subtract 15 minutes from 4:50, putting me at 4:35. I can check my answer by adding the minutes back to 4:35 to see if I come out at 5:45.

4. Work with a Partner

If the problem is not on a test, you can talk over the problem with a partner. Each of you can help the other by sharing ideas, notes, and sketches. Putting your ideas into words can help make them clearer to both of you.

Summing Up

- Use a four-step plan to solve word problems: read, plan, solve, and check.

- Draw a picture and think aloud to help you keep track of the information.

- Try different methods of solving problems, such as using a calculator, estimating, working backward, and working with a partner.

Elements of Textbooks

As you study various textbooks, you see that they have many different elements. You notice headings, photos and illustrations with captions, glossaries, indexes, and other items that are designed to help you learn the material being presented. Some textbooks have a greater variety of elements than others do.

To get the most out of your reading, you need to know what these elements are, what they are designed to do, and how you should use them. Though you have probably seen these elements many times, take a few minutes to review them.

Elements of Textbooks

Chapter Previews

Most textbooks have a preview at the beginning of each chapter. It is a quick summary of all the important points in the chapter.

EXAMPLE

List of the themes in the chapter

World map showing highlighted area

Mini table of contents

Map showing important locations

DESCRIPTION

Take a few minutes to go through **chapter previews.** You might feel like jumping in and starting to read the chapter, but don't skip the previews. They are like a road map, in a way. They give you goals and a sense of direction.

DEFINITION

Chapter previews are brief sections at the beginning of chapters. They can be part of a page, or they may go on for several pages. Their purpose is to give you an idea of what you will be reading.

Charts and Graphs

Like maps, charts and graphs use pictures and symbols to present information.

EXAMPLE

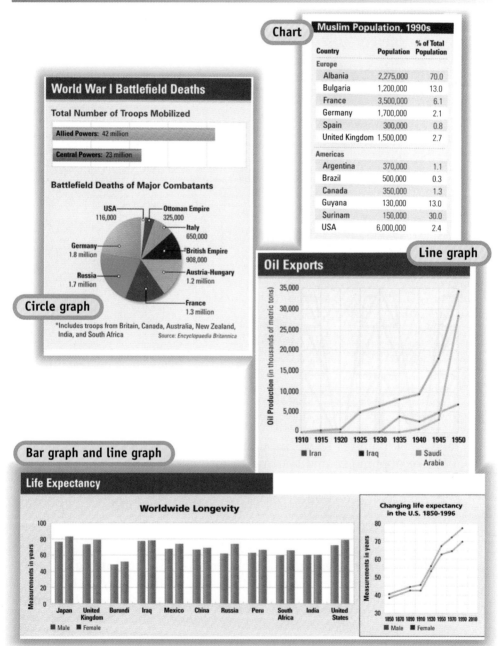

Chart

Muslim Population, 1990s

Country	Population	% of Total Population
Europe		
Albania	2,275,000	70.0
Bulgaria	1,200,000	13.0
France	3,500,000	6.1
Germany	1,700,000	2.1
Spain	300,000	0.8
United Kingdom	1,500,000	2.7
Americas		
Argentina	370,000	1.1
Brazil	500,000	0.3
Canada	350,000	1.3
Guyana	130,000	13.0
Surinam	150,000	30.0
USA	6,000,000	2.4

World War I Battlefield Deaths

Total Number of Troops Mobilized

Allied Powers: 42 million

Central Powers: 23 million

Battlefield Deaths of Major Combatants

USA 116,000
Ottoman Empire 325,000
Italy 650,000
Germany 1.8 million
British Empire 908,000
Russia 1.7 million
Austria-Hungary 1.2 million
France 1.3 million

Circle graph

*Includes troops from Britain, Canada, Australia, New Zealand, India, and South Africa
Source: Encyclopaedia Britannica

Line graph

Oil Exports

Oil Production (in thousands of metric tons)

1910 1915 1920 1925 1930 1935 1940 1945 1950

■ Iran   ■ Iraq   ■ Saudi Arabia

Bar graph and line graph

Life Expectancy

Worldwide Longevity

Measurements in years

Japan | United Kingdom | Burundi | Iraq | Mexico | China | Russia | Peru | South Africa | India | United States

■ Male   ■ Female

Changing life expectancy in the U.S. 1850-1996

Measurements in years

1850 1870 1890 1910 1930 1950 1970 1990 2010

■ Male   ■ Female

Charts and Graphs, continued

DESCRIPTION

Charts and graphs are efficient ways to show a lot of information. You are not expected to remember every bit of information in a chart or graph. Use charts and graphs more as resources.

Each chart or graph has a main point. Read the title to determine the main point. One way to do this is to turn the title of the chart or graph into a question, and then answer that question by reading the chart. For example, after looking at the circle graph, you might ask yourself, "Which nation suffered the most battlefield deaths in World War I, and which suffered the fewest?" The answer to the question is a way of summarizing the main idea of the graph, which you might want to include in your notes.

SUMMARY NOTES

During World War I, Germany suffered the largest number of battlefield deaths, and the United States suffered the fewest.

When you look at a line graph or a bar graph, read the title, the labels on the vertical and horizontal axes, and any other text. Also pay attention to any colors, patterns, or symbols. Then summarize the main point of the graph in your own words.

DEFINITION

Charts give information, show processes, or make comparisons, usually in column form. **Graphs** use lines, symbols, and pictures to show information.

Footnotes

A footnote is used to give additional information about a point made, a word used, or an idea presented in the text.

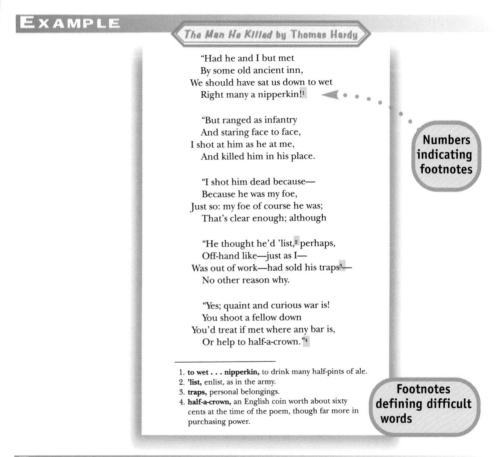

The Man He Killed by Thomas Hardy

"Had he and I but met
By some old ancient inn,
We should have sat us down to wet
Right many a nipperkin![1]

"But ranged as infantry
And staring face to face,
I shot at him as he at me,
And killed him in his place.

"I shot him dead because—
Because he was my foe,
Just so: my foe of course he was;
That's clear enough; although

"He thought he'd 'list,[2] perhaps,
Off-hand like—just as I—
Was out of work—had sold his traps[3]—
No other reason why.

"Yes; quaint and curious war is!
You shoot a fellow down
You'd treat if met where any bar is,
Or help to half-a-crown."[4]

1. **to wet . . . nipperkin,** to drink many half-pints of ale.
2. **'list,** enlist, as in the army.
3. **traps,** personal belongings.
4. **half-a-crown,** an English coin worth about sixty cents at the time of the poem, though far more in purchasing power.

Numbers indicating footnotes

Footnotes defining difficult words

DESCRIPTION

Footnotes are signaled by a small raised number in the text. This number corresponds to a number at the bottom or side of the page, which precedes the explanation or reference. Often, footnotes are used to define and pronounce difficult words, as in this example. Footnotes are also used to cite references or sources for the material in the text or to give further explanation of the material.

DEFINITION

Footnotes are numbered notes or comments at the bottom or side of a page, referring to something on the page.

Glossaries

A glossary is a mini-dictionary, listing the specialized terms of the subject. Glossaries are usually located at the end of a textbook but before the index. Boldface words throughout the book are defined in the glossary.

EXAMPLE

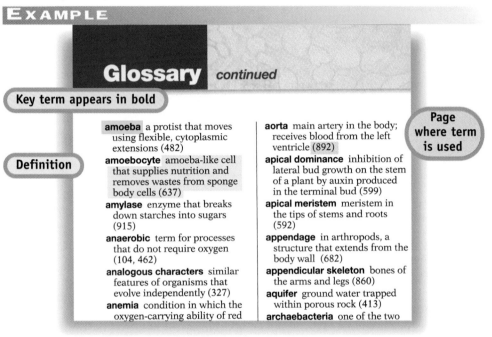

Glossary *continued*

Key term appears in bold

Definition

Page where term is used

amoeba a protist that moves using flexible, cytoplasmic extensions (482)

amoebocyte amoeba-like cell that supplies nutrition and removes wastes from sponge body cells (637)

amylase enzyme that breaks down starches into sugars (915)

anaerobic term for processes that do not require oxygen (104, 462)

analogous characters similar features of organisms that evolve independently (327)

anemia condition in which the oxygen-carrying ability of red

aorta main artery in the body; receives blood from the left ventricle (892)

apical dominance inhibition of lateral bud growth on the stem of a plant by auxin produced in the terminal bud (599)

apical meristem meristem in the tips of stems and roots (592)

appendage in arthropods, a structure that extends from the body wall (682)

appendicular skeleton bones of the arms and legs (860)

aquifer ground water trapped within porous rock (413)

archaebacteria one of the two

DESCRIPTION

Glossaries are listings, dictionary-style, of the specialized vocabulary of a subject. Usually, every word in the glossary is defined when it is first used in the text. But what if you encounter the word again and can't remember the meaning? Rather than look back through the text for the definition, check in the glossary. It's faster and more efficient.

DEFINITION

Glossaries are alphabetical lists of the key terms in the text. They might include names of people, events, and places as well. They are useful tools to help you understand the specialized language of the subject.

Indexes

The index is at the very back of a textbook, after the glossary. It lists every important idea, term, definition, person, and place mentioned in the text, telling the pages on which it is found.

EXAMPLE

Index

Explanation of symbols

An *i* preceding a page reference in italics indicates that there is an illustration, and usually text information as well, on that page. An *m* or a *c* preceding an italic page reference indicates a map or a chart, as well as text information on that page.

Entry

Page where word appears

Abbasid Dynasty, 240, 279
Abbas the Great (Safavid shah), *i 449*
Aborigines, 367, 665, 667
Abraham, 72, 234, 235, 237
absolute monarchs, 517, 540. *See also* monarchy.
absolute ruler, 147, 532
absolutism. *See also* monarchy.
    causes and effects of, *c 540*
Abu-Bakr (caliph), 238
accommodation, 961
acropolis, 115
Addams, Jane, 652
Adulis, 200
Adulyadej, King Bhumibol (Thailand), *i 525*
Aegean Sea, 67
Aeschylus, 123
Afghanistan, 875
Africa, *m 190, 191, m 194, m 364, m 368, i 502, m 974. See also* South Africa; Africa, East; Africa, North; Africa, West.
    age-set system, 369
    Christianity in, *m 191,* 200–201
    civilizations of, 190–205, *c 206*
    comparative size of, *m 207*
    cultural developments of, 197, 200–201
    democracy in, 916–920
    desertification, 195

in World War II, 824, 835
Africa, East, 190–205, *m 379. See also* Africa.
    cultural blending in, *c 448*
    Islamic influences on, 379–380
    slavery in, 380
    Swahili, 378
    trade in, 378–379
Africa, North, *m 789. See also* Africa.
    Islam, 369–374
    Maghrib, 369
    Muslim reformers, 368
    in World War II, 824–825, 835–836
Africa, West, 197–198, *m 372, m 383. See also* Africa.
    empires of, *m 364*
    gold-salt trade, 371
    societies in, 197–198
Afrikaners, 468
afterlife. *See* burial rites.
Age of Faith, 341, 343
    death of, 361
Age of Reason. *See* Enlightenment.
agricultural revolution, 14–16, 633–634
agriculture, *m 15, c 215. See also* farming.
    in Africa, 195–196
    in Americas, 213–215
    beginnings, *m 15*
    in ancient China, 290
    in China, 473

Algeria
    early art of, *i 13*
    FLN, 899
    independence of, 899, *c 906*
Allah, 234, 236, *c 248*
Allies
    World War I, 748
    World War II, 829, *m 836*
almanac, *c 986,* 987–989
Almohad Dynasty, 364, 370, *c 382*
Almoravid Dynasty, 364, 369–370, *c 382*
alphabet
    ancient and modern, *i 69*
    Cyrillic, 273
    Greek, 69
    Phoenician, *c 79*
Amazons, 116
ambergris, 378
"America," 484. *See* the Americas; United States.
American Revolution, *c 568,* 563–569
    causes of, 563–564
    effects of, 567, *c 598*
    Enlightenment, role of, 564
    French influence on, 565
Americas, the, *c 224, c 412, i 502. See also* Aztec Civilization; Mayan Civilization; North America.
    African influence on, 499
    agriculture's effect on, 213–215

Subentry under main entry

DESCRIPTION

Indexes are search tools, similar to "search engines" on the Internet but located at the end of a book. An index is very useful when you are looking for specific terms or names.

DEFINITION

Indexes are alphabetical listings of a book's contents, indicating the pages on which each topic, term, name, or place is discussed.

Maps

This map shows Europe just before the start of World War I. By "reading" the map, you can determine which countries were allies, which were enemies, and which were neutral.

EXAMPLE

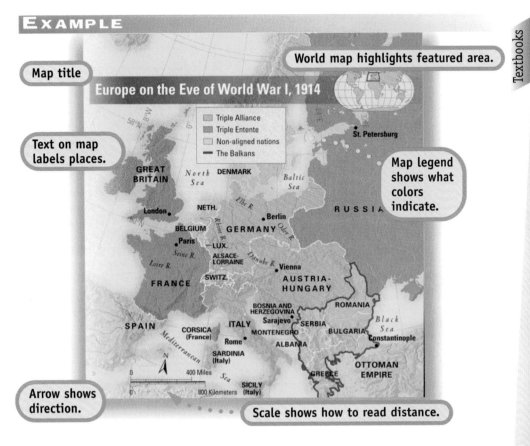

World map highlights featured area.

Map title

Europe on the Eve of World War I, 1914

Text on map labels places.

Map legend shows what colors indicate.

Triple Alliance
Triple Entente
Non-aligned nations
The Balkans

St. Petersburg

GREAT BRITAIN   *North Sea*   DENMARK   *Baltic Sea*   R U S S I A

London   NETH.   *Elbe R.*   Berlin
BELGIUM   *Rhine R.*   GERMANY   *Oder R.*
Paris   LUX.
ALSACE-LORRAINE   *Danube R.*   Vienna
Seine R.
Loire R.   SWITZ.   AUSTRIA-HUNGARY
FRANCE

BOSNIA AND HERZEGOVINA   ROMANIA
SPAIN   ITALY   Sarajevo   SERBIA   *Black Sea*
CORSICA (France)   MONTENEGRO   BULGARIA   Constantinople
Rome   ALBANIA
Mediterranean
SARDINIA (Italy)
N
0   400 Miles   *Sea*   GREECE   OTTOMAN EMPIRE
0   800 Kilometers   SICILY (Italy)

Arrow shows direction.

Scale shows how to read distance.

DESCRIPTION

Maps are visual presentations of an area. Maps can show political boundaries (such as borders separating countries) and natural features (such as lakes, rivers, and seas). The title of a map tells the main idea, and the legend (or map key) tells you what the symbols on the map mean. As you read a map, try to put into your own words what the map is depicting.

DEFINITION

Maps present information in visual form and show where something is or where something happened.

Photos and Illustrations

Photos and illustrations can give you a quick idea of what you will find in a chapter.

EXAMPLE

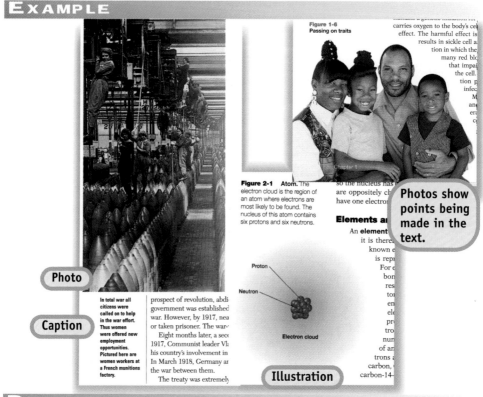

Photo

Caption

Photos show points being made in the text.

Illustration

DESCRIPTION

When you look at the **photos and illustrations** in a textbook, you can get an idea of the unit or chapter content. Photos and illustrations can tell you quickly what it might take many words to explain. The text below or next to the photo or illustration is called the *caption*. A caption explains the reason the photo or illustration has been included. A caption will also describe the content of a photo or illustration.

DEFINITION

The photos and illustrations in a textbook not only add visual interest but also emphasize important points. Use them to find out the content of the chapter.

Special Features

Special features elaborate on or clarify material in the text.

EXAMPLE

Caribbean

Pullout box

Locomotives began to crisscross the eastern **United States** in the **1840s**. At that time, train tracks started to connect some American cities. Railroads enabled raw materials and finished goods to move back and forth between mines, factories, cities, and ports.

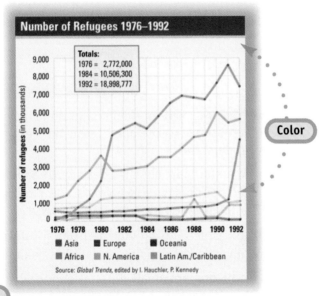

Number of Refugees 1976–1992

Totals:
1976 = 2,772,000
1984 = 10,506,300
1992 = 18,998,777

Number of refugees (in thousands)

9,000
8,000
7,000
6,000
5,000
4,000
3,000
2,000
1,000
0

1976 1978 1980 1982 1984 1986 1988 1990 1992

Color

■ Asia ■ Europe ■ Oceania
■ Africa ■ N. America ■ Latin Am./Caribbean

Source: *Global Trends*, edited by I. Hauchler, P. Kennedy

Symbols and icons

ChemSafety

◆ ⬟ CAUTION: Always wear safety goggles and a lab apron to protect your eyes and clothing.

◆ CAUTION: Do not touch or taste any chemicals. Know the location of the emergency shower and eyewash station and how to use them. If you get a chemical on your skin or clothing, wash it off at the sink while calling to the teacher. Notify the teacher of a spill. Spills should be cleaned up promptly, according to your teacher's directions.

◆ CAUTION: Glassware is fragile. Notify the teacher of broken glass or cuts. Do not clean up broken glass or spills with broken glass unless the teacher tells you to do so.

Special Features, continued

EXAMPLE

Crisis in the Balkans

Nowhere was that dispute more likely to occur than on the Balkan Peninsula. This mountainous peninsula in the southeastern corner of Europe was home to an assortment of ethnic groups. With a long history of nationalist uprisings and ethnic clashes, the Balkans were known as the "powder keg" of Europe.

Europe's Powder Keg By the early 1900s, the Ottoman Empire—which included the Balkan region—was in rapid decline. While some Balkan groups struggled to free themselves from Ottoman rule, others already had succeeded in breaking away from their Turkish rulers. These peoples had formed new nations, including Bulgaria, Greece, Montenegro, Romania, and Serbia.

Nationalism was a powerful force in these countries. Each group longed to extend its borders. Serbia, for example, had a large Slavic population. Serbia hoped to absorb all the Slavs on the Balkan Peninsula. On this issue of Serbian nationalism, Russia and Austria-Hungary were in direct conflict. Russia, itself a mostly Slavic nation, supported Serbian nationalism. Austria, which feared rebellion among its small Slavic population, felt threatened by Serbia's growth. In addition, both Russia and Austria-Hungary had hoped to fill the power vacuum created by the Ottoman decline in the Balkans.

In 1908, Austria annexed, or took over, Bosnia and Herzegovina.

> **Sidebar**

SPOTLIGHT ON

The Armenian Massacre
One Balkan group that suffered greatly for its independence efforts was the Armenians. By the 1880s, the roughly 2.5 million Christian Armenians in the Ottoman Empire had begun to demand their freedom. As a result, relations between the group and its Turkish rulers grew strained.

Throughout the 1890s, Turkish troops killed tens of thousands of Armenians. When World War I erupted in 1914, the Armenians pledged their support to the Turks' enemies. In response, the Turkish government deported nearly 2 million Armenians. Along the way, more than 600,000 died of starvation or were killed by Turkish soldiers.

The Great War **745**

DESCRIPTION

Special features—such as sidebars, pullout boxes, symbols and icons, and color—are used to elaborate on the text or to make the text easier to understand.

- A **sidebar** is a short article that deals with a sidelight of the text. It usually supports or expands a point made in the text and is set off by being put in a box.

- A **pullout box** is used to provide additional information related to a photo or illustration. It is more detailed than a caption.

- **Symbols and icons** are small illustrations used to call attention to a recurring feature in a textbook.

- **Color** is used for visual interest, to make charts and graphs easier to read, and to make some type stand out.

DEFINITION

Special features are used for visual interest, to provide extra information, and to clarify the main text.

Study Questions and Reviews

Most textbooks include study questions and reviews. These are usually placed at the end of each chapter.

EXAMPLE

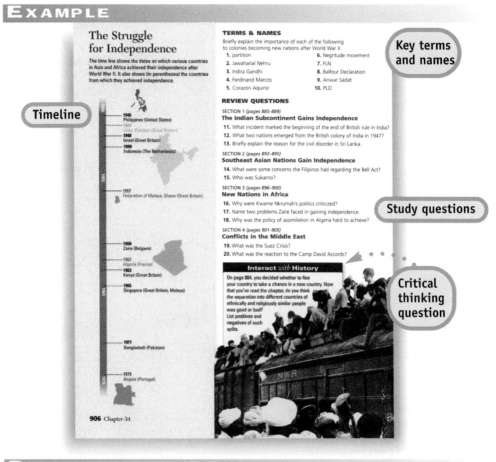

The Struggle for Independence

The time line shows the dates on which various countries in Asia and Africa achieved their independence after World War II. It also shows (in parentheses) the countries from which they achieved independence.

Key terms and names

Timeline

TERMS & NAMES
Briefly explain the importance of each of the following to colonies becoming new nations after World War II.
1. partition
2. Jawaharlal Nehru
3. Indira Gandhi
4. Ferdinand Marcos
5. Corazón Aquino
6. Negritude movement
7. FLN
8. Balfour Declaration
9. Anwar Sadat
10. PLO

REVIEW QUESTIONS

SECTION 1 (pages 885–889)
The Indian Subcontinent Gains Independence
11. What incident marked the beginning of the end of British rule in India?
12. What two nations emerged from the British colony of India in 1947?
13. Briefly explain the reason for the civil disorder in Sri Lanka.

SECTION 2 (pages 892–895)
Southeast Asian Nations Gain Independence
14. What were some concerns the Filipinos had regarding the Bell Act?
15. Who was Sukarno?

SECTION 3 (pages 896–900)
New Nations in Africa
16. Why were Kwame Nkrumah's politics criticized?
17. Name two problems Zaire faced in gaining independence.
18. Why was the policy of assimilation in Algeria hard to achieve?

Study questions

SECTION 4 (pages 901–905)
Conflicts in the Middle East
19. What was the Suez Crisis?
20. What was the reaction to the Camp David Accords?

Critical thinking question

Interact with History
On page 884, you decided whether to flee your country to take a chance in a new country. Now that you've read the chapter, do you think the separation into different countries of ethnically and religiously similar people was good or bad? List positives and negatives of such splits.

Timeline entries:
1946 Philippines (United States)
1947 India, Pakistan (Great Britain)
1948 Israel (Great Britain)
1949 Indonesia (The Netherlands)
1957 Federation of Malaya, Ghana (Great Britain)
1960 Zaire (Belgium)
1962 Algeria (France)
1963 Kenya (Great Britain)
1965 Singapore (Great Britain, Malaya)
1971 Bangladesh (Pakistan)
1975 Angola (Portugal)

906 Chapter 34

DESCRIPTION

Study questions and reviews at the end of each chapter often reflect the purpose-setting questions, if any, at the beginning of the chapter. But they are usually more detailed, focusing on key terms, main ideas, and critical thinking.

DEFINITION

Study questions and reviews at the end of a textbook chapter help you recall and remember information and often ask you to apply what you know.

Table of Contents

The table of contents is located in the first few pages of a textbook. It is a general outline, or overview, of the contents of the book. As you look it over, you will see the topics you'll be reading about and how they're organized. Notice all the information you can find on a single page:

EXAMPLE

Table of Contents, continued

DESCRIPTION

A **table of contents** is an excellent study outline. In fact, you can copy the table of contents in outline form into your notebook as you read through the text.

> **OUTLINE**
>
> Unit 2: Africa
> III. Geography and Early History of Africa
>   A. The Shape of the Land
>   B. Climate and Diversity
>   C. Early Civilizations of Africa
> IV. Heritage of Africa
>   A. Trading States and Kingdoms
>   B. Patterns of Life
>   C. The Slave Trade
>   D. Age of European Imperialism
>   E. Effects of European Rule

Then, you can add several details under each part to summarize the contents of the chapter. This makes a useful study guide to which you can refer later.

> **OUTLINE**
>
> III. Geography and Early History of Africa
>   A. The Shape of the Land
>   1. A Vast Continent
>   2. Landforms
>   3. Rivers
>   4. Natural Resources
>   B. Climate and Diversity

DEFINITION

The **table of contents** is a list of the major chapters and parts of a book, including the page numbers on which each section can be found. The purpose of a table of contents is to help you find specific sections of the book quickly and easily.

Timelines

A timeline is a special kind of chart that shows a sequence of events within a certain time frame.

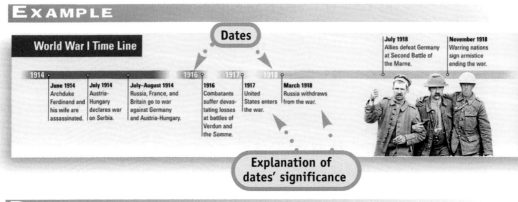

Dates

Explanation of dates' significance

DESCRIPTION

Timelines include a printed line that represents a certain length of time. This line is subdivided into smaller time units, along which historical events are listed in order at the point they occurred. Sometimes timelines include photos or art appropriate to a particular period.

A timeline can help you preview or review a lesson, understand a sequence of events, and help to fix dates in your mind.

DEFINITION

Timelines are visual representations of the events that occurred from one date to another.

Typography

The word *typography* refers to the type styles, or fonts, used on the page. Special fonts, such as **boldface** and *italic,* are used to call attention to certain types of information.

EXAMPLE

Theme
4

Homeostasis

All living organisms must maintain a stable internal environment in order to function properly. Organisms respond to changes in their external environment, adjusting their processes accordingly. The maintenance of stable internal conditions in spite of changes in the external environment is called **homeostasis** *(hoh mee oh STAY sihs).* An organism unable to balance its internal conditions with its environmental conditions could become ill and die. Arctic seals, such as the one in **Figure 1-5,** are able to maintain a constant body temperature in spite of their cold environment because of their thick layer of body fat.

Larger type for heading

Boldface

Italic

DESCRIPTION

Textbooks put certain words, quotations, headings, or captions in **boldface**. This change in **typography** is a signal that the information is more important than the text around it. Boldface is another way of saying, "Look at me! I'm important."

Italics are often used to set words apart from the rest of the text. Italic type might be used for pronunciations, as in the example. It is also used to indicate the title of a book, movie, work of art, or name of a ship. Color is also used sometimes to set off some type so that it stands out.

DEFINITION

Boldface type is heavier and darker than the typography in surrounding text, like this. It is used to help signal that a word, term, or event is more important and to make it stand out. Italic type is slanted, like *this*. It is used to set a word, phrase, or sentence apart.

Unit, Chapter, and Section Headings

The headings or titles in a textbook announce the topics that are covered.

EXAMPLE

Unit heading

UNIT 6
Industrialism and the Race for Empire
1700–1914

Chapter heading

CHAPTER 25
The Industrial Revolution, 1700–1900

PREVIEWING THEMES

Science & Technology
From the spinning jenny to the locomotive train, there was an explosion of inventions and technological advances. These improvements paved the way for the Industrial Revolution.

Empire Building
The global power balance shifted after the Industrial Revolution. This shift occurred because industrialized nations dominated the rest of the world.

Economics
The Industrial Revolution transformed economic systems. In part, this was because nations dramatically changed the way they produced and distributed goods.

EUROPE AND THE U.S. IN THE 1800s

— U.S. Railroads 1840

CANADA

PACIFIC OCEAN

INTERNET CONNECTION
Visit us at www.mhworldhistory.com to learn more about the Industrial Revolution.

Section heading

1 The Beginnings of Industrialization

TERMS & NAMES
• Industrial Revolution
• enclosure
• crop rotation
• industrialization
• factors of production
• factory
• entrepreneur

MAIN IDEA
The Industrial Revolution started in England and soon spread elsewhere.

WHY IT MATTERS NOW
The changes that began in Britain paved the way for modern industrial societies.

SETTING THE STAGE In the United States, France, and Latin America, political revolutions brought in new governments. A different type of revolution now transformed the way people did work. The **Industrial Revolution** refers to the greatly increased output of machine-made goods that began in England during the 18th century. Before the Industrial Revolution, people wove textiles by hand. Beginning in the middle 1700s, machines did this and other jobs as well. The Industrial Revolution started in England and soon spread to Continental Europe and North America.

Part heading

The Industrial Revolution Begins

By 1700, small farms covered England's landscape. Wealthy landowners, however, bought up much of the land that village farmers had once worked. Beginning in the early 1700s, large landowners dramatically improved farming methods. These agricultural changes amounted to an agricultural revolution. They eventually paved the way for the Industrial Revolution.

Subheading

The Agricultural Revolution After buying up the land of village farmers, wealthy landowners enclosed their land with fences or hedges. The increase in their landholdings enabled them to cultivate larger fields, using new seeding and harvesting methods. Within these larger fields, called **enclosures**, landowners experimented to discover more productive farming methods to boost crop yields. The enclosure movement had two important results. First, landowners experimented with new agricultural methods. Second, large landowners forced small farmers to become tenant farmers or to give up farming and move to the cities.

Jethro Tull was one of the first of these scientific farmers. He saw that the usual way of sowing seed by scattering it across the ground was wasteful. Many of the seeds failed to take root. He solved this problem with an invention called the seed drill in about 1701. The seed drill allowed farmers to sow seeds in well-spaced rows at specific depths. A larger share of the seed germinated, boosting crop yields.

THINK THROUGH HISTORY

A. Recognizing Effects What were some of the effects of enclosure and crop rotation?

Crop Rotation The process of **crop rotation** proved to be one of the best developments of the scientific farmers. The process improved upon older methods of crop rotation, such as the medieval three-field system. One year, for example, a farmer might plant a field with wheat, which exhausted soil nutrients. The next year he planted a root crop, such as turnips, to restore nutrients. This might be followed in turn by barley, then clover.

Livestock breeders improved their methods, too. In the 1700s, for example, Robert Bakewell increased his mutton output by allowing only his best sheep to breed. Other farmers followed Bakewell's lead. Between 1700 and 1786 the average weight for lambs climbed from 18 to 50 pounds.

Agricultural Revolution

Jethro Tull's Seed Drill

The seed drill enabled farmers to plant methodically. They abandoned the wasteful broadcast method of scattering handfuls of seed across the fields.

The Industrial Revolution **633**

Unit, Chapter, and Section Headings, continued

DESCRIPTION

The **headings** in a textbook start with the broadest and proceed to the narrowest. The order follows this pattern:

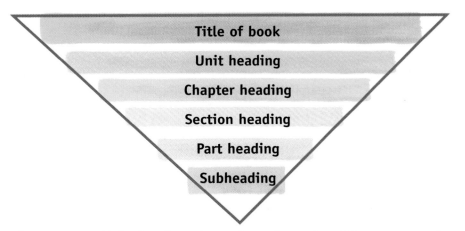

Title of book

Unit heading

Chapter heading

Section heading

Part heading

Subheading

The purpose of the headings is to show the order of importance of the material. For the broadest ideas, the headings are set in larger type. As the ideas get more and more specific, the type gets smaller.

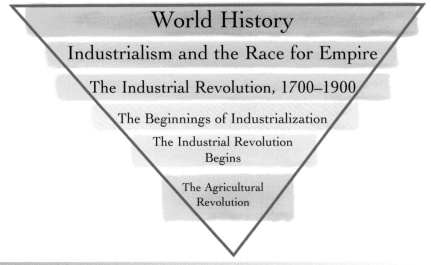

World History

Industrialism and the Race for Empire

The Industrial Revolution, 1700–1900

The Beginnings of Industrialization

The Industrial Revolution Begins

The Agricultural Revolution

DEFINITION

The **headings** in a textbook list the ideas, from broadest (the title of the book) to narrower (unit headings, chapter headings, and section headings) to narrowest (part headings and subheadings).

151

Reading
Nonfiction

Introduction to Reading Nonfiction

A world without nonfiction is unimaginable. When you read to find out what happened in the nation's capital yesterday, what the weather will be, or when a game or performance is scheduled, you're reading nonfiction. When you read to learn the words, thoughts, and experiences of those who live today and of those who have vanished, you're reading nonfiction.

Nonfiction is a record of real people, places, events, thoughts, and times. There are two basic types of nonfiction.

Expository nonfiction *is factual and informative writing.*

Articles, news stories, persuasive essays, and editorials are expository nonfiction. You probably read some factual and informative writing every day, either on the Internet or in a newspaper or magazine. The desire to know what's happening and what people think about it is a powerful motive for readers.

Narrative nonfiction *tells a true story.*

At some time, you've probably been curious about historical figures, movie and sports stars, or artists, writers, and musicians and their lives and times. Biographies, autobiographies, memoirs, and some personal essays are narrative nonfiction. They satisfy our curiosity about others' lives.

Nonfiction, perhaps more than any other type of writing, requires that you read critically. Make judgments about what seems accurate, biased, or just plain wrong when reading a news story or an editorial. Try to discover a writer's intention when reading an autobiography, biography, or personal essay.

Reading a Personal Essay

An essay is a short work that deals with one topic. Essays are often classified as *formal* or *informal*. A formal essay is highly structured. The author usually follows a clear, logical plan. A formal essay deals with a serious subject. An informal essay is not as tightly structured as a formal essay. It addresses a less serious topic and provides insight into the personality of the writer.

A **personal essay** is informal and may deal with any subject. You have probably been writing personal essays in school for many years. In the following personal essay, N. Scott Momaday first describes an event and then explains how it affected him. The essay is part recollection and part reflection.

Nonfiction

Goals

Here you'll learn how to:
✔ recognize the subject and main idea of an **essay**
✔ use the reading strategy of **outlining**
✔ identify the **three main parts of an essay:** introduction, body, and conclusion

A Set a Purpose

When you read a personal essay, you first want to find out what the essay is about. That's the subject. Then you want to find out what point the author's making about the subject. Then you need to decide how you feel about the main idea. These questions can help you think about your purpose as you read.

Setting a Purpose

■ **What is the subject of the essay?**

■ **What does the writer say about the subject?**

■ **How do I feel about what the writer says?**

B Preview

Previewing an essay gives you important information. It can alert you to the subject and perhaps even give you some clues about the author's message. When you preview an essay, look carefully at these key elements:

Preview Checklist

✔ the title and author
✔ the first and last paragraphs
✔ any key words or any words in boldface or italics
✔ any repeated words or phrases

Now preview "The Indian Dog" by N. Scott Momaday. Watch for items on your checklist. Make notes about anything you think is important or interesting.

The Indian Dog

by N. Scott Momaday

PREVIEW
Title and author

PREVIEW
First paragraph

Nonfiction

When I was growing up I lived in a pueblo in New Mexico. There one day I bought a dog. I was twelve years old, the bright autumn air was cold and delicious, and the dog was an unconscionable bargain at five dollars.

PREVIEW
Repeated words

It was an Indian dog; that is, it belonged to a Navajo man who had come to celebrate the Feast of San Diego. It was one of two or three rangy animals following in the tracks of the man's covered wagon as he took leave of our village on his way home. Indian dogs are marvelously independent and resourceful, and they have an idea of themselves, I believe, as knights and philosophers.

NOTE
End of introduction

The dog was not large, but neither was it small. It was one of those unremarkable creatures that one sees in every corner of the world, the common denominator of all its kind. But on that day—and to me—it was noble and brave and handsome.

NOTE
Body

It was full of resistance, and yet it was ready to return my deep, abiding love; I could see that. It needed only to make a certain adjustment in its lifestyle, to shift the focus of its vitality from one frame of reference to another. But I had to drag my dog from its previous owner by means of a rope. It was nearly strangled in the process, its bushy tail wagging happily all the while.

That night I secured my dog in the garage, where there was a warm clean pallet, wholesome food, and fresh water, and I bolted the door. And the next morning the dog was gone, as in my heart I knew it would be; I had read such a future in its eyes. It had squeezed through a vent, an opening much too small for it, or so I had thought. But as they say, where there is a will there is a way—and the Indian dog was possessed of one indomitable will.

I was crushed at the time, but strangely reconciled, too, as if I had perceived intuitively some absolute truth beyond all the billboards of illusion.

NOTE
End of body, beginning of conclusion

The Indian dog had done what it had to do, had behaved exactly as it must, had been true to itself and to the sun and moon. It knew its place in the scheme of things, and its place was precisely there, with its right destiny, in the tracks of the wagon. In my mind's eye I could see it at that very moment, miles away, plodding in the familiar shadows, panting easily with relief, after a bad night, contemplating the wonderful ways of man.

PREVIEW
Words in italics

Caveat emptor. But from that experience I learned something about the heart's longing. It was a lesson worth many times five dollars.

PREVIEW
Last paragraph

C Plan

What did you learn on your preview? You may have noticed that Momaday:

- describes a dog
- writes in the first person
- describes his relationship to the "Indian dog" of the title
- focuses on a lesson he learned

When you finish your preview, make a reading plan. How can you get more out of a personal essay? The reading strategy of outlining can help.

Reading Strategy: Outlining

Many readers find **outlining** helpful as they are reading a personal essay. Outlining forces you to decide what information is important and how it is related to the subject and main idea, or message, of the writing. In addition, outlining requires you to express facts and ideas in your own words. This, in turn, helps you process the information and remember what you've read.

To use the strategy, set up a simple Topic or Sentence Outline in your notebook or on a separate piece of paper before you begin reading. List three Roman numerals—one for the introduction, one for the body, and one for the conclusion of the essay. Leave plenty of room between the Roman numerals so that you can add or change details as you go. Here is a sample of the kind of Outline you might create:

Nonfiction

OUTLINE

I. Introduction (the writer's recollections)
    A. Introductory detail
    B. Introductory detail
    C. Introductory detail

II. Body (the writer's recollections)
    A. Detail
      1.
      2.
    B. Detail
      1.
      2.
    C. Detail
      1.
      2.

III. Conclusion (the writer's reflections)
    A. Main idea (if it appears here)
    B. Explanation of main idea
    C. Explanation of main idea

During Reading

Stay focused when you read a personal essay. Try not to let unfamiliar vocabulary or long, complex sentences distract you from your reading purpose.

D Read with a Purpose

From your preview of "The Indian Dog," you know that the essay involves N. Scott Momaday's recollections about a dog. Now that you have previewed the essay, go back and read it carefully. Look for the author's feelings about the dog and how his experiences with the dog changed his feelings about himself or his outlook on life.

Finding the Main Idea

What does Momaday say about the dog and what he learned? When you figure that out, you've got the main idea. The **main idea** is what the writer wants you to remember most after reading the essay. In some cases, the author will state the main idea directly. In personal essays, however, the main idea is usually implied. Follow these steps to find an implied main idea in a personal essay.

1. Reread parts of the essay in which the writer reflects on the experience he or she has described. (This is usually toward the end of the essay.)

2. Watch for words and phrases that signal the author is going to say something important. For example: "This experience taught me . . . ," "Now I realize that . . . ," "My point is that. . . ."

3. Ask yourself two important questions:

How did the experience change the author's view of self or the world?

What did the author learn from the experience described?

Look again at the final three paragraphs of Momaday's essay.

Nonfiction

from "The Indian Dog"

NOTE
Words and phrases that signal the main idea

I was crushed at the time, but strangely reconciled, too, as if I had perceived intuitively some absolute truth beyond all the billboards of illusion.

The Indian dog had done what it had to do, had behaved exactly as it must, had been true to itself and to the sun and moon. It knew its place in the scheme of things, and its place was precisely there, with its right destiny, in the tracks of the wagon. In my mind's eye I could see it at that very moment, miles away, plodding in the familiar shadows, panting easily with relief, after a bad night, contemplating the wonderful ways of man.

Caveat emptor. But from that experience I learned something about the heart's longing. It was a lesson worth many times five dollars.

NOTE
Main idea

In the final paragraph, Momaday inserts a familiar Latin phrase, *Caveat emptor* ("Let the buyer beware"), and explains that the experience with the dog taught him that what one really wants provides a strong motive for action.

He writes that he "learned something about the heart's longing." His main idea is not stated, because he doesn't tell the reader what exactly he learned. You have to infer what he learned about "the heart's longing" that was worth "many times more than five dollars."

Finding Supporting Details
Has Momaday supported his main idea? Supporting details may be facts, examples, statistics, or quotations. Or they may be the writer's own experiences.

On the next page is one Outline a reader made. Notice that points I. A., B., and C. are taken from the first two paragraphs. Point II. A. comes from the third and fourth paragraphs. Point II. B. and C. come from the fifth and sixth paragraphs. Point III. comes from the last two paragraphs.

I. Introduction
    A. Momaday establishes time and place.
        1. He tells a story that happened when he was twelve.
        2. He lived in New Mexico.
    B. Momaday describes the dog he buys.
        1. Dog is Indian.
        2. It belongs to a Navajo man.
        3. It walks behind a wagon with other dogs.
    C. He describes Indian dogs in general.
        1. They are "independent and resourceful."
        2. They think of themselves as "knights and philosophers."
II. Body
    A. Momaday describes his dog.
        1. It is "unremarkable" in appearance.
        2. To Momaday, it was "noble and brave and handsome."
        3. He has to drag it from its owner.
    B. Momaday takes the dog home.
        1. He makes a home for it in the garage.
        2. Upon reflection, he knew in his heart that the dog
           would not stay.
    C. He finds the dog has run away.
        1. He knows the dog has a strong will.
        2. He is crushed but "strangely reconciled."
III. Conclusion
    A. Main idea: Momaday now understands something about the
       heart's longing.
    B. Buying a dog fulfilled one longing.
    C. The dog needed to leave to fulfill its own longing.

This is a detailed Outline. You can make yours simpler, if you like. However, if the essay is a challenging one, you may find that listing many details on the Outline can help you better think through what you read. In this essay, the supporting details come from the writer's own experiences.

How Personal Essays Are Organized

Knowing how most personal essays are organized can make it easier for you to find the main idea and pick out supporting details. You'll have a better idea of where to look if you know beforehand what to expect.

Most personal essays are organized in what is called a *funnel pattern*. A funnel pattern looks like this:

FUNNEL PATTERN

Although personal essays are not all organized in the same way, a writer usually introduces the topic in the first few paragraphs. Then, she or he expands on that topic in the body. The body is the longest part of the essay. The conclusion is usually quite short. It might be one paragraph or one sentence. These three parts add up to the main idea.

E Connect

What personal ideas or memories came to mind as you were reading Momaday's essay about the dog? Have you had an experience with a dog? If so, what did you learn from that experience? Making a personal connection to what an author describes can help you process important details and remember what you've read.

For example, look at how one reader reacted to this part of Momaday's essay.

> I know exactly what he means. My dog is totally independent and thinks he is in charge of me, rather than the other way around.

from "The Indian Dog"

Indian dogs are marvelously independent and resourceful, and they have an idea of themselves, I believe, as knights and philosophers.

Another reader had this to say in a journal entry.

JOURNAL ENTRY

I like the way Momaday showed that he understood that the dog, like a human being, had to be true to itself. Even though Momaday hated that the dog ran away, he knew all along that the dog wasn't going to be his dog.

After Reading

When you finish reading a personal essay, reflect for a moment or two on what you've learned.

F Pause and Reflect

These questions can help you think carefully about what you've read. Each question touches on one part of your reading purpose.

Looking Back

- **Can I name the subject of the essay?**
- **Do I know what the author says about the subject?**
- **Can I tell how I feel about the author's main idea?**

G Reread

If you cannot answer "yes" to each question on the checklist above, you haven't fully met your reading purpose. In that case, it might be a good idea to do some rereading.

Rereading Strategy: Questioning the Author

Questioning the author as if he or she were right in the room is an excellent strategy to use when you're not sure you've understood an essay. When you question the author, you hold a "conversation" with the writer about parts of the selection you didn't understand.

To use the strategy, imagine that the writer is sitting next to you. Then ask some questions that help you zero in on important or confusing parts of the reading. For example, you might ask questions like these:

AFTER-READING QUESTIONS

What does this detail mean?

What is the message of this essay?

How does this part of the essay relate to this other part?

What is the significance of this paragraph?

Nonfiction

Answering your questions

After you've made your list of questions for the author, you can begin answering them. Do this in a way that makes the most sense to you. Write in your reading journal, or discuss the questions with a friend. Raise some of these questions in class and let the group answer them. A Double-entry Journal helps you keep track of what you learn during your question-and-answer session.

> **DOUBLE-ENTRY JOURNAL**
>
> **QUESTION:** Does the dog want to go or not?
>
> | QUOTE | MY THOUGHTS |
> |---|---|
> | "But I had to drag my dog from its previous owner by means of a rope. It was nearly strangled in the process, its bushy tail wagging happily all the while." | At first I thought the dog wanted to leave, but now I'm not so sure. Now that I know how things turn out, I see that this might be a clue that Momaday is setting himself up for trouble with this dog. |

Asking questions and thinking about the answers can help you discover how you feel about an essay. Ask yourself whether you liked Momaday's topic. Consider how you felt about the dog's urgent need to escape.

H Remember

Of course, there's no point in spending all this time on a selection if you don't figure out a way to remember what you've read. Here are two ways to help you retain what you've learned.

1. Read Some More

Find another short piece by the same author and read it carefully. Then, compare the second selection to the first. Work toward an understanding of the author's beliefs and ideas. Make a few quick notes in your reading journal.

2. Create an Organizer

Make a graphic organizer that explores some aspect of the essay. A Main Idea Organizer such as the one below can help you get at the heart of the author's message.

MAIN IDEA ORGANIZER

"The Indian Dog" MAIN IDEA: The heart's longings can be extremely powerful.		
DETAIL #1	**DETAIL #2**	**DETAIL #3**
As a boy, Momaday buys a dog.	The dog longs for freedom.	The boy recognizes that the dog's longings and his own are not the same.

Nonfiction

Summing Up

When you read a personal essay, remember to use the reading process and the reading strategy of **outlining**. Note the **three main parts of the essay: introduction, body,** and **conclusion.** You may need to refer to these notes or organizers later for a test or class discussion:

- Outline
- Double-entry Journal
- Main Idea Organizer

Use the strategy of **questioning the author** when you reread a personal essay.

Reading an Editorial

An **editorial** is a kind of persuasive writing that is published in a newspaper or magazine or on a website. The purpose of most editorials is to advance an argument or discuss important issues of the day.

Good editorials make concise, thoughtful arguments and support those arguments with facts, figures, statistics, and examples. As a critical reader, your job is first to understand the argument presented and then to evaluate and decide how you feel about the argument.

Here you'll learn how to read and respond to an editorial called "College Sports Myth Versus Math."

Goals

Here you'll learn how to:

✔ recognize the **author's viewpoint** or **assertions**

✔ use the strategy of **questioning the author**

✔ understand **how an editorial is organized**

Before Reading

The reading process can help you sift through the information presented in an editorial and discover the most important ideas. It can also help you evaluate the writer's opinion and form your own ideas about the topic.

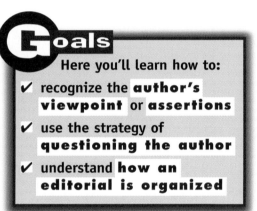

A Set a Purpose

Sometimes you'll read editorials for insight and sometimes for an assignment. In either case, your purpose will be more or less the same: understand the author's viewpoint, evaluate how persuasively the point is supported, and then decide how you feel about it.

In most cases, you can use the headline of an editorial to help you set your purpose for reading. Ask yourself three key questions about the headline.

College Sports Myth Versus Math

Nonfiction

Setting a Purpose

■ **What is the college sports myth versus math?**

■ **How do I feel about it?**

■ **How persuasive is the editorial?**

B Preview

Editorials are easy to preview because they're written for readers who are in a hurry. When you preview an editorial, look carefully at these items:

Preview Checklist

✔ the headline and date
✔ any repeated words
✔ the writer's assertions
✔ the first and last paragraphs

The items on the checklist can provide important clues about the topic of the editorial and the argument the writer is making. Now preview the editorial. Watch for information about the topic and the writer's argument.

College Sports Myth Versus Math

FEBRUARY 3, 2001

When it comes to preferential treatment in college admissions, minorities, musicians, and the children of alumni have nothing on varsity athletes.

It will surprise no one that football and basketball players are heavily recruited and coddled by colleges.

The common wisdom is that colleges covet brawny athletes because they bring in money by filling the stands.

But news that players of squash, tennis, lacrosse and every other varsity sport have an edge on admissions, and bring down the overall academic achievement levels of the student body, may raise a few eyebrows.

That's one of the findings of a new study, "The Games of Life," by the Andrew W. Mellon Foundation.

There is a growing gap between student athletes and their classmates in aptitude, values, interests, and academic achievement, according to the study, authored by James L. Shulman, a Mellon officer, and William G. Bowen, the foundation president and former president of Princeton. They find the contributions varsity athletics make to campus life have been seriously overrated.

The study evaluated the entering classes of 1951, 1976, and 1987 at 32 selective public and private colleges and universities, and found the gap in SAT scores between athletes and other students has grown considerably. In 1951, the scores of athletes and non-athletes were virtually the same.

The performance gap between athletes and their fellow students is not limited to big-time university football or basketball programs. Varsity tennis players at coed liberal arts colleges, for example, slipped 140 points behind their classmates' SAT scores in the study's most recent

"College Sports Myth Versus Math," continued

year. Student athletes earned lower grades than their fellow students. Is it that athletes just don't have time to study? Well, students engaged in other time-consuming extracurricular activities tended to produce higher-than-average grades.

NOTE
Assertion

The study also found that big, expensive campus sports programs generate surprisingly little profit even for the big bowl-winners.

NOTE
Supporting details

Winning seasons don't appreciably increase alumni contributions. And the alumni-athletes themselves give less than their former classmates, and, when they do give, are more likely to limit their donation to the athletic program.

None of that is likely to make much of a difference in the feverish enthusiasm Americans tend to give to college sports. "Jock culture" seems to have become almost everyone's culture on campus. College administrators should take a little time out to ask themselves how much of a contribution their varsity sports programs are making to the ideals of academic excellence, not just athletic excellence.

PREVIEW
Last paragraph

NOTE
Recommendation

Nonfiction

Plan

What did you learn from your preview? From your preview of the title and first two paragraphs, you probably discovered that the topic of this editorial is college sports. The words *college* and *athletes* are repeated throughout the editorial.

Next, the writer usually makes one or more **assertions.** These assertions are statements about the topic. To find the assertions (and the writer's support for the assertions), you need a strategy. When reading editorials, the best strategy to use is questioning the author.

Reading Strategy: Questioning the Author

Questioning the author is a strategy to help you figure out what the author is saying. It involves asking such questions as, "What does the author mean here?" What's his or her message?" and "Does this idea or opinion make sense?" These questions (and your answers to them) can help you think critically about a text.

Questioning the author can help you identify an author's assertions and the support for those assertions. Think about these questions during your reading of an editorial.

1. Why does the author begin this way?

2. What point is the author making?

3. Why does the writer mention this detail?

4. What does the writer want me to believe?

5. What action can I take, or what am I supposed to do?

List these questions in your journal, or use sticky notes to record your questions. Jot down answers as you read.

During Reading

If you're asking questions of the writer, you're reading actively. Questioning the writer helps you focus on the writer's ideas, sort through your own feelings on the subject, and figure out how the writer's ideas relate to what you already know about the topic.

D Read with a Purpose

Start your questioning by thinking carefully about your purpose questions.

■ What is the college sports myth versus math?

■ How persuasive is the editorial?

■ How do I feel about it?

Keep these questions in mind as you do a careful reading of "College Sports Myth Versus Math." Notice the notes one reader made.

Nonfiction

---

from "College Sports Myth Versus Math"

But news that players of squash, tennis, lacrosse and every other varsity sport have an edge on admissions, and bring down the overall academic achievement levels of the student body, may raise a few eyebrows.

Question:
What does the author mean by this?

Answer: I think this means that this information will surprise some people.

Now go back to the editorial and read it carefully with your questions in mind.

Analyze

Here's how one reader asked and answered questions to the writer of the editorial about college athletes.

QUESTIONS	MY THOUGHTS
1. Why does the author begin this way?	The first paragraph makes the reader want to read more about "preferential treatment."
2. What point is the author making?	College athletes of those sports besides football and basketball also get "preferential treatment" and bring down academic achievement levels.
3. Why does the writer mention the detail about alumni-athletes?	This detail supports the idea that an athlete's contributions to college life are overrated.
4. What does the writer want me to believe?	I'm to believe that athletes don't benefit colleges as much as was thought.
5. What action can I take, or what am I supposed to do?	The writer isn't clear about what readers can do.

Evaluate

A Critical Reading Chart helps you evaluate information. Record your thoughts in the second column.

CRITICAL READING CHART

MY QUESTIONS	MY THOUGHTS
1. Is the main idea or assertion clear?	very clear
2. What evidence is presented?	gap in achievement, SAT scores, little profit
3. Are the sources authoritative and reliable?	Mellon Foundation probably OK
4. Is the evidence convincing?	seems to be
5. Is there another side to the story?	more recent survey might be different

How Editorials Are Organized

Reading and responding to an editorial is easier if you understand how the information is organized. Most editorials contain three parts: the author's *assertions,* the *support,* and the *recommendation.*

The three parts of an editorial can appear in any order. But more often than not, editorial writers follow this order.

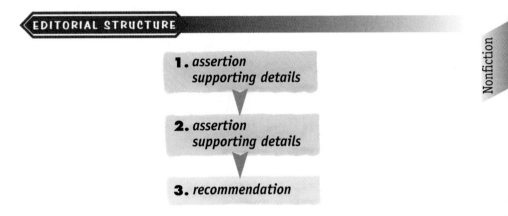

EDITORIAL STRUCTURE

1. *assertion*
    supporting details

2. *assertion*
    supporting details

3. *recommendation*

Nonfiction

The writer of "College Sports Myth Versus Math" used this organization. Look back at the beginning of the editorial on page 170. The editorial opens with an attention-grabbing fact about preferential treatment in college admissions. In the third paragraph, the writer makes an *assertion:* the players of all varsity sports "have an edge on admissions, and bring down the overall academic achievement levels of the student body."

After the assertion, the writer cites a study in *support* of this assertion and begins with the most important fact: declining SAT scores of varsity athletes over the last 50 years. The writer then makes another *assertion:* sports programs don't generate much profit. The writer supports this assertion by saying that winning seasons don't do much to increase contributions from alumni, and alumni-athletes give less money than other alumni do. Again, the support is from the study cited earlier.

At the end comes the writer's *recommendation,* the writer's suggestion for how the problem should be solved. Editorial recommendations often contain such words as *should, could,* or *might.*

E Connect

Connecting with an editorial means deciding how you feel about the writer's argument.

What were your reactions as you read the editorial? Did you feel strongly about any of the points the writer made? Note how one reader responded to the conclusion of the editorial.

from "College Sports Myth Versus Math"

"Jock culture" seems to have become almost everyone's culture on campus. College administrators should take a little time out to ask themselves how much of a contribution their varsity sports programs are making to the ideals of academic excellence, not just athletic excellence.

There's definitely enthusiasm about college sports in my house.

But what should they do once they ask themselves this question?

Write a quick evaluation of the editorial in your journal so that you can refer to it later. On the next page is one reader's response.

JOURNAL

I think the argument this editorial writer makes is very clear. There is good support for the assertions.

Sometimes, you may want to analyze what a writer implies. <u>Use an Inference Chart when you want to look a little closer at part of a reading.</u>

INFERENCE CHART

TEXT	WHAT I CONCLUDE
The "gap in SAT scores between athletes and other students has grown."	Athletes are recruited for their athletic ability, but other students have to have high SAT scores to get into college.

After Reading

When you finish reading an editorial in a newspaper, you probably turn the page in search of sports news, the comics, or a movie review. But stop! Two more activities will be helpful if you're reading an editorial for a school assignment.

F Pause and Reflect

Go back to your reading purpose and see whether you can answer these questions.

Looking Back

- Do I know what the college sports myth is?
- Can I explain how the writer refutes or challenges the myth?
- Do I know how I feel about the editorial?

G Reread

After reading, you may feel the need to reread an editorial. You might want to go back to find out where the writer got his or her facts. You might want to make sure you can pull together all the facts to form your own opinion about the subject.

Rereading Strategy: ▶ Synthesizing

Synthesizing means taking all the facts, ideas, or assertions in a piece of writing and pulling them together to show how they add up. To do this, create an organizer that shows what you've learned.

Here's how one reader used Summary Notes to pull together all the ideas in the editorial.

SUMMARY NOTES

Nonfiction

TOPIC: college sports
MAIN POINT: College athletes and expensive sports programs don't benefit schools as much as people thought.
1. College athletes have lower SAT scores than other students. 2. College athletes have lower grades than other students. 3. Alumni contributions don't increase even when teams win. 4. Former college athletes give less money to colleges than their former classmates do.

H Remember

Use the information you read to help you remember it. Here are two ways you can recall "College Sports Myth Versus Math."

1. Discuss with a Friend

Sometimes the best thing you can do after you read something is talk about it with a friend. Mention what you learned in an email or over lunch. Talk about the editorial with a classmate who has also read it. Exchange ideas and discuss differences of opinion. By sharing what you read, you are more likely to remember it.

2. Write a Letter

Newspapers are full of letters agreeing or disagreeing with editorials. Maybe you don't agree with the study the writer used as a basis for the editorial. You think the study may be flawed. Or maybe you do agree with the writer. Write a letter expressing your opinion.

Summing Up

When you read an editorial, find the three main parts: **viewpoint** or **assertions**, **support**, and **recommendation.** Use the strategy of **questioning the author.** Use one or all of these tools:

- ■ **Double-entry Journal**
- ■ **Critical Reading Chart**
- ■ **Inference Chart**
- ■ **Summary Notes**

To improve your understanding of an editorial, use the rereading strategy of **synthesizing.**

Reading a News Story

Why do you read a newspaper, news magazine, or Internet news site? You read it to find out what's happening in the world. **News stories** tell you about events that are occurring around the world and in your backyard.

When do you read a news story? You read the news when you have a little extra time. Sometimes a major event makes you want to read whatever you can as the news comes in. You may also read news stories for class assignments.

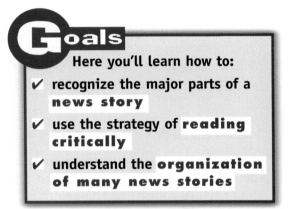

G **oals**

Here you'll learn how to:

✔ recognize the major parts of a **news story**

✔ use the strategy of **reading critically**

✔ understand the **organization of many news stories**

Nonfiction

Here you'll read a newspaper story about the effect of violence in the media on kids.

Before Reading

The reading process can help you evaluate information in a news story and form your own opinions about what you read.

A Set a Purpose

Very rarely will you sit down and read a newspaper from beginning to end. Instead, you'll scan the headlines and read only those stories that catch your eye. In general, your purpose for reading will be to find out what the story has to say about a subject. To frame your purpose, ask a *who, what, where, when, why,* or *how* question about the headline. For example, think about the headline "Violent Images May Alter Kids' Brain Activity." Then set a purpose for reading this story.

■ **How do violent images alter kids' brain activity?**

or

■ **Why do violent images alter kids' brain activity?**

Wanting to learn about either of these two purpose questions is a good reason for reading. Of course, once you begin reading the story, you may find that your purpose changes a bit. You might think of other questions you'd like to have answered, or you may decide to focus on a slightly different aspect of the subject. In that case, simply make a note of your new purpose question and continue reading.

B Preview

News stories are easy to preview because they're usually organized in the same predictable way. The most important information in the story usually appears at the beginning, called the story's **lead.** The lead can vary in length from one sentence to several paragraphs.

When you preview a news story, begin by skimming the lead. It can tell you what to expect from the rest of the story. Now, preview the headline and first paragraph of the news story "Violent Images May Alter Kids' Brain Activity." See how many of the six questions you can answer. Look for these items:

Preview Checklist

✔ the headline
✔ the reporter's name (appears in what is called the byline)
✔ the lead
✔ any key or repeated words and phrases

PREVIEW
Headline

Violent Images May Alter Kids' Brain Activity

PREVIEW
Byline

PREVIEW
Lead

PREVIEW
Key words

BY MARILYN ELIAS

Media violence may trigger aggression in kids by stimulating brain regions involved in fighting for survival and storing readily recalled traumatic memories, a scientist will report Friday.

Functional magnetic resonance imaging (MRI) scans show that violent film clips activate children's brains in a distinctive, potentially violence-promoting pattern, says Kansas State University psychologist John Murray. He will speak at the Society for Research in Child Development meeting in Minneapolis.

The brain scans were done on eight youngsters, ages 8 to 13, as they watched TV for 18 minutes, six minutes each of boxing sequences from *Rocky IV*, non-violent PBS clips and just a blank screen marked with an "X."

Compared with MRIs done before the study, and scans taken during non-violent scenes, the boxing images evoked much greater activation of three brain regions:

NOTE
Fact

- The amygdala, which registers emotional arousal and detects threats to survival.

- The premotor cortex, an area believed to rev up when a person thinks about responding to a threat.

- The posterior cingulate, reserved for storing long-term memory of important, often troubling events. For instance, this area activates when Vietnam combat veterans and rape victims recall their trauma.

Although children may consciously know violence on the screen isn't real, "their brains are treating it as real, the gospel truth," Murray says. There's no proof this brain activation will spur aggression,

NOTE
Quote

Nonfiction

NOTE
Opinion

"but it does give us great reason for concern."

Flashbacks readily occur after post-traumatic stress; images of on-screen aggression also may recur and influence kids, he says.

PREVIEW
Repeated words

One Yale University study showed a delayed effect a few days after youngsters watched aggressive TV spots. When prompted with cues similar to those in the TV scene, they, too, behaved aggressively.

NOTE
Opposing viewpoint

But Murray's study "is way too small to make a case" for the brain-aggression link, says Yale psychologist Dorothy Singer, an expert on how TV affects children. "It's very important stuff, but we need larger numbers."

And kids' TV viewing habits don't promote belligerent behavior nearly as much as exposure to real violence and parents' failure to monitor their youngsters' activities, a recent study of 2,245 students showed.

Still, "if your child is watching lots of TV, then you have reason to be concerned," says Mark Singer of Case Western Reserve University in Cleveland. "Many, many studies show it isn't healthy."

NOTE
Opinion

C Plan

What did you learn from your preview of the headline and first paragraph? You probably discovered that this news story explains an important scientific study about media violence and its effect on kids' brains. You probably picked up on some key words such as *aggression, violence,* and *brain regions.*

You may want to jot down some basic facts about the news story in a 5 W's and H Organizer.

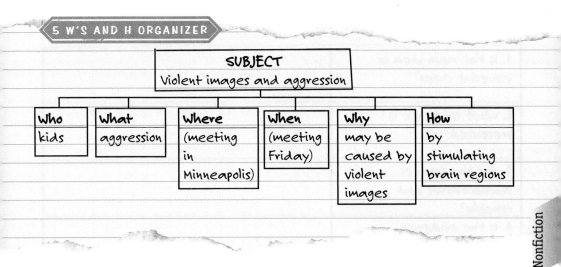

SUBJECT
Violent images and aggression

Who	What	Where	When	Why	How
kids	aggression	(meeting in Minneapolis)	(meeting Friday)	may be caused by violent images	by stimulating brain regions

Nonfiction

That first paragraph in the news story may have raised some questions in your mind. To read the article carefully, you need a plan.

Reading Strategy: Reading Critically

A good strategy to use with a news story is **reading critically.** In fact, you may already use this strategy without being aware of it. It means looking at the facts presented by a writer and then deciding what those facts mean and how believable they are. It also means evaluating evidence, deciding whether it is convincing, and recognizing that important information may be left out of a story.

Perhaps the most important aspect of reading critically is asking yourself questions. You need to be skeptical as a reader, doubting, asking questions, and demanding proof. To help you do that, set up a Critical Reading Chart that you can fill in later.

1. Is the main idea or viewpoint clear?	
2. What evidence is presented?	
3. Are the sources authoritative and reliable?	
4. Is the evidence convincing?	
5. Is there another side of the story?	

During Reading

Once you finish your preview, you can begin your careful reading.

D Read with a Purpose

Remember that your purpose is to find out how or why violent images alter kids' brain activity. As you read the rest of the story, note any facts and details that help you answer your purpose question. Also watch for opinions. Consider whether or not they are well supported.

If you've read this story simply because you're interested, you probably don't need to write anything down. If you've read it for a class assignment, however, you should pause for a moment after you finish reading and think about what you've learned. Completing the Critical Reading Chart can help you sift through the material you've read and locate the most important details.

CRITICAL READING CHART

MY QUESTIONS	MY THOUGHTS
1. Is the main idea or viewpoint clear?	Yes. Violence can alter brain activity in kids.
2. What evidence is presented?	MRI scans, flashback information, Yale University study
3. Are the sources authoritative and reliable?	Yes, they seem to be. She quotes doctors from good universities.
4. Is the evidence convincing?	It's pretty convincing. Television images can be powerful.
5. Is there another side of the story?	Singer says study is too small. Another study says real violence causes more trouble than TV violence.

Nonfiction

Of course, you won't take the time to create a chart like this one for every news story you read. Even so, you'll still need to think through what you read in this way and consider whether the evidence a writer provides is reliable and persuasive.

How News Stories Are Organized

Finding important details in a news story is easier if you understand how the information is organized. Many news stories follow a standard organization called an *inverted pyramid*. It looks like this:

INVERTED PYRAMID

Lead

Most important details

Less important details

Least important details

The lead establishes what the story is all about. In addition, it can answer several or all of the most important journalistic questions: *who, what, where, when, why, how.* At the same time, the writer attempts to "hook" readers and convince them to continue reading.

Some news stories open with what is called an *indirect lead,* or *soft lead.* An indirect lead draws readers into the story with an interesting story or quotation. It too can answer some or all of the six questions. For example, if the reporter who wrote about violent images had opened with an anecdote about a specific person who exhibited aggressive behavior after watching a violent film, that would have been a soft lead. An indirect, or soft, lead can be three or four paragraphs long.

E Connect

If you connect your own life in some way to the information in a news story, you will find the information more meaningful and interesting. As you read, ask yourself, "How does this apply to me?" "What else have I read on this subject?"

CONNECT

For example, notice how one reader marked these paragraphs from the TV violence news story. Did you have any of the same reactions?

---

from "Violent Images May Alter Kids' Brain Activity"

Although children may consciously know violence on the screen isn't real, "their brains are treating it as real, the gospel truth," Murray says. There's no proof this brain activation will spur aggression, "but it does give us great reason for concern."

Flashbacks readily occur after post-traumatic stress; images of on-screen aggression also may recur and influence kids, he says.

I don't get this. If you know something is fake, then why doesn't your brain know it too?

I can't believe that TV can cause this kind of stress!

The connections you make while you read may lead to some important questions. These questions, in turn, can shape your overall response to the story. If you're left with many questions, maybe the reporter failed to support the main idea adequately or investigate the story thoroughly.

After Reading

Although you may thumb through a newspaper quickly, as a critical reader you know that it's important to reflect on what you've read.

F Pause and Reflect

After you read a news story, pause for a few minutes to think about what you've learned. Ask yourself these questions:

Looking Back

- **Have I met my reading purpose?**
- **Can I restate the reporter's main idea?**
- **Do I understand the facts in the story?**
- **Can I give my own opinion of what was written?**

If you find yourself unable to answer "yes" to one or more of these questions, you may need to do a little rereading.

G Reread

Sometimes one quick reading of a news story will be enough. Other times—especially if you're doing research for a paper or a debate in class—you'll want to do some rereading to be sure you understand the main idea and supporting details.

Rereading Strategy: Summarizing

Summarizing is a strategy that you can use with any type of newspaper story. When you summarize, you use your own words to retell the most important ideas in the story. Making Summary Notes can greatly improve your ability to understand and remember what you've read.

Use a paragraph-by-paragraph summary when summarizing a news story. Set up a chart that looks like the one on the next page. Skim each paragraph. Then restate the idea of the paragraph in your own words. The result is a quick and accurate summary of the story.

Nonfiction

SUMMARY NOTES

1. Violence in the media may cause aggression in kids.
2. MRI scans show that violent film clips activate a violence-promoting mechanism in children's brains.
3. For the study, scientists had eight children watch violent and non-violent TV for 18 minutes.
4. The violent show caused a reaction in three brain regions: the amygdala, premotor cortex, and posterior cingulate.
5. A child's brain thinks the violence on TV is real.
6. The result may be post-traumatic stress in kids.
7. One study showed kids reacting aggressively after an aggressive TV show.
8. Some researchers question whether media violence really does trigger aggression in kids.
9. They say that exposure to real violence has a far worse effect on children.
10. Most studies show that too much TV is bad for kids.

H Remember

Here are two things you can do to help you remember a news story.

1. Make a Graphic Organizer

Refer to the summary you created. Then make a Cause-Effect Organizer, using your notes.

Write a cause in the left box. Write one or more effects that come from that cause in the boxes at the right.

CAUSE-EFFECT ORGANIZER

CAUSE	EFFECT	EFFECT
violent images	activate • amygdala • premotor cortex • posterior cingulate	result in aggressive or violent behavior

191

2. Find Out More

Use the Internet to find out more about what you read in a news story. If you read the story in a newspaper, go first to the website of that paper. Publishers often include links for further investigation.

Summing Up

When you read a news story, use the strategy of **reading critically.** It can help you understand and evaluate the facts and details the reporter offers. Looking for the **lead** and an **inverted pyramid organization** will help you find the most important information. Keep track of the information and your ideas by using one of these tools:

- 5 W's and H Organizer
- Critical Reading Chart
- Summary Notes
- Cause-Effect Organizer

After reading, use the rereading strategy of **summarizing.**

Reading a Biography

If you're like most people, you probably enjoy hearing stories about someone's life. It's fun to learn how and why someone is important and then compare that person's life to your own.

A **biography** is the story of a person's life written by another person. The writer of a biography is called the *biographer*. The person the biographer writes about is the *biographical subject*.

How do biographers find out about their subject? They may interview the person they want to write about. They may interview people who know or knew that person. They may consult public records, diaries, letters, newspapers, and histories. Biographers often list their sources at the end of a biography.

A good biography makes readers feel that they know the subject inside and out. Here you'll read an excerpt from a biography about the renowned baseball player Jackie Robinson and the general manager of the Brooklyn Dodgers, Branch Rickey, who signed Robinson.

Nonfiction

Goals

Here you'll learn how to:

✔ appreciate the **two major goals of a biography**

✔ use the strategy of **looking for cause and effect**

✔ understand the **organization biographers use** in telling the story

Before Reading

A good biographer has two goals in mind when writing:

- tell an interesting story
- create a "portrait," or impression, of the biographical subject so that readers can understand what he or she is or was really like

A Set a Purpose

Imagine yourself looking over the biography shelves at your library. What drives you to choose one book over another? Most likely it's your curiosity about the biographical subject. Two questions that may come to mind as you thumb through the pages of a biography are:

What kind of life has he or she had?

What was he or she really like?

These two questions apply to any biography you read—whether for a school assignment or for pleasure. Finding answers to these two questions can be your purpose for reading.

Setting a Purpose

- **What kind of life has this person had?**
- **What was he or she really like?**

B Preview

Before you begin your preview of the book about Jackie Robinson, consider what you already know. Who was Jackie Robinson? What did he do that made him famous? What stories have you heard about him? Keep this information—called "prior knowledge"—in mind as you preview.

If the biographical subject is completely new to you, your preview takes on added importance. It will be your first introduction to someone that you will get to know very well. When you preview, pay attention to the items on this checklist:

Nonfiction

Preview Checklist

✔ the title and author
✔ the front, back, and inside covers
✔ the table of contents and chapter titles
✔ any photographs or illustrations
✔ any dedication, preface, introduction, or note to the reader
✔ the first paragraph or two of the text
✔ any repeated words

Now preview the covers and table of contents of John C. Chalberg's biography *Rickey & Robinson*. Use sticky notes or a highlighter to keep track of important details.

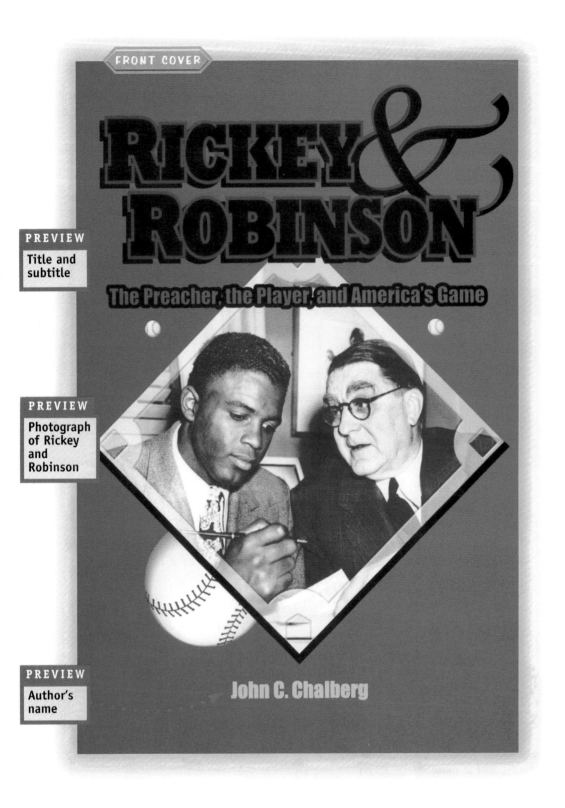

RICKEY & ROBINSON

PREVIEW

Title and subtitle

The Preacher, the Player, and America's Game

PREVIEW

Photograph of Rickey and Robinson

PREVIEW

Author's name

John C. Chalberg

BACK COVER

RICKEY & ROBINSON
The Preacher, the Player, and America's Game

John C. "Chuck" Chalberg

teaches American history at Normandale Community College in Bloomington, Minnesota. He has written *Emma Goldman: American Individualist* and edited *American Isolationism*. In his other lives he performs one-man shows as Teddy Roosevelt, H. L. Mencken, G. K. Chesterton, and Branch Rickey.

PREVIEW

Information about the author

Advance Praise for *Rickey & Robinson*:

"Chalberg knows his men. This sprightly written dual biography breathes life into two fascinating men forever joined in our historical imagination."

> *Larry R. Gerlach*
> *Professor of History, University of Utah*

"...a deft and entertaining account of the Rickey and Robinson saga. Based on a thorough knowledge of the secondary sources and great enthusiasm for the subject, this book should appeal to baseball historians and general readers alike."

> *Steve Gietschier*
> *The Sporting News*

PREVIEW

Critics' comments about the book

"A striking, provocative, and interesting book about two of the baseball giants of the 20th century.... The changing world of baseball, the civil rights movement, and the American social landscape provide the canvas on which the lives of these two men unfold."

> *Richard C. Crepeau*
> *Professor of History, University of Central Florida*

U.S. History/Sport History

Harlan Davidson, Inc.
Wheeling, Illinois 60090-6000

ISBN 0-88295-952-2

9 780882 959528

Contents

PREVIEW

Chapter titles

NOTE

Chapter titles suggest Robinson's story will be told chronologically.

Warm-ups

PREVIEW

First few paragraphs

August 1945 was a month of seismic shocks. On August 6 an atomic bomb obliterated Hiroshima. Three days later Nagasaki was hit with the same terrible weapon. Hiroshima and Nagasaki . . . the names of those two Japanese cities immediately became part of the permanent vocabulary of people everywhere, for what happened on those two devastating August days guaranteed a rapid end to the second great war of the twentieth century. It also proved a very unsettling start to what would soon prove to be a postwar filled with shocks and aftershocks all of its own.

A few weeks later a bombshell of a different sort reached an advanced state of readiness in an American city far removed from the carnage of war.

C Plan

What did you learn on your preview?

1. This is a "dual" biography, meaning it is about two people.
2. The author is a history teacher.
3. Rickey and Robinson were "baseball giants who met in 1945."
4. Robinson was African American, and Rickey was white.

You probably found other clues about Rickey and Robinson or noticed how the book is organized. The facts and details you found on your preview will serve as background for your careful reading.

Since your purpose is to find out about the life of the biographical subject, you'll want to mark, highlight, or take careful notes about facts and details. Pay attention to key events. Think about how those events shaped the life of the person you're reading about.

Nonfiction

Reading Strategy: Looking for Cause and Effect

All biographers try to show how the life experiences of the biographical subject affected that person. Watch for these experiences and their effects as you read.

To use the strategy of **looking for cause and effect,** draw one or more Cause-Effect Organizers in your journal, and make notes on the major events (the causes) side as you read. After reading, think about the effects of these causes, and write them in the Effects boxes. You can vary the number of Effects boxes.

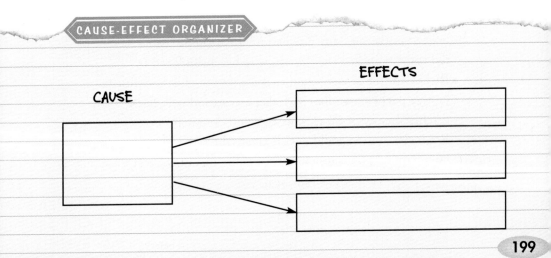

CAUSE-EFFECT ORGANIZER

EFFECTS

CAUSE

During Reading

Here are some questions that can keep you focused and on track as you read a biography:

- What are the key events of the person's life?
- What effects did these events have on him or her?
- What words would I use to describe the person?
- What is my opinion of him or her?

D Read with a Purpose

Now read an excerpt from Chalberg's biography. As you read, keep your purpose in mind. Be sure to take notes that help you meet this purpose. Track major events in your Cause-Effect Organizer.

This excerpt from the chapter titled "The Fifth Inning" focuses on Jackie Robinson's first season with the Brooklyn Dodgers. Robinson was the first African American to play major league baseball. Notice the highlighting and the Cause-Effect Organizer that follows.

> NOTE
> Robinson's reaction to discrimination

> NOTE
> Words signal time.

from *Rickey & Robinson* by John C. Chalberg

During that pathbreaking 1947 season there were many things that Jackie Robinson had to make himself do—and not do. He had to put up with the humiliation of staying alone in black hotels while his white teammates were housed in the best any city had to offer. On occasion, he did room with Wendell Smith, who had been hired by Rickey for the season. Smith's role was not clearly defined; he was part companion, part chaperone, and part flack catcher. In any of these roles he could do much for Robinson, but he could not eliminate the sense of humiliation and disappointment Jackie often felt.

from *Rickey & Robinson*, continued

Not the least of his pains concerned the failure of his white teammates to protest his being subjected to segregated housing arrangements whenever the Dodgers were on the road. And more often than not he had to eat alone, though on occasion he was joined by another Dodger rookie, centerfielder Duke Snider.

NOTE
Words signal place.

At bat, Robinson quickly learned that one of Branch Rickey's warnings had to be taken to heart. He also learned that Gene Benson hadn't been entirely right: the majors were not necessarily easier, at least not for their lone black player. By the end of May, Robinson had been thrown at— or close to—countless times and hit six times. On each of those half-dozen occasions he could only do what he had promised Rickey he would do: shake off the sting and trot stoically to first base. Though he probably did not know this, that sixth HBP (hit by a pitch) tied the individual mark for the whole of the 1946 season. There would be only three more such incidents during the rest of the 1947 season. Did National League pitchers suddenly grow kinder and gentler? Not really: two months of the season was enough to teach them that they didn't want the explosive Jackie Robinson dancing off first base and charging into second if they could possibly help it.

NOTE
Pitchers throw ball *at* instead of *to* Robinson.

NOTE
Words signal time.

Nonfiction

. . . There were also incidents that cut the other way. One day in Boston—or possibly Cincinnati, since the accounts vary—the foul language and general abuse was particularly offensive. This time some of the taunts seem to have been directed at Robinson's keystone partner, "Pee Wee" Reese. Of course, both Reese and Robinson knew who the real target of the animosity was. In the midst of the verbal abuse, Reese left his position, walked over to first base, and put his hand on Robinson's shoulder. Suddenly the hecklers in the stands and in the dugout grew silent. For the first time in anyone's memory a white player had touched a black player fondly—and deliberately—on a baseball diamond. Another turning point had been reached. And the season was not yet half over.

NOTE
Robinson is target of abuse.

NOTE
Reese puts his hand on Robinson's shoulder— why?

EFFECTS

CAUSE

became the only black player in baseball

→ stayed alone in black hotels

→ had to eat alone

→ hit by a ball six times

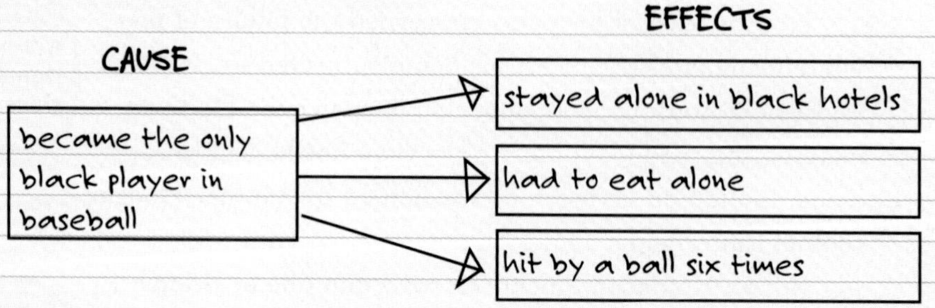

As you can see from the Cause-Effect Organizer, the fact that Robinson was the only black player had serious effects. What can you tell about how these events shaped his life?

Sometimes you have to read between the lines, or make some inferences about the influence of events on a person. If so, it's helpful to make an Inference Chart.

With it you can gather ideas about a character or situation to see what conclusions you can draw.

TEXT	WHAT I CONCLUDE
1. He had to stay alone in black hotels and eat alone.	He was probably lonely and angry because of segregation.
2. He was hit by pitches.	He must have been bruised and realized how dangerous this was.
3. He was insulted on the field.	It must have been hard for him to keep his temper.
4. Reese puts his hand on Robinson's shoulder.	Robinson was probably surprised and grateful.

Details about Key Events

Making Sequence Notes can help you keep track of important events. Look again at the excerpt for some of the events the reader marked. The reader then created this simple organizer.

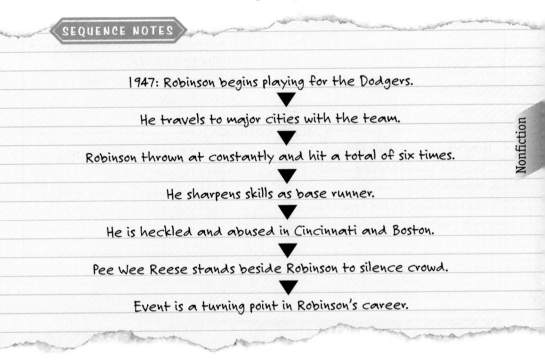

SEQUENCE NOTES

1947: Robinson begins playing for the Dodgers.

▼

He travels to major cities with the team.

▼

Robinson thrown at constantly and hit a total of six times.

▼

He sharpens skills as base runner.

▼

He is heckled and abused in Cincinnati and Boston.

▼

Pee Wee Reese stands beside Robinson to silence crowd.

▼

Event is a turning point in Robinson's career.

Nonfiction

Keeping track of events and when they occur can help you understand cause and effect.

Details about the Subject

In addition to watching for details about time, place, and key events, you'll want to search carefully for details about the biographical subject. As you read, ask yourself:

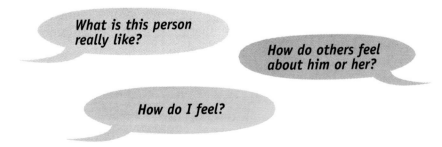

What is this person really like?

How do others feel about him or her?

How do I feel?

Use a Character Map to create a portrait of the subject and record your impressions.

WHAT HE SAYS AND DOES	WHAT OTHERS THINK ABOUT HIM
1. He's "explosive" and fast. 2. He "dances" and "charges."	1. Fans and opposing teams heckle him because he's black. 2. Management is confident enough in him to hire him. 3. Only Pee Wee Reese tries to defend him.

JACKIE ROBINSON

HOW HE LOOKS AND FEELS	HOW I FEEL ABOUT HIM
1. Picture shows him as a young man. 2. humiliated by racism 3. disappointed in his teammates 4. tries not to let insults bother him	1. I think he was brave. 2. In a lot of ways, he was a hero.

How Biographies Are Organized

Many biographies are written in **chronological** (time) **order.** This means that the biographer begins with the birth of the subject and continues telling the story in order through the subject's whole life.

1. Details about Time
2. Details about Place

Take another look at the table of contents for Chalberg's book (page 198). Notice that the chapter titles are named for the innings of a baseball game. They progress from the "first inning" to the "ninth." This important clue tells you Chalberg has used chronological order to tell Rickey and Robinson's story.

As you read a biography, look for changes in the subject's life. Sometimes the changes have to do with school, family, or jobs. Sometimes the changes are internal. They involve a transformation in the subject's feelings about himself or herself. When looking for these changes, pay attention to details about time, place, and key events.

adulthood

young
adulthood

school-age years

early years

Reader forms
opinion of subject.

completed portrait

Nonfiction

Details about Time

Look back at the excerpt. Notice that one reader highlighted these words:

- end of May
- 1946 season
- 1947 season
- season "not yet half over"

Highlighting these words helps you understand the sequence of events in Robinson's life.

Details about Place

Details about place are equally important in a biography. Where a person lives and works can have a profound effect on how that person thinks and feels. Consider, for example, how different Jackie Robinson's life would have been had he refused to travel with his team to the South. Did you notice these phrases as you were reading the excerpt?

- segregated housing
- on the road
- Boston or Cincinnati

The highlighting and notes you made while reading can help you understand what the subject was like and what kind of life he or she led. In addition, your notes can help you consider your own impressions of the subject.

E Connect

When you read a biography, think about your impression of the person described. How do you feel about the portrait the writer has created? Ask yourself:

> **Do I like this person? Why or why not?**

> **Would I want to be like this person?**

> **Do I admire him or her? Why or why not?**

One way to connect with a biography is to record your own thoughts as you read. Make predictions, comment on your reactions, and connect the events described to your own experiences. For example, look at the notes this reader made while reading *Rickey & Robinson:*

---

from *Rickey & Robinson*

> *I'm surprised that he didn't quit.*

Though he probably did not know this, that sixth HBP (hit by a pitch) tied the individual mark for the whole of the 1946 season. There would be only three more such incidents during the rest of the 1947 season. Did National League pitchers suddenly grow kinder and gentler? Not really: two months of the season was enough to teach them that they didn't want the explosive Jackie Robinson dancing off first base and charging into second if they could possibly help it.

> *I like the lesson Robinson taught them. He was a great base runner.*

After Reading

When you finish reading a biography, take a moment to consider what you've learned.

F Pause and Reflect

At this point, it's a good idea to return to your reading purpose. Ask yourself: "Have I met my purpose, or do I need to find out more about the biographical subject?" Use questions like these to help you decide if there's more you need to do.

Nonfiction

Looking Back

■ Can I name several important events in the subject's life?

■ Do I understand how these events affected the subject?

■ Do I have a sense of what the person was really like?

■ Can I say how I feel about the subject?

■ Can I support how I feel with evidence from the text?

G Reread

If you can't answer "yes" to all of the questions on the checklist, you may need to do some rereading. Of course, you won't have time to reread the entire biography. Instead, zero in on the parts that you thought were most important or most puzzling. Concentrate on making some thorough notes about these key parts of the biography.

For example, you might begin by listing some key areas of the subject's life that you would like to know more about.

 childhood

school and education

family

personality traits

first real accomplishments

Outlining can help you look at one part of the subject's life. To use the strategy, create an Outline with the Roman numerals I–IV. Leave plenty of room between the numerals for details. For an example, see the Outline below. This form will work for almost any biography you read.

Then page through the book and add to your Outline the most important events from the subject's life. If there's a part of the subject's life you'd like to study more, make additional notes on the Outline. For example, the Outline below focuses on Robinson's adult years and his time with the Dodgers.

TOPIC OUTLINE

Title or Subject
  I. Early Years
    A. important event
    B. important event
  II. School-age Years
    A. important event
    B. important event
  III. Young Adulthood
    A. important event
    B. important event
  IV. Adulthood
    A. important event
    B. important event
    C. important event

IV. Adulthood: Robinson's 1947
    season with the Dodgers
  A. encounters racism on the
     field and off
    1. insults
    2. forced to obey unfair
       segregation laws
  B. ignores taunts and jeers of
     the crowd
    1. stays quiet but refuses to
       back down
    2. must prove himself
  C. Reese incident
    1. crowd silent
    2. turning point

H Remember

Of course, no one expects you to remember every detail of every biography you read. Still, you'll often need to remember the important parts. Here are a couple of suggestions.

1. Make a Timeline

To help you remember key events from the subject's life, try making a Timeline. Begin by skimming the table of contents. Write key events in your reading journal. Then look at your during-reading notes. Pay particular attention to life-altering events in the subject's life, and add drawings to your timeline.

2. Make a Map

Draw a map showing the places that were important in the subject's life. Start with his or her birthplace, and then show where the subject went to school, worked, married, traveled, and died.

Nonfiction

Summing Up

The reading strategy of looking for **cause and effect** can help you understand how the key events shaped a biographical subject. Remember that most biographies are organized in **chronological** (time) **order.** Within this structure, the biographer describes one, two, or more key events from each phase of the subject's life. You can use one of these tools to keep track of what you're learning:

- ■ Cause-Effect Organizer
- ■ Inference Chart
- ■ Sequence Notes
- ■ Character Map
- ■ Outline

The rereading strategy of **outlining** can help you process what you've learned and focus on important parts of the subject's life.

Reading a Memoir

A **memoir** is a type of autobiographical writing. In an autobiography, the writer usually tells the story of his or her whole life in some detail. A memoir, however, focuses on only part of the writer's life, often a part that shaped his or her life most significantly.

Memoirs, like autobiographies, contain reflections on the meaning of various happenings in the writer's life, and they also provide insight into a particular time or place or describe the people with whom the writer was closely associated.

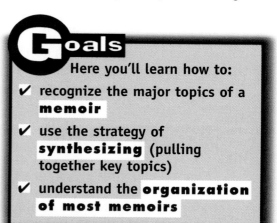

G oals

Here you'll learn how to:

✔ recognize the major topics of a **memoir**

✔ use the strategy of **synthesizing** (pulling together key topics)

✔ understand the **organization of most memoirs**

Here you'll use the reading process to help you read and understand an excerpt from Isak Dinesen's memoir *Out of Africa*. Isak Dinesen (1885–1962) was the pen name of Baroness Karen Blixen.

Before Reading

What compels some people to write a memoir? What do they hope to accomplish? Most people who write memoirs write with two goals in mind:

▉ to tell the story of part of their life in an interesting and dramatic way

▉ to provide insight into the people, places, times, and events that influenced them

Use the reading process to help you understand the writer's experiences and how those experiences shaped the person he or she became.

A Set a Purpose

Picture yourself standing in your local library. What makes you choose one autobiography, diary, collection of letters, or memoir over the others? Most likely, it's your interest in the person who wrote the book. You want to find out about this person's life. What exactly do you want to find out from the book you've chosen? Your answer to this question can help you set your purpose.

Nonfiction

Setting a Purpose

■ **What kind of life did this person have at this time?**

■ **How do I feel about him or her and the places, times, and events described?**

Finding answers to these two questions can be your purpose for reading. Keep them in mind as you read through a memoir.

B Preview

After you set your purpose, preview the memoir. Look carefully for these items.

Preview Checklist

✔ the title and author
✔ front and back cover
✔ any summaries, quotations, or reviews
✔ any dedication, preface, introduction, or note to the reader
✔ the title of each chapter
✔ any photographs or illustrations
✔ the opening paragraph or two of the first chapter

Now preview the front and back covers and inside jacket flap of Isak Dinesen's *Out of Africa*.

FRONT COVER

PREVIEW

Photo of author

ISAK DINESEN

PREVIEW

Title and author

OUT OF AFRICA

BACK COVER

THE MODERN LIBRARY OF THE WORLD'S
BEST BOOKS

◆

"I HAD A FARM IN AFRICA, AT THE FOOT OF
THE NGONG HILLS....IT WAS AFRICA DIS-
TILLED UP THROUGH SIX THOUSAND FEET, LIKE
THE STRONG AND REFINED ESSENCE OF A CON-
TINENT....IN THE HIGHLANDS YOU WOKE UP IN
THE MORNING AND THOUGHT: HERE I AM,
WHERE I OUGHT TO BE."

—ISAK DINESEN, "THE NGONG FARM"

PREVIEW

Quotation from book

PREVIEW

Summary

FROM INSIDE DUST JACKET

Out of Africa is Isak Dinesen's memoir of her years in Africa, from 1914 to
1931, on a four-thousand-acre coffee
plantation in the hills near Nairobi.
She had come to Kenya from Denmark with her husband, and when
they separated she stayed on to man-
age the farm by herself, visited frequently by . . . the big-game
hunter Denys Finch-Hatton, for
whom she would make up stories
"like Scheherazade." In Africa, "I
learned how to tell tales," she
recalled many years later. "The
natives have an ear still. I told stories
constantly to them, all kinds." Her
account of her African adventures,
written after she had lost her beloved
farm and returned to Denmark, is
that of a master storyteller, a woman
whom John Updike called "one of
the most picturesque and flamboy-
ant literary personalities of the
century."

PREVIEW

Reviewer comments

Plan

What did you notice on your preview?

- Dinesen lived on a coffee plantation in Africa from 1914 to 1931.
- *Out of Africa* is her memoir of that time.
- Dinesen managed the plantation by herself after she and her husband separated.

Did you learn anything else? Perhaps you already know something about Dinesen or have seen a movie about this part of her life. If so, add what you know to your preview notes. Your knowledge will come in handy when it is time to do a careful reading.

When you've finished previewing, make a reading plan. What strategy can help you get the most from reading a memoir?

Reading Strategy: Synthesizing

Use **synthesizing** to pull together key topics in a memoir and then look at them as a whole. Synthesizing helps you get a feel for the big picture. Synthesizing is like gluing several photographs onto a piece of paper. When you've finished, you have a completed "portrait" of a person, time, place, idea, or event.

Synthesizing works well with memoirs because most memoirs cover the same general topics:

KEY TOPICS IN A MEMOIR

1. reasons for the focus on this particular period in the writer's life

2. physical surroundings

3. actions and personalities of people the writer knew

4. work and major achievements

5. major problems and how they were overcome

6. opinions and actions that reveal the writer's character and personality

Finding Key Topics

As you read, watch for facts and details about each of these topics. Pay particular attention to the anecdotes (little stories) the writer tells. These can help sharpen your impression of the writer.

To use the strategy, make a Key Word or Topic Notes chart. List key topics on the left side. Use the right side for your during-reading notes. Key Word or Topic Notes help you remember main ideas.

KEY WORD OR TOPIC NOTES

Nonfiction

KEY TOPICS	NOTES
reasons for the focus on this period in the writer's life	
physical surroundings	
work and major achievements	
major problems	
personality and character traits	

Your notes in the right column will come from all parts of the memoir. Some notes may be quite long, so leave plenty of room between each key topic.

You may find as you're reading that you need to add a topic or two to the left side of the organizer. For example, if the writer does a lot of traveling, you might make "travels" a key topic and then take notes on that topic in addition to the others. You might also want to make notes on what the writer seems to value most in life.

During Reading

After you set up the organizer for your Key Topic Notes, you can begin your careful reading of the memoir.

D Read with a Purpose

Keep your reading purpose in mind. Remember that your first reading goal is to find out about the kind of life Dinesen had in Africa. Your second reading goal is to decide how you feel about her and the people, places, times, and events described.

As you read, take notes in your key topic organizer. Jot down important or interesting details, as well as any questions you have for the author. If you're not sure where something belongs in the organizer, write it on a sticky note, and leave it in the book for later.

Now read these excerpts from Chapter 1 of *Out of Africa*.

---

from *Out of Africa* by Isak Dinesen

I had a farm in Africa, at the foot of the Ngong Hills. The Equator runs across these highlands, a hundred miles to the North, and the farm lay at an altitude of over six thousand feet. In the day-time you felt that you had got high up, near to the sun, but the early mornings and evenings were limpid and restful, and the nights were cold.

Physical surroundings

The geographical position, and the height of the land combined to create a landscape that had not its like in all the world. There was no fat on it and no luxuriance anywhere; it was Africa distilled up through six thousand feet, like the strong and refined essence of a continent. The colors were dry and burnt, like the colors in pottery. The trees had a light delicate foliage, the structure of which was different from that of the trees in Europe; it did not grow in bows or cupolas, but in horizontal layers, and the formation gave to the tall solitary trees a likeness to the palms, or a heroic and romantic air like fullrigged ships with their sails clewed up, and to the edge of a wood a strange appearance as if the whole wood were faintly vibrating.

She describes the land.

from *Out of Africa*, continued

We grew coffee on my farm. The land was in itself a little too high for coffee, and it was hard work to keep it going; we were never rich on the farm. But a coffee-plantation is a thing that gets hold of you and does not let you go, and there is always something to do on it: you are generally just a little behind with your work.

She was determined.

In the wildness and irregularity of the country, a piece of land laid out and planted according to rule, looked very well. Later on, when I flew in Africa, and became familiar with the appearance of my farm from the air, I was filled with admiration for my coffee-plantation, that lay quite bright green in the gray-green land, and I realized how keenly the human mind yearns for geometrical figures. All the country round Nairobi, particularly to the north of the town, is laid out in a similar way, and there lives a people, who are constantly thinking and talking of planting, pruning or picking coffee, and who lie at night and meditate upon improvements to their coffee-factories.

She was proud of her farm.

Coffee-growing is a long job. It does not all come out as you imagine, when, yourself young and hopeful, in the streaming rain, you carry the boxes of your shining young coffee-plants from the nurseries, and, with the whole number of farm-hands in the field, watch the plants set in the regular rows of holes in the wet ground where they are to grow, and then have them thickly shaded against the sun, with branches broken from the bush, since obscurity is the privilege of young things. It is four or five years till the trees come into bearing, and in the meantime you will get drought on the land, or diseases, and the bold native weeds will grow up thick in the fields—the black-jack, which has long scabrous seed-vessels that hang on to your clothes and stockings.

Problem: drought, diseases, weeds

Nonfiction

Place: near Nairobi

Nairobi was our town, twelve miles away, down on a flat bit of land amongst hills. Here were the Government House and the big central offices; from here the country was ruled.

When I first came to Africa, there were no cars in the country, and we rode in to Nairobi, or drove in a cart with six mules to it, and stabled our animals in the stables of *The Highland Transport*. During all my time, Nairobi was a motley place, with some fine new stone buildings, and whole quarters of old corrugated iron shops, offices and bungalows, laid out with long rows of eucalyptus trees along the bare dusty streets. The Offices of the High Court, the Native Affairs Department, and the Veterinary Department were lousily housed, and I had a great respect for those government officials, who could get any work at all done in the little burning hot, inky rooms in which they were set.

Sympathizes with workers

The colony is changing and has already changed since I lived there. When I write down as accurately as possible my experiences on the farm, with the country and with some of the inhabitants of the plains and woods, it may have a sort of historical interest.

Her purpose for writing the memoir

What did you learn about Dinesen from reading these parts of *Out of Africa*? Sort out the information in your Key Topic Notes.

KEY WORD OR TOPIC NOTES

KEY TOPICS	NOTES
reasons for the focus on this period in the writer's life	experiences may be of historical interest
physical surroundings	• plantation near the equator • over six thousand feet high
work and major achievements	• successfully ran a coffee plantation
major problems	• drought, weeds, and diseases • transportation difficult
personality and character traits	• feels pride in her achievements • loves the beauty of Africa • is strong and determined

Nonfiction

Key Word or Topic Notes can help you keep track of important details from the writer's life. Keep in mind that you have two parts to your reading purpose. The second part includes forming an opinion about the author. To do this, use a Web. An organizer like this one can sharpen your understanding of the author.

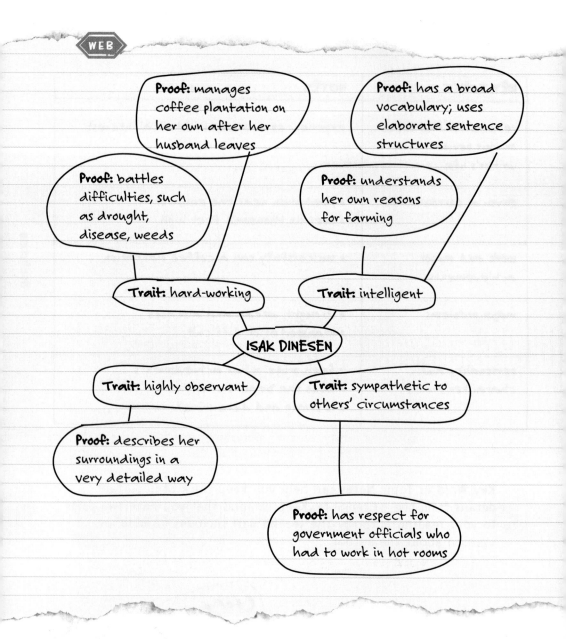

Proof: manages coffee plantation on her own after her husband leaves

Proof: has a broad vocabulary; uses elaborate sentence structures

Proof: battles difficulties, such as drought, disease, weeds

Proof: understands her own reasons for farming

Trait: hard-working

Trait: intelligent

ISAK DINESEN

Trait: highly observant

Trait: sympathetic to others' circumstances

Proof: describes her surroundings in a very detailed way

Proof: has respect for government officials who had to work in hot rooms

Add traits and proofs as you read the memoir. Each time you add a new trait, try to supply at least two pieces of proof. If you can't support a trait, it may not be very important in the writer's life.

You might also collect your feelings about the author in an Inference Chart. Making inferences as you read is a good way to learn about the author.

INFERENCE CHART

TEXT	WHAT I CONCLUDE
Writer She took over management of the coffee plantation after her husband left.	She was determined and brave. It probably wasn't easy to run that plantation on her own.
Places She describes her farm in detail. Nairobi, where the government offices were, was the nearest town.	Her descriptions of the farm and the surrounding countryside make them sound beautiful. Nairobi must have been where she bought supplies.
Times When she first arrived (1914), there were no cars there.	It must have been hard to run a farm without a car, and it must have taken a long time to travel the twelve miles to town.

Nonfiction

An Inference Chart helps you draw conclusions about important aspects of a subject's life. Note how each inference is based on fact, a quote, or an event from the memoir.

How Memoirs Are Organized

Every memoir you read will be organized a little differently. Still, most memoirs share several features.

Almost all memoirs are written in the first-person. Watch for pronouns such as I, we, and our.

A memoir often focuses on one or more major periods in the writer's life. Look for them.

Memoirs are not always told in chronological order, so you may want to create a Timeline of events. You can add events as you read the whole book.

TIMELINE

Dinesen goes to Africa.
Dinesen returns to Denmark.

| 1914 | | no cars yet | separates from husband | grows coffee | later flew in Africa | 1931 |

Connect

As you read about the kind of life Dinesen led in Africa, consider the second part of your reading purpose—to form impressions of the writer and the people, places, times, and events described. As you read, make notes in your reading journal about your impressions or ideas.

JOURNAL

This was obviously a major period in Dinesen's life, one that deeply affected her. Maybe this was because her life in Africa was so different from her life in Europe.

After Reading

After you finish a memoir, take a minute to think about the portrait the writer has created. Begin with a check to see whether you've met your reading purpose.

F Pause and Reflect

After you finish reading, you probably should review your reading purpose. Then ask yourself questions like these:

Looking Back

- Do I have a good portrait of the writer?
- Do I have a clear impression of the people, places, times, and events?
- Do I know how I feel about the writer?
- Do I understand the purpose of the memoir?

If you feel you cannot answer "yes" to each, you may need to do some rereading.

G Reread

Sometimes you need to "see" something in your mind or say it aloud in order to understand it. Suppose that after reading the memoir you still don't have a clear idea of the places Dinesen describes. As you reread, look for details that describe the settings.

Rereading Strategy: Visualizing and Thinking Aloud

When you **visualize,** you make mental pictures of what you are reading. When you **think aloud,** you talk to yourself about what you are reading. To use the strategy, make some quick sketches of the places Dinesen describes. While you sketch, talk to yourself about what you're doing. This can help you make sense of a passage.

Nonfiction

H Remember

If you've read a complete memoir for a class assignment, you need to find a way to remember the important facts and details. Here are two suggestions that can help you remember what you've read.

1. Give an Oral Summary

Think of a friend, classmate, or family member who would be interested in hearing a summary of the memoir. Use the chapter titles in the book and your notes to prepare a summary. End with your opinion of the memoir.

2. Write a Book Review

Try writing a review of the memoir. You might just write it in your reading journal. Or, you might try to publish it in your school newspaper or literary magazine. Open the review with your overall impression of the author and the book. Here is an example of the opening of one reader's review:

> **BOOK REVIEW**
>
> Isak Dinesen's Out of Africa is the story of the seventeen years she managed a coffee plantation near Nairobi and of her love for the land and the people. Dinesen is honest about the difficulties she faced from 1914 until 1931, and she describes both her strengths and her weaknesses. Her descriptions of daily life on the farm help you see, hear, and feel what life was like for her and for the many people she knew.

Summing Up

Remember that many memoirs are **organized in chronological order.** Use the reading process and the strategy of **synthesizing** (pulling together major topics) to help you get more out of a memoir. These reading tools can help you get a sense of the writer's life and personality:

- Web
- Inference Chart
- Key Topic Notes
- Timeline

Remember, too, that **visualizing and thinking aloud** when you reread can help you "see" key passages in a memoir.

Focus on Persuasive Writing

On any given day, you probably read dozens of examples of persuasive writing. Radio, television, the Internet, posters, and signs all contain persuasive messages. You may even see an airplane trailing a long banner with a message intended to persuade.

Persuasive writing makes an argument or attempts to prove something is true. It attempts to convince you to adopt the viewpoint of the writer. Among other things, persuasive writing can ask you to:

- take action
- spend money
- accept an opinion
- consider an idea
- support a cause
- change your mind

Here you'll read an essay called "Appearances Are Destructive." As you read, think about what the author is persuading you to do.

Goals

Here you'll learn how to:

✔ **recognize the topic and the author's assertion and viewpoint**

✔ **identify the three parts of an argument**

✔ **use the strategy of reading critically to evaluate the argument**

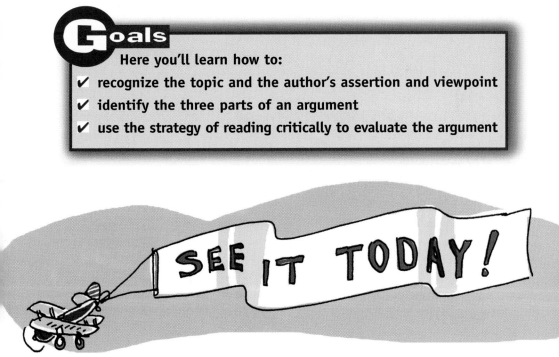

SEE IT TODAY!

Nonfiction

Here's a three-step plan for focusing on persuasive writing:

THREE-STEP PLAN

Step 1. Find the topic.

Step 2. *Find what the writer says about the topic (his or her assertion or viewpoint).*

Step 3. *Decide what you think about the writer's argument.*

The **assertion** is a statement of belief that the writer explains and supports. In most persuasive writing the assertion is brief and direct—sometimes only one sentence long. The assertion may include such phrases as, "You should . . . ," "The point is . . . ," or "What I'm trying to say is. . . ."

A writer's assertion can appear anywhere in the essay, article, or editorial. In some persuasive writing, the assertion appears at the beginning of the piece. It is then usually followed by three or more pieces of support. In other persuasive writing, the assertion comes at the end and is preceded by three or more pieces of support.

Look for the topic and assertion in this essay "Appearances Are Destructive" by Mark Mathabane. As you preview, look for:

Preview Checklist

✔ the title or headline
✔ the first and final paragraphs
✔ any repeated words and phrases

After your preview, take a moment to organize what you've learned. Notice the notes one reader collected in a Preview Chart.

PREVIEW

Title

"Appearances Are Destructive" by Mark Mathabane

PREVIEW

First paragraph

As public schools reopen for the new year, strategies to curb school violence will once again be hotly debated. Installing metal detectors and hiring security guards will help, but the experience of my two sisters makes a compelling case for greater use of dress codes as a way to protect students and promote learning.

NOTE

Mathabane's topic = dress codes

Shortly after my sisters arrived here from South Africa I enrolled them at the local public school. I had great expectations for their educational experience. Compared with black schools under apartheid, American schools are Shangri-Las, with modern textbooks, school buses, computers, libraries, lunch programs and dedicated teachers.

Nonfiction

NOTE

Support #1 from writer's life

But despite these benefits, which students in many parts of the world only dream about, my sisters' efforts at learning were almost derailed. They were constantly taunted for their homely outfits. A couple of times they came home in tears. In South Africa students were required to wear uniforms, so my sisters had never been preoccupied with clothes and jewelry.

PREVIEW

Repeated words

They became so distraught that they insisted on transferring to different schools, despite my reassurances that there was nothing wrong with them because of what they wore.

I have visited enough public schools around the country to know that my sisters' experiences are not unique. In schools in many areas, Nike, Calvin Klein, Adidas, Reebok and Gucci are more familiar names to students than Zora Neale Hurston, Shakespeare and Faulkner. Many students seem to pay more attention to what's on their bodies than in their minds.

NOTE

Support #2

Teachers have shared their frustrations with me at being unable to teach those students willing to learn because classes are frequently disrupted by other students ogling themselves in mirrors, painting their fingernails, combing

NOTE

Support #3

their hair, shining their gigantic shoes, or comparing designer labels on jackets, caps and jewelry.

The fiercest competition among students is often not over academic achievements, but over who dresses most expensively. And many students now measure parental love by how willing their mothers and fathers are to pamper them with money for the latest fads in clothes, sneakers and jewelry.

Those parents without the money to waste on such meretricious extravagances are considered uncaring and cruel. They often watch in dismay and helplessness as their children become involved with gangs and peddle drugs to raise the money.

When students are asked why they attach so much importance to clothing, they frequently reply that it's the cool thing to do, that it gives them status and earns them respect. And clothes are also used to send sexual messages, with girls thinking that the only things that make them attractive to boys are skimpy dresses and gaudy looks, rather than intelligence and academic excellence.

The argument by civil libertarians that dress codes infringe on freedom of expression is misleading. We observe dress codes in nearly every aspect of our lives without any diminution of our freedoms—as demonstrated by flight attendants, bus drivers, postal employees, high school bands, military personnel, sports teams, Girl and Boy Scouts, employees of fast-food chains, restaurants and hotels.

In many countries where students outperform their American counterparts academically, school dress codes are observed as part of creating the proper learning environment. Their students tend to be neater, less disruptive in class and more disciplined, mainly because their minds are focused more on learning and less on materialism.

It's time Americans realized that the benefits of safe and effective schools far outweigh any perceived curtailment of freedom of expression brought on by dress codes.

PREVIEW
Repeated words

NOTE
Support #4

NOTE
Addresses opposing viewpoint

NOTE
Support #5

PREVIEW
Final paragraph

PREVIEW CHART

Title:	"Appearances Are Destructive"

CLUES ABOUT THE TOPIC	CLUES ABOUT THE ASSERTION
repeated words: clothing, jewelry, shoes His topic = dress codes	Assertion appears in first and final paragraphs. He is in favor of dress codes for students.

Nonfiction

After you've made some notes about the topic and assertion, you can begin reading critically. Reading critically is a valuable strategy to use with persuasive writing.

Reading Strategy: **Reading Critically**

Reading critically means understanding and evaluating what a text has to say. Once you know the subject of the essay and the author's assertion, you can evaluate the quality of the argument and decide how you feel about it. Now you're ready to read the essay slowly and critically.

During Reading

When you read writing intended to persuade, don't decide right away how you feel about it. First, be sure you understand the point the writer is making and how he or she makes it.

Every good argument has three parts.

229

Assertion	Support	Opposing Viewpoint
A statement of belief that the author explains and then supports	The facts, figures, statistics, and examples the author gives that prove the assertion is correct	The "other side" of the argument. Since every argument has at least two sides, the writer must anticipate objections to the assertion and then refute or answer those objections.

The three parts of an argument can appear in any order. They can also be mixed together. Your job as a critical reader is to check that all three parts are present. If one part is missing, the argument is flawed. Here is how one reader used an Argument Chart to sort Mathabane's argument.

ARGUMENT CHART

ASSERTION	SUPPORT	OPPOSING VIEWPOINT
Dress codes benefit students in many ways.	#1 Mathabane's story about his sisters' view of dress codes	#1 limits personal freedom of what you can wear
	#2 his observations in schools around the world	#2 students' opposition to dress codes
	#3 his discussions with teachers about dress codes	
	#4 his thoughts about students pressuring parents for nice clothes	
	#5 his thoughts about more disciplined students	

After Reading

Think about the points Mathabane makes in his essay. Ask yourself:

> **What's my opinion of Mathabane's assertion?**

> **Is his support strong and convincing?**

> **Has his argument changed my view of the topic?**

Nonfiction

1. Connect to the Topic

How does the topic relate to your own life? Have you had any experiences that are similar to the ones the author has described? Make some notes. Here are one reader's thoughts about a paragraph from Mathabane's essay.

from "Appearances Are Destructive"

The fiercest competition among students is often not over academic achievements, but over who dresses most expensively. And many students now measure parental love by how willing their mothers and fathers are to pamper them with money for the latest fads in clothes, sneakers and jewelry.

This is really true! Kids in our school spend a lot of time worrying about who's best dressed.

2. Evaluate the Argument

Do you find Mathabane's argument persuasive? Do you feel that his support is convincing? What other evidence might have strengthened his point?

Evaluate the essay in your reading journal. Do you agree with this reader's response?

I think Mathabane's argument is clear. I could tell right away how he feels about dress codes and why he thinks they are necessary. I like the fact that he told about an experience from his own life to begin his argument. That makes his assertion more convincing.

But maybe you disagree. Let's say that you feel the writer's argument is *not* effective. If this is the case, you need to figure out why. Begin by checking for fallacies or **bias** in the writer's argument.

Understanding Propaganda Techniques

Writers use all kinds of techniques to make their arguments persuasive. Some of these techniques are effective, and some aren't. If an argument fails to persuade, it may be a "flawed" argument.

On the next page are some of the most common propaganda techniques. Think about the number of times you've seen them in ads, speeches, editorials, or essays.

1. Appeal to Ignorance *Suggesting that if no one has ever proved a particular claim, then it must not be true:* "Show me a study that proves violence on TV is bad for children."

2. Either/Or *Analyzing a complex situation as if it has only two sides:* "Either we buy a dishwasher today, or we live with dirty dishes for the rest of our lives."

3. Bandwagon Appeal *Suggesting that if everyone does it or believes it, it must be right or good:* "If everyone is fooling around in class, it must be OK for me to do it too."

4. Loaded Words *Using emotionally charged words that will produce strong positive or negative feelings:* "Our miraculous new vitamin will change your life forever."

5. Broad Generalization *Making a broad statement that something is true about all members of a group:* "Kids who don't play a sport are lazy."

6. Red Herring *Changing the subject to distract you from the real argument:* "Too much TV is bad for you, but video games are even worse." *(The second half of this statement has nothing to do with the dangers of too much TV, but it manages to soften the edges of the real argument.)*

7. Circular Thinking *Beginning with the very point you're trying to prove:* "That's a stupid idea because it makes no sense."

8. Straw Man *Exaggerating or oversimplifying the other side so that it can be rejected as* ridiculous: "Those citizens who oppose the war care nothing about democracy."

Nonfiction

Take another look at Mathabane's essay. Does he support his statement that "Many students now measure parental love by how willing their mothers and fathers are to pamper them. . . ."? No, he really doesn't. What about his use of the words *gangs, drugs,* and *gaudy looks?* Are these loaded words? Many people would consider them so. When you read writing intended to persuade, be on the lookout for propaganda techniques.

3. Decide How You Feel

After you decide whether an argument is convincing, consider how *you* feel about the author's assertion. Do you personally agree with the point the author is making? Why or why not?

One way to decide how you feel about a topic is to form your own argument about it. Organize your thoughts in an opinion chart. Your notes will come in handy if you're asked to make an oral or written presentation.

OPINION CHART

MY VIEWPOINT	SUPPORT	OPPOSING VIEWPOINT
I agree with Mathabane's idea that schools should have a dress code, but I think students should be allowed to decide what that dress code should be.	#1 In our school, there is a lot of competition to be "best dressed." #2 This causes hurt feelings and fights and distracts students from their real purpose for going to school. #3 A dress code could put a stop to these problems. #4 If students are allowed to decide what the code will be, there will be a better chance that everyone will follow it.	Parents and students who believe clothing is a form of self-expression and sign of status might object to a dress code.

Summing Up

- Good persuasive writing has three parts: an assertion, support for the assertion, and acknowledgment of opposing viewpoints.

- Use the strategy of reading critically to analyze an argument and evaluate its effectiveness.

Focus on Speeches

Most of the time you listen to speeches, but sometimes you'll need to read one. You may have to give a speech, analyze one, or do a dramatic reading. Other times, you may want to read an interesting political speech that has been reprinted in a newspaper.

Using the reading process when you read a speech will help you understand and evaluate the speaker's message.

Goals

Here you'll learn how to:
- ✔ find the speaker's purpose
- ✔ use the strategy of reading critically
- ✔ understand how speeches are organized
- ✔ recognize common stylistic devices

Nonfiction

Before Reading

Reading a speech is like reading any piece of nonfiction. Your job as reader is to find out what the speaker says. Some of the first questions to ask yourself are these: What is the subject, and what is the speaker's purpose?

Think about the reason for the speech. Most speakers have one of two purposes in mind: to inform or to persuade. The purpose of an informative speech is to explain something. The purpose of a persuasive speech is to convince the audience to adopt the viewpoint of the speaker. This diagram shows common characteristics of each type of speech.

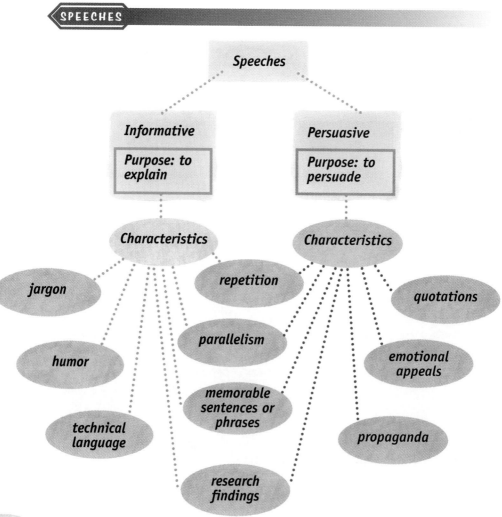

Reading a Speech

Here's a four-step plan for focusing on a speech:

FOUR-STEP PLAN

Step 1.
Figure out the occasion or purpose of the speech.

▶

Step 2.
Understand the organization.

▶

Step 3.
Find out the speaker's main idea or viewpoint and support for that idea or viewpoint.

▶

Step 4.
Evaluate the speech.

Nonfiction

Previewing

Previewing can help you find the occasion for the speech. Previewing can also give you important information about the organization of the speech, the speaker's main idea or viewpoint, and the support for the main idea or viewpoint.

Most published speeches include some background information about the speaker and the historical significance of the speech. Pay careful attention to this information. It often will give you clues about the subject and purpose.

Preview Checklist

✔ the title
✔ the topic
✔ the context (time, place, and audience)
✔ the introduction and conclusion
✔ any repeated words and phrases

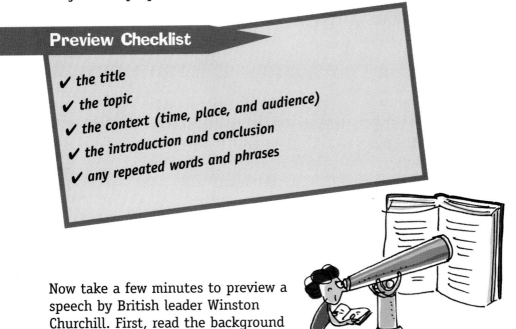

Now take a few minutes to preview a speech by British leader Winston Churchill. First, read the background section.

"Blood, Toil, Tears, and Sweat" by Winston Churchill

This speech was given May 13, 1940, only three days after Churchill first became prime minister of Britain. The speech was given in the House of Commons, the lower house of Parliament, in London. Churchill's speeches were often repeated on the radio at night and served to strengthen the British resolve to defeat Hitler's advancing armies during World War II. In 1940, the Nazis were threatening to invade England.

It must be remembered that we are in the preliminary stage of one of the greatest battles in history, that we are in action at many points in Norway and in Holland, that we have to be prepared in the Mediterranean, that the air battle is continuous and that many preparations have to be made here at home. In this crisis I hope I may be pardoned if I do not address the House at any length today. I hope that any of my friends and colleagues, or former colleagues, who are affected by the political reconstruction, will make all allowance for any lack of ceremony with which it has been necessary to act. I would say to the House, as I said to those who have joined the Government: "I have nothing to offer but blood, toil, tears, and sweat."

We have before us an ordeal of the most grievous kind. We have before us many, many long months of struggle and of suffering. You ask, what is our policy? I will say: It is to wage war, by sea, land, and air, with all our might and with all the strength that God can give us: to wage war against a monstrous tyranny, never surpassed in the dark, lamentable catalogue of human crime. That is our policy. You ask, What is our aim? I can answer in one word: Victory— victory at all costs, victory in spite of all terror, victory, however long and hard the road may be; for without victory, there is no survival. Let that be realized; no survival for the British Empire; no survival for all that the British Empire has stood for, no survival for the urge and impulse from "Blood, Toil, Tears, and Sweat," continued

of the ages, that mankind will move forward towards its
goal. But I take up my task with buoyancy and hope. I feel
sure that our cause will not be suffered to fail among men.
At this time I feel entitled to claim the aid of all, and I say,
"Come then, let us go forward together with our united
strength."

PREVIEW

Conclusion

What did you find out from previewing Churchill's speech? You
probably learned more than you expected.

Step 1. Look at the Occasion or Purpose of the Speech

The italic background before the speech makes it clear that Churchill
delivered this speech because he feared that Hitler would soon
invade England. You probably also learned from the repeated words
that Churchill had victory on his mind. Clearly, a part of Churchill's
purpose was to persuade the government and people of Great Britain
that they *could* win a fight against Hitler.

Before you begin your careful reading, choose a reading strategy.
Since you know Churchill's purpose was to persuade, you'll want to
use a reading strategy that works well with persuasive writing.
Reading critically can help because your task will be to evaluate
Churchill's argument.

Reading Strategy: Reading Critically

Reading critically means understanding and evaluating a text. When
reading a speech, you must know the purpose and subject of the
speech. Then you must understand the organization, speaker's
viewpoint, and support for the viewpoint. Finally, you'll decide how
you feel about the speech.

Now you're ready to read Churchill's speech slowly and carefully.

Step 2. Understand the Organization

The standard way to organize a speech is to divide it into an introduction, body, and conclusion. The speaker usually explains the purpose in the introduction and offers the main idea or viewpoint and support in the body of the speech. In the conclusion, the speaker restates the purpose or calls for action. The three parts are marked in Churchill's speech.

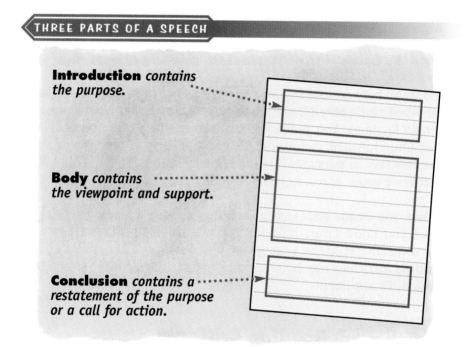

THREE PARTS OF A SPEECH

Introduction *contains the purpose.*

Body *contains the viewpoint and support.*

Conclusion *contains a restatement of the purpose or a call for action.*

Of course, not all speakers follow this organization. However, enough speakers do follow the standard organization that you should get into the habit of looking for the three main parts of the speech as you read. Identifying these parts can make it easier for you to understand the speaker's message.

One way of identifying the three parts of a speech is by making an Outline with three Roman numerals. Another option is to create a simple Nonfiction Organizer. It shows the three basic parts of Churchill's speech.

NONFICTION ORGANIZER

TITLE "Blood, Toil, Tears, and Sweat"
SUBJECT War against Hitler
INTRODUCTION • says the battle is just beginning • apologizes for his informality • stresses the importance of the situation
BODY • says long struggle ahead • emphasizes that victory is the aim
CONCLUSION • urges audience to join him in seeking victory against Hitler

Nonfiction

Step 3. Find out the Viewpoint and Support

Knowing how the speech is organized can make it easier to figure out the speaker's viewpoint and support. Sometimes a speaker will state the viewpoint directly ("Now is the time to forgive past grievances. . . . "). More often, however, the viewpoint is implied.

To find an implied viewpoint, use this formula:

> *Subject of the speech*
> *+ Speaker's opinion of the subject*
> _____
> *= Speaker's main idea or viewpoint*

(Churchill's subject)	war against Hitler
(Churchill's opinion of the subject)	+ victory is possible
(Churchill's viewpoint)	= Great Britain can win a war against Hitler.

All good speakers know that they must support their viewpoint.

| facts and statistics | firsthand experiences or examples | opinions of experts | logical reasoning |

| comparisons and contrasts | research results | appeals to emotion |

Some speakers will offer several different types of support. Others will rely heavily on one type—appeals to emotion or logic, for example. Your job as reader is to find the support and then decide whether or not it's convincing. An Evidence Organizer like the one shown here can help.

EVIDENCE ORGANIZER

VIEWPOINT: Great Britain can win a war against Hitler.			
SUPPORTING DETAIL #1	SUPPORTING DETAIL #2	SUPPORTING DETAIL #3	SUPPORTING DETAIL #4
We will wage war everywhere.	God will give us strength.	We will win because we must. There will be no British Empire without victory.	Churchill himself feels confident of victory.

Churchill doesn't offer the support you might expect to see in a persuasive speech. He gives no facts or statistics. Instead, he makes an appeal to the audience's emotions.

Appealing to the audience's emotions is a common persuasive technique. Good speakers know that if they can make the audience feel sad or angry or enthusiastic, they can persuade the audience to take action. Notice how Churchill does this.

from "Blood, Toil, Tears, and Sweat"

You ask, what is our policy? I will say: It is to wage war, by sea, land, and air, with all our might and with all the strength that God can give us: to wage war against a monstrous tyranny, never surpassed in the dark, lamentable catalogue of human crime. That is our policy. You ask, What is our aim? I can answer in one word: Victory— victory at all costs, victory in spite of all terror, victory, however long and hard the road may be; for without victory, there is no survival. Let that be realized; no survival for the British Empire; no survival for all that the British Empire has stood for, no survival for the urge and impulse of the ages, that mankind will move forward towards its goal. But I take up my task with buoyancy and hope. I feel sure that our cause will not be suffered to fail among men. At this time I feel entitled to claim the aid of all, and I say, "Come then, let us go forward together with our united strength."

NOTE

Appeals to sense of right and wrong

Nonfiction

NOTE

Appeals to a noble cause and sense of united purpose

In the body of the speech, Churchill calls Hitler's advance a "monstrous tyranny" and uses the words *dark* and *lamentable,* words designed to make the audience feel anger. Then he marshals the enthusiasm of the audience by proclaiming that victory is within their grasp. He ends the speech by inviting the people of Great Britain to join him and "go forward together with our united strength." With almost every sentence of the speech he appeals to the audience's emotions.

After Reading

Are you one of those people who can recognize a great speech the minute you read it? If you aren't (and most of us aren't), you'll need a plan that you can follow when it comes time to evaluate a speech.

4. Evaluate the Speech

First, notice and then analyze the speaker's stylistic devices.

Next, judge how well they work.

COMMON STYLISTIC DEVICES

Device	Example	What it does
Figurative language (similes, metaphors, hyperbole, and personification)	Churchill compares Hitler's aggression to "a monstrous tyranny, never surpassed in the dark, lamentable catalogue of human crime."	Adds freshness and vibrancy to the writing.
Repetition (repeated words or phrases)	"Victory—victory at all costs, victory in spite of all terror, victory however long and hard the road may be. . . ."	Adds emphasis and strength to the argument. Repetition can also make the speech memorable.
Parallelism (repeated grammatical structure)	"You ask, what is our policy? . . . You ask, What is our aim?"	Adds rhythm to the writing. Makes the speaker seem "eloquent" and therefore convincing.
Memorable sentences or phrases	"I have nothing to offer but blood, toil, tears, and sweat."	Makes the speaker seem joined with the common people of Britain.
Propaganda techniques (see page 233)	"Come, then, let us go forward together with our united strength." (bandwagon)	Makes the speech all the more persuasive and convincing. Enlists the help of everyone.

Copy the form on the next page and evaluate Churchill's speech.

Evaluation Form

Speaker's Name _____

Speaker's Topic _____

	Poor	Fair	Good	Very Good	Excellent
1. Clear organization	❏	❏	❏	❏	❏
2. Clear viewpoint	❏	❏	❏	❏	❏
3. Use of support	❏	❏	❏	❏	❏
4. Language appropriate to audience	❏	❏	❏	❏	❏
5. Topic appropriate to audience	❏	❏	❏	❏	❏

Nonfiction

Very often the power of a speech comes through its appeals not just to our intelligence but to our hearts. If the speech touches you on some emotional level, then it is effective.

A speech is also effective if the support the writer offers is strong and convincing. Think again about Churchill's speech. To support his claim that Great Britain can win the war, he explains that God, humankind, and he himself are united in an effort to defeat Hitler. What could be more convincing than that?

Summing Up

■ Find out when and why the speech was given and who the audience was.

■ Use the strategy of reading critically to help you identify the speaker's viewpoint and support.

■ Understand the organization of the speech.

■ Evaluate the quality of the stylistic devices.

Elements of Nonfiction

In high school and beyond, you'll be expected to respond to all different kinds of nonfiction. For this reason, it's important that you become familiar with the terms people use when discussing nonfiction. Turn to this glossary of elements as needed. Look up the term, read the example, study the definition, and then apply what you've learned.

Elements of Nonfiction

Allusion

Writers often rely on the reader's knowledge of other works, such as poems, stories, novels, paintings, and musical works. Here is one example:

EXAMPLE from "Neighbors" by Dan Jacobson

Jamie was younger than the two girls. He was a victim of Down's syndrome; not so much a Scot, therefore, as a member of a nation to which people like himself belonged. He was big for his age, and plump, and invariably wore on his close-cropped head the cap of a local high school — which he would never be able to attend. The cap, and his girth, and the circularity of his features, and the trousers he wore pulled as high up his waist as they could go, made him look like Tweedledum or Tweedledee in Tenniel's illustrations to *Alice in Wonderland*.

Reference to another literary work

DESCRIPTION

An **allusion** to a well-known work serves as a point of reference for a reader. Here it establishes very specifically a point of comparison for the reader, who can look up Tenniel's illustration. Writers use allusions in their writing not primarily to show that they have read widely but also to suggest meaning without directly stating it.

Here, in the example, Dan Jacobson is describing his neighbors in South Africa and suggests Jamie's appearance by referring to the well-known pen and ink drawings in Lewis Carroll's classic novel. The allusion serves as a kind of shortcut, allowing a writer to suggest a lot more than he or she actually says.

DEFINITION

An **allusion** is a reference to another literary, artistic, or musical work.

Nonfiction

Analogy

Writers often grapple with the problem of how to explain something that is unfamiliar. Here a veteran news reporter explains the far-off events of the Vietnam War to his television audience.

EXAMPLE

from "We Are Mired in a Stalemate" by Walter Cronkite

Tonight, back in more familiar surrounds in New York, we'd like to sum up our findings in Vietnam, an analysis that must be speculative, personal, subjective. Who won and who lost in the great Tet offensive against the cities? I'm not sure. The Vietcong did not win by knockout, but neither did we. The referees of history may make it a draw. Another standoff may be coming in the big battles expected south of the Demilitarized Zone. Ke Sanh could well fall, with a terrible loss in American lives, prestige and morale, and this is a tragedy of our stubbornness there; but the bastion no longer is a key to the rest of the northern regions, and it is doubtful that the American forces can be defeated across the DMZ with any substantial loss of ground. Another standoff. On the political front, past performance gives no confidence that the Vietnamese government can cope with its problems, now compounded by the attack on the cities. It may not fall, it may hold on, but it probably won't show the dynamic qualities demanded of this young nation. Another standoff.

> Comparison to boxing match

DESCRIPTION

The writer compares the fighting in Vietnam to a boxing match. Key words such as *knockout, draw,* and *referees* tip you off. An **analogy** is a comparison of something unfamiliar to something much more familiar. By explaining the faraway war in terms of a boxing match, Cronkite cloaks the events in familiar terms.

DEFINITION

An **analogy** is a comparison of something unfamiliar with something that is better known.

Anecdote

As you read, you'll often find writers pausing for a moment to tell a brief story, as in this example.

EXAMPLE from *Kaffir Boy* by Mark Mathabane

I was out in the streets playing soccer one weekday afternoon when Florah came running up to me, crying. She told me that something terrible had happened at home and I was wanted immediately. When I reached home I found my mother pacing mechanically about the shack, murmuring helplessly, desperately, uncontrollably, clasping and unclasping her hands.

"It cannot be! No it cannot be! Not my husband! Not my husband!" She was saying to herself.

"What happened to Papa, Mama?" I said with fright as I flung myself at her. I thought that maybe he had been killed. For a while my mother did not answer; but finally she controlled her emotions and between sobs told me what had happened. My father had been arrested that morning at the bus stop—for being unemployed.

Story of his mother's distress

DESCRIPTION

An **anecdote** is a brief story told to entertain or make a point. In the example above, Mark Mathabane tells of his mother's reaction to the arrest of his father. The story helps make the point about the injustice of apartheid, a time in South Africa when blacks could be arrested simply for not having a job.

DEFINITION

An **anecdote** is a brief story told to make a point or to entertain.

Assertion or Viewpoint

To assert something means to state or declare it. An assertion expresses a viewpoint or opinion. Usually an assertion is backed up with ample evidence. Notice the way the statement below is supported in the sentences that immediately follow.

EXAMPLE

from *The Edge of the Sea* by Rachel Carson

Statement The edge of the sea is a strange and beautiful place. All through the long history of Earth it has been an area of unrest where waves have broken heavily against the land, where the tides have pressed forward over the continents, receded, and then returned. For no two successive days is the shore line precisely the same. Not only do the tides advance and retreat in their eternal rhythms, but the level of the sea itself is never at rest. It rises or falls as the glaciers melt or grow, as the floor of the deep ocean basins shifts under the increasing load of sediments, or as the earth's crust along the continental margins warps up or down in adjustment to strain or tension. Today a little more land may belong to the sea, tomorrow a little less. Always the edge of the sea remains an elusive and indefinable boundary.

Supporting details or evidence

DESCRIPTION

An **assertion** or **viewpoint** can be an author's opinion, claim, hypothesis, or conclusion. The essential element of an assertion is that it makes a statement followed by supporting evidence.

In the example above, Rachel Carson asserts the premise of her book *The Edge of the Sea*. In the first line of her book, she makes the assertion that "the edge of the sea is a strange and beautiful place." Carson's assertion attempts to hook the reader into the book and establish why the reader should continue on through the next 200-plus pages.

DEFINITION

An **assertion** or **viewpoint** is a claim, statement, or declaration that the writer supports with evidence or detail.

Author's Purpose

In 1963, Dr. Martin Luther King, Jr., was jailed for leading a Civil Rights protest in Birmingham, Alabama. From his jail cell, King wrote an open letter to the ministers of Birmingham. In the first paragraph of his letter, he reveals his purpose.

EXAMPLE

> from "Letter from Birmingham Jail" by Martin Luther King, Jr.
>
> My Dear Fellow Clergymen,
> While confined here in the Birmingham city jail, I came across your recent statement calling our present activities "unwise and untimely." Seldom, if ever, do I pause to answer criticism of my work and ideas. If I sought to answer all of the criticisms that cross my desk, my secretaries would be engaged in little else in the course of the day, and I would have no time for constructive work. But since I feel that you are men of genuine good will and that your criticisms are sincerely set forth, I would like to try to answer your statement in what I hope will be patient and reasonable terms.

King's purpose: to explain

DESCRIPTION

An author's reason for writing is called the **author's purpose.** The author's purpose is the stated or implied goal for writing.

An author might choose to write an essay, article, book, or other work of nonfiction for four basic reasons:

- to explain or inform
- to entertain
- to persuade
- to enlighten or reveal an interesting truth

Sometimes a writer will have two or more purposes in mind. However, one purpose is usually more important than the others.

DEFINITION

An **author's purpose** is his or her reason for writing. Authors generally write with one or more of these purposes in mind: to explain or inform, to entertain, to persuade, or to enlighten.

Nonfiction

251

Bias

Bias is a leaning in one direction, a partiality toward one view over another. You may think the word *bias* has negative connotations and that having a bias is a fault. But everyone has a bias of one sort or another. The problem lies with readers who aren't careful to detect it. What bias can you identify in the example below?

EXAMPLE

from *Coming into the Country* by John McPhee

Meanwhile the sight of the bear stirred me like nothing else the country could contain. What mattered was not so much the bear himself as what the bear implied. He was the predominant thing in that country, and for him to be in it at all meant that there had to be more country like it in every direction and more of the same country all around that. He implied a world. He was an affirmation to the rest of the earth that his kind of place was extant. There had been a time when his race was everywhere in North America, but it had been hunted down and pushed away in favor of something else. For example, the grizzly bear is the state animal of California, whose country was once his kind of place; and in California now the grizzly bear is extinct.

Feeling of writer

Makes contrast with California

DESCRIPTION

The passage above appears in John McPhee's account of his travels throughout Alaska. From it, you can probably infer McPhee's opinions about other environmental issues, such as logging, oil drilling, and a number of others. McPhee tells you of his **bias,** or partiality, by explaining how powerfully he was moved by seeing the grizzly bear. Then, he immediately contrasts that with the situation in California, where the grizzly bear, the state animal, is now extinct. A clear bias toward preserving the environment and our natural resources rings through this passage.

DEFINITION

A **bias** is a mental leaning, inclination, prejudice, or bent.

Connotation and Denotation

What's the difference between the words *home, house,* and *mansion?* What's different between a compact car and a gas-guzzler? Words have specific definitions, but they also suggest additional meanings. The choice of words in the example convey the author's feelings about Saddam Hussein and American weaponry in the Gulf War.

EXAMPLE

from "War and Remembrance" by Scott Simon

Strong words

Nonfiction

The repugnance I felt over this kind of remote control, slaughter-by-keystroke was more a moral misgiving than disapproval. Saddam Hussein was a bad man who had made his own citizens the main casualties of his mad, immoral, imperialist venture. But it was difficult to root for all of the extraordinary instruments the U.S. military was dedicating to Saddam's defeat. One day, an Air Force colonel showed me the guts of the bomb known as the Bouncing Betty—a diabolical basketball in appearance, round and brown but studded. It was designed to be dropped onto the desert floor, then bounce up two and a half feet to explode in a shower of shrapnel in all directions.

Words with moral overtones

DESCRIPTION

The **denotation** of a word is its dictionary definition. The **connotation** of a word is its emotional associations or what it implies.

The words *dislike, hate,* and *repugnance* carry the same denotation of extreme distaste, but *repugnance* has the strongest connotation. *Slaughter* has a stronger connotation than *destroy* or *kill. Diabolical* suggests evil. When you explore the connotative meanings of the words Simon uses, you feel his moral objections.

DEFINITION

The **denotation** of a word is its dictionary definition. The **connotation** of a word is the surrounding emotional feelings associated with it.

Deductive Reasoning

Writers will often begin with a general statement, or assertion, and then give several specific examples. Note the generalization that begins this paragraph:

EXAMPLE

from *On the Origin of Species* by Charles Darwin

There is no exception to the rule that every organic being naturally increases at so high a rate, that if not destroyed, the earth would soon be covered by the progeny of a single pair. ❶ Even slow-breeding man has doubled in twenty-five years, and at this rate, in a few thousand years, there would literally not be standing room for his progeny. ❷ Linnaeus has calculated that if an annual plant produced only two seeds—and there is no plant so unproductive as this—and their seedlings next year produced two, and so on, then in twenty years there would be a million plants.

> **Begins with general statement**

> **Moves to specific examples**

DESCRIPTION

The above example shows **deductive reasoning** because it goes from the general to the specific. The paragraph begins with a broad, general premise. Then it takes up two specific examples that demonstrate that it is valid.

- Example of how fast people multiply
- Example of how fast plants multiply

The term *deductive reasoning* refers to a way of thinking that begins with the general and goes to the specific or moves from a premise to a logical conclusion.

DEFINITION

Deductive reasoning is a pattern of thought that proceeds from the known to the unknown, from the general to the specific, or from a premise to a logical conclusion.

Inductive Reasoning

Have you ever heard the expression "Start small"? It refers to leading up to what's important or building up to bigger things, which is what inductive reasoning is. Note the points that lead up to the conclusion of this famous speech:

EXAMPLE

from "I Will Fight No More" by Chief Joseph

Tell General Howard I know his heart. What he told me before, I have it in my heart. I am tired of fighting. Our chiefs are killed; Looking-Glass is dead, Ta-Hool-Shute is dead. The old men are all dead. It is the young men who say yes or no. He who led on the young men is dead. It is cold, and we have no blankets; the little children are freezing to death. My people, some of them, have run away to the hills, and have no blankets, no food. No one knows where they are—perhaps freezing to death. I want to have time to look for my children, and see how many of them I can find. Maybe I shall find them among the dead. Hear me, my chiefs! I am tired; my heart is sick and sad. From where the sun now stands I will fight no more forever.

Series of details

Moves from specifics to general conclusion

DESCRIPTION

The term **inductive reasoning** refers to a way of thinking that begins with specific details and goes to a general or logical conclusion.

In the example, Chief Joseph uses inductive reasoning, beginning with specific details and moving toward a general (and inevitable) conclusion. As in this example, inductive reasoning is often used in persuasive writing.

DEFINITION

Inductive reasoning is a pattern of thought that proceeds from small, specific details or reasons to a broader, more general conclusion.

Nonfiction

Irony

As a way of joking or adding a touch of humor, writers will occasionally say the opposite of what they mean. Here, in a letter to his editor, novelist Frank O'Connor reacts to being addressed as "Mr. O'Connor."

EXAMPLE

from *The Happiness of Getting It Down Right* edited by Michael Steinman

Frank O'Connor to Gus Lobrano, May 22, 1952

False sense of being hurt

Dear Mr. Lobrano,

I am naturally deeply hurt at not being addressed as "professor." "Full Professor" itself would not be amiss. However as they've invited me back next year you'll have further opportunities.

Continues irony in next few sentences

Listen, I shall be deserting my professorship with indecent haste the week after next and hope to get to New York on Tuesday 3rd with good luck and a bit of wangling—now don't ask me what wangling is.

DESCRIPTION

You probably joke with friends all the time. You say one thing but mean another, because your friends *know* the truth. The obvious difference between "what is said" and "what is meant" is what creates the humor. **Irony** occurs when the intended meaning is the direct opposite of the stated meaning.

Frank O'Connor says he is "deeply hurt" at not being addressed as "professor," but he doesn't really mean it. As a reader, you can see clues to his irony in the following sentences. O'Connor implies that his editor could even address him as "full professor" and that there will be future opportunities for him to do so.

DEFINITION

Irony is a humorous or sarcastic way of saying the exact opposite of what is really meant.

Jargon

Some nonfiction contains jargon. Jargon refers to the technical language of a certain group, occupation, or class. Doctors, sports writers, actors, and scientists, for example, all use the jargon of their particular field. It can also refer to meaningless or unintelligible talk or writing.

EXAMPLE

from "Freshman Shows the Way" by Bob Sakamoto

. . . Samantha Findlay was born to play ball. When she's not taking extra ground balls after practice, she's in a batting cage perfecting a compact, powerful swing that's the envy of college players.

Findlay is batting .415 as Lockport heads into Friday's Class AA quarterfinals in East Peoria, and she has ten doubles, four triples, five home runs, 40 RBIs and 19 stolen bases.

DESCRIPTION

Although it is usually very technical, **jargon** is easily understood by members of a particular group—sports fans, for example. For people outside of that group, however, jargon can be confusing.

You can use two methods to make sense of jargon or technical vocabulary in a reading: guess/go and context clues.

- **Guess/go** Not every technical term will be essential to your understanding. Make a quick guess about a word you don't know, and then move on. If it turns out you need a clear understanding of the term, you can check a dictionary later.

- **Context clues** Use context clues to help you define tricky technical words. Check surrounding sentences for words that can help you understand the term in question.

DEFINITION

Jargon is the specialized or technical vocabulary of a particular group. Some authors use jargon to give "weight" to their writing. Others use jargon because these words best describe what they are discussing.

Nonfiction

Lead

To lead means "to guide or direct the course of." A lead is also the beginning of a news story, which in most instances contains all of the essential information of the story.

EXAMPLE

from "Terrorism Is Not the Only Scourge"

What
Who
When
How

Where
Why

Terrorism is like a hideous disease, and sensible countries seek to eradicate it. But it should not be forgotten that hideous diseases, of the non-metaphorical sort, kill and cripple far more people, especially in poor countries. Encouragingly, recent decades have seen huge progress in the struggle against sickness. Between 1960 and 1995, life expectancy in poor countries rose by 22 years, largely because modern medicine prevented millions of premature deaths. In the 1950s, 15% of children died before their fifth birthday; now only 4% do.

DESCRIPTION

A **lead** tries to answer the key questions in the first few paragraphs—*who, what, where, when, why*, and *how*. Sometimes a news story will begin with an attention-grabbing opening in the first paragraph or two and then explain the essential details. Most journalists, however, use the lead to help readers decide quickly whether or not they want to read a story by putting the key information right at the beginning. Then, a reader can decide to read more or stop after getting the gist of a story.

DEFINITION

A **lead** is the opening paragraphs of a news story and contains essential information. It usually tells *who, what, where, when, why,* and *how.*

Main Idea

In this paragraph, a writer describes her relationship with her parents. Can you tell what her main idea is?

EXAMPLE

from "To Be Young, Gifted and Black" by Lorraine Hansberry

Of love and my parents there is little to be written: their relationship to the children was utilitarian. We were fed and housed and dressed and outfitted with more cash than our associates and that was all. We were also vaguely taught certain vague absolutes: that we were better than no one but infinitely superior to everyone; that we were the products of the proudest and most mistreated of the races of man; that there was nothing enormously difficult about life; that one *succeeded* as a matter of course. . . . But of love, there was nothing ever said.

Main idea

Details supporting the main idea

DESCRIPTION

The **main idea** is the "big idea" of a single paragraph or an entire work. It is the central point the author makes. Identifying the main idea (also called a "thesis" or "controlling idea") will help you understand what the writing is about. When an author states the main idea, it may be in the first or last sentence. If the main idea is not stated directly, you have to infer the main idea by studying the details.

DEFINITION

The **main idea** is the central idea in a piece of writing. It is what the author wants you to remember most. Some writers state the main idea directly. Others expect you to infer it.

Nonfiction

Rhetorical Questions

Have you ever noticed that some writers ask questions that they don't expect you to answer? The questions are for effect and are, in fact, statements. Note the questions in this essay.

EXAMPLE   from "Benjamin Franklin" in *Studies in Classic American Literature* by D. H. Lawrence

The Perfectibility of Man! Ah heaven, what a dreary theme! The perfectibility of the Ford car! The perfectibility of which man? I am many men. Which of them are you going to perfect? I am not a mechanical contrivance.

Education! Which of the various me's do you propose to educate, and which do you propose to suppress?

Anyhow, I defy you. I defy you, oh society, to educate me or to suppress me, according to your dummy standards.

The ideal man! And which is he, if you please? Benjamin Franklin or Abraham Lincoln? The ideal man! Roosevelt or Porfirio Díaz?

There are other men in me, besides this patient ass who sits here in a tweed jacket. What am I doing, playing the patient ass in a tweed jacket? Who am I talking to? Who are you, at the other end of this patience?

Who are you? How many selves have you? And, which of these selves do you want to be?

Questions asked to make a point

DESCRIPTION

The explosion of questions in the above example shows the power of **rhetorical questions,** which are asked only for effect—to emphasize a point—and for which no answer is expected. In the example above, D. H. Lawrence is writing about Benjamin Franklin, who attempted to work toward the "perfectibility of man." Lawrence asks, "The perfectibility of which man?" He clearly expects no answer, because for him the answers are obvious.

DEFINITION

A **rhetorical question** is a question asked for effect and to make a statement or point. No answer is expected.

Satire

Writers use satire to poke fun at human vices or weaknesses. Who or what is Dave Barry's target in this excerpt from his column about a bus museum?

EXAMPLE

from "Budget Surplus Crisis Solved . . .
Build a Bus Museum" by Dave Barry

> **URGENT TAXPAYER BULLETIN:** The Federal Budget Surplus Crisis has become so severe that there is now serious talk in Washington of letting you keep slightly more of your own money.
>
> That is correct: The government has been taking in so much of your money that EVEN CONGRESS is having a hard time spending it all. Not that Congress isn't trying! In fact, in recent years Congress, faced with the alarming buildup of your money, has come up with some truly creative things to spend it on. My favorite is the Greyhound Bus Museum. . . .

Subject or "target" of the satire

Nonfiction

DESCRIPTION

Satire is a literary device used to ridicule or make fun of a human weakness or vice (for example, greed). Writers also use satire to poke fun at large institutions or society in general. In the example, note how Dave Barry uses satire to attack Congress for what he believes is wasteful spending.

In most cases, the purpose of a satire is to correct or change the subject of the satiric attack. Here the writer uses humor, irony, or sarcasm to make the target seem ridiculous and to show readers why change is needed.

DEFINITION

Satire is a literary device used to ridicule or make fun of human vices or weaknesses. The usual purpose of satire is to correct or change the subject of the satiric attack.

Supporting Details

Nonfiction writers develop their topics by providing supporting details. The details may consist of facts, statistics, expert opinion, or directions. Or, they may be descriptive and appeal to the senses. Notice the sensory details in this example.

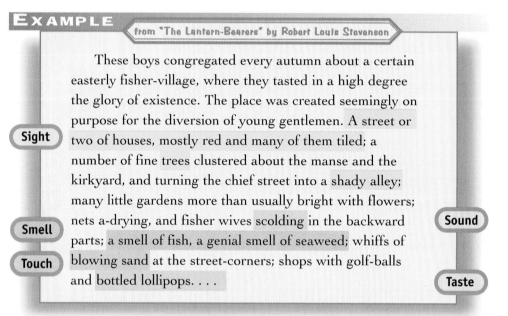

EXAMPLE

from "The Lantern-Bearers" by Robert Louis Stevenson

These boys congregated every autumn about a certain easterly fisher-village, where they tasted in a high degree the glory of existence. The place was created seemingly on purpose for the diversion of young gentlemen. A street or two of houses, mostly red and many of them tiled; a number of fine trees clustered about the manse and the kirkyard, and turning the chief street into a shady alley; many little gardens more than usually bright with flowers; nets a-drying, and fisher wives scolding in the backward parts; a smell of fish, a genial smell of seaweed; whiffs of blowing sand at the street-corners; shops with golf-balls and bottled lollipops. . . .

Sight

Smell

Touch

Sound

Taste

DESCRIPTION

Writers often use facts, statistics, expert opinion, or directions as **supporting details** to back up their opinions or describe a process.

Details that appeal to the senses are often used to create a clear description of a person, place, time, object, or action. Some writers use both types of details in a single selection.

DEFINITION

Supporting details are used to furnish evidence, describe a process, or create an impression. They help make writing vivid and believable.

Understatement

Sometimes writers exaggerate to get their point across or to make people laugh. Other times they say less than they mean, as in this example.

EXAMPLE

> from *The Universe* by Isaac Asimov

> In fact, if we go back 2,500 years to, say, 600 B.C., we find that the entire Universe known to man was but a patch of flat ground, and not a very large patch either.
> That is still all that man is directly aware of today; just a patch of flat ground and, of course, the sky overhead with small luminous objects shining in it. Nor does the sky seem to be very far above our heads.

> Making something sound less than it is

DESCRIPTION

In the passage above, science writer Isaac Asimov makes it sound as if humans know very little about the universe. He mentions two examples, that people are aware only of a patch of ground and of a sky that seems nearby. He deliberately uses **understatement** to emphasize how little many people still understand.

Understatement is the opposite of exaggeration. Writers use it to get their point across, open readers' eyes, and add humor or an element of surprise.

DEFINITION

Understatement is a technique in which writers intentionally say less than is complete or true.

Nonfiction

Reading Fiction

Introduction to Reading Fiction

Reading Kinds of Fiction

Reading a Short Story
Reading a Novel

Ways of Reading Fiction

Focus on Plot
Focus on Setting
Focus on Characters
Focus on Theme
Focus on Dialogue
Focus on Comparing and Contrasting

Elements of Fiction

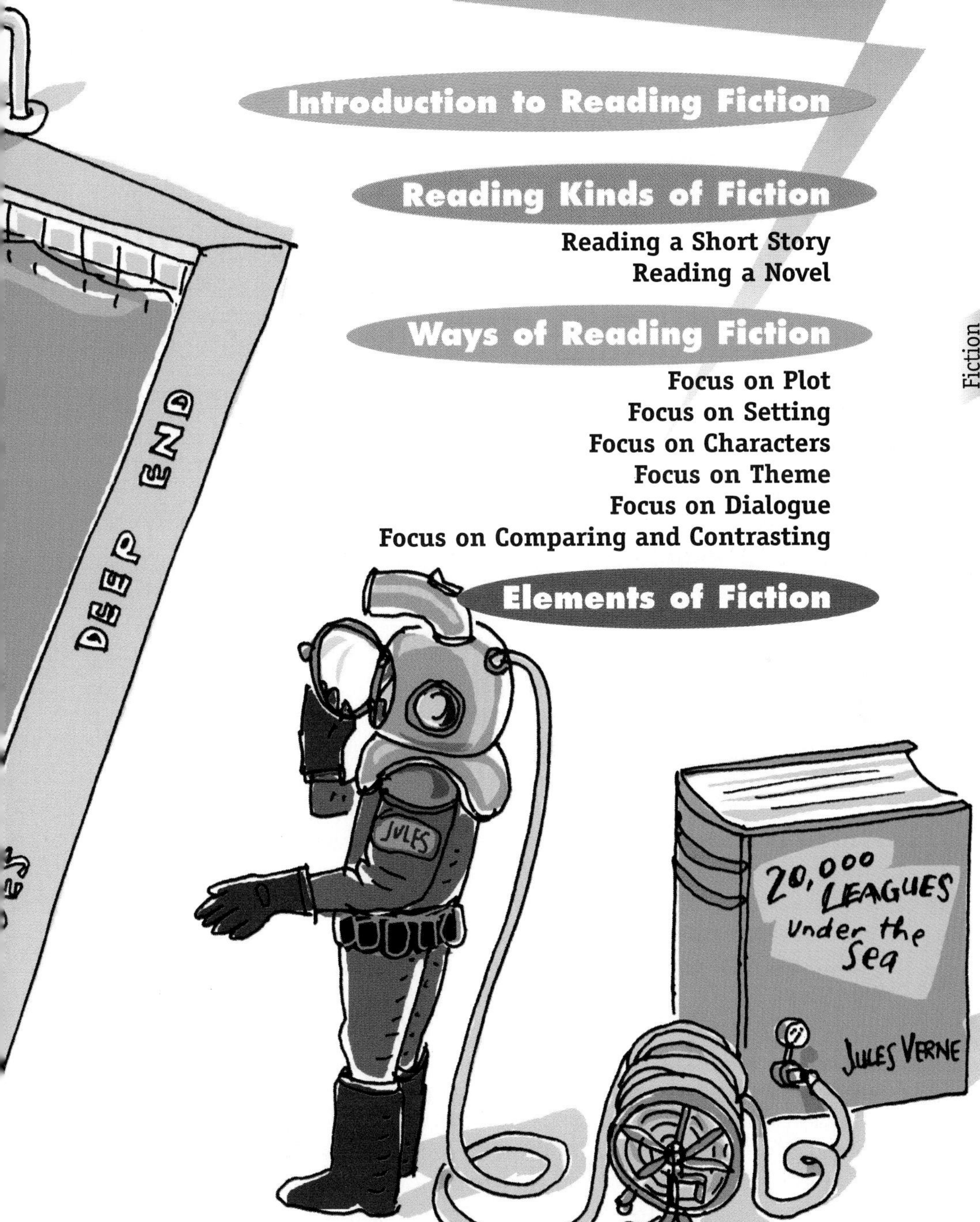

DEEP END
JULES
20,000 LEAGUES Under the Sea
JULES VERNE

Introduction to Reading Fiction

We need fiction. Through novels and stories we learn how the world works. In science classes you examine the lives of cells. Through fiction you come to understand your own life and the lives of others. Writer Muriel Rukeyser said that "the universe is made of stories." Writer Willa Cather wrote, "There are only two or three human stories, and they go on repeating themselves as fiercely as if they had never happened before." What are these stories? William Faulkner, in his Nobel Prize address, said that they are the old "truths of the heart . . . without which any story is doomed—love and honor, and pity and compassion and sacrifice." Based on what these writers and others have said over time, we might say these things about fiction:

Fiction is true. Huh? You think to yourself, "I thought it was fake, made up out of some writer's imagination." It is, which is why it can take place in the past or present, in a forest or a space station. If it's good fiction, you read it and think, "Wow, that's so true."

Fiction is incomplete. Writing a story is only half the process. You bring a story to life by using your imagination. You make the story in your head by being an active reader.

Fiction is complex. People are complex. No one is entirely good or bad. Fiction explores the human heart. A Native American chief said that "the longest journey is the one from the head to the heart." Literature takes us on that journey.

Fiction is dangerous. Philosopher Henry David Thoreau wrote, "Many a man has dated a new era in his life from the reading of a book." One day, if you are lucky, you read a book, you meet a character you care about or an idea that challenges your view of the world, and you are changed. If books were safe, people would not ban them.

Fiction is fun. It's fun to imagine different lives and realities from the corner of your own couch or classroom. Physicist Albert Einstein said that, through education, students should develop a childlike capacity for play and imagination in order to prepare them for the world ahead. Fiction is a fun way to do that before you decide what character you want to play in the story of your life.

Reading a Short Story

A short story is not about a life so much as a moment in someone's life. A short story can be as long as 30 pages or as short as 500 words. How does a writer bring a character or a world to life within so few pages? How can you as the reader understand that character and that world? Consider the following opening lines from three short stories. What questions do they bring to mind?

"I read about it in the paper, in the subway, on my way to work."
  ("Sonny's Blues" by James Baldwin)

"In walk these three girls in nothing but bathing suits."
  ("A & P" by John Updike)

"There's a man outside the door."
  ("Birthday" by David Wong Louie)

Fiction

Each of these lines contains some mystery. They confuse you even as they draw you in. You want to know what is going to happen or who is outside the door. The key to understanding a short story is to set some goals.

Goals

Here you'll learn how to:

✔ appreciate the **short story** genre

✔ use the reading strategy of **synthesizing**

✔ understand the **structure of a short story**

Before Reading

You read better if you know what to expect. You don't want to know everything, because that would steal the pleasure of reading the story. You can take some steps, however, to prepare to read.

A Set a Purpose

Your teacher often determines why you read. For example, he or she might tell you to focus on the relationship between two characters or on how a story expresses a certain theme. You, on the other hand, might want to find an additional reason to read. Suppose that you are assigned the short story "Powder" by Tobias Wolff. You might begin with these questions:

Setting a Purpose

- **What kind of powder is this story about?**
- **Who are the main characters, and what are they like?**
- **What is the setting?**
- **What are the main events?**

The title of the story is the obvious place to start. Gather your thoughts about the title. Here's a Web that one reader made before reading "Powder."

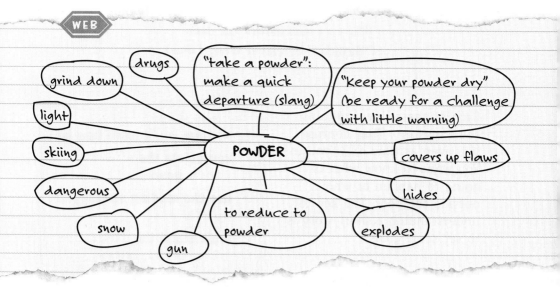

WEB

drugs — grind down — light — skiing — dangerous — snow — gun — "take a powder": make a quick departure (slang) — "keep your powder dry" (be ready for a challenge with little warning) — POWDER — covers up flaws — hides — to reduce to powder — explodes

Your purpose, of course, often changes as you read. Sometimes, in fact, it is best to begin by previewing the text and *then* setting a purpose. Setting a purpose after previewing is helpful when reading fiction because you do not usually know what a story will be about. When reading articles or other nonfiction texts, you generally have a purpose in mind before previewing them.

B Preview

When you preview a story, you do not read every word. Instead, skim through the story. Here are a few things to look for:

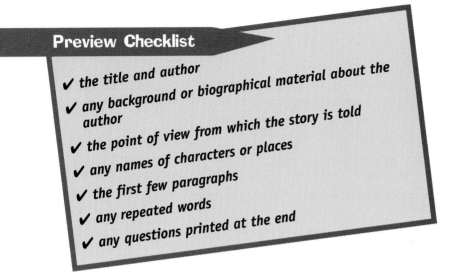

Preview Checklist

✔ the title and author

✔ any background or biographical material about the author

✔ the point of view from which the story is told

✔ any names of characters or places

✔ the first few paragraphs

✔ any repeated words

✔ any questions printed at the end

Now preview "Powder" by Tobias Wolff.

Fiction

Powder

by

Tobias Wolff

The Author Tobias Wolff was born in Alabama in 1945. His parents divorced when he was five. After dropping out of high school, he enlisted in the special forces and became an advisor to the South Vietnamese from 1964 to 1968. He later graduated from Oxford University. *This Boy's Life* is his memoir about his youth. The book was made into a 1993 movie of the same name starring Ellen Barkin and Robert DeNiro. He has published a second memoir, several short story collections, and a novel. His short stories have won the O. Henry Prize and the Rea Award. He was writer-in-residence at Syracuse University from 1980 to 1997 and now teaches at Stanford University.

The Selection "Powder" was first published in the *New York Times Magazine* and later collected in *The Night in Question* (1996), along with 14 other Wolff stories.

Further Reading "Mortals" by Tobias Wolff

"Powder," continued

Just before Christmas my father took me skiing at Mount Baker.[1]

He'd had to fight for the privilege of my company, because my mother was still angry with him for sneaking me into a nightclub during his last visit, to see Thelonious Monk.[2]

He wouldn't give up. He promised, hand on heart, to take good care of me and have me home for dinner on Christmas Eve, and she relented. But as we were checking out of the lodge that morning it began to snow, and in this snow he observed some rare quality that made it necessary for us to get in one last run. We got in several last runs. He was indifferent to my fretting. Snow whirled around us in bitter, blinding squalls, hissing like sand, and still we skied. As the lift bore us to the peak yet again, my father looked at his watch and said, "Criminy. This'll have to be a fast one."

By now I couldn't see the trail. There was no point in trying. I stuck to him like white on rice and did what he did and somehow made it to the bottom without sailing off a cliff. We returned our skis and my father put chains on the Austin-Healey[3] while I swayed from foot to foot, clapping my mittens and wishing I was home. I could see everything. The green tablecloth, the plates with the holly pattern, the red candles waiting to be lit.

We passed a diner on our way out. "You want some soup?" my father asked. I shook my head. "Buck up," he said. "I'll get you there. Right, doctor?"

I was supposed to say, "Right, doctor," but I didn't say anything.

---

1 **Mount Baker,** a ski resort in Washington State.

2 **Thelonious Monk,** famous jazz pianist.

3 **Austin-Healy,** English sports car.

PREVIEW
Names of characters and places

PREVIEW
First-person narrator

PREVIEW
Repeated word

PREVIEW
First three paragraphs, the exposition

NOTE
The relationship between the father and son

Fiction

271

PREVIEW
Character

A state trooper waved us down outside the resort. A pair of sawhorses were blocking the road. The trooper came up to our car and bent down to my father's window. His face was bleached by the cold. Snowflakes clung to his eyebrows and to the fur trim of his jacket and cap.

"Don't tell me," my father said.

NOTE
Obstacle increases tension, rising action

The trooper told him. The road was closed. It might get cleared, it might not. Storm took everyone by surprise. So much, so fast. Hard to get people moving. Christmas Eve. What can you do.

My father said, "Look. We're talking about five, six inches. I've taken this car through worse than that."

The trooper straightened up. His face was out of sight but I could hear him. "The road is closed."

NOTE
Father's frustration and son's tone

My father sat with both hands on the wheel, rubbing the wood with his thumbs. He looked at the barricade for a long time. He seemed to be trying to master the idea of it. Then he thanked the trooper, and with a weird, old-maidy show of caution turned the car around. "Your mother will never forgive me for this," he said.

"We should have left before," I said. "Doctor."

He didn't speak to me again until we were in a booth at the diner, waiting for our burgers. "She won't forgive me," he said. "Do you understand? Never."

PREVIEW
Repeated word

"I guess," I said, but no guesswork was required; she wouldn't forgive him.

"I can't let that happen." He bent toward me. "I'll tell you what I want. I want us all to be together again. Is that what you want?"

"Yes, sir."

He bumped my chin with his knuckles. "That's all I needed to hear."

When we finished eating he went to the pay phone in the back of the diner, then joined me in the booth again. I figured he'd called my mother, but he didn't give a report. He sipped at his coffee and stared out the window at the empty road. "Come on, come on," he said, though not to me. A little while later he said it again. When the trooper's car went past, lights flashing, he got up and dropped some money on the check. "Okay. Vamanos."[4]

The wind had died. The snow was falling straight down, less of it now and lighter. We drove away from the resort, right up to the barricade. "Move it," my father told me. When I looked at him he said, "What are you waiting for?" I got out and dragged one of the sawhorses aside, then put it back after he drove through. He pushed the door open for me. "Now you're an accomplice," he said. "We go down together." He put the car into gear and gave me a look. "Joke, son."

Down the first long stretch I watched the road behind us, to see if the trooper was on our tail. The barricade vanished. Then there was nothing but snow: snow on the road, snow kicking up from the chains, snow on the trees, snow in the sky; and our trail in the snow. Then I faced forward and had a shock. The lay of the road behind us had been marked by our own tracks, but there were no tracks ahead of us. My father was breaking virgin snow between a line of tall trees. He was humming "Stars Fell on Alabama." I felt snow brush along the floorboards under my feet. To keep my hands from shaking I clamped them between my knees.

My father grunted in a thoughtful way and said, "Don't ever try this yourself."

"I won't."

"That's what you say now, but someday you'll get your license and then you'll think you can do anything. Only you

NOTE
Climax

Fiction

PREVIEW
Repeated word

---

4 **Vamanos,** Spanish for "Let's go."

won't be able to do this. You need, I don't know—a certain instinct."

"Maybe I have it."

"You don't. You have your strong points, but not this. I only mention it because I don't want you to get the idea this is something just anybody can do. I'm a great driver. That's not a virtue, okay? It's just a fact, and one you should be aware of. Of course you have to give the old heap some credit, too. There aren't many cars I'd try this with. Listen!"

I did listen. I heard the slap of the chains, the stiff, jerky rasp of the wipers, the purr of the engine. It really did purr. The old heap was almost new. My father couldn't afford it, and kept promising to sell it, but here it was.

I said, "Where do you think that policeman went to?"

"Are you warm enough?" He reached over and cranked up the blower. Then he turned off the wipers. We didn't need them. The clouds had brightened. A few sparse, feathery flakes drifted into our slipstream and were swept away. We left the trees and entered a broad field of snow that ran level for a while and then tilted sharply downward. Orange stakes had been planted at intervals in two parallel lines and my father steered a course between them, though they were far enough apart to leave considerable doubt in my mind as to exactly where the road lay. He was humming again, doing little scat riffs[5] around the melody.

"Okay then. What are my strong points?"

"Don't get me started," he said. "It'd take all day."

"Oh, right. Name one."

"Easy. You always think ahead."

True. I always thought ahead. I was a boy who kept his

---

5 **scat riffs,** free-form style of jazz singing.

clothes on numbered hangers to ensure proper rotation. I bothered my teachers for homework assignments far ahead of their due dates so I could draw up schedules. I thought ahead, and that was why I knew that there would be other troopers waiting for us at the end of our ride, if we even got there. What I did not know was that my father would wheedle and plead his way past them – he didn't sing "O Tannenbaum," but just about – and get me home for dinner, buying a little more time before my mother decided to make the split final. I knew we'd get caught; I was resigned to it. And maybe for this reason I stopped moping and began to enjoy myself.

NOTE
Resolution

Fiction

Why not? This was one for the books. Like being in a speedboat, only better. You can't go downhill in a boat. And it was all ours. And it kept coming, the laden trees, the unbroken surface of snow, the sudden white vistas. Here and there I saw hints of the road, ditches, fences, stakes, but not so many that I could have found my way. But then I didn't have to. My father was driving. My father in his forty-eighth year, rumpled, kind, bankrupt of honor, flushed with certainty. He was a great driver. All persuasion, no coercion. Such subtlety at the wheel, such tactful pedalwork. I actually trusted him. And the best was yet to come—switchbacks and hairpins impossible to describe. Except maybe to say this: if you haven't driven fresh powder, you haven't driven.

NOTE
Son's reaction to father

Questions to Consider

1. What are the causes of some of the difficulties between the father and son?
2. The father doesn't say whom he called from the diner. What is your guess, and on what do you base your guess?
3. Who has changed the most by the end of the story?
4. What do you think will be the future relationship between the father and son?

PREVIEW
Textbook questions

C Plan

What did a preview of "Powder" tell you?

■ The son tells the story.

■ The story takes place just before Christmas.

■ The story is about snow and driving in it.

All this you can learn within a few minutes at the most, simply by reading several paragraphs and then skimming through the story. If study questions or other useful information is included, you can create an even more complete impression of what the story is about.

What you learned from the preview will help you make a plan. Then, you can discover what kind of powder the story refers to, who the main characters are, and what they are like. Here are four ways to plan:

1. Use Your Prior Knowledge

You probably know something about snow and father-son relationships. Think about what you already know to make some predictions about the conflicts in the story.

WAYS TO PLAN
✔ Use Your Prior Knowledge
✔ Focus on One Part
✔ Watch What Changes
✔ Appreciate the Story

2. Focus on One Part

Stories have many different aspects worth studying. You could, for example, focus on an author's language. You might look for words or details that relate to the title or the themes. Another approach is to concentrate on one character. You could, for example, focus on the father, looking at not only what he says and does but why.

This plan works best when you have a very specific reason for reading a story. You can often learn more from a story by reading for a specific purpose than from trying to read for everything—plot, character, theme, style—all at once.

3. Watch What Changes

Look for changes. Some changes may take place within a character. Some changes may occur in the setting. The mood of a story may change from time to time. When reading for changes, ask not only *what* changes but *why* it changes and how those changes affect other aspects of the story. Once you know all that, you'll be a lot closer to understanding the story.

4. Appreciate the Story

To appreciate a story you don't know much about, look at a number of elements. Plot, setting, characters, theme, style, and point of view are the elements that make up a story.

By looking at a number of story elements at once, you'll gain a better appreciation of the writer's craft. You are, in a sense, reading as a writer. To examine at least some of these, you'll need a reading strategy such as synthesizing.

Fiction

Reading Strategy: Synthesizing

When you synthesize, you look at a number of parts or elements and pull them together to form something new. It's like assembling cheese, tomato, and other ingredients, putting them together, and coming up with a tasty pizza. **Synthesizing** is a good reading strategy to use to answer the purpose questions on page 268. Synthesizing will help you:

- identify the key events in a story
- evaluate the information about the characters, and then decide what is important to know
- determine how one event relates to another
- figure out the narrator's motive for telling the story
- organize the essential details and events into a summary of what happens and what it means

Use a Fiction Organizer to help you direct your attention to the important details. A Fiction Organizer helps you collect all the key information about a story.

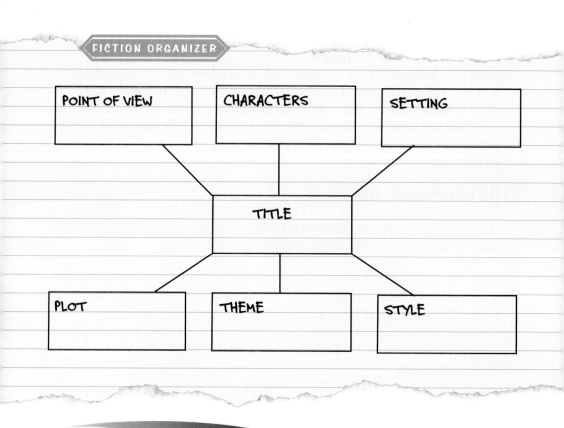

During Reading

You've established a purpose, previewed the story, and decided on a strategy. Now it's time to read "Powder."

D Read with a Purpose

How you read a story depends on your purpose. Synthesizing demands that you pay attention to many different aspects of a story at the same time and evaluate their importance. As you read slowly and carefully, record your notes in one or more graphic organizers.

Here's how one reader started to make notes in a Fiction Organizer.

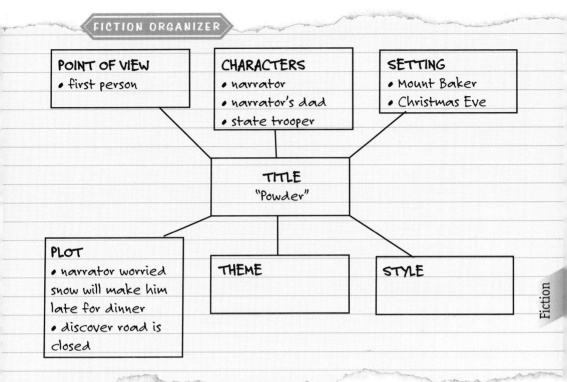

FICTION ORGANIZER

POINT OF VIEW
• first person

CHARACTERS
• narrator
• narrator's dad
• state trooper

SETTING
• Mount Baker
• Christmas Eve

TITLE
"Powder"

PLOT
• narrator worried snow will make him late for dinner
• discover road is closed

THEME

STYLE

Fiction

As you read, consider two other useful tools for reading a short story. A Cause-Effect Organizer can help you determine the reason something happens.

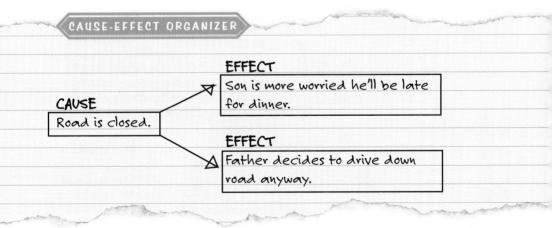

CAUSE-EFFECT ORGANIZER

CAUSE
Road is closed.

EFFECT
Son is more worried he'll be late for dinner.

EFFECT
Father decides to drive down road anyway.

A Character Development Chart can help you understand a character.
Create a Character Development Chart like the one on the next page to help you focus on how characters change. Notice that the reader came up with a possible theme based on the changes in the narrator.

279

BEGINNING	MIDDLE	END
Narrator wants to be home and is annoyed with father.	Narrator worried they won't be home in time and is afraid.	Narrator learns to trust and like his father during the drive.

POSSIBLE THEME
Learning to trust can sometimes result in a better understanding of oneself and others.

How Stories Are Organized

Short story plots fall into a somewhat predictable pattern. Return to "Powder," and look for these parts of the story, noted in the margins. These five parts are common to most short stories.

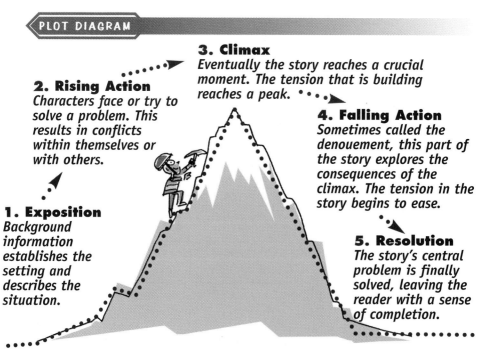

PLOT DIAGRAM

3. Climax
Eventually the story reaches a crucial moment. The tension that is building reaches a peak.

2. Rising Action
Characters face or try to solve a problem. This results in conflicts within themselves or with others.

4. Falling Action
Sometimes called the denouement, this part of the story explores the consequences of the climax. The tension in the story begins to ease.

1. Exposition
Background information establishes the setting and describes the situation.

5. Resolution
The story's central problem is finally solved, leaving the reader with a sense of completion.

Sometimes it helps to draw the story's action. Drawing the plot allows you to see the shape of the story better.

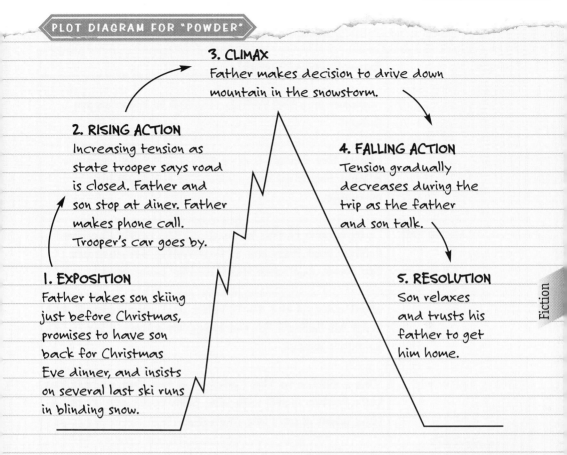

PLOT DIAGRAM FOR "POWDER"

3. CLIMAX
Father makes decision to drive down mountain in the snowstorm.

2. RISING ACTION
Increasing tension as state trooper says road is closed. Father and son stop at diner. Father makes phone call. Trooper's car goes by.

4. FALLING ACTION
Tension gradually decreases during the trip as the father and son talk.

1. EXPOSITION
Father takes son skiing just before Christmas, promises to have son back for Christmas Eve dinner, and insists on several last ski runs in blinding snow.

5. RESOLUTION
Son relaxes and trusts his father to get him home.

Fiction

E Connect

Reading is more interesting if you can connect it to your own life and relationships. Of course, sometimes you think it's impossible to connect to a story. You or your experiences are just too different. But connecting to a story just calls for a little imagination. You may not have driven down the side of a mountain in a snowstorm, but have you ever been on a roller coaster? Your father might be a quiet man who would never break the law, but do you know kids at school who can be wild? Or do you have an uncle who does crazy things like the father in "Powder"? Here are some prompts that helped one reader connect to the story.

Prompts	Example from "Powder"
I wonder why . . .	I wonder why the father wanted to take his son skiing?
I think . . .	I think the father is very nervous. Maybe he is afraid this is his last chance to patch up his marriage.
I can relate to this because . . .	I can relate to this because I know people like the father, and they are so frustrating because you like them and hate them at the same time.
What caused . . .	What caused the son to relax and enjoy himself and trust his father? For one thing, he admired his father's driving.
This is similar to . . .	This is similar to The Catcher in the Rye, except this kid's father is still with him. Both books are about a time when a son's life changed.
This reminds me of . . .	This reminds me of a trip I took with my mom when I was twelve.

Here is what another reader wrote when trying to connect her own life to this story:

JOURNAL ENTRY

This story reminds me of just last year when I went skiing with my dad around Christmas. My parents had just gotten divorced, and my dad wanted to get away and spend some time just with me. For a while I felt really awkward, especially when we were driving there. I didn't know what to talk about, and he just kept talking his head off about all sorts of stuff. By the next day he settled down, and I started to see him in a new way, more as my friend. This was important because I knew I wasn't going to see him much after that because he was moving to another state.

After Reading

"Powder" leaves you with several questions and ideas to think about. For most of the story the son has been clearly frustrated with his father. We can imagine him rolling his eyes and sighing each time his father goes too far once again. What changes as they are going down the mountain? Is it just the experience the son is learning to enjoy, or something else? Why does the son suddenly trust this man?

F Pause and Reflect

Throughout the story certain details helped you complete one or more of your graphic organizers. Now check on your understanding of the story by asking yourself questions like these:

Looking Back

- **Can I describe the main characters?**
- **What do the main characters want most?**
- **How does the title fit the story?**
- **How is the setting significant?**
- **Does the ending make sense? Why or why not?**
- **What is the theme of the story?**

Any of these questions might prompt you to go back to the story and do some rereading.

G Reread

Because of their length and depth, short stories often invite rereading. When you know what happens, you can pay more attention to how or why it happens. Rereading allows you to establish a new or revised purpose and look for the answers to other questions. It's best to use a new strategy as you reread because you probably have new questions in mind this time around.

Fiction

Close Reading

Synthesizing allows you to bring together the many different aspects of a story. **Close reading,** on the other hand, can help you answer questions like the ones on the Looking Back checklist. To start with, take some time to reread the opening of the story more closely. As you do, use a Close Reading Organizer like this one.

CLOSE READING ORGANIZER

Text of "Powder"	What I Think about It
"Just before Christmas my father took me skiing at Mount Baker."	"Christmas" immediately creates a situation. Many people find the holidays stressful. This also immediately establishes the time and place setting. The word <u>took</u> has a different feeling than if he'd said, "My father and I went skiing." <u>Took</u> suggests that the son might not have wanted to go or even that he went against his will.
"He'd had to fight for the privilege of my company, because my mother was still angry with him for sneaking me into a night-club during his last visit, to see Thelonious Monk."	"Fight for the privilege of my company" has a sarcastic tone. The son doesn't sound excited about the idea. The mother clearly isn't. That the father sneaked his son into a night-club shows me that he can be irresponsible. The father might think he should show his son the adult world. The words "his last visit" tell us that the parents are not living together.
the title "Powder"	When you bring fire and powder together, they explode; the parents seem explosive. "Powder" also implies covering up something, especially a blemish. The father seems to want to ignore his past actions.
"He wouldn't give up. He promised, hand on heart, to take good care of me and have me home for dinner on Christmas Eve, and she relented."	"He wouldn't give up" raises the question, "Why?" Maybe he wants to win his way back into his wife's heart by showing her what a great dad he can be.

Look at Setting

The time and place of the story affect the plot. A snowstorm on Christmas Eve sets up the conflict in the story. As you reread, take note of the setting, as this reader did.

SETTING CHART

TITLE: "POWDER"

CLUES ABOUT TIME	CLUES ABOUT PLACE
season	first place
"Just before Christmas"	Mount Baker
time of day	second place
Christmas Eve	blocked road
	third place
	diner
	fourth place
	snowy road down the mountain

Fiction

The time—Christmas Eve—is the most important detail of the setting. It's often a tense time of the year.

Compare Characters

As you reread and go deeper into the story and its ideas, character emerges as one of the more important aspects of the story. Is the son like his father, the man he found so frustrating through the early part of the story? Use a Venn Diagram like the one on the next page to help you compare the ways in which the father and son are similar and different.

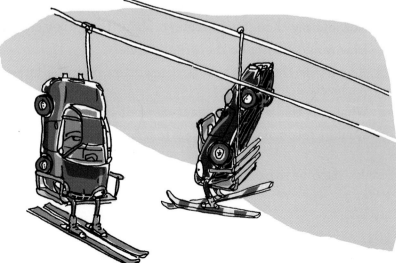

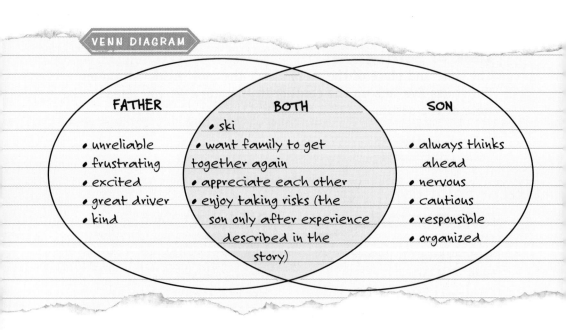

FATHER
- unreliable
- frustrating
- excited
- great driver
- kind

BOTH
- ski
- want family to get together again
- appreciate each other
- enjoy taking risks (the son only after experience described in the story)

SON
- always thinks ahead
- nervous
- cautious
- responsible
- organized

Rereading the story to examine characters helps you realize that, by the end of the story, the son has in all likelihood become more like his father.

H Remember

Here are two suggestions to help you remember what you've read.

1. Talk about It

Use some of the following questions to help you discuss the story:

- What did this story make me think about?
- What were my first thoughts when I finished reading it?
- What do I think the father would say if he read this story?
- How might the mother respond to this story?
- How did my thoughts or feelings about the father change?
- How would I describe the writer's style?
- How would the story change if rewritten from the father's perspective?
- What was the most important moment in the story?
- Would I recommend this story to a friend? Why or why not?

Discuss some of these questions with a partner.

2. Write a Sequel to the Story

What happens after the end of the story? In your journal, write a short sequel to the story telling what happens next. For example, you might start with the boy's arrival home. Through this writing exercise, you can extend your understanding of the characters by seeing how they would react in new situations.

Summing Up

When you read short stories, use the reading process and apply the strategy of **synthesizing.** Organizers can help you sort out information and understand **plot structure.** Remember these useful tools when reading short stories:

- Web
- Fiction Organizer
- Cause-Effect Organizer
- Character Development Chart
- Plot Diagram
- Making Connections Chart
- Close Reading Organizer
- Setting Chart
- Venn Diagram

Remember that **close reading** can be an effective rereading strategy.

Fiction

Reading a Novel

Novelists are like painters who need a large canvas to express their ideas. The length of a novel allows a writer to follow one or more characters across a longer period of time than a short story permits. It also allows a novelist to examine a character or event in greater depth.

Here, you will study about a novel through Erich Maria Remarque's *All Quiet on the Western Front*. You won't read the whole book, but you will read passages that illustrate what it was like for Paul Bäumer and his German schoolmates during World War I.

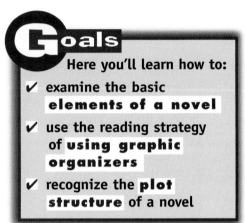

Goals

Here you'll learn how to:

✔ examine the basic **elements of a novel**

✔ use the reading strategy of **using graphic organizers**

✔ recognize the **plot structure** of a novel

Before Reading

Whether you read a novel to learn more about World War I or the human heart, it helps to follow the reading process. Novels are long. The reading process offers you a road map to make sure that you don't get lost and that you understand what you read along the way.

A Set a Purpose

With so much detail and so many characters in a novel, it can be difficult to know what matters most. The basic elements of a story help determine what is important. Your initial purpose when reading a novel is to answer several general questions.

Setting a Purpose

■ **Who is telling the story?** *(point of view)*

■ **Who are the main characters, and what are they like?** *(characters)*

■ **Where and when does the story take place? What is this place, culture, or historical period like?** *(setting)*

■ **What happens?** *(plot)*

■ **What is the author's central idea or message?** *(theme)*

■ **How does the author express his or her ideas?** *(style)*

Fiction

B Preview

Try not to just jump into the novel and start reading. If you have your own copy of the book, keep a pencil or highlighter nearby for annotating. If your book belongs to the school, have a reading journal or pad of sticky notes handy so you can make notes as you read. Then, preview these parts of the book to get a sense of what to expect:

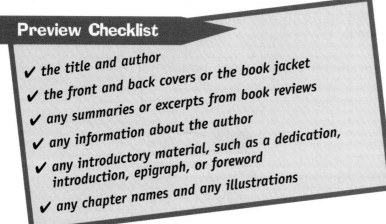

Preview Checklist

✔ the title and author

✔ the front and back covers or the book jacket

✔ any summaries or excerpts from book reviews

✔ any information about the author

✔ any introductory material, such as a dedication, introduction, epigraph, or foreword

✔ any chapter names and any illustrations

Take a moment to think about the novel's title. Use Webs to explore what it means.

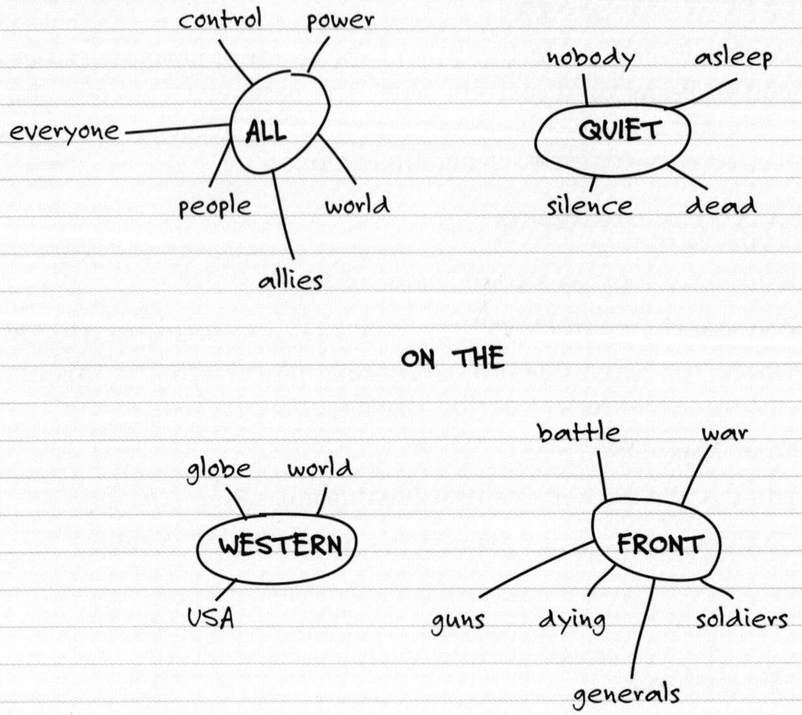

control   power

nobody   asleep

everyone —— ALL

QUIET

people | world

silence   dead

allies

ON THE

battle   war

globe   world

WESTERN

FRONT

USA

guns   dying   soldiers

generals

Above are Webs that show the different associations one reader made for the title *All Quiet on the Western Front*. Not all of your ideas will ultimately be right, but an activity like this gets you thinking about what the book *could* be about.

Book covers also offer useful clues. Notice how much you can learn from previewing the front cover and book jacket.

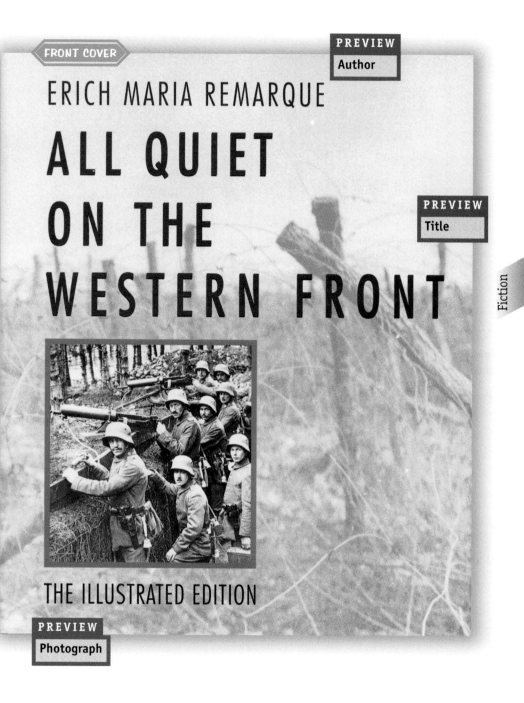

FRONT COVER

ERICH MARIA REMARQUE

ALL QUIET ON THE WESTERN FRONT

Fiction

THE ILLUSTRATED EDITION

LITERATURE $29.95 FPT
$39.95 in Canada

ALL QUIET ON THE WESTERN FRONT
THE ILLUSTRATED EDITION

ERICH MARIA REMARQUE

PREVIEW

Publication date

Little, Brown and Company first published Erich Maria Remarque's *All Quiet on the Western Front*, arguably the greatest war novel of all time, in 1929. Subsequently, the book has been translated into 45 languages and has sold more than 50 million copies. Though a fictional account, it is a timeless document of the devastation and human tragedy of World War I.

PREVIEW

Summary

The story, told from the perspective of a young German soldier, is extraordinarily detailed and realistic and thus lends itself well to the amplification of an illustrated edition. Sixty compelling, previously unpublished black-and-white photographs from the Liberty Memorial Museum in Kansas City, Missouri—the only World War I museum in the United States—are used to illustrate this clas-

60 black-and-white illustrations
09962945

sic narrative. These photographs, showing German soldiers in the trenches, gathered around the cookhouse, guarding Russian prisoners, convalescing in the hospital, and so forth—all experiences described by Remarque's thoughtful and sensitive protagonist, Paul Bäumer—provide a fascinating visual and historical context for this exceptional novel.

ERICH MARIA REMARQUE (1898–1970) was born and raised in Germany. He gained literary prominence in 1929 with the publication of *All Quiet on the Western Front*. The Nazis eventually burned the book and stripped Remarque of his German citizenship. He then became a United States citizen, though he lived primarily in Switzerland. Remarque's diaries, letters, and other archival materials are now located at New York University.

Jacket design by Peter M. Blaiwas

A Bulfinch Press Book
Little, Brown and Company
Boston • New York • Toronto • London

PREVIEW

Information about author

PRINTED IN THE UNITED STATES OF AMERICA

From previewing the front cover and book jacket, you learn that the 1929 novel focuses on World War I from the perspective of a German soldier, Paul Bäumer. You also found a few brief facts about the author.

Now preview the author's note, which is on an opening page.

AUTHOR'S NOTE

This book is to be neither an accusation nor a confession, and least of all an adventure, for death is not an adventure to those who stand face to face with it. It will simply try to tell of a generation of men who, even though they may have escaped its shells, were destroyed by the war.

PREVIEW
Author's purpose

Fiction

C Plan

Now you have a rough idea of the story. As you begin to read, you will take in a lot more information. You need a way to organize that information.

Reading Strategy: Using Graphic Organizers

Using a graphic organizer like the one below is especially helpful if you prepare it before you begin. Keep it handy so you can organize the information about point of view, characters, setting, plot, theme, and style as you read.

FICTION ORGANIZER

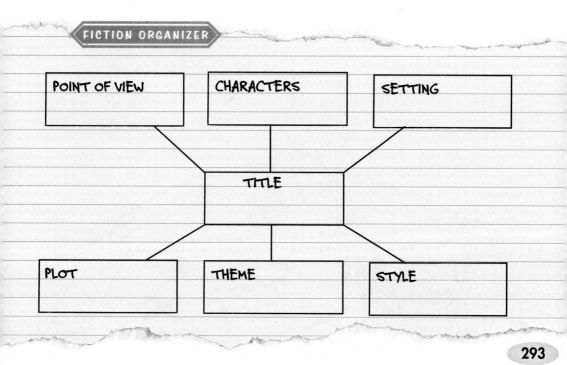

POINT OF VIEW   CHARACTERS   SETTING

TITLE

PLOT   THEME   STYLE

During Reading

Depending on the length of a novel, you might read it in a few days or in a few weeks. Some readers get swept up in a novel and can't put it down, but novels you study in school require time and attention. You are studying the book, not devouring it.

D Read with a Purpose

Recall the questions you want to answer about the novel:

- Who is telling the story? *(point of view)*
- Who are the main characters, and what are they like? *(characters)*
- Where and when does the story take place? What is this place, culture, or historical period like? *(setting)*
- What happens? *(plot)*
- What is the author's central idea or message? *(theme)*
- How does the author express his or her ideas? *(style)*

Novels are more complicated than textbooks in some ways. Textbooks have heads and subheads such as "Causes of World War I" that offer clues to content. Textbooks provide maps, lists of key terms or people, and timelines. Novels do not. In a novel, you may find information about setting, characters, and point of view all within one paragraph. Here, you'll look at these elements of novels one at a time.

1. Point of View

The **point of view** is the perspective from which an author tells a story. The person telling a story, the *narrator,* is your guide. The novel's opening quickly establishes Paul's voice and his point of view.

NOVEL ELEMENTS
- ✔ Point of View
- ✔ Characters
- ✔ Setting
- ✔ Plot
- ✔ Theme
- ✔ Style

Fiction

from *All Quiet on the Western Front* by Erich Maria Remarque

We are at rest five miles behind the front. Yesterday we were relieved, and now our bellies are full of beef and haricot beans. We are satisfied and at peace. Each man has another mess-tin full for the evening; and, what is more, there is a double ration of sausage and bread. That puts a man in fine trim. We have not had such luck as this for a long time. The cook with his carroty head is begging us to eat; he beckons with his ladle to everyone that passes, and spoons him out a great dollop. He does not see how he can empty his stew-pot in time for coffee. Tjaden and Müller have produced two washbasins and had them filled up to the brim as a reserve. In Tjaden this is voracity, in Müller it is foresight. Where Tjaden puts it all is a mystery, for he is and always will be as thin as a rake.

NOTE
Narrator is a male character in the novel.

NOTE
First-person pronouns

By the end of the first paragraph, you know a good deal about the point of view. The pronouns (*we, our, us*) indicate that the point of view is first person. The narrator is one of the characters in the story.

2. Characters

To read a novel successfully, you have to keep track of the **characters.** As you meet each new character, you have to know how he or she is connected to those you already know. Remarque distinguishes the characters through their names, their abilities and desires, and their actions and speech. You can imagine the camera slowly shifting from one face to the next as Paul's voice tells us about them.

from *All Quiet on the Western Front*

NOTE
Gives information about each character

NOTE
Eight characters

. . . Half an hour later every man had his mess-tin and we gathered at the cook-house, which smelt greasy and nourishing. At the head of the queue of course were the hungriest—little Albert Kropp, the clearest thinker among us and therefore only a lance-corporal; Müller, who still carries his school textbooks with him, dreams of examinations, and during a bombardment mutters propositions in physics; Leer, who wears a full beard. . . . And as the fourth, myself, Paul Bäumer. All four are nineteen years of age, and all four joined up from the same class as volunteers for the war.

Close behind us were our friends: Tjaden, a skinny locksmith of our own age, the biggest eater of the company. He sits down to eat as thin as a grasshopper and gets up as big as a bug in the family way; Haie Westhus, of the same age, a peat-digger, who can easily hold a ration-loaf in his hand and say: Guess what I've got in my fist; then Detering, a peasant, who thinks of nothing but his farm-yard and his wife; and finally Stanislaus Katczinsky, the leader of our group, shrewd, cunning, and hard-bitten, forty years of age, with a face of the soil, blue eyes, bent shoulders, and a remarkable nose for dirty weather, good food, and soft jobs.

CLASSIFICATION NOTES

After only a few pages you've already met eight characters including the narrator, some of whom have unusual European names such as Haie and Tjaden. You need a way to understand their relationship to each other. Classification Notes can help you keep track of lots of characters. You can add to the notes as new characters enter the story. In the following example, you see the characters you have just met in black. Those you have yet to meet but who will play an important role later appear in red.

CLASSIFICATION NOTES

Main Character: Paul Bäumer

School Friends	Teacher	Army Friends
Albert Kropp	Kantorek	Tjaden
Müller		Haie Westhus
Leer		Detering
Franz Kemmerich		Stanislaus Katczinsky (Kat)

Officer	Family	"Enemies"
Himmelstoss	Mother	Russians
	Father	French Girls
	Sister	Gérard Duval

Fiction

CHARACTER MAP

You need to get to know what the main characters are like so you can understand how they respond to one another, the war, and their own circumstances. The notes above reveal that the characters fall into groupings—school friends, army friends, officer, teacher, family, enemies—that are connected to different settings throughout the novel. Certain characters matter more than others. Study major characters closely, for they influence the story and other characters. Katczinsky, whom Paul and the others call "Kat," is such a character in *All Quiet on the Western Front*. As you read the first chapter, you might start an organizer like this one for Kat.

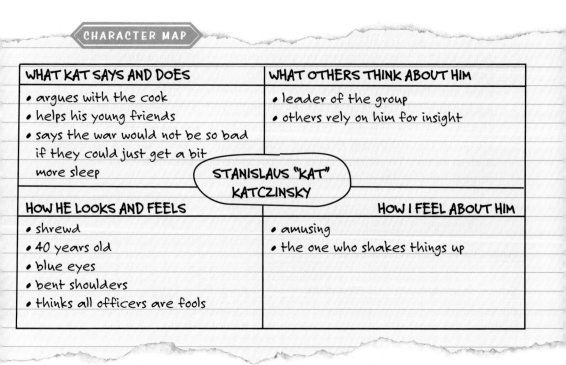

WHAT KAT SAYS AND DOES	WHAT OTHERS THINK ABOUT HIM
• argues with the cook • helps his young friends • says the war would not be so bad if they could just get a bit more sleep	• leader of the group • others rely on him for insight

STANISLAUS "KAT" KATCZINSKY

HOW HE LOOKS AND FEELS	HOW I FEEL ABOUT HIM
• shrewd • 40 years old • blue eyes • bent shoulders • thinks all officers are fools	• amusing • the one who shakes things up

Katczinsky's character takes shape early on as you see how he reacts to the war and how he cares for his young friends. The way Paul describes him and the way others respond to him clearly show that he is their leader in more than just fighting. Keep a Character Map as you read a novel, and you will understand the story and its characters much better.

3. Setting

The **setting** tells you about the time and place in which a story happens. Time refers to the year (for example, 1917) and also the historical period (for example, near the end of World War I). These *general setting* details are accompanied by *immediate settings* that focus more on the time and place of individual events. In *All Quiet on the Western Front,* Paul's hometown, the front, and the base are all immediate settings of the war and his experience.

GENERAL SETTING: LOCATION

The title of Remarque's novel places the story on the Western Front during World War I. A "front" is the forward-most position of the soldiers in a war. They are up front where the fighting is. Although the specific location is rather vague, the Western Front was in Western Europe. A description of the front itself comes in Chapter Four.

from *All Quiet on the Western Front*

Our faces are neither paler nor more flushed than usual; they are not more tense nor more flabby—and yet they are changed. We feel that in our blood a contact has shot home. That is no figure of speech; it is fact. It is the front, the consciousness of the front, that makes this contact. The moment that the first shells whistle over and the air is rent with the explosions there is suddenly in our veins, in our hands, in our eyes a tense waiting, a watching, a heightening alertness, a strange sharpening of the senses. The body with one bound is in full readiness.

It often seems to me as though it were the vibrating, shuddering air that with a noiseless leap springs upon us; or as though the front itself emitted an electric current which awakened unknown nerve-centers.

Every time it is the same. We start out for the front plain soldiers, either cheerful or gloomy: then come the first gun-emplacements and every word of our speech has a new ring.

When Kat stands in front of the hut and says: "There'll be a bombardment," that is merely his own opinion; but if he says it here, then the sentence has the sharpness of a bayonet in the moonlight, it cuts straight through the thought, it thrusts nearer and speaks to this unknown thing that is awakened in us, a dark meaning—"There'll be a bombardment." Perhaps it is our inner and most secret life that shivers and falls on guard.

To me the front is a mysterious whirlpool. Though I am in still water far away from its center, I feel the whirl of the vortex sucking me slowly, irresistibly, inescapably into itself.

NOTE
The front seems to be alive.

Fiction

NOTE
Setting is further described by their reaction.

NOTE
Setting is described as a metaphor.

These details about the setting and the men's reactions to bombardment convey the general atmosphere of the front, and they help create an overall mood in the novel.

GENERAL SETTING: TIME PERIOD

Remarque begins the novel in 1916, at a point when the company has lost half its men in its latest battle with the British. At this point the German momentum in the war had stalled. The time period also determines the conditions in which the men would have fought: in trenches, with guns, gas, and the first tanks and planes used in a war. Throughout the novel, Remarque shows what war did to people. The war emptied whole towns of their young men. Note how the following passage shows what it was like for many during the war:

from *All Quiet on the Western Front*

Our early life is cut off from the moment we came here, and that without our lifting a hand. We often try to look back on it and to find an explanation, but never quite succeed. For us young men of twenty everything is extraordinarily vague, for Kropp, Müller, Leer, and for me, for all of us whom Kantorek calls the "Iron Youth." All the older men are linked up with their previous life. They have wives, children, occupations, and interests, they have a background which is so strong that the war cannot obliterate it. We young men of twenty, however, have only our parents, and some, perhaps, a girl—that is not much, for at our age the influence of parents is at its weakest and girls have not yet got a hold over us. Besides this there was little else— some enthusiasm, a few hobbies, and our school. Beyond this our life did not extend. And of this nothing remains.

Kantorek would say that we stood on the threshold of life. And so it would seem. We had as yet taken no root. The war swept us away. For the others, the older men, it is but an interruption. They are able to think beyond it. We, however, have been gripped by it and do not know what the end may be. We know only that in some strange and melancholy way we have become a waste land. All the same, we are not often sad.

> **NOTE**
> Setting sets mood of loss and confusion.

On the next page is an example of the kind of notes you might make about setting. Such information helps you to understand how setting influences plot, theme, and characters.

ALL QUIET ON THE WESTERN FRONT	
TIME:	**PLACE:**
• toward end of World War I • many soldiers in their twenties	• Western Front in World War I • opens with them at camp behind the front (to rest) • not under attack but can hear and see the war

Fiction

IMMEDIATE SETTING: DETAILS

Novels, like murals, are large, but they are also, like murals, made of many smaller details. These details often depict specific scenes related to the larger setting. A scene like the one that follows, for instance, helps you understand a bit better what the setting looked like on a typical day when the men were not fighting. Can you notice a change in mood?

from *All Quiet on the Western Front*

These are wonderfully care-free hours. Over us is the blue sky. On the horizon float the bright yellow, sunlit observation-balloons, and the many little white clouds of the anti-aircraft shells. Often they rise in a sheaf as they follow after an airman. We hear the muffled rumble of the front only as very distant thunder, bumble-bees droning by quite drown it. Around us stretches the flowery meadow. The grasses sway their tall spears; the white butterflies flutter around and float on the soft warm wind of the late summer. We read letters and newspapers and smoke. We take off our caps and lay them down beside us. The wind plays with our hair; it plays with our words and thoughts. The three boxes stand in the midst of the glowing, red field-poppies.

NOTE
Pleasant images contrast with the war's horrors.

NOTE
Details set a mood of peace, rest, and calm.

4. Plot

The **plot** is what happens in the story. Novels usually have one main plot and many subplots. The story typically focuses on conflicts and how the characters respond to them.

The plot in *All Quiet on the Western Front* is at times confusing because Remarque wrote it as a series of episodes. You might be reading about what is happening at camp between battles, and then Paul will suddenly reflect on his school days for several pages. Choosing a way to follow a plot is especially useful in a complex story. One possibility is to write a brief summary about what happens in each chapter. Summary Notes like the ones below are helpful when trying to find your way back to a moment in the story later, when you are writing about it. Another possibility is to make a short note in your book—at the top of the page if you own the book, on a sticky note if you do not—that identifies an important event, such as, "Paul gets wounded and sent home."

SUMMARY NOTES

CHAPTER ONE

Paul Bäumer and his friends have come from the front, where they have been fighting for two weeks. They lost 80 men. Paul introduces us to his friends. They go to visit Kemmerich, whose leg has been amputated.

CHAPTER TWO

Paul remembers life before the war. He visits Kemmerich, who dies. Paul tells about joining the army and training under Corporal Himmelstoss. The men hate Himmelstoss, who hates them.

Sequence Notes like the ones shown on the next page are a more graphic way of summarizing a story. They show how one event leads to another and how the story is organized.

SEQUENCE NOTES

Paul and friends join the army at age 19. → Himmelstoss is attacked for humiliating Tjaden. → They go to training camp for ten weeks.

→ assigned to Second Company (150 men) → Assigned to No. 9 platoon under Himmelstoss for six weeks of training → Second Company loses 80 men in battle with British.

→ Kemmerich dies from wounds. → New recruits arrive to replace the dead. → Second Company returns to front.

→ major bombardment: five killed, eight wounded → Himmelstoss arrives to serve as commanding officer. → Tjaden and Kropp are punished for disrespecting Himmelstoss.

Fiction

Sequence Notes work better for this novel than for some others. These notes for *All Quiet on the Western Front,* for example, show the order in which events happen, although they contain very few dates or other suggestions about the time.

How Novels Are Organized

As you read novels, watch for the moments that seem to show changes in the characters or the tension in the story. In *All Quiet on the Western Front,* for example, you might pay attention to how Paul's feelings about the war change as his friends are killed, or as the war continues. Making a Plot Diagram is a good way to remember the structure of a novel.

PLOT DIAGRAM

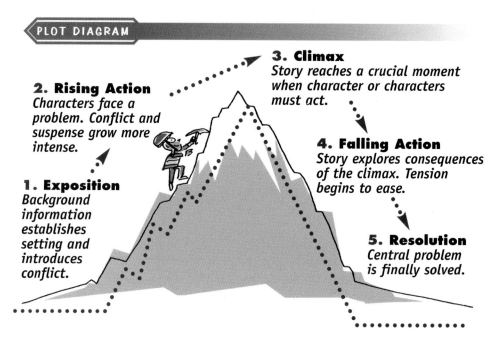

3. Climax
Story reaches a crucial moment when character or characters must act.

2. Rising Action
Characters face a problem. Conflict and suspense grow more intense.

4. Falling Action
Story explores consequences of the climax. Tension begins to ease.

1. Exposition
Background information establishes setting and introduces conflict.

5. Resolution
Central problem is finally solved.

The organization of novels varies. Many of them open in the present and then, after a few comments, go back in time. Some novels start in the middle of the story. Still other novels start in the beginning and are called *linear* because they go in a straight line from point A to B to C. One event is followed by another. *All Quiet on the Western Front* follows this pattern. It does have a slight but somewhat common variation. Paul periodically has a *flashback* to some event in the past—at home, earlier in the war, or while at school. These memories usually offer insight or comment about whatever he is currently feeling or doing.

On the next page is one possible Plot Diagram for *All Quiet on the Western Front.*

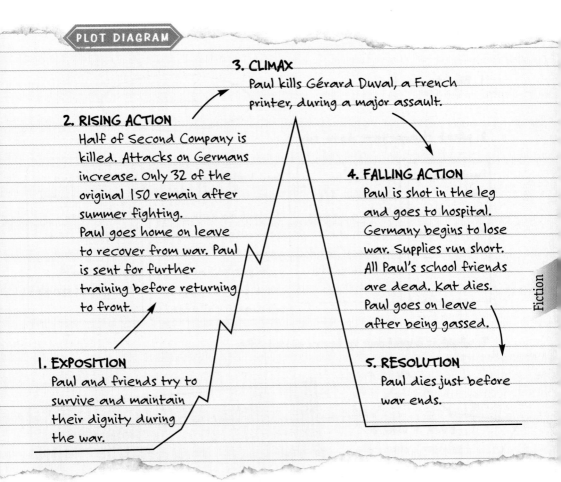

PLOT DIAGRAM

3. CLIMAX
Paul kills Gérard Duval, a French printer, during a major assault.

2. RISING ACTION
Half of Second Company is killed. Attacks on Germans increase. Only 32 of the original 150 remain after summer fighting. Paul goes home on leave to recover from war. Paul is sent for further training before returning to front.

4. FALLING ACTION
Paul is shot in the leg and goes to hospital. Germany begins to lose war. Supplies run short. All Paul's school friends are dead. Kat dies. Paul goes on leave after being gassed.

1. EXPOSITION
Paul and friends try to survive and maintain their dignity during the war.

5. RESOLUTION
Paul dies just before war ends.

Fiction

5. Theme

Theme is the main idea (or ideas) an author develops throughout a literary work. You can form ideas about themes by noting some of the major topics. Ask yourself these questions to help you identify themes:

What are the big ideas in this novel?

What events, actions, or remarks in the novel relate to these topics?

What does the author say—through these events, actions, or remarks—that makes a statement about life?

On the next page is an organizer one reader completed to identify a theme.

1. Big idea or topic:

Compassion

2. What characters do or say:

| Paul stays with Kemmerich to keep him company while he dies. | Paul lies to Kemmerich's mother, saying her son died "at once" and did not suffer. | Paul tells the Frenchman he killed, "I want to help you. Comrade, comrade, comrade—" and promises to take care of the man's wife and children. | He shares his cigarettes with the Russian "enemies" he is told to guard. He talks with those who speak German. |

3. What is important to learn about life:

Even in war, a soldier can feel compassion toward his friends and especially toward his enemies.

A novel may have many themes, some the author intended and some you perceive on your own. This three-step process helps you develop a clear theme statement. For example, if you choose what you think is an important topic but can't find many ideas that relate to that topic, then choose another topic. Look for details related to your new topic.

306

6. Style

An author's **style,** just like that of a singer or filmmaker, is based on how he or she expresses ideas. Authors use words and literary devices to create their own distinctive styles. Asking questions such as the ones below will help you analyze an author's style:

AUTHOR'S STYLE

Sentence Structure: *Does the author use mostly short sentences or long, complex sentences?*

Word Choice: *Does the author use simple words or long, formal ones?*

Tone: *What sort of feeling do you have about the writing? Is it loose and casual, formal and proper, or something different?*

Dialogue: *Do the characters speak in slang or dialect? Does their language seem realistic and believable?*

Sensory Details: *Does the author use words that appeal to your five senses?*

Figurative Language: *Does the author use words to paint pictures? Are similes and metaphors an important part of the author's style?*

You might use a Double-entry Journal to help you examine a writer's style.

DOUBLE-ENTRY JOURNAL

QUOTES	MY THOUGHTS
Paul Bäumer describing the front: "The front is a cage in which we must await fearfully whatever may happen. We lie under the network of arching shells and live in a suspense of uncertainty."	I like the way Remarque keeps coming up with different metaphors for the front. I also like Paul's voice. It sounds so serious.
Opening of Chapter 6: "We go up to the front two days earlier than usual. On the way, we pass a shelled school-house. Stacked up against its longer side is a high double wall of yellow, unpolished, brand-new coffins."	The visual image of new coffins piled up against a bombed-out school is powerful. He has already said repeatedly that school is made meaningless by the war.

Fiction

Good readers connect what they read to themselves and the world in which they live. To help you connect to what you read, ask yourself questions such as these:

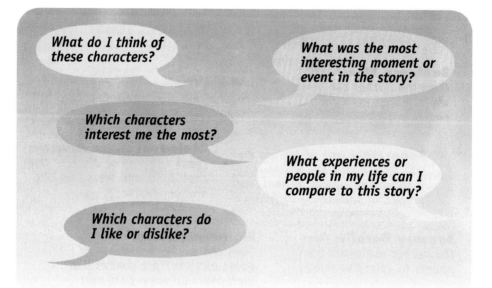

What do I think of these characters?

What was the most interesting moment or event in the story?

Which characters interest me the most?

What experiences or people in my life can I compare to this story?

Which characters do I like or dislike?

In this passage from *All Quiet on the Western Front,* Paul talks about the Russian soldiers he must guard and whom he is supposed to hate because they are the "enemy." Read the notes one reader made about this passage.

> from *All Quiet on the Western Front*
>
> I now know a few of those who speak a little German. There is a musician amongst them, he says he used to be a violinist in Berlin. When he hears that I can play the piano he fetches his violin and plays.

It is so easy not to like people we do not know. We think we know what they are really like, but we don't.

Even people who are supposed to be enemies are a lot like us.

After Reading

Reading a novel is an achievement, one in which you have probably invested a lot of time and energy. Finishing it, however, is only part of the accomplishment. Take a little more time to reflect on the novel, its ideas, and your own thoughts before you move on to other books.

F Pause and Reflect

Return to the questions you first asked about the basic parts of a novel.

Looking Back

- **Do I know the point of view?**
- **Can I describe the characters?**
- **Can I visualize the setting?**
- **Do I understand the plot?**
- **Do I know the central idea or theme?**
- **Can I describe the author's style?**

Your notes and the various graphic organizers you've used while reading should help you answer some of the questions, but what if you can't answer a few of them? Take the time then to reread portions of the book.

G Reread

Rereading parts of a novel helps you notice details you may have missed the first time and clarify anything that confused you. You might reread to examine the author's style or a character's motivation. You might go back into the novel with a different question or two. With *All Quiet on the Western Front*, for instance, you could go back and challenge the novel's reputation, asking why people should still read a work originally published in 1929. Or you might ask what made Katczinsky such a memorable character or why his relationship with Paul was so important to him.

Fiction

When you are **synthesizing,** you are looking at all the parts of a book and deciding how they fit together. A short story, a poem, and an article are all short enough to reread in one sitting. A 300-page novel is different. It tests your memory, your intelligence, and your patience.

Look at the Whole Novel

Look at all elements. Go back to your Fiction Organizer and fill it in. If there are gaps in your understanding, you can reread any notes you made during your reading of the novel. Here is an organizer one reader made to synthesize, or pull together, the main details.

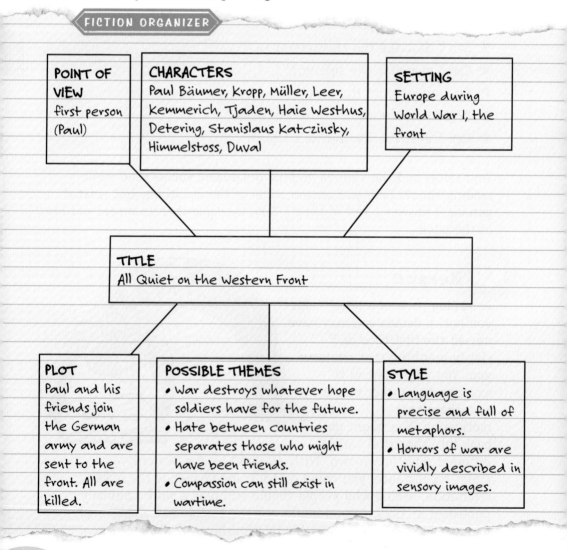

FICTION ORGANIZER

POINT OF VIEW
first person
(Paul)

CHARACTERS
Paul Bäumer, Kropp, Müller, Leer, Kemmerich, Tjaden, Haie Westhus, Detering, Stanislaus Katczinsky, Himmelstoss, Duval

SETTING
Europe during World War I, the front

TITLE
All Quiet on the Western Front

PLOT
Paul and his friends join the German army and are sent to the front. All are killed.

POSSIBLE THEMES
• War destroys whatever hope soldiers have for the future.
• Hate between countries separates those who might have been friends.
• Compassion can still exist in wartime.

STYLE
• Language is precise and full of metaphors.
• Horrors of war are vividly described in sensory images.

Look at a Major Character

Let's say you get to the end of the novel and realize that Katczinsky's death and Paul's relationship with Kat are crucial to the story. They are among the most memorable moments in the book, and surely Kat's death is the final blow for Paul. It makes sense, as part of your study of the novel, to reread the parts of the book that focus on Kat so you can appreciate what he means to the story and the other characters. Use a Character Map like the one below to help you organize information about Kat.

CHARACTER MAP

WHAT KAT SAYS AND DOES	WHAT OTHERS THINK ABOUT HIM
• steals food to keep himself and friends strong • shares with others—food, cigarettes, stew • knows when there will be a bombardment	• has all the soldiers' trust • Paul has a close friendship with him. • He is their leader.

STANISLAUS "KAT" KATCZINSKY

HOW HE LOOKS AND FEELS	HOW I FEEL ABOUT HIM
• feels sympathy for innocent new recruits • feels compassion for wounded soldiers • hates the generals and emperors • says they need a war to become famous	• respect him for his strength and character • depressed when he dies • trust him because he is honest and cares about people • would want him with me if I were in a war

Fiction

When you pull together the various parts of a novel in graphic form, you can easily review for a test or prepare to write a paper on the novel.

H Remember

After reading and studying an entire novel, you can't help having an opinion about it. Try not to reduce the whole book to a good or bad evaluation. Try one of the suggestions below to help you think a bit more critically about the book.

1. Make a Recommendation

Imagine your teacher has asked whether students should read the novel next year, or a friend emails you to ask if he or she should read it. Give your opinion and support it with a few points. Give only enough background so readers can get a sense of the story. Then, mention one or two reasons you did or did not like the novel.

2. Compare the Novel with the Film

All Quiet on the Western Front was made into a movie, first shown in 1930. Rent the movie, and write a comparison of the book with the film.

3. Extend Your Interpretation

Design a new book jacket for *All Quiet on the Western Front* or for whatever novel you are studying. Get some quotes recommending the book from classmates, and include those on the back of the jacket. Add a short plot summary, and make a drawing for the front cover.

Summing Up

When you read a novel, use **graphic organizers** to help you keep track of the essential elements: point of view, characters, setting, plot, theme, and style. The tools listed below can help you read a novel successfully:

- Web
- Fiction Organizer
- Classification Notes
- Character Map
- Setting Chart
- Summary Notes
- Sequence Notes
- Plot Diagram
- Topic and Theme Organizer
- Double-entry Journal

Remember, too, to look for the **organization of the plot.** Use the rereading strategy of **synthesizing** to help you decide how the parts of the novel fit together.

Focus on Plot

In his book *On Writing*, Stephen King says that he tends to depend on "situation rather than story." He goes on to explain: "I want to put a group of characters (perhaps a pair; perhaps just one) in some sort of predicament and then watch them work their way free. . . . The situation comes first. The characters . . . come next." How these characters respond to their predicament is the plot. The **plot** is what happens.

Most plots move in *chronological order*. This is also called a *linear* design because a plot moves from point A to point B. Some writers believe there are only two basic plots: a stranger came to town, or a person went on a journey. The plot then describes what happened when the stranger came to town or the person went on a journey. The other elements—theme, characters, setting, point of view—all influence the plot and the story's meaning.

Fiction

Goals

Here you'll learn how to:

✔ **follow the events of a plot**

✔ **identify the story's subplots and how these relate to the main plot**

✔ **consider how plot contributes to a story's theme**

Before Reading

Before you ever begin reading, it helps to know the parts of a plot. When you know these parts, you know how stories work. Whether you realize it or not, you are probably pretty familiar with the structure of a story.

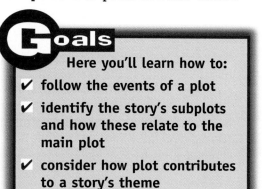

Identifying Parts of a Plot

Plots are traditionally divided into five parts. Most, but not all, fictional works have all five of these parts.

◀ PLOT PARTS

1. Exposition: *This is the background information that establishes the setting and describes the situation in which the main characters find themselves.*

2. Rising Action: *One or more characters face or try to solve a problem. This results in conflicts within the characters or with others. These conflicts grow more intense and complicated as the story unfolds.*

3. Climax: *Eventually the story reaches a crucial moment when the characters must act.*

4. Falling Action: *Sometimes called the* denouement, *this part of the story explores the consequences of the climax. The reader feels the tension in the story begin to ease.*

5. Resolution: *The story's central problem is finally solved, leaving the reader with a sense of completion, although the main character may not feel the same way.*

Using a Plot Diagram allows you to organize the story as you read it. It's like a map that tells you where you are in the action of the story.

◀ PLOT DIAGRAM

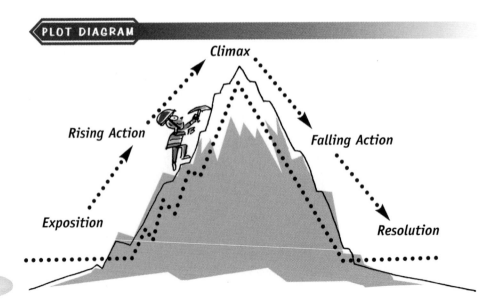

Climax

Rising Action

Falling Action

Exposition

Resolution

Getting Background Information

Authors give you a lot of valuable information in the first few pages of a story. In fact, you may not realize how important the first few paragraphs are until you finish the story and reread the opening. The beginning of most stories will tell you something about these story elements:

■ setting (time and place)

■ character (names and descriptions)

■ source of the conflict or problem in the story

If you can mark your book, make notes about these details in the margins. If you should not write in your book, use sticky notes to jot down your observations. See how much information you can glean from the opening of a story. Here is how one reader marked the exposition of Toni Cade Bambara's short story "Blues Ain't No Mockinbird."

Fiction

from "Blues Ain't No Mockinbird" by Toni Cade Bambara

The puddle had frozen over, and me and Cathy went stompin in it. The twins from next door, Tyrone and Terry, were swingin so high out of sight we forgot we were waitin our turn on the tire. Cathy jumped up and came down hard on her heels and started tap-dancin. And the frozen patch splinterin every which way underneath kinda spooky. "Looks like a plastic spider web," she said. "A sort of weird spider, I guess, with many mental problems." But really it looked like the crystal paperweight Granny kept in the parlor. She was on the back porch, Granny was, making the cakes drunk. The old ladle dripping rum into the Christmas tins, like it used to drip maple syrup into the pails when we lived in the Judsons' woods, like it poured cider into the vats when we were on the Cooper place, like it used to scoop buttermilk and soft cheese when we lived at the dairy.

"Go tell that man we ain't a bunch of trees."

"Ma'am?"

Characters introduced are the narrator, Cathy, Tyrone, Terry, Granny, and a man with a camera.

Setting is cold weather and outside a house.

Description of ladle shows family has moved a lot.

"I said to tell that man to get away from here with that camera." Me and Cathy look over toward the meadow where the men with the station wagon'd been roamin around all mornin. The tall man with a huge camera lassoed to his shoulder was buzzin our way.

Man with a camera may be the source of the conflict.

During Reading

Once you begin reading, start to figure out how the events relate to one another as well as to the theme and characters. One way you can do this is by choosing a good reading strategy to help you accomplish your purpose.

Reading Strategy: Using Graphic Organizers

Since stories are organized into a sequence of events, **graphic organizers** are useful tools when it comes to remembering a plot. For example, a Story String helps you keep track of the events in a story. Each frame shows an important event in the story. Draw each box, and then make a note describing the event. When you finish, you have a visual summary of the complete story.

Certain words, called transitional words, signal movement in time throughout a story. Watch for words such as *next, later, then,* or other words that indicate time passing. These words help you keep track of what is happening and signal that the story may be moving from one stage (exposition) to another (rising action).

On the next page is a possible Story String for "Blues Ain't No Mockinbird."

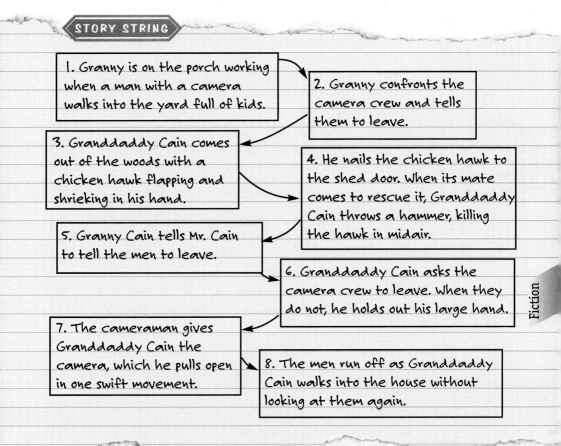

STORY STRING

1. Granny is on the porch working when a man with a camera walks into the yard full of kids.

2. Granny confronts the camera crew and tells them to leave.

3. Granddaddy Cain comes out of the woods with a chicken hawk flapping and shrieking in his hand.

4. He nails the chicken hawk to the shed door. When its mate comes to rescue it, Granddaddy Cain throws a hammer, killing the hawk in midair.

5. Granny Cain tells Mr. Cain to tell the men to leave.

6. Granddaddy Cain asks the camera crew to leave. When they do not, he holds out his large hand.

7. The cameraman gives Granddaddy Cain the camera, which he pulls open in one swift movement.

8. The men run off as Granddaddy Cain walks into the house without looking at them again.

Fiction

Understanding Flashbacks

Although most stories happen in chronological order, there are exceptions. Writers often use a device called a *flashback*. When you look at a Story String of "Blues Ain't No Mockinbird," you see a story organized in chronological time. But that is not the complete story. To explain why Granny was so upset by the camera crew, Bambara gives more information about Granny's background. She does this by using a flashback to an incident that occurred years before.

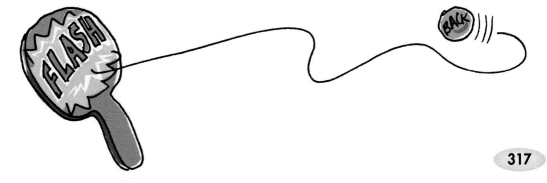

Me and Cathy were waitin, too, cause Granny always got somethin to say. She teaches steady with no let-up. "I was on this bridge one time," she started off. "Was a crowd cause this man was goin to jump, you understand. And a minister was there and the police and some other folks. His woman was there, too."

NOTE

Flashback to an earlier time

"What was they doin?" asked Tyrone.

"Trying to talk him out of it was what they was doin. The minister talkin about how it was a mortal sin, suicide. His woman takin bites out of her own hand and not even knowin it, so nervous and cryin and talkin fast."

"So what happened?" asked Tyrone.

"So here comes . . . this person . . . with a camera, takin pictures of the man and the minister and the woman. Takin pictures of the man in his misery about to jump, cause life so bad and people been messin with him so bad. This person takin up the whole role of film practically. But savin a few, of course."

This author uses a flashback here to explain why Granny reacts to a later situation in the way she does. Sometimes flashbacks distract you for a moment from the main action. When you return to the main story, you might find things have changed in some important way. You can evaluate the importance of a flashback by asking how the story or your understanding of it would change if the author had not included the flashback. In some cases, much of a story is a flashback. For example, much of Homer's *Odyssey*—the whole middle part of it—is a flashback that explains where Odysseus has been and how he escaped.

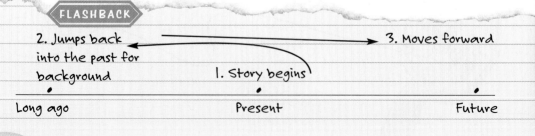

FLASHBACK

2. Jumps back into the past for background

1. Story begins

3. Moves forward

Long ago   Present   Future

Understanding Subplots

Subplots are other, smaller stories within a story. Subplots are related to the main plot, but they explore some aspect of the plot that is less important than the primary plot. Think of them as smaller plots that orbit around the main plot. The main plot in "Blues Ain't No Mockinbird" is about the conflict between the Cains and the camera crew. There is another story, however, that focuses on the relationship between Granny and Granddaddy Cain. This relationship is symbolized by the chicken hawk's efforts to save its captive mate.

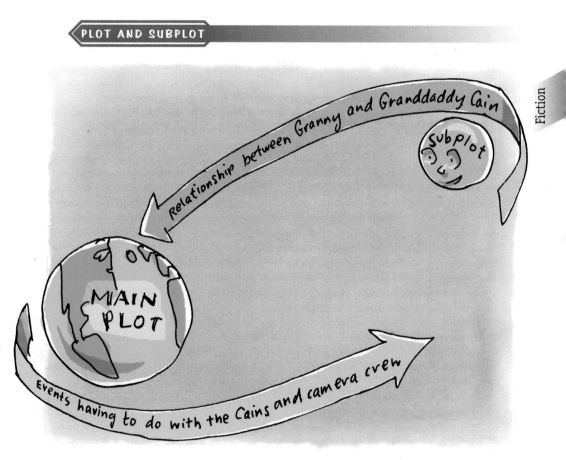

PLOT AND SUBPLOT

Relationship between Granny and Granddaddy Cain

Subplot

MAIN PLOT

Events having to do with the Cains and camera crew

Fiction

Keep track of any subplots as you read. Once you find the beginnings of a subplot, consider starting a separate set of notes or graphic organizers. By keeping track of it, you will most likely find that the subplot reinforces or expands on the theme of the story.

After Reading

When you finish reading a story and a friend asks you, "What happened?" you should be able to answer. If you cannot give the basics—the main characters, their conflict, how they responded to it, how things turned out in the end—you probably did not understand the story very well. First, try to identify the five parts of a story— exposition, rising action, climax, falling action, and resolution. This allows you to check your understanding and to build a good plot summary.

Knowing what happened is the crucial first step of this process. The next step involves thinking about what the plot meant. Use one of the following methods to extend your understanding of the plot.

1. Ask Questions

Ask the obvious questions that will lead you to new insights about a story. In the case of "Blues Ain't No Mockinbird," you might ask (and answer) these kinds of questions:

> *Why did Bambara begin her short story with a bunch of kids playing around and talking about cracks in the ice?*

> *Why did she describe all the different ways Granny used the ladle over the years?*

> *Why did she have Granddaddy Cain come out of the forest with a squalling chicken hawk in his hand and then nail it to the shed door?*

> *Why did the author have a flashback to the scene on the bridge where Granny saw a photographer come to film a possible suicide?*

Questions like these will lead to a deeper understanding of stories and also of the writer's craft. Once you ask these kinds of questions, you need to infer answers to them. Write down possible ideas in a journal entry like the one on the next page.

When I first saw Granddaddy Cain come out of the forest with that chicken hawk in his hand, I didn't know what to think. I assumed it was just to make him look scary, which it does! But then I realized that a chicken hawk is the female, and Cain was trying to get the male hawk. When one of the kids says the hawk is coming to claim his mate, I remembered the way the author talked about how Granddaddy Cain took care of Granny in the past anytime she felt threatened or disrespected. Then I understood that Bambara was comparing the hawks to Granny and Granddaddy Cain. When he threw that hammer and killed the hawk in midair, he was telling the camera crew to leave his wife alone. Also, his manner commands respect, which the camera crew did not show when they trespassed on the property.

Fiction

This journal entry explores one question. You do not need to compose a journal entry for every question that comes to you after reading. But you will find that coming up with questions and trying to answer a few of them will lead you to a deeper, more insightful understanding of a story.

2. Consider the Climax

Attentive readers can usually feel the climax of a story coming. Tension is mounting, and you know the characters cannot hold on much longer before they do something. Returning to the scene in which Granddaddy Cain kills the hawk, you might ask how this climax relates to the theme of the story. Here's where a Plot Diagram can help.

The diagram on the next page shows the climax in "Blues Ain't No Mockinbird." Notice how the *rising action* differs from the *falling action*. The difference reveals important clues about the theme of the story.

CLIMAX: Granddaddy Cain comes into the yard with a chicken hawk, which he nails to the shed door. When the mate comes, he kills it with a hammer while the camera crew watches.

RISING ACTION: Camera men show no respect for Granny.

FALLING ACTION: Granddaddy Cain asks for the camera and then destroys the film they took of Granny.

RESOLUTION: The men run away. Granddaddy enters the house without looking back, and Granny goes back to humming and working on her cakes.

EXPOSITION: The camera crew comes into Granny's yard without being invited.

Note how the incident with the chicken hawk fits perfectly in the context of the overall plot. But by itself, it seems odd and at first unrelated to the main conflict—the disrespect shown by the cameraman. The theme of the story might be stated as "Privacy has to be defended, especially against those who don't respect it."

Summing Up

- Plots are usually divided into five parts: exposition, rising action, climax, falling action, and resolution.
- Some stories contain flashbacks that tell about an earlier time.
- Many stories and novels have a main plot and one or more subplots.
- Understanding the action of the plot can help you understand how the theme is developed.

Focus on Setting

Stories and novels take place in a particular time and place. Some stories are about places that exist only in an author's imagination or, in the case of science fiction, on other planets. They may be set in the morning, during the day, or in the evening. They may take place in the past, present, or future.

General settings are the overall locations and time periods in which a work takes place—Pennsylvania in the 1700s, for example. *Immediate settings* are more specific—for example, a room in a house on Walnut Street in Philadelphia on August 7, 1753. Both general and immediate settings can change one or more times in a novel or story.

"Time" also refers to the historical period in which a story is set. A novel set in South Africa, for example, might take place *before* the country created policies, called apartheid, that segregated nonwhites and whites. The novel could also be set *during* the era of apartheid when conflict between nonwhites and whites was at its worst. Or the novel could be set more in the present time, after apartheid was dismantled. Where *and* when the author sets a work obviously matters.

Fiction

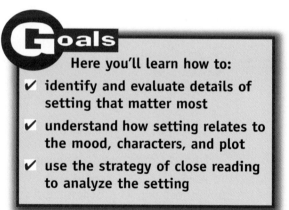

Goals

Here you'll learn how to:

✔ **identify and evaluate details of setting that matter most**

✔ **understand how setting relates to the mood, characters, and plot**

✔ **use the strategy of close reading to analyze the setting**

Before Reading

When focusing on setting, look first for those clues that tell you when and where the story happens. Writers usually put this information early in a story. Some stories are set in more than one time and place. In such cases, you begin your reading knowing you must constantly determine where and when the events described are set. Now take a look at a passage from Alan Paton's novel *Cry, the Beloved Country*, which is set in South Africa in 1946.

from *Cry, the Beloved Country* by Alan Paton

Physical details

Where you stand the grass is rich and matted, you cannot see the soil. But the rich green hills break down. They fall to the valley below, and falling, change their nature. For they grow red and bare; they cannot hold the rain and mist, and the streams are dry in the kloofs. Too many cattle feed upon the grass, and too many fires have burned it. Stand shod upon it, for it is coarse and sharp, and the stones cut under the feet. It is not kept, or guarded, or cared for, it no longer keeps men, guards men, cares for men. The titihoya does not cry here any more.

Conditions have changed.

The great red hills stand desolate, and the earth has torn away like flesh. The lightning flashes over them, the clouds pour down upon them, the dead streams come to life, full of the red blood of the earth. Down in the valleys women scratch the soil that is left, and the maize hardly reaches the height of a man. They are valleys of old men and old women, of mothers and children. The men are away, the young men and girls are away. The soil cannot keep them any more.

Human relationship to setting

Setting is important in this novel, for Paton looks at the relationship between the people who live in the country and in the big city of Johannesburg. The description tells you a story about the land, which was once green and fertile and now is dry and barren. The details of the setting paint a picture of the poor land and set the mood of the novel. Small, seemingly unimportant details reveal a great deal about life in this country and set the stage for the rest of the novel.

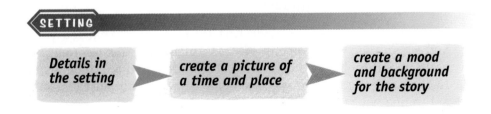

SETTING

Details in the setting ➤ create a picture of a time and place ➤ create a mood and background for the story

Reading Strategy: Close Reading

Setting is all about details. Writers use them to paint a picture of the time or to help you feel the mood of a story. Writers do not put details in stories without a purpose. **Close reading** helps you take time to examine a writer's choices and the ways they affect the story.

Highlighting or keeping notes about the setting helps you pay attention to these details. Putting sticky notes on the pages also helps you read closely. Such notes are especially useful when a novel has several different settings. A chart like the one below gives you a way to organize these different details.

Fiction

INFERENCE CHART

TITLE: Cry, the Beloved Country	
DETAILS ABOUT SETTING	POSSIBLE MEANINGS OR IMPORTANCE
• rich, thick grass	• beautiful land • people there probably well-off
• hills change and grow red and bare	• Soil near the valley is washing away, and crops don't grow well.
• too many cattle and fires • soil not "kept"	• people there probably poor
• Only old men and women there	• Young people have gone because the land cannot support them.

325

During Reading

Setting contributes significantly to mood and to a reader's understanding of characters and plot. If a writer ignores the importance of setting, the story will not hold together. You will not be able to fully enter into the story because you will lack the details you need to imagine the scene and sense the mood.

Setting and Mood

Mood is the feeling the story creates in you. To understand it better, think about how movies use music to create a feeling of anxiety (fast, high-pitched violins), sadness (slow, low notes on a solo saxophone), or excitement (loud rock band or full orchestra).

When you read this next excerpt from *Cry, the Beloved Country*, pay attention to how the setting helps to create the mood. Note the words and phrases that convey emotion.

---

from *Cry, the Beloved Country*

Have no doubt it is fear in the land. For what can men do when so many have grown lawless? Who can enjoy the lovely land, who can enjoy the seventy years, and the sun that pours down on the earth, when there is fear in the heart? Who can walk quietly in the shadow of the jacarandas, when their beauty is grown to danger? Who can lie peacefully abed, while the darkness holds some secret? What lovers can lie sweetly under the stars, when menace grows with the measure of their seclusion?

There are voices crying what must be done, a hundred, a thousand voices. But what do they help if one seeks for counsel, for one cries this, and one cries that, and another cries something that is neither this nor that.

NOTE
Describes the atmosphere of fear

Use one key word to organize the words and phrases that convey the feeling, or mood, of this passage.

Fear is a major topic in this novel. The author creates the feeling of fear by carefully choosing a few key words and phrases in creating the setting.

Writers also use sensory details to create a mood through the setting. Here is a short excerpt from the scene in *Cry, the Beloved Country* when the main character, a village priest named Stephen Kumalo, finds his sister, Gertrude, who is living in an area with a bad reputation.

Fiction

> **from *Cry, the Beloved Country***
>
> There is laughter in the house, the kind of laughter of which one is afraid. Perhaps because one is afraid already, perhaps because it is in truth bad laughter. A woman's voice, and men's voices. But he knocks, and she opens.
>
> —It is I, my sister.
>
> Have no doubt it is fear in her eyes. She draws back a step, and makes no move towards him. She turns and says something that he cannot hear. Chairs are moved, and other things are taken. She turns to him.
>
> —I am making ready, my brother.
>
> They stand and look at each other, he anxious, she afraid. She turns and looks back into the room. A door closes, and she says, Come in, my brother.
>
> Only then does she reach her hand to him. It is cold and wet, there is no life in it.

NOTE
Sounds of laughter

NOTE
Sounds of movement

NOTE
Sight details

NOTE
Touch

The mood here is one of fear and anxiety.

Setting and Characters

Setting affects our perception of characters or suggests how characters will act in the story. Kumalo's sister, Gertrude, is living in a bad area. Her own despair and failure are part of the setting. Her life reflects the lives of hundreds of thousands of blacks who came to the city from the country only to find no housing and little opportunity for work. An Inference Chart can help you better understand the way setting and characters influence each other.

INFERENCE CHART

WHAT THE CHARACTER SAYS OR DOES	WHAT I CONCLUDE
Gertrude keeps the door closed so Kumalo cannot see into her house.	She is afraid and ashamed. Her brother is a priest, and she knows he will not approve of her life.
Kumalo knocks, even though he knows he will not like what he sees.	He cares about his sister. That's why he came, to save her. He is anxious but strong. He does not avoid the truth about people.

The setting reveals Gertrude in her environment, the kind of problems she has, and how she has responded to life in the city. You learn about characters by seeing how they react in various settings. Are they strong and courageous and able to rise above their circumstances? Or are they defeated by them? Gertrude is afraid and ashamed. Her brother, Stephen, is strong and unafraid.

Setting and Plot

Writers change the setting for different reasons, but a change usually affects the plot somehow. Active readers notice such shifts and ask, "Why did the author suddenly change the setting here?"

For example, at one point Stephen Kumalo goes to Ezenzeleni, a community of blind people. As you read the following description of that place, try to determine why the author might have shifted the story away from the shantytown and big city to this community.

---

from *Cry, the Beloved Country*

It was a wonderful place, this Ezenzeleni. For here the blind, that dragged out their days in a world they could not see, here they had eyes given to them. Here they made things that he for all his sight could never make. Baskets stout and strong, in osiers of different colors, and these osiers ran through one another by some magic he did not understand, coming together in patterns, the red with the red, the blue with the blue, under the seeing and sightless hands. He talked with the people, and the blind eyes glowed with something that could only have been fire in the soul. It was white men who did this work of mercy, and some of them spoke English and some spoke Afrikaans. Yes, those who spoke English and those who spoke Afrikaans came together to open the eyes of black men that were blind.

NOTE New setting— new mood

NOTE Hopeful tone

Fiction

If you were plotting the tension in the story, the shift to this setting at Ezenzeleni would signal a major drop. The setting becomes gentle, light, even hopeful. It provides a break from the previous despair and shows both the reader and Kumalo that there is cause for hope. This setting is a reminder to Kumalo and to you as a reader that other people can live lives different from Gertrude's in the shantytown.

After Reading

When you finish reading and begin thinking about the meaning of a story or novel, take time to think about the role setting plays. The setting of *Cry, the Beloved Country,* for example, alternates between the countryside and the city. By the novel's end, the word *country* has come to mean not just the countryside but the country of South Africa. It is a country in which Kumalo and James Jarvis, the father of a man Kumalo's son murdered, realize black and white can and must learn to live together.

If you have a hard time drawing conclusions about the setting in a novel, try one of the following ideas.

1. List Key Settings

Take time to make a Setting Chart like the one below to help you appreciate the role setting plays.

SETTING CHART

TITLE: Cry, the Beloved Country	
GENERAL TIME: • period when segregation policies were enforced by the government • wide differences in income and housing between blacks and whites	**GENERAL PLACES:** • Johannesburg, South Africa • South African countryside
IMMEDIATE TIME: • not given	**IMMEDIATE PLACES:** • place where Kumalo's sister lives • Ezenzeleni

The Setting Chart, for example, helps point out the contrast between the city and the country. It also helps remind you of Ezenzeleni, so that you take the time to ask yourself, "What was the point of that part of the story?"

2. Sketch the Setting

Visualizing the setting allows you to see the story much better. You get a sense of what a place looks like. Using a Storyboard allows you to do just what movie directors do: see where one scene begins and another takes over. After you've made a sketch of the setting, make some notes about what you've learned from it.

STORYBOARD

1. small, poor village halfway up a hill in African countryside

2. train coming into a chaotic big city near nighttime, and a black elderly priest looking out

3. the same elderly priest standing before his sister's barely open door in a shantytown and her scared eyes looking out at him

Fiction

Summing Up

- A general setting is the overall location and time period of the whole story.

- An immediate setting is the specific location and time at which an event takes place.

- Writers often give clues about the time, place, and atmosphere in the early pages of the story to orient the reader.

- Setting can help you understand the mood, characters, and plot.

- Changes in setting usually signal a change in action and atmosphere, or mood.

Focus on Characters

Plot is *what* happens; setting deals with *where* and *when* a story happens; **characters** are the people *who* do things or have things done to them.

You usually remember the characters long after the plot and setting have left your memory. Characters often determine how and why you read a story. Your ability to "read a character" in a piece of writing affects a lot:

- your view of the plot
- your opinions of the other characters
- your understanding of the theme

Here you'll examine characters in Guy de Maupassant's story "The Necklace." De Maupassant tells the story of an unhappy married woman whose desire for luxury leads to trouble.

Goals

Here you'll learn how to:

✔ **identify and understand different character types**

✔ **recognize how characters affect plot, other characters, and theme**

✔ **use graphic organizers to analyze characters and track changes in them**

Before Reading

Not all characters are created equal. Some are more important than others. Some are more complete, or *round,* than others. Characters who are less important are called *flat* characters. One way of classifying characters is according to their role in the story. Stories typically have a **protagonist,** who is the main character, and an **antagonist,** who is the person or thing working against the protagonist. Here, you will look at characters by focusing on major and minor characters.

Major and Minor Characters

The *main character* is the one you watch when you read. Often you can best understand a character by asking, "What does this character want more than anything else?" Asking this question focuses your attention on what a character does and why. You won't always get this kind of information about *minor characters*. Understanding their role may not require knowing what they think or why they act as they do. You do need to understand the relationship among the major and minor characters, because the relationships can affect the action in important ways.

You can usually identify the main character or characters easily. The title may offer information about who the main character is, or a quick skim through the story will reveal the names most frequently used. For example, after previewing "The Necklace," you learn that Matilda Loisel is the main character.

Clues about Characters

The process of creating a character is called *characterization*. Writers create characters by making them say and do things and by having them react to one another. When reading, pay attention to these 5 kinds of clues about character:

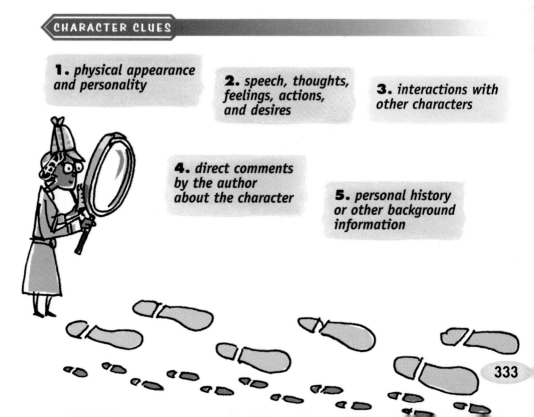

CHARACTER CLUES

1. *physical appearance and personality*

2. *speech, thoughts, feelings, actions, and desires*

3. *interactions with other characters*

4. *direct comments by the author about the character*

5. *personal history or other background information*

Fiction

What is there to say about a character in a story? What do you talk about, for instance, when you discuss Matilda Loisel in "The Necklace"? The strategy of **using graphic organizers** can help you identify the different aspects of a character.

<u>Use a Character Map to help you identify and organize details about a specific character.</u> It will help you understand a character and his or her role in a story or novel. Make a Character Map before you begin to read, and fill it in as you read.

CHARACTER MAP

WHAT CHARACTER SAYS AND DOES	WHAT OTHERS THINK ABOUT CHARACTER
CHARACTER'S NAME	
HOW CHARACTER LOOKS AND FEELS	HOW I FEEL ABOUT CHARACTER

During Reading

Keep in mind the questions that help you think about characters. Much of your understanding of a story comes through asking yourself questions. So, as you read, look for details about what characters say and do. Notice also how gestures reveal and develop characters. Then, ask yourself what these details mean, and answer your questions by making inferences. For example, read these three short excerpts from "The Necklace," in which the author describes Matilda, the main character.

from "The Necklace" by Guy de Maupassant

She was one of those pretty, charming young ladies, born, as if through an error of destiny, into a family of clerks. She had no dowry, no hopes, no means of becoming known, appreciated, loved, and married by a man either rich or distinguished; and she allowed herself to marry a petty clerk in the office of the Board of Education.

NOTE
How she looks

She suffered incessantly, feeling herself born for all delicacies and luxuries. She suffered from the poverty of her apartment, the shabby walls, the worn chairs, and the faded stuffs. All these things, which another woman of her station would not have noticed, tortured and angered her.

NOTE
How she feels

Fiction

"Here," he said, "here is something for you."

She quickly tore open the wrapper and drew out a printed card on which were inscribed these words:

The Minister of Public Instruction and Madame George Ramponneou ask the honor of M. and Mme. Loisel's company Monday evening, January 18, at the Minister's residence

Instead of being delighted, as her husband had hoped, she threw the invitation spitefully upon the table, murmuring:

"What do you suppose I want with that?"

"But, my dearie, I thought it would make you happy. You never go out, and this is an occasion, and a fine one! I had a great deal of trouble to get it Everybody wishes one, and it is very select; not many are given to employees. You will see the whole official world there."

She looked at him with an irritated eye and declared impatiently:

"What do you suppose I have to wear to such a thing as that?"

NOTE
What she does

NOTE
What she says

Here's how one reader used a Character Map to understand Matilda.

WHAT CHARACTER SAYS AND DOES	WHAT OTHERS THINK ABOUT CHARACTER
• throws invitation on table • says doesn't want invitation • says she has nothing to wear • sounds sarcastic and angry	• husband surprised she's not pleased

CHARACTER'S NAME
Matilda

HOW CHARACTER LOOKS AND FEELS	HOW I FEEL ABOUT CHARACTER
• pretty and charming • suffers from poverty • feels tortured and angered	• feel a little sorry for her • must be hard to live with

Matilda's husband gives up his savings to buy her a new dress. In a later passage, they are having a discussion.

from "The Necklace"

NOTE
How she feels

NOTE
What she wants

NOTE
What she says

The day of the ball approached, and Mme. Loisel seemed sad, disturbed, anxious. Nevertheless, her dress was nearly ready. Her husband said to her one evening:

"What is the matter with you? You have acted strangely for two or three days."

And she responded: "I am vexed not to have a jewel, not one stone, nothing to adorn myself with. I shall have such a poverty-laden look. I would prefer not to go to this party."

He replied: "You can wear some natural flowers. At this season they look very chic. For ten francs you can have two or three magnificent roses."

She was not convinced. "No," she replied, "there is nothing more humiliating than to have a shabby air in the midst of rich women."

from "The Necklace," continued

Then her husband cried out: "How stupid we are! Go and find your friend Madame Forestier and ask her to lend you her jewels. You are well enough acquainted with her to do this."

She uttered a cry of joy. "It is true!" she said. "I had not thought of that."

The next day she took herself to her friend's house and related her story of distress. Mme. Forestier went to her closet with the glass doors, took out a large jewel case, brought it, opened it, and said: "Choose, my dear."

She saw at first some bracelets, then a collar of pearls, then a Venetian cross of gold and jewels and of admirable workmanship. She tried the jewels before the glass, hesitated, but could neither decide to take them nor to leave them. Then she asked:

"Have you nothing more?"

"Why, yes. Look for yourself. I do not know what will please you."

Suddenly she discovered in a black satin box a superb necklace of diamonds, and her heart beat fast with an immoderate desire. Her hands trembled as she took them up. She placed them about her throat, against her dress, and remained in ecstasy before them. Then she asked in a hesitating voice full of anxiety:

"Could you lend me this? Only this?"

"Why, yes, certainly."

She fell upon the neck of her friend, embraced her with passion, then went away with her treasure.

NOTE
What she does

Fiction

NOTE
How she feels

Another way of organizing what you know about a character is to make a Character Web, such as the one on the next page, for Matilda.

gets a new dress

refuses her husband's first suggestion

feels sad, disturbed, and anxious

MATILDA

would prefer not to attend the party without a jewel

borrows necklace

visits friend

Note how the reader collected further details about Matilda. A Character Web also offers a fast way to gather all you know about minor characters, who can also be important to a story. Here is a Character Web for Matilda's husband.

CHARACTER WEB

clerk at the Board of Education

goes to great trouble to get an invitation to the ball

tries to make Matilda happy

MATILDA'S HUSBAND

sensitive to Matilda's feelings

Character and Plot

Characters make the plot happen. The plot is often about what characters do or how they respond to what happens. The plot also shapes what characters do, how they feel, or what they say.

Plot relies on conflicts or problems to create tension. Much of that tension comes from our curiosity about how the characters will respond to each new plot development.

As you read, ask yourself these sorts of questions:

What is this character's role in the plot?

How do the events in the plot affect this character?

How would the plot change if this character were taken out of the story?

Character and Other Characters

In "The Necklace," there are three characters: Matilda, her husband, and the friend from whom Matilda borrows a necklace to wear to the party. The loss of that necklace is what drives the plot. Matilda is the protagonist. The antagonist are the envy and pride of Matilda. They are behind the ten-year struggle she and her husband wage to pay for the necklace that they purchase to replace the lost one. The author keeps the reader in suspense, wondering whether the struggle will be successful and how it will affect Matilda.

Characters' comments about and reactions to other characters provide important insights. In this example, watch how Matilda, the main character, and her husband respond to each other. Consider what such responses say about them and their relationship.

Fiction

from "The Necklace"

She removed the wraps from her shoulders before the glass for a final view of herself in her glory. Suddenly she uttered a cry. Her necklace was not around her neck. Her husband, already half undressed, asked: "What is the matter?"

NOTE
How Matilda reacts

She turned toward him excitedly:

"I have—I have—I no longer have Madame Forestier's necklace."

He arose in dismay: "What! How is that? It is not possible."

NOTE
How her husband reacts

And they looked in the folds of the dress, in the folds of the mantle, in the pockets, everywhere. They could not find it.

He asked: "You are sure you still had it when we left the house?"

NOTE
How they react together

"Yes, I felt it in the vestibule as we came out."

"But if you had lost it in the street we should have heard it fall. It must be in the cab."

"Yes. It is probable. Did you take the number?"

"No. And you, did you notice what it was?"

"No."

They looked at each other, utterly cast down. Finally Loisel dressed himself again.

"I am going," said he, "over the track where we went on foot, to see if I can find it."

NOTE

How they feel

In this one short scene we see Matilda and her husband reacting to the loss of the necklace.

A tool such as an Inference Chart can help you interpret what characters reveal about themselves.

INFERENCE CHART

WHAT CHARACTERS SAID OR DID	WHAT I CAN CONCLUDE ABOUT THEM
• Matilda discovers her necklace is missing. • She says she had it when she left the party.	• Matilda is in a panic. • She tries to reassure her husband.
• Her husband questions her. • He says it must be in the cab. • He leaves to look for the necklace.	• Her husband is also in a panic. • He doesn't blame her, however. • He takes action.

Character and Theme

Characters act out a story's themes. If a main character has a need for money, you can be sure one of the central themes involves money. The themes of a story will typically mirror the themes running through the main character's life. Two clues, if you watch them closely, can help you understand the themes in any story.

1. Characters' Actions, Feelings, or Thoughts about Life

Be on the lookout for what the characters say about life in general or for what they reveal about their actions or feelings. These comments often relate to or even develop a story's theme. For example, many years later, Matilda meets the friend from whom she borrowed the necklace. Matilda's remarks reinforce the story's theme, which adds more information about the characters themselves.

from "The Necklace"

"You recall the diamond necklace that you loaned me to wear to the Minister's ball?"

"Yes, very well."

"Well, I lost it."

"How is that, since you returned it to me?"

"I returned another to you exactly like it. And it has taken us ten years to pay for it. You can understand that it was not easy for us who have nothing. But it is finished, and I am decently content."

NOTE
Statement about her actions

NOTE
Statement about her feelings

Fiction

Matilda's conversation suggests that she and her husband have endured a hard life to pay for replacing the necklace. This information adds to our understanding of the story and of the main characters.

2. A Change in a Character

Characters change as they experience new things and learn from those experiences. Aside from major and minor characters, you have two other useful ways of describing characters: *static* and *dynamic*. A *static character* remains the same throughout the story; he or she does not change. A *dynamic character,* on the other hand, does change and grow over the course of the story. How can you tell the difference between them? Ask yourself these questions as you read:

Does the character feel different about herself or himself at the end of the story?

Do other characters notice differences in him or her?

Does the character's appearance, condition, or status change?

Does the character learn anything by the story's end?

Change is part of any story. Read the following passage, which appears near the end of "The Necklace." As Matilda approaches her friend, note how she has changed.

She approached her. "Good morning, Jeanne."

Her friend did not recognize her and was astonished to be so familiarly addressed by this common personage. She stammered:

"But, Madame — I do not know — You must be mistaken."

"No, I am Matilda Loisel."

Her friend uttered a cry of astonishment: "Oh! My poor Matilda! How you have changed."

"Yes, I have had some hard days since I saw you, and some miserable ones — and all because of you."

"Because of me? How is that?"

At the end of the story, the author shows that Matilda's life has changed, along with her appearance. But the author has a trick up his sleeve.

"You say that you bought a diamond necklace to replace mine?"

"Yes. You did not perceive it then? They were just alike?"

And she smiled with a proud and simple joy. Mme. Forestier was touched and took both her hands as she replied:

"Oh, my poor Matilda! Mine were false. They were not worth over five hundred francs!"

Because "The Necklace" ends with a surprising revelation about Mme. Forestier, you are forced to look again at how this will affect Matilda Loisel.

After Reading

When you finish reading, what do you know about the characters and their roles? Use the following questions to assess your understanding at this point:

Can I identify the major and minor characters?

Do I know what the main characters want most of all and why?

Do I know why they act the way they do?

Do I know which characters change by the end of the story?

Can I tell how the main characters affect the plot, other characters, and themes?

Fiction

When you finish a story, you often have questions that you cannot answer. For example, you have to infer Matilda's feelings after the last line of the story. How does she feel after learning the diamonds were fake? You have few clues because the story ends so suddenly. Use a Character Development Chart such as the one on the next page to reflect on how a character changes from the beginning to the end of the story.

BEGINNING	MIDDLE	END
Matilda is unhappy with her life. She longs for beautiful things, which her husband cannot afford. She borrows and loses a necklace.	Matilda works hard for ten years to help her husband pay for the new necklace.	Matilda is proud of the results of her efforts. She is "decently content."

POSSIBLE THEMES:

1. People can change.
2. Hardship can both ruin and rescue one's life.
3. Life's events are determined by fate.

Summing Up

- Characters can be major or minor, static or dynamic.
- The process of creating a character is called *characterization*.
- Understanding characters helps you understand plot, other characters, and themes.
- Graphic organizers can help you keep track of your ideas about characters.
- Change in a main character often points to the themes in a story or novel.

Focus on Theme

Themes are the interwoven ideas that hold a story or novel together. If you compare a novel to a piece of fabric, the story (or plot) would be the threads that run one way, and the ideas (themes) would be the strands woven the other way. Many works have more than one theme, some major and some minor.

Sometimes you might confuse a story's theme with its topic or subject. The *subjects* of *All Quiet on the Western Front,* for example, are a war and the young men who fought in it. The *themes* of that novel are larger, more abstract ideas that comment on that subject. For example, possible themes might be that "Young men in combat can lose their faith in the future" or "Soldiers on opposite sides in a war can still feel compassion for one another."

Some stories and novels have obvious themes. Alan Paton, for example, says throughout *Cry, the Beloved Country,* "Have no doubt it is fear . . . " and discusses different types of and reasons for fear throughout the book. *All Quiet on the Western Front* focuses on youth from the beginning, examining what youth is all about and when and how the soldiers lost their youth by fighting in the war.

In some stories, however, the themes may not be so obvious, or they are more complex. An author might develop a theme but may never come right out and say what the theme is. This section focuses on not only what themes are but how authors develop them.

Fiction

Goals

Here you'll learn how to:

✔ **identify and understand themes in fiction**

✔ **find details that develop themes in a literary work**

✔ **see the difference between a subject or topic and a theme**

Before Reading

You can follow this three-step plan when focusing on the themes of a literary work:

Plan for Understanding Theme

Step 1 Identify the big ideas or central topics.

Step 2 Find out what the characters do or say that relates to the central topics.

Step 3 State what the author says about life that relates to the central topics.

Step 1: Identify the "big ideas" or central topics.

Think about a piece of music. Notice how certain sound patterns keep returning throughout the piece? This is how themes work in a story. They appear as ideas throughout the story and are expressed through what different characters do, think, or say.

Themes are often introduced through a story's title, although you may not realize the connection until you finish reading. A title such as *To Kill a Mockingbird,* for example, gives you little information about the themes, but when you finish reading, you realize that it relates to one of the book's big ideas.

How can you identify a central topic? Many stories have certain topics in common. Here are a number of topics you will find in many books. You can identify a central topic by noting the chief conflicts in a work or by concentrating on what characters do, say, and want.

COMMON TOPICS FOR THEMES

ambition	*friendship*	*loyalty*
change	*future*	*money*
childhood	*growing up*	*power*
choices	*hope*	*prejudice*
courage	*human needs*	*relationships*
culture	*identity*	*secrets*
differences	*independence*	*success*
faith	*justice*	*trust*
family	*loss*	*truth*
freedom	*love*	*war*

During Reading

Now that you know what possible topics to look for, these big ideas should be easier to find, right? As you take notes during your reading, you might simply list the topics that keep coming up. This technique helps you pay attention while you read and prepares you for figuring out the theme later on. Looking for recurring topics also gives you an additional purpose while reading, which helps you read with greater focus and insight.

Step 2: Find out what the characters do or say that relates to the central topics.

Once you identify a topic, see what the author says about it and how the characters' actions relate to the idea. These provide clues to understanding theme. In a short story such as Tim O'Brien's "On the Rainy River," for example, making decisions is an important topic. The main character struggles with decisions about whether to run away to Canada or fight in Vietnam, and what to believe and what not to believe about the war, his country, and even himself.

You will know if you choose a good topic to investigate. If you choose well, you will find examples and details relating to this topic throughout a story. Clues about the theme appear in several forms:

- repeated words, ideas, or symbols
- images and metaphors
- important plot events or dialogue
- changes in characters' actions, beliefs, or values

Reading Strategy: Using Graphic Organizers

Graphic organizers, such as Summary Notes and Double-entry Journals, are a useful way of keeping track of details related to a topic.

Bharati Mukherjee's novel *Jasmine,* for example, features many central topics. Any one of them can lead to a theme. The novel tells the story of a young Indian woman who flees her country after her husband's death. She changes identities and locations throughout the novel in an effort to find out who she is. Summary Notes show how a theme develops chapter by chapter.

Fiction

BOOK:	JASMINE
TOPIC:	IDENTITY
CHAPTER 1	In India a fortune-teller says Jasmine will be a widow and live in exile. The chapter ends with her living in Iowa years later.
CHAPTER 4	She compares herself as a girl in India with herself as a woman in America.
CHAPTER 12	Prakash, her Indian husband, changes her name from Jyoti to Jasmine.

A Double-entry Journal can help you look at specific lines and passages to see what they mean and how they relate to a topic.

DOUBLE-ENTRY JOURNAL

BOOK: JASMINE
TOPIC: IDENTITY

QUOTES	WHAT I THINK ABOUT IT
"Masterji, you are here to tell me that there is a lotus blooming in the middle of all this filth, no?" (p. 50)	Jasmine's teacher comes to tell her father that she is not a common village girl and should not be married off. They have a discussion about Jasmine's future and what she really is. This is important because identity is based not only on what you are or where you are from, but on what you know and can do.
"Yogi's in a hurry to become all-American, isn't he?" (p. 28)	"Yogi" is the nickname school friends give to Jasmine and Bud's adopted Vietnamese son. His real name is Du. This quote brings up the question of what it means to be American now. Kids like Du change identities to meet the needs of the situation. Jasmine is always saying Du does whatever he must to survive. Changing names, identities—these are not big problems or sacrifices for him.

After Reading

Now it's time to use your notes and organizers to help you write about the themes the author explores.

Step 3: State what the author says about life that relates to the central topics.

Use a Topic and Theme Organizer to identify the themes in a story or novel. You can make an organizer for each big idea in a novel. First, list the big idea or main topic. Then, tell the details of what the characters say or do that relates to that topic. Next, write what is important to learn about this topic. Here's an organizer one reader made for *Jasmine*.

Fiction

> **TOPIC AND THEME ORGANIZER**
>
> **I. BIG IDEA**   (Identity)
>
> **2. WHAT CHARACTERS DO OR SAY**
>
> | Jasmine keeps changing her name every time she moves to a new place: Jasmine, Jane, Jazzy, Jase, and Jyoti. | Many different characters leave one place to go to another where they think they can be their "real" selves. People resist these changes: Taylor won't let Jasmine be "Jane." Prakash won't let Jasmine be "Jyoti," and Jasmine's teacher won't let her drop out of school. | Identity is also what you do: Darrel has always been a farmer; Prakash was born to be an engineer; Lillian Gordon lives to help immigrants; Bud is a banker. |
> |---|---|---|
>
> **3. WHAT IS IMPORTANT TO LEARN**
>
> Who we are depends on where we are and the people we are with.

Note that the organizer includes several different examples, each of which relates to a different aspect of identity. Jasmine is the main character in the novel, but the topic of identity relates to all the characters. A good theme statement will not limit you to talking only about the main character.

Tip 1. State your idea. *Try not to summarize the story. Your theme statement should be a complete sentence that expresses the story's theme. Try completing the following sentence: "The point the author makes is that _____."*

Tip 2. Use precise words. *Vague words—such as* good *or* important *or* bad—*make it hard to get your point across.*

Tip 3. Avoid using characters' names. *Good theme statements are about the whole story and its ideas, not just one particular character.*

Summing Up

- A theme is different from a subject or topic. The topic is the big idea in a story or novel. Theme is the author's ideas about that subject.

- Follow the three-step plan for understanding theme: 1) Identify the "big ideas" or central topics. 2) Find out what the characters do or say that relates to the central topics. 3) Make a statement about life that relates to a central topic.

- Different readers will have different interpretations of a work. Readers bring their own experiences and ideas to a text, and these influence their interpretation. So long as you or another reader can provide evidence—examples and details—that supports your interpretation, you are reading well.

Focus on Dialogue

How characters speak, as well as what they talk about, tells us a lot about their background, personality, and culture. If you think about it, that makes perfect sense. You learn about your friends by what they say and what others say about them, and the same thing happens with characters. Through dialogue, you come to know what characters are like and, just as important, how you feel about them.

Dialogue refers specifically to what characters say to each other in a work of literature. Some works contain a lot of dialogue. Others contain very little, but dialogue can still:

- provide clues about the characters
- affect the mood
- explain and advance the plot

Goals

Here you'll learn how to:

✔ **understand the forms of dialogue**

✔ **see how dialogue affects the characters, mood, and plot of a literary work**

✔ **understand the different ways dialogue is shown**

Fiction

Before Reading

Not all dialogue is actually spoken in a story. Sometimes characters are speaking, and sometimes they are merely thinking to themselves. It is important to recognize when characters are speaking aloud and when they are speaking to themselves, in their head. One sure way to know the difference is to learn the rules for how dialogue is shown.

Quotation Marks and Speech Tags

Dialogue is typically indicated by quotation marks. What falls between those quotation marks is what the character is saying. But some writers use different ways to indicate speech. Alan Paton, for example, in *Cry, the Beloved Country,* uses dashes to indicate speech (—How can I help you? asked the clerk). The speaker of the lines is indicated by *speech tags.* These are the words that indicate who spoke and how they spoke.

Read this passage from Toni Cade Bambara's story "Blues Ain't No Mockinbird" to see how dialogue works. This passage shows several different ways that writers use dialogue.

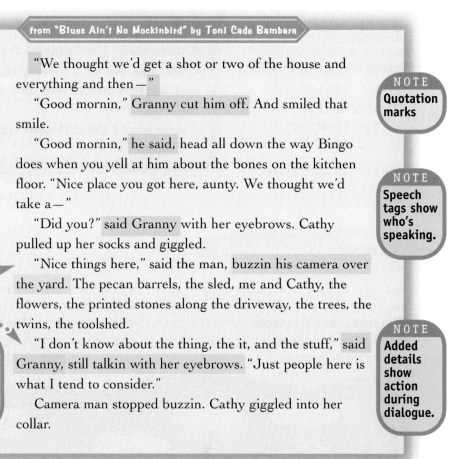

from "Blues Ain't No Mockinbird" by Toni Cade Bambara

"We thought we'd get a shot or two of the house and everything and then—"

"Good mornin," Granny cut him off. And smiled that smile.

NOTE Quotation marks

"Good mornin," he said, head all down the way Bingo does when you yell at him about the bones on the kitchen floor. "Nice place you got here, aunty. We thought we'd take a—"

"Did you?" said Granny with her eyebrows. Cathy pulled up her socks and giggled.

NOTE Speech tags show who's speaking.

"Nice things here," said the man, buzzin his camera over the yard. The pecan barrels, the sled, me and Cathy, the flowers, the printed stones along the driveway, the trees, the twins, the toolshed.

NOTE New paragraph used for new speaker

"I don't know about the thing, the it, and the stuff," said Granny, still talkin with her eyebrows. "Just people here is what I tend to consider."

Camera man stopped buzzin. Cathy giggled into her collar.

NOTE Added details show action during dialogue.

You probably noticed that the writer begins a new paragraph each time a different character speaks. This practice, used by most writers, helps you keep track of who is speaking. Try also to keep the following points in mind.

1. Extended Quotations: If a speaker's words extend beyond one paragraph, there will be no closing quotation marks until that speaker stops talking, although the opening quotation marks will appear at the beginning of each new paragraph. If you get confused, stop and simply ask, "Who is talking, and how can I be sure?"

2. Embedded Quotations: Sometimes a character will quote what another character said. These quotations can be confusing, since single quotation marks are embedded within double quotation marks, as in this example from "Blues Ain't No Mockinbird."

from "Blues Ain't No Mockinbird"

NOTE

Main quotation

"Get them persons out of my flower bed, Mr. Cain," say Granny moanin real low like at a funeral.

"How come your grandmother calls her husband 'Mr. Cain' all the time?" Tyrone whispers all loud and noisy and from the city and don't know no better.

NOTE

Embedded quotation

Fiction

3. Representative Dialogue: Some stories include dialogue that is not spoken by any one person in particular. Rather, the dialogue represents what people in general are saying. Here, for example, the speakers represent the many people who have left their villages for the big city of Johannesburg, South Africa, to find work.

The black people go to Alexandra or Sophiatown or Orlando, and try to hire rooms or to buy a share of a house.

—Have you a room that you could let?

—No, I have no room.

—Have you a room that you could let?

—It is let already.

—Have you a room that you could let?

Yes, I have a room that I could let, but I do not want to let it. I have only two rooms, and there are six of us already, and the boys and girls are growing up. But school books cost money, and my husband is ailing, and when he is well it is only thirty-five shillings a week. . . .

NOTE
Statements by no particular person

NOTE
No dash indicates she thinks this but doesn't say it.

4. Internal Dialogue: Some conversations take place in a character's mind but are not spoken. Authors use this internal dialogue for various reasons, but mostly to distinguish between what the character really thinks and what he or she actually says. Authors sometimes use italics to indicate when characters are having such an internal conversation with themselves or an imagined conversation with someone else.

5. No Speech Tags: If the dialogue between two persons consists of short sentences, the writer may omit speech tags after the first couple of lines. If you get confused about which person is speaking, you may have to go back to the first speech tags and reread the words identifying the speakers.

"What's up, Kat?" says Kropp.

"I wish I were back home." Home—he means the huts.

"We'll soon be out of it, Kat."

NOTE
No speech tags given

Reading Strategy: Close Reading

Close reading is an ideal strategy to use when focusing on dialogue because of the different types of information you can gather. Close reading demands that you use your imagination to "hear" what characters say and how they say it.

As you read dialogue, ask yourself some of the following questions:

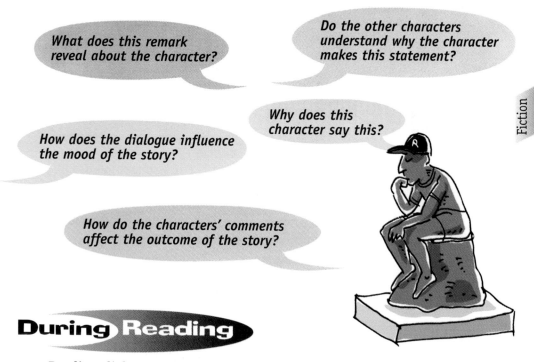

What does this remark reveal about the character?

Do the other characters understand why the character makes this statement?

Why does this character say this?

How does the dialogue influence the mood of the story?

How do the characters' comments affect the outcome of the story?

Fiction

During Reading

Reading dialogue requires that you focus not only on who is talking but also on how they talk and what they say.

Clues about Character

You judge others by how they speak and what they say. Writers know this, of course, which is why a character's speech is never an accident. If characters use slang words, the author intended that. If they speak formally, this, too, is a choice the writer makes for a reason.

Bambara uses the music of her characters' speech to develop their personalities. Read the following examples to see how she uses dialogue to bring her characters to life. What clues about character can you find?

NOTE
Polite but firm

. . . So Granddaddy say above the buzzin, but quiet, "Good day, gentlemen." Just like that. Like he'd invited them in to play cards and they'd stayed too long and all the sandwiches were gone and Reverend Webb was droppin by and it was time to go.

A page later, Granddaddy Cain says to the men:

NOTE
Firmly states ownership

"You standin in the misses' flower bed," say Granddaddy. "This is our own place."

Dialogue also contributes to the mood of a story. If people are angry or anxious, happy or excited, their speech will reveal this. Think about what mood Bambara creates with these lines from Granddaddy Cain. He speaks only two lines in the story, but combined with his actions, they tell a lot about his powerful presence.

Use a journal entry to reflect on what Granddaddy Cain's lines reveal about him. Here's what one reader wrote about him.

JOURNAL ENTRY

So much attention is given to Granddaddy Cain's size and the way he carries himself that he hardly needs to say anything to seem strong and forceful. His "Good day, gentlemen" reflects this dignity. What is really important, though, is his comment, "This is our own place." We know from the first paragraph that the family had to move a lot. So to have a camera crew invade their privacy like they do in this story would be an insult to them.

Clues about Plot

Dialogue can also provide background, emphasize a conflict, and advance the plot. When characters talk, you can get clues about what's going to happen next and explanations of what has happened before. "Listen" to this dialogue between Granny and Smilin man.

---

from "Blues Ain't No Mockinbird"

"Mornin, ladies," a new man said. He had come up behind us when we weren't lookin. "And gents," discoverin the twins givin him a nasty look. "We're filmin for the county," he said with a smile. "Mind if we shoot a bit around here?"

"I do indeed," said Granny with no smile.

> **NOTE**
> **Conflict is shown in two points of view.**

Fiction

Granny's comment, "I do indeed," indicates a conflict, or a problem. That's the beginning of the rising action. Later, Granny tells a story that ends in this way.

---

from "Blues Ain't No Mockinbird"

"So here comes . . . this person . . . with a camera, takin pictures of the man and the minister and the woman. Takin pictures of the man in his misery about to jump, cause life so bad and people been messin with him so bad. This person takin up the whole roll of film practically. But savin a few, of course."

> **NOTE**
> **What Granny saw earlier**

What Granny says suggests one reason for her dislike of strangers taking pictures. Her story confirms her distaste for photographers invading someone's privacy and her distrust of their motives. Granny's story comes at the end of the rising action.

After Reading

When you finish reading a story or novel, look back and reflect on the dialogue in it. What did you learn from it? What lines were memorable? What did the dialogue reveal about the characters?

Double-entry Journals can help you look more closely at dialogue, especially when you are trying to make inferences about a character. Here's what one reader wrote about the following dialogue.

DOUBLE-ENTRY JOURNAL

QUOTE	MY THOUGHTS
"Now aunty," Camera said, pointin the thing straight at her. "Your mama and I are not related."	Granny insists on respect in the way people speak to and treat her. The man's informal tone and familiar use of "aunty" and his pointing his camera right at her show little respect for her.

Summing Up

- Dialogue is traditionally shown by quotation marks and speech tags.

- A new paragraph is started every time that someone new begins speaking.

- Dialogue helps to reveal what the characters are like, the mood, and the plot of a story.

Focus on Comparing and Contrasting

At some time, your teacher will ask you to compare and contrast two or more things in a paper or talk. Sometimes your assignment will have a specific purpose—to compare two characters, for example. Other times, you can choose what to compare and contrast.

How do you start? First, determine what elements you are going to compare and contrast. You will probably write or talk about the following:

- two or more elements within one literary work
- two or more elements in different works by different authors
- two or more elements in different works by the same author

Goals

Here you'll learn how to:

✔ **use the reading process to make strong comparisons and contrasts**

✔ **use different reading tools to analyze works or elements**

✔ **find and organize details from the literary works to support your points**

Fiction

When you *compare*, you focus on how things are similar. When you *contrast*, you focus on how they are different.

Before Reading

When your goal is to compare and contrast, you have to find a number of ways in which things are alike and different. That purpose helps you know what to preview.

Whether you are reading one or two literary works, preview before you begin to read. As you preview, look for these things:

Preview Checklist

✔ the characters and what they are like

✔ when and where the story takes place

✔ the plot

✔ the themes

✔ who tells the story

✔ any words, phrases, or ideas that are repeated throughout the novel

Suppose that your assignment is to compare and contrast two or more elements in different works by the same author. As an example, take two novels by Charles Dickens: *David Copperfield* and *Great Expectations*.

During Reading

Graphic organizers can help you keep track of the details you'll need to make comparisons of two different works.

Reading Strategy: Using Graphic Organizers

As you read *David Copperfield,* you need a way to organize what you learn. Keep track of what you discover by **using graphic organizers,** such as a Fiction Organizer. You may not be able to fill in all the parts of the organizer just by previewing the book covers and the novel itself, but you can add to the organizer as you read. Here are the notes one reader started to make while reading *David Copperfield*.

Fiction

FICTION ORGANIZER

POINT OF VIEW
first person

MAIN CHARACTERS:
David
David's mother
Mr. Murdstone
Miss Murdstone
Steerforth
Mr. Micawber
Uriah Heep
Betsey Trotwood

SETTINGS
England (home, school, London)

PLOT
The story follows David as a boy and a man. He is cruelly treated, has many misfortunes, and longs for happiness.

DAVID COPPERFIELD

STYLE

THEMES

You can do the same kind of organizer for each of the two works you're comparing.

Have a reading notebook handy as you carefully read the works you're comparing. Here's how one reader started to jot down notes on a Two-novel Map in a notebook.

DAVID COPPERFIELD	GREAT EXPECTATIONS
Background	
written 1849-1850	written 1860-1861
somewhat autobiographical	
Main Characters	
David	
David's Mother	Pip
The Murdstones	Joe Gargery
Steerforth	Miss Havisham
Mr. Micawber	Magwitch
Uriah Heep	Estella
Betsey Trotwood	
Main Setting	
London, England	London, England
Main Plot	
• David orphaned at an early age	• Pip orphaned at an early age
• lives with stepfather	• lives with older sister and her husband
Main Events	
Main Themes	
Ending	

A chart like this can show the main similarities and differences between two works. As a reader, your purpose is to collect information to compare the two novels. Your notes and reading strategy ought to help you prepare to write your comparison.

Another useful graphic organizer for comparing and contrasting is a Venn Diagram. Note how the reader used it to compare two characters.

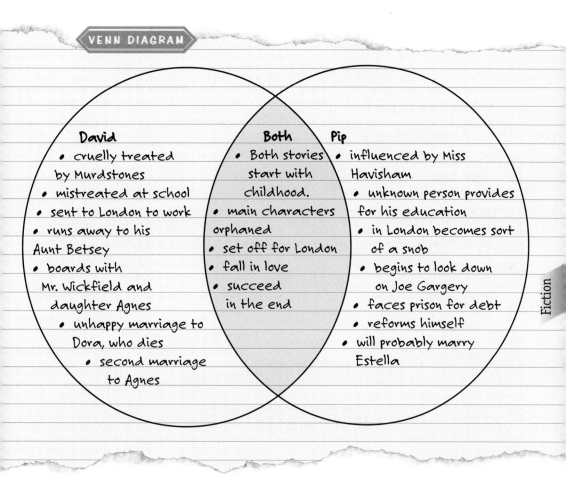

VENN DIAGRAM

David
- cruelly treated by Murdstones
- mistreated at school
- sent to London to work
- runs away to his Aunt Betsey
- boards with Mr. Wickfield and daughter Agnes
- unhappy marriage to Dora, who dies
- second marriage to Agnes

Both
- Both stories start with childhood.
- main characters orphaned
- set off for London
- fall in love
- succeed in the end

Pip
- influenced by Miss Havisham
- unknown person provides for his education
- in London becomes sort of a snob
- begins to look down on Joe Gargery
- faces prison for debt
- reforms himself
- will probably marry Estella

Fiction

If your purpose is to track one or two literary elements through two different selections, think about which elements seem most important to the two works. <u>A Venn Diagram is a good tool to use for comparing a single element.</u> The one above compares two characters, but you could compare settings, style, or themes just as easily using the same tool.

After Reading

After reading two works and taking notes, you still may not be completely ready to write your comparison and contrast paper or speech. Now is the time to look back and reflect on what you need to know. In fact, you may want to think more about what the subject of your comparison and contrast will be. For example, you might want to ask yourself some more questions before you start to write. Answers to these questions can help you decide what about your subject appeals to you most. You may have to reread to answer some of these questions:

Which literary elements did I find most interesting?

Did I find the minor characters, if any, more appealing than the major ones? Why?

Which antagonists were more fully characterized or described?

Which protagonists did I find most realistic?

What were the motives of the characters?

What were some important themes?

Which work gave a clearer picture of immediate settings, and what were these settings?

Was the dialogue realistic?

What were some key aspects of the styles? (sentence structure and figurative language, for example)

How believable were the plots?

Once you have answered these questions, think about how you should organize your ideas for your paper or talk. You will probably have to reread parts of the works before you write a draft. Here's one example of a way to organize your comparison and contrast paper or talk.

MODEL OF COMPARISON AND CONTRAST

Opening

- *Topic Sentence*
  sentence that names what is being compared and/or contrasted and at least two reasons you are going to cite

Body

- *Reason One*
  supporting detail or quote from novel #1
  supporting detail or quote from novel #2
- *Reason Two*
  supporting detail or quote from novel #1
  supporting detail or quote from novel #2

(Continue with as many reasons as you have found.)

Conclusion

- *Conclusion*
  sentence that restates how things are alike and/or different and why these similarities or differences are important

Knowing what you want to write about makes you a more focused reader. That, in turn, can help make you a better writer.

Summing Up

- When you read two or more works, read with the purpose of comparing and contrasting.
- Use graphic organizers to help you collect and remember the information you need.
- Reread parts of the two works to narrow the subject of your paper or talk.

Fiction

Elements of Fiction

Every subject area has its own vocabulary. Science, math, history, and English all use specific words to describe ideas or techniques in these subjects. This vocabulary allows you to discuss the subject. Calling "that guy in the story" a "protagonist" helps everyone understand what you mean. Here, you will learn the terms most commonly used to discuss fiction.

Use this section to clarify what the terms mean. Turn to it as you would a dictionary or glossary.

Antagonist and Protagonist

Fiction often draws its greatest power from the conflict between a main character and someone or something else. In this example from "The Cask of Amontillado," the main character, who is the narrator, vows revenge against an enemy.

EXAMPLE

from "The Cask of Amontillado" by Edgar Allan Poe

The thousand injuries of Fortunato I had borne as I best could; but when he ventured upon insult, I vowed revenge. You, who so well know the nature of my soul, will not suppose, however, that I gave utterance to a threat. *At length* I would be avenged; this was a point definitively settled—but the very definitiveness with which it was resolved, precluded the idea of risk. I must not only punish, but punish with impunity. A wrong is unredressed when retribution overtakes its redresser. It is equally unredressed when the avenger fails to make himself felt as such to him who has done the wrong.

It must be understood, that neither by word nor deed had I given Fortunato cause to doubt my goodwill. I continued, as was my wont, to smile in his face, and he did not perceive that my smile *now* was at the thought of his immolation.

Protagonist

Antagonist

Fiction

DESCRIPTION

The **protagonist** is the main character of a story. He or she typically encounters some problem or obstacle early in the plot. The source of this conflict is the **antagonist.** The antagonist can be a person, a group of people, a force of nature, or something within the protagonist's personality. The protagonist tends to be a sympathetic character. But the antagonist, if opposing a corrupt protagonist, can sometimes be the honorable character.

DEFINITION

The **antagonist** opposes the **protagonist.** The protagonist is the main character, one who is usually sympathetic and respectable.

Character

In this excerpt from "The Adventure of the Speckled Band," the narrator, Dr. Watson, describes a character who has come to seek the help of Sherlock Holmes. She is waiting in their sitting room.

E X A M P L E

from "The Adventure of the Speckled Band" by Sir Arthur Conan Doyle

A lady dressed in black and heavily veiled, who had been sitting in the window, rose as we entered.

"Good morning, madam," said Holmes cheerily. "My name is Sherlock Holmes. This is my intimate friend and associate, Dr. Watson, before whom you can speak as freely as before myself. Ha! I am glad to see that Mrs. Hudson has had the good sense to light the fire. Pray draw up to it, and I shall order you a cup of hot coffee, for I observe that you are shivering."

"It is not cold which makes me shiver," said the woman in a low voice, changing her seat as requested.

"What, then?"

"It is fear, Mr. Holmes. It is terror." She raised her veil as she spoke, and we could see that she was indeed in a pitiable state of agitation, her face all drawn and gray, with restless, frightened eyes, like those of some hunted animal.

How she speaks, how she feels, how she looks

What Holmes observes

D E S C R I P T I O N

A **character** is a person, animal, or imaginary creature in a literary work. Sherlock Holmes was an expert at detecting clues to character. What a person was wearing or carrying, physical characteristics, and actions all gave him insight into the kind of person he was dealing with. You, too, can find clues to character by watching for the ways an author presents characters.

Character, continued

Characterization

An author brings an imaginary person or creature to life through a technique called **characterization.** An author may describe several aspects of a character:

- physical appearance and personality
- speech, thoughts, feelings, actions, and desires
- interactions with other characters
- personal history or other background information

Character Types

Fiction has different types of characters. Like the pieces in a chess game, each character has a part to play. A story or a novel usually has only one *main character*, although there might be several *major characters* around whom the plot revolves. These characters tend to be more complex or *round*. Because such characters often change as a result of their experiences, they are referred to as *dynamic* characters.

Minor characters, on the other hand, often remain the same, which is why they are often called *static* characters. Things happen *to* them but not *within* them. Some of these characters are little more than stereotypes or cardboard cut-outs, appropriately called *flat* characters. Minor characters frequently play a key role in getting the story started or keeping it going.

DEFINITION

A **character** is a person, animal, or imaginary creature in a literary work. A character does things within the story or is the one to whom things are done. Authors create characters by describing physical appearance, gestures, thoughts and feelings, speech and behavior, and interactions with other characters.

Conflict and Complication

In Ernest Gaines's novel *A Lesson Before Dying,* Grant Wiggins, who is a teacher, is asked by Miss Emma to teach her son Jefferson "to be a man" before he is put to death for a crime. Wiggins, the protagonist and narrator, wants to get out of town, but suddenly his plans get more complicated, as the following scene shows.

E X A M P L E

from *A Lesson Before Dying* by Ernest Gaines

"He don't have to do it," Miss Emma said, looking beyond me again.

"Do what?" I asked her.

"You don't have to do it," she said again. It was dry, mechanical, unemotional, but I could tell by her face and by my aunt's face that they were not about to give up on what they had in mind.

> **Conflict between what Miss Emma wants and what Wiggins wants**

"What do you want me to do?" I asked her. "What can I do? It's only a matter of weeks, a couple of months, maybe. What can I do that you haven't done the past twenty-one years?"

"You the teacher," she said.

"Yes, I'm the teacher," I said. "And I teach what the white folks around here tell me to teach — reading, writing, and 'rithmetic. They never told me how to keep a black boy out of a liquor store."

"You watch your tongue, sir," my aunt said.

I sat back in the chair and looked at both of them. They sat there like boulders, their bodies, their minds immovable.

"He don't have to," Miss Emma said again.

"He go'n do it," my aunt said.

"Oh?" I said.

"You go'n do it," she said. "We going up there and talk to Mr. Henri."

Conflict and Complication, continued

DESCRIPTION

One of Wiggins's primary **complications** is his aunt, to whom he owes a debt of loyalty. Such complications are part of the rising action of the plot. Grant will encounter further complications when, for example, the young man he is to "teach" does not want to talk to him. The complication develops from or creates in a character a **conflict** that the novel will resolve by its end. In this case, Grant's conflict is between what Miss Emma and his aunt want him to do and what he himself wants to do.

Five different types of conflict occur in fiction. Although several of them could be present in a novel, most stories draw their tension from one or two of the following conflicts:

1. **person against person** (problem with another character)

2. **person against society** (problem with the laws or beliefs of a group of people)

3. **person against nature** (problem with a force of nature or some aspect of the environment)

4. **person against self** (problem with deciding what to do, think, or feel)

5. **person against fate** (problem that seems beyond the character's control)

DEFINITION

Conflict refers to the struggle between two opposing forces. A conflict may be between a person and one of the following: another person, society, nature, something within himself or herself, or fate. A **complication** causes a plot to become tense or entangled as a result of the conflict. Both conflict and complication are usually resolved at the story's end.

Fiction

Dialogue and Dialect

The following conversation from V. S. Naipaul's story "B. Wordsworth" provides a good example of how dialogue and dialect reveal character. A stranger has just arrived at a house in Trinidad and asked to watch the bees.

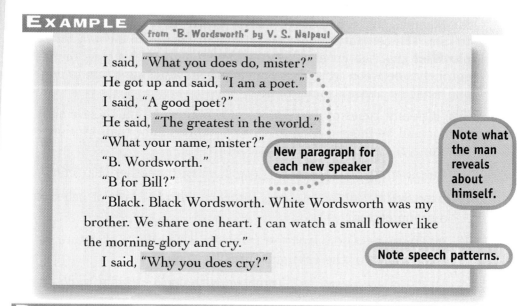

EXAMPLE

from "B. Wordsworth" by V. S. Naipaul

I said, "What you does do, mister?"

He got up and said, "I am a poet."

I said, "A good poet?"

He said, "The greatest in the world."

"What your name, mister?"

"B. Wordsworth."

"B for Bill?"

"Black. Black Wordsworth. White Wordsworth was my brother. We share one heart. I can watch a small flower like the morning-glory and cry."

I said, "Why you does cry?"

New paragraph for each new speaker

Note what the man reveals about himself.

Note speech patterns.

DESCRIPTION

Dialogue can help create character, advance the action, and introduce and reinforce themes. **Dialect** refers to the form of a language spoken by people of a certain region or group. It may differ from the standard language in vocabulary, grammatical structure, or pronunciation. The narrator in the above passage speaks a dialect of English. Many speakers would ask, "What do you do, mister?" The narrator asks, "What you does do, mister?" A character's use of dialect is a clue to his or her educational, family, or regional background.

DEFINITION

Dialogue is the conversation of characters in a literary work. **Dialect** is the form of a particular language. Dialects of English may be spoken in a certain region, such as the southern United States, or within a certain culture.

Flashback

In the following example, the narrator, Paul Bäumer, is thinking back to the time before he enlisted as a German soldier to fight in World War I.

EXAMPLE   from *All Quiet on the Western Front* by Erich Maria Remarque

Our thoughts of a career and occupation were as yet of too unpractical a character to furnish any scheme of life. We were still crammed full of vague ideas which gave to life, and to the war also, an ideal and almost romantic character. We were trained in the army for ten weeks and in this time more profoundly influenced than by ten years at school. We learned that a bright button is weightier than four volumes of Schopenhauer. At first astonished, then embittered, and finally indifferent, we recognized that what matters is not the mind but the boot brush, not intelligence but the system, not freedom but drill. We became soldiers with eagerness and enthusiasm, but they have done everything to knock that out of us.

> How he once felt about the war

> How he now feels about being a soldier

Fiction

DESCRIPTION

A **flashback** interrupts the chronological order of a story. It provides background information that helps the reader understand the current situation. Some stories begin in the middle or near the end of the chronology and then jump back to an earlier time to explain the present situation.

DEFINITION

A **flashback** is an interruption in the narrative to show something that happened before that time. A character in the present may think back to a time in the past or may relate a past event to another character. Information in a flashback can help to explain actions or events in the present.

Foreshadowing

The opening of Flannery O'Connor's famous short story, "A Good Man Is Hard to Find," hints at the tragedy that eventually unfolds. Can you guess what that tragedy might be?

EXAMPLE

from "A Good Man Is Hard to Find" by Flannery O'Connor

The grandmother didn't want to go to Florida. She wanted to visit some of her connections in east Tennessee and she was seizing at every chance to change Bailey's mind. Bailey was the son she lived with, her only boy. He was sitting on the edge of his chair at the table, bent over the orange sports section of the *Journal*. "Now look here, Bailey," she said, "see here, read this," and she stood with one hand on her thin hip and the other rattling the newspaper at his bald head. "Here this fellow that calls himself The Misfit is aloose from the Federal Pen and headed toward Florida and you read here what it says he did to these people. Just you read it. I wouldn't take my children in any direction with a criminal like that aloose in it. I couldn't answer to my conscience if I did."

What she was trying to do

What she says

What she warns

DESCRIPTION

The writer's rule for **foreshadowing** is that if you introduce trouble in a story early on, someone has to be touched by it by the end of the story. O'Connor's story opens with a scene that predicts the outcome. Foreshadowing is a powerful device that creates suspense and contributes to the overall mood of a story.

DEFINITION

Foreshadowing provides hints or clues early in a story that anticipate what is to come. Foreshadowing increases suspense, contributes to mood, and makes the ending seem believable.

Genre

Genre was originally a French word meaning "kind" or "type." Literary genres include novels, short stories, folktales, mythology, poetry, drama, and nonfiction. Within these genres are *subgenres*. For example, there are many different kinds of novels—realistic fiction, mysteries, westerns, science fiction, and fantasy. Within the genre of "thrillers" you will find political, techno, and detective thrillers, each with its own conventions. As you read, ask yourself why an author chose a particular genre. The chart below describes a few of the genres and subgenres.

GENRE	EXAMPLE	CHARACTERS	PLOT	SETTING	THEME
Realistic Fiction	*To Kill a Mockingbird*	*can be people or animals; must be believable*	*highly believable conflict; could happen to anyone*	*present-day setting or recent past*	*any*
Science Fiction/ Fantasy	*Brave New World*	*combination of realistic characters and characters with magical powers*	*realistic conflict or completely imaginary*	*usually realistic world with fantastic qualities*	*often that good wins out in the end*
Myths, Legends, Fairy Tales, and Folktales	*"Theseus and the Minotaur"*	*simple characters; often all good or all bad*	*conflict often person vs. person*	*"Once upon a time"; always long ago; castles and forests*	*that justice is usually important*
Creative Nonfiction	*The Perfect Storm*	*real event and actual participants in the event*	*combines narrative technique and reporting*	*dramatic: "He did not at first notice anything strange."*	*that redemption follows tragedy*

Fiction

DEFINITION

A **genre** is a kind of writing, such as a novel, short story, folktale, myth, poem, play, and nonfiction.

Irony

How would you describe the tone in this passage?

EXAMPLE

from "Indian Education" by Sherman Alexie

The opposite of what one would expect

ELEVENTH GRADE

Last night I missed two free throws which would have won the game against the best team in the state. The farm town high school I play for is nicknamed the "Indians," and I'm probably the only actual Indian to play for a team with such a mascot.

This morning I pick up the sports page and read the headline: INDIANS LOSE AGAIN.

Go ahead and tell me none of this is supposed to hurt me very much.

DESCRIPTION

There are three different types of **irony:** *verbal irony, irony of situation,* and *dramatic irony. Verbal irony* refers to the difference between what a character says and what he or she means. In Shakespeare's play *Julius Caesar,* for example, Brutus refers to the men who killed Caesar as "honorable men," but each time the actor says these words, his tone indicates just the opposite.

Irony of situation occurs when events are contrary to what is expected. Alexie thinks that he's the only Indian to play on a team nicknamed the "Indians," the opposite of what he might expect.

Dramatic irony describes a situation in which the audience or reader of a play knows more about a character's situation than he or she does. In Shakespeare's *Romeo and Juliet,* for example, the audience knows that Romeo, through his secret marriage to Juliet, is now related to Tybalt. Such knowledge intensifies the audience's emotional reaction when Romeo kills Tybalt—an instance of dramatic irony.

DEFINITION

Irony is the contrast between what seems to be and what really is.

Persona

In this opening of a Charles Dickens novel, we meet the main character, who explains his name and begins to tell the story.

EXAMPLE

from *Great Expectations* by Charles Dickens — **Author**

> My father's family name being Pirrip, and my Christian name Philip, my infant tongue could make of both names nothing longer or more explicit than Pip. So I called myself Pip and came to be called Pip.
>
> I gave Pirrip as my father's family name on the authority of his tombstone and my sister — Mrs. Joe Gargery, who married the blacksmith. As I never saw my father or my mother, and never saw any likeness of either of them, my first fancies regarding what they were like were unreasonably derived from their tombstones.

First-person narrator

DESCRIPTION

Persona refers to the voice (or mask) through which an author tells a story. Even when a story or novel has a first-person narrator, this person is *not* the author. Instead, an author takes on the identity of a character to tell the story. In the example above, Charles Dickens is the author, who speaks through the persona of Pip, a young boy when the novel begins. Authors may assume many personas, depending on the main character in the story they wish to create. Male authors may assume the persona of a female character, female authors the persona of a male character. An earth-bound author may take on the persona of an alien from outer space, or an urban-dwelling writer may speak through the persona of a cattle rustler in the old West.

Writers develop a persona in order to help you see events from a particular perspective. By seeing the story through Pip's eyes, a reader naturally sympathizes with him.

DEFINITION

The voice through which an author tells a story is called the persona.

Fiction

Plot and Subplot

Here is a summary of Rudolfo Anaya's novel *Bless Me, Ultima*.

EXAMPLE

> In the beginning, seven-year-old Antonio learns that
> Ultima is coming to live with them during the summer.
> Ultima and Antonio have a special relationship. Ultima has
> powers that lead some people to call her a "<u>bruja</u>," or witch;
> as a <u>curandera</u>, she shares her knowledge with Antonio.
> Throughout the novel, Antonio encounters many strange
> and wonderful things, including the Golden Carp, a crazy
> neighbor, and his first year of school. When Ultima has
> passed on her wisdom to Antonio, she dies.

DESCRIPTION

Plot is what happens in a story. A plot, which usually unfolds in chronological order, has five main parts, described below. A **subplot** is a less important series of events within the main plot. As the paragraph above shows, a simple summary of plot is only the first step in understanding a fictional work.

Parts of Plot

1. **Exposition:** Background information establishes setting and introduces the main character or characters.

2. **Rising Action:** The main character faces or tries to solve a problem. This results in conflicts that grow more intense.

3. **Climax:** The crucial moment occurs when the character must act or make a decision or when fate intervenes.

4. **Falling Action:** Sometimes called the *denouement,* this part of the story explores the consequences of the climactic decision.

5. **Resolution:** The story's central problem is finally solved.

DEFINITION

Plot is what happens in a story. A **subplot** is a less important series of events within the main plot.

Point of View

Every story is told by someone, and that gives the story its vantage point, or point of view.

EXAMPLE — from "Rope" by Katherine Anne Porter

On the third day after they moved to the country he came walking back from the village carrying a basket of groceries and a twenty-four-yard coil of rope. She came out to meet him, wiping her hands on her green smock. Her hair was tumbled, her nose was scarlet with sunburn; he told her that already she looked like a born country woman. His gray flannel shirt stuck to him, his heavy shoes were dusty. She assured him he looked like a rural character in a play.

Had he brought the coffee? She had been waiting all day long for coffee. They had forgot it when they ordered at the store the first day.

Third-person pronouns

EXAMPLE — from "A Telephone Call" by Dorothy Parker

If I didn't think about it, maybe the telephone might ring. Sometimes it does that. If I could think of something else. If I could think of something else. Maybe if I counted five hundred by fives, it might ring by that time. I'll count slowly. I won't cheat. And if it rings when I get to three hundred, I won't stop; I won't answer it until I get to five hundred. Five, ten, fifteen, twenty, twenty-five, thirty, thirty-five, forty, forty-five, fifty. . . . Oh, please ring. Please.

First-person pronoun

Point of View, continued

Point of View is the vantage point from which an author presents a story. Point of view is shaped by the author's choice of *narrator,* the person who tells the story. A story may be told from the **first-person** point of view or the **third-person** point of view. The narrator in the first example is outside the story, observing the characters. The use of the third-person pronouns *she, he, his, they,* and *her* signals that the story is told from the third-person point of view. The narrator in the second example is a character in the story, which is told from the first-person point of view. The use of the pronoun *I* indicates the first-person point of view.

First-person Point of View

Stories told in the *first-person point of view* use *I, me, our, we,* or *my.* The narrator is a character in the story, usually but not always the main character. A story told from one person's point of view limits that character's knowledge to his or her own observations and ideas. Not all narrators are reliable, so they may be biased in their view of characters or events. You must judge whether someone is a reliable narrator based on other details from the story.

Third-person Point of View

Told by a narrator who is not a part of the story's action, the *third-person point of view* uses pronouns such as *he, she,* and *they.* If the third-person narrator appears to know what everyone in the story is thinking and feeling, the point of view is called *omniscient.* Most stories, however, limit the narrator's knowledge to what the protagonist thinks and feels. Such a point of view is called *limited.*

Point of view is the vantage point from which a story is told.

Setting

As you read the passage below, note the sensory details as well as those that describe the general tone and mood.

EXAMPLE

from *1984* by George Orwell

It was a bright cold day in April, and the clocks were striking thirteen. Winston Smith, his chin nuzzled into his breast in an effort to escape the vile wind, slipped quickly through the glass doors of Victory Mansions, though not quickly enough to prevent a swirl of gritty dust from entering along with him.

The hallway smelt of boiled cabbage and old rag mats. At one end of it a colored poster, too large for indoor display, had been tacked to the wall. It depicted simply an enormous face, more than a meter wide: the face of a man of about forty-five, with a heavy black mustache and ruggedly handsome features. Winston made for the stairs. It was no use trying the lift. Even at the best of times it was seldom working, and at present the electric current was cut off during daylight hours. It was part of the economy drive in preparation for Hate Week.

> Time of year

> Place

> What it's like there

Fiction

DESCRIPTION

Details such as "the clocks were striking thirteen," "Hate Week," and a poster of an enormous face establish the setting of *1984* by the end of the first page. You realize that you have entered into a different world. **Setting** tells you what the world of the novel is like by describing its appearance and atmosphere. Setting is about both place and time. Orwell wrote *1984* in the early 1940s, at a time when the year 1984 was the distant future. The setting gives details that help you understand plot, mood, and characters.

DEFINITION

Setting is the time and place in which a literary work takes place.

Style

Note here how the author uses words, sentences, and typography (italicized letters).

EXAMPLE

from *The House on Mango Street* by Sandra Cisneros

Where do you live? she asked.

There, I said, pointing up to the third floor.

You live *there*?

There. I had to look to where she pointed—the third floor, the paint peeling, wooden bars Papa had nailed on the windows so we wouldn't fall out. You live *there*? The way she said it made me feel like nothing. *There*. I lived *there*. I nodded.

I knew then I had to have a house. A real house. One I could point to. But this isn't it. The house on Mango Street isn't it. For the time being, Mama says. Temporary, says Papa. But I know how those things go.

> No quotation marks for dialogue

> Repeated word in italic type

> Short sentence fragments

DESCRIPTION

Style refers to the way a writer uses language. The example above shows a wide variety of style choices. Some writers have more distinctive styles than others, but every writer has a certain style. Writers make careful choices about how they use language. The most useful questions to ask are, "What do I notice about this writer's style?" and "What has this writer accomplished by using language this way?" The three main elements of a writer's style are:

1. word choice
2. sentence structure and length
3. literary devices, such as figurative language, repetition, symbols, dialogue, and imagery

DEFINITION

Style refers to how a writer uses language and literary devices to express ideas and create characters. Style includes the author's word choice and sentence structure as well as use of figurative language, repetition, symbols, dialogue, and imagery.

Symbol

As a reader, you sometimes notice that an object seems to mean something more than it actually is, as in this example.

EXAMPLE

from *The Bean Trees* by Barbara Kingsolver

. . . I bought a car, a '55 Volkswagen bug with no windows to speak of, and no back seat and no starter. But it was easy to push start without help once you got the hang of it, the wrong foot on the clutch and the other leg out the door, especially if you parked on a hill, which in that part of Kentucky you could hardly do anything but. In this car I intended to drive out of Pittman County one day and never look back, except maybe for Mama.

> What the car means to the narrator

The day I brought it home, she knew I was going to get away. She took one look and said, "Well, if you're going to have you an old car you're going to know how to drive an old car." What she meant was how to handle anything that might come along, I suppose, because she stood in the road with her arms crossed and watched while I took off all four tires and put them back on.

> What the mother thinks

Fiction

DESCRIPTION

The narrator thinks that the car represents a ticket to freedom. However, the clue that the car stands for something else as well comes in the mother's comment and the narrator's interpretation of that comment: "What she meant was how to handle anything that might come along. . . ." So the car also stands for the opportunity to have new experiences. A **symbol** is something concrete—an object, a place, or even a person—that represents something abstract and more than itself, such as an idea or an emotion. To determine whether something has symbolic meaning, ask yourself how a character feels about that object, place, or person.

DEFINITION

A **symbol** is a person, place, thing, or event used to stand for something abstract, such as an idea or emotion, in a literary work.

Theme

In the opening paragraph from R. K. Narayan's short story "Like the Sun," the narrator thinks about the meaning of truth.

EXAMPLE

from "Like the Sun" by R. K. Narayan

Truth, Sekhar reflected, is like the sun. I suppose no human being can ever look it straight in the face without blinking or being dazed. He realized that, morning till night, the essence of human relationships consisted in tempering Truth so that it might not shock. This day he set apart as a unique day—at least one day in the year we must give and take absolute Truth whatever may happen. Otherwise life is not worth living. The day ahead seemed to him full of possibilities. He told no one of his experiment. It was a quiet resolve, a secret pact between him and eternity.

Clues about theme

DESCRIPTION

Theme is the main idea in a literary work. Not all works have a theme, and some works have more than one. The words "give and take absolute Truth" are a clue to the theme. That the theme of the story will involve truth in some way is obvious from the beginning of Narayan's story. The topic of the story, then, is truth, but the theme is a statement about truth. Paying attention to what characters say, what key scenes are about, and what the symbols are will help you identify theme in a literary work.

DEFINITION

A **theme** is the author's statement in a literary work. Novels typically have more than one theme, although most short stories focus on only one main theme.

Tone and Mood

How does this excerpt from "The Sniper," a short story set in Ireland, make you feel?

EXAMPLE

from "The Sniper" by Liam O'Flaherty

His actions   He was eating a sandwich hungrily. He had eaten   His feelings
nothing since morning. He had been too excited to eat. He
finished the sandwich, and taking a flask of whisky from his
pocket, he took a short draught. Then he returned the flask
to his pocket. He paused for a moment, considering whether
he should risk a smoke. It was dangerous. The flash might
be seen in the darkness and there were enemies watching.
He decided to take the risk.

His thoughts

DESCRIPTION

Many people use the terms *tone* and *mood* to mean the same thing. **Tone** is usually used to describe an author's attitude toward the subject, characters, or reader. Tone can be described in such terms as formal, informal, intimate, sympathetic, serious, matter-of-fact, satiric, or ironic. **Mood** refers to the atmosphere of a work. The mood of a work might be mysterious, joyous, gloomy, depressing, or peaceful, for example. The tone of the example above from "The Sniper" might be described as serious, and the mood, tense.

DEFINITION

Tone refers to an author's attitude toward the subject, characters, or reader. **Mood** refers to the atmosphere or feeling conveyed by a work.

Reading
Poetry

Introduction to Reading Poetry

Reading a Poem

Ways of Reading Poetry

Focus on Language
Focus on Meaning
Focus on Sound and Structure

Elements of Poetry

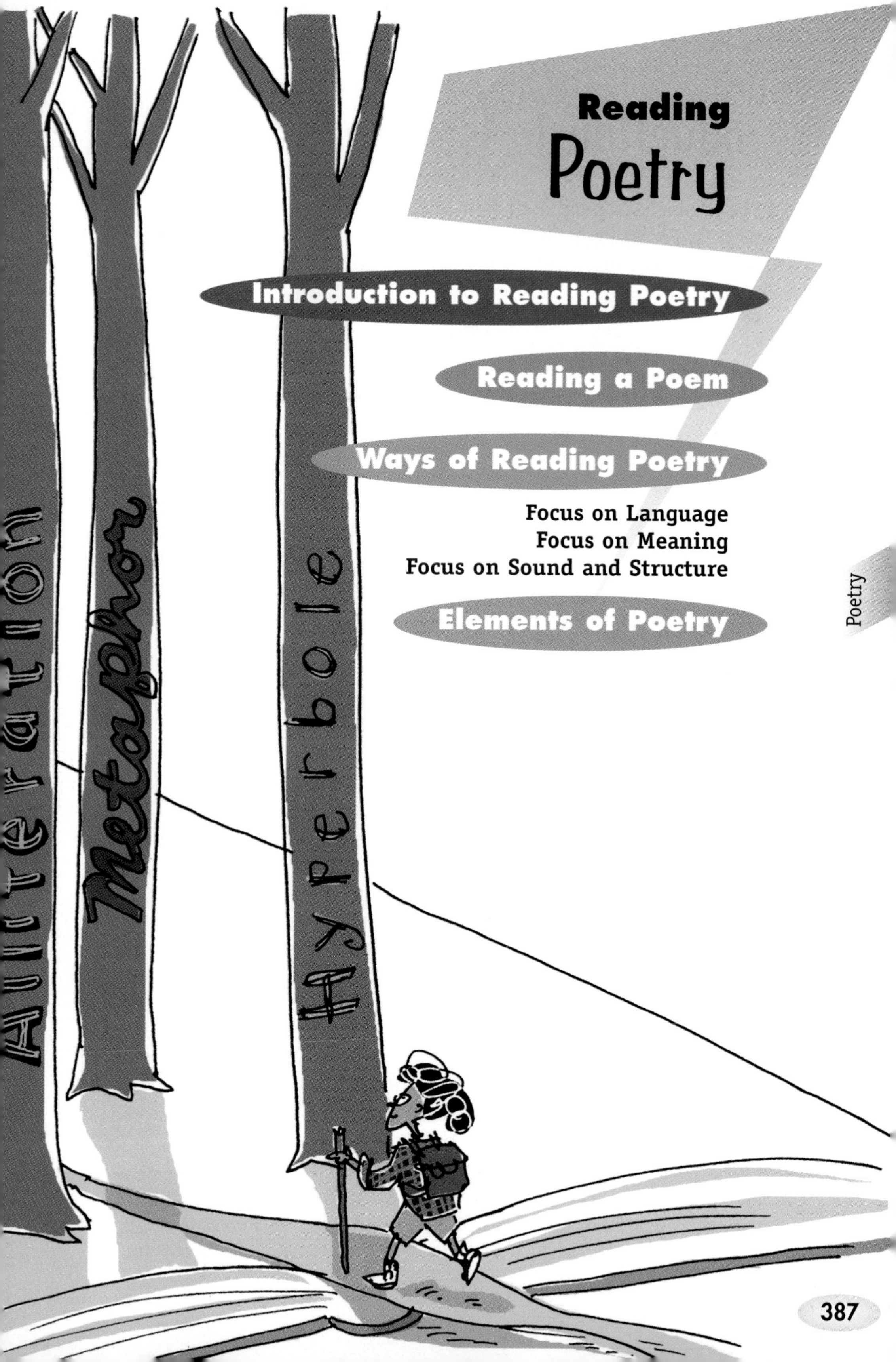

Poetry

Alliteration

Metaphor

Hyperbole

Introduction to Reading Poetry

If you asked six people what a poem is, you'd get six different answers. Poetry is as varied as people's reactions to it, but all poetry has this much in common: it is arranged in relatively short line length, and it says a lot in a few words.

Poetry is one of the oldest art forms in the world. It seems that as soon as people learned to communicate verbally, they wanted to recite or write poems. You're probably aware that you listen to poetry every day in the form of song lyrics. Not all lyrics have poetic qualities, but many do. The ones that are most like poetry are probably the ones easiest to memorize.

The memory of certain poems has sustained people during difficult times. Prisoners of war, when released, said they kept their sanity by spending whole days recalling poems they had learned years before. Thus, poetry is perhaps more powerful because it is often more personal than other forms of literature.

Poetry has a place in our daily society. You see wonderful poems on public transportation. You can hear poet Robert Pinsky reading a poem on the evening news to help the country make sense of a tragic event or to celebrate a national holiday. Poetry slams, events that blend the modern poetry of rap music with ancient oral traditions, are popping up all over the country.

Ultimately, poetry communicates what the heart wants to say, what the society needs to hear. Perhaps this is why the Nobel Prize for Literature is often given to poets in countries where the heart has been silenced.

People are often afraid of poetry, finding its sometimes dense language or symbols difficult to understand. If you are one of these people, this chapter will teach you how to read and enjoy poetry. Not all poems are written to be studied. Still, understanding poetry requires knowing how to read it properly and realizing how a poet is using his or her craft to communicate. In this chapter, you will find several methods and techniques you can follow to make sense of poetry. Poetry can work its magic by helping you hear not only your own heart, but also the world itself and the many songs it sings.

Reading a Poem

If you are like many readers, you probably find it difficult to understand poems right away. Whether they're long or short, rhymed or free verse, poems pack a lot of meaning into a few words. Your problem as a reader is how to unpack them.

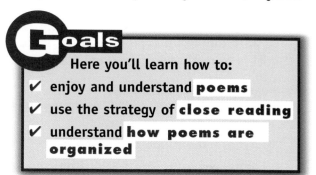

Goals

Here you'll learn how to:

✔ enjoy and understand **poems**

✔ use the strategy of **close reading**

✔ understand **how poems are organized**

Here, you'll read a *sonnet*. A sonnet is only one of many different types of poems. For example, a *narrative poem* tells a story. An *epic* is one kind of long narrative poem that has a hero and often fantastic creatures, such as monsters. *Ballads* are also narrative poems. Ballads have rhyme, and older ballads usually repeat a line or group of lines throughout the poem.

Poetry

A *lyric* is another type of poem. It is a short, personal poem that doesn't tell a story but expresses feelings and thoughts. An *elegy* is a lyric poem mourning someone's death. An *ode* is a lyric poem written to praise someone or something. A sonnet is also a kind of lyric poem.

What makes a sonnet unique? A sonnet is a 14-line poem written according to certain rules. The sonnet form first began in thirteenth-century Italy and has been a favorite type of poetry with poets and readers ever since. Like some other types of poetry, a sonnet can be about any topic, but its specific form and rhythm make it a challenge to poets.

Before Reading

When your teacher assigns a poem, it's useful to ask at that time, "How can I understand this poem?"

A Set a Purpose

As with any other type of reading, start by setting a purpose. Your goal is to read and understand the poem. Try asking these questions:

Setting a Purpose

- **What is the poem about?**
- **What's the mood or feeling of the poem?**
- **What meaning can I take from the poem?**

One good way to discover what a poem means is to preview it.

B Preview

Even though many poems are short, a preview is still helpful and shouldn't take long. Look at the following things when you preview a poem:

Preview Checklist

✔ the title of the poem and name of the poet

✔ the structure and shape of the poem on the page

✔ any rhymes

✔ any words and names that are repeated or that stand out

✔ the first and last lines

Here's how one reader previewed Sonnet 43 by Elizabeth Barrett Browning.

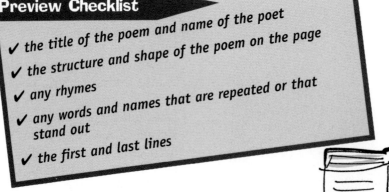

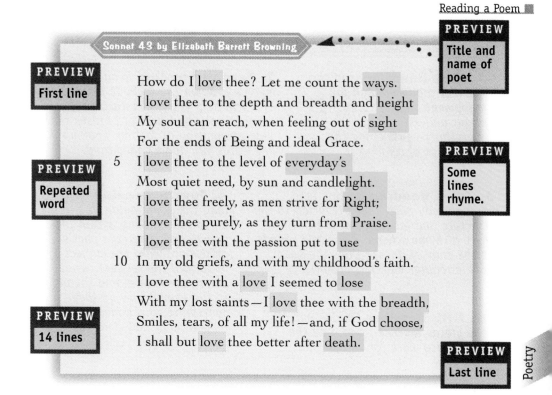

PREVIEW
Title and name of poet

Sonnet 43 by Elizabeth Barrett Browning

PREVIEW
First line

How do I love thee? Let me count the ways.
I love thee to the depth and breadth and height
My soul can reach, when feeling out of sight
For the ends of Being and ideal Grace.

PREVIEW
Some lines rhyme.

PREVIEW
Repeated word

5   I love thee to the level of everyday's
Most quiet need, by sun and candlelight.
I love thee freely, as men strive for Right;
I love thee purely, as they turn from Praise.
I love thee with the passion put to use
10 In my old griefs, and with my childhood's faith.
I love thee with a love I seemed to lose
With my lost saints—I love thee with the breadth,
Smiles, tears, of all my life!—and, if God choose,
I shall but love thee better after death.

PREVIEW
14 lines

PREVIEW
Last line

Poetry

Even from a quick preview, you learned a lot. The sonnet is about how much the speaker loves someone. It was written by Elizabeth Barrett Browning. Many of the 14 lines rhyme, and it has repetition.

Plan

Even though you have learned a lot from your preview, you probably have more questions than answers. For instance, you might ask these questions:

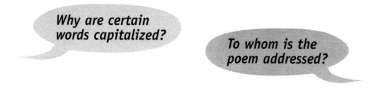

Why are certain words capitalized?

To whom is the poem addressed?

If you can, plan to read a poem several times. Knowing that you're going to read a poem a number of times means that you don't have to think of everything all at once. Repeated readings allow you to focus on a different aspect each time you read.

1. First Reading *Read the poem straight through for enjoyment. Try not to worry about understanding everything—just enjoy the experience of reading it.*

2. Second Reading *Read for meaning. Be on the lookout for clues that will help you understand the poem, especially words or phrases that suggest emotion or feeling. Look up any words you don't understand.*

3. Third Reading *On this read through, pay particular attention to the structure and language of the poem. Is there a rhyme scheme (repeated sounds at the ends of lines)? Does the poem have a regular meter (rhythm)?*

4. Fourth Reading *Now read the poem again for mood (the feeling within the poem) and tone (the poet's attitude toward the subject or toward the reader). What about the images and sounds in the poem? How do they contribute to the meaning? As you read, how does the poem make you feel?*

5. Fifth Reading *Finally, put all the pieces together, and read the poem once more for enjoyment.*

By looking at different parts of a poem each time you read it, you make the task of understanding the whole poem much easier.

Reading Strategy: Close Reading

When you do a **close reading** of a poem, you look at every word and every line. To keep track of your thoughts in a close reading, use a Double-entry Journal. In the left column, write the words, phrases, or lines that you want to focus on. In the right column, write your reactions to the words, tell how you feel about them, or tell what you think the words mean.

DOUBLE-ENTRY JOURNAL

QUOTE	MY THOUGHTS ABOUT IT

You can set up your notes like this in your reading journal to record your reactions to certain lines.

During Reading

Now use your reading plan. Here, you'll see how reading a poem several times can help you unpack its meaning.

READING A POEM
✔ Enjoyment
✔ Meaning
✔ Structure and Language
✔ Mood or Tone
✔ Enjoyment

D Read with a Purpose

Speed reading is not a great technique for reading a poem. If you read a poem slowly, you can think of how the words sound as well as what they mean. Here's what one reader wrote during a first reading of Sonnet 43.

First Reading—Enjoyment

DOUBLE-ENTRY JOURNAL

QUOTE	MY THOUGHTS ABOUT IT
"How do I love thee? Let me count the ways."	I know that the word "thee" is an old-fashioned way of saying "you," and it is used only for people one is close to. I like the second sentence. It hints that there are many ways to love, perhaps too many to count.

The point of a Double-entry Journal is to help you interact with the text as you read. When you read poetry, you are responding to words and lines created by a poet. You might think of reading poetry as receiving a phone call. You don't just listen to what the other person says—you respond to it. Imagine that your response in the right-hand column of your journal is your half of the conversation between you and the poet.

Second Reading—Meaning

One way to grasp the meaning of a poem is to explain the lines in your own words. Look at the example on the next page of how one reader explained lines 2–4 in Sonnet 43.

QUOTE	MY THOUGHTS ABOUT IT
"I love thee to the depth and breadth and height/ My soul can reach, when feeling out of sight/ For the ends of Being and ideal Grace."	I think the speaker means that when she stretches her soul in all directions, the effort she puts forth is the same effort she puts forth in her love.

At this point, try not to worry about whether your explanation agrees with other students' explanations. As long as you can support your view with the text, your "reading" of the poem is probably fine.

Third Reading—Structure and Language

Before you can really understand a poem, you need to consider its structure and language. After all, the poet put considerable thought into arranging the words and lines. Remember that the poem is a means of communication between the poet and you. Asking yourself why the poet chose a certain structure or a certain word will improve your appreciation and deepen your understanding of the poem.

Notice the way one reader commented on the structure and language of Sonnet 43.

Each line begins with a capital letter and has capitals for certain nouns. Browning uses regular punctuation. There are no breaks (stanzas) in the poem. There are 14 lines, and some words rhyme, although some of the rhymes are not exactly perfect.

Browning repeats the phrase "I love thee" many times throughout the poem. She uses abstract words, such as soul, Being, Grace, Right, Praise, and faith. She uses very few concrete words, such as sun and candlelight.

How Poems Are Organized

Some poetry, such as **free verse,** follows no particular rules. It may or may not have rhymes or stanzas or repetition. Some types of poetry, sonnets for example, do follow certain rules. Some sonnets are called Italian, and some are called English, depending partly on how they are rhymed. Sonnet 43 is an Italian sonnet. It follows a certain rhyme pattern or scheme. The rhymes in Sonnet 43 can be marked as follows:

> **from Sonnet 43**
>
> How do I love thee? Let me count the ways.   a
> I love thee to the depth and breadth and height   b
> My soul can reach, when feeling out of sight   b
> For the ends of Being and ideal Grace.   a

This same pattern *(abba)* continues throughout most of the sonnet.

Another characteristic of a sonnet is that most, if not all, lines have a rhythm called *iambic pentameter.* The unit of measurement in a line of poetry is called a *foot.* The word *pentameter* indicates that there are five feet in a line (*penta* means "five"). An *iamb* is an unaccented syllable followed by an accented syllable, as in the word *decide.* Iambic pentameter means that a line has five iambic feet. You can determine the rhythm by reading a line aloud. Accented or stressed syllables are marked with this (/) :

˘ / ˘ / ˘ / ˘ / ˘ /
I shall / but love / thee bet / ter af / ter death.
  1   2   3   4   5

Understanding a Poet's Choices

A poem's rhyme and rhythm add both music and meaning. As you read, you come to anticipate the regular beats and the rhymes, both of which please the ear and make the poem more memorable. You might have noticed, however, that some lines (4 and 13) are not in iambic pentameter. Here the beat changes. Why? You can infer at least two possible answers: Maybe the poet didn't want the rhythm to be too predictable for fear of putting the reader to sleep. Maybe these lines are especially important to the meaning of the poem.

Poetry

Fourth and Fifth Readings—Mood, Tone, and Enjoyment

After you read for meaning and structure, take another look at the poem. This time read it for feeling. Look for words or phrases that express emotion. What mood does the poet create, and how does it affect you? Consider also how the poet achieves this mood. Does the poet use images or allusions? Is the tone of the poem cool and detached, or is it passionate?

Here are one reader's feelings about the poem.

DOUBLE-ENTRY JOURNAL

QUOTE	MY THOUGHTS ABOUT IT
"I love thee with the passion put to use / In my old griefs. . . ."	Recalling sad times of the past gives a serious feeling to the poem. It makes her love sound true and sincere.

Your thoughts about the poem might be quite different from the thoughts above. Maybe you don't like love poems. Maybe you prefer more modern poems. You should, however, be prepared to explain the reasons for your feelings.

E Connect

When you read poetry, try to connect the poem to your own life and experience. React to the words of the poem, and try to find a way to relate to them.

When you connect to a poem, you make it more your own. It will be easier to remember and talk about later. Here are a few of the connections one reader made to Browning's poem.

Sonnet 43

How do I love thee? Let me count the ways.
I love thee to the depth and breadth and height
My soul can reach, when feeling out of sight
For the ends of Being and ideal Grace.
5   I love thee to the level of everyday's
Most quiet need, by sun and candlelight.
I love thee freely, as men strive for Right;
I love thee purely, as they turn from Praise.
I love thee with the passion put to use
10 In my old griefs, and with my childhood's faith.
I love thee with a love I seemed to lose
With my lost saints—I love thee with the breadth,
Smiles, tears, of all my life!—and, if God choose,
I shall but love thee better after death.

I like the repetition of "I love thee" in so many lines. It really emphasizes the point.

The contrast of the sun and candlelight suggests that the love goes on day and night.

This poem was OK, but I'm not sure I like to read "love" poems.

Poetry

You might also find it helpful to your understanding to record your responses to poems in your reading journal. Simply write the title of the poem, the name of the poet, and your response—what the poem made you think and feel.

After Reading

After you read a poem, talk about it with someone else. Exchanging ideas with others helps you understand how others arrive at their interpretations.

F Pause and Reflect

Allow yourself some time to think about the poem. Ask yourself questions like these:

Looking Back

- **Do I have a clear understanding of the poem?**
- **Can I remember any specific words, images, or phrases?**
- **How would I express the "big idea" of the poem?**
- **What mood or feeling did the poet create?**

G Reread

You've already read the poem a number of times. One more reading won't hurt. In fact, if you think of a poem as a work of art (which it is), you'll realize that it's meant to be enjoyed over and over again. As with a painting that you like, you don't look at it just once or even five times. You look at it many times, seeing more in it each time. You will find that you will gain the most by rereading the poems that puzzle you the most.

Rereading Strategy: Paraphrasing

For the lines that you especially enjoyed, or those you didn't quite understand the first time through, the strategy of **paraphrasing** can really help. A paraphrase is a restating of someone else's words in your own words. You can write your paraphrases in a journal.

The point of paraphrasing is to make the ideas your own by expressing them in your own words and in your style. A paraphrase should sound like something you would say if you were expressing the ideas to a friend. On the next page is a Paraphrase Chart that one reader wrote.

PARAPHRASE CHART

LINES	MY PARAPHRASE
"I love thee with the passion put to use / In my old griefs, . . ."	I used to have strong feelings about some sad things, but now my strong feelings are directed toward you. These strong feelings have changed to love.

 Remember

If you really want to remember a poem, follow these tips.

1. Give a Dramatic Reading

Practice reading the poem aloud, and then read it in front of an audience. Your reading might be part of a program or a poetry reading.

2. Write a Poem

Write a poem of your own modeled after Browning's sonnet. Make your poem about any subject, but use the same number of lines and rhyme.

Summing Up

Follow a plan for reading a poem. Read it several times: once for enjoyment, once for meaning, once for the structure and language, once for its mood and tone, and once again for enjoyment. Use the strategy of **close reading** to help you unpack the meaning of the poem. Note how the poem is **organized.** Note also the rhyme scheme and the rhythm. Helpful reading tools to use with poems are these:

■ Double-entry Journal
■ Paraphrase Chart

Use the rereading strategy of **paraphrasing** to put the poem in your own words and help you better understand it.

Poetry

Focus on Language

Poetry is such a complex art that to understand it fully you must appreciate it on many levels. These levels include the meaning of the poem, the sound of the words, the shape and organization of the poem, and the way the poem makes you feel. But you can't appreciate any of these levels without first taking a good look at the language of the poem. Language, after all, is what poetry is made of.

Poets distill their ideas into as few words as possible. That's why you can be sure that each word in a poem has been chosen with great care.

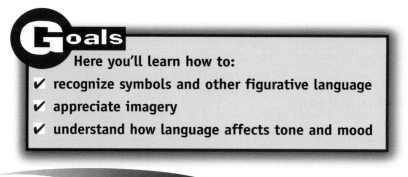

Goals

Here you'll learn how to:

✔ **recognize symbols and other figurative language**

✔ **appreciate imagery**

✔ **understand how language affects tone and mood**

Before Reading

When you focus on the language of a poem, look for the following elements:

- word meanings
- figurative language, such as symbols, metaphors, and similes
- repetition
- imagery that jolts you, surprises you, or makes you say "wow"
- words that convey attitude, tone, or mood

Read the notes one reader made when she began to focus on the language of "Identity" by Julio Noboa Polanco.

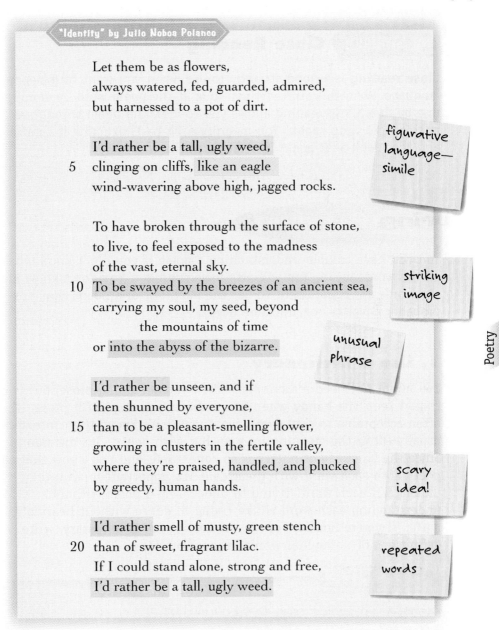

"Identity" by Julio Noboa Polanco

Let them be as flowers,
always watered, fed, guarded, admired,
but harnessed to a pot of dirt.

   I'd rather be a tall, ugly weed,
5 clinging on cliffs, like an eagle
wind-wavering above high, jagged rocks.

figurative language— simile

To have broken through the surface of stone,
to live, to feel exposed to the madness
of the vast, eternal sky.
10 To be swayed by the breezes of an ancient sea,
carrying my soul, my seed, beyond
     the mountains of time
or into the abyss of the bizarre.

striking image

unusual phrase

I'd rather be unseen, and if
then shunned by everyone,
15 than to be a pleasant-smelling flower,
growing in clusters in the fertile valley,
where they're praised, handled, and plucked
by greedy, human hands.

scary idea!

I'd rather smell of musty, green stench
20 than of sweet, fragrant lilac.
If I could stand alone, strong and free,
I'd rather be a tall, ugly weed.

repeated words

Poetry

A quick reading of the poem has revealed great richness of language. The figurative language and striking imagery popped right out. What other things about the poem's language did you notice?

Close reading is a good strategy to use when you want to focus on language. With this strategy, you look at the poem word by word and line by line. Close reading allows you to view the poem through a microscope, so to speak. You magnify each part, examine it carefully, and then look at it again in relation to the whole.

During Reading

You will have trouble understanding a poem if you don't know what all the words mean. You will also have trouble if you don't know how the words are being used. To get the most out of a poem, you'll probably have to look up some words.

1. Use a Dictionary

You might not need a dictionary when you're reading prose, but you should keep one handy when you're reading poetry. With prose, it's often acceptable to skip over a word you don't know; the context can usually fill in the meaning for you. But with poetry, it's different. Since the language of poetry is so condensed, and you know that the poet chose each word with great care, it's important for you to understand each word. Trying to understand a poem without understanding each word is like trying to dance without hearing the music. If you're not sure of a word, look it up. If necessary, write definitions of unfamiliar words in your journal.

JOURNAL ENTRY

guarded—protected from danger; cautious
harnessed—fastened or held in place

The definitions of these two words suggest that the flowers (or the people represented by the flowers) are anything but free. The double meaning of the word *guarded* suggests also that the flowers (or people) have lost all sense of daring, risk-taking, and freedom. You can see from this example the value of looking up words, even if you think you know the definitions. You might have forgotten the second meaning of the word *guarded* and so missed that shade of meaning.

2. Think about Connotations

When you read poetry, spend some time considering the denotations and connotations of words. The *denotation* is the meaning you will find when you look the word up in a dictionary. The *connotation* is the feeling suggested by or associated with the word. For example, consider the following lines from "Identity":

> *from "Identity"*
>
> I'd rather be a tall, ugly weed,
>
> clinging on cliffs, like an eagle
>
> wind-wavering above high, jagged rocks.

What associations do you have for the word *eagle?* The word *eagle* suggests much more than just a large bird of prey.

DENOTATION AND CONNOTATION

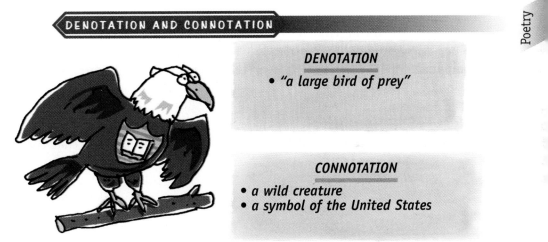

DENOTATION

- *"a large bird of prey"*

CONNOTATION

- *a wild creature*
- *a symbol of the United States*

When you think of an eagle, you think of strength, wildness, and freedom. Eagles are strong flyers, so you think of the exhilaration and fun of flight. Once you're aware of the connotations of the word *eagle,* you can easily see the contrast between the tall, ugly weed the poet wants to be and the "pleasant-smelling flower" he fears he could become.

A **symbol** is something concrete that stands for something abstract, such as the idea of freedom. For example, an eagle is a large bird, but it also stands for and is a symbol of the United States. What does it stand for in this poem? What do you think of when you think of an eagle? You might think of strength, wildness, or freedom.

3. Examine Figurative Language

Figurative language enriches the literal meanings of words. Examples of **figurative language** include similes, metaphors, and symbols. Consider these two examples from "Identity":

Simile

> from "Identity"
>
> Let them be as flowers,
> always watered, fed, guarded, admired,
> but harnessed to a pot of dirt.

The word *as* signals that the poet is using a **simile** to compare "them" to flowers. Of course, the people the poet is referring to are not the same thing as flowers, but they share certain qualities with flowers. Those qualities include being sheltered, cared for, tended, and protected—all in preparation for the big harvest, when they are "plucked/by greedy, human hands." The use of this simile makes a comparison that allows you to see "them" in a new (and perhaps surprising) way.

Metaphor

Another commonly used type of figurative language is a **metaphor,** which the poet uses in this line:

> from "Identity"
>
> I'd rather be a tall, ugly weed.

A metaphor compares two things that are basically unlike each other but that have some qualities in common. Here, the speaker compares himself to a weed. (Notice that this comparison does not use the word *like* or *as.*) A person and a weed are not similar, but what does the weed represent? It represents freedom and independence, something the speaker wants to have.

In fact, this whole poem is an *extended metaphor,* with flowers representing sheltered, "harnessed" people and weeds representing those who value daring and freedom.

4. Look for Imagery

Sometimes you will be startled into imagining a scene, sensation, sound, or taste when you read a poem. Poets use imagery to stimulate your senses. You can probably visualize and smell what the poet describes, but can you see a weed in the "breezes of an ancient sea"? What is an "abyss of the bizarre"? What does this stanza mean? One reader made an inference about the meaning.

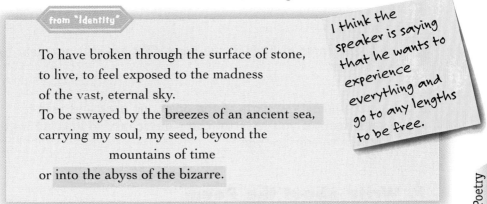

from "Identity"

To have broken through the surface of stone,
to live, to feel exposed to the madness
of the vast, eternal sky.
To be swayed by the breezes of an ancient sea,
carrying my soul, my seed, beyond the
            mountains of time
or into the abyss of the bizarre.

I think the speaker is saying that he wants to experience everything and go to any lengths to be free.

Poetry

5. Look for Repetition

Poets often repeat a word for emphasis. Go back to the text of the poem on page 401. Notice the **repetition** of the phrase "I'd rather" in stanzas two, four, and five. This repetition links parts of the poem so that a single idea is expressed.

6. Look for Tone and Mood

Tone is the author's (and sometimes the **speaker's**) attitude toward the subject or the reader. **Mood** is the atmosphere or feeling the poem conveys. Look for words that convey emotion or feeling. Here's how one reader analyzed the tone and mood of the poem.

JOURNAL ENTRY

I think the tone of "Identity" is firm or determined. The speaker knows who he is and what he wants. The mood is optimistic. He doesn't seem to expect that he could fail in his desires.

After Reading

When you focus on the language of poetry, you pick out key words, look up the meaning of unfamiliar words, and consider connotations, repetition, figurative language, and imagery. There's a lot to consider all at once. So, after you have read a poem, ask yourself questions like these:

■ Do I understand how the language affects the way I read the poem?

■ Are there words or lines in the poem that are still not clear to me?

If you don't understand parts of the poem, go back and read it again—and again if you have to. Use a dictionary to look up words that continue to confuse you.

1. Write about the Poem

Very often, when asked to write about poetry, or the elements of poetry, readers feel stumped. Where can you start?

TIPS FOR WRITING ABOUT POETRY

1. *Decide what the "big idea" is and what the poem says about it.*

2. *The speaker in a poem is not necessarily the poet. Use the term* speaker *unless you want to discuss the poet's technique.*

3. *Figure out what figurative language, if any, and imagery contribute to the poem.*

4. *Examine the structure of the poem, including repetition. Determine how the structure contributes to meaning.*

5. *Decide what the overall mood is and what the speaker's tone is. Is the speaker angry? Depressed? Amused? Look at specific words to "read" the mood.*

6. *Zero in on what you feel about the poem.*

7. *Make an outline before you start to write.*

Here's the first line of a paper about "Identity."

JOURNAL ENTRY

In the poem "Identity" by Julio Noboa Polanco, the speaker declares the kind of person he wants to be, strong and free.

2. Write a Poem of Your Own

So you've read the poem many times. You've taken notes in your journal. You've discussed it with a partner. You've looked up unfamiliar words. You've visualized images. Now what? What does the poem mean to you? Which words and phrases did you especially like? Which images had special meaning for you? One option is to create a poem of your own modeled on the one you just read. Use similar organization, similar content, and some similar language. Here is an example of part of a poem a reader wrote that is modeled on "Identity."

POEM BASED ON "IDENTITY"

Let them be like sheep,
always guided, fed, protected, cared for,
but kept in a pen.
I'd rather be a deer, running free.

Poetry

Summing Up

- Close reading of a poem helps you concentrate on word meaning, figurative language, repetition, and imagery.
- Focusing on specific words and phrases of a poem can help you determine its tone and mood.
- Look especially at unfamiliar words, connotations and denotations of words, similes, and metaphors.

Focus on Meaning

After reading a poem, your first reaction might be to ask yourself, "What does it mean?" This is a natural response to poetry. You've enjoyed the sounds, the rhythm, the imagery, and the feelings stirred up by the words, but now you want to know what idea the poet is communicating.

Sometimes the meaning is clear and straightforward. Other times, it is not so clear, which can frustrate or even discourage you.

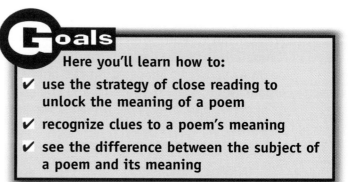

Goals

Here you'll learn how to:

✔ **use the strategy of close reading to unlock the meaning of a poem**

✔ **recognize clues to a poem's meaning**

✔ **see the difference between the subject of a poem and its meaning**

Before Reading

As you prepare to read a poem for the first time, remember to follow a reading plan. The first time you read it, do it just for fun. The second time, keep this question in mind: "What does the poem mean?"

Read for Meaning

As you read, pay particular attention to the following elements:

■ the title

■ any unfamiliar words or words that express emotion or feeling

■ the first and last several lines

Notice how one reader focused on the meaning of "Ex-Basketball Player."

"Ex-Basketball Player" by John Updike

Pearl Avenue runs past the high-school lot,
Bends with the trolley tracks, and stops, cut off
Before it has a chance to go two blocks,
At Colonel McComsky Plaza. Berth's Garage
5   Is on the corner facing west, and there,
Most days, you'll find Flick Webb, who helps Berth out.

describes a neighborhood and introduces a character, Flick Webb

Flick stands tall among the idiot pumps—
Five on a side, the old bubble-head style,
Their rubber elbows hanging loose and low.
10 One's nostrils are two S's, and his eyes
An E and O. And one is squat, without
A head at all—more of a football type.

describes the pumps at a gas station

Once Flick played for the high-school team, the Wizards.
He was good: in fact, the best. In '46,
15 He bucketed three hundred ninety points,
A county record still. The ball loved Flick.
I saw him rack up thirty-eight of forty
In one home game. His hands were like wild birds.

tells about Flick's high-school days, when he was a basketball player

He never learned a trade, he just sells gas,
20 Checks oil, and changes flats. Once in a while,
As a gag, he dribbles an inner tube,
But most of us remember anyway.
His hands are fine and nervous on the lug wrench.
It makes no difference to the lug wrench, though.

tells about Flick's life now, working at the gas station

25 Off work, he hangs around Mae's Luncheonette.
Grease-gray and kind of coiled, he plays pinball,
Sips lemon cokes, and smokes those thin cigars;
Flick seldom speaks to Mae, just sits and nods
Beyond her face towards bright applauding tiers
30 Of Necco Wafers, Nibs, and Juju Beads.

sounds like an empty life

Poetry

Form a First Impression

As you read this poem for the first time, what were your first impressions? The title tells you that the poem is about an ex-basketball player. As you read, you learn that he played in high school and has been working in a gas station ever since.

What else did you notice? The reader observed that Flick's life seems empty now. That's an idea you'll probably want to explore more in later readings.

Reading Strategy: Close Reading

One of the best ways to focus on meaning is to use the strategy of **close reading**. With this method, you go through the poem slowly, line by line and word by word. Try not to rush through this step. This is the time to put on the brakes and enjoy the scenery.

As you go through this process, keep asking yourself, "What does this mean?" Pay attention to how the poem makes you feel. Look for words that show emotion or feeling. Ask yourself, "How do these words help me understand the poet's meaning?" Your feelings and reactions to the poem will help give you some clues to its meaning.

During Reading

When you focus on something, you concentrate your attention on a specific part. If you are looking through binoculars and the image is out of focus, you fiddle around until the image appears more clearly. You do a similar thing when you focus on a poem. If parts of it are fuzzy, unclear, or out of focus, you make adjustments until you understand it more clearly.

Here are four ways to bring the meaning of a poem into focus.

1. Look at Denotations and Connotations

Start by looking up unfamiliar words. To understand the poem, you must know at least the definition (or denotation) of each word. For example, as you read "Ex-Basketball Player," you might want to make notes like these in your journal:

JOURNAL ENTRY

gag—joke
tiers—rows arranged one above another

Often the context will help you figure out what an unfamiliar word means. But it's best to look up a word if you're not sure of the meaning.

Sometimes a word has multiple meanings, some of which can suggest double meanings that might have been intended by the poet. While you're looking up a word in a dictionary, check to see if it has an interesting etymology (word origin). For example, the word *idiot* in line 7 comes from a Greek root that means "one's own, private." Knowing this, you see yet another layer to the sadness of Flick's loneliness.

A word's connotation—the emotional response you have to the word—also offers clues to a poem's meaning. For example, the name of the character, Flick, might suggest interesting connotations to you. You might flick a piece of lint off your jacket or a bug off your arm. The lint or the bug is insignificant, unimportant—something like Flick's life after basketball. His name might imply the ease with which he "flicked" a ball into the basket or something quick that doesn't last long.

Use a Double-entry Journal to focus on the meanings of particular words. In the left column, write the word or phrase that interests you. In the right column, write your thoughts and inferences about it. On the next page is one reader's note about a word that reminded her of Flick's name.

Poetry

WORD OR PHRASE	MY THOUGHTS
Flick	Flick reminds me of flicker. The word flicker can be used as a verb or as a noun. A light flickers, giving off a tiny bit of light before going out. A flicker can also be a sudden brief movement. Both uses of the word remind me of Flick's short moment of fame, the brief time in his life when Flick felt important.

2. Think about the Style

You might think that this poem isn't very "poetic." It reads as if someone had just asked the speaker who Flick Webb is. The speaker then proceeds to tell about Flick in a conversational style. A writer's *style* is achieved through the way he or she uses language—figurative language, imagery, rhythm, word choice, and so on. What makes this poet's style seem conversational, and what does this style contribute to the meaning?

Here are one reader's thoughts about the style of "Ex-Basketball Player."

INFERENCE CHART

TEXT	WHAT I CONCLUDE
first stanza	The rhythm of this stanza reminded me of a basketball player dribbling down the court. At the end of line two, he's stopped by a guard on the opposing team, but by line three, he's off again. The poet sets the scene, but he's also made me think about the action in a basketball game.
second stanza	"Tall" and "Five on a side" suggest basketball; "idiot" and "bubble-head" make me think Flick is surrounded by stupidity.

After Reading

You've read the poem a number of times. You've written comments in your journal. You've looked up words you didn't know. You've thought about the connotations of certain words. Now is the time to ask yourself this question: "Do I understand what this poem means?"

3. Look for the Poet's Attitude

In many poems—but not all—the poet is developing an idea or making some kind of point. As you read, look for that idea. Remember that the subject of the poem is not the same thing as the meaning. The subject of "Ex-Basketball Player" is a particular character, Flick Webb, and what he has done in life. But that is not the meaning of the poem. The meaning comes from the emotion or feeling in the words the poet uses to talk about the subject.

What is the speaker in the poem saying about Flick? How does he feel about how Flick is spending his life? What does he want the reader to think of Flick? Review your notes, the words you considered, and the questions you asked yourself. You will probably find that the meaning of the poem has something to do with the idea that some people are unable to get past their brief moment of fame, either because they have no wish to or because they haven't the ability to do so.

Poetry

Rereading Strategy: Paraphrasing

When you **paraphrase** a line of a poem, you put it into your own words. Here's how one reader paraphrased the last three lines:

PARAPHRASE CHART

QUOTE	MY PARAPHRASE
"Flick seldom speaks to Mae, just sits and nods/Beyond her face towards bright applauding tiers/Of Necco Wafers, Nibs, and Juju Beads."	Flick and Mae don't talk. He just sits there and looks past her at the rows of candy boxes. The phrase "applauding tiers" makes me think maybe he's imagining that they are an audience, clapping for him. Maybe the speaker feels a little sorry for Flick.

4. Listen to Your Own Feelings

How does the poem make you feel? The answer to this question may help you figure out the meaning of the poem. Here are one reader's comments on the last stanza.

from "Ex-Basketball Player"

Off work, he hangs around Mae's Luncheonette.
Grease-gray and kind of coiled, he plays pinball,
Sips lemon cokes, and smokes those thin cigars;
Flick seldom speaks to Mae, just sits and nods
Beyond her face towards bright applauding tiers
Of Necco Wafers, Nibs, and Juju Beads.

He must be remembering the old days. Too bad there's no reason to applaud for him now.

I've seen guys like this. I feel sorry for him. He seems to be wasting his life away.

As you read, consider your own feelings and reactions about the images in the poem. Your personal response can be used as a clue to the poem's meaning.

The meaning you find in a poem will no doubt be different from that found by some other readers. This doesn't matter, since there is no one right answer when it comes to interpreting poetry. The only important thing is that you support your interpretation with specific words and images from the poem.

Summing Up

- Look for the denotations and connotations of words.
- Examine the poet's style.
- Look for the poet's attitude about the subject of the poem.
- Listen to your own feelings about the poem, and support your ideas with specific words or phrases in the poem.
- Use the strategies of close reading and paraphrasing to help you find the meaning of a poem.

Focus on Sound and Structure

The sound and structure of poems can add another dimension to your understanding and enjoyment of poetry. When you read a poem, pay attention to the way it sounds and the way it looks on the page.

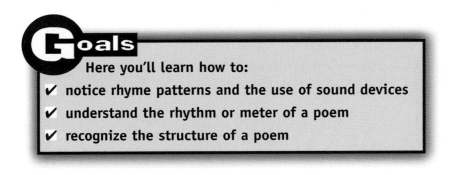

Goals

Here you'll learn how to:

✔ notice rhyme patterns and the use of sound devices

✔ understand the rhythm or meter of a poem

✔ recognize the structure of a poem

Poetry

Before Reading

When you read poetry, pay attention to the sounds of the words and the shape of the poem. For example, you might notice a lot of rhyming words or lines of a certain length, or the poem might be divided into stanzas.

Plan to read a poem more than once. The first time, you'll read the poem just for enjoyment and to get an idea of what it's about. But even during that first reading, listen to the poem's sound and think about its structure.

Preview Siegfried Sassoon's "Suicide in the Trenches." As you read, notice these elements:

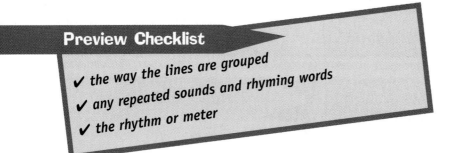

Preview Checklist

✔ the way the lines are grouped

✔ any repeated sounds and rhyming words

✔ the rhythm or meter

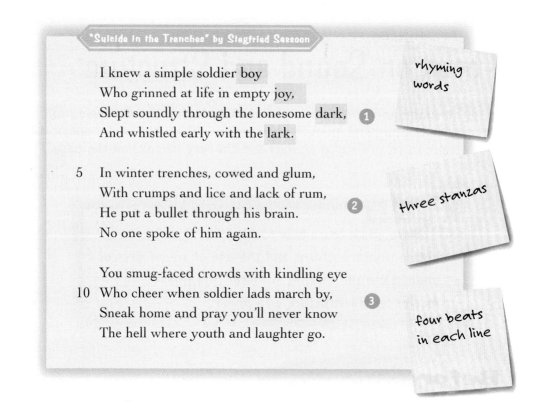

"Suicide in the Trenches" by Siegfried Sassoon

I knew a simple soldier boy
Who grinned at life in empty joy,
Slept soundly through the lonesome dark,   **1**
And whistled early with the lark.

5   In winter trenches, cowed and glum,
With crumps and lice and lack of rum,
He put a bullet through his brain.   **2**
No one spoke of him again.

You smug-faced crowds with kindling eye
10 Who cheer when soldier lads march by,
Sneak home and pray you'll never know   **3**
The hell where youth and laughter go.

rhyming words

three stanzas

four beats in each line

What did you notice about the sound and structure in this poem? Why do you think Sassoon chose to use this particular structure?

Reading Strategy: Close Reading

To understand the sound and structure of a poem, you can use the same strategy that you use when you focus on meaning: **close reading.** This strategy works well with poems because it slows you down and demands that you consider each word and line.

During Reading

As you read poetry, you'll notice great variation in how poems are structured and where the rhymes occur. Some poems have stanzas, and other poems do not. In some poems, rhymes occur in every other line, and in others, pairs of lines are rhymed. You will also see great variations in the use of rhythms and sound devices.

As you focus on sound and structure, look for these four things:

1. organization of lines
2. repeated sounds
3. rhymes
4. rhythm or meter

1. Organization of Lines

The structure of a poem is the way it is organized. What do you notice about the organization of "Suicide in the Trenches"? It has three **stanzas,** and each stanza has four lines. The lines are about the same length. The poet uses standard punctuation and capitalizes the beginning of each line.

Studying stanzas often reveals the meaning of a poem. Like paragraph divisions, stanza divisions help to signal the beginning of a new thought or image. Here is what one reader noticed about the structure of "Suicide in the Trenches":

NOTES

Stanza one
It shows how happy and naive the boy was at one time.

Stanza two
It shows how the war changed the boy and affected his actions.

Stanza three
The poet is now changing gears. This stanza is addressed to the reader directly and tells of the horror of war.

Poetry

2. Repeated Sounds

The sound of a poem may have a definite effect on you. Remember that, like music, poetry is meant to be heard. Listen for the sounds of the words in the poem as you read it aloud. Slow down as you say the words so you can savor them. Think about how the **repetition** of sounds affects both the music and the meaning of the poem.

Alliteration

You may have noticed the repetition of the *s* sound throughout the poem, especially in the first stanza. The repetition of the same sounds at the beginnings of words is called **alliteration**.

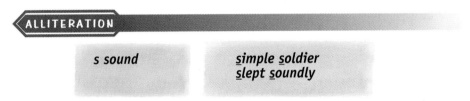

ALLITERATION	
s sound	*s̲imple s̲oldier* *s̲lept s̲oundly*

Did you notice that the *s* sound was repeated in the middle of some words as well? In the first stanza, you see the *s* sound in the words *lonesome* and *whistled*. The sound appears in the second stanza in the words *crumps* (this word is soldiers' slang for exploding shells), *lice*, and *spoke*. It turns up yet again in the third stanza in the words *smug-faced, soldier,* and *sneak*. The *s* sound even appears twice in the first word of the title. Alliteration tends to tie parts of the poem together.

Assonance

The poem includes numerous examples of assonance, too. **Assonance** is the repetition of vowel sounds in accented syllables that are close together. This reader's notes show how Sassoon clustered the words:

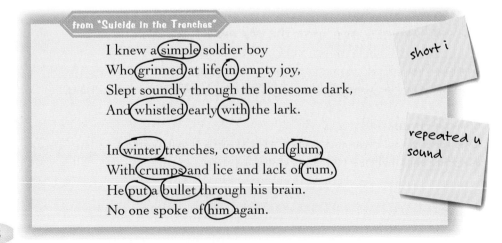

from "Suicide in the Trenches"

I knew a simple soldier boy
Who grinned at life in empty joy,
Slept soundly through the lonesome dark,
And whistled early with the lark.

In winter trenches, cowed and glum,
With crumps and lice and lack of rum,
He put a bullet through his brain.
No one spoke of him again.

short i

repeated u sound

Purpose of Sound Devices

Both alliteration and assonance help to unify ideas in the poem and give it a single effect. They also add to the melodic quality. How would the poem be different if these repeated sounds weren't there? For example, suppose the poet had written these lines: "I knew a handsome soldier boy" or "Slept deeply through the lonesome dark." Some of the alliteration would be lost, and the lines would seem a lot less musical.

3. Rhymes

You probably noticed that the ending sound of each line is the same as the ending sound of another line. This repetition is called **rhyme**. Notice how the rhymes in the first stanza are marked.

> **RHYME SCHEME**
>
> | | |
> |---|---|
> | I knew a simple soldier boy | a |
> | Who grinned at life in empty joy, | a |
> | Slept soundly through the lonesome dark, | b |
> | And whistled early with the lark. | b |

A letter represents the sound at the end of each rhymed word. If the sound is repeated, mark the line with the same letter. Any new sound gets a new letter. If you mark the rhyme scheme of the whole poem, it is *aabb, ccdd, eeff.* When you mark the rhyme scheme of a poem, you can quickly see how much, if any, rhyme the poet used and whether it follows a regular pattern.

After you've considered a poem's rhyme scheme, ask yourself what effect the rhyme scheme has. Note that the rhymes change in each stanza. These changes help to move the poem forward to the end. Does the rhyme make the meaning clearer? Does rhyme affect the mood of the poem? How would a lack of rhyme affect this poem?

Rhyme clarifies the meaning by emphasizing key words, such as *boy, dark,* and *lark.* Rhyme also emphasizes certain words, such as *dark, glum,* and *brain,* all of which contribute to the poem's mood.

Poetry

4. Rhythm or Meter

Like music, language has a beat. This beat is called the poem's **rhythm,** or meter. Rhythm is the pattern of stressed and unstressed syllables in a poem. This pattern creates the beat in the poem. If you count the number of stressed and unstressed syllables in a line, you can determine the meter. Read the following lines aloud, tapping your foot at each strong beat. You will find that there are four beats to each line.

RHYTHM

˘ / ˘ / ˘ / ˘ /
I knew a simple soldier boy

˘ / ˘ / ˘ / ˘ /
Who grinned at life in empty joy,

˘ / ˘ / ˘ / ˘ /
Slept soundly through the lonesome dark,

˘ / ˘ / ˘ / ˘ /
And whistled early with the lark.

As you read, you naturally placed greater emphasis on every second syllable. Did this help you hear the four beats in each line? Does the rhythm suggest anything about soldiers? One reader thought so.

JOURNAL ENTRY

The regular rhythm reminds me of soldiers marching, in this case, probably to their death.

After Reading

Some poems appeal to you more than others. Maybe you like poems that have strong imagery and that use metaphors and similes. You might prefer poems that tell a story. Or perhaps your favorite poems express emotions and create a definite mood. Or maybe you enjoy analyzing the sound and structure of a poem to see how these elements affect the meaning.

Connect to the Poem

No matter what your favorite kind of poetry is, you will get more out of any poem if you make a personal connection to it. The author of "Suicide in the Trenches" fought in World War I and has often been described as an antiwar poet. Knowing the poet's background may help you connect to the poem. You will probably have an opinion about the subject matter and the meaning of the poem, but don't forget to respond to the poem's sound and structure, too.

Here is how one reader reacted to the last two stanzas of "Suicide in the Trenches."

from "Suicide in the Trenches"

In winter trenches, cowed and glum,
With crumps and lice and lack of rum,
He put a bullet through his brain.
No one spoke of him again.

soldier's death

You smug-faced crowds with kindling eye
Who cheer when soldier lads march by,
Sneak home and pray you'll never know
The hell where youth and laughter go.

Speaker is bitter.

Poetry

Another reader connected to the poem in a journal entry.

JOURNAL ENTRY

This space between these two stanzas is very effective. It is almost like a little mourning period for the dead soldier. It also signals that the poet is getting ready to start a new topic—he's getting ready to address the true horrors of war. This poem reminds me of an autobiography I read by a Vietnam veteran.

Write a Poem

To study the sound and structure of a poem in depth, try writing a poem of your own using the same pattern. You don't have to write about the same subject matter, since what you're paying attention to here is sound and structure. As you write, you will appreciate the process the poet went through to create the poem.

Here's how one reader imitated the sound and structure of Sassoon's poem.

She was a girl from Boston town.
Her eyes were blue, her hair was brown.
She liked the feel of Venice Beach,
The cool salt air, the seagull's screech.

She stayed a year, wrote letters home.
Said, "Mom, I'm here and I won't roam.
I like my friends. The surf's not bad.
Good-bye to Boston. Don't be sad."

Summing Up

When you focus on the sound and structure of a poem, you pay attention to:

- organization of lines
- repeated sounds
- rhymes
- rhythm or meter

The sound and structure of a poem can help you see the progression of ideas and how a poet achieves a single effect.

When you read a poem, try to connect to its meaning by exploring the poem's language.

Elements of Poetry

Maybe you've wondered how a poet, using so few words, can evoke such strong feelings. The reason poetry is so powerful is that its language is rich, concentrated, and multi-layered. To get the most out of poetry, you need to consider each word the poet has used. It also helps to understand the many different techniques and styles a poet might use. Once you know about these techniques and styles, you will know how to approach the poems you read.

Use this part of the handbook as a glossary. You can look up a term, read its example, and study its definition.

Poetry

Alliteration

As you read these lines aloud from "The Rime of the Ancient Mariner," take note of the repeated sounds you hear.

EXAMPLE

from "The Rime of the Ancient Mariner" by Samuel Taylor Coleridge

The fair breeze blew, the white foam flew,
The furrow followed free;
We were the first that ever burst
Into that silent sea.

Repeated sounds

DESCRIPTION

As you read Coleridge's lines, did you hear the repeated *f, s,* and *b* sounds? You can see and hear them in the words *fair, foam, flew, furrow, followed,* and *free* and in the words *silent* and *sea* and *breeze, blew,* and *burst.* This technique is called **alliteration.** Alliteration helps to establish mood, provide emphasis, and echo the meaning.

Alliteration is common in English. We use such expressions as "tried and true" and "cool, calm, and collected." In Old English and Middle English poetry, alliteration was one of the most important elements.

DEFINITION

Alliteration is the repetition of sounds at the beginnings of words.

Allusion

The poet alludes to several people and places in this poem.

EXAMPLE

"On First Looking Into Chapman's Homer" by John Keats

Much have I traveled in the realms of gold,
And many goodly states and kingdoms seen;
Round many western islands have I been
Which bards in fealty to Apollo hold.

Reference to the Greek god of music and poetry

5 Oft of one wide expanse had I been told
That deep-brow'd Homer ruled as his demesne;
Yet did I never breathe its pure serene
Till I heard Chapman speak out loud and bold:

Reference to the author of the *Iliad* and the *Odyssey*, two long Greek poems

Then I felt like some watcher of the skies
10 When a new planet swims into his ken;
Or like stout Cortez when with eagle eyes

Reference to translator of Homer

He stared at the Pacific—and all his men
Looked at each other with a wild surmise—
Silent, upon a peak in Darien.

Reference to Spanish explorer

Poetry

DESCRIPTION

Do you understand the **allusions?** Two main ones in the poem above are to a Greek god and to a Greek poet named Homer. Allusions make literature richer by adding extra layers of meaning. Here, the poet connects his and other poets' work with the god Apollo to suggest the honor of being a poet. Recognizing allusions can add to understanding. The more you read, the more allusions you will begin to recognize.

DEFINITION

An **allusion** refers to something with which the reader is likely to be familiar, such as a person, place, or event from history or literature or some aspect of culture.

Consonance

Notice how the consonants at the ends of some lines in this poem sound almost alike.

EXAMPLE

(As Imperceptibly as Grief) by Emily Dickinson

As imperceptibly as Grief
The Summer lapsed away—
Too imperceptible at last
To seem like Perfidy—
5   A Quietness distilled
As Twilight long begun,
Or Nature spending with herself
Sequestered Afternoon—
The Dusk drew earlier in—
10   The Morning foreign shone—
A courteous, yet harrowing Grace,
As guest, that would be gone—
And thus, without a Wing
Or service of a Keel
15   Our Summer made her light escape
Into the Beautiful.

Similar sounds

DESCRIPTION

Poets sometimes use **consonance** instead of rhyme to add variety to their poems. Notice the words "begun/Afternoon," "shone/gone," and "Keel/Beautiful." The words almost rhyme but not quite. Consonance is sometimes called *half rhyme* or *slant rhyme*. It's a softer, more subtle way of adding a musical quality to a poem.

DEFINITION

Consonance is the repetition of identical consonant sounds that are preceded by different vowel sounds.

Figurative Language

One of the great strengths of poetry is that it helps readers see things in a new way. In this excerpt from a poem by Anne Bradstreet, the speaker expresses her feelings about a book that she has published. Note the words she chooses to describe the book.

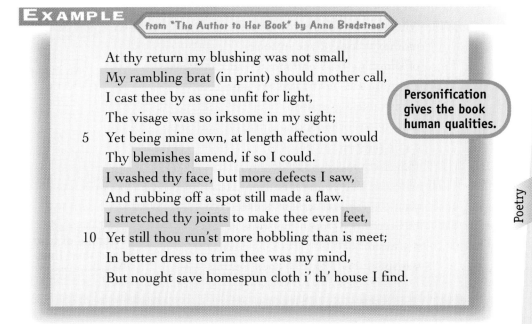

EXAMPLE

from "The Author to Her Book" by Anne Bradstreet

At thy return my blushing was not small,
My rambling brat (in print) should mother call,
I cast thee by as one unfit for light,
The visage was so irksome in my sight;
5 Yet being mine own, at length affection would
Thy blemishes amend, if so I could.
I washed thy face, but more defects I saw,
And rubbing off a spot still made a flaw.
I stretched thy joints to make thee even feet,
10 Yet still thou run'st more hobbling than is meet;
In better dress to trim thee was my mind,
But nought save homespun cloth i' th' house I find.

> Personification gives the book human qualities.

DESCRIPTION

Here, the speaker addresses her book directly, as though it were her own awkward child. She casts herself as a protective mother who tries in vain to improve the appearance and physical health of this child.

Comparing a book to a child or an author to a parent is an example of **figurative language,** or the use of language that goes beyond the words' literal meanings. Poets use figurative language to give freshness and strength to the images they present. The devices for achieving figurative language are called *figures of speech.* The most common ones are *simile, metaphor, personification,* and *hyperbole.*

DEFINITION

Figurative language is language expanded beyond its usual literal meanings.

Free Verse

Some poems, like this one, sound like everyday speech.

EXAMPLE

⟨ (they want me to settle down) by Frances Chung ⟩

they want me to settle down
when I have not yet lived
mother talking to me in songs
of shopping bags and movie star calendars
5 given for free at the grocery store
(she wants a grandson)
with hopes of mooncakes dragon bracelets
and ginger soup
they want me to settle down
10 with the nice young man from Brooklyn
with the car and college degree
but every cockroach that runs across
my mind
whispers that I haven't seen Peking

> No regular punctuation

> No rhymes

> No regular rhythm

> Mixture of long and short lines

DESCRIPTION

Chung's poem is a kind of poetry called **free verse.** Notice that the lines have no set pattern of rhymes or stressed syllables. Lines of various lengths based on the thought, rather than on the number of syllables, are characteristic of free verse.

Free verse often sounds natural, like someone speaking or thinking. Poems written in free verse sometimes cast aside the usual conventions of capitalization and punctuation to give full expression to the ideas.

DEFINITION

Free verse is poetry written without a regular rhyme scheme, meter, or form.

Hyperbole

As you read these lines from a longer poem, notice how the poet exaggerates the time he would spend in praising his love.

EXAMPLE

> from "To His Coy Mistress" by Andrew Marvell

> My vegetable love should grow
> Vaster than empires, and more slow;
> An hundred years should go to praise
> Thine eyes, and on thy forehead gaze;
> 5 Two hundred to adore each breast,
> But thirty thousand to the rest.
> An age at least to every part,
> And the last age should show your heart.
> For, lady, you deserve this state;
> 10 Nor would I love at lower rate.

> Exaggerated amounts of time

Poetry

DESCRIPTION

Often we stretch the truth in our everyday speech to make a point or to inject a little humor. When you say you're starving just before lunchtime, you don't really mean it. You might be hungry, but "starving" is an exaggeration.

Poets use exaggeration, too. Another word for exaggeration is **hyperbole,** and Andrew Marvell used it in his poem. These exaggerated images of time are quite fitting in a poem whose theme is that time is limited and must be used well while we have it.

DEFINITION

Hyperbole, or exaggeration, is the obvious stretching of the truth to emphasize strong feeling or to create a humorous effect.

Imagery

Try to picture what the poet is describing in this poem.

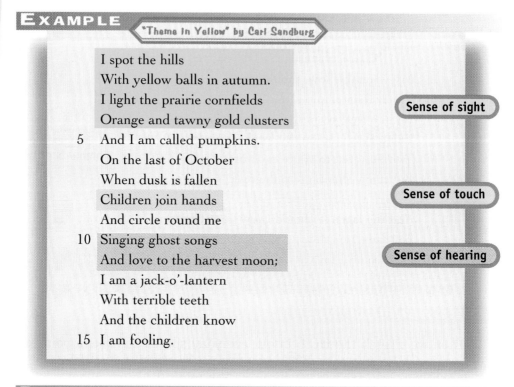

EXAMPLE "Theme In Yellow" by Carl Sandburg

I spot the hills
With yellow balls in autumn.
I light the prairie cornfields
Orange and tawny gold clusters

Sense of sight

5   And I am called pumpkins.
On the last of October
When dusk is fallen
Children join hands

Sense of touch

And circle round me

10   Singing ghost songs
And love to the harvest moon;

Sense of hearing

I am a jack-o'-lantern
With terrible teeth
And the children know

15   I am fooling.

DESCRIPTION

Most of our experiences come to us through our senses. When you think of pumpkins, for example, you think of their color, their smell, their feel, and their taste when baked in a pie. To evoke strong feelings in a reader, writers create **imagery,** or language to appeal to a reader's five senses, as well as to those senses that are felt inside—hunger, pain, sadness, fear, or joy. In the above poem, the various images combine to create a description of an autumn scene.

DEFINITION

Imagery is language that appeals to the five senses. Images help to re-create experiences vividly and add to a reader's enjoyment of what is described.

Inversion

Read these lines from "Kubla Khan," paying attention to the unusual order of the words.

EXAMPLE

from "Kubla Khan" by Samuel Taylor Coleridge

In Xanadu did Kubla Khan · · · · · · · · · · · **Verb**
A stately pleasure-dome decree: **Object comes before the verb.**
Where Alph, the sacred river, ran
Through caverns measureless to man
Down to a sunless sea.

DESCRIPTION

The normal order of sentence parts in English is subject, verb, object. When we change that order, we use **inversion,** a technique that increases emphasis on certain sentence elements by drawing attention to them. The normal order of the first lines of this poem would be as follows:

Normal Order

      S   V   O
Kubla Khan did decree a stately pleasure-dome.

Inverted Order

    V   S   O   V
Did Kubla Khan a stately pleasure-dome decree:

You can see how differently the line reads when you put it in normal order. Suddenly, it sounds flatter and less poetic.

DEFINITION

Inversion means placing a sentence element out of its normal position. Poets use inversion to emphasize, to create a certain mood, and to alter the rhythm of certain lines.

Poetry

431

Lyric

Look for a single unified impression as you read this poem. Try to determine how the poet creates this impression.

EXAMPLE

"When I Heard the Learn'd Astronomer" by Walt Whitman

When I heard the learn'd astronomer
When the proofs, the figures, were ranged in columns
    before me
When I was shown the charts and diagrams, to add,
    divide, and measure them,
How soon unaccountable I became tired and sick,

How speaker felt

5   Till rising and gliding out I wander'd off by myself,
In the mystical moist night-air, and from time to time,
Look'd up in perfect silence at the stars.

Feeling of calm

DESCRIPTION

A **lyric** is a poem that expresses thoughts rather than telling a story. In this lyric, the speaker tells how he felt when he heard the astronomer and where he went after leaving the lecture. The poet's choice of *gliding, wander'd, mystical,* and *silence* creates a feeling of calmness at the end of the poem. The speaker obviously preferred the quiet spiritual experience of being alone with the stars to the charts and diagrams of the astronomer. Notice that the poem is one long sentence, which helps to create a single impression.

DEFINITION

A lyric is a poem that directly expresses the speaker's thoughts and emotions in a musical way. The point of view is usually first person. Marked by imagination, melody, and emotion, a lyric creates for the reader a single unified impression.

Metaphor

What two things are being compared in this poem?

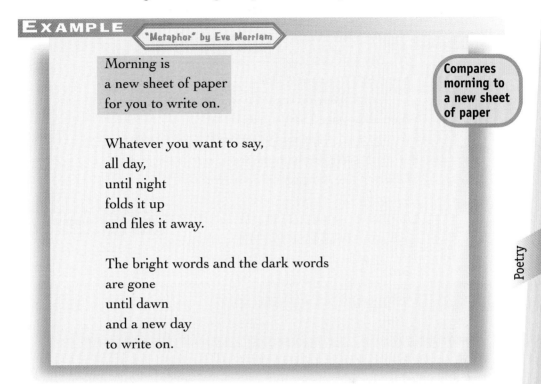

EXAMPLE *"Metaphor" by Eve Merriam*

Morning is
a new sheet of paper
for you to write on.

Whatever you want to say,
all day,
until night
folds it up
and files it away.

The bright words and the dark words
are gone
until dawn
and a new day
to write on.

> **Compares morning to a new sheet of paper**

Poetry

DESCRIPTION

A **metaphor** is a figure of speech in which one thing is compared to something else. In this poem, Eve Merriam compares a clean sheet of paper and a new day. When you have a clean "new sheet of paper," you can put whatever you want on it. When you start a new day, you make choices about what to do that day. A metaphor helps you see the original subject in a new way.

DEFINITION

A **metaphor** is a direct comparison between two unlike things. It does not use the word *like* or *as*.

433

Mood

What kind of feeling do these stanzas from "Daffodils" evoke in you? Look for words that express emotion or feeling.

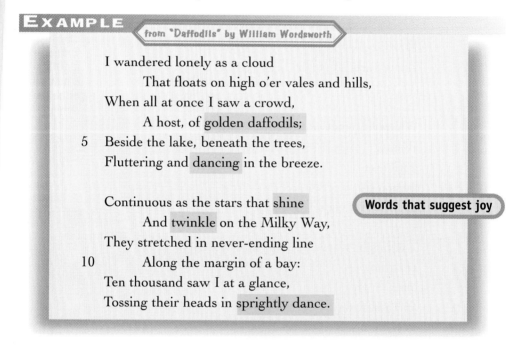

EXAMPLE

from "Daffodils" by William Wordsworth

I wandered lonely as a cloud
    That floats on high o'er vales and hills,
When all at once I saw a crowd,
    A host, of golden daffodils;
5   Beside the lake, beneath the trees,
Fluttering and dancing in the breeze.

Continuous as the stars that shine
    And twinkle on the Milky Way,
They stretched in never-ending line
10   Along the margin of a bay:
Ten thousand saw I at a glance,
Tossing their heads in sprightly dance.

Words that suggest joy

DESCRIPTION

Poets use words, images, and rhythm to create an overall feeling or **mood.** If they are successful, they evoke this feeling in the reader. In this poem about a beautiful sight on a spring day, Wordsworth has created a sunny, joyful mood. Note the words *dancing, shine, twinkle,* and *sprightly dance.* These are happy words. These and other words create a light, airy feeling.

DEFINITION

Mood is the feeling created by a poem or story. Writers use carefully chosen words, phrases, and images to create a mood.

Onomatopoeia

As you read this poem, look for words whose sounds reflect their meanings.

EXAMPLE

"Meeting at Night" by Robert Browning

The gray sea and the long black land;
And the yellow half-moon large and low;
And the startled little waves that leap
In fiery ringlets from their sleep,
5   As I gain the cove with pushing prow,
And quench its speed i' the slushy sand.

Then a mile of warm sea-scented beach;
Three fields to cross till a farm appears;
A tap at the pane, the quick sharp scratch
10 And blue spurt of a lighted match,
And a voice less loud, through its joys and fears,
Than the two hearts beating each to each!

> **Words that sound like what they mean**

Poetry

DESCRIPTION

If you walk through wet sand, you might hear a sound like *slush, slush.* When you read the word *slushy* describing sand, it makes you almost hear the sound. If you've ever lit a match, you've heard sounds like *scratch* and *spurt.*

When writers use words that sound like their meaning, they are using **onomatopoeia.** Other examples of onomatopoetic words are *buzz, bang, plop, crackle, moo, smack, pow, wham,* and *quack.*

DEFINITION

Onomatopoeia is the use of words that imitate the sounds they describe.

Personification

As you read this poem, look for human qualities in unexpected places.

"April Rain Song" by Langston Hughes

Let the rain kiss you.
Let the rain beat upon your head with silver liquid drops.
Let the rain sing you a lullaby.

> **Things humans would do**

The rain makes still pools on the sidewalk.
5 The rain makes running pools in the gutter.
The rain plays a little sleep-song on our roof at night—

And I love the rain.

DESCRIPTION

Here, Langston Hughes speaks of the rain as if it were human. Everyone knows that rain can't actually kiss, sing a lullaby, or play a song, but the rain can remind you of a kiss or a song. This comparison of the rain's actions to things a human being can do is one of the features that makes this poem interesting.

Giving human qualities to nonhuman things adds vitality to writing and helps you see everyday things in a new way. This poetic technique is a kind of figurative language called **personification.** Poets use personification to startle the reader into seeing life in a different way.

DEFINITION

Personification is a figure of speech in which poets give an animal, object, or idea human qualities, such as the ability to love, sing, cry, feel, talk, and make decisions.

Repetition

Have you ever noticed how certain words, phrases, and sounds in poems are sometimes repeated?

EXAMPLE

"Someone" by Walter de la Mare

Someone came knocking
    At my wee, small door;
Someone came knocking,
    I'm sure—sure—sure;

5 I listened, I opened,
    I looked to left and right,
But nought there was a-stirring
    In the still, dark night;
Only the busy beetle

10   Tap-tapping in the wall,
Only from the forest
    The screech owl's call,
Only the cricket whistling
    While the dewdrops fall.

15 So I know not who came knocking,
    At all, at all, at all.

Repeated phrases

Repeated sounds

Repeated words

Poetry

DESCRIPTION

Poets often repeat sounds and words for effect, for the rhythm of it, or just for fun. Rhyming, alliteration, and consonance are all types of **repetition.** You could say the same of meter and stanzas. Repetition helps establish the rhythm in a poem, adds force and clarity, emphasizes ideas, and sets a mood. In this poem, the repetition helps to emphasize the idea of someone knocking on a door.

DEFINITION

Repetition is the use more than once of any element of language—a sound, word, phrase, or sentence.

Rhyme and Rhyme Scheme

As you read "Concord Hymn," listen for words that have the same ending sound.

EXAMPLE

"Concord Hymn" by Ralph Waldo Emerson

By the rude bridge that arched the flood,	a
Their flag to April's breeze unfurled,	b
Here once the embattled farmers stood	a
And fired the shot heard round the world.	b

Similar-sounding words

5 The foe long since in silence slept;
   Alike the conqueror silent sleeps;
And Time the ruined bridge has swept
   Down the dark stream which seaward creeps.

On this green bank, by this soft stream,
10   We set to-day a votive stone;
That memory may their deed redeem,
   When, like our sires, our sons are gone.

Spirit, that made those heroes dare
   To die, and leave their children free,
15 Bid Time and Nature gently spare
   The shaft we raise to them and thee.

DESCRIPTION

In these lines, the words *unfurled* and *world* **rhyme,** as do *sleeps* and *creeps.* They are examples of *end rhyme,* or rhymes that occur at the ends of lines. Sometimes poets use *internal rhyme,* rhyming words within lines. A pattern of repeated rhymes is called the **rhyme scheme.** You can label rhymes with letters, assigning the same letter to all words that rhyme with each other. In the poem above, you can see that the rhyme scheme of these lines is *abab cdcd efef ghgh.*

DEFINITION

Rhyme is the repetition of words that have the same ending
438   sound. A **rhyme scheme** is the pattern of end rhyme in a poem.

Rhythm

As you read these lines, listen for their musical quality, and notice how the poet emphasizes some words more than others.

EXAMPLE "Stopping by Woods on a Snowy Evening" by Robert Frost

Whose woods these are I think I know.
His house is in the village, though;
He will not see me stopping here
To watch his woods fill up with snow.

5   My little horse must think it queer
To stop without a farmhouse near
Between the woods and frozen lake
The darkest evening of the year.

He gives his harness bells a shake
10 To ask if there is some mistake.
The only other sound's the sweep
Of easy wind and downy flake.

The woods are lovely, dark and deep,
But I have promises to keep,
15 And miles to go before I sleep,
And miles to go before I sleep.

> da dúm da dúm pattern

Poetry

DESCRIPTION

The **rhythm** in this poem is quite regular, with a stressed, or accented, syllable following each unstressed one. You can hear the rhythm of a poem by reading it aloud and listening for a pattern of emphasis, such as da dum, da dum, da dum. It looks like this:

Whose woods these are I think I know.

DEFINITION

Rhythm is the musical quality created by a pattern of stressed and unstressed syllables.

Simile

As you read these poems, look for comparisons of things that are mostly unlike but that have some similarities.

EXAMPLES

"Lost" by Carl Sandburg

Desolate and lone
All night long on the lake
Where fog trails and mist creeps,
The whistle of a boat
Calls and cries unendingly,
Like some lost child
In tears and trouble
Hunting the harbor's breast
And the harbor's eyes.

> **Comparison of the whistle to a child's cry**

"Stars" by Gary Soto

At dusk the first stars appear.
Not one eager finger points toward them.
A little later the stars spread with the night
And an orange moon rises
To lead them, like a shepherd, toward dawn.

> **Comparison of the moon to a shepherd**

DESCRIPTION

In "Lost," the poet's comparison of the whistle to a child's cry is effective because everyone has heard a child's cry but not everyone has heard a boat's whistle. The comparison helps the reader understand what the boat's whistle sounds like. In "Stars," the comparison of the moon to a shepherd is a fresh, new way of looking at the progress of the stars across the night sky. Both poems use **similes** to create strong, memorable images.

DEFINITION

A simile compares two unlike things using the word *like* or *as*.

Stanza

Before you begin to read a poem, examine how the poet organized the lines and how the poem looks on the page.

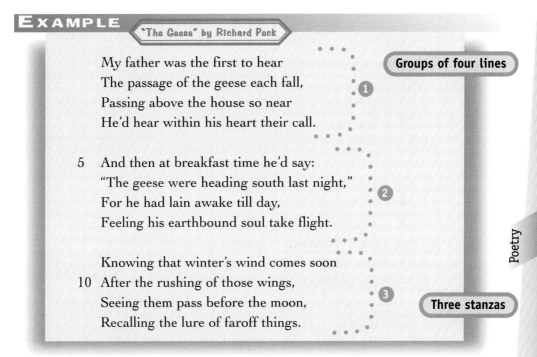

EXAMPLE

"The Geese" by Richard Peck

My father was the first to hear
The passage of the geese each fall,
Passing above the house so near
He'd hear within his heart their call.

1

Groups of four lines

5 And then at breakfast time he'd say:
"The geese were heading south last night,"
For he had lain awake till day,
Feeling his earthbound soul take flight.

2

Knowing that winter's wind comes soon
10 After the rushing of those wings,
Seeing them pass before the moon,
Recalling the lure of faroff things.

3

Three stanzas

Poetry

DESCRIPTION

The word **stanza** comes from a Latin root that means "to stand" or "to stay." You can see the connection if you realize that the lines in a poem's stanza stand together as one unit with its own rhyme scheme. As in the poem above, each stanza often develops a separate idea.

A stanza in a poem is somewhat like a paragraph in prose. Poets use stanzas to give their poems shape on the page and also to help create the poem's meaning. Here are the names of different kinds of stanzas: *couplet* (2-line stanza), *tercet* (3-line), *quatrain* (4-line), *quintet* (5-line), *sestet* (6-line), *septet* (7-line), and *octet* (8-line).

DEFINITION

A **stanza** is an arrangement of two or more lines of poetry into regular patterns of length, rhythm, and often rhyme scheme. Stanzas often indicate separate thoughts and are separated from one another by spaces.

Symbol

Read the poem "Piazza Piece," and ask yourself what the gentleman in the dustcoat represents.

EXAMPLE

"Piazza Piece" by John Crowe Ransom

    —I am a gentleman in a dustcoat trying
    To make you hear. Your ears are soft and small
    And listen to an old man not at all;
    They want the young men's whispering and sighing.
5   But see the roses on your trellis dying   **Words that suggest death**
    And hear the spectral singing of the moon—
    For I must have my lovely lady soon.
    I am a gentleman in a dustcoat trying.

    —I am a lady young in beauty waiting
10   Until my truelove comes, and then we kiss.
    But what gray man among the vines is this
    Whose words are dry and faint as in a dream?
    Back from my trellis, sir, before I scream!
    I am a lady young in beauty waiting.

DESCRIPTION

We see **symbols** around us every day. A flag is the symbol of a country, a logo is a symbol of a company, a tiny clipboard on your computer is a symbol for "paste," a red light is a symbol meaning "stop." A symbol suggests another meaning, depending on the context in which it is found. In this poem, the old man in the dustcoat symbolizes death. The words *old, dying,* and *spectral* support this interpretation. What other clues in the poem indicate that death has come for the young lady? Writers use symbols to express something you cannot see or touch, such as love, hate, fear, or death.

DEFINITION

A **symbol** is something concrete that stands for something else, such as an idea or emotion.

Tone

When you read poetry, think about the speaker's attitude toward the subject.

EXAMPLE

from "The Weary Blues" by Langston Hughes

Droning a drowsy syncopated tune,
Rocking back and forth to a mellow croon,
    I heard a Negro play.
Down on Lenox Avenue the other night
5   By the pale dull pallor of an old gas light
        He did a lazy sway . . .
        He did a lazy sway . . .
To the tune o' those Weary Blues.
With his ebony hands on each ivory key
10 He made that poor piano moan with melody.
        O Blues!
Swaying to and fro on his rickety stool
He played that sad raggy tune like a musical fool.
        Sweet Blues!

Emphasizes the man's skill and talent

DESCRIPTION

The attitude that the poet (or the speaker) takes toward the subject is what gives a poem its **tone.** You have to search for clues in the word choice, the rhythm, and the images to determine what the tone is. The poet won't come right out and tell you. You will have to infer the tone from words or phrases that suggest emotion.

In this poem, you can tell the speaker admires the piano player. He has great respect for the man's talent, and the words "Sweet Blues" suggest that he likes the music. So you could describe the tone in this piece as respectful, or appreciative and enthusiastic.

DEFINITION

Tone is the attitude the writer or the speaker takes toward the audience, the subject, or a character.

Poetry

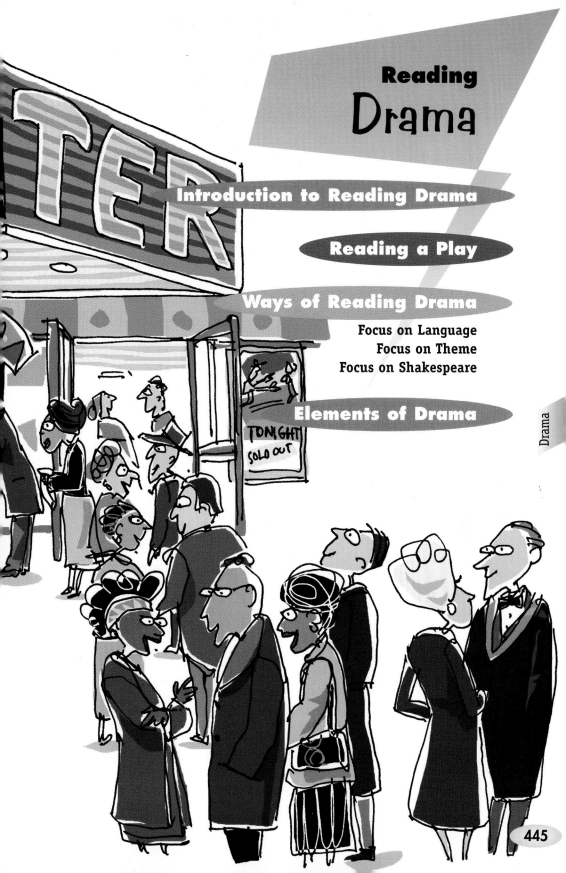

Reading
Drama

Drama

Introduction to Reading Drama

Long before people sat down to read, they gathered to tell and act out stories. As language developed and writing emerged, people began to write these stories down. The tradition of telling and acting out stories evolved into what we now call the theater or drama.

Drama grew from other literary forms. Because plays are written to be performed, they offer the audience a direct, immediate experience. Another unique aspect of drama is its capacity to be interpreted in different ways so that it appeals to different eras, audiences, and cultures.

While it's true that plays are written to be performed, reading a play always comes first, for the director and actors as well as for you in the classroom. Reading a play is one of the easiest reading assignments you will have. Why? With a few exceptions (Shakespeare being one of them), the characters speak in present-day English in short sentences. Even plays once written in other languages have been translated into easily understood English.

If you have seen any kind of play at all or acted in a school play, you already know more about drama than you might think. With this chapter, you will get a little closer look and learn even more.

Reading a Play

Reading plays differs from reading stories and novels in several ways. For one, plays are mostly dialogue and stage directions. Plays are also divided into acts and scenes, not chapters. Each of these characteristics makes reading plays somewhat different from reading stories or novels. But what plays share with fiction is the telling of a story through words.

Here, you'll use the reading process to help you read parts of the play *The Miracle Worker* by William Gibson. This award-winning play tells the story of Helen Keller's childhood and of her teacher, Annie Sullivan, who succeeded in opening the world to Helen, who was deaf and blind.

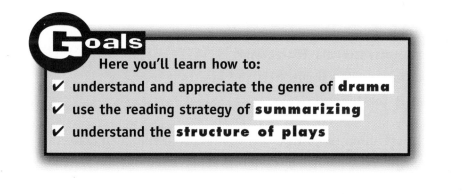

Goals

Here you'll learn how to:

✔ understand and appreciate the genre of **drama**

✔ use the reading strategy of **summarizing**

✔ understand the **structure of plays**

Drama

Before Reading

To read a play, you use a reading process just as you do when reading a novel or short story.

A Set a Purpose

In school, you'll read plays to learn about them as a literary genre. Teachers expect you to understand the plot and characters of individual plays and speak knowledgeably about the elements of drama. Each time you read a play, you'll probably look for answers to these questions:

Setting a Purpose

- **What is the setting?**
- **What are the main characters like, and what is the relationship between them?**
- **What motivates the characters?**
- **What is the central conflict, and how is it resolved?**
- **What is the theme?**

Your purpose, then, is to find out about the setting, characters, conflict, resolution, and theme of the play.

B Preview

As a first step, preview the play. Find out as much as you can about the setting and characters. You'll need this information later to help you with your careful reading. During your preview, look carefully at these items:

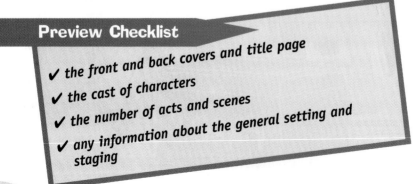

Preview Checklist

✔ the front and back covers and title page
✔ the cast of characters
✔ the number of acts and scenes
✔ any information about the general setting and staging

FRONT COVER

the miracle worker

by william gibson

One of the most beautiful and terrifying dramas of our time — the inspiring story of Helen Keller!

PREVIEW
Title

PREVIEW
Author

Drama

BACK COVER

the wild animal

PREVIEW
Summary of the action

Deaf, blind, and mute twelve-year-old Helen Keller was like a wild animal. Scared out of her wits but still murderously strong, she clawed and struggled against all who tried to help her.

PREVIEW
Clues about characters

Half-blind herself but blessed with fanatical dedication, Annie Sullivan began a titanic struggle to release the young girl from the terrifying prison of eternal darkness and silence.

"An emotional earthquake. . . . a magnificent drama. A play with the power to wrench the heart."
—New York Mirror

PREVIEW
Reviewer comments

the miracle worker

449

PREVIEW
Title

THE MIRACLE WORKER

PREVIEW
Number of acts

A PLAY IN THREE ACTS

PREVIEW
Introductory remarks

"At another time she asked, 'What is a soul?'

"No one knows,' I replied; 'but we know it is not the body, and it is that part of us which thinks and loves and hopes. . . . [and] is invisible. . . .'

'But if I write what my soul thinks,' she said, 'then it will be visible, and the words will be its body.'"

—Annie Sullivan, 1891

CHARACTERS
A DOCTOR
KATE
KELLER
HELEN
MARTHA
PERCY
AUNT EV
JAMES
ANAGNOS
ANNIE SULLIVAN
VINEY
BLIND GIRLS
A SERVANT

OFFSTAGE VOICES

TIME: *The 1880s.*
PLACE: *In and around the Keller homestead in Tuscumbia, Alabama; also, briefly, the Perkins Institution for the Blind, in Boston.*

PREVIEW

Cast of characters

PREVIEW

General setting

Drama

451

Plan

Previewing a play gives you an idea of what to expect during your reading. Drawing on what you already know about the subject of the play can help you get ready to read. After you finish previewing, ask yourself:

■ What do I know about the subject of the play?

■ What do I know about how the play looks on the stage?

Now, make a reading plan. What strategy should you use during your careful reading of *The Miracle Worker*? Most readers find that the strategy of summarizing works well with drama.

Reading Strategy: **Summarizing**

When you summarize, you use your own words to retell the main events or ideas in a play. **Summarizing** helps you keep track of setting changes, character traits and relationships, the sequence of events of the plot, and the themes. In addition, it can greatly improve your ability to understand and remember what you've read.

When you summarize, you retell only the most important ideas and events of the play. If you're not sure what's important and what's not, use a reading tool to help you keep track of the most important ideas. These three tools all work well with the strategy of summarizing:

> SUMMARIZING

1. Summary Notes *help you track important details in the plot.*

2. *A* **Magnet Summary** *organizes information around key concepts, called "magnet words."*

3. *A* **Character Map** *helps you focus on one character and explore his or her motivations.*

Start by preparing a blank chart for Summary Notes, and fill it in as you read.

SUMMARY NOTES

TITLE OR TOPIC	
MAIN POINT	
1. 2. 3. 4.	

During Reading

Now that you have a purpose, a strategy, and a tool, you're ready to start reading carefully.

D Read with a Purpose

Drama

Before you open the play and begin your careful reading, think back to your reading purpose. Remember that one of your goals in reading the play is to find answers to these questions:

■ What is the setting?

■ What are the main characters like, and what is the relationship between them?

■ What motivates the characters?

■ What is the central conflict, and how is it resolved?

■ What is the theme?

As you read, write your thoughts on sticky notes and place them near important lines. If you're allowed to write on the play, use a highlighter to mark information that relates to your purpose.

What follows is part of the first act of *The Miracle Worker*. As you read, look for details about the characters and their relationships, what motivates the characters, the setting, the plot, and any possible ideas about theme.

AUNT EV: How does she stand it? Why haven't you seen this Baltimore man? It's not a thing you can let go on and on, like the weather.

JAMES: The weather here doesn't ask permission of me, Aunt Ev. Speak to my father.

AUNT EV: Arthur, something ought to be done for that child.

KELLER: A refreshing suggestion. What?

(KATE *entering turns* HELEN *to* AUNT EV, *who gives her the towel doll.*)

AUNT EV: Why, this very famous oculist in Baltimore I wrote you about, what was his name?

KATE: Dr. Chisholm.

AUNT EV: Yes, I heard lots of cases of blindness people thought couldn't be cured he's cured, he just does wonders. Why don't you write to him?

KELLER: I've stopped believing in wonders.

KATE (*rocks the cradle*): I think the Captain will write to him soon. Won't you, Captain?

KELLER: No.

JAMES (*lightly*): Good money after bad, or bad after good. Or bad after bad—

AUNT EV: Well, if it's just a question of money, Arthur, now you're marshal you have this Yankee money. Might as well—

KELLER: Not money. The child's been to specialists all over Alabama and Tennessee, if I thought it would do good I'd have her to every fool doctor in this country.

KATE: I think the Captain will write to him soon.

KELLER: Katie. How many times can you let them break your heart?

KATE: Any number of times.

(HELEN *meanwhile sits on the floor to explore the doll with her fingers, and her hand pauses over the face: this is no face, a blank area of towel, and it troubles her. Her hand searches for features, and taps questioningly for eyes, but no one notices. She*

from *The Miracle Worker,* continued

then yanks at her AUNT's *dress, and taps again vigorously for eyes.*)

AUNT EV: What, child?

(*Obviously not hearing,* HELEN *commences to go around, from person to person, tapping for eyes, but no one attends or understands.*)

KATE (*no break*): As long as there's the least chance. For her to see. Or hear, or —

KELLER: There isn't. Now I must finish here.

KATE: I think, with your permission, Captain, I'd like to write.

KELLER: I said no, Katie.

AUNT EV: Why, writing does no harm, Arthur, only a little bitty letter. To see if he can help her.

KELLER: He can't.

KATE: We won't know that to be a fact, Captain, until after you write.

KELLER (*rising, emphatic*): Katie, he can't.

(*He collects his papers.*)

JAMES (*facetiously*): Father stands up, that makes it a fact.

KELLER: You be quiet! I'm badgered enough here by females without your impudence.

(JAMES *shuts up, makes himself scarce.* HELEN *now is groping among things on* KELLER's *desk, and paws his papers to the floor.* KELLER *is exasperated.*)

NOTE

How Helen's mother feels

Drama

NOTE

How Helen's father feels

NOTE

Setting is their home.

Even from a brief passage, you find a great deal of information. You see the conflict developing over seeking help for Helen, who's blind and deaf. You learn how the characters feel about this problem. And, you even glimpse Helen herself through stage directions.

Now look at how summarizing and a few reading tools can help you better understand the play.

1. Summary Notes

Summary Notes can help you keep track of the most important events of the plot. They can also help you focus on the central conflict and the resolution of that conflict. Plus, they are a handy way to keep track of scene changes in the play. Note that scenes within acts in *The Miracle Worker* are not labeled. You might find it helpful to create a summary for each act in a play.

SUMMARY NOTES

TITLE: Act I, scenes 1-4

MAIN POINT: family upset over Helen and how to help her

1. Helen violent

2. arguments about whether to get help

3. Annie Sullivan arrives as teacher.

4. Helen angry

TITLE: Act II, scenes 1-4

MAIN POINT: Annie troubled and discouraged at first

1. tries to fingerspell with Helen

2. struggle with Helen at table

3. mourns brother's death

4. asks and gets permission to take Helen away

2. Magnet Summary

How can you keep track of the plot, the characters, and your ideas about theme? One easy way is through a Magnet Summary. A Magnet Summary organizes information around key concepts called "magnet words." What word or idea stands out most for you as you read? That's your magnet word. The magnet word in the middle of your Web attracts ideas in the same way that a magnet attracts iron or steel. A magnet word can be an idea or feeling. For *The Miracle Worker,* a magnet word could be *conflict,* or *hope,* or *miracle.* Here's a Magnet Summary one reader created for *The Miracle Worker.*

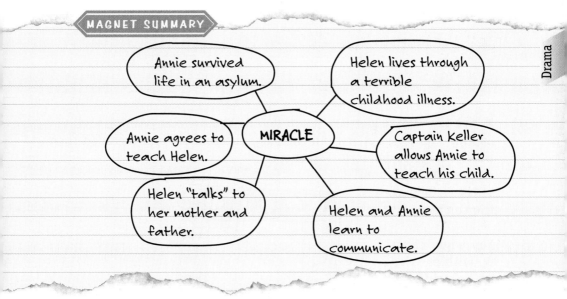

MAGNET SUMMARY

Annie survived life in an asylum.

Helen lives through a terrible childhood illness.

Annie agrees to teach Helen.

MIRACLE

Captain Keller allows Annie to teach his child.

Helen "talks" to her mother and father.

Helen and Annie learn to communicate.

Drama

When you finish your Web around your magnet word, use it to summarize the most important ideas of the play. These ideas can lead you to an understanding of theme. On the next page is a short summary and theme statement one reader wrote after reading *The Miracle Worker.*

In The Miracle Worker, the playwright William Gibson explores various miracles. Gibson's point is that almost everything about Helen Keller's life is a miracle.

At the beginning of the play, the audience learns that it is a miracle that Helen survived a terrible childhood illness. However, because Helen's illness leaves her blind and deaf, her doctor advises the Kellers to put Helen in an institution. The Kellers refuse, which is another small miracle. They decide that they'll find a way to reach Helen themselves.

Another miracle occurs when Annie Sullivan comes to teach Helen. She explains to the Kellers that she knows about miracles because she herself had to struggle to survive life in an asylum. Annie convinces the Kellers that she can teach Helen. When Helen finally learns to communicate with her teacher, it is the greatest miracle of all.

The themes of the play seem to be that miracles can sometimes occur without people knowing that they are miracles and that people are capable of creating miracles.

Notice how the reader has taken details about Helen, Annie, and Captain and Mrs. Keller from the Magnet Summary and included them in the written summary. The theme statement comes out of the details in the summary.

You might come up with an entirely different summary or theme statement based on your ideas about the play. What's important is that you can support your summary and theme statement with specific examples from the play.

3. Character Map

A Character Map can help you analyze a character and see how you and others feel about the character. Here's how one reader started a Character Map for Captain Keller, but you can use a similar map for any character in a play.

⟩ CHARACTER MAP ⟩

WHAT CHARACTER SAYS AND DOES	WHAT OTHERS FEEL ABOUT CHARACTER
• doesn't believe Helen can be helped • refuses to consider other points of view • stands up and collects papers to try to end the argument	• James seems to resent his father. • Aunt Ev thinks he needs her advice. • Kate seems used to putting up with his moods.

CAPTAIN KELLER

HOW CHARACTER LOOKS AND FEELS	HOW I FEEL ABOUT CHARACTER
• annoyed, stubborn, and sure of himself • has given up trying to find help for Helen	• seems to feel the household should revolve around him and his wishes • maybe annoyed because Helen is really the center of the household • probably typical of a nineteenth-century father

Drama

Often as you read a play, you'll discover that it makes sense to create more than one Character Map. For instance, as you read further into this play, the character of Annie Sullivan becomes increasingly important. One way to get a grasp of her character is through making a Character Map. It's a quick, easy way to zoom in on her character.

WHAT CHARACTER SAYS AND DOES	WHAT OTHERS FEEL ABOUT CHARACTER
• determined to get Keller's permission • acts amused • looks him straight in the eye	• Mrs. Keller is unsure at first. • Later, she supports Annie. • Captain Keller argues with her. • Eventually, he sees she is right.

ANNIE

HOW CHARACTER LOOKS AND FEELS	HOW I FEEL ABOUT CHARACTER
• thinks Captain Keller is mostly talk • seems to like and respect Mrs. Keller • not afraid to speak her mind to Captain Keller and Kate	• smart and brave • uses humor even in difficult situations

Create a Character Map for each character you want to focus on. Here's the start of one for Kate Keller.

WHAT CHARACTER SAYS AND DOES	WHAT OTHERS FEEL ABOUT CHARACTER
• wants Keller to get help for Helen • will get help on her own, with his permission	• Keller thinks she will be disappointed again. • not ready at first to listen

KATE KELLER

HOW CHARACTER LOOKS AND FEELS	HOW I FEEL ABOUT CHARACTER
• supports Annie's suggestions if they will help Helen • is firm but polite with her husband	• seems kind • reasonable • determined

Of course, in addition to the characters you need to consider the setting. Often the setting changes with each new act or scene. In the next passage from Act II, the setting is a garden house near the Kellers' home.

from *The Miracle Worker*

KATE (*not looking up*): Miss Annie.

ANNIE: Yes.

KATE (*a pause*): Where would you—take Helen?

ANNIE: Ohh—

(*Brightly*)

Italy?

KELLER (*wheeling*): What?

ANNIE: Can't have everything, how would this garden house do? Furnish it, bring Helen here after a long ride so she won't recognize it, and you can see her every day. If she doesn't know. Well?

NOTE
New setting

KATE (*a sigh of relief*): Is that all?

ANNIE: That's all.

KATE: Captain.

(KELLER *turns his head; and* KATE's *request is quiet but firm.*)

With your permission?

KELLER (*teeth in cigar*): Why must she depend on you for the food she eats?

NOTE
New attempt to teach Helen

ANNIE (*a pause*): I want control of it.

KELLER: Why?

ANNIE: It's a way to reach her.

KELLER (*stares*): You intend to *starve* her into letting you touch her?

ANNIE: She won't starve, she'll learn. All's fair in love and war, Captain Keller, you never cut supplies?

KELLER: This is hardly a war!

ANNIE: Well, it's not love. A siege is a siege.

KELLER (*heavily*): Miss Sullivan. Do you *like* the child?

ANNIE (*straight in his eyes*): Do you?

Drama

461

(*a long pause.*)

KATE: You could have a servant here—

ANNIE (*amused*): I'll have enough work without looking after a servant. But that boy Percy could sleep here, run errands—

KATE (*also amused*): We can let Percy sleep here, I think, Captain?

ANNIE (*eagerly*): And some old furniture, all our own—

KATE (*also eager*): Captain? Do you think that walnut bedstead in the barn would be too—

KELLER: I have not yet consented to Percy! Or to the house, or to the proposal! Or to Miss Sullivan's— staying on when I—

(*But he erupts in an irate surrender.*)

Very well, I consent to everything!

(*He shakes his cigar at Annie.*)

For two weeks. I'll give you two weeks in this place, and it will be a miracle if you get the child to tolerate you.

KATE: Two weeks? Miss Annie, can you accomplish anything in two weeks?

KELLER: Anything or not, two weeks, then the child comes back to us. Make up your mind, Miss Sullivan, yes or no?

ANNIE: Two weeks. For only one miracle?

(*She nods at him, nervously.*)

I'll get her to tolerate me.

> NOTE
> Time and place are set for a miracle.

Note that Annie wants to move Helen to a different setting away from the family. Annie's wish is reflected in the change of setting on the stage.

How Plays Are Organized

Almost all plays are divided into **acts** and **scenes**. Usually a play contains two or three acts and two or three scenes in each act. In many cases, a scene change indicates a change in the setting—either the time or the place or both.

The Miracle Worker has three acts. Although the scenes are not labeled as such, a change in lighting indicates a change in scene.

> from *The Miracle Worker*
>
> *(She pours some water into the basin, dips the handkerchief, and presses it to her mouth. Standing there, bent over the basin in pain—with the rest of the set dim and unreal, and the lights upon her taking on the subtle color of the past—she hears again, as do we, the faraway voices, and slowly she lifts her head to them; the boy's voice is the same, the others are cracked old crones in a nightmare, and perhaps we see their shadows.)*
>
> BOY'S VOICE: It hurts. Annie, it hurts.
> FIRST CRONE'S VOICE: Keep that brat shut up, can't you, girlie, how's a body to get any sleep in this damn ward?

NOTE
Scene changes to the past.

Drama

Here, stage directions are important. They not only indicate Annie's actions but signal the beginning of a flashback to a sad time in Annie's past. Knowing about Annie's life before she arrived in Alabama gives you, and the audience, knowledge about what has made her so determined and brave.

Besides having divisions of acts and scenes, a play, like any story, usually has five parts: *exposition, rising action, climax, falling action,* and *resolution.* In *The Miracle Worker,* the climax, falling action, and resolution all occur within the last few pages of the play. You might want to create a Plot Diagram of William Gibson's play that looks like the one on the next page.

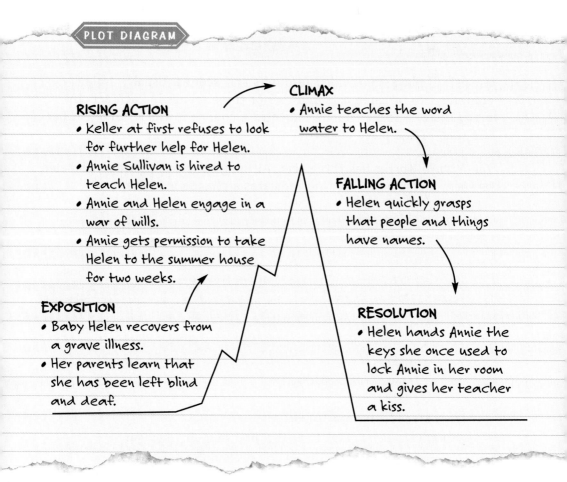

CLIMAX
- Annie teaches the word water to Helen.

RISING ACTION
- Keller at first refuses to look for further help for Helen.
- Annie Sullivan is hired to teach Helen.
- Annie and Helen engage in a war of wills.
- Annie gets permission to take Helen to the summer house for two weeks.

FALLING ACTION
- Helen quickly grasps that people and things have names.

EXPOSITION
- Baby Helen recovers from a grave illness.
- Her parents learn that she has been left blind and deaf.

RESOLUTION
- Helen hands Annie the keys she once used to lock Annie in her room and gives her teacher a kiss.

Drawing a Plot Diagram can help you analyze the events of a play. It can also help you decide which event or events are most critical to the story being told.

E Connect

What are your reactions after finishing a play? Keep track of your thoughts about the characters and plot of a play. Your quick comments can help you think more critically about what you're reading.

For example, here are one reader's reactions to a speech Annie Sullivan makes toward the end of Act III. In an emotional moment, Sullivan worries she has failed in her mission to reach Helen.

from *The Miracle Worker*

ANNIE: I wanted to teach you—oh, everything the earth is full of, Helen, everything on it that's ours for a wink and it's gone, and what we are on it, the—light we bring to it and leave behind in—words, why, you can see five thousand years back in a light of words, everything we feel, think, know—and share, in words, so not a soul is in darkness, or done with, even in the grave. And I know, I *know*, one word and I can—put the world in your hand—and whatever it is to me, I won't take less! How, how do I tell you that *this*— (*She spells.*)

—means a word, and the word means this *thing . . . ?*

I can tell that she's not ready to give up yet.

I feel sympathy for Annie here. She just can't break through to Helen. I wonder if Helen shares some of her frustration?

Drama

After Reading

After you finish reading a play, think about what you've learned. You have probably invested a few hours reading a play, so after you read, take a few extra minutes to collect your thoughts. Ask yourself, "Have I met my purpose for reading?"

F Pause and Reflect

Is there anything about the play that stands out in your mind? What do you feel like discussing? Ask yourself questions such as these:

Looking Back

- Can I describe the setting?
- Can I describe the main characters and their motivations?
- Can I retell the central conflict and summarize the plot?
- Do I understand the main message, or theme, of the play?
- Can I explain what I did and did not like about the play and support my opinion with evidence?

If there are parts of the play that you don't understand or have forgotten, then you may need to do some rereading.

G Reread

Rather than reread the entire play, try zeroing in on the part or parts that you didn't understand. For example, if you're not sure that you fully understand a certain character, reread the part where the character is first introduced to see how other characters react to him or her. If you're not sure you understand the theme, reread for the big ideas and key lines of the play. Look for key speeches from the main characters. Often, these speeches express their strongest emotions and deepest thoughts about life.

Rereading Strategy: Visualizing and Thinking Aloud

Visualizing and thinking aloud is a helpful strategy to use with plays because plays are meant to be seen and heard. Ask yourself, "What does the stage look like? What would the actors look like and sound like?"

To help, you might want to create a Storyboard that reflects your "view" of the play. The sketches you draw can be as simple or as detailed as you like. Drawing a Storyboard also can help you understand the sequence of events in the plot.

STORYBOARD

Act I

An illness leaves Helen Keller blind and deaf.

The Kellers hire Annie to teach Helen, but first Annie must find a way to communicate with her.

Act II

Annie insists that she and Helen be allowed to live away from the Kellers for two weeks.

Annie spells words to Helen, but Helen can't figure out what a word means.

Act III

As soon as Annie brings Helen home, Helen begins misbehaving again.

Helen understands the word <u>water</u>.

Drama

467

H Remember

You may have to take a test on your knowledge of the play, or you may be asked to write about it. For this reason, you need to find a way to remember what you've read. Here are two suggestions.

1. Do an Oral Reading

Get together with a small group. Together, do an oral reading of a key scene from the play. For example, if the play is *The Miracle Worker*, you might read a scene in which all of the main characters are present. Then, discuss with your group what the scene means and why it is important.

2. Watch the Film Version

Most of the plays you read in school will have a film version. Visit your library or local video store, and check out the movie version of the play. Think about differences between the play and movie. Tell the rest of the class what you learned.

Summing Up

When you read a play, use the reading process and the strategy of **summarizing.** You may find these reading tools helpful:

- Summary Notes
- Magnet Summary
- Character Map
- Plot Diagram
- Storyboard

Look for the **organization of plays** as you read. Use the rereading strategy of **visualizing and thinking aloud** to focus on key events.

Focus on Language

Language is the only tool playwrights have. With language, they can set a scene, define a character, and create conflict. Focusing on that language can help you interpret a play.

Goals

Here you'll learn how to:

✔ **find the key lines and speeches in a play**

✔ **understand how the stage directions contribute to a play**

✔ **examine how dialogue reveals character, plot, and theme**

Before Reading

On your first reading of a play, you'll want to find out about the plot and get to know the characters. You will need to reread selected passages, however, to concentrate on the language. When you are rereading, try to read at least a part of the play aloud. Reading aloud is a good way to get a feel for how the lines might be interpreted by actors. Reading the stage directions aloud also helps you imagine what the actors should be doing.

Concentrating on language doesn't necessarily mean focusing on every word. Instead, you'll concentrate on these three elements, all of which can help you understand the language of the play:

- key lines and speeches
- stage directions
- dialogue as a clue to character, plot, and theme

Drama

As you reread, mark passages of dialogue that seem important. Then, return to the places you've marked, and take a careful look at what the characters say and how they say it.

1. Key Lines and Speeches

Every play has a few lines or speeches that stand out. When you are reading a tense scene, you may notice key speeches that emphasize the conflict in a play. Sometimes a humorous line or a sarcastic speech is key because it helps define character. Note the clues about characters and about the conflict in this tense scene from Act II of *The Miracle Worker,* a play about Helen Keller. Moments earlier, Annie, Helen's teacher, was almost fired from her job.

---

from *The Miracle Worker* by William Gibson

KELLER: . . . I have decided to—give you another chance.

ANNIE (*cheerfully*): To do what?

KELLER: To —remain in our employ.

(ANNIE's *eyes widen.*)

But on two conditions. I am not accustomed to rudeness in servants or women, and that is the first. If you are to stay, there must be a radical change of manner.

ANNIE (*a pause*): Whose?

KELLER (*exploding*): Yours, young lady, isn't it obvious? And the second is that you persuade me there's the slightest hope of your teaching a child who flees from you now like the plague, to anyone else she can find in this house.

> **NOTE**
> Sarcastic response from Annie

Notice that Annie has to struggle with Keller as well as with Helen. Annie's one word, *Whose?*, reveals that she is implying that Keller's manner needs to be changed. His explosive speech indicates that this thought hasn't occurred to him.

2. Stage Directions

In some parts of a play, the **stage directions** can be as important as the dialogue itself. Stage directions tell the actors and director how to perform the play, how to arrange the stage, and how the actors should move and talk. In *The Miracle Worker,* stage directions are almost the only clues to what Helen is feeling and doing. For example, read the stage directions in this passage.

from *The Miracle Worker*

ANNIE: All right. Pump.

(HELEN *touches her cheek, waits uncertainly.*)

No, she's not here. Pump!

(*She forces* HELEN's *hand to work the handle, then lets go. And* HELEN *obeys. She pumps till the water comes, then* ANNIE *puts the pitcher in her other hand and guides it under the spout, and the water tumbling half into and half around the pitcher douses* HELEN's *hand.* ANNIE *takes over the handle to keep water coming, and does automatically what she had done so many times before, spells into* HELEN's *free palm:*)

Water. W, a, t, e, r. *Water.* It has a —*name*—

(*And now the miracle happens.* HELEN *drops the pitcher on the slab under the spout, it shatters. She stands transfixed.* ANNIE *freezes the pump handle: there is a change in the sundown light, and with it a change in* HELEN's *face, some light coming into it we have never seen there, some struggle in the depths behind it; and her lips tremble, trying to remember something the muscles around them once knew, till at last it finds its way out, painfully, a baby sound buried under the debris of years of dumbness.*)

HELEN: Wah. Wah.

(*and again, with great effort*)

Wah. Wah.

> NOTE
> **Directions introduce key objects.**

> NOTE
> **Directions show actions of characters.**

> NOTE
> **Directions show character's expressions and movements.**

Drama

In this scene, the stage directions help you understand Helen's dawning realization that words have meaning. This is the "miracle" referred to in the title and part of the major theme of the play.

3. Dialogue

Dialogue is the conversation characters have with each other. In drama, the dialogue serves at least three purposes:

- ■ **Establishes Character** You learn important information about the characters if you "listen" to what they say to each other.
- ■ **Advances the Plot** What the characters say advances the action of the play. Their comments about themselves and others work together to form the plot.
- ■ **Reveals the Theme(s)** You can find clues about the playwright's messages, or themes, within the play's dialogue.

Dialogue and Character

Playwrights spend a lot of time getting dialogue to sound right. Characters have to speak as real people would speak in the same circumstances. Characters also have to sound different from one another. For example, here is a conversation between Annie Sullivan and James, Helen's half brother. What can you infer about each character's personality and the difference between the two?

from The Miracle Worker

NOTE

Difference between James's mild manner and Annie's temper

JAMES: You don't let go of things easily, do you? How will you—win her hand now, in this place?

ANNIE (*curtly*): Do I know? I lost my temper, and here we are!

JAMES (*lightly*): No touching, no teaching. Of course you *are* bigger—

ANNIE: I'm not counting on force, I'm counting on her. That little imp is dying to know.

JAMES: Know what?

ANNIE: Anything. Any and every crumb in God's creation. I'll have to use that appetite too.

(*She gives the room a final survey, straightens the bed, arranges the curtains.*)

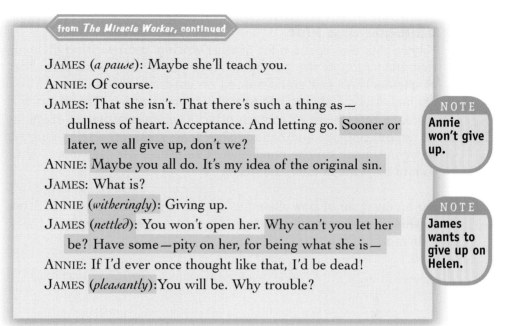

from *The Miracle Worker*, continued

JAMES (*a pause*): Maybe she'll teach you.

ANNIE: Of course.

JAMES: That she isn't. That there's such a thing as — dullness of heart. Acceptance. And letting go. Sooner or later, we all give up, don't we?

ANNIE: Maybe you all do. It's my idea of the original sin.

JAMES: What is?

ANNIE (*witheringly*): Giving up.

JAMES (*nettled*): You won't open her. Why can't you let her be? Have some — pity on her, for being what she is —

ANNIE: If I'd ever once thought like that, I'd be dead!

JAMES (*pleasantly*): You will be. Why trouble?

NOTE

Annie won't give up.

NOTE

James wants to give up on Helen.

In just this one bit of dialogue, you can find several clues about Annie and James.

An Inference Chart can help you keep a record of your conclusions about characters. You can add to the chart as you read the play.

Drama

INFERENCE CHART

TEXT	WHAT I CONCLUDE
"James: Sooner or later, we all give up, don't we?"	James is easily defeated. He is really referring to the fact that he feels defeated by his father.
"Annie: Maybe you all do. It's my idea of the original sin."	Annie is determined and focused.
"James: Why can't you let her be? Have some—pity on her, for being what she is—"	James has given up on Helen and thinks she's learned all she'll ever learn.

Dialogue and Plot

Playwrights also spend a lot of time writing and rewriting dialogue so that the action of the play moves along at a fairly brisk pace. The characters can't just stand around on stage waiting for something to happen. Their dialogue has to make things happen. Characters may speak to themselves or to each other. They may arrive on stage, make an announcement, and depart. They may speak on a telephone and answer a knock on the door, and all the time, the plot moves ahead toward the climax and resolution.

For an example of how dialogue can move the plot forward, "listen" to this dinnertime conversation between Annie Sullivan and the Kellers in Act III.

from *The Miracle Worker*

KATE: Please. I've hardly had a chance to welcome her home—

ANNIE: Captain Keller.

KELLER (*embarrassed*): Oh. Katie, we—had a little talk, Miss Annie feels that if we indulge Helen in these—

> NOTE
> Family may undermine Helen's progress.

AUNT EV: But what's the child done?

ANNIE: She's learned not to throw things on the floor and kick. It took us the best part of two weeks and—

AUNT EV: But only a napkin, it's not as if it were breakable!

> NOTE
> Annie challenges the family.

ANNIE: And everything she's learned *is?* Mrs. Keller, I don't think we should—play tug-of-war for her, either give her to me or you keep her from kicking.

This conversation in the Kellers' dining room is similar to a conversation that occurs earlier in the play. In both scenes, Annie objects that Helen is allowed to do whatever she wishes. In the first scene, she allows herself to be bullied by Helen's parents. In this later scene, Annie speaks up for herself. This illustrates a change in her character and moves the plot forward toward the climax.

Dialogue and Themes

Dialogue also reveals a playwright's themes, or messages. To find the themes, look for passages in which a character, often a main character, makes a strong statement about the world, society, or people in general. Look also for the point at which a character has a deep insight or recognizes a change in himself or herself. For example, read this brief speech that falls at the end of *The Miracle Worker*.

> **from *The Miracle Worker***
>
> ANNIE: I, love, Helen.
>
> (*She clutches the child to her, tight this time, not spelling, whispering into her hair.*)
>
> Forever, and—
>
> (*She stops. The lights over the pump are taking on the color of the past, and it brings ANNIE's head up, her eyes opening, in fear; and as slowly as though drawn she rises, to listen, with her hand on HELEN's shoulders. She waits, waits, listening with ears and eyes both, slowly here, slowly there: and hears only silence. There are no voices. The color passes on, and when her eyes come back to HELEN she can breathe the end of her phrase without fear:*)
>
> —ever.

NOTE
People can create miracles for others.

Drama

In this scene, Annie shows that she has risen above her past to become—for Helen, at least—a true "miracle worker."

After Reading

After you finish studying the language of a play, take a moment to reflect on what you've learned. Ask yourself, "What are the most memorable scenes and speeches from this play?"

To help you remember what you've read, try selecting several passages and creating a Paraphrase Chart. Write a key passage from the play in the left box. Write your paraphrase of the lines in the right box. Then, record your thoughts underneath.

PARAPHRASE CHART

TEXT	MY PARAPHRASE
"Annie: Let me keep her to what she's learned and she'll go on learning from me. Take her out of my hands, and it all comes apart."	Annie tells the Kellers that they must listen to what she says about Helen. Otherwise, Helen will stay locked in her silent world.

MY THOUGHTS
I agree with what Annie says, and I can't understand why the Kellers fight her so much. I think they feel sorry for Helen, but she needs to learn.

Summing Up

■ Key lines and speeches are often what make a play memorable.

■ Stage directions tell you what's happening on the stage and how the characters are to act the lines.

■ Dialogue reveals character, advances the plot, and helps to explain the themes of a play.

Focus on Theme

The **theme** of a play is the playwright's message for the audience. Most plays have one major theme and one or more minor themes. A part of your job as a critical reader is to discover the playwright's themes and think about what they mean.

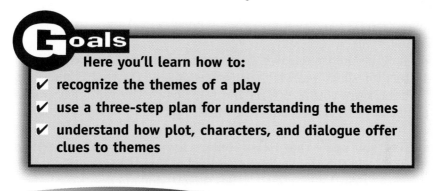

Goals

Here you'll learn how to:

✔ recognize the themes of a play

✔ use a three-step plan for understanding the themes

✔ understand how plot, characters, and dialogue offer clues to themes

Before Reading

Playwrights provide clues to themes in a number of ways. To understand the themes of a play, follow these three steps:

Drama

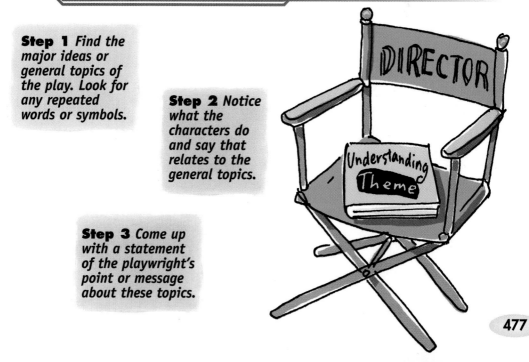

PLAN FOR UNDERSTANDING THEME

Step 1 *Find the major ideas or general topics of the play. Look for any repeated words or symbols.*

Step 2 *Notice what the characters do and say that relates to the general topics.*

Step 3 *Come up with a statement of the playwright's point or message about these topics.*

DIRECTOR

Understanding Theme

Step 1: Find the major ideas, topics, or symbols.

Begin by deciding what topic or big idea the play is generally about. Many times you can figure out the general topic of the play during your preview. The topic is often revealed in:

- the title
- the first several lines of the first scene
- any background information or summaries

If you look at the front cover, back cover, title page, and cast of characters for *The Miracle Worker* (pages 449–451), what clues can you find? Right away you notice on the front cover the sentence in small type that appears underneath the title.

From that, you know that Helen Keller's life is an important topic of the play. But is she the "miracle worker" of the title? On the back cover you notice the words *struggle*, *prison*, and *silence*. Now look again at the description of time and place.

> TIME: *The 1880s.*
> PLACE: *In and around the Keller homestead in Tuscumbia, Alabama; also, briefly, the Perkins Institution for the Blind, in Boston.*

This description reinforces the idea that the play is at least partly about Helen Keller but also about her family. It also raises a new idea—that disabilities ("the Perkins Institution for the Blind") may be an important topic as well. Here is a list of major topics one reader made in a journal while previewing *The Miracle Worker*:

JOURNAL ENTRY

Topics in The Miracle Worker

Helen Keller	Annie Sullivan
disabilities	family relationships
miracles	overcoming adversity

During Reading

While you're reading a play, continue to look for clues about the playwright's message. One of the best ways comes through reading for repeated words or symbols. A **symbol** is a person, place, thing, or event that represents something else.

In *The Miracle Worker,* Annie Sullivan is told before she leaves the Perkins Institution to go to Alabama that "No one expects you to work miracles." In fact, the word *miracle* appears quite often in the play.

Here's the Web that one reader made about some key words, major ideas, or symbols.

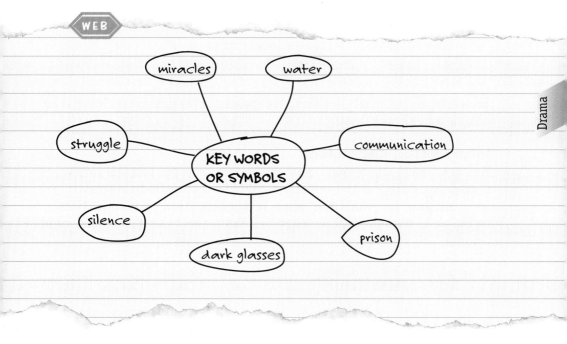

WEB

miracles water

struggle communication

KEY WORDS OR SYMBOLS

silence

dark glasses prison

Drama

Look for repeated words as you read. They can be important clues to the playwright's intention. That a miracle may eventually have to do with water is apparent to the perceptive reader. You know that because water, water pitchers, and a water pump appear or are mentioned several times in dialogue or stage directions.

Step 2: Find out what the characters do and say that relates to the general topics or symbols.

Once you have your list of topics and your Web, think carefully about what the characters do and say that relates to these topics. Pay attention to parts of the play in which the characters learn something about themselves, others, or life in general.

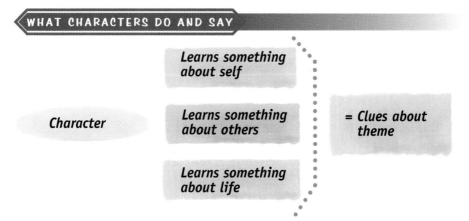

To keep track of what you find, try making a Double-entry Journal or a Topic and Theme Organizer.

Interpreting Characters

You can "read" characters by what they say and do. List the key passages you find in the left-hand column of your Double-entry Journal. Look for words that show or suggest strong emotion. Then, record your thoughts about what the characters have said in the right column.

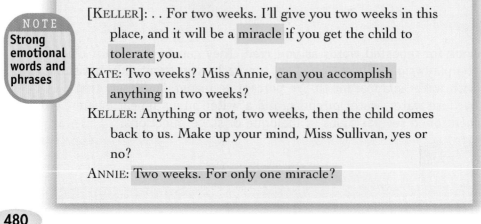

from *The Miracle Worker*

NOTE
Strong emotional words and phrases

[KELLER]: . . For two weeks. I'll give you two weeks in this place, and it will be a miracle if you get the child to tolerate you.

KATE: Two weeks? Miss Annie, can you accomplish anything in two weeks?

KELLER: Anything or not, two weeks, then the child comes back to us. Make up your mind, Miss Sullivan, yes or no?

ANNIE: Two weeks. For only one miracle?

QUOTE	MY THOUGHTS
"I'll give you two weeks in this place, and it will be a miracle if you get the child to tolerate you."	Keller wants a miracle, and Annie seems to think she can deliver. I think she might be "The Miracle Worker."

You might have noticed the word *miracle* in this passage and realized that it relates to one of the big ideas of the play. That the word *miracle* appears in the title as well is an important clue.

Interpreting Theme

Good readers gather information as they go and adjust their ideas accordingly. For example, you may decide halfway through your reading of a play that one of the general topics you listed for the work is not very important at all. So you cross that one off your list and concentrate on the remaining ones. The key is to leave yourself open to new thoughts and ideas as you read.

You can use a Topic and Theme Organizer to keep track of your thoughts about the big ideas in a play. Write the general topic at the top of the organizer. Then, write details about what the characters say and do in the middle. At the bottom in the star, write the statement of theme. For example, on the next page is the beginning of an organizer one reader created while reading *The Miracle Worker*.

Drama

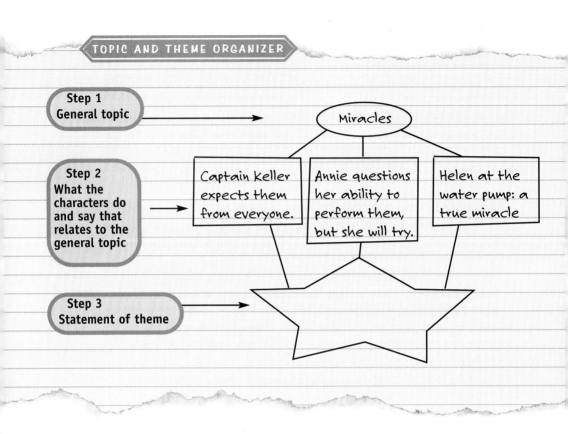

Step 1
General topic → Miracles

Step 2
What the characters do and say that relates to the general topic →

Captain Keller expects them from everyone.

Annie questions her ability to perform them, but she will try.

Helen at the water pump: a true miracle

Step 3
Statement of theme →

Keep adding to your Topic and Theme Organizer as you read. For example, the reader who created this organizer will probably add boxes to the center, because the word *miracle* comes up a half-dozen or more times in Gibson's play. The result will be a careful study of the big idea of "miracles."

The benefit of taking notes as you read is that once you decide on the theme, you have several good reasons to support it. That will make discussing the theme easier when it is time to write a paper or essay about the play.

After Reading

By the time you finish a play, you should have an excellent understanding of the events of the plot and what the characters are like. Look at the notes and organizers you made while reading. Now think about possible themes. Ask yourself again and again, "What is the playwright's point or message about the general topic?"

Step 3: Come up with a statement of the playwright's point or message about the topic.

Review the theme clues you've found and draw a conclusion about what they mean. Try not to make the mistake of confusing a play's topic with its theme. The topic is what the play is about. The theme is the point the playwright wants to make *about* the topic.

> topic = what the play is about

> theme = the author's point or message about the topic

For example, you know that an important topic in *The Miracle Worker* is "miracles." So ask yourself, "What is the playwright telling me about miracles?"

ORGANIZER

topic = miracles

theme = People can make their own miracles.

To check that you've found a major theme in the work, you might create a Main Idea Organizer. Look for at least three details from the play that support the theme.

THEME: People can make their own miracles.		
DETAIL #1	DETAIL #2	DETAIL #3
Annie manages to overcome her past and becomes a happy, successful adult.	Annie uses her wits and hard work to give language to Helen.	Helen overcomes challenges and learns how to communicate with the world.

Many works have more than one theme. If you find plenty of supporting details for your theme statement, chances are good that you've found a major theme in the play. On the other hand, if you have trouble locating support, you may want to rethink your ideas about the major theme. Return to your notes to see whether you find a theme that is more readily supported with details from the play. If that's the case, then this is probably the major theme.

Summing Up

- The theme is a general statement or point about life. Most plays have a major theme and one or more minor themes.

- Use a three-step plan to find the themes of a play:

  1. Find the major ideas or general topics. Look for any recurring words or symbols.

  2. Find out what the characters do and say that relates to the general topic.

  3. Come up with a statement of the playwright's point or message.

- Look for theme clues as you read. Pay attention to parts of the play in which the characters learn something about themselves, others, or life in general.

Focus on Shakespeare

To read Shakespeare's plays, you'll need the sharpest reading tools in your tool box. Once you get the hang of it, however, you'll understand why he is considered such a great playwright.

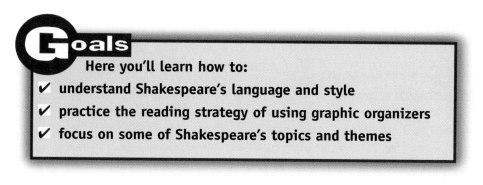

Goals

Here you'll learn how to:

✔ **understand Shakespeare's language and style**
✔ **practice the reading strategy of using graphic organizers**
✔ **focus on some of Shakespeare's topics and themes**

Before Reading

You may read a Shakespeare play before you go to see it performed. Or you may have to read one for a school assignment. Whatever your reason, your purpose for reading is the same: to understand and appreciate Shakespeare's writing.

If your assignment is to read and respond to a Shakespeare play, allow plenty of time to read the entire play once and key scenes more than once. Shakespeare's plays have five acts, so you will be spending a lot of time with a play. You need a plan that can help strengthen your understanding and enjoyment of Shakespeare's work. Here is a reading plan that will work for all of his plays.

Drama

1. *First, read the entire play. Read the first time for sense.*

2. *Reread key scenes. This time, read for specifics.*

Before you read the entire work, get a sense of what the play is about. As always, begin with a preview. Pay particular attention to the items on this checklist:

Preview Checklist

✔ the title

✔ any background information, summaries, or illustrations

✔ the cast of characters (here called the dramatis personae)

✔ the location and numbering of notes

✔ the characters in capital letters

✔ the stage directions in italic type

For practice, preview the title page for *Romeo and Juliet* and part of the Prologue, which appears just before Act I, scene 1.

from *Romeo and Juliet* by William Shakespeare

Romeo and Juliet

PREVIEW
Title

A PLAY IN FIVE ACTS BY WILLIAM SHAKESPEARE
1594

PREVIEW
Number
of acts

Dramatis Personae

CHORUS

ESCALUS, Prince of Verona.

PARIS, a young Count, kinsman of the Prince.

MONTAGUE, head of two houses at variance with each other.

CAPULET, head of two houses at variance with each other.

AN OLD MAN, of the Capulet family.

ROMEO, son to Montague.

TYBALT, nephew to Lady Capulet.

PREVIEW
List of
characters

MERCUTIO, kinsman to the Prince and friend to Romeo.

BENVOLIO, nephew to Montague and friend to Romeo.

FRIAR LAURENCE, Franciscan.

FRIAR JOHN, Franciscan.

BALTHASAR, servant to Romeo.

ABRAM, servant to Montague.

SAMPSON, servant to Capulet.

GREGORY, servant to Capulet.

PETER, servant to Juliet's nurse.

AN APOTHECARY.

THREE MUSICIANS.

AN OFFICER.

LADY MONTAGUE, wife to Montague.

LADY CAPULET, wife to Capulet.

JULIET, daughter to Capulet.

NURSE, to Juliet.

CITIZENS OF VERONA, Gentlemen and Gentlewomen of both houses, Maskers, Torchbearers, Pages, Guards, Watchmen, Servants, and Attendants.

Drama

PREVIEW
Setting

PREVIEW
Plot summary

SCENE: Verona; Mantua

PLAY SUMMARY: Juliet, a Capulet, and Romeo, a Montague, fall in love at a masked ball held by the Capulets. Because the Montagues and Capulets are sworn enemies, the couple is married secretly by Friar Laurence. Unaware of this secret marriage, Juliet's father promises Count Paris that he may marry Juliet. Soon after, Tybalt— a Capulet—kills Romeo's friend Mercutio in a quarrel. Romeo kills Tybalt and is banished to Mantua. So that she does not have to marry Paris, Friar Laurence gives Juliet a potion that will make it appear that she has died in the night. Romeo returns to Verona and learns that Juliet has "died." He goes to her burial vault, gives her a last kiss, and kills himself with poison. Juliet awakens, sees that Romeo is dead, and kills herself with a dagger. The families learn what has happened and end their feud.

The Prologue

(*Enter Chorus*)

CHORUS

Two households, both alike in dignity,   1
In fair Verona, where we lay our scene,
From ancient grudge break to new mutiny,   3

PREVIEW
How notes are indicated

    Where civil blood makes civil hands unclean. 4
From forth the fatal loins of these two foes
    A pair of star-crossed lovers take their life;   6
Whose misadventured piteous overthrows   7
    Doth with their death bury their parents' strife.

PREVIEW
Location of notes

1 **dignity** rank, status

3 **mutiny** strife, discord

4 **Where . . . unclean** where citizens' hands are stained with their
   fellow citizens' blood

6 **star-crossed** ill-fated

7 **misadventured** unlucky

During Reading

Remember that first, you read the entire play all the way through. Read to learn what happens in the play, what the characters are like, and what their motivations are. Of course, before you can figure out what a scene is about, you need to be able to understand what the characters are actually saying.

Read for Sense

To modern ears and eyes, the language of a Shakespeare play (called Elizabethan English) seems more than a little odd. At first, it seems that the characters say strange things and that some of their sentences sound out of order. Look at the following speech spoken by Juliet's Nurse to Romeo. (We would call her a nursemaid or a nanny.)

Drama

from *Romeo and Juliet*, Act II, scene 4

NURSE: Well, sir, my mistress is the sweetest lady—
      Lord, Lord! When 'twas a little prating thing—O,
      there is a nobleman in town, one Paris, that would
      fain lay knife aboard; but she, good soul, had as lief   198
      see a toad, a very toad, as see him. I anger her
      sometimes, and tell her that Paris is the properer man,   200
      but I'll warrant you, when I say so, she looks as pale as
      any clout in the versal world. Doth not rosemary and   202
      Romeo begin both with a letter?   203

NOTE
Elizabethan English

---

198 **fain lay knife aboard** like to assert his claim; **lief** willingly

200 **properer** handsomer

202 **clout** cloth; **versal** universal

203 **a letter** the same letter

One key to reading Shakespeare is to rely on context clues. When you come to an unfamiliar word, think about the meaning of the sentence as a whole. For example, look again at the speech above. Even if you don't know what *fain, lief,* and *versal* mean, you can still figure out the overall sense. The Nurse is saying that her beloved Juliet is growing up and now has a will of her own.

Focus on Speeches

Sometimes you'll arrive at a passage that you know is important. It may be a highly emotional speech, one that signals a turning point in the action, or one that reveals a character's future plans. You'll want to take a little extra time to understand each word of every line. Use the notes to help you with unfamiliar words.

from *Romeo and Juliet,* Act II, scene 5

Enter Juliet

NOTE

Juliet is alone on the stage.

NOTE

Juliet impatiently awaits to hear what Romeo has told the Nurse.

JULIET: The clock struck nine when I did send the Nurse;
   In half an hour she promis'd to return.
   Perchance she cannot meet him. That's not so.
   O, she is lame! Love's heralds should be thoughts,
      Which ten times faster glides than the sun's beams
   Driving back shadows over louring hills.   6
   Therefore do nimble-pinion'd doves draw Love, 7
   And therefore hath the wind-swift Cupid wings.
   Now is the sun upon the highmost hill
      Of this day's journey, and from nine till twelve
   Is three long hours, yet she is not come.
   Had she affections and warm youthful blood,
   She would be as swift in motion as a ball;
   My words would bandy her to my sweet love,   14
      And his to me,
   But old folks, many feign as they were dead—   16
   Unwieldy, slow, heavy, and pale as lead.

---

6 **louring** dark, threatening

7 **Love,** a reference to the Roman mythological goddess Venus, whose chariot was pulled by swift-winged horses

14 **bandy** toss to and fro, as in tennis

16 **feign as** act as though

After reading the footnoted definitions, return to the text and skim the lines once more. Knowing the definitions of the unfamiliar words as you reread should help you understand the passage as a whole.

Shakespeare's Language

Shakespeare's language sounds so different because the English language has significantly changed in the more than 400 years since his plays were first written. Words that were common in the late 1500s have fallen out of use. It may help you to learn what some of these words mean.

SHAKESPEARE'S LANGUAGE

Pronouns

thou, thee, ye = you
thy or *thine* = your or yours

Verbs

hast or *hath* = has
ist = is
canst = can
dost = does
art = are
wilt = will
dost = do or does
wert = were

Contractions

't = it
'tis = it is
o'er = over
e'er = ever
ne'er = never

Common Words

anon = soon
conceit = opinion
cousin or *coz* = friend
cuckold = the husband of an unfaithful wife
cur = a bad person
fain = gladly
feign = pretend
forsooth = in truth or for sure
hap or *haply* = perhaps
hence = away from here

hither = here
mistress = female head of a household
tarry = wait
thence = away from there
troth = faithfulness or faith
wench = girl or young woman, often used for a servant
wherefore = why
whither? = where to?

Besides following Shakespeare's language, you'll need to keep track of the characters and plot.

Reading Strategy: Using Graphic Organizers

Summary Notes can help you keep track of the characters and the plot. As you read, summarize each scene in each act. On the next page are one reader's notes on a scene from Act I.

Drama

ACT AND SCENE: Act 1, scene 2

MAIN POINT: Capulet agrees that Paris can marry Juliet if she accepts the match.

1. Capulet invites Paris to a feast.
2. Romeo and Benvolio find out about the feast.
3. Capulet's servant says they can attend if they are not Montagues, but Romeo is a Montague.
4. Benvolio and Romeo decide to attend, Romeo in hopes of seeing Rosaline, his beloved.

Shakespeare's Style

You might also find Shakespeare's plays challenging because most of the dialogue is written in verse. Servants and commoners often speak in prose, but everyone else speaks in verse. Shakespeare wrote blank verse, which is poetry with a regular rhythm. In blank verse, each line has ten syllables, and every other syllable is accented. However, this rhythm does vary from time to time. Very often, the couplet (two lines) at the end of a speech is rhymed. Notice that the last two lines in Juliet's speech rhyme. This rhyming couplet makes a definite ending to Juliet's speech just before the Nurse enters.

from *Romeo and Juliet*, Act II, scene 5

> My words would bandy her to my sweet love,
>   And his to me.
> But old folks, many feign as they were dead—
> Unwieldy, slow, heavy, and pale as lead.

NOTE
Couplet

Here are a few other tips for understanding Shakespeare's style.

TIPS FOR UNDERSTANDING SHAKESPEARE

1. *Read some dialogue aloud, and pay attention to the punctuation. Don't pause at the end of a line if there's no punctuation. Where there's a comma, pause slightly. Where there's a semicolon, make your pause longer.*

2. *Some lines are inverted. That is, the verb or object may come before the subject. If you can't make sense of an inverted line, find the verb or verbs and then the subject, and reword the sentence. In the following line,* is *is the verb and* sun *the subject.*

Juliet's words in line 9:
"Now is the sun upon the highmost hill. . . ."

Rewritten sentence:
Now the sun is upon the highmost hill. . . .

What does she mean?
It is getting on toward noon.

3. *Shakespeare often makes allusions to myths. Note those allusions. Look up names you don't know in a dictionary. For example, you probably already know that, in myth, Cupid is the god of love and is always pictured with wings. It is a perfect allusion in line 8 of Juliet's speech shown on page 490 because she is anxiously waiting to hear where she and Romeo are to be secretly married.*

Drama

After Reading

When you've finished your first reading, if you are like most readers, you probably will want to clarify a few points about the play.

Read for Specifics

Refresh your memory about character names, important events, and so on. At this point, reread to make certain you understand the settings, characters' motivations, plot, and theme. Graphic organizers can help you understand and remember how each of these elements works.

Take a moment to thumb through the Reading Tools section at the back of this handbook. Look for organizers that can help you explore setting, characters, plot, and theme. On the next page are three other useful organizers that will help you keep track of some of the elements in a Shakespeare play.

CLUES ABOUT TIME	CLUES ABOUT PLACE
• People fight with swords. • Some of the vocabulary is from past times.	Verona, Mantua, Friar Laurence's cell, and a tomb

PLOT DIAGRAM

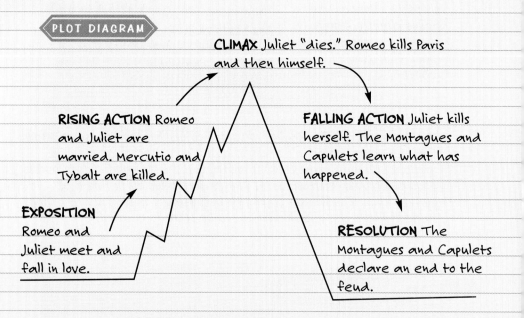

CLIMAX Juliet "dies." Romeo kills Paris and then himself.

RISING ACTION Romeo and Juliet are married. Mercutio and Tybalt are killed.

EXPOSITION Romeo and Juliet meet and fall in love.

FALLING ACTION Juliet kills herself. The Montagues and Capulets learn what has happened.

RESOLUTION The Montagues and Capulets declare an end to the feud.

CHARACTER DEVELOPMENT CHART

ROMEO

BEGINNING	MIDDLE	END
He seems young and maybe a little silly in the way he carries on about Rosaline and Juliet at first.	His love for Juliet seems to make him more thoughtful, but this love is forbidden.	He is a little out of control and not so gentle anymore. He kills Paris and then himself.

POSSIBLE THEME: Hate between families can destroy what they love most.

Shakespeare's Topics

Like the drama of today, Shakespeare's plays are about people and their problems. To explore these problems, Shakespeare created 38 plays, each with a different plot. Within these 38 plots, however, you can find at least two recurring topics: love and revenge.

Love

Shakespeare's favorite topic was love. Around this topic, he wrote plays with themes that deal with forbidden love, love that's not returned, familial love, love between friends, and love at first sight. Quite often in Shakespeare's work, the love between the two main characters drives the action of the play. In some plays (*Measure for Measure,* for example), the result is comic. In others (such as *Romeo and Juliet*), the result is tragic.

To understand how the topic of love works in a given play, create a Web with the name of a topic in the center. On the spokes, write words or lines that you think relate to the topic. This can help you come up with a statement of theme like the one at the bottom of the Web.

Drama

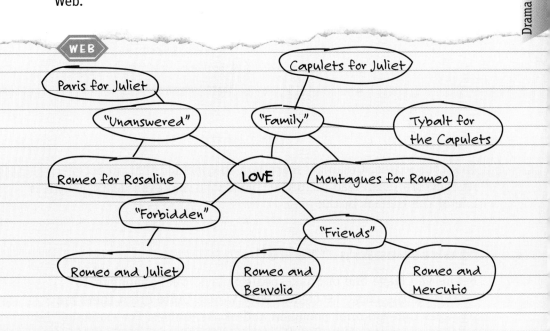

POSSIBLE THEME: Love for others is no guarantee of a happy ending.

Revenge

Revenge is another topic that pops up again and again in Shakespeare's plays. In some works (for example, *Hamlet* and *Macbeth*), the central theme revolves around revenge. In other plays (such as *Romeo and Juliet*), it is a subplot.

To explore themes about revenge in a play, watch for clues about why someone seeks revenge and how he or she goes about getting it. Then, think about the effect of the revenge. For example, make an organizer that helps you remember how revenge works in a play.

CAUSE-EFFECT ORGANIZER

CAUSE
Romeo seeks revenge.

EFFECT
Romeo stabs Tybalt.

EFFECT
Romeo is forced to flee.

This Cause-Effect Organizer leads you to conclude that an act of revenge can often lead to further bloodshed and even death, which is one of the themes in the play.

Shakespeare's "Voice"

Before you leave one of Shakespeare's plays, take a moment to "listen" to the music he creates with words. Quite often there are passages that are brief poems in and of themselves. For example, the following speeches from Act II, scene 5, are famous ones.

from *Romeo and Juliet*, Act II, scene 5

JULIET (*to herself*): O Romeo, Romeo! wherefore art thou
    Romeo?
    Deny thy father and refuse thy name!
    Or, if thou wilt not, be but sworn my love,
    And I'll no longer be a Capulet.
ROMEO (*aside*): Shall I hear more, or shall I speak at this?
JULIET: 'Tis but thy name that is my enemy;
    Thou art thyself, though not a Montague.
    What's Montague? It is nor hand, nor foot,
    Nor arm, nor face, nor any other part
    Belonging to a man. O, be some other name!
    What's in a name? That which we call a rose
    By any other word would smell as sweet;

You can record your reactions to your favorite lines in a play in a Paraphrase Chart.

Drama

PARAPHRASE CHART

LINE	MY PARAPHRASE
"Deny thy father and refuse thy name!"	Juliet is telling Romeo to ignore the fact that he's a Montague.
"What's in a name? That which we call a rose / By any other word would smell as sweet."	The name itself makes no difference. What matters is the thing itself.

MY THOUGHTS
Juliet is a romantic, but her ideas are not very practical.
I agree that a name should make no difference.

Your first Shakespeare play will be the most challenging to read. The next play will be a little bit easier, and the ones after that easier still. As with many worthwhile things, reading Shakespeare takes time but offers great rewards in the end.

Summing Up

Reading Shakespeare takes practice and a little patience.

- On your first reading, read for sense.
- Reread for specifics.
- Concentrate on Shakespeare's language and major speeches.
- Notice how the topics of love and revenge work in the play.
- Use graphic organizers to help you keep track of the literary elements:
  - Summary Notes
  - Setting Chart
  - Plot Diagram
  - Character Development Chart
  - Web
  - Cause-Effect Organizer
  - Paraphrase Chart

Elements of Drama

A drama, or play, is a literary work told in dialogue. Like novels and short stories, a drama has a setting, characters, plot, and a theme. The chief difference between a drama and other works of fiction is that a drama is meant to be performed in front of an audience.

The written version of a drama is called a *script,* and the author is called a *playwright.* You should know these terms because they will help you discuss and write about drama. You'll find other drama terms here, along with examples and definitions.

Use this section of the handbook as you would a glossary. Look up a term, read the example, review the definition, and apply what you've learned to your own reading.

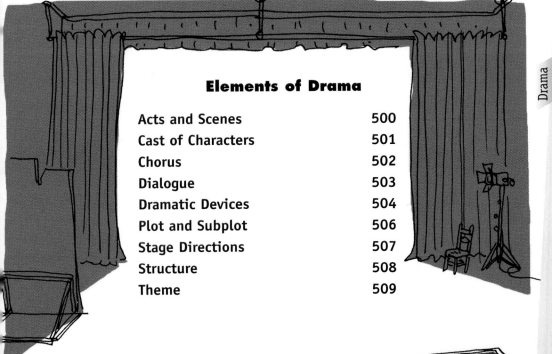

Elements of Drama

Drama

Acts and Scenes

Plays have one or more acts, the major divisions in the action. Scenes are smaller divisions within an act.

EXAMPLE

from *The Man Who Came to Dinner* by George S. Kaufman and Moss Hart

The scene is the home of Mr. and Mrs. STANLEY, in a small town in Ohio.

ACT I:	Scene 1. A December morning.
	Scene 2. About a week later.
ACT II:	Another week has passed. Christmas Eve.
ACT III:	Christmas morning.

DESCRIPTION

This opening from *The Man Who Came to Dinner* shows the two major divisions of a play: **acts** and **scenes.** Most modern plays have one to three acts. Older plays may have four or five acts. In performance, the end of an act is often signaled by the lowering of the curtain as the house lights are turned up, followed by an intermission.

Within each act of a play, you will find several scenes. Act and scene changes usually mean that the setting—either the time or place or both—will change. *The Man Who Came to Dinner* has one physical setting, the living room of the Stanley house, but the time setting changes with each act and scene. Each scene change may also involve a different actor or actors than were in the previous scene.

DEFINITION

Acts are the major divisions in a dramatic work. **Scenes** are smaller divisions within an act. Either time or place, or both, may change with each act and scene.

Cast of Characters

At the beginning of most plays, the playwright lists major and minor characters.

EXAMPLE from *Langston Hughes: Poet of the People* by Mary Satchell

CAST OF CHARACTERS	EXTRAS
Langston Hughes, black American writer	Waiter
Mr. James Hughes, his father	Longshoreman
Señora Garcia, housekeeper	Young Couple
Thad, medical student	Four Men
Mrs. Mary McLeod Bethune, Bethune-Cookman College founder	Young Woman
Helen, her secretary	Passersby
Mrs. Jones	
Johnny Jones	
Alice Jackson	
Jean Baxter } College students	
Kevin Daniels	

DESCRIPTION

The **cast of characters** lists everyone in the play and may identify the major characters. Some scripts list characters in order of importance, as this one does. Others list characters by order of appearance on stage. *Extras,* who are unnamed characters, are always listed in order of appearance.

DEFINITION

A cast of characters is a list that tells who is in the play. The list may also describe the characters.

Drama

Chorus

The chorus of a play is one or more actors who speak together with one voice. In classical Greek drama, the chorus is often as important as the chief actors of the play. In Shakespeare's drama, the chorus, if it is included, is less important.

EXAMPLE

from *Oedipus Rex* by Sophocles

OEDIPUS. Thou villain born!

CREON. And if thy mind is darkened . . .?

OEDIPUS. Still obey!

CREON. Not to a tyrant ruler.

OEDIPUS. O my country!

CREON. I, too, can claim that country. 'Tis not thine!

CHORUS. Cease, O my princes! In good time I see Jocasta
    coming hither from the house; And it were well with her
    to hush this strife.

DESCRIPTION

In Greek drama, the **chorus** is a group of actors who speak together with one voice and describe and comment on the main action of the play. Members of a chorus use song, dance, and chants to explain the action and characters of a play. In the above excerpt, the chorus orders Oedipus and Creon to stop fighting and then cues the audience that Jocasta is about to enter the scene.

Occasionally, as in *Romeo and Juliet,* a single character may act the part of a chorus, usually coming to the front of the stage to comment on the action. Although a few modern playwrights still experiment with using a chorus, the practice has mostly died out.

DEFINITION

The chorus is a group of actors who speak together with one voice and describe and comment on the main action of a play.

Dialogue

Dialogue is the chief element of a play.

EXAMPLE

from *The Glass Menagerie* by Tennessee Williams

AMANDA (*faintly*): Things have a way of turning out so
badly. . . . The gentleman caller has made an early
departure. What a wonderful joke you played on us!

TOM: How do you mean?

AMANDA: You didn't mention that he was engaged to be
married.

TOM: Jim? Engaged?

AMANDA: That's what he just informed us.

> Stage directions tell how a line is spoken.

> Speech tags tell who's talking.

DESCRIPTION

Dialogue is the conversation the characters have with one another. As in other kinds of fiction, dialogue in a play can:

- establish character
- advance the plot
- help to establish theme(s)

In a play, dialogue is accompanied by *speech tags*. In the above example, the speech tag in the first line tells you that Amanda is speaking, and the *stage direction* "faintly" indicates how she is to say the line. Playwrights may also indicate a character's actions with such stage directions as "smiles," "turns around," or "slams the door."

DEFINITION

Dialogue is the conversation among characters in a play. *Speech tags* indicate the speaker, and *stage directions* indicate any action the speaker is to perform. Analyzing dialogue can help you understand the characters, track the events of the plot, and discover clues to theme.

Drama

Dramatic Devices

Playwrights use several types of dramatic devices that add interest to a play. The most important of these include *monologues* or *soliloquies* and *asides*. Here is an example of a monologue.

EXAMPLE

from *Abingdon Square* by Maria Irene Fornés

MARION. I need my child. I need my child, Minne. I need that child in my arms and I don't see a way I could ever have him again. He has been irrevocably taken from me. There is nothing I could do that would bring him back to me. I have begged him to let me see him. I have gone on my knees. I have offered myself to him. I have offered my life to him. He won't listen. He won't forgive me. I'm at his mercy. . . .

Here is an example of an aside.

EXAMPLE

from *Romeo and Juliet* by William Shakespeare

JULIET (*to herself*): O Romeo, Romeo! wherefore art thou Romeo?
Deny thy father and refuse thy name!
Or, if thou wilt not, be but sworn my love,
And I'll no longer be a Capulet.
ROMEO (*aside*): Shall I hear more, or shall I speak at this?

DESCRIPTION

The **dramatic devices** *monologue* and *soliloquy* mean essentially the same thing. In a monologue or soliloquy, a character speaks when he or she is alone on the stage. Occasionally, other characters may be present. If this is the case, however, the other characters are unaware of what is being said.

Monologues and soliloquies are often important, dramatic moments in a play, because they focus on one character's thoughts. In the first example above, Marion tells her innermost thoughts and reveals the grief she feels after having been separated from her child.

Dramatic Devices, continued

In an *aside,* a character turns to the audience to say something that the other characters on stage are not supposed to hear. Asides sometimes add humor to a play. In *Romeo and Juliet,* Romeo asks himself (or the audience) if he dares interrupt Juliet's impassioned speech. Juliet is not supposed to hear him say this.

DEFINITION

Dramatic devices are tools a dramatist may use to add interest to a play. In a *monologue* or a *soliloquy,* a character speaks when alone on the stage or apart from any other actors. An *aside* is a remark not intended to be heard by other characters.

Drama

Plot and Subplot

This diagram shows the relationship between the main plot and subplots in *Romeo and Juliet*.

EXAMPLE

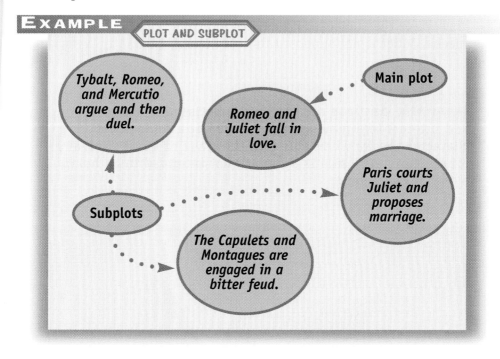

PLOT AND SUBPLOT

Tybalt, Romeo, and Mercutio argue and then duel.

Romeo and Juliet fall in love.

Main plot

Paris courts Juliet and proposes marriage.

Subplots

The Capulets and Montagues are engaged in a bitter feud.

DESCRIPTION

Plot is what happens in a play. A **subplot** is less important than the main plot. Understanding the events of one or more subplots can strengthen your understanding of the main plot. Sometimes the action of the subplot will mirror, or imitate, the action of the main plot. For example, Paris's courting of Juliet mirrors Romeo's courting of Juliet.

Quite often, the action of a subplot will somehow influence the action of the main plot. For example, the feud between the Capulets and the Montagues complicates the love affair between Romeo, a Montague, and Juliet, a Capulet.

DEFINITION

The main **plot** contains the central action of the play. Some plays have one or more **subplots.** These are less important than the main plot and can enhance your understanding of the action and theme.

Stage Directions

Stage directions help the actors interpret a scene. They can help readers interpret a scene as well. Note how these characters show their dislike for each other.

EXAMPLE

from *The Importance of Being Earnest* by Oscar Wilde

CECILY: . . . May I offer you some tea, Miss Fairfax?

GWENDOLEN (*with elaborate politeness*): Thank you. (*Aside.*)
   Detestable girl! But I require tea!

> **How the character sounds**

CECILY (*sweetly*): Sugar?

GWENDOLEN (*superciliously*): No, thank you. Sugar is not
   fashionable any more. (CECILY *looks angrily at her, takes
   up the tongs and puts four lumps of sugar into the cup.*)

CECILY (*severely*): Cake or bread and butter?

GWENDOLEN (*in a bored manner*): Bread and butter,
   please. Cake is rarely seen at the best houses nowadays.

CECILY (*cuts a very large slice of cake and puts it on the tray*):
   Hand that to Miss Fairfax.

> **What the character does or feels**

MERRIMAN *does so, and goes out with footman.*

GWENDOLEN *drinks the tea and makes a grimace. Puts down
   cup at once, reaches out her hand to the bread and butter, looks
   at it, and finds it is cake. Rises in indignation.*

DESCRIPTION

Stage directions are instructions to the actors and director. They tell how to perform the play, including how the stage should look and how the actors should move and talk. In almost all scripts, stage directions are written in italics and often enclosed in parentheses. In the example above, notice that how the characters are directed to act and speak indicates their feelings for each other.

DEFINITION

Stage directions are instructions by a playwright to the actors and director that tell how to stage and perform a play.

507

Structure

Here is the traditional way that the action of a play is organized, using *Romeo and Juliet* as an example.

EXAMPLE

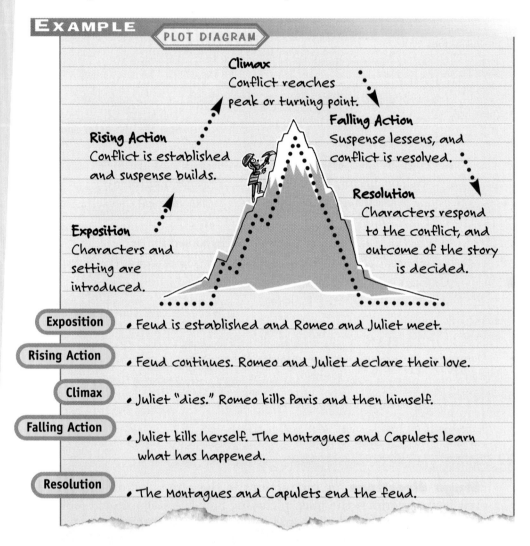

PLOT DIAGRAM

Climax
Conflict reaches peak or turning point.

Rising Action
Conflict is established and suspense builds.

Falling Action
Suspense lessens, and conflict is resolved.

Resolution
Characters respond to the conflict, and outcome of the story is decided.

Exposition
Characters and setting are introduced.

Exposition • Feud is established and Romeo and Juliet meet.

Rising Action • Feud continues. Romeo and Juliet declare their love.

Climax • Juliet "dies." Romeo kills Paris and then himself.

Falling Action • Juliet kills herself. The Montagues and Capulets learn what has happened.

Resolution • The Montagues and Capulets end the feud.

DESCRIPTION

The organization of a play is called its **structure.** Almost all plays are structured around a plot. The plot itself usually has five parts: exposition, rising action, climax, falling action, and resolution.

DEFINITION

The **structure** of a play is its organization.

Theme

In this short excerpt from Act II, scene 2 of *Romeo and Juliet,* Juliet tells Romeo what it means to love.

EXAMPLE

from *Romeo and Juliet* by William Shakespeare

ROMEO: Lady, by yonder blessèd moon I swear,
    That tips with silver all these fruit-tree tops—
JULIET: O, swear not by the moon, th' inconstant moon,
    That monthly changes in her circled orb.
    Lest that thy love prove likewise variable.
ROMEO: What shall I swear by?
JULIET: Do not swear at all. . . .

Clue
to theme
statement

DESCRIPTION

Theme is the central idea of a work, or the playwright's message for the audience. Some plays have many themes, but one is usually more important or more fully developed than the others. This is called the *major theme*. The others are called the *minor themes*.

To find a theme, first look at the general topic or big idea of the play. (Very often this big idea relates to the central conflict of the plot.) Then, look for what the characters say and do that relates to the big idea. Finally, make a theme statement that explains the author's point about a topic. In Act II, Juliet says that she does not want Romeo's love to be like the moon. Her speech foreshadows a major theme: True love does not change as the moon does monthly but remains steadfast.

DEFINITION

Theme is a statement about life around which the playwright builds the play.

Drama

509

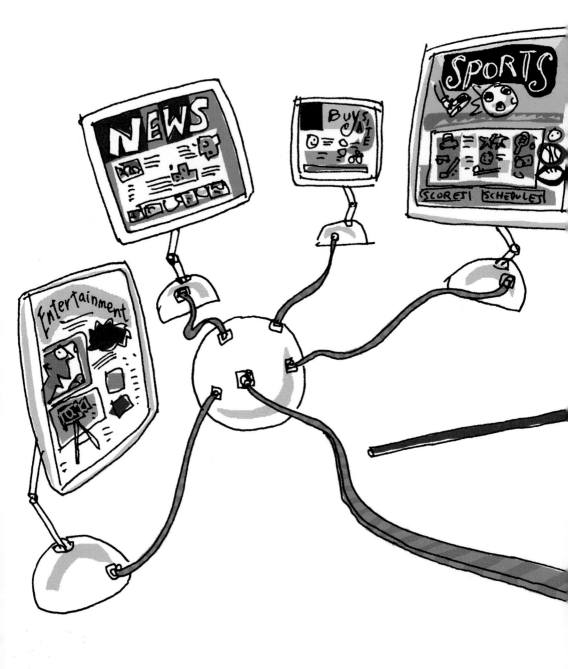

Reading on the Internet

- Introduction to Reading on the Internet
- Reading a Website
- Elements of the Internet

CLICK

Internet

Introduction to Reading on the Internet

The Internet is a vast network that connects computers all over the world. Originally developed by the U.S. Department of Defense in the 1970s and meant for scientists, universities, and government, it did not become readily available to the general public until the 1990s. The **World Wide Web** became part of the Internet in 1991.

Today millions of people have access to the Internet through computers in businesses, homes, schools, and libraries, and at Internet cafes, which are places where people can access the Web for a small fee.

This chapter provides information about the World Wide Web, how to find what you want on the Web, and how to evaluate the information you find. It also provides definitions of terms you might have run across in your explorations.

You begin to look at any site on the Web with the home page. Look on this book page as your home page for starting your exploration of strategies and tools for reading on the Internet.

Reading a Website

Many of the skills you use to read textbooks will help you read a website. The sidebars, bold typefaces, icons, and color-coded terms that link you to other pages in your textbooks resemble websites more than they do regular book pages.

Of course, websites work differently from books. You read books in the order in which the information appears. Websites, on the other hand, resemble . . . a web! You can follow the information in any direction, clicking on a link to take you wherever it and your curiosity want to take you.

Websites differ from books and other publications in another important way: quality of information. Books, while subject to error, are carefully edited, and publishers try to uphold high standards of accuracy and expertise. Anyone can have a website. Once you click your way into a website, whether it's a reputable one or a random site you've never heard of before, you need to know how to evaluate what you find there. Reading a website demands that you use the reading process and your critical eye.

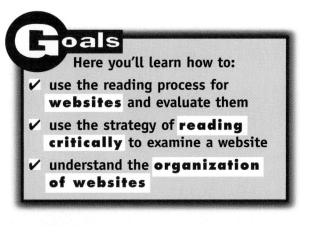

Goals

Here you'll learn how to:

✔ use the reading process for **websites** and evaluate them

✔ use the strategy of **reading critically** to examine a website

✔ understand the **organization of websites**

Internet

Before Reading

Think of a bird that flies over a lake, checks everything out, and then dives toward what it wants to see. That's how most people use a website. They scan it for information and then click on what they want to see. Jakob Nielsen, one of the world's experts on the Internet, found that people do three things when they use the Web: *collect* and *compare* multiple pieces of information (about websites, products, services, information) in order to *choose* which item to use or buy.

A Set a Purpose

Very few people log on to the Web without a purpose. They might log on to check their email or grab some information from an encyclopedia, but in either case they have a purpose. The first step to effective use and reading of the Web is to set a purpose for yourself.

Suppose that your teacher has asked you to write a paper about the life and work of a major European painter. Your teacher provides you with a list of artists, but none is familiar. When you ask someone about the list, he or she immediately spots the Dutch artist "Johannes Vermeer" and starts talking with great passion about the Vermeer exhibit at the National Gallery of Art in Washington, D.C. You decide to check out Vermeer.

The first general questions to ask yourself are these:

What terms should I use to conduct my search?

How can I find the information I need?

What kind of website is most likely to offer what I need?

Then, begin your investigation by asking these more specific questions:

■ **When and where did Johannes Vermeer live?**

■ **What kind of life did he have?**

■ **What kind of pictures did he paint?**

■ **What are some of his most important paintings?**

Obviously other questions will arise as you begin to answer these first ones. Keep a pad of paper handy so you can write down these further questions or the other information that you find.

◀NOTES▶

VERMEER PROJECT
1. When and where did he live?
2. What kind of life did he have?
3. What kind of pictures did he paint?
4. What are some of his most important paintings?

These questions might include, "How do I copy one of his paintings to use in a presentation I might want to make?" This brings up another question to keep in mind when using the Web: "Is it legal to copy and use material from people's websites?" The quick answer is that it depends. In most cases, sites will tell you whether it is okay or not. Use your notepaper to keep track of various addresses on the Internet. These addresses are called URLs. (URL stands for *U*niform *R*esource *L*ocator.)

Internet

See What's Out There

The first step in researching a project with the Web is to see what's out there. For this, use a **search engine,** a program that helps you find information on a computer. It helps to know the strengths and weaknesses of various search engines. For example, some allow you to look for images. Some require that you search by asking questions instead of typing in key words. Other search engines offer brief descriptions of what you will find on a site if you click on a link. Others just offer the site's name and link.

Here is one page of a search for the topic "Johannes Vermeer" using the Google search engine. Note that there are several links that look useful.

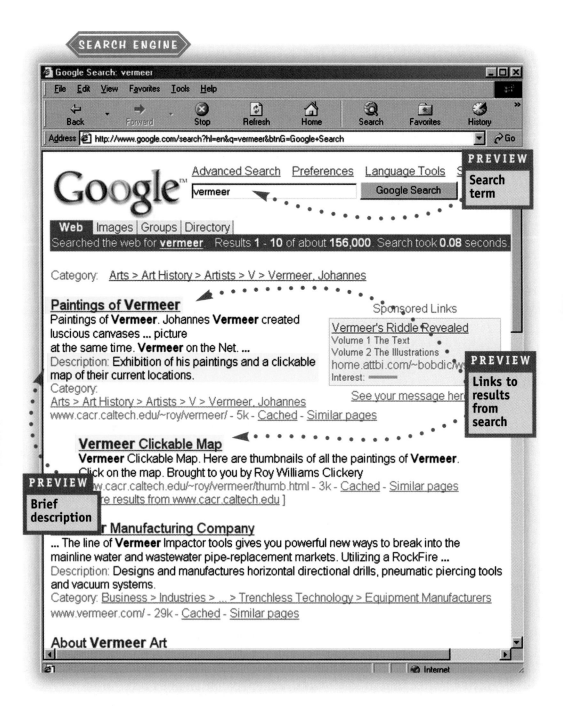

PREVIEW
Search term

PREVIEW
Links to results from search

PREVIEW
Brief description

Stay Focused

The results of your initial search will show you enough information to decide where you should start. Some sites exist to sell, others to inform, and others to exhibit or display. Some descriptions are in languages other than English. You can waste a lot of time clicking on links that look interesting but are not related to your purpose. Take some time to look at the site and decide on the most useful links before you start off in all kinds of directions.

B Preview

When you preview a website home page, look for these things:

Preview Checklist

✔ the name and overall appearance
✔ the main menu or table of contents
✔ the source or sponsor
✔ any description of what it contains
✔ any images or graphics that create a feeling
✔ the purpose of the site

Internet

Start with a site that looks like it will have a lot of information, such as the National Gallery of Art.

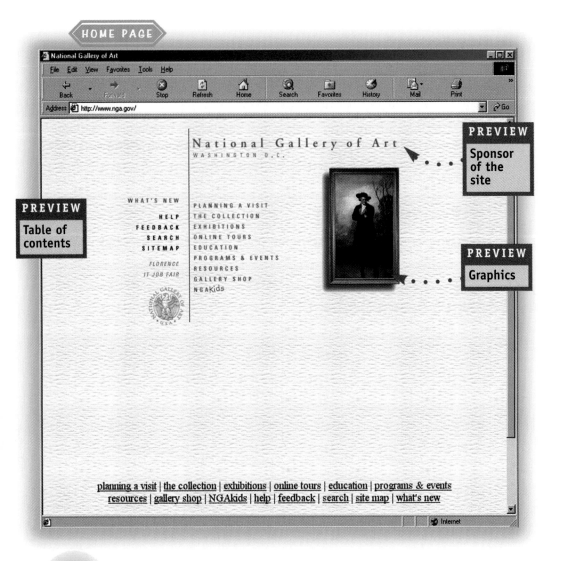

National Gallery of Art

File Edit View Favorites Tools Help

Back Forward Stop Refresh Home Search Favorites History Mail Print

Address http://www.nga.gov/ Go

PREVIEW
Sponsor of the site

National Gallery of Art
WASHINGTON D.C.

PREVIEW
Table of contents

WHAT'S NEW   PLANNING A VISIT
        HELP   THE COLLECTION
    FEEDBACK   EXHIBITIONS
      SEARCH   ONLINE TOURS
      SITEMAP   EDUCATION
                    PROGRAMS & EVENTS
    FLORENCE   RESOURCES
    IT JOB FAIR   GALLERY SHOP
                    NGAKids

PREVIEW
Graphics

planning a visit | the collection | exhibitions | online tours | education | programs & events
resources | gallery shop | NGAkids | help | feedback | search | site map | what's new

Internet

C Plan

Even though the National Gallery home page does not contain a lot of words, it offers several potentially useful categories. It tells you nothing about Vermeer, but such categories as "Exhibitions" and "Online Tours" suggest this site provides useful resources.

You could try "Exhibitions," but the exhibition for Vermeer was a long time ago. What if you search "The Collection" to see what they have by or about Vermeer?

COLLECTION PAGE

Johannes Vermeer

File Edit View Favorites Tools Help

Back   Forward   Stop   Refresh   Home   Search   Favorites   History   Mail   Print   Edit

Address http://www.nga.gov/cgi-bin/psearch

the collection

NATIONAL GALLERY OF ART

WHAT'S NEW
HELP
FEEDBACK
SEARCH
SITEMAP

FLORENCE
IT JOB FAIR

planning a visit
the collection
exhibitions
online tours
education
programs & events
resources
gallery shop
nga kids

Artist

Johannes Vermeer
Also known as Jan Vermeer; Vermeer van Delft
Dutch, 1632 - 1675

Biography
Works by associated artists (2)
Works after this artist (2)

Painting

- Girl with a Flute, probably 1665/1670, (Attributed to), 1942.9.98 (image available)
- Girl with the Red Hat, c. 1665/1666, 1937.1.53 (image available)
- A Lady Writing, c. 1665, 1962.10.1 (image available)
- Woman Holding a Balance, c. 1664, 1942.9.97 (image available)

Done   Internet

Internet

When you search for Vermeer, you find a whole page devoted to him. Now think back to the questions you are trying to answer:

■ When and where did Johannes Vermeer live?

■ What kind of life did he have?

■ What kind of pictures did he paint?

■ What are some of his most important paintings?

The results of your preview confirm that this is a useful site, one that will provide all the information you need for this assignment. Now you can begin following promising links to find answers to your research questions.

Reading Critically

One of the most important questions to answer as you begin to read a website is, "How much can I trust the information on this site?" In this case, you can assume that the National Gallery of Art is a reliable source. Its only motivation is to promote art and maintain its reputation as one of the leading museums in the United States. Still, it's easy to jump from one site to another when surfing the Web, so stay alert and take time to evaluate each site's credibility. That's why you need to **read critically.**

READING INTERNET SITES

1. *Preview the site.*

2. *Evaluate the type and quality of the material, as well as the organization of the site. Will it be easy to use?*

3. *Review your purpose. Does the site appear to have the information you need for your assignment?*

4. *If the information you want is contained on a few pages, you might consider printing them so you can take notes from them or highlight passages.*

5. *Write down the URL (address) of the site and the date on which you accessed it. You may need to provide a bibliography for your report, which should include this information.*

6. *Finally, create a profile of the site by looking critically into its sponsor(s), its most recent update, its point of view, and its level of expertise.*

WEBSITE PROFILER

URL:	
SPONSOR	DATE
POINT OF VIEW	EXPERTISE
REACTION/EVALUATION	

During Reading

Let's say you clicked on "Biography" from the National Gallery "Collection" page. That takes you to a two-page summary of Vermeer's life, which contains answers to some of your questions. It might be a good idea to print this biography so you can make notes or highlight the information that addresses your questions.

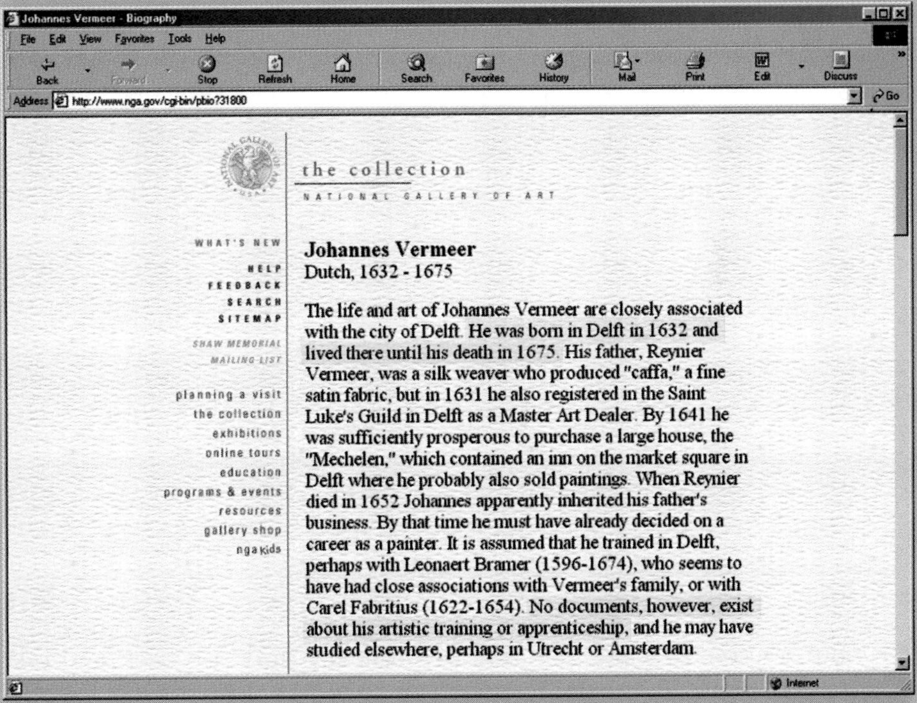

D Read with a Purpose

Keep your research questions in mind as you read. Once you find a promising site, collect all the information you can from it. You might want to take notes on each of your major research questions:

- ■ Vermeer's life
- ■ Vermeer's paintings
- ■ important works

Take Notes

After reading the entire Vermeer biography section of the website, you have the answers to several of your questions. Take notes on information with a note-taking tool such as a Web. Here's how one reader started to fill in a Web.

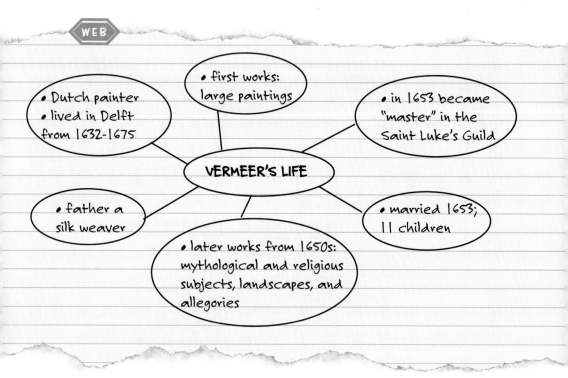

WEB

- first works: large paintings
- Dutch painter
- lived in Delft from 1632-1675
- in 1653 became "master" in the Saint Luke's Guild

VERMEER'S LIFE

- father a silk weaver
- married 1653; 11 children
- later works from 1650s: mythological and religious subjects, landscapes, and allegories

But you haven't yet seen any of Vermeer's work. Go back and take another look at the "Collection" on page 519. Notice that there are four available images of his paintings. Better check those out! They will give you a good idea about some of his works.

Don't Plagiarize

It's easy to copy and paste what you find on a website. The problem is that those words *are not your words.* Plagiarism means you are stealing someone else's words and ideas and offering them as your own. At times, you will want to use a direct quotation. Use quotation marks to indicate any words that are not yours but are taken from your source. Be sure to mark where you found the quote so you can add the information to your bibliography. But the best policy is to paraphrase the information you find and put it into your own words.

How Websites Are Organized

Think for a minute about how websites are organized. This knowledge will not only help you use the site better, but it will keep the information organized in your head and notes. Nearly all website designers start by using pencil and paper to outline their sites. They spend a lot of time figuring out how to categorize information. If they don't come up with the right categories, users will be confused, give up, and not return to the site.

If you draw a diagram of the National Gallery of Art home page, it will certainly not look like a book. The pages in a book follow an orderly chronological sequence. Instead, a website will look like what it is called: a web. You can click on a navigation link at the bottom or side of a page and jump off to any one of several directions. It's like being able to beam yourself anywhere in space with the click of a mouse.

ORGANIZATION OF A WEBSITE VS. A BOOK

A website almost resembles a solar system, with each "planet" providing more and more information through its links. Some home pages offer a site map or other organizational view of its design. This is often worth taking a look at because it can sometimes help you locate information.

E Connect

Eventually you need to do with the Web what you try to do with everything else you read: connect with its ideas and content. Take a moment to consider the point of view offered by the site. Then, consider your own opinion of Vermeer and his work.

Part of connecting with a site means deciding whether you want to return to it again in the future. Web browsers have a list of "Favorites" or "Bookmarks." These are websites you like so much that you want to be able to get back there again. Completing a Website Profiler allows you to form an intelligent opinion about the overall site, and it has a place for you to give your own reaction to the site.

WEBSITE PROFILER

NATIONAL GALLERY OF ART

URL: http://www.nga.gov

SPONSOR United States	DATE has a 2002 copyright date
POINT OF VIEW The gallery promotes the work of classical and modern artists. Masters such as Vermeer have a featured place within the museum and on the website.	EXPERTISE The museum is run by experts in the field.

REACTION/EVALUATION Site was excellent. Very nicely designed; you can move around quickly. Includes quality information and images. Like the viewing, interactive options for the images. Would come back just to take more of the virtual exhibit tours.

By adding a Website Profiler to your notebook, you will have a complete record of the site if you want to return to it again. You do not have to create such detailed notes for every site you visit, but doing so will help you to have a record of any site you want to include in a bibliography.

After Reading

The Internet offers you only one vehicle to get you to your destination. You have now spent some time researching Vermeer online for an art or history class. You might also have consulted books and magazine articles about him. Could you write a paper on Vermeer now?

F Pause and Reflect

Here are a few good questions to ask before you leave a website:

Looking Back

- Did I find the information I was looking for?
- Was I confused or puzzled by anything I read?
- What else would I like to know about this subject?

G Reread

Rereading a website does not always make sense, but delving further into the material on a site often does. Use new search terms and questions as you reread. Each time you read research, you are able to pay attention to something different: a fact, a date, a connection, something you didn't notice before but which now inspires new questions.

Rereading Strategy: Skimming

Skimming is a good way to evaluate the quality of information on a website and also to find information on a site once you get there. Here are some tips to help with skimming a website.

Internet

525

1. Look for general ideas.
Pay attention to these elements:

❏ *the source and purpose of the site*

❏ *major headings in boldface type*

❏ *subheadings that show categories of information*

❏ *repeated words*

❏ *any links to visuals*

❏ *domain names, such as .edu, .org, and .com. (Only educational institutions have the domain name .edu.)*

2. Don't read everything.
Skip over information that doesn't meet your needs or seems to be inaccurate or inappropriate. This information might include these things:

❏ *sites in a language you can't read*

❏ *sites that exist only to advertise something, such as a restaurant, hotel, or product*

❏ *sites whose purpose seems likely to promote hate*

❏ *sites with grammatical or spelling errors*

❏ *sites with "dead" links (that is, links that are discontinued or not working)*

H Remember

If the site is a good one, you'll want to remember it. Use your browser to create a bookmark so you can find it easily in the future. Despite the millions of websites out there, good ones are invaluable because they save you time and you can trust them. You can also create folders within your browser's "Favorites" section. If you regularly look for information about a topic, you should organize these links into a folder (for example, Art Links) for quick reference.

In addition to bookmarking the sites you like, you also need to remember the material you find. Here are a couple of ways to do that.

1. Email a Friend

Email the URL to a friend, and describe the site. Compare what you find on a site with what your friends find. This may even help you better understand your subject. When you correspond with others, you also make new connections that allow you to understand the material in new ways.

2. Organize What You Learned

You may have taken hurried notes while reading a site, but organizing your information forces you to remember it even more. Here's one way you might organize the information you discovered about Johannes Vermeer.

TIMELINE

1632	after 1652	April 1653	Dec. 29, 1653	1675
born and baptized Oct. 31	inherited father's business	married Catharina Bolnes	became a master in St. Luke's Guild	died in debt, leaving wife and 11 children

Summing Up

Use the reading process and the strategy of **reading critically** when you read a website. Search to find out what sites might be useful. Because of the **organization of a website,** remember to stay focused. To evaluate and get the most from a website, use such tools as these:

■ Website Profiler

■ Web

■ Timeline

Try the rereading strategy of **skimming** to find specific information and to evaluate a website.

Internet

Elements of the Internet

The Internet works differently from the way a book does. Once you type in a website address (URL), you have the feeling you are traveling to a place. When you arrive at that virtual place, you are part of a community that shares an interest in what that online location offers. That place might be a chat room, a discussion area, or a site that offers a virtual theme park of ideas and smaller communities. You could say the Internet is to a book what a mall is to one store.

To use the information on the Internet well, however, you need to know what the different elements are, what they offer, and how they work. In short, you need to know how to find what you need and how to read it once you find it. Here, you will learn about some of these elements.

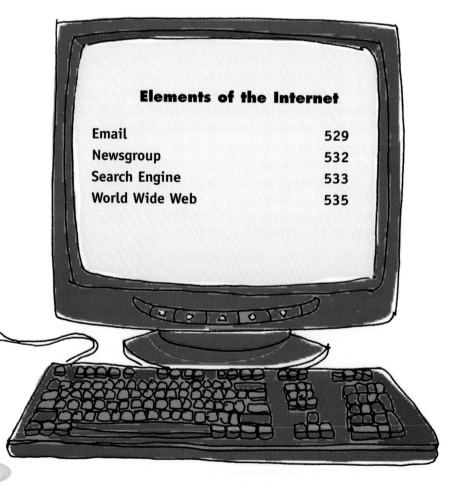

Elements of the Internet

Email

Here is a typical email message or letter.

EXAMPLE   EMAIL

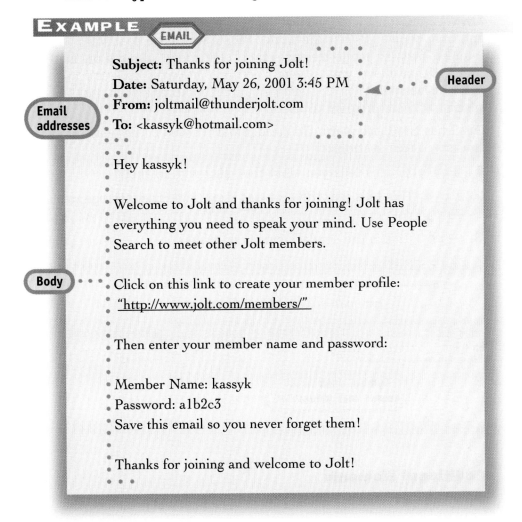

Header

Email addresses

Subject: Thanks for joining Jolt!
Date: Saturday, May 26, 2001 3:45 PM
From: joltmail@thunderjolt.com
To: <kassyk@hotmail.com>

Hey kassyk!

Welcome to Jolt and thanks for joining! Jolt has everything you need to speak your mind. Use People Search to meet other Jolt members.

Body

Click on this link to create your member profile: "http://www.jolt.com/members/"

Then enter your member name and password:

Member Name: kassyk
Password: a1b2c3
Save this email so you never forget them!

Thanks for joining and welcome to Jolt!

Internet

529

Email, continued

DESCRIPTION

Email (electronic mail) allows you to send and receive messages to and from people all over the world. People who have common interests may exchange messages in a "chat room," a place on the Internet that allows you to send electronic messages back and forth. "Instant messaging" is similar to email but requires a separate, special software program to use it.

Email has two basic parts: the header and the body. The header consists of four sections:

1. Subject: This tells you what the email will be about.

2. Date: This tells you the date and exact time the message was sent to you.

3. From: This is the sender's email address.

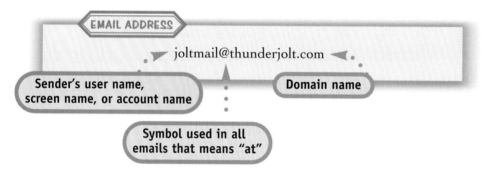

4. To: This is your email address.

Additional Elements

Fwd: This abbreviation means the message was forwarded, or sent on, from another address.

Attachment: When you send an email, you can attach different types of files (for example, documents and digital photos) that the recipient can open. Be sure recipients have the program they need to open any files you send them.

Signature: This appears at the bottom of an email message. Signatures include phone numbers and other contact information.

Email, continued

Using Email Wisely

Email is one of the most useful applications of the Internet, but it can also cause problems. You can avoid these if you use email wisely. Here are a few suggestions:

● Don't send messages you will regret. Angry emails, called "flames," are often written in ALL CAPS, which is the online equivalent of screaming.

● Think twice before sending information that could embarrass you or others. You can't control who sees an email message. Your friend might accidentally forward your private note to others who might not be as careful to respect your privacy.

● Omit any details about where you live or how to reach you. Never agree to meet anyone you don't know. While you usually know who you are writing to or hearing from, you can't always be sure about people you meet online. So, play it safe and don't give out any personal information.

● Be cautious about opening email or downloading attachments from someone you don't know. Your computer could be infected with a virus. So, if you don't know who sent you a message, be sure you have virus protection software on your computer before opening emails from people you don't know.

DEFINITION

Email is an electronic message sent from one computer to another. Its two basic parts are the header and the body.

Internet

Newsgroup

A newsgroup is a discussion group for people with the same interests who can participate online.

EXAMPLE

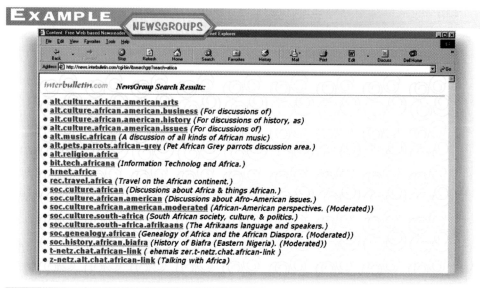

DESCRIPTION

A **newsgroup** topic consists of several different pieces of information. Here is one example from the list above:

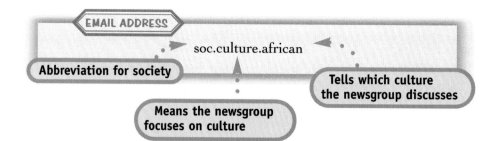

If you were investigating South Africa's culture, you could type in "soc.culture.african" or "soc.culture.south-africa" and post your questions to the newsgroup. Participants in that discussion group could then respond to you directly through email or post their comments to the newsgroup.

DEFINITION

A **newsgroup** is an online discussion area created for people with a specific interest in common.

Search Engine

Before searching for information on the Internet, ask yourself whether it is the most effective way of finding what you want. Often a good dictionary or encyclopedia will provide the answer you seek in half the time. You might find information you need through specialized online databases, such as Newsbank or Infotrac, to which your school or public library subscribes. In other words, *you* are the most important search engine.

When you do decide to use the Internet to track down information, a search engine can help you.

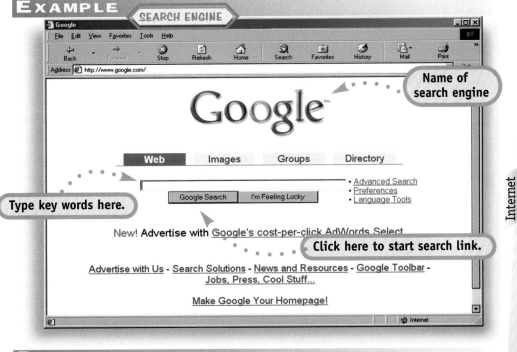

EXAMPLE

Type key words here.

Click here to start search link.

Name of search engine

DESCRIPTION

A **search engine** is an online tool that helps you find information on the Internet. After you type in search terms, the search engine returns addresses that match your request.

Each search engine has different rules. Some search engines ask you to type in a question. Others want you to type in key words and use AND (for example, women AND sports or women + sports). The most important aspect of a search, however, is the precision of your search terms. You cannot conduct an efficient or successful search if your terms are too general.

533

Search Engine, continued

When you finally do get results from your search, you must evaluate the quality and reliability of the results. Here are a few samples from a Google search for "physics and roller coasters:"

EXAMPLE · SEARCH ENGINE

Once you find sites and search engines you trust, create bookmarks for them so you can find them quickly when you need them.

DEFINITION

A **search engine** is an online tool that helps you find information and other specific online resources.

World Wide Web

Many people believe that the Web is the most important discovery since television.

EXAMPLE — EXPLORATORIUM WEB PAGE

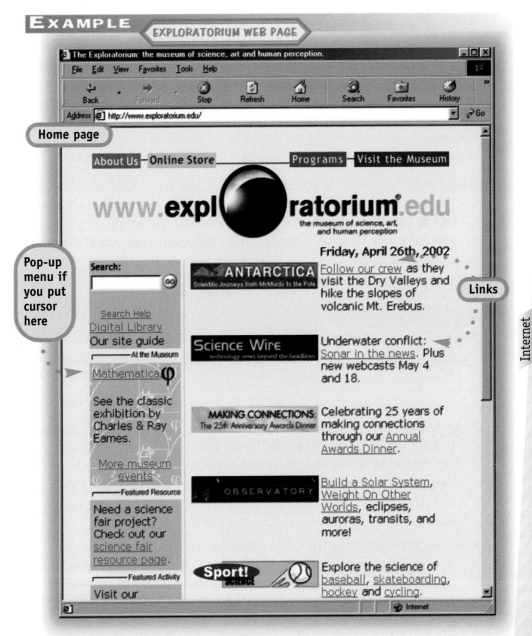

Home page

Pop-up menu if you put cursor here

Links

Internet

World Wide Web, continued

DESCRIPTION

The **World Wide Web** is a system of computers around the world that are linked and able to share files. The home page for the Exploratorium gives you a good idea of what the World Wide Web offers. Through the Exploratorium website, you can read, listen to, or view scientific information about almost anything. The *home page* serves as a table of contents for the site, which is made up of individual, linked screens or web pages. The home page gives you a sense of what is on the site and offers different ways to navigate the site.

Here is a list of the most common elements of a website:

Browser: A browser is software that you use to explore websites. The key features of a browser are arranged in the navigation bar at the top of a window. The most important elements are probably the back and forward buttons. These help you navigate the site. Additional, more advanced features appear in the pull-down menus.

Navigation bar

Features: Websites include various features such as pop-up menus to help you navigate the site, boxes into which you can enter search terms or your email address, and various arrows and buttons to help you navigate a site more easily. Take time to identify the different features in each site and learn how each site uses them.

Links: Links take you from one place to another. They are usually indicated by underlining or highlighting. They can take you to a different page within the website you are viewing or to a different website altogether. This highlighted information is called *hypertext*. When you move the cursor, look for the little icon of the hand to tell you when a word or image is a link.

World Wide Web, continued

Plug-in Applications: These programs allow you to access files and use your browser's multimedia capabilities. With the right plug-ins, you can play movies, listen to music, and play games on the Web.

URL (Uniform Resource Locator): This is the term used to describe the address of a website (for example, http://www.exploratorium.edu). You type this in to go to a website. The last part of it—.com, .org, .edu—indicates the type of site. The ending of the Exploratorium URL signals that it is educational. *Org* refers to an organization, and *com* refers to a business or commercial enterprise.

DEFINITION

The **World Wide Web** is the system of computers around the world that are joined and able to share files.

Internet

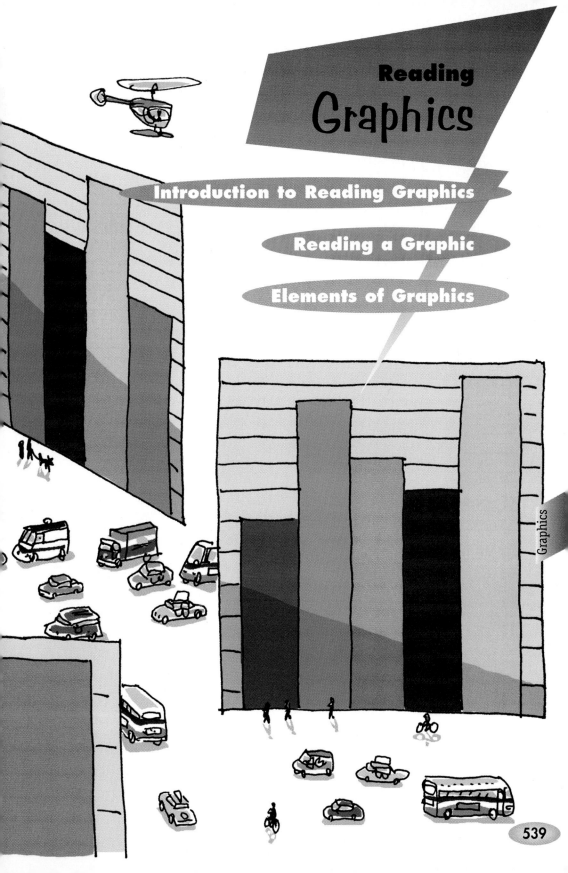

Reading
Graphics

Graphics

Introduction to Reading Graphics

Much information you read every day is in visual form. Graphics are a kind of shorthand for showing what it would take many words to tell. For example, you can see right away how a sports figure in a news photo is feeling without ever reading the news story. A cartoon portrays a point of view more quickly than an essay can. Pie charts, tables, and diagrams show facts or statistics that would take pages of text to explain. This handbook even shows you how to make simple graphic organizers to record and organize information.

You have been looking at graphics all your life, but can you truly "read" them? If you want to learn how to get the most from the visuals you encounter every day, read up on them here.

Reading a Graphic

You read different kinds of information all day long. Often this information appears in the form of graphs, charts, timelines, maps, photographs, or illustrations. Graphics are used for at least three purposes: to explain, to persuade, and to tell stories. Just because graphics are "visual pictures" doesn't mean you can relax when you read them. Each graphic makes unique demands on you as a reader, who must choose the strategy that will work best.

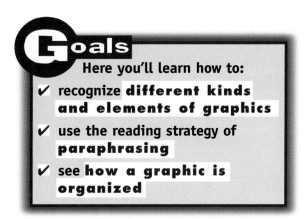

Goals

Here you'll learn how to:

✔ recognize **different kinds and elements of graphics**

✔ use the reading strategy of **paraphrasing**

✔ see **how a graphic is organized**

Before Reading

The process you use to read other texts can help you read graphic information as well. Many graphics contain words as well as visuals. Don't ignore the words or the smaller details such as the color or symbols used. Using the reading process can direct your attention to all the details you must "read" if you are to understand.

Graphics

A Set a Purpose

In most cases, you already have a purpose when you encounter a graphic. For instance, you might be reading a newspaper article about the latest predictions for college graduates. Your purpose in reading this article is to learn how it might affect you. Or you might be reading a magazine article about the new census, which says that the structure of the American family has changed dramatically since the last census. Or you might be studying a chart in your history book.

Two specific questions can help you set your purpose when reading a graphic:

Setting a Purpose

- What is the graphic about?
- What does it say about the subject?

B Preview

When you first look at a page of words, you know where to begin: the top left corner. Graphics often lack such structure. As you preview a graphic, look for:

Preview Checklist

✔ the title or heading
✔ any captions or background text
✔ any labels and column and row headings
✔ any colors, patterns, icons, or other symbols
✔ any keys or legends
✔ the scale or unit of measurement
✔ the source of both the graphic and its data

Now use this checklist to preview "Digital Kids."

1.

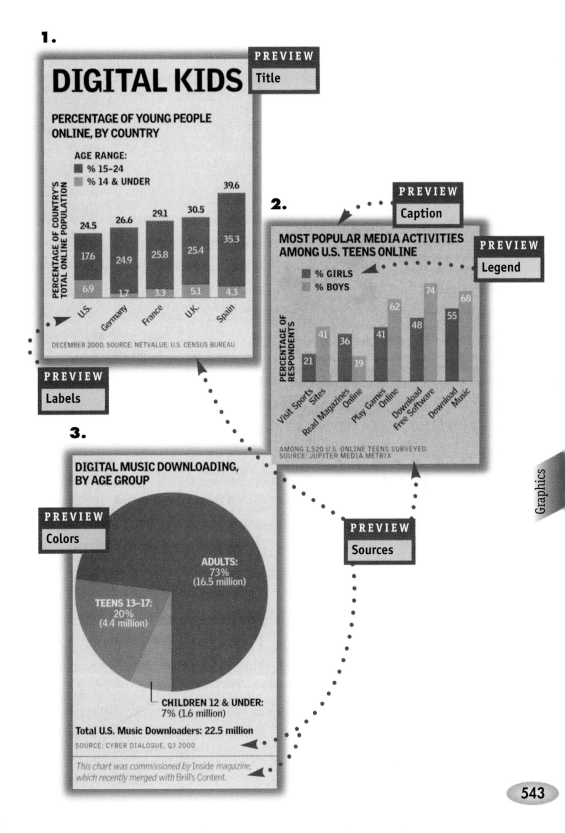

DIGITAL KIDS

PREVIEW **Title**

PERCENTAGE OF YOUNG PEOPLE
ONLINE, BY COUNTRY

AGE RANGE:
■ % 15–24
■ % 14 & UNDER

PERCENTAGE OF COUNTRY'S
TOTAL ONLINE POPULATION

	U.S.	Germany	France	U.K.	Spain
	24.5	26.6	29.1	30.5	39.6
	17.6	24.9	25.8	25.4	35.3
	6.9	1.7	3.3	5.1	4.3

DECEMBER 2000. SOURCE: NETVALUE; U.S. CENSUS BUREAU

PREVIEW **Labels**

2.

PREVIEW **Caption**

MOST POPULAR MEDIA ACTIVITIES
AMONG U.S. TEENS ONLINE

PREVIEW **Legend**

■ % GIRLS
■ % BOYS

PERCENTAGE OF
RESPONDENTS

	Visit Sports Sites	Read Magazines Online	Play Games Online	Download Free Software	Download Music
	21	36	41	48	55
	41	19	62	74	68

AMONG 1,520 U.S. ONLINE TEENS SURVEYED.
SOURCE: JUPITER MEDIA METRIX

3.

DIGITAL MUSIC DOWNLOADING,
BY AGE GROUP

PREVIEW **Colors**

ADULTS:
73%
(16.5 million)

TEENS 13–17:
20%
(4.4 million)

CHILDREN 12 & UNDER:
7% (1.6 million)

Total U.S. Music Downloaders: 22.5 million

SOURCE: CYBER DIALOGUE, Q3 2000

PREVIEW **Sources**

This chart was commissioned by Inside *magazine,
which recently merged with Brill's Content.*

Graphics

Plan

A quick preview gives you a good sense of the information presented. The three graphics provide a visual explanation of our increasingly digital world, one that reveals several surprises.

■ Spain has the greatest percentage of young people online.

■ In the U.S. more boys than girls download free software.

■ Adults download more music than teens do.

Now take a closer look at what the graphics show. Use the following five-step plan to help you read any graphic:

PLAN FOR READING A GRAPHIC

1. *Scan the graphic to develop an overall impression of its content and possible meaning.*

2. *Read all of the text, including any captions or other text.*

3. *Tell in your own words what the graphic shows.*

4. *Think about the quality, meaning, and purpose of the information. Ask yourself, "Is the information in this graphic from a reliable source? Does the information seem unbiased and complete?"*

5. *Make a connection with the graphic. What are the implications for your own life? How does the graphic relate to other information in the chapter, article, or book?*

The key strategy for reading graphics is paraphrasing, or restating the information in your own words.

Reading Strategy: **Paraphrasing**

Paraphrasing means that you put the information in a graphic into your own words. This strategy, which can also help you understand articles, poems, and reports, makes you a more active reader. As you read, ask, "How would I explain that in my own words?" Paraphrasing not only increases your understanding, it improves your ability to remember what you read later on when you need to write about or discuss the information.

Use a Paraphrase Chart like the one below to walk you through this process.

PARAPHRASE CHART

TITLE	MY PARAPHRASE
MY THOUGHTS	

Graphics

During Reading

Now go back and take a closer look at the graphics on page 543. Remember to read the text included with them. One common mistake readers make with graphics is that they "look at," rather than "read," what's there. Say the title aloud. Then, read and say the captions and labels. That way you'll be sure not to skip them. Remember to concentrate on what the information says. Get ready to react to it so that you see how it relates to your original purpose.

D Read with a Purpose

Remember that your purpose is to find out what a graphic is about and what it means. As a first step, read the graphic more closely. The heading for each graphic may be clearer if you restate it as a question. Instead of "Percentage of Young People Online, by Country," ask yourself, "What percentage of kids around the world is online?" and "Which countries have the most kids online?"

As you try to answer your questions, you'll find that others arise. For example, maybe you wonder why the bars in the first graph are wider than those in the second or what the different colors represent. If the graphic is really complex, consider making notes right on the page or on a sticky note.

What would it look like if you jotted down your interpretation of the first graph? Here's how one reader paraphrased the information:

PARAPHRASE CHART

TITLE	MY PARAPHRASE
"Digital Kids"	Out of five major western countries, Spain has the highest percentage of "young people" online. Young people in this case means under age 24. Spain has a total of 39.6% of its young people online, compared to only 24.5% of America's youth (which earns us a fifth place ranking behind the U.K., France, and Germany). I noticed that the U.S. does have the most kids under 15 (6.9%) online. Spain has almost 10% more young people ages 15–24 online than the next country (U.K.), which has 25.4%.

MY THOUGHTS
I was surprised that of the five countries, the U.S. had the lowest percentage of young people online.

How Graphics Are Organized

You will understand graphics better if you learn the different elements and parts in them. Color might be used one way in a chart and another way in a map. How graphics are organized or even which type of graphic—chart, graph, timeline—is used depends on the point the text is making.

1. Finding the Axes

2. Finding the Legend

Most graphics include some written content. Words appear in the title or header. They also usually appear in the legend and in captions. Look first at the words in a graphic. They are your starting points. First, find the title and caption. Then, find the legend that explains the color coding. Finally, notice the information on each axis.

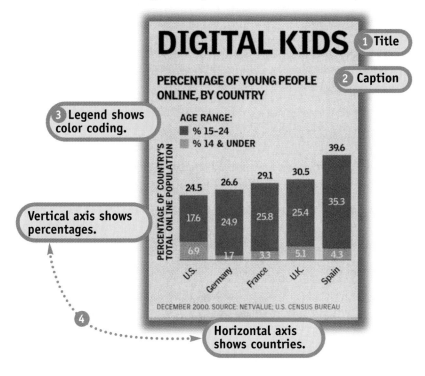

DIGITAL KIDS

1 Title

PERCENTAGE OF YOUNG PEOPLE ONLINE, BY COUNTRY

2 Caption

3 Legend shows color coding.

AGE RANGE:
■ % 15–24
□ % 14 & UNDER

Vertical axis shows percentages.

PERCENTAGE OF COUNTRY'S TOTAL ONLINE POPULATION

Country	% 15–24	% 14 & UNDER
U.S.	24.5	17.6 / 6.9
Germany	26.6	24.9 / 1.7
France	29.1	25.8 / 3.3
U.K.	30.5	25.4 / 5.1
Spain	39.6	35.3 / 4.3

DECEMBER 2000. SOURCE: NETVALUE; U.S. CENSUS BUREAU

4 Horizontal axis shows countries.

Graphics

Finding the Axes

Graphics are often used to compare such things as groups, eras, countries, or products. In the first two "Digital Kids" graphics, the bottom rule, or line, is called a *horizontal axis*. Most graphs have a rule running up the left side, the *vertical axis,* though sometimes the line is implied and reinforced by the vertical text. In the first graph, the unit of measurement for the vertical axis is a percentage. The horizontal axis shows the different countries. Be sure you understand the labels on the two axes because they form the basis of the comparison shown in the graph. In fact, you should always ask yourself, "What's being shown in this graphic?"

Finding the Legend

The *legend,* sometimes called the *key,* explains the different colors, abbreviations, symbols, shapes, icons, or line patterns. On maps and certain other graphics, the legend might also tell you the units of measurement (for example, miles, tons, frequency of use, minutes). Color is often used to code the information in graphics. In the graph on the previous page, the blue and gold refer to the age ranges. If you did not know what the colors stood for, you would not understand what the graph shows.

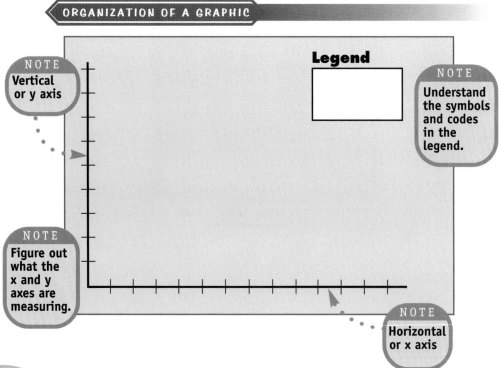

ORGANIZATION OF A GRAPHIC

Legend

NOTE
Vertical
or y axis

NOTE
Understand
the symbols
and codes
in the
legend.

NOTE
Figure out
what the
x and y
axes are
measuring.

NOTE
Horizontal
or x axis

E Connect

Graphics help you make several kinds of connections. First, they make a visual connection among various numbers, groups, and trends. In this way, they connect what often seem to be unrelated items and, by comparing them, show you something that words alone could not. As a reader, you should also connect the information to your original reading purpose. As you read, ask, "What does this information mean?" or "Why is it important?" You might also ask a more personal question, such as, "What surprised me most about this information?" or "How does this information relate to my life?"

Here's how one reader made a personal connection to the second graphic on page 543.

PARAPHRASE CHART

CAPTION	MY PARAPHRASE
Most Popular Media Activities Among U.S. Teens Online	• About twice as many boys visit sports sites online as girls do. • Girls read magazines online almost twice as much as boys do. • Boys play games online more than girls do, but the gap is not as important as in other areas. • Both download free software. More boys than girls do this. • Both download a lot of music.

MY THOUGHTS

This was based on a pretty big number of people—1,520 teens through an online survey. Still, is that representative of all teens? Did they all come through one website? How did they find the kids to answer the questions? The information might depend on what site was used to survey these teens.

I wonder whether the number of boys and girls online is equal now? This survey tells us what those who are online do, but maybe there were more boys than girls answering the questions. Of my friends, more girls do the music downloading.

Graphics

After Reading

At this point, you should have a good idea of what a graphic shows. Still, you may want to reread it, especially if it is part of a textbook chapter or newspaper or magazine article. You may find other information that will help you make additional connections or help you better understand the graphic.

F Pause and Reflect

Before rereading a graphic, think again about your original reading purpose questions. Ask yourself these questions:

Looking Back

■ **Do I understand what the graphic is about?**

■ **Can I explain in my own words what I learned?**

■ **Is there anything about the graphic that confuses me?**

Sometimes you may feel confident that you have fulfilled your reading purpose. Other times you might want to go back and patch up your understanding by finding additional details. That's when you need to go back and reread using another reading strategy.

G Reread

If you are like most readers when reading graphics in textbooks, you often do not give the same attention to the graphic and its captions as you do to the main text. As you read along, check out the graphics. Then, return to the text and see how it relates to the graphics. The text and the graphics are meant to complement each other. Rereading might also involve comparing one graphic to other graphics or evaluating the information in a graphic.

Rereading Strategy: Reading Critically

Reading information in a graphic demands that you always challenge it, question the results, and consider the implications. Such skepticism is essential for a critical reader. **Reading critically** can help you draw conclusions from the graphics you read.

For example, the first question that arises as you reread the graphs on page 543 is the date. Some of this information is from the year 2000. Is that important? Does it mean the information here is no longer valid or reliable? Some of it, perhaps the statistics about online access by young people, is probably out of date. Much information is "time sensitive," meaning that it's valid for a week, a month, a year, but probably not much longer. Here's how one reader drew some conclusions about information in the third graph.

CRITICAL READING CHART

Example: Digital Music Downloading, by Age Group	
1. What is being compared?	compares how many kids versus adults download digital music
2. What similarities and differences do I see?	Both groups, and even kids under 12, are downloading a ton of music. Adults have access to high-speed lines at work, which probably accounts for the higher numbers for adults.
3. Is there anything unusual about the way the data are presented?	The graph does not show where they are downloading the music—at home or at work? And what is the source of the music? The graph doesn't compare the groups by gender. This information I can get, however, from the other graph that compares what boys and girls do online.
4. What trends or other relationships do I see?	The obvious question is, "What will this do to the recording industry? Will companies buy these online sites and sell their music through these sites?" New laws and delivery systems will be coming, but downloading music is here to stay.

Graphics

Reading a Graphic Critically

As a reader, you want to evaluate the quality of the information you find in graphics and decide whether that information is presented fairly. The information in the three graphs comes from various sources: the U.S. Census Bureau and three separate companies. These various companies gathered their information by different means: online surveys, market research, and individual interviews. Keep in mind that another company—a magazine—created these graphs using the data provided by these various groups.

Evaluating the Sources

You need to ask yourself, "Are these good sources?" You can trust the U.S. Census Bureau. After all, it has no motive for gathering false information or painting a biased picture. You can probably trust the other sources, too. Still, it's important to ask. If a magazine hires a company to gather information, that might put pressure on the company to provide the "right" numbers so it gets hired again. You just have to be skeptical when reading information. You might also ask, for example, whether an online survey is reliable. Who answered the questions? How many answered? Perhaps the anonymity of the online survey allowed kids to be more honest, in which case this might be better information than you usually find.

H Remember

Graphics help you organize a lot of information into an understandable package. Graphics also help you visualize the information and understand the relationships among the data, which makes it more likely you will remember that information. Still, you need to make connections with the material if you are to remember it. Paraphrasing is a start, but here are two other activities to try.

1. Conduct Your Own Survey

If the information in a graphic relates to current trends in society, conduct your own survey on the same topic. Survey some of your friends and family. Put your findings in a graph, and compare the information to what's shown in the graphics you studied.

2. Make a List

Lists help you organize information, making it easier for you to remember the details later. On the next page is a list one reader made after reading the three graphics about "Digital Kids":

"Digital Kids"

What surprised me most:

1. I was very surprised to see Spain listed as number one.
2. I assumed that kids downloaded much more music than adults.
3. It's interesting that girls use the web to read magazines. This will cost the publishers a lot of money in lost sales and subscriptions. Maybe this kind of thing will force publishers to charge for use of their websites soon?

Summing Up

When reading graphics, use the reading process and the strategy of **paraphrasing.** This strategy helps you understand the different comparisons and types of information in graphics. Be sure to pay close attention to **how the graphic is organized.** You can find most of these clues in the title, the legend, and in the labels used on the axes of any graphs. Three tools can help you understand the information in any graphic:

- ■ Paraphrase Chart
- ■ Critical Reading Chart
- ■ Summary Notes

Last, remember to use the rereading strategy of **reading critically** to help you evaluate the reliability of the information.

Graphics

553

Elements of Graphics

Graphics are used not only to explain but to tell stories and persuade. Here you will learn to read the graphics most commonly found on the Internet, in textbooks, in other informational books, and in newspapers and magazines.

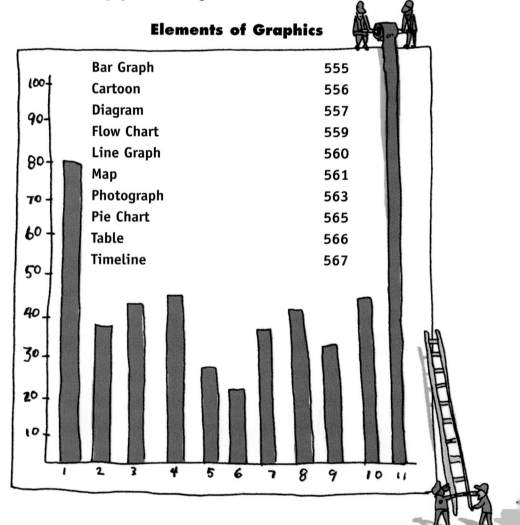

Elements of Graphics

Bar Graph	555
Cartoon	556
Diagram	557
Flow Chart	559
Line Graph	560
Map	561
Photograph	563
Pie Chart	565
Table	566
Timeline	567

Bar Graph

As you read the bar graph below, ask yourself, "What can I learn from it?" With all graphs, it is always good to ask why this particular type of graph was chosen. What does it communicate, for example, that a line graph or a pie chart does not?

EXAMPLE

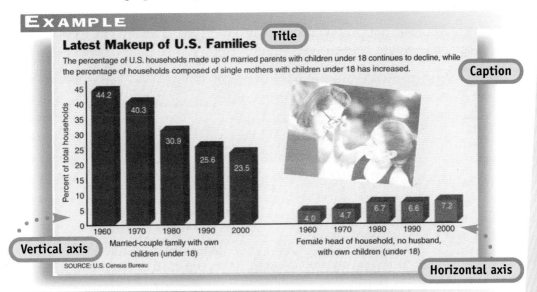

Latest Makeup of U.S. Families — Title

The percentage of U.S. households made up of married parents with children under 18 continues to decline, while the percentage of households composed of single mothers with children under 18 has increased. — Caption

Percent of total households

44.2, 40.3, 30.9, 25.6, 23.5

1960 1970 1980 1990 2000

Married-couple family with own children (under 18)

Vertical axis

4.0 4.7 6.7 6.6 7.2

1960 1970 1980 1990 2000

Female head of household, no husband, with own children (under 18)

Horizontal axis

SOURCE: U.S. Census Bureau

DESCRIPTION

A **bar graph** compares quantities or amounts, groups, or periods of time. Horizontal and vertical axes represent this information. Some graphs use symbols or small pictures instead of bars to represent the data. They are called *pictographs*. To read a graph, follow these steps:

1. Read the title and any captions. These give you the subject of the graph.

2. Then look at each axis. Read the labels and units of measurement to understand what is being measured or compared.

3. Use your own words to paraphrase what the graph says.

DEFINITION

A **bar graph** uses vertical or horizontal bars to show or compare information.

Graphics

Cartoon

Cartoons comment in timely and humorous ways on current events and culture. Cartoonists help us laugh at ourselves and things that are happening around us. While some cartoonists are talented artists, it is not their artistic skill that you notice but the ideas behind what they draw and say.

Ask yourself not only what the cartoon below is about but why someone would think it was funny.

EXAMPLE

"Go ask your search engine."

DESCRIPTION

A **cartoon** requires only a moment to make its point. If you have to look at it very long, the cartoonist obviously failed to communicate the point.

If a cartoon has a caption, read it first. Then, notice such details as the setting, the clothes, and people's expressions. You may have to make some inferences. For example, who is speaking in this cartoon? The point is that adults no longer have to answer kids' questions.

DEFINITION

A **cartoon** is a drawing that makes humorous but meaningful comments about life and society by using words and images.

Diagram

Sometimes you just can't understand something—a process, an event, or the way something works—until you see it. Visual explanations reveal how one thing relates to another and what it looks like. A diagram illustrates the whole process for you.

EXAMPLE

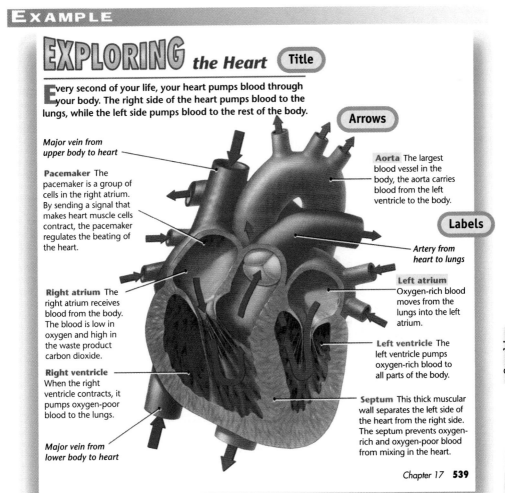

EXPLORING *the Heart*   (Title)

Every second of your life, your heart pumps blood through your body. The right side of the heart pumps blood to the lungs, while the left side pumps blood to the rest of the body.

(Arrows)

Major vein from upper body to heart

Pacemaker The pacemaker is a group of cells in the right atrium. By sending a signal that makes heart muscle cells contract, the pacemaker regulates the beating of the heart.

Right atrium The right atrium receives blood from the body. The blood is low in oxygen and high in the waste product carbon dioxide.

Right ventricle When the right ventricle contracts, it pumps oxygen-poor blood to the lungs.

Major vein from lower body to heart

Aorta The largest blood vessel in the body, the aorta carries blood from the left ventricle to the body.

(Labels)

Artery from heart to lungs

Left atrium Oxygen-rich blood moves from the lungs into the left atrium.

Left ventricle The left ventricle pumps oxygen-rich blood to all parts of the body.

Septum This thick muscular wall separates the left side of the heart from the right side. The septum prevents oxygen-rich and oxygen-poor blood from mixing in the heart.

Chapter 17 **539**

Graphics

Diagram, continued

DESCRIPTION

Diagrams offer so much to look at that it's hard to know where to start. Follow these steps when reading a **diagram:**

1. First, read the heading or title and any text that tells what the diagram shows.

2. Read each label and look at the part it identifies. Start at the top. Then, read each label clockwise until you have read all around the diagram.

3. Follow any arrows or numbers. Pay attention also to the color of arrows, line patterns, or symbols because they might be meaningful.

4. A diagram clarifies and explains. Do more than just look at it. Take time to reflect on it or draw a conclusion about it.

5. Diagrams add to, or supplement, the written text so you need to know how the diagram relates to the text in your textbook or magazine article. As you read, switch back and forth between the graphic and the text.

6. Diagrams often use key vocabulary words. Write these words in your vocabulary journal, and be sure you know their meaning.

To clarify the diagram, try to redraw it yourself. This can help you remember and better understand the different parts of it.

DEFINITION

A **diagram** is a drawing with labels that shows or explains something.

Flow Chart

A flow chart shows a process or sequence of steps. Flow charts are essential tools for people in business and for those who design software and other systems.

EXAMPLE

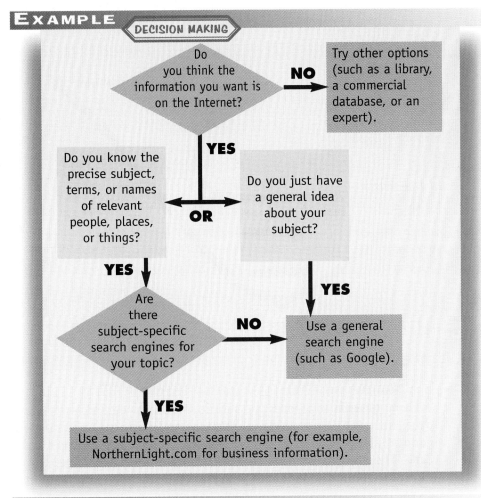

DESCRIPTION

Read the title of a **flow chart** and follow the arrows. This one shows a process for making decisions. Sometimes a flow chart is called a decision-making tree.

DEFINITION

A flow chart is a visual picture of the order of operations used to create a product, make a decision, or complete a process.

Graphics

559

Line Graph

A line graph shows patterns and relationships between types of information or groups. It may show, for example, how the temperature goes up or down during a day or week. A line graph helps you see the big picture by providing a visual explanation that words cannot match.

EXAMPLE

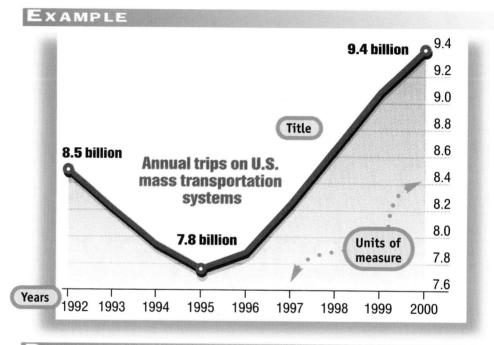

DESCRIPTION

A **line graph** expresses the relationship between different data over time. A line graph shows changes and patterns and is especially good at showing a lot of small changes or several patterns at one time. The steeper the line is, the faster the rate of change. Using different colored lines and line styles (dotted, solid, dashed), it may show information about the past, the present, and even the future. This graph, for example, shows how U.S. ridership on public transit changed over eight years.

DEFINITION

A **line graph** shows points that represent amounts, times, or places. These points are plotted and then connected by one or more lines that show change.

Map

A map can serve many purposes, only one of which is to help you get from one place to another. Often a map shows information in the context of a specific place and time.

EXAMPLE

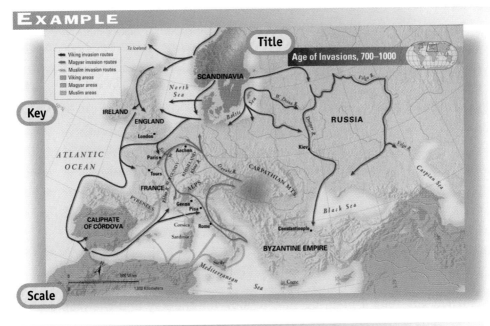

Title

Age of Invasions, 700–1000

Key

Scale

- Viking invasion routes
- Magyar invasion routes
- Muslim invasion routes
- Viking areas
- Magyar areas
- Muslim areas

DESCRIPTION

A **map** can show population patterns, locations, physical features, climates, and distances from one place to another. The map above uses colors to show which people invaded an area of Europe in a 300-year period and from which areas they came. This map of a continent's invasion patterns becomes a visual narrative of a specific time and place. You will come across many different kinds of maps in your reading.

Maps are also very common on tests. Before you take any social studies tests, review the parts of a map and be sure you know how to read it.

1. First, read the title.

2. Then, read the labels to get an overall sense of what the map shows.

3. Then, try to restate to yourself one or two things the map shows.

Graphics

Map, continued

KINDS OF MAPS

Kind of Map	What It Mainly Shows
Demographic	Who lives where (by race, by age, by culture); how they vote; what they earn; what they do for a living
Historical	Events and political boundaries: where they were, where they moved
Physical	Physical features, such as land elevations, rivers, and lakes
Political	Political units, such as boundaries between one congressional district and another
Road or Travel	Roads and highways
Thematic	Information on specific topics, such as climate, population density, or natural resources

When you read a map, be sure to look for the key and the map scale. The key describes the color-coding and symbols used on the map. The map *scale* shows you how to judge distance on the map and how it reflects the actual distance in miles or kilometers.

DEFINITION

A **map** is a representation of part or all of the heavens or the earth's surface. It usually shows places, such as planets and constellations, boundaries between countries, bodies of water, cities, or geographic regions.

Photograph

Photographs can move you in ways you do not always understand. They capture a moment, freeze it in time, and give it back to you to consider over and over. Some photographs capture historical truths, such as moments at which great leaders made heroic or awful decisions. Photographs tell stories with images instead of words. What a writer does with words, a photographer does with light and shadow, color, and arrangement. Photographs can do more than tell stories: they can offer visual arguments that urge you to act, to help, to speak out, or to change.

EXAMPLE

President Richard Nixon and Mrs. Nixon leave the White House in 1974.   (Caption)

Graphics

Photograph, continued

DESCRIPTION

When you "read" a **photograph,** read any title or caption and identify the subject. Photographers, like writers, create their images by making choices. The photograph of former President Richard Nixon on the previous page would be entirely different if it were shot from a different angle. But its perspective from inside the helicopter, with the White House in the background, makes a powerful statement. It shows President Nixon, who resigned from office, and Mrs. Nixon saying good-bye to Vice-president and Mrs. Gerald Ford, who became the new President and First Lady.

When reading photographs, keep in mind one thing: Has this image been changed in any way? Thanks to software programs and improved digital technology, creating visual lies is now as easy as clicking your mouse.

When reading a photograph or other image, think about these questions:

1. Why are you looking at this photo?
2. Is this image in its original state (that is, no "doctoring") or in a digital version?
3. Who took this picture and why?
4. What was the photographer trying to do (for example, narrate, explain, describe, persuade, or some combination of these purposes)?
5. Why did the photographer choose this angle or perspective?
6. Where in the photograph do you look first?
7. What do you need to know to read the image successfully?

DEFINITION

A **photograph** is a picture taken from real life with a camera. Photographs are stored on film or digital media, which can possibly be enhanced or otherwise changed on a computer.

Pie Chart

A pie chart (sometimes called a *circle graph*) is related to a bar graph but gives the reader a different perspective on data. For example, these various pie charts all describe students from one high school.

EXAMPLE

DESCRIPTION

A **pie chart** works especially well to show the parts or shares of a whole in percentages. The "pieces" of the pie show relative size of one piece versus other pieces.

1. When reading a pie chart, first read the title, all captions, and any other related text.

2. Identify what the different pieces of the pie chart represent. Do this by looking for labels or a legend that explains the different colors or patterns.

3. Then, compare the sizes of the pieces of the pie. Be aware that pie charts show major factors very well but tend to minimize the smaller details. This is why you will commonly see a slice on the chart that says, for example, "10% Other."

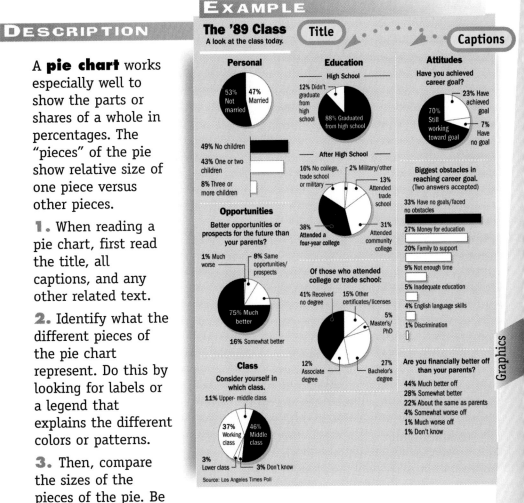

The '89 Class
A look at the class today.

Title

Captions

Personal
53% Not married
47% Married

49% No children
43% One or two children
8% Three or more children

Opportunities
Better opportunities or prospects for the future than your parents?
1% Much worse
8% Same opportunities/ prospects
75% Much better
16% Somewhat better

Class
Consider yourself in which class.
11% Upper- middle class
37% Working class
46% Middle class
3% Lower class
3% Don't know

Source: Los Angeles Times Poll

Education
High School
12% Didn't graduate from high school
88% Graduated from high school

After High School
16% No college, trade school or military
2% Military/other
13% Attended trade school
38% Attended a four-year college
31% Attended community college

Of those who attended college or trade school:
41% Received no degree
15% Other certificates/licenses
5% Master's/ PhD
12% Associate degree
27% Bachelor's degree

Attitudes
Have you achieved career goal?
23% Have achieved goal
70% Still working toward goal
7% Have no goal

Biggest obstacles in reaching career goal.
(Two answers accepted)
33% Have no goals/faced no obstacles
27% Money for education
20% Family to support
9% Not enough time
5% Inadequate education
4% English language skills
1% Discrimination

Are you financially better off than your parents?
44% Much better off
28% Somewhat better
22% About the same as parents
4% Somewhat worse off
1% Much worse off
1% Don't know

Graphics

DEFINITION

A **pie chart** is a graph in the form of a circle. Pie charts show parts that make up a whole. They show the relative size or importance of different factors.

Table

Tables organize different types of information into categories for easy reference. Tables are an easy way to compare the performance of different players, products, or services over time.

EXAMPLE

BASKETBALL HALL OF FAME PLAYERS — Title

Headings

Player	Year Elected	Points	FG%	FT%	Rebs.	Assts.
Rick Barry*	1987	18,395	0.449	0.900	5,168	4,017
Elgin Baylor	1976	23,149	0.431	0.780	11,463	3,650
Bill Bradley	1982	9,217	0.448	0.840	2,533	2,363
Wilt Chamberlain	1978	31,419	0.540	0.511	23,924	4,643
Julius Erving*	1993	18,364	0.507	0.777	5,601	3,224
Walt Frazier	1987	15,581	0.490	0.786	4,830	5,040
Hal Greer	1981	21,586	0.452	0.801	5,665	4,540
John Havlicek	1983	26,395	0.439	0.815	8,007	6,114
Connie Hawkins*	1992	8,233	0.467	0.785	3,971	2,052
Elvin Hayes	1990	27,313	0.452	0.670	16,279	2,398
Dan Issel*	1993	14,659	0.506	0.797	5,707	1,804
Kareem Abdul Jabbar	1995	38,387	0.559	0.721	17,440	5,660
Bob Lanier	1992	19,248	0.514	0.767	9,698	3,007
Pete Maravich	1987	15,948	0.441	0.820	2,747	3,563

*NBA stats only

Read down the "Points" column and across.

DESCRIPTION

A **table** packs a lot of information into a small space. The purpose of a table is usually for reference and to make comparisons. For example, which Hall of Fame player in the table above scored the most points?

When you read a table, first look at the title and any captions. Then, look at the headings for the different columns so you know what is being compared and how it is being measured. Make sure you know what each column contains. Use a ruler or your finger to help you line up a column or row of data. First, find the column you want to know about. Then, go down the column to the row you want to know about. Then, move across that row to find the information you need. Who did score the most points?

DEFINITION

A **table** is a list of statistics or information on a subject, usually arranged in columns and rows.

Timeline

A timeline shows a series of events and the dates on which they occurred.

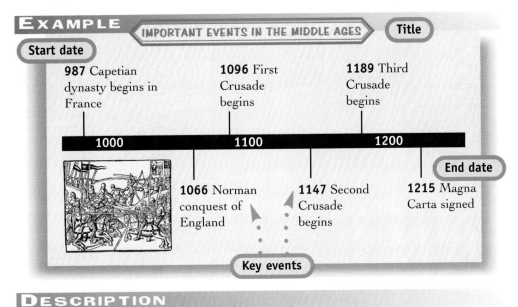

EXAMPLE

IMPORTANT EVENTS IN THE MIDDLE AGES — Title

Start date

987 Capetian dynasty begins in France

1096 First Crusade begins

1189 Third Crusade begins

1000   1100   1200

End date

1066 Norman conquest of England

1147 Second Crusade begins

1215 Magna Carta signed

Key events

DESCRIPTION

Textbooks often put a **timeline** at the beginning of a chapter or section to provide an overview of the events and era you are about to study. These timelines can prepare your mind for what you will read.

1. Read the title of the timeline first.

2. Identify a question that the timeline can help you answer—for example, "What are two important events in the Middle Ages?"

3. Take time to evaluate what is on the timeline. This will help you understand the importance of the events shown.

4. Look at the beginning and end dates of the timeline. Often the span or cutoff dates are important.

5. As you read the timeline, think about the effect one event might have had on another. Timelines offer you a glimpse of how one event might cause others.

DEFINITION

A **timeline** shows a series of events organized in chronological, or time, order.

Graphics

Reading for the Everyday World

Introduction to Reading for the Everyday World

Reading a Driver's Handbook

Kinds of Everyday Reading

Focus on Reading Instructions
Focus on Reading for Work

Everyday

Introduction to Reading for the Everyday World

The reading you do in school is not the only kind of reading that you need to do well. Your "real world" or "everyday world" reading can be just as important as your school assignments. The information you get from this type of reading can help you get a driver's license, keep a job, or use a new cell phone.

Real-world writing comes in different formats and appears in many different places. Instructions are packed with a game or something you have to put together. On the job, you may receive memos or updated safety procedures. Sometimes rules are attached to a wall in your workplace or in the gym at school. Leases, credit card agreements, and insurance papers are other examples of real-world writing you may encounter now or in the future. While this kind of writing isn't exactly thrilling, you will have to know some reading strategies to stay informed about all you need to know in the everyday world.

Reading a Driver's Handbook

If you're like most students, you'll be reading a driver's handbook published by the state you live in to prepare for a driver's test. Since you don't want to have to take the test twice, you'll want to prepare well for the questions you'll be asked and the driving you'll have to do.

Here you'll apply the reading process to part of a driver's handbook.

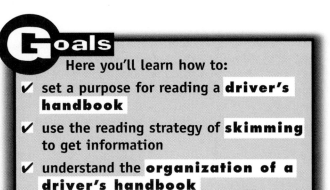

Goals

Here you'll learn how to:

✔ set a purpose for reading a **driver's handbook**

✔ use the reading strategy of **skimming** to get information

✔ understand the **organization of a driver's handbook**

Before Reading

Although you have probably never read a driver's handbook before you needed to, you can bet that when you do see it, it will tell you all you ever wanted to know about tests, laws, signs, signals, crashes, and safe driving. In fact, a handbook may contain up to 100 pages of material your state thinks you should know before you get behind the wheel. How are you going to attack this handbook? Start by setting a purpose.

Everyday

A Set a Purpose

Often your purpose will be clear when you begin and determined by what you are reading. For example, let's say you're reading a handbook to prepare for a written examination for your driver's license. Your goal is to pass the test so you'll get your license.

Start by being as clear as possible about what you want to find out.

Setting a Purpose

■ **What do I need to know to pass the written examination for a driver's license?**

Once that is clear, you can begin. You have a clear target, or goal, for your reading.

B Preview

When you preview, you open your mind to the information you're about to read. Previewing gives you an idea about the subject and how it is organized. As you preview, look for organizational features like these:

Preview Checklist

✔ the table of contents

✔ any headings

✔ any words in large type, boldface type, or all capital letters

✔ any numbered or bulleted lists

✔ any graphic elements, such as illustrations and diagrams

Now preview a section from a driver's handbook, beginning with the table of contents.

from *Rules of the Road*

PREVIEW
Topics in table of contents

PREVIEW
Key topic

Table of Contents

By previewing the topics in the table of contents, you can zero in on the information that concerns you the most: the driver's license tests. Look there first.

PREVIEW
Key information

from *Rules of the Road*

Chapter Two: The Driver's License Tests

When you apply for your driver's license, you will be asked questions about your general health and will take vision, written and driving tests. You are allowed three attempts to pass each of these tests within one year from the date you paid your application fee. The information for the written test is given in this manual. This chapter will give you information on the following:

- Organ Tissue Donor Central Registry
- voter registration
- the vision screening
- the written test
- the driving test

Organ Tissue Donor Central Registry

When you apply for or renew your driver's license or identification card, driver services personnel will ask if you intend to sign an organ donor card and wish to be a part of the organ donor registry. The registry helps document your intention to become an organ donor. The registry does not replace, but supplements, the organ donor card on the back of the driver's license or identification card. It is important to discuss your wishes with your family as final permission must be granted by next of kin.

Voter Registration

Driver Services personnel ask all applicants if they wish to register to vote under the National Voter Registration Act, which enables them to vote in all elections. License renewal applicants qualifying for the Safe Driver Renewal program can request that voter information be mailed to their home address.

The Vision Screening

Your vision will be screened to determine if you see well enough to drive. This screening is not a professional eye exam. In place of this screening, you may submit a vision specialist report or a letter completed by a licensed optometrist, ophthalmologist or physician. Forms for this report are available at your local driver services facility. If you need to wear glasses or contact lenses, a restriction will be noted on your license. Then you *must always wear your glasses or contact lenses* when you drive. Here is some information you should know about vision restrictions:

- The minimum requirement for visual acuity is 20/40 acuity with or without corrective lenses. Drivers with acuity between 20/41 and 20/70 are limited to daylight driving only.
- You must have at least 140 degree peripheral vision (the ability to see to the side) to have a license without restrictions. This is with or without corrective lenses.

18

- If you wear telescopic lenses, you must meet special requirements and undergo additional testing to receive your license.

If you need more information, contact your local driver services facility.

The Written Test

The questions for the basic written test, which will allow you to operate passenger cars, are taken from the information given in this manual. There will be additional questions for other classifications. The test requires you to:

- identify *traffic signs* by shape, color or symbol (Chapter 7).
- identify *signals* and *pavement markings* (Chapter 8).
- answer multiple choice and true/false questions about *traffic laws, safety rules, accident prevention* and *vehicle equipment* (Chapters 3, 4, 6, 9, 10, 11).

The study questions that appear at the end of each chapter are similar to questions that are included on the driver's license written test. Studying these questions will help you prepare for the test. If you apply for a license to drive a motorcycle, truck or bus, you may obtain an operator's manual from any driver services facility. Study the manual before taking the test. Written and driving tests vary for different classifications of drivers' licenses.

The Driving Test

The driving test will allow you to demonstrate your ability to drive. You must provide a vehicle that is licensed and properly equipped for the driver's license classification you are seeking. If the vehicle is registered in Illinois, it must display valid license plates as required by Illinois law. If the vehicle is registered outside of Illinois, it must meet the registration requirements of the respective state. The vehicle, unless exempt, must comply with the Illinois Mandatory Insurance law. You will *automatically fail the test* if you violate any traffic law or commit any dangerous action while taking your test. You and the examiner are required to wear *safety belts* during the driving test.

The vehicle must be driven to the facility by a driver who has a valid license or permit. No one but the examiner will be with you during the test. If you bring children with you, please bring someone along to take care of them. During the basic test, which will allow you to drive passenger cars, you will be graded on your ability to do the following:

- start the vehicle. Check your vehicle controls, such as parking brake and mirrors. All the *required equipment* listed in Chapter 11 must be working properly. Make all adjustments to seats, safety belts, mirrors and other equipment before you move your vehicle.
- back the vehicle. You will back the vehicle about 50 ft. at a slow speed, straight and smoothly. Turn your head to the right and watch to the rear as you back.

19

The headings help you locate the information you want. The bullets, too, list specific areas of the written test that you need to read:

■ traffic signs

■ signals and pavement markings

■ traffic laws, safety rules, accident prevention, and vehicle equipment

A quick check of Chapter 8 will show you graphic elements to help you understand signals and pavement markings.

C Plan

Your quick preview of the driver's handbook told you quite a bit:

■ The written test will focus on traffic signs, laws, and safety.

■ Signals, pavement markings, accident prevention, and vehicle equipment also seem important.

By previewing the material, you have found out where the other information you might need is. Next you need to plan how to get the information that will help you prepare for the test.

Because you previewed the material, you can more easily make a plan to find answers to your questions. Now you need a strategy for reading.

Reading Strategy: Skimming

When you skim, you sort out the information you need from the parts that you don't need. Instead of reading each word or sentence carefully, you move your eyes quickly over the page. You can use your finger or a ruler to guide your eyes along. **Skimming,** like previewing, can help you get a general sense of the content. It can also help you locate the specific information you are looking for.

In this case, you know the key subjects that will be on the test. If you can't mark up a driver's handbook, make Key Word or Topic Notes to help you find out what you need to remember.

KEY WORD OR TOPIC NOTES

KEY WORDS OR TOPICS	NOTES

Everyday

During Reading

Now that you have a plan and a strategy, the next step is to read.

D Read with a Purpose

Start skimming the chapters that contain information likely to be on the test. To stay on track, you may even want to write key words or topics you want to take notes on. Keep track of them with notes like this.

KEY WORD OR TOPIC NOTES

KEY WORDS OR TOPICS	NOTES
traffic signs	• Key signs include Stop, Yield, Wrong Way, and Do Not Enter. • Note U-sign for "No U-Turn" and the arrow sign that means "No Right Turn."
signals	Signals are like the red, green, and yellow lights.
pavement markings	These are the marks in the middle of a road. • Two solid lines mean "no passing." • Broken yellow lines mean "passing allowed." • Two-way turn lanes are like the lanes we have in front of school.

Finding details about your key words or topics is the goal of skimming. Look for your key topics. Read carefully when you find them, and ignore everything else. Once you have found the specific information about your key topics, take notes on them so that you can review quickly and easily before you take the examination.

You might also use a Web as a way to take notes about a few key areas.

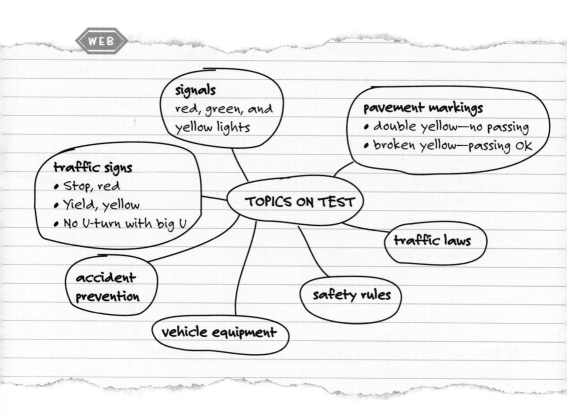

The value of collecting notes around a common subject is that it helps you remember. In other words, reading tools such as a Web and Key Word or Topic Notes serve as memory aids as much as aids to help you read for a specific purpose.

E Connect

When you do everyday reading, you will have a better chance of remembering what you read if you connect the material to your own life. Active readers respond, react to, and even comment on what they read. Much of what you read can seem boring and irrelevant if you don't interact with what you read and tie it to something meaningful in your life. Passing the written test to get a driver's license is obviously important for most people. For example, note how one reader responded to this part of the handbook.

Everyday

from *Rules of the Road*

You may not make a U-turn:

- Where you cannot see 200 feet in each direction because of a curve, hill, rain, fog, or other reason.
- Where a "NO U-TURN" sign is posted.
- When vehicles may hit you.
- On a one-way street.
- In front of a fire station. Never use a fire-station driveway to turn around.

This is a good point. If you can't see ahead, you can't see possible danger.

Two serious accidents happened on the curving road just south of school.

After Reading

You may do everyday reading very quickly without taking time to reflect on what you read. But if you want to remember the information and use it later, you'll need to take a few minutes to think about what you've read. First, you'll want to see if you met your reading purpose and are ready for the test.

F   Pause and Reflect

After you've finished the everyday reading that you needed to do, take a moment to look back over it. Have you accomplished your reading purpose? Ask yourself a few questions like these:

Looking Back

- ■ Do I know what I need to know to pass the driver's exam?
- ■ Is there anything that confuses me?

Perhaps you got everything the first time through the driver's handbook. But most of the time, you will find it helpful to do a little rereading.

G Reread

You may want to go back and read more carefully to find more information about a specific area, such as the special rules about railway crossings or school buses. As you reread for these key words, take the time to paraphrase the material, or put it into your own words. This will not only make the information clearer to you, but it will also help you remember it.

Rereading Strategy: Visualizing and Thinking Aloud

Sometimes you have to "see" something mentally or say it aloud to understand it. To help you with this, try writing down your thoughts.

THINK ALOUD

I have to stop when the school bus stops and puts out the arm to stop. I can't drive ahead on either side of the street until the bus does. I always have to stop at a railroad crossing when there's a stop sign, a flag person, or the gates are down.

H Remember

If you really want to remember your everyday reading material, here are two suggestions to help.

1. Ask, "What If?"

Ask yourself what would happen if you didn't follow the instructions, rules, or advice you were reading about. For example, consider the driving advice that you should use a hand signal as well as a light signal if the sun is very bright. Ask, "What happens if the sun is very bright?" You will soon realize that the turning light on a car is hard to see in bright light. A hand signal is easier to see.

You can even take "What If" a step further and create your own questions for a driver's test. Asking your own questions and answering them is a great way to prepare for tests.

2. Write Summary Notes

Another way to remember your everyday reading material is to make Summary Notes. They can be as detailed as you like. You can create a summary for each chapter or each page.

Everyday

TOPIC: left turn from a two-way street
1. Start turn at left edge of lane closest to middle of street.
2. If signs or markings say it's okay, you can start turn from a different lane.
3. Complete the turn into any lane that is safe.
4. If there's a left-turn lane, you must use it.

Summing Up

When you do everyday reading, remember to use the reading process and the reading strategy of **skimming.** Use reading tools like these to help yourself remember what you read:

- ■ Key Word or Topic Notes
- ■ Web
- ■ Summary Notes

Then, after you read, remember to look back, reread, and use the strategy of **visualizing and thinking aloud** to make sure you understand all of the information you've read.

Focus on Reading Instructions

One type of everyday reading that you'll probably have to do sometime is to read instructions. Maybe you've bought a new cell phone with special features that you want to use. Maybe you have to set up a new DVD player. Whether the instructions explain some kind of complex electronic gadget or simply how to put together a chair or bookshelf, you will need to read instructions at some time in your life. To put together the item, you take out the instruction sheet and begin reading.

Goals

Here you'll learn how to:

✔ **identify a purpose for reading instructions**

✔ **use the strategy of close reading to learn what the instructions explain**

✔ **understand the organization of instructions**

Everyday

581

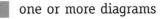

Before Reading

Many of the instructions you'll read involve two things:

- one or more diagrams
- a process or series of steps

Previewing the instructions will help you get an idea of what to do. Diagrams can be especially helpful when you read instructions. They show you various parts and how the item will look once it's assembled.

Here's what to preview with instructions:

Preview Checklist

✔ the title and headings
✔ the steps in the process
✔ any diagrams or graphics
✔ any key words in boldface or capital letters
✔ any bulleted lists

Before you start to read instructions, it is important to have a specific purpose in mind.

READING PURPOSES

Instructions Example	Reading Purpose
1. Cell Phone Instructions	How do I change the cover on the phone?
2. DVD Player Instructions	How do I set up the language features for audio and subtitles?

Now, preview these two examples of instructions.

1. Cell Phone Instructions

Changeable Color Covers (2800 Series Only)

This cell phone's attractive Changeable Color Covers give your phone a colorful personal touch.

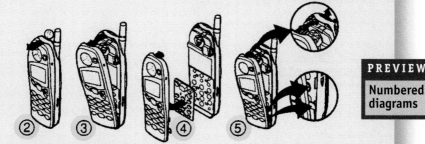

Caution: When changing covers, don't use the phone's antenna as leverage.

1. Switch off the power and disconnect the phone from the charger or any other device.

2. Using a coin, depress the colored tab on the top of the phone and slide out the color cover forward.

3. Remove the cover.

4. Remove the rubber keypad from the back of the cover. Place it into the back of the new cover.

5. Place the bottom of the cover against the bottom of the phone. Make sure all three sets of plastic tabs line up with their respective slots, as shown above. Close the cover and snap it shut all the way around the edge of the phone.

For operation, safety, care and maintenance—see your **Owner's Manual.**

Everyday

2. DVD Player Instructions

PREVIEW

Title

Setting Up the Language Features

PREVIEW

Headings

Setting up in ENGLISH

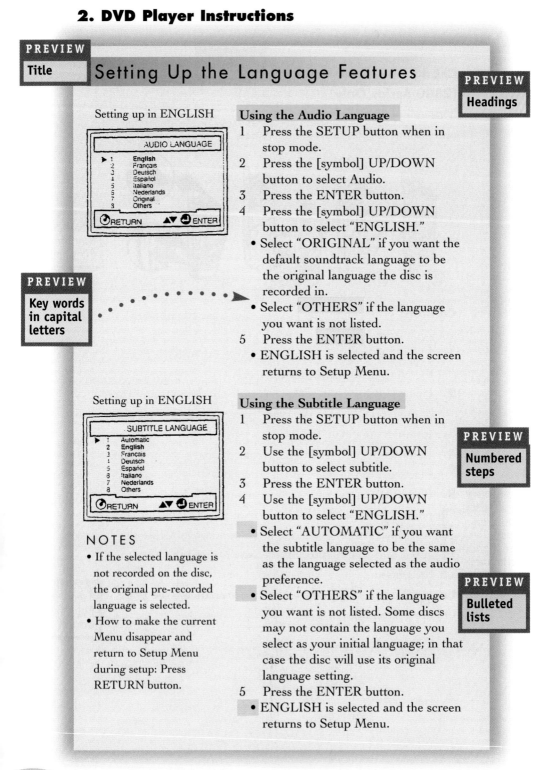

AUDIO LANGUAGE

▶ 1   English
   2   Français
   3   Deutsch
   4   Español
   5   Italiano
   6   Nederlands
   7   Original
   8   Others

RETURN   ▲▼ ENTER

Using the Audio Language

1   Press the SETUP button when in stop mode.
2   Press the [symbol] UP/DOWN button to select Audio.
3   Press the ENTER button.
4   Press the [symbol] UP/DOWN button to select "ENGLISH."
- Select "ORIGINAL" if you want the default soundtrack language to be the original language the disc is recorded in.
- Select "OTHERS" if the language you want is not listed.
5   Press the ENTER button.
- ENGLISH is selected and the screen returns to Setup Menu.

PREVIEW

Key words in capital letters

Setting up in ENGLISH

SUBTITLE LANGUAGE

▶ 1   Automatic
   2   English
   3   Français
   4   Deutsch
   5   Español
   6   Italiano
   7   Nederlands
   8   Others

RETURN   ▲▼ ENTER

Using the Subtitle Language

1   Press the SETUP button when in stop mode.
2   Use the [symbol] UP/DOWN button to select subtitle.
3   Press the ENTER button.
4   Use the [symbol] UP/DOWN button to select "ENGLISH."
- Select "AUTOMATIC" if you want the subtitle language to be the same as the language selected as the audio preference.
- Select "OTHERS" if the language you want is not listed. Some discs may not contain the language you select as your initial language; in that case the disc will use its original language setting.
5   Press the ENTER button.
- ENGLISH is selected and the screen returns to Setup Menu.

NOTES

- If the selected language is not recorded on the disc, the original pre-recorded language is selected.
- How to make the current Menu disappear and return to Setup Menu during setup: Press RETURN button.

PREVIEW

Numbered steps

PREVIEW

Bulleted lists

584

Reading Strategy: Close Reading

When you use the strategy of **close reading,** you read word for word, sentence by sentence, or line by line. The steps on an instruction sheet are written in the order in which they are to be performed. When you're reading instructions, close reading is an effective strategy because it ensures that no important step will slip by without notice.

During Reading

Once you have decided on your strategy, you're ready to begin reading. Look back at the instructions on pages 583 and 584 and do a close reading. As you do, follow these steps.

1. Highlight or Mark

Use a highlighter or pen to mark the most important words and phrases. If you're not allowed to mark the instructions permanently, use sticky notes to mark key parts.

2. Think Aloud

As you read the instructions, think aloud about the steps. Say them aloud, so you can hear as well as read the steps. By thinking aloud, you also put the directions in your own words.

THINK ALOUD

So, as a first step, I turn everything off and unplug the phone. Then I need to get the cover off. Don't use the antenna. I should use a coin or something like that to get the cover off.

Everyday

3. Reread

Almost no one understands directions the first time through, so why should you? That's the reason for going back again and again and rereading. In fact, go back as often as you need to reread and understand.

4. Go Step by Step

You may find the best method for reading directions is to do one step at a time. Read a step and then do it. Go back and read another step. Then try to do it. By going one step at a time, you can figure out all of the puzzling terms or language used in directions. By working one step at a time, you might save yourself the trouble of doing all the steps over again, if you've done them out of order.

5. Read the Diagram

Instructions often have a series of numbered steps and diagrams to help you identify terms the instructions are using. They instruct you to make sure "all three sets of plastic tabs line up," but you can't do it unless you note in the diagram where the tabs and slots are located. You'll find it helpful to go back and forth between looking at the diagram and the object itself.

6. Ask Yourself Questions

With instructions, asking questions can help you carry out the steps. Why did they call these "slots" when before they used the word "tabs"? Or maybe you ask yourself, "Did it work?" or "Is this worth a try?" By asking yourself questions, you help clarify what the instructions are saying. They give you another way to think through the reading.

After Reading

When you read instructions, you're looking for information that will tell you how to do something. If you're able to accomplish what you set out to do, you know that the instructions have been useful. Sometimes, however, you do not accomplish your goal. When this happens, you have to go back and see what you did wrong.

1. Ask a Friend for Help

Sometimes when you read instructions, you may get distracted and miss something. Maybe a friend could help. Ask the friend to read the instructions aloud as you carry them out. Or you read the instructions aloud and let your friend try to follow them.

2. Check Off the Steps

It can be easy to skip a step. One way to make sure you've done everything is to check off the steps as you perform them. When you get to the end of the list, check to see if you've accomplished what you wanted. If you've checked off each step, you should have no problem.

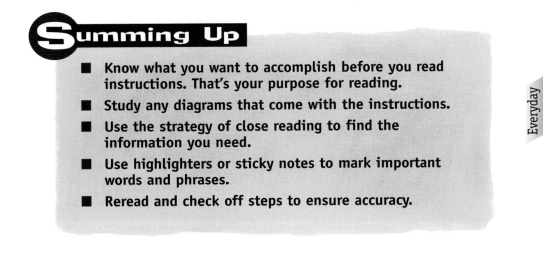

Summing Up

- **Know what you want to accomplish before you read instructions. That's your purpose for reading.**
- **Study any diagrams that come with the instructions.**
- **Use the strategy of close reading to find the information you need.**
- **Use highlighters or sticky notes to mark important words and phrases.**
- **Reread and check off steps to ensure accuracy.**

Everyday

Focus on Reading for Work

Work-related reading is important for a number of reasons, especially if you want to do well, advance, or even just keep your job. As an employee, you will need to do a variety of reading, from an employee handbook or job description, to work schedules and memos about workplace safety.

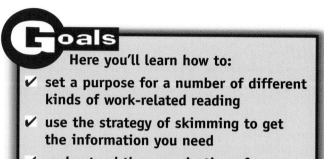

Goals

Here you'll learn how to:

✔ **set a purpose for a number of different kinds of work-related reading**

✔ **use the strategy of skimming to get the information you need**

✔ **understand the organization of different types of work-related writing**

Before Reading

If you have a summer job or after-school job, you are probably doing more work-related reading than you realize. Follow a few easy steps to get the most out of your workplace reading.

STEPS FOR UNDERSTANDING WORKPLACE READING

Step 1 *Identify the reason you're reading.*

Step 2 *Understand the way the writing is organized.*

Step 3 *Find what you need to know.*

Step 4 *Apply the information to your own life to help you remember it.*

588

Identifying a Reading Purpose

Think about what you want to know before you begin reading work-related materials. Are you looking for the company policy concerning breaks, vacation days, or sick pay? Do you want to find out if the company will pay for any of your education expenses?

Know *what* you're looking for so you have a purpose for reading. Then, look at the organization of the material so you'll know *where* to look. Various steps may be numbered, for example, or information may be organized by times or dates.

Let's say you want to know these two things: your work hours and the company's vacation and sick day policies. To find out your work hours, do you have to read everyone's work schedule? No, of course you don't. All you have to read is the work schedule that applies to you.

Note how the material itself often gives you the purpose for reading. Note, too, that your purpose changes depending on what you are reading.

READING PURPOSES

Workplace Reading	Reading Purpose
1. Memo on Workplace Safety	When do I have to wear safety goggles or a mask?
2. Job Description	Will I have to run errands in a part-time job I'm considering?
3. Work Schedule	When is the spaceship kit to be loaded for delivery?

Everyday

Now, preview these examples of everyday writing. As you do so, look for the information you need to fulfill your reading purpose. Here, you'll read:

■ a Memo on Workplace Safety

■ a Job Description

■ a Work Schedule

1. Memo on Workplace Safety

CREATIVE PRODUCTIONS, INC.

Creative Productions, Inc.
1167 Watershed Avenue
Willowbrook, Illinois 60202

Telephone 555-893-1000
email: creative@moonbeam.net
Fax 555-893-2000

PREVIEW
To whom
it is
written

PREVIEW
Who
wrote the
memo

Memo

To: Warehouse part-time staff	From: Bill Griffiths
Fax:	Pages: 1
Tel: 877-893-1000, ext. 2332	Date: November 30
Subject: New safety rules	CC: Supervisors

PREVIEW
Date sent

PREVIEW
Subject
of memo

To all part-time Warehouse staff:

Starting this week, the following **new safety rules go into effect.** Please observe these rules at all times while on company property.

1. Wear plastic safety goggles when in the packing room and near any equipment with moving parts.
2. Keep shirts tucked in and do not wear loose-fitting clothing around any of the machinery.

PREVIEW
Specific
information
for reading
purpose

3. Contact a supervisor if you see or are responsible for anything spilled on the factory floor, especially water or any oil-based products.
4. Report all injuries that occur at work within 15 minutes of the time they occur. Fill out a report for the nurse in your supervisor's office or at the main personnel office.
5. Wear safety masks when unpacking materials, especially any inventory packed in foam pellets, sawdust, or shredded paper.

These safety rules are to be observed at all times while employees are on company property. Thank you for your help.

Think safety first!

2. Job Description

Office Assistant Job Description

The office assistant manages all operations in the office and ensures that they run smoothly at all times. In addition, the office assistant helps the president. Applicants need excellent language skills, familiarity with computers, and a high school diploma.

1. Answer the phone when people are out of the office, away from their desks, or on the phone.
2. Prepare packages for mail, overnight delivery, or messenger services.
3. Drop off the mail and overnight delivery packages at Give Us Your Packages (at corner of Wilhelm and Lincoln streets) at the end of the day (about 20 minutes before your workday ends).

4. Photocopy jobs as soon as you can.
5. Make sure the photocopier and fax machine have plenty of paper and are working.
6. Keep the office clean.
7. Take out the trash when it accumulates.
8. Buy miscellaneous items (see list on refrigerator) from the grocery store as needed.
9. Water the plants once a week (on a day of your choosing).
10. Unload the books and packages that arrive and place them on the shelves. File catalogues and brochures as well, and put mail in reception desk in-basket.

Everyday

3. Work Schedule

PREVIEW — Title
PREVIEW — Key for color coding
PREVIEW — List of steps
PREVIEW — Specific information for reading purpose

Kit-building Schedules

Color key: Building | Packing | Storing

Kit	4/5	4/6	4/7	4/8	4/9	4/12	4/13	4/14	4/15	4/16	4/19	4/20	4/21	4/22	4/23	4/26	4/27	4/28	4/29	4/30	5/3	5/4
Racing Kit	1	1	2	3	4	5	5	6	7	7	8	8	9	9	9	10	11	12				
Sailing Kit	1	1	2	3	4	5	5	6	7	7	8	8	9	9	9	10	11	12				
Make-up Kit	1	1	2	3	4	5	5	6	7	7	8	8	9	9	9	10	11	12				
Truck Kit	1	1	2	3	4	5	5	6	7	7	8	8	9	9	9	10	11	12				
Spaceship Kit	1	1	2	3	4	5	5	6	7	7	8	8	9	9	9	10	11	12				
Battleship Kit	1	1	2	3	4	5	5	6	7	7	8	8	9	9	9	10	11	12				
Earring Kit			1	1	2	3	4	5	5	6	7	7	8	8	9	9	9	10	11	12		
Necklace Kit			1	1	2	3	4	5	5	6	7	7	8	8	9	9	9	10	11	12		
Painting Kit			1	1	2	3	4	5	5	6	7	7	8	8	9	9	9	10	11	12		
T-shirt Painting Kit			1	1	2	3	4	5	5	6	7	7	8	8	9	9	9	10	11	12		
Music-making Kit					1	1	2	3	4	5	5	6	7	7	8	8	9	9	9	10	11	12
Rock Painting Kit					1	1	2	3	4	5	5	6	7	7	8	8	9	9	9	10	11	12
Book-making Kit					1	1	2	3	4	5	5	6	7	7	8	8	9	9	9	10	11	12
Pumpkin-carving Kit					1	1	2	3	4	5	5	6	7	7	8	8	9	9	9	10	11	12
Easter Egg Kit					1	1	2	3	4	5	5	6	7	7	8	8	9	9	9	10	11	12

Steps	Tasks	Days	
1	Create initial drawing of kit	2	
2	List key items in kit	1	
3	Find source for each item in kit	1	Stage 1: Building
4	Create model kit	1	
5	Set up kit items for assembly	2	
6	Run test assembly of kit	1	
7	Build boxes for kits	2	
8	Pack items in boxes	2	Stage 2: Packing
9	Wrap kits in shipping paper	3	
10	Move kits for storage	1	
11	Load kits for delivery	1	
12	Delivery of kits to warehouse	1	Stage 3: Storing
		18 days	3.8 weeks

Reading Strategy: Skimming

When you're looking for specific information, the best reading strategy to use is **skimming.** When you skim, you run your eyes quickly over the material, looking for headings, boldface type, bulleted lists, and other elements that call attention to themselves. You slow down to read the parts that contain key words you are looking to find and read those parts more closely. Then, you go back to the skimming.

Skimming is like channel-surfing with your TV remote control. You just keep on going until you find something that's interesting. Then you focus in on what you want to see.

During Reading

Once you have a plan and a strategy, the next step is to read. Look back at the memo, job description, and work schedule on pages 590–592. Note how key words and features have been highlighted.

These highlighted parts hold the most interest for you as a reader. Often you need to find just a small bit of information buried within a document. Here are a few tips to help you find what you need.

Tip #1: Read Titles or Headings

As you skim the material, pay attention to the headings. They usually tell you the subject, or what the material is about. Think about your purpose.

For example, look at the kit-building schedule. On what day should you begin loading the spaceship kits? To answer that question, you need to read all of the titles and headings. First, find out which task loading kits is (step 11). Next, read down the column with the names of the kits to find the spaceship kit. Then, read over to step 11 and up to the date (4/27).

Everyday

Tip #2: Highlight

Sometimes, if you can, you may want to use a highlighter to mark important parts. It makes key words stand out. That way, the next time you're looking for the same information, it will be easy to find.

For example, by highlighting key words in the job description, you read actively through the list. The act of highlighting keeps you involved with what you are reading, and that can help you remember more of what you read.

Tip #3: Connect the Information to Yourself

A large amount of work-related reading may seem a little boring. Reading at work is not like reading for fun. You may even need to connect it to yourself just to make the material understandable.

For example, you might imagine what your day would be like if you came to work and performed each of the responsibilities listed in the job description. How would you feel about that job?

After Reading

When you do everyday reading, you're usually looking for specific information. If you find it, you're done. You don't have to read any more. If, however, you don't find it, you have to keep looking. Here are a few suggestions if you don't find the information you want the first time through the material.

1. Reread

Maybe you skimmed the material too quickly. Go back and reread it, this time a little more slowly. Look again at the headings, the boldface type, and words in capital letters. If there's a table of contents or an index, take a closer look at it. Maybe you were looking in the wrong place for the information you wanted.

2. Ask for Help

Sometimes the information is right where you were looking, but you just didn't see it. Maybe your mind was wandering or not fully tuned in to the task of understanding what you read. Whatever the reason, you need some help. Ask a friend to take a look at the material too. A friend might help you to see the material in a new way and get more from it.

Summing Up

- Set a purpose before you begin reading work-related material.
- Be aware of the organization of the material.
- Use the strategy of skimming to find the information you need.
- Use a highlighter to help you remember more of what you read.
- Look back to see if you found what you were looking for.

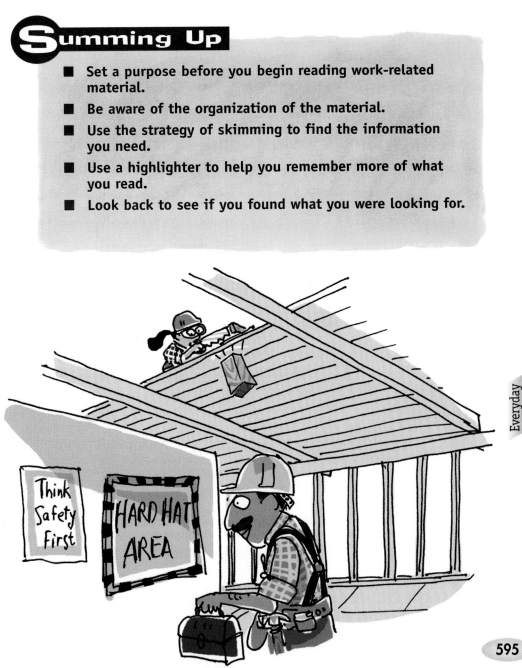

Think Safety First

HARD HAT AREA

Everyday

Reading
for Tests

Introduction to Reading for Tests

Reading Tests and Test Questions

Ways of Reading Tests

Focus on English Tests
Focus on Writing Tests
Focus on Standardized Tests
Focus on History Tests
Focus on Math Tests
Focus on Science Tests

English Test
Results

Tests

Introduction to Reading for Tests

Who, if anyone, actually *likes* taking tests? The answer is probably no one. But your job is not necessarily to *enjoy* the tests you take but to do well on them.

Over the course of one year, you'll take a number of tests in your courses and perhaps one or more standardized tests. The tests in your classes evaluate how well you have learned a particular subject, such as algebra or English. Your scores will be compared with others in your class or in your grade.

Standardized tests examine your knowledge of a range of subjects, such as math, history, and English. You also may be asked to take state- or district-level standardized tests, called "exit exams." Like the nationwide standardized tests, exit exams also test your knowledge of a range of subjects. Your scores on these tests will be compared with the scores made by students across your state or across the country.

Although every test you take will be a little different, the way you take the test can be almost the same. You can use the reading process to help you read and score well on the tests you take, and you can apply the strategies and tips you'll learn in this chapter.

Reading Tests and Test Questions

You can improve your test-taking abilities by remembering one simple tip: read the directions, questions, and answer choices carefully.

All too often, you are in a hurry, pressured by having a limited time for the test, or flustered by a difficult question. You begin reading but rush through the reading selection or test questions. Then, none of the answers seems to make sense. Suddenly, the entire test seems really difficult, and you begin to panic. What if you can't answer the questions?

You can avoid this "test anxiety" by using the reading process and some good reading strategies and by preparing a little in advance.

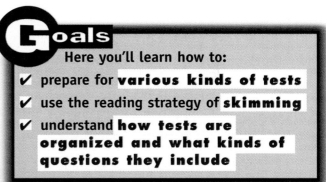

Goals

Here you'll learn how to:

✔ prepare for **various kinds of tests**

✔ use the reading strategy of **skimming**

✔ understand **how tests are organized and what kinds of questions they include**

Before Reading

The key to doing well on any type of test is to be well prepared. It makes no sense to wait until the last minute and then cram, cram, cram. You simply cannot process and understand a large amount of material in a short amount of time. What you need to do, then, is begin preparing for important tests at least a week in advance. Make a test-taking plan, and then stick to it up to the day of the test.

A good test-taking plan will include a method for reviewing the information, memorizing what you need to know, and using that knowledge on the test itself.

In the days before the test, learn everything you can about the kind of test you'll be taking and the types of questions that you can expect to see. Use class notes, textbooks, study guides, old quizzes, and any other related material to help you prepare.

Tests

A Set a Purpose

You should have a plan for what to do when the test is in front of you. First, you need to find out what the test questions are asking. Next, decide question by question what information you need for the answer.

Setting a Purpose

■ **What is the test question asking?**

■ **What information is needed to answer it?**

B Preview

On the morning of the test, review your notes one last time before school. Focus on the areas that gave you the most trouble while preparing for the test. Then, gather the materials you'll need for the test: pencils, highlighters, calculator, ruler, or whatever else you need to bring.

As soon as your teacher passes out the test, preview the entire exam. (On some standardized tests, you are not allowed to flip through the entire booklet. On these tests, preview the first page only.)

Read the directions and at least three or four of the questions. Your goal is to get a general sense of what the test is about and what the questions are like. Look for the following:

Preview Checklist

✔ the amount of time you have to take the test

✔ the instructions about how to mark answers

✔ whether or not there is a penalty for wrong answers

✔ the types of questions, such as multiple-choice, true-false, short answer, or essay

✔ any test passages, maps, diagrams, or other graphics

Now preview the sample English test that follows. Use the Preview Checklist to guide you as you skim the pages of the test.

PREVIEW

Amount of time and question type

Midyear English Test

60 Minutes—5 Questions, 1 Essay

DIRECTIONS: Answer each question. Choose the correct answer and then fill in the corresponding oval on your answer sheet. Write your essay in the blue test booklet.

Do not linger over problems that seem too difficult. Skip these and return to them later. You will not be penalized for wrong answers.

PREVIEW

Special instructions

PREVIEW

No penalty for guessing

Passage

"The Laugher"

Read this short story. Think about the writer's message for readers. Then answer the questions that follow.

PREVIEW

Type of reading

NOTE

Story title and author

"The Laugher" by Heinrich Böll

When someone asks me what business I am in, I am seized with embarrassment: I blush and stammer, I who am otherwise known as a man of poise. I envy people who can say: I am a bricklayer. I envy barbers, bookkeepers, and writers the simplicity of their avowal, for all these professions speak for themselves and need no lengthy explanation, while I am constrained to reply to such questions: I am a laugher. An admission of this kind demands another, since I have to answer the second question: "Is that how you make your living?" truthfully with "Yes." I actually do make a living at my laughing, and a good one too, for my laughing is—commercially speaking—much in demand. I am a good laugher, experienced, no one else laughs as well as I do, no one else has such a command of the fine points of my art. For a long time, in order to avoid tiresome explanations, I called myself an actor, but my talents in the field of mime and elocution are so meager that I felt this designation to be too far from the truth: I love the truth, and the truth is: I am a laugher. I am neither a clown nor a comedian. I do not make people gay, I portray gaiety: I laugh like a Roman

NOTE

Important detail

NOTE

How he makes a living

Tests

emperor, or like a sensitive schoolboy, I am as much at home in the laughter of the seventeenth century as in that of the nineteenth, and when occasion demands I laugh my way through all the centuries, all classes of society, all categories of age: it is simply a skill which I have acquired, like the skill of being able to repair shoes. In my breast I harbor the laughter of America, the laughter of Africa, white, red, yellow laughter—and for the right fee I let it peal out in accordance with the director's requirements.

I have become indispensable; I laugh on records, I laugh on tape, and television directors treat me with respect. I laugh mournfully, moderately, hysterically; I laugh like a streetcar conductor or like a helper in the grocery business; laughter in the morning, laughter in the evening, nocturnal laughter and the laughter of twilight. In short: wherever and however laughter is required—I do it.

It need hardly be pointed out that a profession of this kind is tiring, especially as I have also—this is my specialty—mastered the art of infectious laughter; this has also made me indispensable to third- and fourth-rate comedians, who are scared—and with good reason—that their audiences will miss their punch lines, so I spend most evenings in night clubs as a kind of discreet claque, my job being to laugh infectiously during the weaker parts of the program. It has to be carefully timed: my hearty, boisterous laughter must not come too soon, but neither must it come too late, it must come just at the right spot: at the pre-arranged moment I burst out laughing, the whole audience roars with me, and the joke is saved.

But as for me, I drag myself exhausted to the checkroom, put on my overcoat, happy that I can go off duty at last. At home I usually find telegrams waiting for me: "Urgently require your laughter. Recording Tuesday," and a few hours later I am sitting in an overheated express train bemoaning my fate.

I need scarcely say that when I am off duty or on

NOTE
Subject of paragraph

NOTE
How he feels

NOTE
Important details

vacation, I have little inclination to laugh: the cowhand is glad when he can forget the cow, the bricklayer when he can forget the mortar, and carpenters usually have doors at home which don't work or drawers which are hard to open. Confectioners like sour pickles, butchers like marzipan, and the baker prefers sausage to bread; bullfighters raise pigeons for a hobby, boxers turn pale when their children have nose-bleeds: I find all this quite natural, for I never laugh off duty. I am a very solemn person, and people consider me—perhaps rightly so—a pessimist.

> **NOTE**
> **Important details**

During the first years of our married life, my wife would often say to me: "Do laugh!" but since then she has come to realize that I cannot grant her this wish. I am happy when I am free to relax my tense face muscles, my frayed spirit, in profound solemnity. Indeed, even other people's laughter gets on my nerves, since it reminds me too much of my profession. So our marriage is a quiet, peaceful one, because my wife has also forgotten how to laugh; now and again I catch her smiling, and I smile too. We converse in low tones, for I detest the noise of the night clubs, the noise that sometimes fills the recording studios. People who do not know me think I am taciturn. Perhaps I am, because I have to open my mouth so often to laugh.

I go through life with an impassive expression, from time to time permitting myself a gentle smile, and I often wonder whether I have ever laughed. I think not. My brothers and sisters have always known me for a serious boy.

So I laugh in many different ways, but my own laughter I have never heard.

> **NOTE**
> **Main point?**

Tests

Multiple-choice Questions

1. What is the narrator's profession?
   - A. comedian
   - B. actor
   - C. clown
   - D. laugher

> **PREVIEW**
> **Several multiple-choice questions**

603

NOTE
Vocabulary
question

2. At one point, the narrator says his job involves "laughter in the morning, laughter in the evening, nocturnal laughter and the laughter of twilight." What does *nocturnal* mean?

    A. afternoon

    B. daybreak

    C. nighttime

    D. never

NOTE
Fact
question

3. What is the narrator unable to do for his wife?

    A. smile

    B. speak in a loud voice

    C. laugh

    D. make money for fine things

4. Which of these words would you say best describe the narrator?

    A. timid and nervous

    B. talkative and jolly

    C. somber and serious

    D. warm and loving

NOTE
Inference
questions

5. What do you think the narrator means when he says, "So I laugh in many different ways, but my own laughter I have never heard."

    A. He can laugh, but he cannot smile.

    B. He is hearing impaired.

    C. He's afraid to show his wife that he can laugh.

    D. He seems happier on the outside than he is on the inside.

PREVIEW
Essay
question

Essay Question

What do you think is the main idea of this story? Write a one-paragraph summary. Support what you say with evidence from the text. Then proofread your work.

C Plan

Be sure to spend part of your preview time looking at the test questions you need to answer. Some questions ask for recall of facts, and others will require you to make an inference or draw a conclusion. Get into the habit of putting a check mark or star next to questions that you think you know how to answer. These are the questions you'll answer first when it comes time to take the test.

Reading Strategy: Skimming

Skimming means letting your eyes roam down the page in search of key words. Most tests require you to return to the passage or test item again and again to find answers to specific questions. Skimming can help you to do this quickly and efficiently.

Skimming does not replace doing a careful first reading. But few readers can remember all of the details in a passage after one reading. Skimming is the strategy you use after you've read the passage and begun answering the questions.

STEPS TO ANSWER TEST QUESTIONS

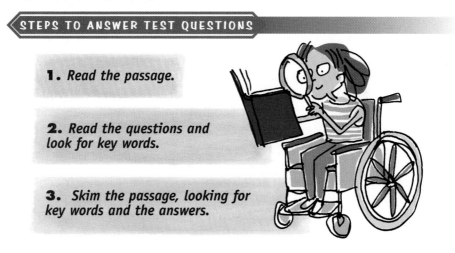

1. *Read the passage.*

2. *Read the questions and look for key words.*

3. *Skim the passage, looking for key words and the answers.*

Tests

You can skim in many different ways. Most readers find it helps to skim with a tool, such as a pencil, note card, or student I.D. Run the tool down the center of the page and let your eyes follow along. Watch for key words or phrases from the questions. With a little practice, you'll find that you're able to skim an entire selection in about 30 seconds.

During Reading

A slow and careful reading of the passage or test items is essential. If you rush, you run the risk of missing important information or misunderstanding important facts.

D Read with a Purpose

Remember to follow the steps in your plan when reading a test.

1. Read the Passage

When you read a test passage, use a highlighter if you're allowed. (Most standardized tests allow you to mark the test booklet as much as you like.) Make notes about key words or information that seems important. Remember that in many paragraphs the first sentence and the last sentence

TEST PLAN
✔ Read the Passage
✔ Read the Questions
✔ Skim for Answers

often have special importance, so read them with extra care.

Look back at the highlighted details one reader marked while reading "The Laugher." Sometimes, as is the case with the first paragraph, you'll find many important details. In other paragraphs, you'll find just a few. Keep in mind that too much highlighting can end up distracting you. Mark only the details that you think are significant to the overall meaning.

2. Read the Questions

On your preview, you skimmed the questions to get an idea of the types of questions and what you'll be expected to know. After you finish your careful reading of the passage, read the test questions again.

Probably the easiest way to raise your test scores is to read each question and the possible answers *very carefully*. Be sure you understand what information the question is asking you to find.

As you read each question, underline or highlight the key words in the question. Each question will have a few key words that tell you what to find out, as in this example.

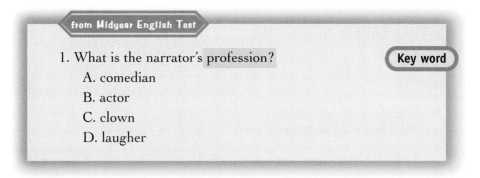

1. What is the narrator's profession?
   A. comedian
   B. actor
   C. clown
   D. laugher

Key word

Read all possible answers to the question, even if you're sure you know the correct answer.

Although it might seem like a waste of time to read every answer, read them anyway. Sometimes the first answer you see will look right, when in fact the third or fourth answer is the correct one. For instance, you might be tempted to mark the first answer above until you read down to the best answer.

3. Skim for Answers

Sometimes you will be able to find the exact words of an answer in the passage itself. That's usually easy to find. If the question is "What motivated John Brown?" and one of the answers reads, "to serve the cause of liberty," skim for that quote in the passage. But often answers will paraphrase or reword what's in the passage. One answer might be that John Brown "fought for freedom." So sometimes you have to look for answers that paraphrase what's in the passage.

Take another look at the test questions for "The Laugher." Of the five multiple-choice questions, two ask for factual recall, and three require critical thinking. You will see these types of questions frequently.

KINDS OF TEST QUESTIONS

Factual recall
The answer is right there, in the passage.

Critical thinking
You must make inferences or draw conclusions.

Essay
You must answer a question by writing a short essay.

Tests

607

FACTUAL RECALL QUESTIONS

You can find the answer to a factual recall question "right there" within the passage itself. This is where the strategy of skimming comes in.

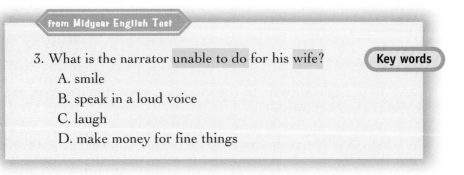

from Midyear English Test

3. What is the narrator unable to do for his wife?   **Key words**
   A. smile
   B. speak in a loud voice
   C. laugh
   D. make money for fine things

To answer, begin by skimming the story for the key word *wife*. Most questions will have one or two key words that can help you zero in on the correct answer. *Wife* appears in paragraph six. Once you find the key word, you need to:

1. read the sentence that contains the key word.

2. read the *sentence before* and the *sentence after* the one with the key word.

If you do that, you'll know the answer is "C. laugh."

CRITICAL THINKING QUESTIONS

Many test questions will ask you to make inferences about the reading passage. Inference questions might ask about the main idea, style, tone, mood, main character, author's purpose, and so on.

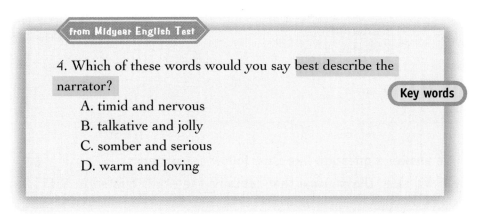

from **Midyear English Test**

4. Which of these words would you say best describe the narrator?

Key words

   A. timid and nervous
   B. talkative and jolly
   C. somber and serious
   D. warm and loving

To answer this question, you'll need to make inferences about the narrator's personality using clues that you find in the passage. Look for words you highlighted, and skim for words in the passage that describe the narrator. Look, too, for things the narrator says or does. For example, the last sentence states, "but my own laughter I have never heard." These can be clues. Then, take what you learned and put it with what you already know. Use what you find to answer the question.

INFERENCE QUESTIONS

WHAT I LEARNED	+ WHAT I ALREADY KNOW	= ANSWER
"my own laughter I have never heard"	doesn't sound happy	probably "C. somber and serious"

Test questions frequently point you to a specific part of the passage and ask you to examine a word or line, as in this example:

Tests

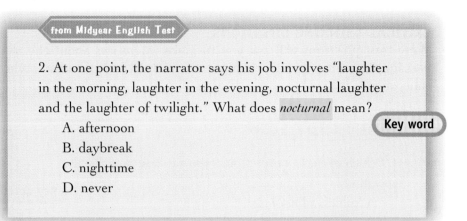

2. At one point, the narrator says his job involves "laughter in the morning, laughter in the evening, nocturnal laughter and the laughter of twilight." What does *nocturnal* mean?

    A. afternoon

    B. daybreak

    C. nighttime

    D. never

Key word

To answer a question like this, follow these steps:

First, skim the passage that contains the words quoted in the question.

Then, read three or more sentences surrounding the word you are asked to define. Look for context clues that can help you find the meaning of the word.

from "The Laugher"

    I have become indispensable; I laugh on records, I laugh on tape, and television directors treat me with respect. I laugh mournfully, moderately, hysterically; I laugh like a streetcar conductor or like a helper in the grocery business; laughter in the morning, laughter in the evening, nocturnal laughter and the laughter of twilight. In short: wherever and however laughter is required—I do it.

Read the part before.

Read the part after.

When you return to the paragraph and sentence in which the word *nocturnal* appears, you see the context. The words around *nocturnal* are *evening, twilight,* and *morning.* You'll also find that in the next paragraph the narrator says he spends much of his time working in "night clubs." This helps to confirm for you that the correct answer is "C. nighttime."

ESSAY QUESTIONS

The key to essay questions is to read them carefully, plan what you'll say, write, and check your work. In short, you need to use the writing process.

> **from Midyear English Test**
>
> What do you think is the main idea of this story? Write a one-paragraph summary. Support what you say with evidence from the text. Then proofread your work.

The essay question asks you to do four things. Now read the question again and note what it asks.

> **from Midyear English Test**
>
> **①** What do you think is the main idea of this story? Write a
> **②** one-paragraph summary. **③** Support what you say with
> evidence from the text. Then **④** proofread your work.

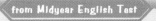

A Main Idea Organizer can help you sort out your thoughts.

> **MAIN IDEA ORGANIZER**
>
> | MAIN IDEA | | |
> |---|---|---|
> | It's possible to laugh and still be serious. | | |
> | **DETAIL #1** | **DETAIL #2** | **DETAIL #3** |
> | He bemoans his fate. | Although the narrator is a laugher by profession, he says he is a "very solemn person." | His brothers and sisters "have always known" him to be "serious." |
> | **CONCLUSION** A person who seems happy may actually be quite serious on the inside. | | |

Tests

Write your essay using this organizer, and afterward check your work. Read the essay word for word to yourself, check punctuation and spelling, and you're done.

611

How Tests Are Organized

In most cases, the questions on a test will progress from easy to somewhat more difficult ones.

ORDER OF QUESTIONS

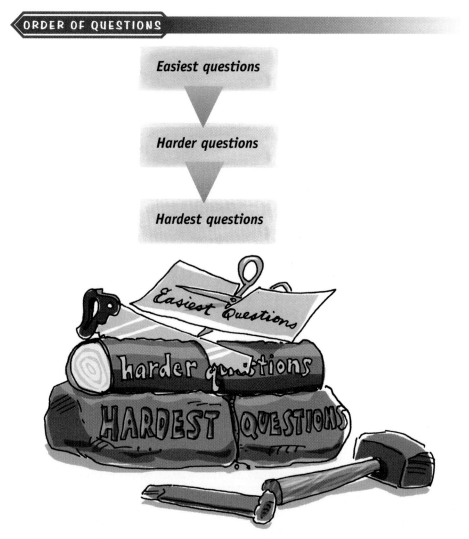

Easiest questions

Harder questions

Hardest questions

Furthermore, the questions about a reading passage also tend to follow the order of the reading. This means that you should look for the answer to question 1 in the beginning of the passage, the answer to question 2 slightly after that, and so on.

For example, in the test shown earlier, the answer to question 1 can be found in the first paragraph. The answer to question 2 comes in the second paragraph.

E Connect

You're probably asking yourself, "Why would I want to make a connection to the questions on a test?" After all, your main focus is to answer the questions correctly. But if you think about it, connecting to a test question makes a whole lot of sense. You can use these personal connections to help raise your score.

from "The Laugher"

I go through life with an impassive expression, from time to time permitting myself a gentle smile, and I often wonder whether I have ever laughed. I think not. My brothers and sisters have always known me for a serious boy.

So I laugh in many different ways, but my own laughter I have never heard.

This kind of thing happens in life. Lots of times kids laugh, but they really don't think things are funny.

After Reading

Always try to leave three to five minutes at the end of the test to check your answers. Mistakes on tests can result because you don't fill in the answer sheet correctly. Be sure your name is correctly printed at the top of the page. If you're asked to fill in ovals, be sure you do so with a pencil, rather than a pen. Be sure also that you fill in the entire oval. Most standardized tests are machine-graded, and machines have no sympathy for students who fail to fill in the answer ovals completely.

Tests

F Pause and Reflect

Spend a moment checking to see which questions you've answered and which ones you've left blank or made guesses on. Check the clock to see how much time remains. Take another look at the hard questions to see whether you want to make any changes in the answers.

■ **Have I answered every question to the best of my ability?**

■ **Are there answers that I need to rethink or spend more time on?**

■ **Is my writing in the essay answer neat and free of spelling and grammatical errors?**

You've met your purpose only if you've found the information needed to answer each question. This means that you may need to return to some of the questions you had trouble with and do some rereading. Sometimes rereading a question a second or even a third time will clarify what's needed, and suddenly you'll know the correct answer.

G Reread

You'll probably need a new strategy to help you find information that is relevant to these tougher questions. Many test-takers use the strategy of visualizing and thinking aloud to help them answer the hardest questions.

Rereading Strategy: Visualizing and Thinking Aloud

Return to the most difficult questions and try **visualizing and thinking aloud.** Reread the question, and then talk your way through the answers. Try talking quietly to yourself as you would if you were explaining something to a friend.

---

from Midyear English Test

5. What do you think the narrator means when he says, "So I laugh in many different ways, but my own laughter I have never heard."

    A. He can laugh, but he cannot smile.

    B. He is hearing impaired.

    C. He's afraid to show his wife that he can laugh.

    D. He seems happier on the outside than he is on the inside.

Here's the part of the story that contains the quote in the question, as well as the paragraph before it:

from "The Laugher"

I go through life with an impassive expression, from time to time permitting myself a gentle smile, and I often wonder whether I have ever laughed. I think not. My brothers and sisters have always known me for a serious boy.

So I laugh in many different ways, but my own laughter I have never heard.

By returning to the selection and rereading, you can probably eliminate one or more answers that are clearly wrong. Talk to yourself about each possible answer. Visualize what the narrator is saying here and what he has said throughout the story.

THINK ALOUD

I'm not really sure what he means when he says that he laughs a lot, but that he's never heard his own laughter. I know from what he said earlier that he does in fact smile, so I can cross out answer A. I also know from what I've read that this guy is not hearing impaired. He can hear the night club jokes and knows the right moment to laugh, so I am sure answer B. is also wrong.

from Midyear English Test

A. He can laugh, but he cannot smile.

B. He is hearing impaired.

C. He's afraid to show his wife that he can laugh.

D. He seems happier on the outside than he is on the inside.

Tests

Now that you've crossed out two choices, you have a better chance at figuring out the answer to the question. Again, use the strategy of thinking aloud:

It's possible that C. is the correct answer, but the word afraid bothers me. This doesn't seem like a guy who is scared. He seems like a guy who is depressed. So I'm going to say D. is correct.

H Remember

Sometimes after you finish a test, you want to forget about it. Try to resist this urge. You might be surprised how much more you can learn if you spend a few minutes discussing and reflecting on the test questions. Here are a few ways to do that.

1. Ask a Classmate

After the test is finished, talk about the questions with other students. See how they answered the tough questions, and ask about questions you had trouble with. Remember that knowing the answer to some of these challenging questions might help on a future test.

2. Test Yourself

After a test, ask yourself questions like these:

What helped me most to answer the test questions?

What would I do differently for the next test?

How well prepared was I?

Summing Up

Use the reading process to help you read a test. First, preview the test to find out what the questions are asking. Then, read the passage and each question. Use the strategy of **skimming** to locate answers to specific questions. Remember that test questions can often be divided into **three basic types:**

■ factual recall

■ critical thinking

■ essay

When you reread test questions, **visualizing and thinking aloud** can help you decide on the correct answers.

Focus on English Tests

As a high school student, you'll take lots of English tests. Many of these will be course exams, since almost all school districts require four years of English. Almost any standardized test or exit exam you take will have an English or reading component.

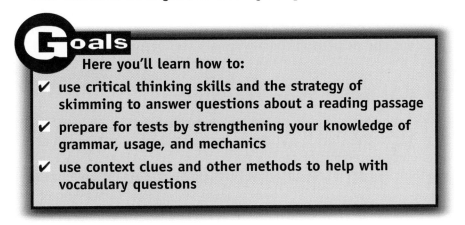

oals

Here you'll learn how to:

✔ **use critical thinking skills and the strategy of skimming to answer questions about a reading passage**

✔ **prepare for tests by strengthening your knowledge of grammar, usage, and mechanics**

✔ **use context clues and other methods to help with vocabulary questions**

Before Reading

Most English exams will test your knowledge of:

▪ reading

▪ grammar, usage, and mechanics

▪ vocabulary

Some tests will also look at your writing ability.

One of the best ways to study for an English test is to read, because reading can improve your vocabulary and your knowledge of grammar. It can also sharpen your ability to make inferences and draw conclusions—two critical thinking skills that you'll use often.

During a test, take what you've learned from your own reading, and put it with what you've learned in class. Here are a few tips that can help you to be better prepared.

Tests

Tip #1: Make Note Cards

You can use Study or Note Cards to help you prepare for an English test. Write grammatical terms (such as *appositive*) on the front and definitions with examples on the back.

Tip #2: Take a Practice Test

Ask your teacher what the test will cover. Then, create a practice test of your own. Exchange tests with a classmate. You'll find that writing questions and answering them will help you prepare.

Tip #3: Build Your Vocabulary

Try to learn the meaning of some new words before each test. Look for words in the stories and books you're reading. Put them in a vocabulary notebook or on file cards. Then learn them. Vocabulary questions are on many different tests, so start preparing yourself.

By using tests as one more reason to learn new vocabulary, you'll help yourself gear up for the test and build your vocabulary at the same time.

Tip #4: Learn Key Rules

English tests tend to be about a few subjects over and over again. For example, they will test to see if you can identify a sentence fragment and a run-on sentence. They will test to see if you can use commas and quotation marks. And they will see whether you understand the rules for subject-verb agreement. If you learn the rules about these few things, you'll start scoring better on English tests, because questions on these topics are almost always on them.

Before you begin answering questions, preview the test. Look for the kinds of questions included. Are there vocabulary questions? Questions asking you about punctuation and usage? Questions about a reading passage? After seeing what's on the test, you can plan how you will handle the various parts.

During Reading

After a preview of the passage and questions, begin working through the test. First, answer the easiest questions. You are likely to find at least three different kinds of questions on English tests:

- reading passage questions
- grammar, usage, and mechanics questions
- vocabulary questions

Reading Passage Questions

Most standardized English exams begin with two passages for you to read. Usually one passage will be fiction and the other one will be nonfiction.

Use the reading process described in this handbook to help you read the passage. Take notes on the test booklet if you can. Watch especially for sentences that sound important, such as those at the beginning or end of the passage. These may relate to the author's theme or main idea.

Then, begin answering the questions. Use the strategy of skimming. Because most reading passage questions tend to follow the order of the passage itself, skim the first paragraph for question 1, the next few paragraphs for question 2, and so on.

Some questions will require you to make inferences. To answer these questions, skim to find the part of the passage that contains the key words in the question. Then, reread carefully several sentences or even paragraphs in the area of those key words. Ask yourself, "What is the author telling me here?" Your answer to this question might be the answer to the test question. Now read the sample passage and question on the next page.

Tests

Reading Passage #1
from *A Tale of Two Cities* by Charles Dickens

Along the Paris streets, the death-carts rumble, hollow and harsh. Six tumbrils carry the day's wine to La Guillotine. All the devouring and insatiate monsters imagined since imagination could record itself, are fused in the one realization, Guillotine. And yet there is not in France, with its rich variety of soil and climate, a blade, a leaf, a root, a sprig, a peppercorn, which will grow to maturity under conditions more certain than those that have produced this horror. Crush humanity out of shape once more, under similar hammers, and it will twist itself into the same tortured forms. Sow the same seed of rapacious license and oppression over again, and it will surely yield the same fruit according to its kind.

DIRECTIONS: Use Reading Passage #1 to help you answer the following questions.

1. When Dickens says, "Crush humanity out of shape once more, under similar hammers, and it will twist itself into the same tortured forms," he is saying that . . .

   A. People rarely make the same major mistakes twice.
   B. History can repeat itself.
   C. Revenge is impossible for the worst crimes of all.
   D. The era of the Guillotine is long past and best forgotten.

Try thinking aloud to help you answer this question.

THINK ALOUD

The sentence after the quote says that if you "sow the same seed" the yield will be the same. That shows that answers D. and A. cannot be right. Since there is no mention of revenge in the passage, C. must also be wrong. So B. is probably the correct answer.

Grammar, Usage, and Mechanics Questions

Some English tests assess your knowledge of the rules of the language. The key to doing well with these questions is to read carefully and come to the test prepared. You can assume your English test will be like most others and ask about the rules of:

■ capitalization

■ punctuation

■ usage

■ subject-verb agreement

First, examine the word or sentence in the question. Then, decide for yourself what's wrong with it. Next, read the possible answers. See if one of the answers matches your thoughts. For example, here is a typical question:

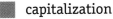
SAMPLE QUESTION

DIRECTIONS: Read the sentence. Look at the words and phrases underlined. If the word or phrase is incorrect, mark the choice that makes the statement appropriate for standard English. If the word or phrase is correct, mark NO CHANGE.

2. The three children, <u>whom were all</u> dressed exactly alike, carried in their hands the papier-mâché airplanes they made at school last week.

    A. NO CHANGE

    B. who were all

    C. they were all

    D. all of whom were all

The question asks about "whom were all." The answers tell you to focus on *whom,* because they all have "were all." So, focus on the pronoun *whom.* Is this usage correct? *Were* is a verb, and a verb needs a subject. But you may remember learning that *whom* is not used as a subject. You'll probably see you need *who,* not *whom,* in this sentence. That means B. is correct.

Vocabulary Questions

The vocabulary part of a test will include questions about word definitions, parts of speech, and word relationships (word analogies). Use context clues to help you figure out the meaning of a word or an analogy you don't understand.

For example, read the test question below. What context clues can help you figure out the meaning of the underlined word?

To answer, look at the second half of the sentence. The rain has "created little rivers" in the ground. The context tells you the answer must be "D. soaked."

Word analogies test your knowledge of word relationships. To solve an analogy, first look at the pair of words given (for example, *color* : *green* ::) and decide how they are related. Here are seven common relationships explored in word analogies:

COMMON KINDS OF WORD ANALOGIES

1. synonyms *(SCARY : FRIGHTENING)*	**2. antonyms** *(ASLEEP : AWAKE)*	**3. set and subset** *(COLOR : GREEN)*
4. succession or pattern *(ZIG : ZAG)*	**5. a part of** *(MILK : DAIRY)*	**6. relative size** *(SKYSCRAPER : HOUSE)*
7. relationship to each other *(LION : CUB)*	**8. homophones** *(AIR : HEIR)*	**9. forms of a word** *(CURIOUS : CURIOSITY)*

Now try to complete this analogy:

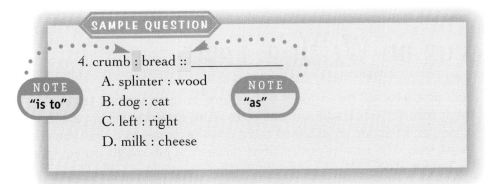

SAMPLE QUESTION

4. crumb : bread :: _____

NOTE "is to"

NOTE "as"

A. splinter : wood
B. dog : cat
C. left : right
D. milk : cheese

The first colon in an analogy stands for the words "is to." The double colon stands for the word "as." Read an analogy this way: *Crumb is to bread as _____*. To answer this question, you first need to figure out that *crumb* is a subset, or small part of, *bread*. Then, look for a choice that shares this same relationship. The correct answer is "A. splinter : wood" because *splinter* is a subset of *wood*.

After Reading

With any test, leave a few minutes at the end to check your work. Proofread any writing you did, and be sure you haven't made any obvious errors on the answer sheet. Return to questions that gave you the most trouble, and look at those answers again.

No matter what, be confident and don't doubt yourself or your answers. If you still can't figure out an analogy or grammar problem, stick with your original answer. In most cases, your first choice will probably be your best one.

Summing Up

- **Use the strategy of skimming to help you answer questions about a reading passage.**
- **With grammar questions, answer the question on your own first, and then read the choices given.**
- **Use context clues to help you with vocabulary questions.**
- **To solve an analogy, figure out the relationship between the pair of words given.**

Tests

Focus on Writing Tests

You probably will be required to take one or more writing tests in high school. Your challenge will be to write an essay within a specific time period about an assigned topic or in response to a text you first must read. The time pressure alone makes the job tough, so you need to be prepared.

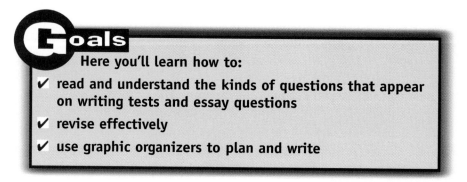

Goals

Here you'll learn how to:

✔ **read and understand the kinds of questions that appear on writing tests and essay questions**

✔ **revise effectively**

✔ **use graphic organizers to plan and write**

Before Reading

In the days leading up to test day, find out what you can about the test. Some districts and states have websites that you can use to prepare yourself mentally for what's to come. The more you know about the test ahead of time, the more confident you'll feel on test day.

When you hear the words "writing test," you can expect to be tested on a few basic areas:

 correcting sentence errors

 improving sentences and paragraphs

 responding to essay questions in timed writings

Here are some tips to help you get ready for a writing test.

Tip #1: Prepare for a Writing Test

Review the basics. Know the basic rules for correcting errors in sentences, such as fragments and run-ons, subject-verb agreement, and placement of modifying phrases and clauses.

Complete one or more practice tests or test questions. Practice tests and questions are often available on the test's website, or you can make up test questions on your own.

Talk to others who have taken the test in the past. The questions will change from year to year, of course, but the form of the test will likely stay the same. So, learn from others who've already taken the test.

Get a plan. Go into the test with a plan for how essays on essay tests should be structured. Memorize that plan, so you can concentrate on answering the essay question instead of wondering *how* your essay should be written.

Tip #2: Preview a Writing Test

As soon as you receive your copy of the test, preview it to see what kinds of questions are on it and what sort of essay you will have to write. For most of the writing tests you take, you'll need to answer either one or two essay questions. You'll probably have a set amount of time for each essay. That means you'll need to decide how many minutes to spend on each part of the exam.

Test writers often put the easiest questions first and progress to the more challenging questions. Consider that as you preview the test.

During Reading

The first few minutes of a writing test are probably your most important. Collect your thoughts. Try not to let the first puzzling question shake your confidence. Keep your cool, take a deep breath, relax, and then get to work.

Tests

Tip #3: Read the Directions

Read the directions carefully. If you can, use a highlighter or pencil to mark the most important parts of the directions. This is also where most test-takers make their first critical mistake. They tend to rush through reading the directions and questions and misunderstand them.

Tip #4: Read the Possible Answers Carefully

You will find more clues than you think by reading the possible answers carefully. Often you can rule out one or more answers just by reading them with care. Especially on writing tests, you need to read the answers with as much or even more care than the questions themselves. A single comma or period might be the only difference between two answers, so slow down enough to read each choice before trying to answer the question.

Tip #5: Read the Writing Prompt

The writing prompt for the essay question sets up the situation to write about and gives instructions about exactly what kind of response to write. Here are the three different types of prompts that you'll see over and over again on writing tests:

COMMON KINDS OF PROMPTS

Prompt #1: Personal
You are asked to write about a personal experience or belief. For example:
Write about an experience that changed your life.

Prompt #2: Social *You are asked to give your opinion about a social problem or issue. For example:*
Discuss illiteracy in America and what you can do to help.

Prompt #3: Academic *You are asked to write about a piece of literature, an event in history, or something else you've learned about in school. For example:*
Discuss the topics of remorse and revenge in Charles Dickens's *A Tale of Two Cities*.

Tip #6: Use a Writing Plan

To do well on timed writings, you need to go into the test with an idea of how you will organize your essay.

1. Writing the Topic Sentence

For example, you have to begin with a topic sentence, so get a plan for writing one.

The [subject of the essay] is both A) _____ and B) _____.

Example: The character of Markham is both eerie and wacky.

This very simple model can be an effective way to begin almost any essay. By saying the subject is two things, you make your responses seem thoughtful, and you sound clear and to the point. If you describe the subject only one way, your essay might sound simplistic.

2. Supporting Your Topic Sentence

Organize your essay in a clear, simple way. Support your topic sentence point by point using examples from the reading.

3. Concluding the Essay

At the end of your essay, you want to leave your reader with something memorable. Close by saying the most important reason the subject was *eerie* and *wacky*. One model of a well-organized essay looks like the organizer shown here. This is not the *only* model, but it's an effective one.

MODEL ESSAY RESPONSE

Topic Sentence
Subject is A and B.
Body of Essay
1. Support for A
2. Support for A
3. Support for B
4. Support for B
Conclusion
Reason subject is A and B.

Now look at the directions and prompt from a state writing test.

Writing Examination

This is an assessment of your writing. You will have 22 minutes to write an essay. Your essay will be evaluated on its central idea, organization, clarity of expression, and use of the conventions of written English.

DIRECTIONS

- Read both the Writing Prompt and the Writing Directions carefully.
- Plan your essay before you begin writing. Use the space on this page.
- Address the central idea outlined in the assignment. Develop your thesis with specific supporting details and examples.
- Allow time to check your essay for errors in spelling, punctuation, grammar, and sentence formation. These types of errors will count against and may lower your final score.
- Write your essay on the lined pages of the test booklet. Writing that appears in the margins or on this page will not be scored.

WRITING PROMPT

Think of a unique building or monument you have seen or know about. It might be nearby or far away or have an unusual architectural style. How would you describe this building or monument?

WRITING DIRECTIONS

Write a brief essay describing this building or monument in detail. Explain what makes it unique and why it has captured your attention. Then proofread your writing.

What did you learn from reading the directions? What are you supposed to write about? Look for key words. These key words tell you everything you need to know about the assignment.

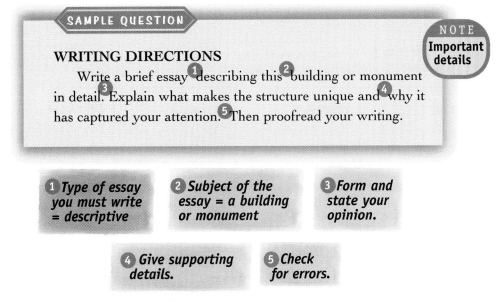

NOTE
Important details

WRITING DIRECTIONS

Write a brief essay describing this building or monument in detail. Explain what makes the structure unique and why it has captured your attention. Then proofread your writing.

1 *Type of essay you must write = descriptive*

2 *Subject of the essay = a building or monument*

3 *Form and state your opinion.*

4 *Give supporting details.*

5 *Check for errors.*

Planning the Essay

Before you do any type of writing, you need a good plan. This is doubly important for timed writing. Take a few minutes to put together a graphic organizer to sort out what you need to say. A graphic organizer can stop you from just writing whatever pops into your head—another common mistake that test-takers make.

Here is an all-purpose organizer that you can use for nearly any test.

MAIN IDEA ORGANIZER

TOPIC SENTENCE:			
DETAIL 1	DETAIL 2	DETAIL 3	DETAIL 4
CONCLUDING SENTENCE:			

Tests

A Main Idea Organizer works well with a timed writing test. In a matter of minutes, you can fill it in and begin writing your essay. Using an organizer allows you to focus on writing a clear, unified essay, not the form it will take.

TOPIC SENTENCE: To me, the most fascinating monument in the world is the Statue of Liberty because it is both a landmark and a symbol.

DETAIL 1	DETAIL 2	DETAIL 3	DETAIL 4
The Statue of Liberty symbolizes everything that is great about the United States: freedom, democracy, and safety for all people.	The statue, which is of a woman holding a torch, was a gift from another nation, which shows that the world knows what the United States has to offer.	The statue also has personal meaning to me and my family, since it was the landmark we searched for as our plane landed on U.S. soil for the first time.	The Statue of Liberty has stood for years at the tip of New York, the first of many landmarks a visitor to that great city will see.

CONCLUDING SENTENCE: The Statue of Liberty is important not only as a monument with personal meaning for me but also as a symbol of the freedom we have in the United States.

After Reading

After you write your essay, you'll need to go back and edit it carefully. First, look at the "big picture"—the content and organization of the essay. Ask yourself this important question: "Does my essay say what I want it to say?" Then, read what you've written. Use questions like these to help you revise:

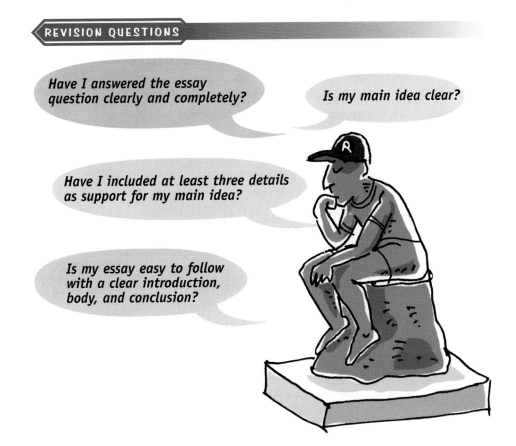

REVISION QUESTIONS

Have I answered the essay question clearly and completely?

Is my main idea clear?

Have I included at least three details as support for my main idea?

Is my essay easy to follow with a clear introduction, body, and conclusion?

After you've checked your content and organization, take a few minutes to look at the spelling, grammar, punctuation, and sentence structure. Remember that even the smallest mistakes can count against you and weaken the overall effect of the essay.

Summing Up

- Read each test question carefully. Look for key words that tell you what to write.
- Use a Main Idea Organizer to plan your essay.
- Leave five or more minutes at the end to proofread for content and organizational errors, as well as spelling or grammatical errors.

Tests

Focus on Standardized Tests

You will probably take a few different standardized tests in high school, so get ready. These tests measure your skills, progress, and achievement in all different subjects, including English, math, science, history, and foreign languages. Some of the tests will be required as district and state proficiency exams. Others will be optional, including the PSAT, SAT, and ACT.

You can do several things beforehand to prepare yourself for a standardized test. In addition, you can use a number of test tips to help raise your score.

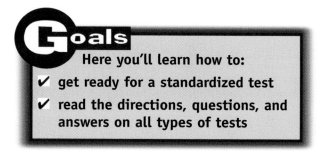

Goals

Here you'll learn how to:

✔ **get ready for a standardized test**

✔ **read the directions, questions, and answers on all types of tests**

Before Reading

Although every standardized test is different, many follow basically the same format. Most are divided into two or three parts. Almost all of them contain a verbal or writing part. Many contain math, and some include questions on science and history. Here are some tips that can help you prepare:

Tip #1: Visit the Test Website

Most states maintain a test website that offers information about the standardized tests you can expect to take over the course of a school year. Your state or school district may do the same. Important information will include test dates, test content, sample test items, information about time restrictions, and how the test is scored.

Tip #2: Take a Practice Test

Your state or district may offer downloadable sample tests on their websites. The major test-writing companies do this, and bookstores are loaded with standardized test preparation books. Print out a couple of practice tests, and do them alone or with a study group. Learn your areas of weakness, and concentrate on those in the days leading up to the test.

Tip #3: Prepare Yourself Mentally and Physically

Standardized tests can be exhausting. That's why taking practice tests helps, because you build up endurance and strength to take the test. Eat well and get plenty of rest the day before the test. You will concentrate better if you are well rested the day of the exam.

Tip #4: Relax

One reason to prepare well before the test is that it helps you *as* you take the test. You will relax knowing that you are as well prepared as you can be.

During Reading

On the day of the test, gear yourself up for it. Stay positive and relaxed. You have a chance to show what you know. Remind yourself that it's only a test. The test won't "determine" the rest of your life. You determine your own destiny by how you study and prepare day by day as a student.

Tests

Tip #5: Preview the Test

Your test monitor will let you know if you are allowed to preview the entire test before the time period begins. If you are *not* allowed to do so, take two minutes of the test period to preview the first section. Mark the easiest questions so you can come back to them first. Note any graphics or visuals. You may need a little extra time to complete these questions.

Tip #6: Listen to the Instructions

You need to listen very carefully to the verbal instructions. Most standardized tests have strict rules about time limits, penalties for guessing, working ahead, materials you can use to answer the questions, and so on.

Tip #7: Read the Directions and Questions

Each part of a standardized test will usually have its own set of directions. Take the time in between sections to read the directions carefully. If you're allowed, mark the most important points with a highlighter. You may need to refer to these directions later. Practice by reading the sample directions below.

> ◤ SAMPLE DIRECTIONS ◥
>
> **DIRECTIONS:** Mark only one answer to each question. Only responses marked on the answer sheet will be scored. You will NOT be penalized for guessing. It's in your best interest to answer every question on the test, even if you must make a guess.

Next, remember to take a deep breath and read the questions carefully. Block out distractions and think only about the question you're reading. If something distracts you, start reading the question again. With test questions, your reading purpose is, "What is this question asking me to find?" Read the entire question, *even if you think you know the answer*. Every word in a test question is important, so you must take every word into consideration. A careful reading of each question can help you a lot.

Tip #8: Read Every Answer

Read all answer choices for a test question, even if you know the right answer. This will only take a few seconds and is well worth the effort. Many students make careless mistakes because they choose the first answer that seems right. Beware of answers that are *only half true*. If you don't read all of the answers, you may settle for an answer that's only partially true.

SAMPLE QUESTION

13. In our log cabin, we have <u>neither TV or</u> computers.
    A. NO CHANGE
    B. no TV, and we have no
    C. neither TV nor
    D. either TV nor computers

Thinking aloud, or talking to yourself, while you're taking a test is a useful strategy because it helps you sort out your thoughts. Here are the thoughts of one reader who answered the sample question.

THINK ALOUD

To answer, I have to figure out if "neither TV or" is grammatically correct. I don't think it is, but look at these four choices.
A. No, it needs to be changed. There is something wrong with the sentence. It doesn't sound right.
B. This might be right.
C. Actually, I think this is correct.
D. This seems clearly wrong.
    Answer C. seems to me to be the most correct. I'll go with that answer.

Tests

Tip #9: Eliminate Wrong Answers

After reading all the answers, cross out the ones you know are wrong. If you are left with only two choices, you should make a guess between the two of them, even if there is a penalty for guessing. You have as good a chance of answering correctly as you do answering wrong, so take a chance. Here are some tips for spotting wrong answers. Look for:

- ones that "sound wrong" to you

- ones that are only partially true

- ones that don't "fit," so if you substitute, the answer doesn't work

- ones that, even though they sound true, don't have the information called for in the question

Tip #10: Make Educated Guesses

Making a guess doesn't mean filling in ovals on the answer sheet at random. If you really don't know the answer to a question, try to make a knowledgeable guess. Begin by looking for clues in the question itself. Then talk your way through the answers. Eliminate those that are wrong, and then go with your instincts.

SAMPLE QUESTION

37. Which of the following is an irrational number?
   A. 1/3
   B. 0.304
   C. $\sqrt{0.9216}$
   D. $\pi/10$

THINK ALOUD

I know that an irrational number is one that can't be represented by a ratio of two integers. A. is wrong because it has an integer numerator and denominator. I'm pretty sure B. is also wrong because a decimal can be written as a rational number. But C. and D. could both be right. I've seen square roots that are rational numbers like $\sqrt{4}$. I'm going to guess D., because I know that pi alone is an irrational number.

After Reading

Try to leave two or more minutes at the end of the test period to check your work. Since you probably won't have time to return to the questions themselves, use these few minutes to check for any errors on your answer sheet. If there is no penalty for guessing, be sure you have answered every single question. Erase any marks that could confuse the machine that scores the answer sheets.

If you still have time remaining, check a few questions. Take a second look at the harder questions to be sure you have answered them correctly.

Summing Up

- ▪ **Prepare yourself mentally and physically for a standardized test.**
- ▪ **Take the first few minutes of the test period to preview each section of the test that you are allowed to look at.**
- ▪ **Read each question and every answer carefully.**
- ▪ **Eliminate answers that are incorrect, and use the strategy of thinking aloud to talk your way through the questions.**
- ▪ **Plan ahead so that you have time to make educated guesses rather than just guessing at random.**

Last Question

Tests

Focus on History Tests

History tests examine your knowledge of important historic events and the people, places, and dates connected with those events. The students who do well on history tests are the ones who have kept up with their reading over the course of the school year. But even they sometimes need a little extra help in taking a test. Here you'll find a reading plan that works well with all kinds of history tests—for tests in your history class and on state tests that include history.

Goals

Here you'll learn how to:

✔ **prepare for a history test**

✔ **preview common elements on a history test**

✔ **use test-taking tips that can help raise your test score**

Before Reading

Your first step when preparing for a history test is to reread the material you are going to be tested on. Pay attention to the study guides or chapter preview boxes that open each new chapter of the book. Memorize definitions for key terms and study:

Names, dates, people, and places Make a list of three or four from each chapter.

End-of-chapter questions Try to answer each one of these questions. Use them as a kind of practice test.

Maps, timelines, graphs, primary sources, and political cartoons Learn how to read, understand, and respond to the graphics in your book.

After you review your history text, begin reviewing your class notes. If your teacher has given you a study guide, use that to determine which parts of your notes are most important. Be sure you know every name, date, and event listed on the study guide.

Here are some additional test-taking tips that may help:

Tip #1: Create a Top Ten List

If the history test is a mid-term or final, you can't study absolutely everything you've done in a year. Instead, you'll need to pick and choose your topics. Working alone or with a study partner, create a "top ten" list of the most important topics to study. Show the list to your teacher to see if you've missed anything important. For example, here's a top ten list of Civil War topics:

TOP TEN LIST

1. African-American slavery
2. Abolitionism
3. Abraham Lincoln
4. Secession
5. Confederate Army
6. Union Army
7. Battle of Bull Run
8. Gettysburg
9. Emancipation Proclamation
10. Reconstruction

You can use a top ten list for any course or part of a course. Learn a little bit about each item on the list. It's a way of keeping yourself focused in the days leading up to the test.

Tip #2: Learn How to Read Graphics

Most history tests will include at least one map, timeline, chart, table, or graph. Review the part in this handbook on how to read graphics. Look in the back of your history text, which may offer additional tips on reading graphics. Keep in mind that in most visuals, the graphics and text are equally important.

Tip #3: Use Graphic Organizers

The strategy of using graphic organizers can help you both before and during a test. Know how to create both Main Idea Organizers and Sequence Notes, because they can help you with readings and essays.

Tests

Tip #4: Preview

Always begin by previewing the test you're about to take. Read the directions for any special instructions and any information about how much time you'll have to take the exam. Then glance through the rest of the test pages. Take special note of questions that involve graphics. You'll need to allow extra time for these.

After your preview, begin answering the easiest questions. Even if the question seems ridiculously easy, take the time to read it carefully. Highlight key words or phrases. If the question is multiple choice, read each of the choices before making your final selection of the answer. Now try a sample test question.

> **SAMPLE QUESTION**
>
> 14. The Homestead Act of 1862 offered:
>   A. houses for Southerners displaced by the final battles of the Civil War.
>   B. emigration papers for all Native American tribes.
>   C. land to any settler who would farm it for five years.
>   D. financial aid for New York City orphans traveling west.

Tip #5: Eliminate Incorrect Answers

If you're not sure of the answer to a question, begin by crossing out the answers that you know are wrong. See if you can reduce your choices to two—rather than four or five—answers to choose from. For example, you may remember that the Homestead Act wasn't about orphans in New York City, so you can rule answer D. out.

Tip #6: Beware of Partially True Answers

Some answer choices may look right, but they are only half true.

> **THINK ALOUD**
>
> Answer A. is partly true, but the Civil War hadn't ended by 1862. Papers might have been given to Native American tribes, but I don't think they wanted to move. Financial aid may have been given to orphans, but that's not what the Homestead Act offered. So, "C. land to any settler" seems right.

Talking through the answers, using all you know about that period in history, is the best way to get the answer.

Tip #7: Look at the Big Picture

When you come to a graphic on a test, pause for a moment and look at the "big picture." Ask yourself, "What can this graphic tell me?" Make notes in the margin of your test booklet if you can, and then do a careful reading of the graphic. Finish by drawing conclusions about the information and answering the question, as in this example:

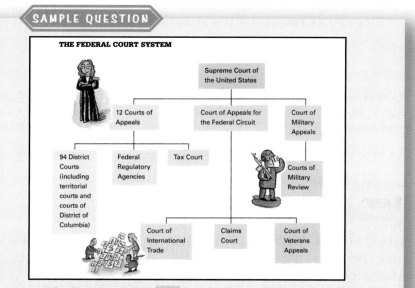

SAMPLE QUESTION

THE FEDERAL COURT SYSTEM

10. Which statement is not supported by information in the diagram?

    A. The Supreme Court has ultimate authority over all federal courts.

    B. Defendants in a U.S. Claims Court have the right to take their case to a Court of Appeals for the Federal Circuit.

    C. Defendants in a Court of Veterans Appeals have the right to take their case to a Court of Military Review.

    D. A case that begins in a Court of International Trade may ultimately end up in the Supreme Court.

What is the "big picture" of this diagram? Read from top to bottom. Work on understanding the graphic before you tackle the question. This question challenges you to first read the question, then the graphic, and then the answer choices, so take your time.

Tests

I need to look at each possible answer before I decide which one is not supported by the diagram.

Answer A. is supported. The Supreme Court clearly has the most authority.

B. is supported. I see the line connecting Claims Court with the Federal Circuit Court of Appeals.

C. is not supported. The next step after Veterans Appeals is a Court of Appeals for the Federal Circuit.

D. is supported. A line connects these two courts.

Note that you must read all four possible answers to find the correct one at the end. The correct answer is C. That's the one that's *not* supported.

After Reading

Save the last five minutes of the test period for a quick check of your work. Be sure you've answered every question and that your handwriting is neat and easy to read.

Next, spot-check several answers. Reread the question to be sure you understood it the first time around. Then, read the possible answers and see if you really did choose the right one.

Summing Up

- **Use your textbook and class notes to prepare for a history test.**

- **Preview the test before you begin working. Mark easy questions and do these first.**

- **Read the directions, questions, and answers very carefully. Don't rush!**

- **Get a sense of the "big picture" of a graphic before tackling the questions. Be sure to read all three parts of the question with care—the question, the answers, and the graphic.**

Focus on Math Tests

If you're like most students, you can succeed on any math test, even if math is not your best subject. The key is preparing beforehand.

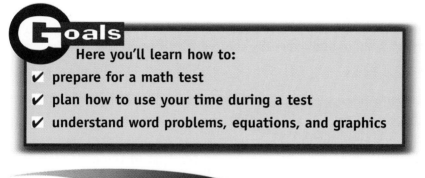

Goals

Here you'll learn how to:

✔ **prepare for a math test**

✔ **plan how to use your time during a test**

✔ **understand word problems, equations, and graphics**

Before Reading

Preparing for a math test takes some time and effort. You're not magically going to become a math whiz. The more time that you prepare, the better off you'll be. Learning math is a building process. If you've been studying all along, preparing for the test should be a snap. If you haven't, then the test offers a chance to catch up on what you've missed.

Getting Ready

First, review old homework assignments, quizzes, and tests. Rework the practice problems to make sure you still know how to do them. "Correct" the errors that you made on previous exams so that you don't end up making the same mistakes again.

Next, thumb through your math text. Look at the charts, graphs, and diagrams. Read the captions and think through the example problems. Learn how to read and understand the different types of visuals presented in your book, because one or more are sure to appear on the test.

Finally, sit down and memorize key terms, rules, and formulas. This is particularly important if the test is for algebra, geometry, or calculus. You need to have all of the important formulas memorized so that you can call upon them to help you solve the test problems.

Tests

Previewing

As soon as your teacher hands out the test, begin previewing. This is an essential step. Many students forget about it in their rush to begin working. Take two minutes to skim the entire test.

The purpose of your preview is to find out what kind of math questions to expect. Look for questions that you think will be easy, and mark these with a star. When it's time to begin working, you'll start with these and leave the more difficult questions for the end.

During Reading

After your preview, begin working on the first of the easy problems. Read the question slowly and carefully. Underline or highlight what you need to find out. If you're not sure of an answer, note your ideas in the margin and move on to the next problem. Try solving the problem below. Write down your thoughts as you work through the problem.

Solving the Easy Problems

SAMPLE QUESTION

On August 1, Kim opened a savings account with a deposit of $500. On the first day of each month thereafter, she withdrew $60. Write a formula that will give the total of Kim's savings after n months. How many withdrawals of $60 each could Kim make?

Problem Notes
I'll let S stand for savings. $S = 500 - 60n$. I divide 60 into 500 to get 8 withdrawals. $S = 500 - 60 \cdot 8$. She withdrew $480 in 8 months, giving her a total of $20 after 8 months.

Remember, some problems only look difficult. A careful reading of each word in the problem may give you clues about how to solve it.

Solving the Challenging Problems

You may need help with the most challenging math questions. Here are some test-taking tips that help.

Tip #1: Eliminate Wrong Answers

Begin by using number sense and mental math to eliminate answers that are clearly wrong. In most cases, a problem will offer one or two choices that can be ruled out. Find those and cross them out. Try using this tip with this sample question.

SAMPLE QUESTION

DIRECTIONS: Use the table below to answer the question.

x	2	6	8	12	14
y	3	27	39	63	75

17. Which equation shows the relationship between x and y in the table?

A. $y = -6x - 9$

B. $y = 6x - 9$

C. $y = 9x - 6$

D. $y = -9x + 6$

Problem Notes

I can rule out A. and D. because what you're multiplying x by is a negative number. That means larger values of x would give smaller values of y. That's not what the table shows. So, B. and C. are left. I'm pretty sure B. is the correct answer. If I plug in the answers, I see that C. doesn't work.

Use the strategy of thinking aloud to help you rule out wrong answers.

Tip #2: Plug in Answers

When you have a choice of answers, try plugging some of the given values into the equation. This strategy would not work on a test without multiple choices, of course, but you can usually find the correct answer on a test that does have them.

SAMPLE QUESTION

19. William Penn High School chartered buses for 60 students to go on a field trip. Council Rock High School chartered buses for 80 students. The total cost of the buses was the same for the two schools. Students from Council Rock High paid $5 less than students from William Penn High. What was the cost per student for William Penn High School?

    A. $5   B. $15

    C. $20   D. $40

First, decide what the question is asking you to find out. Then, write an equation that will find the information.

THINK ALOUD

I need to find the cost per ticket for Penn High students (x). The total cost of the buses (y) is the same. So, an equation is:

price for Penn = price for Council Rock

$$60 \cdot x = 80 \cdot (x - 5)$$

I'll start by plugging in choice A. That gives me 0 on the right but not on the left. A. is wrong. Now let me try choice B.

$$60 \cdot 15 = 80 \cdot 10$$
$$900 \neq 800$$

So, B. is wrong. Now try C., $20.

$$60 \cdot 20 = 80 \cdot 15$$
$$1,200 = 1,200$$

That means C. is correct. Answer D. can't be right because

$$60 \cdot 40 = 80 \cdot 35$$
$$2,400 \neq 2,800$$

Tip #3: Visualize the Answer

Use a sketch or drawing to help make math problems clearer and to help you organize your work.

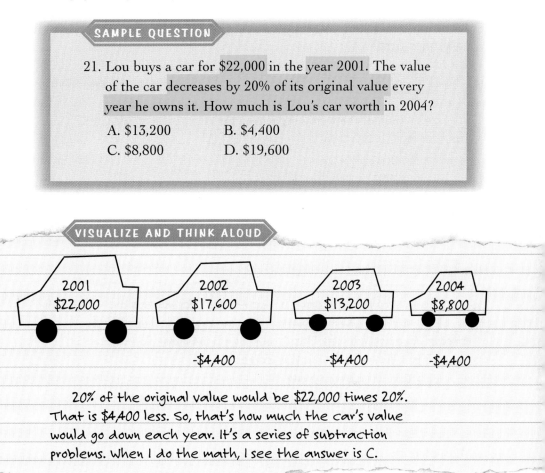

SAMPLE QUESTION

21. Lou buys a car for $22,000 in the year 2001. The value of the car decreases by 20% of its original value every year he owns it. How much is Lou's car worth in 2004?

　　A. $13,200　　　B. $4,400
　　C. $8,800　　　D. $19,600

VISUALIZE AND THINK ALOUD

| 2001 | 2002 | 2003 | 2004 |
| $22,000 | $17,600 | $13,200 | $8,800 |

　　　　　　-$4,400　　　　　-$4,400　　　-$4,400

20% of the original value would be $22,000 times 20%. That is $4,400 less. So, that's how much the car's value would go down each year. It's a series of subtraction problems. When I do the math, I see the answer is C.

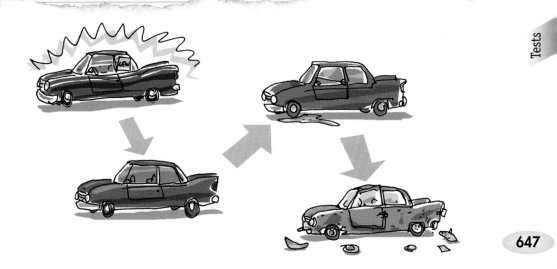

Tip #4: Try Easier Numbers First

Sometimes you'll need to use the answers to solve a math problem. When you do, begin with the easiest answers and work your way up to the hard ones. After all, why solve an equation with a bunch of hard numbers when you might have gotten the answer by trying the easy ones first?

24. Which of the following is true for all possible values of x?
   A. $3(x + 1) = 3x + 1$
   B. $2(x + 3) = 2x + 6$
   C. $7(2x + 1) = 7x + 5$
   D. $5(3x - 2) = 15x - 7$

THINK ALOUD

The key to this question is the phrase "for all possible values of x." I'll solve the equations with easy numbers like 1 or 0 first. I'll choose an easy number like 0 and plug it into one formula at a time until I figure out which is correct:

$3(0 + 1) = 0 + 1$ Wrong
$2(0 + 3) = 2(0) + 6$ Correct. But I better check the others.
$7(0 + 1) = 7(0) + 5$ Wrong
$5(0 - 2) = 15(0) - 7$ Wrong

B. is correct.

After Reading

Perhaps, like most students, you leave the problems involving figures (triangles, rectangles, and cubes), graphs, charts, and diagrams for the end. You may tend to think of these questions as the most challenging, when often they can be the easiest ones on the test.

To solve most problems with figures or graphics, you'll need to use the formulas you've learned in class. This is why it's so important to study *before* the test to memorize key formulas and rules you might need. If you're not sure which formulas are most important for the upcoming test, ask your teacher.

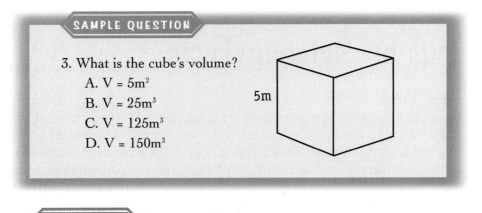

SAMPLE QUESTION

3. What is the cube's volume?
   A. $V = 5m^2$
   B. $V = 25m^3$
   C. $V = 125m^3$
   D. $V = 150m^3$

5m

THINK ALOUD

I know the formula for the volume of a cube is $V = s^3$, where s is the length of each side. So, for this cube, $s = 5$. The volume of this cube would be 5^3 or 125 cubic meters. Answer C. is correct.

You may feel that you don't have very much time at the end of the test to check your work, but try to leave just a few minutes before the bell rings. Look back on a math test as you would any other kind of reading. Try to check the problems that gave you the most difficulty.

Avoid leaving answers blank unless you know there is a penalty for guessing. If there *is* a penalty for guessing, make a guess only if you can narrow your choices down to two. Then, you have a fifty-fifty chance of getting the question right.

Summing **Up**

- ▪ **Prepare for the test ahead of time by studying your notes and textbook.**
- ▪ **Memorize any key rules and formulas you've covered in class.**
- ▪ **During the test, work the easiest problems first. Then, tackle the challenging ones.**
- ▪ **Use good test-taking techniques, such as plugging in the answers, visualizing, ruling out wrong answers, and trying easier choices first.**

Tests

Focus on Science Tests

Most science tests ask you to recall important concepts and use your reasoning skills. When preparing for a science test, spend part of your time learning the language of science—key terms, abbreviations, formulas, and theories. Spend the other part of your time reviewing the scientific method as shown in problems and experiments in your textbook.

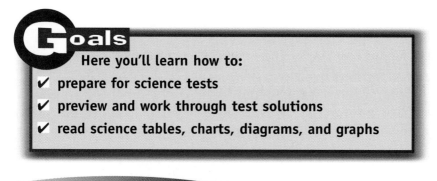

Goals
Here you'll learn how to:
- ✔ **prepare for science tests**
- ✔ **preview and work through test solutions**
- ✔ **read science tables, charts, diagrams, and graphs**

Before Reading

Much of the vocabulary in science is different from your everyday vocabulary. As a result, you need to learn new terms as you go, rather than wait until the night before the test.

Here are some tips that you can use to prepare for science tests.

Tip #1: Learn Science Terms

Add a few new science terms to your vocabulary each week. Note terms in your textbook, and write them in your science notebook. Look up their meanings in the glossary of the textbook or in a dictionary. You don't have to learn *every* term, but try to learn a few each week. That way you'll be prepared when test time comes.

Tip #2: Read and Review

Read your textbook, and review before the test. Pay particular attention to the study guide or "chapter-at-a-glance" box that opens each chapter in your textbook. That section is a tip-off that tells you, "Hey, this is important."

Tip #3: Make Yourself Diagrams

To understand the steps in a scientific process, make a diagram. In most cases, a picture is easier to remember than written notes, as with this example:

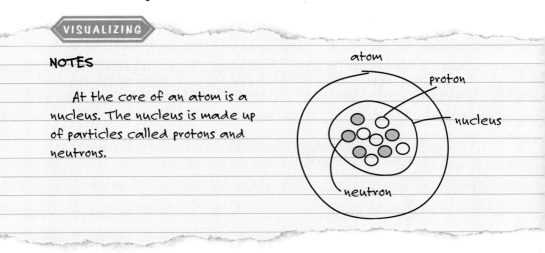

VISUALIZING

NOTES

At the core of an atom is a nucleus. The nucleus is made up of particles called protons and neutrons.

atom

proton

nucleus

neutron

Tip #4: Learn How to Read Graphics

Your science textbooks will contain charts and graphs in just about every chapter. Learn how to read and understand these graphics before taking any test. It may help to review the pages on reading graphics in this handbook (pages 539–553).

Tip #5: Preview

With science tests, as with any kind of reading, always begin the test with a preview. Skim the directions to find out how much time you have. Then, do a quick reading of a few questions. Mark the easy ones and answer them first. Glance at any charts, graphs, or diagrams. Chances are good that these graphics will take a bit more time during the test, so budget your time accordingly.

Tests

During Reading

On a science test, you will find all types of questions—multiple choice, true-false, short answer, and essay. You'll also find that many of the science tests you take will be divided into two parts: science knowledge and science reasoning.

Science Knowledge

The science knowledge part of the exam tests your recall of scientific terms, facts, and formulas. You'll probably answer the science knowledge questions on the exam first. They often are easier than the scientific reasoning questions. Remember to read each question carefully. Then reread it. Many times the simple step of rereading a question will help you answer it. As you read each question, look for key words that remind you of something you read or learned about in class. Then, talk yourself through the answers, eliminating any that are clearly wrong. Finish by choosing the answer that makes the most sense.

SAMPLE QUESTION

1. The sun is only one of billions of
   A. stars
   B. galaxies
   C. quasars
   D. light rays

THINK ALOUD

The sun is a star, but is it one of billions of galaxies? No. The Milky Way is a galaxy. Answer C. might be true, but I remember that quasars emit blue light, so C. is wrong. D. can't be right. The sun emits light rays. So I think the right answer must be A.

Science Reasoning

Some standardized tests, such as the ACT, include a part called "Science Reasoning." Science reasoning measures your ability to draw conclusions from a set of data. To answer a science reasoning question, you call on your knowledge of scientific terms and formulas. You use what you know to analyze and interpret the data. Here's how you do it:

HOW TO ANSWER A REASONING QUESTION

1. *Read the data. If you can, highlight key terms and what you need to find out.*

2. *Come up with a hypothesis. Decide what you think the answer should be before reading the choices.*

3. *Then, read the possible answers. One may be similar to your hypothesis. If so, that's probably the answer.*

SAMPLE QUESTION

DIRECTIONS: Use the information in the box to answer the question.

Carla took a plastic cup half-filled with sand, covered it, punched a hole in the cover, inserted a thermometer, and recorded the temperature of the cup's contents. She then shook the cup for 5 minutes and again recorded the temperature. She recorded the following temperature data:

Reading #1: 20°C   Reading #2: 24°C

14. The most likely explanation for these data is:
   A. The heat from Carla's hand was transferred to the contents of the cup to increase the temperature.
   B. The sand particles in the cup reacted chemically, giving off heat.
   C. The friction of the sand particles moving against each other in the cup produced heat.
   D. The warm air from the room entered the cup through the hole in its cover.

Tests

THINK ALOUD

I need to figure out why the temperature of the sand went up after Carla shook it. My hypothesis is that friction caused the temperature to rise. Friction can increase temperature. My hypothesis is the same as answer C., so I'll mark that as the answer.

Some science reasoning questions require you to read and interpret a graphic. Read the question and any words that explain it.

Beaufort Scale of Wind Velocity

Beaufort Number	Mph	Description
0	below 1	Calm
1	1-3	Light air movement
2	4-7	Light breeze
3	8-12	Gentle breeze
4	13-18	Moderate breeze
5	19-24	Fresh breeze
6	25-31	Strong breeze
7	32-38	Near gale
8	39-46	Gale
9	47-54	Strong gale
10	55-63	Storm
11	64-72	Violent storm
12-17	73+	Hurricane

6. Wind speed recorded at 41 mph would be assigned what Beaufort number?

To answer, read down the "Mph" column to the row for 39-46 mph. Move your finger left to the Beaufort number column to find that this wind would be given an 8 on the Beaufort scale.

After Reading

After you've answered every easy question, you'll need to return to the more challenging questions. Read each challenging question again. If you can, make notes to yourself in the margin of the test sheet or booklet. Ask yourself, "What is this question asking me?"

Use the same strategies to answer the challenging questions that you used to answer the easy questions: make a diagram if it would help, read the question and answer choices carefully, eliminate wrong answers, and think aloud to work your way through to the correct answer. If you find that you still can't answer the question, you'll need to make an educated guess.

Make a Guess

When you make an educated guess, you need to put some thought into it. Random guessing won't help you. Eliminate all of the answers except two in order to make guessing a worthwhile option. Remember that test writers often give you clues within the question itself.

Remember also that some answers sound right but are only half true. Try not to be fooled by these answers. Read each answer carefully.

Check Your Work

Save the last few minutes of the test period to reread each question and each answer. Be sure you've marked the best answer to each question. If you make a correction, do so neatly.

Summing Up

- **Begin studying for science tests well in advance. Review class notes, handouts, and your textbook.**
- **When you receive the test, begin with a preview. Read and highlight key words in the directions. Star the easiest questions and save the more challenging ones for last.**
- **Make diagrams to help you think through some questions.**
- **Make educated guesses if you're not certain of the answers.**

Tests

Improving Vocabulary

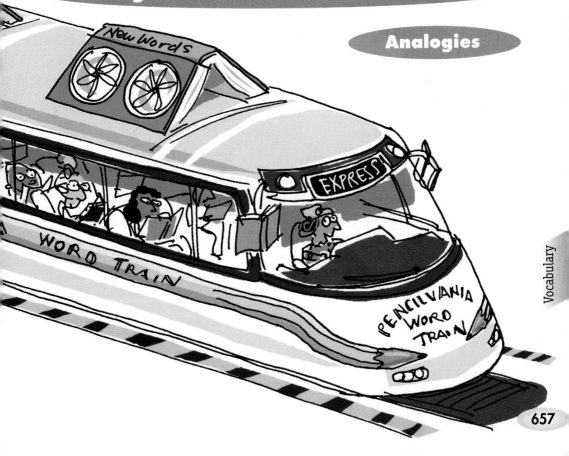

Vocabulary

657

Introduction to Improving Vocabulary

You have the ability to speak and to make language. That's what sets you apart from animals and other species. You think in words, read with words, and write with words. They are an essential part of what makes you a distinct individual. They are a resource, a source of wisdom and strength.

Improving your vocabulary means learning to use the right word at the right time. Improving your vocabulary also means learning new words and their meanings and adding these words to the wealth of words you already know. In fact, improving your vocabulary is probably one of the surest ways of gaining insight into the world around you.

Improving Vocabulary

When you were very young, you quickly learned the importance of vocabulary. You knew it was easier to get what you wanted if you could name it. You learned that if you said *juice*, you'd get juice and not milk. You probably don't remember the excitement of making this discovery. But the day you realized that certain sounds actually meant something was the day you started to build your vocabulary. Now, of course, the words you are learning are much more complicated and specialized.

Goals

Here you'll learn how to:

✔ keep a **vocabulary journal**

✔ learn the meanings of **prefixes, suffixes, and word roots**

✔ learn different kinds of **context clues**

✔ use **dictionaries and thesauruses**

✔ understand **analogies**

Learning New Words

Each year you take new or more advanced classes in various subject areas. Each course assumes you remember all the vocabulary you previously learned. Your teachers also build on that foundation by introducing new terms in each of your subjects.

Vocabulary

Why Build a Strong Vocabulary?

Your vocabulary tells someone a great deal about you. The right words used at the right time tell other people that you are intelligent, well informed, and persuasive. The wrong words, however, tell others that you are not well spoken or educated. You take time with your appearance, knowing that being stylish and well dressed makes a good impression. You should also take time with your vocabulary, for a good vocabulary not only makes a good impression but also helps you think more clearly.

Have you ever heard someone say, "I know what I mean, but I just don't know how to say it"? Well, that person was probably wrong. The truth is that if you don't know how to express something, you may feel something but you don't fully understand it. You use words not only to express your thoughts, but also to form them. The greater your vocabulary, the more you are able to translate your ideas into words.

Think of your vocabulary as the foundation of your ability to think clearly. It is also the foundation of your ability to communicate your thoughts to others.

Collecting New Words

When you read newspapers, magazines, and books, you are likely to come across unfamiliar words from time to time. Are you tempted to skip over them and just keep on reading? Try not to do that, and your vocabulary will improve as a result.

Take time to collect those words, and make them part of your own vocabulary. Why should other people have those words and not you? Grab them for yourself.

Here are seven ways to make new words your own.

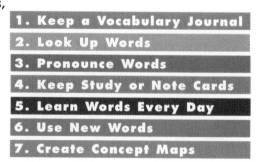

1. **Keep a Vocabulary Journal**
2. **Look Up Words**
3. **Pronounce Words**
4. **Keep Study or Note Cards**
5. **Learn Words Every Day**
6. **Use New Words**
7. **Create Concept Maps**

1. Keep a Vocabulary Journal

Get a notebook, and set aside separate parts of it for each category of new words that you'll be recording. You might want to divide the notebook into parts for science, English, math, social studies, computer technology, prefixes, suffixes, and word roots.

As you read or hear a new word that is important to know, write it down in the appropriate part of your notebook. If you read the word in a book, include the title and the page on which the word appears. If you hear the word, include a note about the source. After recording the word, write the sentence or phrase in which it occurs.

> **VOCABULARY JOURNAL**
>
> ENGLISH
> Oct 15
> from The Great Gatsby by F. Scott Fitzgerald
> vulnerable, page 7: "In my younger and more vulnerable years my
> father gave me some advice...."
>
> imperceptibly, page 14: "...she nodded at me almost imperceptibly,..."
>
> Oct 16
> from class
> aspirations: "Fitzgerald's family had high social aspirations but not
> much money."
>
> extravagant: "He and his wife, Zelda, soon became part of the
> extravagant society of the 1920s."

Be sure to leave enough room around each entry for the definition of the word and any other notes you might want to make later.

Your goal with a vocabulary journal is to become familiar with the 2,000 most commonly used words because they make up about 80 percent of all the words you will probably see. So, focus on words such as *commerce* and *intentional*, not words like *silviculture* and *valerian*, which you may never hear of again.

Vocabulary

2. Look Up Words

Many textbooks have glossaries, so you can look up some of your new words there. For other words (those that you hear and those that you get from books without glossaries), you will have to check a dictionary. Read the definitions and choose the one that fits the way the word was used when you came across it.

DICTIONARY ENTRY

vul • ner • a • ble (vul' nər-ə-bəl) *adj.*: **1.a.** Susceptible to physical injury. **b.** Susceptible to attack. **c.** Open to censure or criticism. **2.** Liable to succumb, as to persuasion or temptation.

If you go back to the way the word was used in the sentence from *The Great Gatsby,* you can see that definition 1.b. fits in this case. Your next step, then, is to write this definition in your journal.

VOCABULARY JOURNAL

vulnerable, page 7: "In my younger and more vulnerable years my father gave me some advice. . . ."
susceptible to attack

You might also want to write a sentence of your own using the word. This will give you more practice with it and is just one more step toward making the word your own. Experts say that you need to see a word used or hear it about eight times before you learn it.

3. Pronounce Words

Saying words aloud can help you fix them in your mind. Check the pronunciation, usually in parentheses, in a glossary or dictionary. Then, note which syllable or syllables have the most stress. In the example above, the first syllable is stressed, or accented.

Some words can be pronounced in more than one way, depending on the part of speech. For example, *excuse* can be pronounced as (ik skyooz) or (ik skyoos). If there is more than one pronunciation, note which one applies to the way the word is used.

4. Keep Study or Note Cards

Another method of keeping track of new words is to use index cards. Put the word on one side and its definition and an example of how it is used on the back. Then, carry the cards with you and read them until you learn the word and its meaning. You'll need the following supplies:

 lined 3 x 5 cards

 index-card box

(front of index card)
vulnerable

(back of index card)

susceptible to attack

5. Learn Words Every Day

A word will become part of your vocabulary when you see it and use it. You'd be surprised at how easy it is to learn a word. Here's a plan for learning the words you've added to your vocabulary journal.

Vocabulary

REMEMBERING WORDS

1. *Set aside eight to ten minutes each day for reviewing your new words. Try to schedule this at the same time every day, so you won't forget. The time you choose doesn't really matter—what matters is that you make this part of your regular routine.*

2. *Choose several vocabulary words to review.*

3. *Read the word. Try to remember the definition and the example of how it was used when you first saw it or heard it.*

4. *Check the meaning of the word to see if you remembered it correctly. If you were correct, put a check by that word and go on to the next word.*

5. *If you were not correct, highlight the word in your journal or on your note card so you can go over it again.*

6. *If you were unable to recall the meaning, reread the word, its definition, and the example two or three times.*

7. *Try to use the word in a sentence. Then write or say the sentence.*

6. Use New Words

For the words to be part of your vocabulary, you need to begin to use them in conversation or in writing. Look for safe ways to try out new words. Try following these tips:

■ When you answer in class or when you speak to friends and family, try to find ways to include the new words.

■ Use the new words when you are doing a writing assignment for school or writing a letter or email.

7. Create Concept Maps

To learn about the "big ideas" in your school subjects, create Concept Maps for key terms. Concept Maps do two things: 1) help you remember a lot of words connected to a single idea, and 2) build your understanding of abstract ideas or concepts.

Concept Maps, such as the one on the next page, are built around details, definitions, and examples.

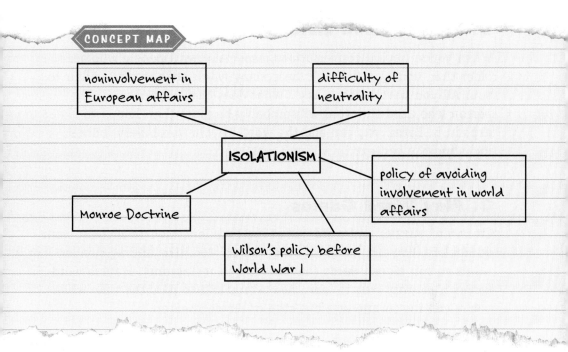

CONCEPT MAP

noninvolvement in European affairs

difficulty of neutrality

ISOLATIONISM

policy of avoiding involvement in world affairs

Monroe Doctrine

Wilson's policy before World War I

Create Concept Maps in your vocabulary journal for key terms, such as *democracy, socialism, virus, evolution,* and *genetics,* that you find in your textbooks. You'll find Concept Maps can increase your understanding of these important ideas.

Ways to Make Vocabulary-building Fun

Learning new words can be fun, if you want it to be. Here are a few ways to have fun while also building your vocabulary.

1. Read in Your Leisure Time

The reading you do on your own—magazines, newspapers, stories—provides the best opportunity for collecting words. As you read, be alert for new words. If you come across a word you don't know, don't just skip over it. Ask yourself, "Have I ever seen this word before? Can I guess what it means, based on the text around it?" If you aren't sure of the meaning, write the word in your vocabulary journal. You don't have to look it up right away. Jot it down, continue with your reading, and look up the word later.

Vocabulary

2. Be an Active Listener

When you're having conversations, especially with people who are older than you, you probably hear many words that aren't familiar to you. All you have to do is ask, "What does that word mean?" The person who used the word will probably be more than happy to explain it. Later, you can add the word to your vocabulary journal, including the context in which it was used.

3. Play Word Games

Crossword puzzles and word games are excellent ways to increase your vocabulary. You can make up other games, too, like finding smaller words within bigger words (*rest* and *ant* in restaurant). Playing word games is an easy way to learn new words and to pass the time while you're waiting in line at a bus stop or movie theater.

Skills for Learning New Words

Keeping track of new words as you find them is one way of increasing your vocabulary. But you need some skills to help you add new words to your vocabulary. One such skill is using context clues.

Context Clues

You're bound to come across words that you don't know while you're reading. Sometimes it's not practical to look the word up in a dictionary. For one thing, a dictionary might not be handy. For another, you might be too engrossed in what you're reading to want to stop. Another way to find out the meaning of a word is to look for clues the author left behind—the context clues.

Recognizing Context Clues

Context clues are the words, phrases, and sentences around the word that is unfamiliar. Very often, you'll find enough information in the surrounding text to figure out the meaning of a new word. In this example, look for clues that suggest the meaning of *pestilence*.

The "Red Death" had long <u>devastated</u> the country. No pestilence had ever been so <u>fatal</u>, or so <u>hideous</u>. Blood was its Avatar and its seal—the redness and the horror of blood. There were sharp <u>pains</u>, and sudden <u>dizziness</u>, and then profuse <u>bleeding</u> at the pores, with dissolution. The scarlet stains upon the body and especially upon the face of the victim, were the pest ban which shut him out from the aid and from the sympathy of his fellow men. And the whole seizure, progress and termination of the <u>disease</u>, were the incidents of half an hour.

Clues in this passage tell you that *pestilence* means "a contagious disease that becomes an epidemic." The fact that it has devastated the country is one clue. That it is fatal and hideous are other clues. The description of the symptoms—pains, dizziness, and bleeding—are still more clues. The final clue is the use of the word *disease*. In the next example, look for clues to the word *mendicant*.

Mr. Medbourne, in the vigor of his age, <u>had been a prosperous merchant</u>, but had <u>lost all</u> by a frantic speculation, and was now little better than a mendicant.

The fact that Mr. Medbourne had once been "prosperous" but had "lost all" are the clues in the passage that tell you *mendicant* has something to do with being poor. In fact, the word means "beggar."

Here's another example in which context clues tell you the meaning of a difficult word. Look for clues to the meaning of *incumbent*.

Vocabulary

> He could not force her to do anything. If she wanted to
> lie and pretend, he would have to pretend to believe her.
> And yet a great sadness settled down upon him. He was
> not to win her after all—that was plain. He turned, and
> she, being convinced that he felt that she was lying now,
> felt it incumbent upon herself <u>to do something about it</u>—to
> win him around to her again.

From the context, you can see that this is a turning point in a
relationship. The man is convinced the woman is lying, and the
woman wants to convince him otherwise. She will have to do
something or say something to change his mind. You get the feeling
from the context that she really *must* do something. That's one of the
meanings of *incumbent*—"imposed as a duty or an obligation." You
can understand the meaning of *incumbent* simply by replacing it with
words that fit the context, like "a duty or obligation."

Kinds of Context Clues

Writers usually provide clues that help you figure out the meanings of
difficult words. Knowing the types of context clues writers use will
help you better understand what you read. It will also help you do
better on standardized vocabulary tests.

1. DEFINITIONS OR SYNONYMS

Writers often give a synonym or a definition of a difficult word. One
clue that a synonym or definition will follow is a comma or a dash.
Other clues might include such words as *or, is called, that is,* and *in
other words.*

This kind of clue is often found in textbooks, especially science,
history, and mathematics textbooks. Here is an example:

> **from *The Aztecs* by Michael E. Smith**
>
> The Aztecs are long gone, yet we know quite a bit about them today. Our knowledge comes from two sources: ethnohistory, the study of written documents, and archaeology, the study of material objects or artifacts.

You will also find this kind of clue in fiction, but not as often as in textbooks. Here is an example from a novel:

> **from *The Sea Wolf* by Jack London**
>
> But Wolf Larson seemed voluble, prone to speech as I had never seen him before.

2. CONCRETE EXAMPLES

Writers sometimes give examples that illustrate and clarify a difficult concept. The example helps you determine the meaning of a new word. Writers use signal words—*such as, including, for instance, to illustrate, are examples of*, and *for example*—to alert you that an example will follow.

> **from *Essentials of Anatomy and Physiology***
>
> Antigens can be divided into two groups: foreign antigens and self antigens. Foreign antigens are introduced from outside the body. Components of bacteria, viruses, and other microorganisms are examples of foreign antigens that cause disease.

3. CONTRAST CLUES

Sometimes authors will include the opposite meaning to clarify the meaning of a challenging word. The underlined phrases in this example hint at the opposite of *elegance*.

Vocabulary

from *Midnight In the Garden of Good and Evil* by John Berendt

Williams was wearing gray slacks and a blue cotton shirt turned up at the sleeves. His heavy black shoes and thick rubber soles were oddly out of place in the elegance of Mercer House, but practical; Williams spent several hours a day on his feet restoring antique furniture in his basement workshop. His hands were raw and callused, but they had been scrubbed clean of stains and grease.

If you were not sure of the meaning of *elegance,* the surrounding text gives you a hint of what it is *not.* Since "heavy black shoes and thick rubber soles were oddly out of place," you can infer that *elegance* refers to tasteful, refined beauty. This meaning is further reinforced when you read about Williams's hands, "raw and callused"—another detail that would have been "oddly out of place" because they are the opposite of *elegance.*

Here is another example of a contrast clue. In this excerpt, the two characters have been on a ship for a long time, and they are just coming onto land. Note how the underlined words are contrast clues for the word *stable.*

from *The Sea Wolf*

I sprang out, extending my hand to Maud. The next moment she was beside me. As my fingers released hers, she clutched for my arm hastily. At the same moment I swayed, as about to fall to the sand. This was the startling effect of the cessation of motion. We had been so long upon the moving, rocking sea that the stable land was a shock to us. We expected the beach to lift up this way and that, . . .

Since the stable land is so surprising to the characters, you can determine that *stable* means "fixed, stationary, not moving," the opposite of being in motion.

4. DESCRIPTION CLUES

Sometimes an author will use context clues that describe what a word means. In this example, look for clues to the meaning of *liaison*.

> **from "Deep in the Woods" by David Remnick**
>
> In Vermont, Natalia was Solzhenitsyn's liaison with the world; she retains that function here, <u>dealing with publishers, reporters, readers, harassers</u>. I doubt if Aleksandr Isayevich [Solzhenitsyn] has picked up a ringing telephone in decades.

If you didn't know the meaning of the word *liaison*, you can figure out what it means based on what Natalia does. A liaison is a contact person, a go-between, someone who eases communication between two or more people.

5. WORDS OR PHRASES THAT MODIFY

Modifiers—such as adjectives, adverbs, or phrases and clauses—often provide clues to the meaning of an unfamiliar word. Note how the underlined words in this example elaborate on the meaning of the word *remote*.

> **from *House Made of Dawn* by N. Scott Momaday**
>
> It is a remote place, and <u>divided from the rest of the world by a great forked range of mountains on the north and west; by wasteland on the south and east, a region of dunes and thorns and burning columns of air; and more than these by time and silence.</u>

Based on the underlined part of the passage, you can infer that *remote* means "isolated, out of the way," or "distant."

Vocabulary

6. CONJUNCTIONS SHOWING RELATIONSHIPS

Writers often provide context clues that begin with conjunctions showing the relationships between words. These context clues allow readers to link unfamiliar words to familiar ones. Coordinating conjunctions include *and, but, or, nor, for,* and *yet.* Common subordinating conjunctions include *since, because, even though, if, just as, when, whenever, until,* and *although.* In this example, note how the writer uses the subordinating conjunction to join the meaning of the word *discipline* to the rest of the sentence.

from "Talent" by Annie Dillard

People often ask me if I discipline myself to write, if I work a certain number of hours a day on a schedule.

Based on the clause that begins with *if,* you have strong clues suggesting that the meaning of *discipline* is "to impose an orderly pattern of behavior upon, to exercise self-control."

7. UNSTATED OR IMPLIED MEANINGS

Many times you can figure out the meaning of an unfamiliar word by drawing on your own experience of similar situations. In this example, look for clues to the meaning of the word *chaos.*

from "Zlateh the Goat" by Isaac Bashevis Singer

Through the window Aaron could catch a glimpse of the chaos outside. The wind carried before it whole drifts of snow. It was completely dark, and he did not know whether night had already come or whether it was the darkness of the storm.

If you have ever observed a storm, even if from the comfort of your home, you have some idea of what it would be like to be out in it. It would be wild and frightening. You might lose sight of familiar landmarks and be confused about where to go to be safe, and that's exactly what *chaos* means—"a state of utter confusion."

Beyond Context Clues

What happens if you encounter a word that has few or no context clues? When this happens, you have several options:

■ You can check in a dictionary immediately.

■ You can ask your reading partner or a family member.

■ You can jot down the word and the sentence in which it appears. Then you can look it up in a dictionary or ask someone later.

Not all words will have context clues. Don't give up if you can't figure out every word from its context. You have a lot of resources to use in unlocking the meaning of these unfamiliar words. Think of them as challenges that will only make your word collection bigger and better.

Understanding Roots, Prefixes, and Suffixes

Another method of acquiring more words is to learn the meanings of word roots, prefixes, and suffixes.

Word Roots

A *word root* is the part of the word that carries its meaning. If you know the meanings of common Greek and Latin roots, you will be able to determine the meanings of dozens of related words. For example, the Latin roots *ped* and *pod* mean "foot." Knowing this, you might be able to figure out the meaning of each of these words:

■ podiatrist = person who treats foot ailments

■ pedestrian = person who walks

■ pedicure = care of the feet

■ pedometer = instrument for recording the number of steps taken

■ pedal = lever worked by the foot

You have to beware of relying too heavily on knowledge of word roots to figure out word meanings. If you looked at the word *pediatrician,* for example, you might think it has something to do with feet. However, this word is based on a different Greek root, *paid* or *pais,* which means "child." Working with roots is one good method of acquiring new words, but it's not always foolproof. For a list of word roots, see the Reader's Almanac on page 763.

Vocabulary

Prefixes

Prefixes are word parts that are added to the beginning of some words to change their meaning. If you know the meaning of the prefix, you have a clue to the meaning of the whole word. For example, the prefix *pre-* means "before." Knowing this, and with some knowledge of word roots, you can probably figure out the meanings of words like these:

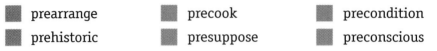

- prearrange
- precook
- precondition
- prehistoric
- presuppose
- preconscious

Another example is the prefix *dis-,* which means "the opposite of." Knowing this prefix gives you a head start on figuring out words like these:

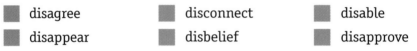

- disagree
- disconnect
- disable
- disappear
- disbelief
- disapprove

For a list of prefixes, see the Almanac on page 758.

Suffixes

A *suffix* is a letter or group of letters added to the end of a word. When you add a suffix to the end of a word, you change its meaning and usually its part of speech. Here are some examples of words with one or more suffixes. The Latin roots *sens* and *sent* mean "to feel" or "to think."

SUFFIXES AND PARTS OF SPEECH

Word	Part of Speech	Meaning
sensation	*noun*	*a feeling caused by stimulation of a sense organ*
sensitive	*adjective*	*able to receive stimulation of the senses*
sentiment	*noun*	*an attitude or thought prompted by feeling*
sentimental	*adjective*	*resulting from feeling rather than reason*
senseless	*adjective*	*lacking sense*
sensitize	*verb*	*to make sensitive*
sensor	*noun*	*a device that responds to a physical stimulus*
sensory	*adjective*	*relating to sensation or to the senses*
sensational	*adjective*	*arousing a quick, intense emotional reaction*

For a list of suffixes, see the Almanac on page 760.

Putting Word Parts Together

One of the best ways to build your vocabulary is to learn the meanings of word parts.

TIPS ABOUT WORD MEANINGS

1. *Most words in English are based on at least one root:*
annual, credible, inject, negate, phonics

2. *Words do not always have both a prefix and a suffix.*
Words with no prefix or suffix:
night, port, sound, time, wish

Words with one prefix:
pronoun, regress, disturb, exclaim, mistake

Words with one suffix:
final, awful, nation, liberate, formless

3. *Words can have more than one root, prefix, or suffix.*
Words with two roots:
cosmology, thermometer, seismograph, telephone

Words with two prefixes:
disentangle, unexplainable, semiconductor, reprogram

Words with two suffixes:
endlessly, gracefulness, softened, generosity

4. *When a base word is combined with a prefix or suffix, the base word often changes.*
Words in which the spelling of the base word changes:

prime	primitive
proclaim	proclamation
remit	remission

Vocabulary

Word Families

A word family is a collection of words that are built on the same root. Here are a few examples of word families:

WORD FAMILY FOR *MOVE*

mov, mob, mot = "move"

movie	moveable	mobile
moving	moved	remove
mobility	motility	motive
motivation	motile	motif
automobile	motor	motorcycle

WORD FAMILY FOR *SOUND*

phon, phono = "sound"

telephone	megaphone	phonics
symphony	cacophony	cacophonous
euphony	euphonious	saxophone
sousaphone	phonograph	phonetics
phonology	phoneme	

WORD FAMILY FOR *SEND, LET GO*

mis, miss, mit ="send," "let go"

admission
dismiss
intermission
missile
permit
promise
transmit

Diving into Dictionaries and Thesauruses

Dictionaries are to reading as maps are to driving. You can get along without them, but you might waste a lot of time not knowing where you're going.

Using Different Dictionaries

Just as you don't need a map of the world if you're driving across your own state, you don't need to carry a 12-pound unabridged dictionary around with you all the time. But you'll want to get a hardbound dictionary to use at home. Keep it near your desk or wherever you do your homework.

Carry a smaller paperback dictionary with you in your backpack to school. This way it will be handy whenever you need to find the meaning of a word or check its spelling. If the paperback dictionary doesn't list the word you're looking for, jot it down in your vocabulary journal, and look it up later in your larger dictionary.

Why Use a Dictionary?

What can you find in a dictionary? Well, you can find a lot more than just the word and its definition. Open any dictionary and you'll find:

■ the correct spelling of a word

■ the correct pronunciation of a word

■ how a word can be divided at the end of a line of writing

■ how the word is spelled when an ending is added

■ synonyms of the word, if applicable

■ the part or parts of speech of a word

■ the definition or definitions of a word

■ a pronunciation key

■ sometimes, the history of a word

■ sometimes, a sentence or phrase showing how a word is used

■ sometimes, photographs or diagrams

Vocabulary

Focus on Using a Dictionary

Dictionaries are not all created equal. Some dictionaries have more words than others; many include the history of a word, and others do not; others include example sentences showing how a word is used, and others do not. Some dictionaries include photographs, diagrams, maps, and charts to explain various words. Some dictionaries have biographical and geographical names at the back of the book. It's a good idea to take some time to explore the many parts of whatever dictionary you use. Although dictionaries are not all alike, almost all dictionaries can answer the most common kinds of questions you'll have about words.

Take a look at these three dictionary entries, and note the differences in how they treat the word *personify*.

---

from *Webster's Tenth New Collegiate Dictionary*

per • son • i • fy \pər-'sä-nə-ˌfī \ *vt* **-fied; -fy • ing**
(ca. 1741) **1:** to conceive of or represent as a person or as having human qualities or powers **2:** to be the embodiment or personfication of: INCARNATE <a teacher who *personified* patience>—**per • son • i • fi • er** \-ˌfī(- ə)r\ *n.*

---

from *Oxford American Dictionary*

per • son • i • fy (pĕr-son-ĭ-fı) *v.* (**per-son-i-fied, per-son-i-fy-ing**) **1.** to represent (an idea) in human form or (a thing) as having human characteristics, *justice is personified as a blindfolded woman holding a pair of scales.* **2.** to embody in one's life or behavior, *he was meanness personified.* **per • son • i • fi • ca • tion** (pĕr-son-ĭ-fĭ-kay-shŏn) *n.*

from *The American Heritage Dictionary of the American Language*

per • son • i• fy (pər-sŏn'ə-fī´) *tr. v.* **-fied, -fying, -fies. 1.** To think of or represent (an inanimate object or abstraction) as having personality or the qualities, thoughts, or movements of a living being. **2.** To represent (an object or abstraction) by a human figure. **3.** To represent (an abstract quality or idea): *This character personifies evil.* **4.** To be the embodiment or perfect example of: *"Stalin now personifies bolshevism in the eyes of the world."* (A.J.P. Taylor). [French *personnifier,* from *personne,* person, from Old French *persone,* PERSON.] **—per • son´i • fi´er** *n.*

Any one of these entries might be sufficient, depending on why you were looking up *personify*. You should know that sometimes you have to look up a word in more than one dictionary. Dictionaries do not all include the same information.

Notice that the word *personify* is pronounced the same way in all three dictionaries shown here, but the way the pronunciation is shown differs. In the first entry, the primary accent mark comes before the accented syllable. In the second entry, the accented syllable is in boldface type. In the third entry, the primary accent mark comes after the accented syllable.

In addition, only the first entry shows a date in the first line. This is the date of the earliest recorded use of *personify* in English.

All three entries include a phrase or sentence showing how the word is used. At the end of the third entry is the history of the word. This history, or etymology, shows that *personify* came from a French word into English.

Vocabulary

Parts of a Dictionary

Being familiar with the parts of a dictionary can help you look up words. On page 681 is a list of some of the most important parts of a dictionary. Those numbers correspond to the circled numbers on the dictionary page below.

from *The American Heritage College Dictionary*

1 **runabout**

runny

2 **run•a•bout** (rŭn´ə-bout´) *n.* **1.a.** *Naut.* A small motorboat. **b.** A light aircraft. c. A small open automobile or carriage. **2.** A vagabond or wanderer.

3 **run•a•gate** (rŭn´ə-gāte´) *n.* **1.** A renegade or deserter. **2.** A vagabond. [Alteration of obsolete *renegate,* renegade (influenced by RUN + *agate,* on the way < ME, straight way : ME *a,* on, var. of *on*; see ON + ON *gata,* way; see **ghē-***) < ME < Med.Lat. *renegātus.* See RENEGADE.]

4 **run•a•way** (rŭn´ə-wā´) *n.* **1.** A person who has run away. **2.** Something that has escaped control or proper confinement. **3.** *Informal.* An easy victory. —*adj.* **1.** Escaping or having escaped restraint, captivity, or control: *runaway horses.* **2.** Out of control: *runaway inflation.* **3.** Easily won. **5**

6 **run•down** (rŭn´ doun´) *n.* **1.** A point-by-point summary. **2.** Baseball. A play in which a runner is trapped between bases and is pursued by fielders. —*adj.* also run-down (run´-down´). **1.a.** In poor physical condition; weak or exhausted. **b.** Dirty and dilapidated. **2.** Unwound and not running. **7**

8 **run•ny** (rŭn´ ē) *adj.* —**ni•er, -ni•est.** Inclined to run or flow.

1 Guide Words

Two guide words appear at the top of each dictionary page. They tell you what the first and last words on that dictionary page are. The guide words make it easier to locate the word you're looking for.

2 Entry Word

Entry words are listed in boldface type and in alphabetical order. They show how the word can be divided into syllables, how the word is spelled, and whether the word should be capitalized.

3 Word History

Some entries have information about the origin, or *etymology*, of the word. This part tells you where the word originally came from.

4 Definitions

A number identifies each definition of a word, if there is more than one. When you look up a word, always read *all* the meanings and apply the one that is most appropriate to your purpose.

5 Illustrative Example

Often you will find an example of the word used in a phrase or sentence for one or more definitions. These examples show you exactly how the word can be used with that particular meaning.

6 Pronunciation

The pronunciation appears immediately after the entry word. The respelling shows you how to say the word. It also shows which syllable is stressed or accented. Most dictionaries have a pronunciation guide, or key, on every two-page spread or in the front of the dictionary. This guide tells you how each symbol in a pronunciation should sound.

7 Part of Speech

Right after the pronunciation respelling, you'll find the abbreviation for the part of speech of the word. When other forms of the entry word are given after the definition, the parts of speech, syllabication, and pronunciation respelling are also included.

8 Inflected Forms

When the spelling of inflected forms (plural forms, past-tense forms) might give you trouble, these are included at the end of the entry.

Vocabulary

Focus on Using a Thesaurus

A thesaurus, like a dictionary, is a tool that can help you expand your vocabulary. Unlike a dictionary, it does not have a pronunciation guide, elaborate definitions, or illustrative examples of how a word is used.

A thesaurus is a collection of synonyms—words that have the same or nearly the same meaning. All the words that mean "beautiful" are grouped together (*lovely, attractive, appealing, pleasing, pretty, admirable, good-looking*) as are all the words that mean "govern" (*command, administer, reign, rule, oversee, dictate, tyrannize*). Many entries in a thesaurus also list antonyms. For example, the antonyms of "beautiful" might be listed as *ugly, deformed,* and *hideous*.

from *Roget's II, the New Thesaurus*

Entry word | **Word meanings**

Part of speech

Synonyms

fake *verb* **1.** To contrive and present as genuine : counterfeit, feign, pretend, simulate. *Idioms:* make believe, put on an act. *See* TRUE. **2.** To make a fraudulent copy of : counterfeit, falsify, forge. *See* TRUE. **3.** To impart a false character to (something) by alteration : doctor, fabricate, falsify, fictionalize, fictionize. *See* TRUE. **4.** To take on or give a false appearance of : affect, assume, counterfeit, feign, pretend, put on, sham, simulate. *Idiom:* make believe. *See* TRUE. **5.** To behave affectedly or insincerely or take on a false or misleading appearance of : act, counterfeit, dissemble, feign, play-act, pose, pretend, put on, sham, simulate. *See* HONEST, TRUE. **6.** To compose or recite without preparation : ad-lib, extemporize, improvise, make up. *Idiom:* wing it. *See* PLANNED, PREPARED.

Notice that the entry for *fake* shows six definitions and four idioms that mean about the same thing as *fake*. The entry also refers you to other entries in the same thesaurus. These entries, such as *true* and *honest*, are antonyms for *fake*.

Connotation and Denotation

Let's say that you want to describe someone. Suppose that the first word that comes to your mind when describing that person is *loud*. Being a very careful writer, you decide to see whether *loud* is the best word you can use in this situation. After all, *loud* can describe many things, from sounds to people to colors.

In a thesaurus, you find this entry:

from *Roget's II, the New Thesaurus*

loud *adjective* **1.** Marked by extremely high volume and intensity of sound : blaring, deafening, earsplitting, roaring, stentorian. *See* SOUNDS. **2.** Tastelessly showy : brummagem, chintzy, flashy, garish, gaudy, glaring, meretricious, tawdry, tinsel. *Informal:* tacky. *See* STYLE.

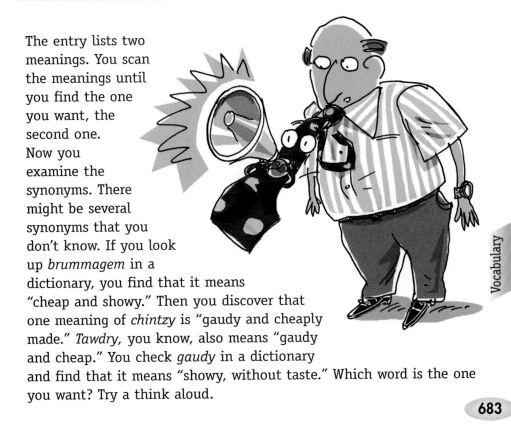

The entry lists two meanings. You scan the meanings until you find the one you want, the second one. Now you examine the synonyms. There might be several synonyms that you don't know. If you look up *brummagem* in a dictionary, you find that it means "cheap and showy." Then you discover that one meaning of *chintzy* is "gaudy and cheaply made." *Tawdry*, you know, also means "gaudy and cheap." You check *gaudy* in a dictionary and find that it means "showy, without taste." Which word is the one you want? Try a think aloud.

Vocabulary

BRUMMAGEM Will anyone else know what this means? I don't think this is the word I want.

CHINTZY This word has several meanings, so I'm not sure the meaning I want would be clear.

FLASHY This one is okay, but it doesn't go far enough.

GARISH This is not exactly how I want to describe the person.

GAUDY This one is a little closer because this person wears bright or showy outfits.

What you've just done is consider the denotation and connotation of words until you found the most accurate adjective to describe the person. The *denotation* of a word is the dictionary definition. The *connotation* of a word is all the associations surrounding the word. The synonyms you found in the thesaurus all mean about the same thing, but they have slightly different connotations. *Brummagem* probably doesn't call up many associations for most people. But the connotations you have for *gaudy* help you decide that this is the word you want to use.

Think about the connotations and denotations next time you're reading and considering the meanings of descriptive words. The writer probably chose the words very carefully.

Analogies

Analogies are expressions that show similarities between two things. On standardized tests, analogies show up quite often. An analogy question has two sets of words that share a common relationship. Your job as a reader is to figure out the relationship of the pair of words that is given. Then, you apply that same relationship to the other pair of words and complete the analogy.

How to Read Analogies

Analogies can be expressed in several ways. They can be completely written out, as in this example:

> **SAMPLE ANALOGY**
>
> *huge* is to *enormous* as *tiny* is to *minuscule*

They can use colons [:] and double colons [::] as symbols for "is to" and "as," as in this example:

> **SAMPLE ANALOGY**
>
> huge : enormous :: tiny : minuscule

You would read this: *huge* "is to" *enormous* "as" *tiny* "is to" *miniscule*. Or analogies can be a mixture of words and symbols, as in these examples:

> **SAMPLE ANALOGY**
>
> *huge* is to *enormous* :: *tiny* is to *minuscule*
> huge : enormous as tiny : minuscule

When you encounter an analogy question, your job is to find the missing word or pair of words. Each word is important and must be considered carefully. First, read the analogy slowly. Next, figure out the relationship between the first pair of words. How are they related?

Sample Analogy Questions

1. hat : head :: shoe : _____
   - a. leather
   - b. shoelace
   - c. foot
   - d. leg
2. fear : courage :: timidity : _____
   - a. bravery
   - b. boldness
   - c. shyness
   - d. love
3. knight : night :: reign : _____
   - a. rule
   - b. write
   - c. rain
   - d. right
4. calm : composed :: kind : _____
   - a. build
   - b. considerate
   - c. slow
   - d. eager

Try using the strategy of thinking aloud to work through these analogies. In your head, talk your way through the relationship between each pair of words.

THINK ALOUD

1. OK. A hat goes on my head, and a shoe goes on my foot. So the analogy must be "hat is to head as shoe is to foot."

2. Fear and courage are opposites. So I need to find a word that is the opposite of timidity. The only word that will work here is boldness.

3. Knight and night sound the same but are spelled differently. So I need to find a word that sounds the same as reign but is spelled differently. That word would be rain.

4. Calm and composed are synonyms. I need to choose a word that means the same as kind. The only word that works is considerate.

Types of Analogies

Analogies present many kinds of relationships. When you encounter an analogy on a standardized test, identify exactly what is being compared in the completed pair before choosing your answer. Here are some examples.

1. Analogies in Which Word Order Is Not Important

RELATIONSHIPS IN ANALOGIES

1. Synonyms

omit : skip :: choose : _____

  a. chosen   b. reject   c. pick   d. delete

2. Antonyms

jolly is to *gloomy* as *elation* is to _____

  a. depression   b. happiness   c. darkness   c. laugh

3. Rhyming Words

chair : lair :: poise : _____

  a. pose   b. noise   c. noisy   d. grace

4. Homophones

crews : *cruise* as _____ : _____

  a. beech : beach   b. run : ran

  c. four : fort   d. knot : knots

5. Parts of the Same Thing

stem : petal :: _____ : _____

  a. TV : radio   b. trunk : leaf

  c. knife : spoon   d. train : plane

6. Two Examples from the Same Class

lake is to *river* as *hill* is to _____

  a. view   b. trees   c. climb   d. mountain

(Answers: 1. c, 2. a, 3. b, 4. a, 5. b, 6. d)

Vocabulary

687

2. Analogies in Which Word Order Is Important

1. Different Forms of the Same Word
apply : application :: evaluate : _____
a. evaluating   b. evaluated   c. evaluation   d. value

2. Name and Location
country : England :: continent : _____
a. Atlantic   b. borders   c. Spain   d. Asia

3. Class and Example of that Class
offspring : colt :: _____ _____
a. fish : school   b. singer : soprano
c. football : basketball   d. cloud : puffy

4. Item and Who Uses It
plane is to *pilot* as *stage* is to _____
a. performer   b. audience   c. curtain   d. director

5. Item and What It Is Designed to Do
hammer : pound :: _____ _____
a. faucet : drip   b. shower : water
c. car : steering wheel   d. knife : cut

6. Item and a Word that Describes It
thorn is to *sharp* :: *comedian* is to _____
a. stage   b. funny   c. laughter   d. routine

7. Whole and Part
dresser : drawer :: sweater : _____
a. sleeve   b. knit   c. pants   d. coat

RELATIONSHIPS IN ANALOGIES, continued

8. Action and Where It Takes Place

run is to *track* as *swim* is to _____

a. race   b. dive   c. pool   d. spa

9. Result and Who Does It

house : *builder* :: _____ _____

a. sonnet : poet   b. photograph : picture
c. movie : film   d. whale : mammal

10. Sequence

infancy : *childhood* :: _____ _____

a. tree : seed   b. children : babies
c. first : last   d. bud : flower

(Answers: 1. c, 2. d, 3. b, 4. a, 5. d, 6. b, 7. a, 8. c, 9. a, 10. d)

 **umming Up**

You can follow several methods to build your vocabulary. One is to keep a vocabulary journal in which you write down the new words you read or hear. To determine the meaning of new words, use context clues, a dictionary, and a thesaurus. You can also use knowledge of word roots, prefixes, suffixes, and word families to learn new words. Then, learn the various kinds of analogies so you'll be prepared when you see them on a standardized test.

Vocabulary

Reader's
Almanac

- Doing Research
- Strategy Handbook
- Reading Tools
- Word Parts: Prefixes, Suffixes, and Roots

Doing Research

Knowing how to research *effectively* should be one of your personal goals. Effective researchers know how to find the *most* and *best* information in the *least* amount of time.

Here you'll learn how to find useful material, keep track of information, and evaluate and document sources. Take what you learn here and use it to help you complete your next research project.

Why do research? Here are eight good reasons. Maybe you can think of more.

> REASONS FOR RESEARCH

1. To find answers or information you need
Let's say you're going to buy a stereo and want to know which one is the best deal.

2. To write a paper or essay for class
How else will you learn the causes for the French Revolution?

3. To prepare a talk or presentation
Perhaps you want to give a talk on hiking the Appalachian Trail.

4. To give yourself that extra edge on an upcoming test
Find out about Sigmund Freud before you take a test about his theories.

5. To write a news story or editorial for the school paper
Imagine your assignment: to find out how a school board member voted at the last three board meetings.

6. To take part in a debate
Gather the facts to argue your point about the scientific value of cloning.

7. To take part in a class discussion
Researching Kate Chopin's life can help you understand the settings, characters, plots, and themes in her book The Awakening.

8. To satisfy your curiosity
Discover what other people have said about your favorite movie.

Almanac

691

The Basics of Research

Every step of the reading process described in this handbook—set a purpose, preview, plan, and so on—has a similar step in the research process. Think of this process as the two sides of a mountain.

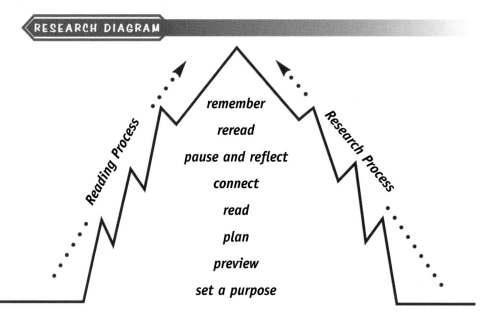

RESEARCH DIAGRAM

Reading Process

Research Process

remember
reread
pause and reflect
connect
read
plan
preview
set a purpose

Here are some ideas of how to use the reading process when you research.

A Set a Purpose

Always begin by thinking about the purpose of your research. Why are you there, at the library or in front of the computer screen? What are you looking for? Be as clear and specific in your purpose as you can:

I need to find information about _____.

B Preview

Before you begin your search, get a sense of what materials are available to you and which you'll want to use first. What kinds of sources will you look for? Will you start out at the library or begin with an Internet search? Gather your materials and then make a plan.

C Plan

Choose a reading strategy that can help you meet your research purpose. Use different strategies depending on what you're reading and what you're looking for. If the topic is complex, plan on using two or more strategies.

STRATEGIES TO USE WHILE RESEARCHING

Close Reading	*Note-taking*	*Looking for Cause and Effect*
Outlining	*Paraphrasing*	*Questioning the Author*
Reading Critically	*Skimming*	*Using Graphic Organizers*
Summarizing	*Synthesizing*	*Visualizing and Thinking Aloud*

See pages 713-737 for a discussion of these strategies.

D Read with a Purpose

Some researchers end up buried in an avalanche of sources. You can avoid this problem by reminding yourself of your purpose again and again as you research. Write your purpose on an index card and keep your research questions in front of you as you move from source to source.

E Connect

Keep your interest alive as you research. Relate what you're reading to your own life and to your previous knowledge. If possible, choose materials that you enjoy working with. If you come to a book, article, or website that doesn't spark your interest, choose another. There's plenty of information out there.

F Pause and Reflect

When you've completed your research, take a moment to reflect on the information you've found. Ask yourself, "Do I know enough now to write a good report or give a knowledgeable talk about the topic?" If your answer is *no,* go back to the stacks or to a computer for more research.

Almanac

G Reread

Rereading is an important part of researching. You'll reread when you double-check facts, evaluate sources, and prepare to present what you've learned. Use one of the reading strategies to help you reread.

H Remember

It's essential that you find a way to remember what you've learned, especially if your research time is spread out over several days. Most researchers use the strategy of note-taking to help them remember. They use index cards to keep track of important information, key sources, and notes.

Finding Sources

You'll use two different types of sources when you research: primary and secondary sources. Both are important.

Here's an example of the primary and secondary sources you might use to research a topic.

SOURCES

TOPIC: The Food and Drug Administration (FDA) approval process for a new medication	
PRIMARY SOURCES	SECONDARY SOURCES
• interview with a pharmaceutical executive • pharmaceutical company documents • FDA documents, survey of new drugs brought to the market over the last ten years	• encyclopedia entry about the FDA • newspaper article that tracks the approval process from start to finish • television documentary about the FDA

Primary Sources

A **primary source** is an original source. This means that the source informs you directly, rather than through another person's explanation or interpretation.

You're working with primary sources when you:

- read someone's diary
- get information firsthand by observing an event
- survey or interview people to collect their ideas and opinions
- do experiments to prove a point or understand a theory
- analyze original documents, such as the Declaration of Independence

Most readers enjoy using primary resources because they offer a way to get personally involved in the research. Here are the most common primary sources. You will probably use each at least once during your high school career.

TYPES OF PRIMARY SOURCES

autobiographies	*memoirs*	*diaries*
journals	*logs*	*experiments*
observations	*surveys*	*polls*
interviews	*panels*	*letters*
shows		*speeches*

Secondary Sources

A **secondary source** is one that contains information that *other people* have gathered and interpreted. A secondary source is different from a primary source in that it is not an *original* source. Secondary sources extend, analyze, interpret, or evaluate primary information.

You're working with a secondary source if you:

- read a newspaper article
- examine an encyclopedia entry
- study a science text
- watch a documentary on TV
- visit a website

Almanac

Types

Books: *nonfiction, informational or how-to books, biographies, plays, and poetry*

Reference Works: *dictionaries, thesauruses, encyclopedias, atlases, maps, handbooks, indexes, directories, almanacs, and catalogs*

Periodicals: *newspapers, magazines, and journals*

Audiovisual Resources: *television, radio, film, cassettes, CDs, videotapes, and DVDs*

Electronic Media: *web pages, on-line databases, news sites (webcasts), hotlines, news broadcasts, TV and radio broadcasts*

Government Publications: *journals, guides, programs, records, statistics, reports, pamphlets, and brochures*

Business Publications: *journals, annual reports, newsletters, press releases, pamphlets, handbooks, manuals, presentations, displays, and educational programs*

Where to Find Them

Libraries: *public, school, and special libraries (ones that specialize in legal, medical, government, business, and research)*

Mass Media: *radio, television, film, and print*

Learning Sites: *museums, zoos, science centers, parks, nature centers, historical sites, plants and facilities, colleges, and universities*

Computer Resources: *personal computers (for files and programs) and networks (for email, Internet, and online services)*

Government: *municipal, state, and federal offices*

Research Sites: *laboratories, testing centers, and think tanks*

Conference Sites: *shows, fairs, exhibits, and conventions*

Workplaces: *corporate databases, company files, bulletin boards, and websites*

The Internet and the Library

Researching is a little like going on a scavenger hunt. You know what the "treasure" is (the information you want), but you may need to complete a series of steps before you can find it.

Student researchers have two important sources at their disposal: the Internet and the library. Both are enormously helpful and can be a starting point for almost any research project.

Using the Internet

What would we do without the Internet? It's an amazing information source that links tens of thousands of computers all over the world. With just a few keystrokes, you can find out almost anything you need to know. It's a fast and convenient source of information.

As great as it is, however, the Internet presents some problems to researchers. First, there's so much information on the Internet that it's easy to get lost. Second, a lot of information on the Internet is not reliable, meaning it cannot always be checked or supported with facts. Many websites appear to be research sites but in truth offer nothing more than unfounded claims and unsupported opinions.

So surf the Internet wisely. Use the reading process to help you understand and evaluate each site that you visit. For more information on using search engines and reading websites, see "Reading on the Internet," pages 511–537.

Almanac

Using the Library

If you think going to the library is old-fashioned, think again. The library offers reliable information and presents it in many easy-to-use formats. The key to researching in the library is understanding what a library offers and how to find it.

THE COMPUTER CATALOG

When you enter the library, your first stop should be the computer catalog. A computer catalog contains information about the library's holdings. This means that every book, video, cassette, and software program that the library owns is listed in the computer catalog. In addition, sometimes you can use your library's computer to find out what other libraries in the area have in their collections. This is useful for books that you need to borrow on interlibrary loan.

The first time you use the computer catalog, you may need to ask a librarian for help. If not, log on and begin at the library's "welcome," or start-up, screen.

START-UP SCREEN

For library searches

Levin County Public Libraries
Connect to Knowledge

Welcome to the Levin County Library Network!

For magazine and newspaper searches

Databases:
1. author, title, subject searches
2. general periodical index
3. information about libraries in our system

To search other libraries in the system

To make a selection, type a number and then press [RETURN]>>>

This web page is maintained by the Levin County Public Library Web Team.

webmaster@levinlib.org
Copyright © 2002 The Levin County Library System

When you locate a book, the computer catalog entry will look something like this:

COMPUTER CATALOG ENTRY

Book title

The author's name

Publisher information

Call number or shelving information

Descriptive information

Location information— which libraries have the book

Request: Title.
Title: The call of the wild / Jack London.
Author: London, Jack, 1876-1916.
Publisher: New York : Signet, c.1960.
Description: xiv, 176 p. ; 21 cm.
Holdings : Item Holdings
Location Call number Available Franklin Park
Circulation 813.52 L847
Unavailable, On Loan Montgomery
Pbk. J FICTION Available
Help window

After leaving the home page, you will be prompted to make a series of choices. Eventually you will end up on a screen that gives the same information you would find on a catalog card. Print the information if you can, or take quick notes on a note card.

KEY WORD SEARCHES
When you do a computer catalog search, you'll begin by typing in a *key word*. A key word is one, two, or more words that tell the computer what you are looking for.

SEARCHES FOR TITLES
You can search for a book by typing in the entire title. But if you don't know the whole title, you can use just one word as your key word. The computer will show you all the titles in the system that contain this key word. Then, you scan the list to find the title you're looking for. (If the key word is a common one, such as *wild*, then you'll have a lot of titles to scan. It's best to give as many key words as you can to help the computer narrow the search.)

TITLE: CALL WILD

SEARCHES FOR AUTHORS
If you know an author's last name, use this as your key word. If you can only remember the first couple of letters of the author's last name, try using these as your key word.

AUTHOR: LOND

Almanac

SEARCHES FOR SUBJECTS

Very often you'll know the subject, but not the book title or the author's name. When this is the case, use the subject as your key word. It's important to be as specific as possible. For example, *wolves* is more specific than *mammals; Alaskan wolves* is more specific than *wolves.* If your key word is not specific enough, you'll end up with hundreds of titles to search through.

SUBJECT: ALASKAN WOLVES

REFINING A SEARCH

Your library computer will probably allow you to refine (broaden or narrow) your search. Refining your search can save tremendous amounts of time.

Most library computers encourage you to use what are called "Boolean operators." Boolean operators are the words *and, or, not,* and *with.* Here are several examples of Boolean searches.

BOOLEAN OPERATORS

Key words you enter	The computer will show you
fiction	listings that contain the word fiction
fiction and *wild*	listings that contain the words fiction *and* wild
wild or *call*	listings that contain either wild *or* call
wild not *animal*	listings that contain the word wild, *but not the word* animal
wild with *London*	listings that contain the word wild *and the name* London

Using Call Numbers

Learning how to read a call number is an important step in learning how to use a library effectively.

Call numbers are based on the classification system libraries use to organize their materials. Most public and school libraries use what is called the Dewey decimal system, named for Melvil Dewey, the American librarian who invented it.

The Dewey decimal system divides books into 10 major subject classes, with 100 numbers assigned to each class.

DEWEY DECIMAL SYSTEM

Call numbers	What you'll find there
000-099	*General Works:* encyclopedias, atlases, handbooks, and other books that cover many subjects
100-199	*Philosophy*
200-299	*Religion*
300-399	*Social Sciences:* books on education, government, law, economics, and other social sciences
400-499	*Languages:* dictionaries and books about grammar
500-599	*Sciences:* books about biology, chemistry, all other sciences, and math
600-699	*Technology:* books about computers, engineering, inventions, medicine, and cooking
700-799	*Arts and Recreation:* books about painting, music, and other arts, plus sports and games
800-899	*Literature:* poetry, plays, essays, famous speeches, and literary criticism
900-999	*History, Travel, and Geography*

The ten major subclasses in the Dewey decimal system are broken down into divisions, sections, and subsections. Each has its own topic and number, as in this example:

900 History /Class
970 History of North America /Division
970.004 History of North American Indians /Subsection
970.00497 History of the Sioux Indians /Sub-subsection

Almanac

IN THE STACKS

The call number tells you where the book is located in the library. When you search the stacks, or shelves, begin at the end of the stack and look at the directional signs. These tell you the range of call numbers shelved in a particular stack.

FICTION AND BIOGRAPHIES/AUTOBIOGRAPHIES

The only exception to the call number system is fiction and biographies/autobiographies. Fiction is usually located in its own section of the library. The books are shelved alphabetically according to the author's last name. Biographies and autobiographies are usually located in a section near fiction. They are shelved alphabetically by the last name of the person the book is written about. For example, the biography of Tecumseh written by John Sugden will be alphabetized under "T."

Using Reference Works

After you check the library's computer catalog, you may want to take a look in the general reference section of the library. Here you'll find dictionaries, encyclopedias, atlases, and so on.

In most cases, books in the reference section do not circulate, which means that you cannot check them out. Sometimes a library will shelve older copies of a reference book in the general collection. These books do circulate, but their information will not be completely current.

It's a good idea to familiarize yourself with the reference section of your library. Walk through the stacks and take a look at the books available. Talk to a reference librarian about works that may assist you with a particular research topic. Most librarians love to help you find what you need, and they can help you become an efficient researcher. Most reference sections contain some or all of these helpful resources:

Almanacs These regular (usually annual) publications are filled with facts and statistics:

   The World Almanac and *Information Please Almanac* offer information on various subjects, such as business, politics, history, religion, sports, education, and the arts.

Atlases These are books of maps and related facts. Most atlases contain information on countries, transportation, languages, climate, and more.

- *Hammond World Atlas and Book of Facts* includes maps of countries as well as information about major cities.
- *The Rand McNally Commercial Atlas and Marketing Guide* includes maps of the United States and its major cities.
- *Street Atlas USA* or *Street Finder Index* on CD-ROM lets you call up street maps for any place in the United States.

Biographical Dictionaries These contain short biographies of famous people. Many subject areas have their own biographical dictionaries, such as the *Dictionary of Scientific Biography* or the *Oxford Companion to African American Literature*.

- *Current Biography* has articles containing a photo of the individual and a biographical sketch.
- *Dictionary of Literary Biography* contains useful information on authors past and present.

Directories These contain lists of people and groups. The most useful directories are found on the Internet, since these are updated constantly. In your library, look for *The National Directory of Addresses and Telephone Numbers*. It includes listings for companies, associations, schools, and churches around the country.

Guides and Handbooks These provide guidelines and models for exploring a topic, an area of knowledge, or a profession.

- *The Kids' Guide to Summer Jobs* offers information about summer employment around the country.
- *Occupational Outlook Handbook* explores the job market and how to prepare for a future career.

Yearbooks These cover major developments in specific areas of interest during a previous year.

- *Congressional Yearbook* offers a yearly review of Congress.
- *Statistical Abstract of the United States: The National Data Book* gives statistical information about the United States, including information about population, geography, politics, and employment.

Almanac

Finding Articles in Periodicals

You can use two ways to find an article in a periodical (newspaper, magazine, or journal). The first is to use a periodical database, such as EBSCO or Proquest. The second is to use a periodical index, such as the *Reader's Guide to Periodical Literature*. Most libraries offer only one of these two methods of research. So your first step will be to ask the reference librarian which system your library has.

PERIODICAL DATABASES IN THE LIBRARY

You can access a library's periodical database through the online catalog. Some libraries charge a fee for this service. In others, the search is free, but they charge a small fee for printing an article.

The advantage of using a database such as EBSCO or Proquest is that the entire text of the article has already been downloaded. This means that you won't need to wait while a librarian pulls a back issue of a magazine or newspaper.

PERIODICAL DATABASES ON THE INTERNET

Many newspaper and magazine websites will allow you to search their archives, but they may charge a fee for this service. Remember also that most of the periodicals in the Internet archives will be fairly recent. Very few newspapers and magazines store articles for more than ten years. Use a search engine to find a website that lists Web periodicals.

USING THE *READER'S GUIDE TO PERIODICAL LITERATURE*

The *Reader's Guide to Periodical Literature* is a print index to articles published in more than 200 magazines, newspapers, and journals. Volumes of the index are arranged by time period. You can search a time period by topic or author's last name. Articles are arranged alphabetically.

Remember that your library will not subscribe to every periodical listed in the *Reader's Guide*. The reference librarian can give you a list of the periodicals available in your library. It's a good idea to check the list before you start using the *Reader's Guide*. It can be frustrating to find an article that seems to be just what you want only to discover your library doesn't have it and that it would take weeks to receive it through an interlibrary loan.

LOCATING ARTICLES FROM THE *READER'S GUIDE*

Once you've found the listing you're looking for in the *Reader's Guide,* use the "call slips" located at the periodical desk. The person who pulls the periodical for you will need this information:

 name of the periodical

 issue date of the periodical

 title and page number of the article

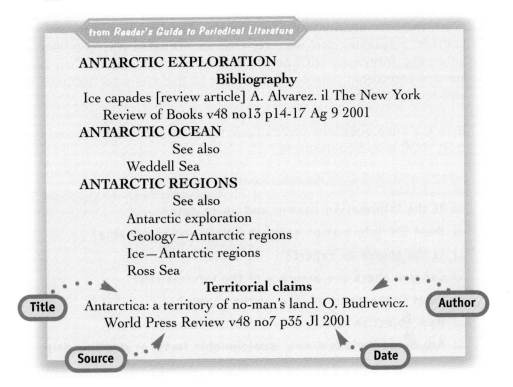

from *Reader's Guide to Periodical Literature*

ANTARCTIC EXPLORATION
Bibliography
Ice capades [review article] A. Alvarez. il The New York
Review of Books v48 no13 p14-17 Ag 9 2001
ANTARCTIC OCEAN
See also
Weddell Sea
ANTARCTIC REGIONS
See also
Antarctic exploration
Geology—Antarctic regions
Ice—Antarctic regions
Ross Sea
Territorial claims

Title — Antarctica: a territory of no-man's land. O. Budrewicz. — Author
World Press Review v48 no7 p35 Jl 2001

Source — Date

Some libraries allow you to find your own periodical, but in most a librarian finds the magazine for you. More and more often, libraries are storing periodicals on CD-ROM or microfilm. Ask the reference librarian for help if it is your first time researching periodicals electronically.

OTHER PERIODICAL INDEXES

The *Reader's Guide to Periodical Literature* is the most commonly used periodical index, but there are other indexes available as well. For example, you might use the *General Periodical Index*, which is similar to the *Reader's Guide* but published on CD-ROM. Or you might use a single-publication index, such as the *New York Times Index*.

Almanac

Evaluating Sources

Not all information sources are equally reliable. Before you spend a lot of time carefully reading a source, evaluate it. If you intend to use it, it's your responsibility to decide whether a source is a good one.

Sometimes it's fairly easy to determine which sources are more reliable. For example, newspapers and magazines that have a long and well-respected publishing history *(Time, Newsweek, Fortune, Sports Illustrated)* are usually fairly trustworthy. This is also true for journals, magazines, and websites that are affiliated with a college or university. Interviews with people who are professionals in their field are also considered reliable. The point is to find the most accurate and authoritative source you can.

Here are some questions you can ask to determine which sources are most reliable and appropriate:

Checklist for Evaluating a Source

❏ **Is the information current and up-to-date?**

❏ **Does the information seem complete and reasonable?**

❏ **Is the source an expert?**

❏ **Can you check the accuracy of the information?**

❏ **What is the point of view of the source?**

❏ **How objective does the information seem?**

❏ **Are there obvious errors, questionable facts, or sloppy writing?**

Use an organizer called a Source Evaluator to pull together your notes about a major source. Here's an example of what one looks like:

SOURCE EVALUATOR

RESEARCH PURPOSE	Write the purpose of your research here.
SOURCE TYPE	Write whether source is primary or secondary here.
TITLE OR LOCATION	Write the title or location of research here.
DATE	Write the date of your finding here.
EXPERTISE	Comment on whether source is authoritative here.
BIAS?	Write comments on whether source is biased here.
REACTIONS	Write your reactions to your findings here.

Keeping Track of Information

Unless you simply needed to look up one or two facts in just one or two sources, you will probably find yourself at a table with a collection of books, periodicals, and printouts scattered in front of you. You've checked to be sure that your sources are reliable and that the information is up-to-date. What do you do now? How should you begin? How can you find and keep track of the specific information you need without drowning in a sea of reference materials?

Reading Sources

Your first step should be to remind yourself of your research purpose. Then, preview the sources you have in front of you. Skim the table of contents for each book, glance at the headings of every article, and look for key words on every printout. Place sticky notes by information that is relevant to your purpose. Create a "discard" pile for any books, magazines, printouts, or photocopies that do not help you meet your purpose.

Your next step is to work your way systematically through each source. Use the strategy of skimming to make the job easier. As you read, look for information that you know is important. When you come to an important fact or detail, read slowly. If you've found information you need in a source, it's time to take some notes.

Taking Notes

Taking notes as you read is the best way to keep track of what you're learning. Sometimes you may prefer to photocopy or print out material you find and read and highlight it later. But having a clear note-taking system will not only help you organize your information more easily but also help you when it's time to create your research report.

Figure out a note-taking system that works best for you. One of the most popular methods is to take notes on index cards. The basic idea is to make a separate *bibliography card* for each source you read. Then, record important details—summaries, paraphrases, or direct quotes—on *note cards*. You give each card a heading.

Almanac

Index Cards

Below are samples of four different kinds of cards you will probably use to complete most research projects.

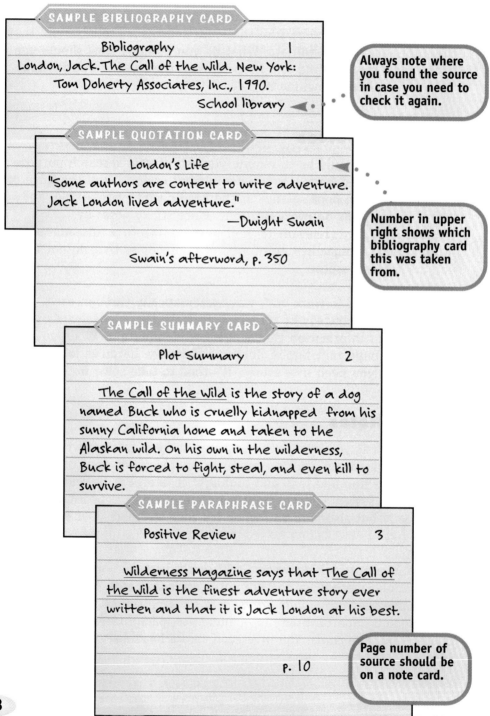

SAMPLE BIBLIOGRAPHY CARD

Bibliography   1
London, Jack. The Call of the Wild. New York:
Tom Doherty Associates, Inc., 1990.
                              School library

> Always note where you found the source in case you need to check it again.

SAMPLE QUOTATION CARD

London's Life   1

"Some authors are content to write adventure.
Jack London lived adventure."
                              —Dwight Swain

Swain's afterword, p. 350

> Number in upper right shows which bibliography card this was taken from.

SAMPLE SUMMARY CARD

Plot Summary   2

The Call of the Wild is the story of a dog
named Buck who is cruelly kidnapped from his
sunny California home and taken to the
Alaskan wild. On his own in the wilderness,
Buck is forced to fight, steal, and even kill to
survive.

SAMPLE PARAPHRASE CARD

Positive Review   3

Wilderness Magazine says that The Call of
the Wild is the finest adventure story ever
written and that it is Jack London at his best.

                              p. 10

> Page number of source should be on a note card.

Paraphrasing

In your haste to complete your research paper, you may unintentionally use an author's words as if they were your own, especially when you paraphrase. Remember to make the words sound like your style when you are paraphrasing. You can use quotes within your paraphrase, but always put quotation marks around an author's words. Here are examples of paraphrases based on an author's words.

AUTHOR'S WORDS

Although some critics have dismissed *The Call of the Wild* as the worst kind of anthropomorphism, the fact is that London succeeded in portraying the wilderness experience and the courage necessary to survive.

POOR PARAPHRASE

Some critics have said that The Call of the Wild is the worst kind of anthropomorphism, but the truth is, London "succeeded in portraying the wilderness experience..." (Samuelson 15).

This paraphrase uses too many of the author's words.

GOOD PARAPHRASE

While some scholars charge that anthropomorphism makes the novel unworthy of serious consideration, "London succeeded in portraying the wilderness experience..." (Samuelson 15).

If you leave out part of a quotation, use an ellipsis (three periods with a space before and after) to show the omission. Be fair, however. Don't change the author's meaning by quoting only part of his or her statement. Be sure to credit the author by name, and include the page number.

Before you hand in your research paper, reread any paraphrases and compare them to the sources you found. If any of your words are the same as an author's and are not in quotes, you need to revise your work, either by rewriting your paraphrase or by adding quotation marks. Plagiarism, or passing off someone else's work as your own, is stealing.

Almanac

Documentation

Your readers are going to want to know where you found your information. Therefore, you'll need to document each source you use. Your goal here is to make the documentation specific enough so that a person could double-check your research if he or she wanted to do so. For that reason, it's not enough simply to say, "I found my information on the Internet." You need to record the site name, when you visited, what links you followed, and so on. The same is true for any books, periodicals, or other sources you use.

Remember that all uses of source material—summaries, paraphrases, and direct quotations—need to be properly documented. The full quote and the author's name should be recorded on a numbered quotation card. The author's full name and full source should be recorded on a bibliography card that carries the same number as the quotation card. The information from the bibliography card will be included in the documentation for your paper. The only exception is information that's considered to be *common knowledge*. That means factual information that's easy to find and about which there is no disagreement (such as what team won the 1999 World Series or where Thomas Jefferson was born).

Informal Documentation

You can use either of two types of documentation: informal and formal. Your teacher will specify the type required for your presentation or report.

Informal documentation usually means naming a source or sources within the text of the presentation or report. For example:

> Many parents are unhappy with what they call the "over-vaccination" of their children. There are numerous parenting books on this topic, such as Shots in the Dark and Your Child and Disease.

Formal Documentation

Formal documentation of sources is a bit more involved. Pay attention as your teacher outlines his or her specific requirements. Some teachers will ask for parenthetical references and a "works cited" page. Others may assign a formal bibliography. Always follow your teacher's specific directions. The *form* of your documentation is usually very important.

Different academic disciplines use different styles of formal documentation. Two of the most widely used are those recommended by the Modern Language Association (MLA) and the American Psychological Association (APA). Instructors in English and history, for instance, usually prefer MLA style, while instructors in science or psychology often prefer APA style. Both combine some sort of *parenthetical* (in-text) *references* with a separate list of all the sources you used.

PARENTHETICAL REFERENCES

MLA
In *Norman Castles in Britain*, Jeremy Crown says that one of William the Conqueror's first tasks was to build a system of castles beginning at Hastings (27).

APA
The Bayeux Tapestry shows the building of the castle at Hastings (Crown, 1967, p. 12).

LIST OF WORKS CITED OR REFERENCES

MLA
Crown, Jeremy. *Norman Castles in Britain*. London: Lenox, 1967.

APA
Crown, J. (1967). *Norman castles in Britain*. London: Lenox.

The information you need and how you present it varies, depending on the type of source. The format for a book entry shown above is different, for example, from the format for a newspaper article or a website. For a full presentation of the different styles of documentation, see one of the following sources on the next page.

Books

Writers INC: A Student Handbook for Writing and Learning. Boston: Great Source Education Group, 2001.

The Chicago Manual of Style, Fourteenth Edition. Chicago: University of Chicago Press, 1993.

Websites

www.mla.org The official Modern Language Association website.

www.apa.org The official website of the Publication Manual of the American Psychological Association.

www.thewritesource.com The website of the publishers of the *Writers INC* handbook. Check here for sample research papers and MLA and APA documentation updates.

Strategy Handbook

This part of the handbook describes reading strategies that can help you become a more effective reader. Use these reading strategies to help you tackle almost any kind of reading. The descriptions tell you what strategies work best with which types of reading material. Choose one of the strategies before you start to read, and watch your reading improve!

Key Strategies

Almanac

Close Reading

Close reading means reading word for word, sentence by sentence, or line by line. It means paying close attention to how words, sentences, and even punctuation contribute to meaning.

Close reading is a good strategy to use with poetry or with small parts of a longer work. For longer works, choose a part that you know is important, such as directions on a test, steps for conducting a science experiment, or the conclusion of an essay.

Using the Strategy

To do a close reading, first read the selection slowly and carefully.

1. Select and Read Choose a few lines or a key passage. Mark important parts, either by using a highlighter or by using small sticky notes.

2. Analyze Look at each line or passage you marked. Ask yourself questions like these:

- Why did the writer use this particular word?
- What does this mean?
- What am I supposed to do?
- Why is this important?
- What do these words suggest?
- What is the connection between these two sentences?
- What is the significance of this detail?
- Why does this begin (or end) this way?

By answering these questions, you'll unlock the meaning of the passage.

3. React Make connections to what you've read. Your personal reactions to words or phrases can help you understand meaning. Your prior knowledge can often help you figure out what you're supposed to do.

Record your thoughts in a Double-entry Journal. For example, here is one reader's reaction to the first part of a poem by William Shakespeare.

DOUBLE-ENTRY JOURNAL

QUOTE	MY THOUGHTS AND FEELINGS
"Weary with toil, I haste me to my bed, The dear repose for limbs with travel tirèd; But then begins a journey in my head, To work my mind when body's work's expirèd."	The speaker is tired from work ("toil") and travel and is anxious to rest. The "journey" in his head starts, however, which must mean that he can't sleep for thinking. I like how "journey" fits with "travel," in line 2.

You can use what you gathered from a close reading to back up your ideas about a work. By telling what specific words and phrases mean, you will have the reasons you need to support your views.

DEFINITION

Close reading means reading word for word, sentence by sentence, or line by line. Use close reading when a work is short or when you come to a paragraph or section in a longer work that you know is important. Assume that every word you read carries meaning and contributes to the mood, tone, or message of a selection.

Almanac

Looking for Cause and Effect

Writers often tell why things happen. The events or situations that happen first are the *causes*. The events or situations that happen as a result are the *effects*.

Looking for cause and effect is a good strategy to use with textbooks, fiction, or biography.

Using the Strategy

You often make connections as you read and as you see relationships among ideas and events.

1. Read First, read the selection all the way through. Highlight or use sticky notes to record your comments or questions, including any thoughts about cause-effect relationships.

2. Create an Organizer Next, create an organizer showing the cause-effect relationships you noticed. Of the different organizers that follow, choose the one that seems to work best for you.

ONE CAUSE AND SEVERAL EFFECTS

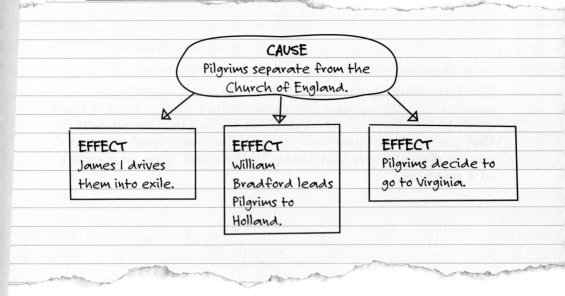

CAUSE
Pilgrims separate from the Church of England.

EFFECT
James I drives them into exile.

EFFECT
William Bradford leads Pilgrims to Holland.

EFFECT
Pilgrims decide to go to Virginia.

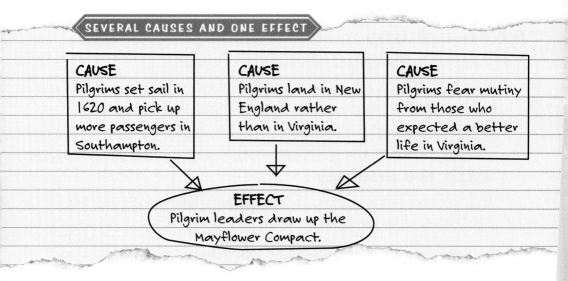

SEVERAL CAUSES AND ONE EFFECT

CAUSE
Pilgrims set sail in 1620 and pick up more passengers in Southampton.

CAUSE
Pilgrims land in New England rather than in Virginia.

CAUSE
Pilgrims fear mutiny from those who expected a better life in Virginia.

EFFECT
Pilgrim leaders draw up the Mayflower Compact.

3. Revise the Organizer As you read or reread, you may want to add to or revise your organizer. For instance, sometimes as you read, you'll discover that a cause-effect relationship you thought was simple is actually more complicated. A will cause B and C, and then B and C will cause D.

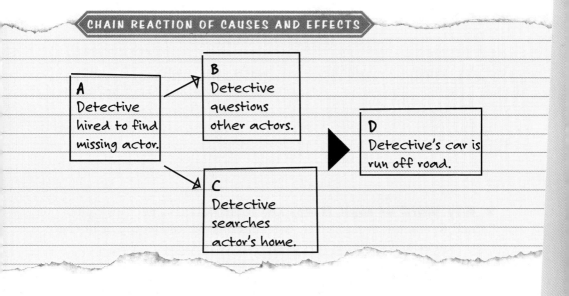

CHAIN REACTION OF CAUSES AND EFFECTS

A
Detective hired to find missing actor.

B
Detective questions other actors.

C
Detective searches actor's home.

D
Detective's car is run off road.

DEFINITION

Looking for cause and effect means concentrating on the process by which one event brings about another. The event or events that happen first are the causes. The event or events that happen as a result are the effects.

Almanac

Note-taking

DESCRIPTION

Taking notes is a good way to remember what you read, especially if you're preparing for a test. You can take notes on anything that seems important or interesting.

Using the Strategy

After you preview a reading, choose the note-taking tools you will use. Here are five that work well:

1. 5 W's and H Organizer This tool answers the questions *who, what, where, when, why,* and *how.* They work well when you are reading a chapter or article or when you are listening to a class lecture. You can organize the notes into a Web for easy reference later.

5 W'S AND H ORGANIZER

			SUBJECT: Early English Colonization				

WHO	WHAT	WHERE	WHEN	WHY	HOW
Pilgrims	left England	went to Massachusetts	1620	didn't like Church of England	sailed on the Mayflower

2. Key Word or Topic Notes Key Topic Notes, sometimes called Cornell Notes, are organized in two columns. Write the topics in the first column and explanations of the topics in column two.

KEY WORD OR TOPIC NOTES

KEY WORDS	NOTES FROM "EARLY ROADS"
Philadelphia-Lancaster Turnpike	Toll road completed in 1794.
Zane's Trace	started in 1794. first road through Ohio.
Cumberland Road	built 1811-1816. connected Cumberland, MD., with Wheeling, OH.

3. Summary Notes Jot down the most important terms, events, or details in Summary Notes. Chapter-by-chapter notes work well with longer works. You may even want to divide your notes into three or four parts, as in the example.

SUMMARY NOTES

Chapter 12: "Early Roads"
Problem
Settlers moving westward in 1800s had to contend with poor roads.
Dates and Places
• 1811-1816 Cumberland Road constructed by federal government from Cumberland, Maryland, to Wheeling, Ohio.
• 1825-1838 Road extended to Vandalia, Illinois.
Total Cost
$1.75 million
Outcome
Road later called National Road.

4. Timeline When you need to remember a series of events, simply make notes that show times and events in order.

TIMELINE

1801	1803	1809	1811
Jefferson becomes President.	Louisiana Purchase	Madison becomes President.	Cumberland Road begun.

DEFINITION

Note-taking is a way of remembering key events and details from a reading or lecture. It makes it easy to review for a test.

Almanac

Outlining

DESCRIPTION

Outlining is an efficient way to organize information into topics and subtopics. General ideas are written as main headings. Each general idea is then divided into two or more smaller topics or subtopics. Subtopics can be divided even further into smaller subtopics.

<OUTLINE>

NORTH AMERICAN INDIANS

I. Cherokees
   A. homeland at time of European contact
     1. parts of the Carolinas, the Virginias, Kentucky, Tennessee, Alabama, and Georgia
     2. about 22,000 acres
   B. location today
     1. western North Carolina
     2. Cherokee Reservation in Oklahoma

II. Wampanoag
   A. in 1600s
     1. lived in parts of Massachusetts and Rhode Island
     2. people numbered over 20,000
   B. location today
     1. Mashpee, Massachusetts
     2. Martha's Vineyard

NOTE These heads correspond with major heads in chapter.

NOTE Important details are listed under subtopics.

The chapter headings in your textbook can often serve as main headings in an outline. As you read the chapter, note the main ideas under each heading (shown as A and B above) and the smaller details given about each main idea (shown as points 1 and 2 in the Outline above).

Using the Strategy

When you outline, focus on only the most important facts and details. You can use either Topic or Sentence Outlines. Outlining can help you to understand and remember textbook chapters.

1. Topic Outlines A Topic Outline lists major topics in a reading. As in the example on the previous page, topics are stated briefly in words or phrases rather than in complete sentences.

2. Sentence Outlines A Sentence Outline contains the major points, along with specific details. Points are written in complete sentences. Use Sentence Outlines when you read longer selections to give you a more complete record of what the selection is about.

FROM A SENTENCE OUTLINE

NORTH AMERICAN INDIANS

1. The Cherokees were living in eastern and southern lands at the time of the first European contact.
   - A. They lived in parts of the Carolinas, the Virginias, Kentucky, Tennessee, Alabama, and Georgia.
   - B. They lived on about 22,000 acres.
   - C. Today they live in western North Carolina and on a reservation in Oklahoma.
2. The culture of the Cherokees is still strong.

3. Outlines and Textbooks You can often use the major headings and subheadings in a textbook or reference work to decide what's important. These headings can become major topics or subtopics in your Outline. Take notes directly in outline form as you read. Paraphrase facts and details and write them in the appropriate sections. Take special note of key terms and their definitions.

DEFINITION

Outlining will help you organize the most important topics and details in your reading, especially in textbooks and reference works. Topic Outlines use words or phrases to describe vital information. Sentence Outlines use complete sentences to list major points and supporting details.

Almanac

Paraphrasing

When you paraphrase, you use your own words to record what you've heard, read, or seen. Paraphrasing is a good strategy to use when reading graphics, math problems, essays, and poems because it lets you put pictures and sentences into your own words.

When you have a hard time understanding something, state the meanings of difficult terms, sentences, or problems in words that make sense to you.

Using the Strategy

Expressing in your own words what somebody else wrote or drew gives you a new way to understand the meaning.

1. Preview Start to paraphrase by getting a general idea of the main topic of a reading or graphic. Look at headings and skim the reading. Ask yourself questions like these:

- What is this graphic or selection about?
- What are some clues to the meaning or main idea?
- What other facts and details stand out?

At this time, you are looking only for the general idea.

2. Take Notes To paraphrase a graphic, start by reading the title and any text. With a long reading or a poem, focus on a difficult passage or an important group of lines. Write your thoughts or questions in the margins or on sticky notes while you read. If you don't know the meaning of a word, look it up in a dictionary.

Notice how one reader wrote a question about the meaning of a word in this part of a poem by Matthew Arnold.

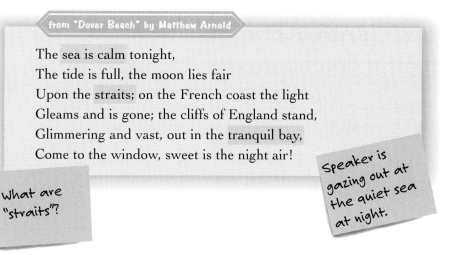

from "Dover Beach" by Matthew Arnold

The sea is calm tonight,
The tide is full, the moon lies fair
Upon the straits; on the French coast the light
Gleams and is gone; the cliffs of England stand,
Glimmering and vast, out in the tranquil bay,
Come to the window, sweet is the night air!

What are "straits"?

Speaker is gazing out at the quiet sea at night.

3. Put the Material in Your Own Words Remember that you are restating meaning in your own way, using your words. Think about how you would answer the questions, "What does this mean?" or "What is this about?" You can use a Paraphrase Chart to help organize your thoughts. Quote as little as possible, but when you do quote, put quotation marks around anything from the source.

PARAPHRASE CHART

LINES	MY PARAPHRASE
"The tide is full, the moon lies fair	It is high tide, and the moon shines on the bay.

MY THOUGHTS
The scene is beautiful, and the mood is peaceful.

DEFINITION

Paraphrasing is using your own words to describe what you've seen, heard, or read.

Almanac

Questioning the Author

When you read, you probably have questions about why an author chose a certain subject, used a particular word, made a character do or say something, or selected a particular setting.

If you can figure out the answers to some of these questions, you'll have a better understanding of a work.

Using the Strategy

Questioning the author is a key strategy to use to understand an author's ideas, especially in fiction and poetry.

1. Read and Ask Questions To use this strategy, imagine that you have a chance to question an author. Start asking questions the moment you begin to read. Write them down. Here are some questions you might ask:

- Why did you begin the way you did?
- Why did you have the character act this way?
- Why did you arrange the details in this order?
- Why did you use this particular word or phrase?
- Why is this point important?
- Is the time or place setting particularly significant?
- What am I supposed to think of the ending?
- What is the main idea?
- Why did you choose this subject to write about?

By asking questions, you activate your brain. The questions engage you as you read and get your thought processes working. You may not know the entire answer to each question you ask. That's OK. The purpose of the strategy is to start you making inferences about the text.

2. Infer the Answers Since the author won't actually answer your questions, you will have to make some inferences. Chances are that you will find clues somewhere in the text that will help you. Maybe the author set a story in a particular period in history because there were significant political changes during that time. Maybe a character changes because of some crisis in his or her life. Write down your answers, and do a little rereading if you're still puzzled. If you can't infer answers to all your questions, try asking someone who has read the same material for his or her thoughts on your questions. Often another reader may have some further information or another point of view that may be helpful.

3. Evaluate As a last step, ask what the author's purpose was and how well that purpose was met.

EVALUATING AUTHOR'S PURPOSE

Author's Purpose	Questions to Ask
To explain	Have I learned something I didn't know before?
To entertain	Did I enjoy the selection? Did it make me want to keep reading?
To persuade	Have I changed my mind because of what I read? If not, why not?
To enlighten	Did the topic make me think about something in a new way, or give me some new insights?

DEFINITION

Questioning the author is the strategy of asking questions as you read about why an author made particular choices.

Reading Critically

Reading critically means reading with a close eye on what a writer says and doesn't say. It means evaluating the points a writer makes. It also means thinking about what facts and details mean and what might have been left out.

Critical readers are skeptical readers. They know to ask the following questions:

■ Is the writer knowledgeable about his or her subject?

■ Is all evidence presented trustworthy?

■ Has the writer considered one or more opinions on a topic?

■ Has the writer left out any crucial facts or points of view?

Reading critically doesn't mean that you should mistrust everything you read. It just means that you should decide whether a writer is reliable and whether you should accept what he or she says.

Speeches, editorials, news stories, websites, biographies, and autobiographies all demand that a reader use a critical eye.

Using the Strategy

Follow these steps to use the strategy of reading critically:

1. List First, write out a list of critical reading questions to ask yourself as you're reading:

■ What is the main idea or major viewpoint of the writing?

■ Is the writer an expert in his or her field?

■ How well does the writer support the main idea with evidence?

■ Do the writer's sources seem authoritative and reliable?

■ Is the evidence convincing?

■ Could there be other viewpoints that are not mentioned? If so, what are they?

■ What seems to be the writer's motivation for writing?

2. Be an Active Reader While you are reading, look for answers to your critical reading questions. Always consider a writer's motives. This question is particularly important if you're reading documents you found on the Internet.

3. Evaluate Make a Critical Reading Chart to help you assess the reading. Write questions in the first column and your evaluations in the second column.

CRITICAL READING CHART

My Questions	My Thoughts
1. Is the main idea or viewpoint clear?	
2. What evidence is presented?	
3. Are the sources authoritative and reliable?	
4. Is the evidence convincing?	
5. Is there another side to the story?	

Make Critical Reading Charts like the one above, and put them in your notebook or journal. They will help you read some nonfiction texts better and more critically.

DEFINITION

Reading critically means finding and evaluating a writer's main idea. It involves examining the evidence and the writer's motivation.

Almanac

Skimming

Skimming is a strategy that works well with almost any kind of reading. Skimming can give you a sense of what a reading is about. It is a particularly effective strategy when you encounter a long or challenging selection, such as the passages you find on tests. Skimming is also useful when you are looking to find a specific bit of information.

Good readers know that skimming has a number of uses:

1. It helps familiarize you with the general topic and important ideas.

2. It gives you a head start on understanding challenging words or concepts.

3. It helps you locate a particular detail quickly.

4. It helps you review material you need to know for a test or presentation.

Using the Strategy

When you skim, you don't read every word or even every sentence. Instead, you let your eyes move down each page of a selection.

1. Skimming for General Ideas To get a general idea of what a reading is about, pay particular attention to these text elements:

- the title
- the table of contents or list of chapter features
- the length and difficulty of a selection
- any graphics
- any captions
- any headings or bulleted or boldface terms
- any repeated words
- the first and last paragraphs

2. Skimming for Specific Information Sometimes you need to look for a fact, a detail, a name, or a date in an article or on a test. Use skimming to help you sift through all the material. If you come upon a page or a paragraph that doesn't contain what you need, move on. If you've already read the material once, you may have a pretty good idea about where that specific detail is in a selection. Look for headings that can help you zoom in on the detail you need.

3. Skimming Paragraphs Many paragraphs, particularly in textbooks, have a stated main idea. Make it a habit to underline or note that main idea. If the main idea is implied, jot down a note about it. Then, you will know whether you need to skim the ideas in that paragraph or skip them.

4. Skimming on Tests Many times you will have to skim a selection to answer test questions about it. If you can write on the test, on your first reading of a selection, circle a key word or phrase that states or suggests the subject of each paragraph. That will help you later. For example, if a test question asks about Viking settlements in Britain, you can skip the information about Vikings in Scandinavia.

With tests, you also need to skim for the key words in questions.

SAMPLE QUESTION

Why did Britain pass the Intolerable Acts?

For this question, the key words are "Intolerable Acts." Go back to the chapter or test passage, and skim for those key words. Once you locate them, read at least *one sentence before* and *one sentence after* the sentence that mentions the key words. Usually, then, you can answer the question.

DEFINITION

Skimming means glancing quickly through a selection. You might skim to get a general sense of the major topics, vocabulary, and ideas in a selection. You can also skim for details or for a quick review of material before a test.

Almanac

Summarizing

Summarizing is a strategy that helps you recap main ideas or events in a selection. It works well with any type of reading. Summarizing involves briefly stating main ideas, details, or events in your own words and is useful for remembering these main points.

Using the Strategy

The key to summarizing is knowing how to pick out what's important.

1. Summarizing Fiction or Drama As you read a selection, take some notes. A good summary will include these things:

- title and author
- characters
- setting
- point of view (if fiction)

- plot
- theme
- style

Knowing what you are looking for as you read will help you summarize. You can also create a simple organizer such as the one below to help you take notes. Although this organizer is labeled "fiction," you can use the same organizer for drama.

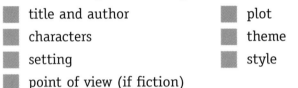

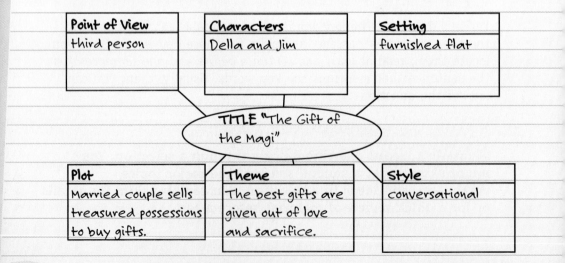

Point of View	Characters	Setting
third person	Della and Jim	furnished flat

TITLE "The Gift of the Magi"

Plot	Theme	Style
Married couple sells treasured possessions to buy gifts.	The best gifts are given out of love and sacrifice.	conversational

2. Summarizing Nonfiction When you want to summarize nonfiction, first ask yourself what the subject is. Next, ask yourself what the writer says about the subject and what things stand out. Look for these things when you read nonfiction:

- the general subject
- the writer's main idea or viewpoint
- the supporting details
- definitions or explanations

Use this kind of organizer to help you summarize a nonfiction selection:

NONFICTION ORGANIZER

SUBJECT
INTRODUCTION
BODY
CONCLUSION

DEFINITION

Summarizing is telling the main events or ideas in a selection as briefly as possible using your own words. Summarizing can help you remember main points.

Synthesizing

DESCRIPTION

When you synthesize, you look at several parts, facts, or elements and pull them together. You consider these parts and figure out how they make a whole.

Synthesizing works well for long works, both fiction and nonfiction, because it helps you keep track of a lot of details from an entire work.

Using the Strategy

Synthesizing is like being a detective who gathers all the clues to a crime and then puts them together to solve it.

1. Using Synthesizing with Fiction To evaluate a novel or story, you look at many different elements, such as the plot, characters, setting, themes, and style. Use synthesizing to look closely at certain details throughout a work to see how the different elements work together. Take notes on each element as you read. Use an organizer like the one below to keep track of your ideas.

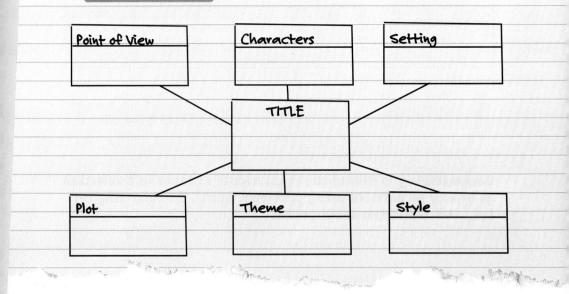

FICTION ORGANIZER

Point of View

Characters

Setting

TITLE

Plot

Theme

Style

2. Using Synthesizing with Nonfiction When you read nonfiction, you focus on a number of things at once. In a biography or memoir, for example, you note how a person grew up, what events shaped the person's life, what character and personality traits the person has, and so on. When you've finished reading, you can put together all the information to get a clear picture of the person. You should also synthesize when you read a news story or an editorial. Pulling all the facts and opinions together can help you come up with the main idea of a reading.

MAIN IDEA ORGANIZER

MAIN IDEA		
British laws infuriated Colonial America.		
DETAIL	DETAIL	DETAIL
set high tariffs on goods colonists needed	required colonists to feed and lodge British troops	taxed newspapers and marriage licenses
CONCLUSION		
It became necessary for colonists to revolt.		

3. Evaluating What You Learn When you finish reading, pull together all the different elements of the selection that you've noted. Ask yourself the meaning of the combined elements. How does the beginning fit with the end? What story do they add up to? Try to point out the strongest and the weakest parts of the reading.

DEFINITION

Synthesizing means considering all the different parts of a text and combining them to come up with an understanding and evaluation of the whole work.

Almanac

Using Graphic Organizers

Graphic organizers are visual pictures of ideas. You create them to help you organize, see, and interpret important ideas in a reading. You can use graphic organizers with fiction, nonfiction, drama, and poetry. Use graphic organizers to keep track of events in a plot, understand cause and effect, appreciate a character, or unlock the meaning of lines of poetry.

Using the Strategy

Most readers have some dependable tools they can use for different reading assignments. As a reader, you need to know a number of different types of organizers. Here are several useful ones.

1. Cause-Effect Organizer A Cause-Effect Organizer works well with history, biographies, and essays.

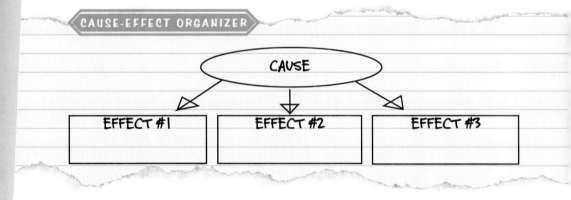

CAUSE-EFFECT ORGANIZER

CAUSE

EFFECT #1   EFFECT #2   EFFECT #3

2. Double-entry Journal A Double-entry Journal can help you understand parts of a text.

DOUBLE-ENTRY JOURNAL

QUOTE	MY THOUGHTS

3. Character Map A Character Map helps you understand characters in fiction or drama.

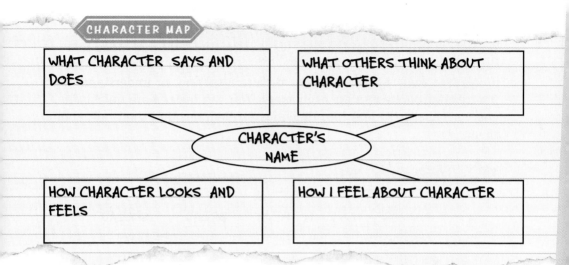

4. 5 W's and H Organizer A 5 W's and H Organizer helps you collect key information about nonfiction, such as essays, news stories, and textbooks.

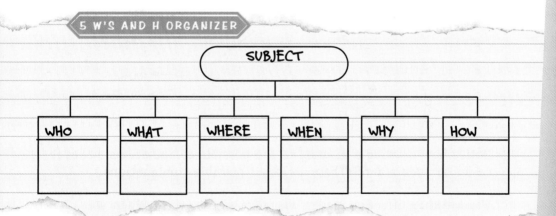

Try Different Organizers

Try different kinds of organizers to help you understand and remember what you read. Keep them in your notebook. See "Reading Tools" on page 738 for a list of more graphic organizers.

DEFINITION

Graphic organizers are visual pictures of ideas. They are the charts, webs, diagrams, and any other visuals you draw that can help you understand and remember what you read.

Almanac

Visualizing and Thinking Aloud

Sometimes you need to picture something in your mind or say it aloud in order to understand it. Visualizing and thinking aloud is a strategy that can help you do that. It can help you figure out a math problem, answer a test question, picture a setting, or understand poetry that contains a lot of imagery. You can learn more quickly if you turn abstract ideas into drawings or diagrams and then talk about them.

EXAMPLE

A deli shop offers two kinds of meat, ham and turkey. You can get the meat either on white or wheat bread. You can have either mayonnaise or mustard as a spread. How many possible combinations of meat, bread, and spread are there?

MEAT	BREAD	SPREAD	
Ham →	White →	Mayo	1
		Mustard	2
	Wheat →	Mayo	3
		Mustard	4
Turkey →	White →	Mayo	5
		Mustard	6
	Wheat →	Mayo	7
		Mustard	8

Notice how drawing a diagram of the possible combinations makes it easier to understand. (There are eight possible combinations.)

Visualizing Effective readers visualize as they read. When you visualize, you make mental pictures of the text as you read. Focus on the pictures that appear in your mind and draw what you see.

Thinking Aloud Talk to yourself about what you're reading. Ask yourself questions or keep a record of your ideas and reactions. You can help yourself "hear" the ideas in your head by saying them quietly to yourself. Often, thinking aloud and visualizing go together.

Using the Strategy

Follow these steps to visualize and think aloud:

1. Read and Sketch You may want to make a quick sketch of a math problem, science concept, setting, or character as you read. Make space in your notebook for sketches.

You can use visualizing with almost any kind of reading. Even if your science text shows the parts of a cell, make your own sketch to help you remember. With fiction or autobiography, you may want to create a map to help you keep track of a character's travels. When reading drama, you may want to make a sketch of a stage setting as described at the beginning of a play.

2. Listen to Your Thoughts As you read, talk to yourself about what you're doing. Often, this can make a process or a passage clearer. This way you're using two of your senses (sight and hearing) instead of just one.

3. Review and Reflect When you have a notebook of sketches— some of which only you can figure out—you can use them to jog your memory. Recall what you were thinking when you sketched that polar journey across Antarctica or the life cycle of a moth. Review your sketches and talk to yourself about them.

DEFINITION

Visualizing and thinking aloud means making a mental picture or sketch of the words you read and talking through your ideas about what you're reading or drawing.

Almanac

Reading Tools

This part of the Almanac lists reading tools that can help you get more out of your reading. Think of this section as your toolkit. Look through it, and decide which tool can help you most.

Reading Tools

ARGUMENT CHART

An Argument Chart is a tool that helps you examine and analyze persuasive writing, such as a speech, editorial, or magazine article.

Viewpoint	Support	Opposing Viewpoint
Put the writer's viewpoint or assertion here.	*Write three or four ways the writer supports the position here.*	*Note if the writer considers other viewpoints here.*

See an example on page 230.

CAUSE-EFFECT ORGANIZER

A Cause-Effect Organizer is a tool to help you figure out what are causes and what are the effects resulting from those causes. It shows the relationship between them.

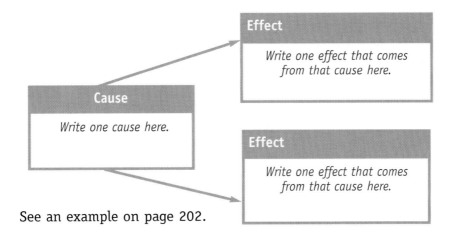

See an example on page 202.

CHARACTER DEVELOPMENT CHART

A Character Development Chart is useful for tracing the changes in a character throughout a story, novel, or play. A chart like this one may also help you discover one or more themes of a work.

Beginning	Middle	End
Write how the character feels or acts at the beginning.	*Write how the character feels or acts in the middle.*	*Write how the character feels or acts at the end.*

Possible Themes:	
	Write what you think a theme of the work might be here.

See an example on page 280.

CHARACTER MAP

A Character Map helps you understand and analyze a character in a story, biography, play, or novel. This tool helps you organize what you know and think about a character.

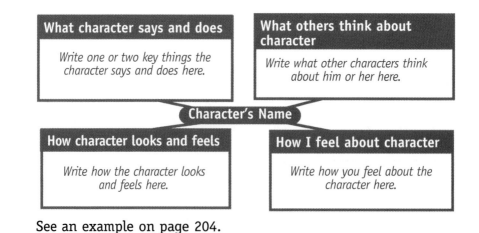

What character says and does

Write one or two key things the character says and does here.

What others think about character

Write what other characters think about him or her here.

Character's Name

How character looks and feels

Write how the character looks and feels here.

How I feel about character

Write how you feel about the character here.

See an example on page 204.

CHARACTER WEB

A Character Web can help you organize what you know about a character. You may want to make a Character Web for each major character in a story or novel.

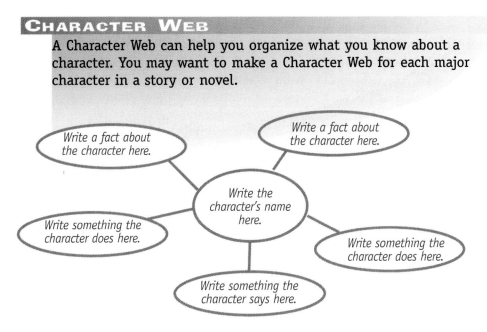

See an example on page 338.

CLASSIFICATION NOTES

Classification Notes can help you organize separate groups or types and categorize the characteristics of each of them.

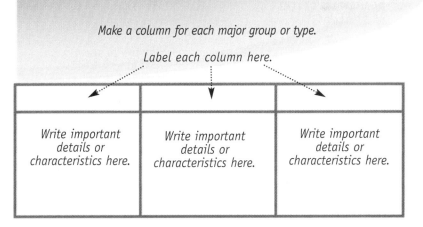

See an example on page 67.

CLOSE READING ORGANIZER

A Close Reading Organizer is a good tool to use when you want to focus on the meaning of words, phrases, and sentences.

Text	What I Think About It
Write the ideas, words, phrases, or sentences you want to analyze in this column.	*Write your analysis of the words or the passages here.*

See an example on page 284.

CONCEPT MAP

A Concept Map helps you keep track of everything you know about a concept or idea. It works well with big ideas, such as *feudalism, ecology,* or *impressionism.*

Create an organizer with one box surrounded by five to seven boxes.

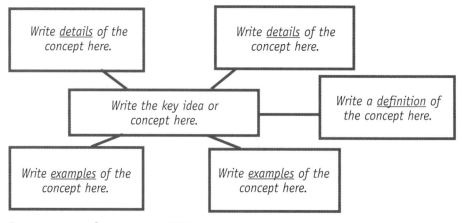

See an example on page 665.

CRITICAL READING CHART

A Critical Reading Chart can help you analyze information in a nonfiction text or a graphic. The chart can help you distinguish between fact and opinion, discover evidence, and identify the main idea or viewpoint.

	My Questions	My Thoughts
Create an organizer with these five questions.	1. Is the main idea or viewpoint clear?	Record the main point here.
	2. What evidence is presented?	Note the evidence here.
	3. Are the sources authoritative and reliable?	List and comment on sources here.
	4. Is the evidence convincing?	Evaluate the evidence here.
	5. Is there another side of the story?	Write another possible viewpoint here.

See an example on page 187.

DOUBLE-ENTRY JOURNAL

A Double-entry Journal helps you interpret a line of poetry, decide how you feel about a character's words or actions, or react to a writer's main idea.

Quote	My Thoughts
Write a key quote or several lines here.	Write what you think or feel about the lines of text here.

See an example on page 166.

EVIDENCE ORGANIZER

You can use an Evidence Organizer to record the evidence or support for a viewpoint or assertion in persuasive writing. This chart helps you analyze whether the supporting details are convincing.

Viewpoint		
Record the writer's viewpoint here.		
Supporting Detail	**Supporting Detail**	**Supporting Detail**
Write a detail here.	*Write a detail here.*	*Write a detail here.*

See an example on page 242.

FICTION ORGANIZER

A Fiction Organizer helps you collect all of the key information about a story, novel, or play.

Fill in the information from the text in the boxes of the organizer.

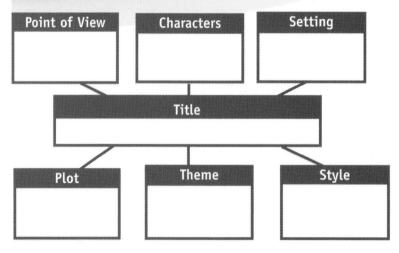

See an example on page 310.

5 W's AND H ORGANIZER

A 5 W's and H Organizer helps you gather important information about a subject.

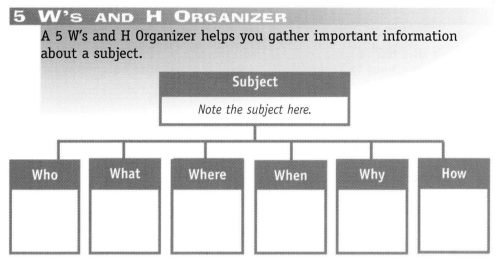

Label each box below the subject with one of the 5 W's and the H. Write notes that answer each question in the boxes.

See an example on page 185.

FLOW CHART

A Flow Chart shows a sequence of operations. It is useful for helping you remember the steps in an experiment or the stages of a process.

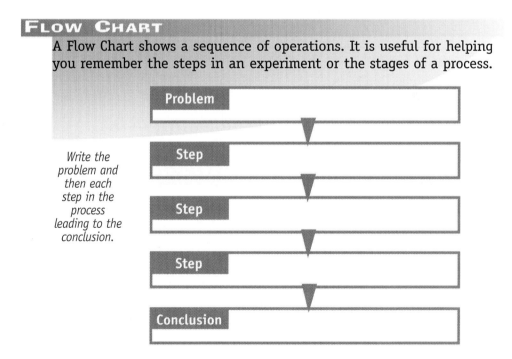

See an example on page 123.

INFERENCE CHART

An Inference Chart can help when you have to figure out from the clues in a text what a writer is telling you. Use an Inference Chart when you have to take a closer look at a character, a detail or event, or a setting.

Text	What I Conclude
Write part of the text, a detail, or an event here.	*Write the conclusions you draw about the meaning of it here.*

See an example on page 202.

KEY WORD OR TOPIC NOTES

Use Key Word or Topic Notes to record main ideas from your reading. Key Word or Topic Notes work well for taking notes on textbooks or during a class presentation.

Divide your notebook into two columns. Make the right side wider than the left side.

Key Words or Topics	Notes
Note the key words or main topics here. These are the main things to study.	*Take notes about each key word or topic here.*

See an example on page 219.

MAGNET SUMMARY

To help you organize your thoughts after reading, use a Magnet Summary. Choose one word that is important to your reading. Then, gather all the other words, ideas, and details you can think of around it. Finally, summarize your ideas about the magnet word. A Magnet Summary works with any kind of reading.

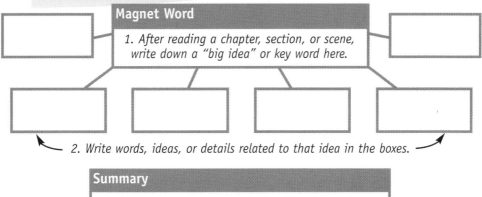

Magnet Word

1. *After reading a chapter, section, or scene, write down a "big idea" or key word here.*

2. *Write words, ideas, or details related to that idea in the boxes.*

Summary

3. *Use what you've written to create a short summary about the importance of the magnet word here.*

See an example on page 457.

MAIN IDEA ORGANIZER

Use a Main Idea Organizer to help you distinguish between the big ideas and the details. This tool works well with nonfiction, such as biography, magazine articles, persuasive writing, textbooks, and speeches.

Main Idea	*Write what you think is the biggest, most important idea here.*		
Detail	**Detail**	**Detail**	
Next write details here.	*Next write details here.*	*Next write details here.*	
Conclusion	*Finally, write the conclusion the author makes here.*		

See an example on page 63.

MAKING CONNECTIONS CHART

A Making Connections Chart can help you relate to a written work and increase your understanding. It works best with fiction, but it can be used with nonfiction too.

Create an organizer with questions or statements like these.

I wonder why . . .	*Record your question here.*
I think . . .	*Write your opinion here.*
I can relate to this because . . .	*Write how you can relate to the work.*
This is similar to . . .	*Note what other works you've read or seen that are somewhat the same.*
This reminds me of . . .	*Write what the work reminds you of in your own life.*

See an example on page 282.

NONFICTION ORGANIZER

A Nonfiction Organizer helps you organize what you learn from reading essays, articles, speeches, and editorials. It arranges these works into three parts: introduction, body, and conclusion.

Subject	*Write the general subject here.*
Introduction	*Describe the ideas in the first one or two paragraphs here.*
Body	*Write three or four details, points, or topics from the middle here.*
Conclusion	*Note what happens or what the author says in the last paragraph or two here.*

See an example on page 241.

OUTLINE

Make an Outline to help you understand the organization of a reading. You can use words or phrases (Topic Outline) or full sentences (Sentence Outline) to classify main ideas, topics, and subtopics.

First, find the two, three, or four main topics and write them here.

I. Main Topic 1	
A. subtopic	*Under each main topic,*
B. subtopic	*write two or*
C. subtopic	*more subtopics.*
II. Main Topic 2	
A. subtopic	
B. subtopic	
C. subtopic	

See an example on page 123.

PARAPHRASE OR RETELLING CHART

A Paraphrase or Retelling Chart helps you do two things. It helps you understand parts of a text or graphic by putting them in your own words. It also helps you pull together your own thoughts about a work.

Lines	My Paraphrase
Write two or three lines from a text or facts from a graphic here.	*Tell in your own words what these lines mean here.*

My Thoughts	
	Note your own ideas or reaction to what's said here.

See an example on page 413.

Almanac

PLOT DIAGRAM

A Plot Diagram helps you see how fiction and drama are organized. Use it to analyze the five main parts of a plot.

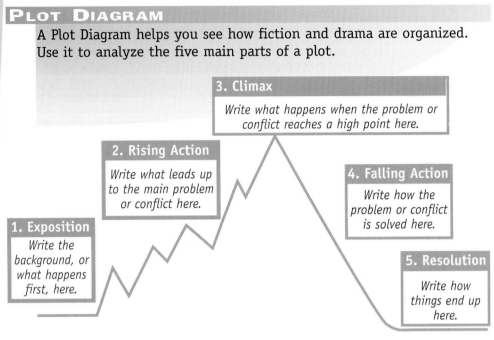

3. Climax
Write what happens when the problem or conflict reaches a high point here.

2. Rising Action
Write what leads up to the main problem or conflict here.

4. Falling Action
Write how the problem or conflict is solved here.

1. Exposition
Write the background, or what happens first, here.

5. Resolution
Write how things end up here.

See an example on page 305.

PREVIEW CHART

A Preview Chart can give you a head start on what a reading might be about. Use it to jot down notes as you skim a persuasive essay, a speech, or an editorial.

Title:	Put the title of the selection here.
Clues about the Topic	**Clues about the Assertion**
Write what you think the selection will be about here.	Write what you think the writer's assertions or viewpoints are here.

See example on page 229.

PROBLEM-SOLUTION ORGANIZER

A Problem-Solution Organizer is a practical tool for recording information from a textbook. It helps you see how problems were or could be solved in history, math, or science. This organizer is also useful for recording information from an editorial or article.

Problem	Solution
Write the problem here.	*Write the solution here.*

See an example on page 96.

SEQUENCE NOTES

Sequence Notes are a lot like Timelines, but they don't always contain dates. They are useful for recording the events in a long work or in a process and are especially helpful when you want to review for a test.

Record what happens first.	*Record what happens next.*	*Record what happens next.*	*Record what happens last.*

See an example on page 61.

SETTING CHART

Create a Setting Chart to keep track of details of the time and place in which a story or play is set. If the work takes place in more than one time or place, you may want to make a box for each major setting or scene.

Clues about First Time	Clues about First Place
Write details about dates, seasons, years, or general time periods here.	*Write details about places, regions, or physical environment here.*
Clues about Second Time	**Clues about Second Place**
Write details about dates, seasons, years, or general time periods here.	*Write details about places, regions, or physical environment here.*

See an example on page 285.

SOURCE EVALUATOR

When you're doing research, a Source Evaluator is a practical tool. It will help you record what you learn from reading or from an interview, along with the date of your finding and your opinion of the source.

Research Purpose	*Write the purpose of your research here.*
Source Type	*Write whether source is primary or secondary here.*
Title or Location	*Write the title or location of research here.*
Date	*Write the date of your finding here.*
Expertise	*Comment on whether source is authoritative here.*
Bias, if any	*Note any bias here.*
Reactions	*Write your reactions to your findings here.*

See an example on page 706.

STORYBOARD

A Storyboard can help you remember major events in fiction. It is useful for reviewing the order of events and understanding why they happened.

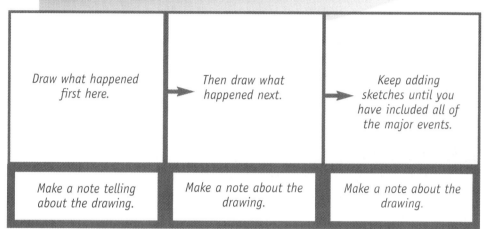

See an example on page 331.

STORY STRING

Use a Story String to take notes on a series of fictional events. It helps you see and remember the order of what happened. Use as many boxes as you need.

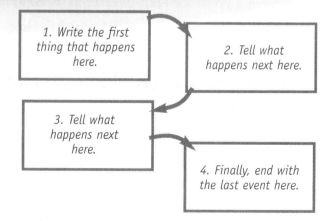

See an example on page 317.

STUDY OR NOTE CARDS

Use Study or Note Cards to help you learn key terms, facts, and ideas from your reading. They are also useful for helping you memorize vocabulary words, study for tests, and keep track of research notes.

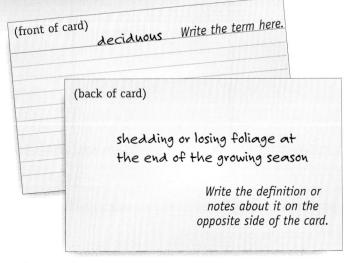

(front of card)

deciduous   Write the term here.

(back of card)

shedding or losing foliage at the end of the growing season

Write the definition or notes about it on the opposite side of the card.

See an example on page 663.

SUMMARY NOTES

Summary Notes are a way of helping you bring together the most important parts of a text, whether it's fiction or nonfiction. You can, for example, summarize each page in a textbook, each scene in a play, each stanza in a poem, or each chapter in a novel.

Title or Topic	Write the title or topic here.
Main Point	Write what you think is the main point or idea here.
1.	List three or four smaller, related points that support the main point here.
2.	
3.	
4.	

See an example on page 179.

TIMELINE

Timelines can help you keep track of dates and events in the order in which they happened. They work well for history textbooks, but they are also useful for stories and plays that jump back and forth in time.

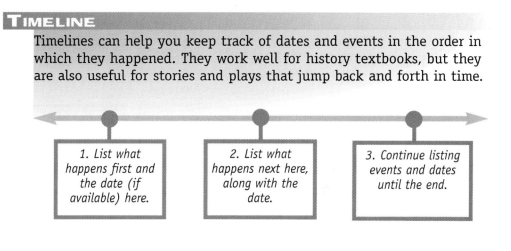

1. List what happens first and the date (if available) here.

2. List what happens next here, along with the date.

3. Continue listing events and dates until the end.

See an example on page 527.

TOPIC AND THEME ORGANIZER

A Topic and Theme Organizer helps you find the theme in a story, novel, poem, or play. Start by listing the big idea or main topic. Then, tell what the characters do and say or what the writer describes that relates to the topic. Finally, write a theme statement that tells the underlying meaning of the work.

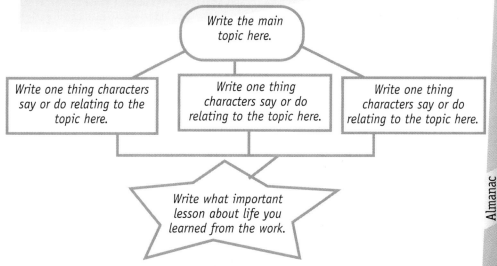

Write the main topic here.

Write one thing characters say or do relating to the topic here.

Write one thing characters say or do relating to the topic here.

Write one thing characters say or do relating to the topic here.

Write what important lesson about life you learned from the work.

See an example on page 349.

Almanac

TWO-NOVEL MAP

A Two-novel Map is useful for comparing and contrasting the major elements of two novels. You can fill in each column as you read a work or when you have finished.

Title	Write the title of the first novel here.	Title	Write the title of the second novel here.

	Characters		Characters	
Record the characters, setting, plot, theme, and so on for the first novel here.	Setting		Setting	Record the characters, setting, plot, theme, and so on for the second novel here.
	Plot		Plot	
	Theme		Theme	

Conclusions	Write your conclusions here.

See an example on page 362.

VENN DIAGRAM

Use a Venn Diagram to compare and contrast two characters, settings, themes, or events. You can also use it to compare and contrast two stories, poems, essays, or plays.

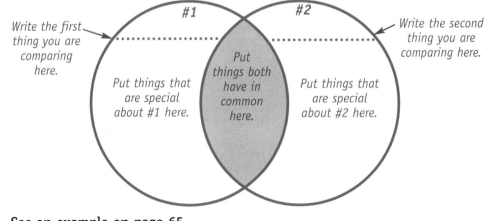

Write the first thing you are comparing here.   #1   #2   Write the second thing you are comparing here.

Put things that are special about #1 here.   Put things both have in common here.   Put things that are special about #2 here.

See an example on page 65.

WEB

A Web is a good tool for organizing notes about almost anything. Use a Web to arrange and brainstorm ideas about an event, a character, an opinion, a word, or an idea. You can add as many ovals to the Web as you need.

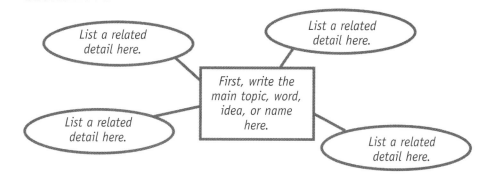

See an example on page 290.

WEBSITE PROFILER

Create a Website Profiler to investigate and record the reliability of a website. A Website Profiler can help you remember what details to check for when you're doing research on the Internet and make it easier for you to assess the value of a site.

Name (URL)	
Write the name and URL here.	
Sponsor	**Date**
Tell who created or pays for the site here.	*Note when the site was last updated here.*
Point of View	**Expertise**
Write the site's point of view here.	*Tell where the information on the site comes from here.*
Reaction	
List your thoughts about the site here.	

See an example on page 524.

Word Parts:

Prefixes, Suffixes, and Roots

Prefixes

Prefixes are word parts added to the beginning of a root or base word to create a new meaning.

Prefixes	Meanings	Examples
a-	not, without	amoral, apart
ab-	away from	abstract, absent
ad-	to, toward, against	addition, additive
ante-	before	antebellum, antecedent
anti-	against, opposite	antiwar, antisocial
arch-	original, chief	archbishop, archangel
auto-	self	automobile, automatic
bi-	two	biped, bilingual
be-	to cause, become	befriend, beneath
circum-	around	circumference, circumnavigate
co-	together	coworker, copilot
con-	with, together	construct, contemplate
contra-	against	contradict, contraband
counter-	against, in opposition	counteract, counterspy
de-	down, away from	descend, detract
demi-	half	demiglaze, demigod
dia-	through, across	diagnosis, diagonal
dis-	the reverse of	disagree, disable
dys-	not normal	dysfunction, dystrophy
en-	to cause, provide	enlighten, enable
epi-	to, against, added on	epicenter, epigram
ethno-	race, nation	ethnic, ethnicity
ex-	out of, away from	expel, external
extra-	outside, beyond	extracurricular, extraordinary
fore-	previously, in front of	forefathers, forefront

Prefixes	Meanings	Examples
hydro-	water	hydroelectric, hydrosphere
hyper-	extra, beyond, over	hypercritical, hyperactive
hypo-	under, below	hypodermic, hypocenter
il-	not	illegal, illegitimate
im-	not	immovable, immobile
infra-	below, underneath	infrastructure, infrared
inter-	between	interstate, interview
intra-	inside of	intramuscular, intramural
ir-	not	irregular, irrelevant
iso-	equal	isobar, isosceles
mal-	bad	maladjusted, malevolent
meta-	change, transform	metacognition, metamorphosis
micro-	small	microwave, microscope
mid-	middle	midterm, midtown
mini-	small	minibus, minivan
mis-	wrongly, badly	mistake, mistrust
mono-	one, single	monopoly, monorail
multi-	many	multimillionaire, multitude
neo-	new, recent	neoclassic, neophyte
non-	not, against	nonplus, nonsense
ob-	in the way of	obstruct, obstacle
octa-	eight	octagon, octet
omni-	all, general	omnipotent, omnipresent
pan-	whole	panacea, panorama
para-	alongside, similar	paramedic, paraphrase
per-	through	percussion, perceive
peri-	all around	perimeter, periscope
poly-	many, more than one	polygon, polytheism
post-	after, later	postmortem, postscript
pre-	earlier, before	prejudge, preview
pro-	in favor of	proclaim, project
proto-	earliest, original	prototype, protoplasm
pseudo-	false, pretend	pseudonym
quadri-	four	quadrant, quadrilateral
re-	back, again	reappear, return
retro-	backward	retroactive, retrospect
self-	by oneself	self-control, self-rule

Almanac

Prefixes	Meanings	Examples
semi-	half	semifinal, semiformal
sub-	under, less than	subhead, subzero
super-	over, more than	superhuman, superstar
tetra-	four	tetralogy, tetrahedron
trans-	across, through	transact, transcend
tri-	three	triangle, tripod
ultra-	beyond	ultrasound, ultraviolet
un-	not, reverse of	unarm, unaware
under-	below, beneath	underground, underwear
uni-	single, one	unicycle, uniform
up-	upper, upward	upheaval, uprising
vice-	in place of	vice president, viceroy

Suffixes

Suffixes are combinations of letters (such as -*ance*) or single letters (such as -*s*) added to the end of base words or word parts. What follows is a sampling of common suffixes. Note the parts of speech they indicate and the examples of words that use them.

Suffixes that form nouns	Examples
-age	garbage, luggage
-al	funeral, portal
-ance	reluctance, allowance
-ant	claimant, attendant
-ee	devotee, employee
-ence	independence, audience
-ent	dependent, student
-er, -or, -ar	peddler, monitor, cellar
-ess	actress, address
-ette, et	kitchenette, booklet
-hood	neighborhood, statehood
-ian, -ion	musician, information
-ism	Buddhism, Communism
-ist	journalist, novelist
-ment	judgment, amusement

Suffixes that form nouns	Examples
-ness	kindness, happiness
-ure	future, creature

Suffixes that form adjectives	Examples
-able	expendable, dependable
-al	personal, optional
-er	messier, better
-est	cutest, smartest
-ful	disdainful, hopeful
-ible	edible, incredible
-ic	bionic, tonic
-ical	historical, tropical
-ish	bluish, skittish
-ive	divisive, pensive
-less	childless, mindless
-ous	joyous, religious
-some	loathsome, worrisome
-y	tasty, worthy

Suffixes that form adverbs	Examples
-erly	easterly, westerly
-fully	beautifully, dutifully
-ly	angrily, merrily
-ward	backward, forward
-ways	sideways, always
-wise	likewise, clockwise

Suffixes that create verb forms	Examples
-ate	congratulate, concentrate
-ed	joked, ripped
-en	brighten, eaten
-fy, -ify	notify, rectify
-ing	frightening, stunning
-ize, -yze	familiarize, analyze
-n	known, grown

Almanac

Greek and Latin Roots

Knowing the meanings of common Greek and Latin roots can help you figure out the meanings of dozens of related words.

Roots	Origins	Meanings	Examples
aero	Greek	air	aerobics, aerate
agri	Latin	field	agriculture, agrarian
alter	Latin	other	alternate, altercation
ambi	Latin	both	ambiguous, ambidextrous
amo	Latin	love	amorous, enamored
ang	Latin	bend	angle, triangle
anim	Latin	life, spirit	animate, animal
ann, enn	Latin	year	annual, biennial
anthropo	Greek	human	anthropology
apt, ept	Latin	fasten	inept, aptitude
aqua	Latin	water	aquarium, aqueduct,
arch	Greek	primitive	archaic, archetype
art	Latin	skill	artisan, artist
aud	Latin	hear	audible, audition
baro	Greek	weight	barometer, isobar
belli	Latin	war	bellicose, rebellion
biblio	Greek	books	bibliography, bible
bio	Greek	life	biology, biosphere
brev	Latin	short	abbreviate, brevity
cam	Latin	field	campus, campaign
cap	Latin	head	captain, decapitate
cardi	Greek	heart	cardiac, cardiogram
cede, ceed	Latin	go, yield	precede, succeed
centr	Latin	center	central, eccentric
cert	Latin	sure	certain, certify
cess	Latin	go, yield	cessation, process
chron	Greek	time	chronic, chronicle
cide, cise	Latin	cut, kill	scissors, suicide
claim, clam	Latin	shout	clamor, exclaim
clar	Latin	clear	clarity, declare
cline	Latin	lean	decline, incline
cogn	Latin	know	incognito, recognize

Roots	Origins	Meanings	Examples
commun	Latin	common	communal, commune
corp	Latin	body	corpse, corporation
cosm	Greek	universe	cosmos, microcosm
crat	Greek	rule	autocrat, bureaucrat
cred	Latin	believe	credit, incredible
cycl	Greek	circle, ring	bicycle, cyclone
dem	Greek	people	democrat, epidemic
dic	Latin	speak	dictate, verdict
div	Latin	separate	divide, division
domin	Latin	rule	dominate, dominion
duc	Latin	lead	conduct, educate
fer	Latin	bear, carry	ferry, transfer
firm	Latin	strong	affirm, confirm
flect	Latin	bend	deflect, reflect
form	Latin	shape	transform, uniform
frag	Latin	break	fragile, fragment
fug	Latin	flee	fugitive, refuge
gen	Greek	birth, race	generate, progeny
geo	Greek	earth	geography, geology
grad	Latin	step, stage	graduate, gradual
gram	Greek	letter	grammar, telegram
graph	Greek	write	autograph, graph
grat	Latin	pleasing	gratify, ungrateful
hab, hib	Latin	hold	habitat, prohibit
hom	Latin	alike	homogeneous, homogenize
hydr	Greek	water	hydrant, hydroelectric
imag	Latin	likeness	image, imagery
init	Latin	beginning	initial, initiate
integ	Latin	whole	integer, integrate
jud, jur, jus	Latin	law	judge, jury, justice
laps	Latin	slip	elapse, relapse
liber	Latin	free	liberate, liberty
log, logy	Greek	word	dialogue, prologue
luc	Latin	light	lucid, translucent
lum	Latin	light	illumine, luminous
luna	Latin	moon	lunar, lunatic
man	Latin	hand	manual, manipulate

Almanac

Roots	Origins	Meanings	Examples
mar	Latin	sea	mariner, submarine
mater, matr	Latin	mother	maternal, matron
mech	Greek	machine	mechanic, mechanize
mens, ment	Latin	mind	demented, mental
migr	Latin	depart	migrate, migrant
miss, mit	Latin	send	missile, submit
mon	Latin	warn	admonish, monitor
mort	Latin	death	mortal, mortician
mot, mov	Latin	move	promote, remove
narr	Latin	tell	narrate, narrative
nat	Latin	born	nation, native
nav	Latin	ship	naval, navigate
not	Latin	mark	denote, note
nun, noun	Latin	declare	enunciate, announce
nov	Latin	new	innovate, novel
numer	Latin	number	enumerate, numeral
ocu	Latin	eye	binocular, oculist
opt	Greek	visible	optic, optician
opt	Latin	best	optimal, optimist
orig	Latin	beginning	aborigine, origin
pater, patr	Latin	father	paternal, patriarch
path	Greek	feeling	empathy, pathos
ped	Latin	foot	pedal, pedometer
pend	Latin	hang	appendix, suspend
phon	Latin	sound	telephone, phonics
photo	Greek	light	telephoto, photograph
phys	Greek	nature	physical, physician
pod	Latin	foot	podiatrist
poli	Greek	city	metropolis, police
pop	Latin	people	populace, popular
port	Latin	carry	import, porter
psych	Greek	mind	psyche, psychology
put	Latin	think	deputy, computer
ques	Latin	ask, seek	quest, question
rect	Latin	straight	erect, rectangle
rid	Latin	laugh	deride, ridicule
rupt	Latin	break	erupt, rupture
san	Latin	health	insanity, sanitary
scend	Latin	climb	ascend, transcend

Roots	Origins	Meanings	Examples
sci	Latin	know	conscience, science
scop	Greek	see	microscope, periscope
scribe	Latin	write	inscribe, describe
script	Latin	written	transcript, script
sect	Latin	cut	dissect, intersect
sed	Latin	settle	sedate, sediment
sens	Latin	feel	sensation, senses
sign	Latin	mark	insignia, signal
sim	Latin	like	similar, simile
sol	Latin	alone	desolate, solitary
solv	Latin	loosen	solvent, resolve
son	Latin	sound	sonar, sonnet
spec	Latin	see	inspect, spectator
sta	Latin	stand	static, stagnant
strict	Latin	draw tight	constrict, restrict
struct	Latin	build	construct, instruct
sum	Latin	highest	summary, summit
tact, tang	Latin	touch	contact, tangent
ten	Latin	hold	tenant, tenure
terr	Latin	land	terrace, terrain
the	Greek	god	monotheism, theology
therm	Greek	heat	thermal, thermos
tract	Latin	pull, drag	attract, tractor
trib	Latin	give	contribute, tribute
turb	Latin	confusion	disturb, turbulence
urb	Latin	city	suburb, urban
vac	Latin	empty	evacuate, vacant
vag	Latin	wander	vagrant, vague
var	Latin	different	variety, vary
ver	Latin	truth	verdict, veracity
vic	Latin	conquer	conviction, victor
vid	Latin	see	evidence, video
voc	Latin	voice	advocate, vocal
void	Latin	empty	avoid, devoid
vol	Latin	wish, will	benevolent, volition
volv	Latin	roll	involve, revolve
vor	Latin	eat	herbivorous, voracious

Almanac

Acknowledgments

439 Stopping by Woods on a Snowy Evening from THE POETRY OF ROBERT FROST edited by Edward Connery Lathem. Copyright 1923, © 1969 by Henry Holt and Co., copyright 1951 by Henry Holt and Company. Reprinted by permission of Henry Holt and Company, LLC

440 From *New and Selected Poems* by Gary Soto © 1995. Reprinted by permission of Chronicle Books, LLC, San Francisco.

441 "The Geese" by Richard Peck, from SOUNDS AND SILENCES: POETRY FOR NOW by Richard Peck, Editor, copyright ©1970, 1990 by Richard Peck. Used by permission of Dell Publishing, a division of Random House, Inc.

442 From SELECTED POEMS, THIRD EDITION, REVISED AND ENLARGED by John Crowe Ransom, copyright © 1924, 1927 by Alfred A. Knopf, Inc. and renewed 1952, 1955 by John Crowe Ransom. Used by permission of Alfred A. Knopf, a division of Random House, Inc.

449–451, 454–455, 461–463, 465, 470,–475, 478, 480 Reprinted with the permission of Scribner, an imprint of Simon & Schuster Adult Publishing Group from THE MIRACLE WORKER by William Gibson. Copyright © 1956, 1957 William Gibson. Copyright (c) 1959, 1960 Tamarack Productions, Ltd., and George S. Klein and Leo Garel as trustees under three separate deeds of trust.

516, 533, 534 © Google, Inc.

518–519, 521, 536 Copyright © 2001 National Gallery of Art, Washington D.C. (www.nga.gov).

532 Interbulletin.com

535 © 2001 Exploratorium, (www.exploratorium.edu)

601–603, 610, 613, 615 Copyright © 1966 by Heinrich Böll. Reprinted here by permission of Verlag Kiepenheuer & Witsch; the Joan Daves Agency of New York; and of Leila Vennewitz.

679–680 Copyright © 1981 by Houghton Mifflin Company. Reproduced by permission from *The American Heritage Dictionary of the English Language*.

PHOTO CREDITS

75 © Tony Waltham/Robert Harding Picture Library

77 © I. Perlman/Stock Boston

78 *bottom* © The ART ARCHIVE

78 *top* © Brocelj Bojan/Corbis

79 © Bruce Forster/Getty Images/Stone

91 *center* © Runk/Schoenberger/Grant Heilmann

91 *top* © Agricultural Research Service/USDA

91 *bottom* © Morgan-Cain and Associates/Holt Rinehart and Winston

92 *bottom* © Ray Pfortner/Peter Arnold, Inc.

92 *top* © Tim Fuller

93 © Frans Lanting/Minden Pictures

113 *background* © Steve Ogilvy/Picture It Corporation

120 *left* © Zig Leszczynski/Animals Animals

120 *right* By Permission of John Harte

121 *left* By Permission of John Harte

121 *right* Jeff Smith/Fotosmith/Holt, Rinehart, Winston

135 *bottom right* Weidenfeld & Nicolson Archives

135 *center* Detail of Vor dem Streik (Before the strike) after a painting by Micahel Munkacsy, © Bildarchiv Preussischer Kulturbesitz, Berlin

136 *top left* Adapted with permission from The New Encyclopædia Britannica, 15th Edition,Volume 29, © 1998 by Encyclopædia Britannica, Inc.

136 *top right* Source: The Cambridge Illustrated History of the Islamic World

142 *right* © Tim Fuller

142 *bottom right* © Kristy Sprott

142 *left* © Roger-Viollet

143 *bottom* Source: Global Trends, edited by I Hauchler, P, Kennedy Reprinted by permission of The Continuum International Publishing Group

145 *right* © Corbis-Bettmann

148 © Hulton Archive/Getty Images

150 *bottom right* © The Granger Collection, New York

150 *left* Photo Courtesy of Peabody Essex Museum. Photo by Jeffrey Dykes.

196 © The Sporting News

212 Courtesy of The Royal Library, Copenhagen

291, 306 © The Liberty Memorial Museum

543 *top/center/bottom,* **547** This graph first appeared in the June, 2001 edition of Brill's Content Magazine. It is reprinted with permission.

555 Reprinted with permission from Education Week Vol. 20 No. 37 Date May 23, 2001

556 The New Yorker Collection 2000 John Caldwell from cartoonbank.com. All Rights Reserved. [for:2000 02 07 038 JCA .HG Search]

557 From Science Explorer Life Science by Michael Padilla, Ph.D., Ioannis Miaoulis, Ph.D., Martha Cyr, Ph.D. © 2001 by Prentice Hall. Used by permission of Pearson Education, Inc.

560 U.S. News & World Report, Source: American Public Transportation Association

561 McDougal Littell 1999

563 Photo by Oliver F Atkins, Nixon Presidential Materials Projet: National Archives and Records Administration

565 Copyright, 2001, Los Angeles Times. Reprinted by permission.

584 © Hitachi

The editors have made every effort to trace the ownership of all copyrighted selections found in this book and to make full acknowledgment for their use. Omissions brought to our attention will be corrected in a subsequent edition.

READERS AND REVIEWERS

Dr. Leslie Adams
Division of Language Arts and Reading
Miami, FL

Ceci Aguilar
Telles Academy
El Paso, TX

Lynn Beale
Irvin High School
El Paso, TX

Jeanie Bosley
West Education
San Francisco, CA

John Brassil
Mt. Ararat High School
Topsham, ME

Doug Buehl
Madison East High School
Madison, WI

Maria Bunge
Austin High School
El Paso, TX

Roseanne Comfort
Westview High School
Portland, OR

Paula Congdon
Rockwood School District
Eureka, MO

Bonnie Davis
Education Park
St. Louis, MO

Lela DeToye
Southern Illinois University
Edwardsville, IL

Kathy Dorholt
New York Mills High School
New York Mills, MN

Steve Edwards
Central High School
Clearwater, FL

Lyla Fox
Loy Norrix High School
Kalmazoo, MI

Jodi Gardner
Assata High School
Milwaukee, WI

Karen Gibson
Appleton North High School
Appleton, WI

Laura Griffo
Jefferson Co. International
Irondale, AL

Carol Hallman
Ross Local School District
Hamilton, OH

Kerry Hansen
Dominican HS
Whitefish Bay, WI

Carol Sue Harless
Stone Mountain High School
Stone Mountain, GA

Rebecca Hartman
Peau-Harris High School
Mishaaka, IN

Christine Heerlein
Rockwood Summit High School
Fenton, MO

Vicky Hoag
Fresno Co. Office of Ed.
Fresno, CA

Jack Hobbs
San Marcos High School
Santa Barbara, CA

Eileen Johnson
Edina Public Schools
Edina, MN

Laurel Key
Central High School
West Allis, WI

Michelle Knotts
Sinagua High School
Flagstaff, AZ

Kathleen Lask
Pattonville Senior High School
Maryland Heights, MO

Jean Lawson
Coronado High School
El Paso, TX

Jean Lifford
Dedham High School
Dedham, MA

Tom Lueschow
University of WI-Whitewater
Whitewater, WI

Maria Manning
Dade County PS
Miami, FL

Jean-Marie Marlin
Mountain Brook High School
Birmingham, AL

Karen McMillan
Miami-Dade County Schools
Miami, FL

Judith Lynn Momirov
Buckeye Trail High School
Lore, OH

Lisa Muller
Castle High School
Newburgh, IN

David P. Noskin
Adlai E. Stevenson High School
Lincolnshire, IL

Cheryl Nuciforo
Enlarged City School District of Troy
Troy, NY

Carolyn Novy
Chicago, IL

Rebecca Romine
Traverse City Central High School
Kewadin, MI

Jeannie Scott
Colorado Springs Dist. 11
Colorado Springs, CO

Susie Schneider
El Paso School District
El Paso, TX

Cathleen Search
Traverse City West High School
Traverse City, MI

Judy Smith
Rockwood School District
Eureka, MO

Leslie Somers
Miami-Dade Public Schools
Miami, FL

Sharon Straub
Joel E. Ferris High School
Spokane, WA

Michael Thompson
Minnesota Dept. of Children, Families, and Learning
Roseville, MN

Mary Ann Wamhoff
Eureka High School
Glendale, MO

Mary Weber
Waterford High School
Waterford, MI

Nancy Wilson
Gladstone High School
Gladstone, OR

Susan Wilson
South Orange Middle School
South Orange, NJ

Sandy Wojcik
Downers Grove High School South
Downers Grove, IL

Fred Wolff
Educational Consultant
Lee, New Hampshire

STUDENT REVIEWERS

Tony Artega,
Burlingame HS
Burlingame, CA

Jessica Batchelor,
Burlingame HS
Burlingame, CA

Laura Belland,
Turpin HS,
Cincinnati, OH

Matthew Brotz,
Dominican HS
Brown Deer, WI

Carissa Clark,
Ross HS
Hamilton, OH

Vera Daciuk,
Burlingame HS
San Mateo, CA

Chelsea Duke,
Edina HS
Edina, MN

Jessica Egler,
Pattonville Senior HS
Maryland Heights, MO

Jessica Friday,
Dominican HS
Brown Deer, WI

Melinda Favreau,
Mt. Ararat HS
Topsham, ME

Lauren Gant,
Pattonville Senior HS
St. Ann, MO

Theresa Gruenke,
Sheboygan North HS
Sheboygan, WI

Marcus Guenther,
Ross HS
Ross, OH

Alexandra Heerlein,
Rockwood Summit HS
Fenton, MO

Melissa Holdorf,
Appleton North HS
Appleton, WI

Michele Jett,
Northwest R1 HS
House Springs, MO

Sarah Kramer,
Loy Norrix HS
Kalamazoo, MI

Danielle R. Lee,
Stone Mountain HS
Stone Mountain, GA

Jason Leeke
Pattonville Senior HS
Maryland Heights, MO

Hillary Line,
Appleton North HS
Appleton, WI

Jillian Lueschow,
Sheboygan North HS
Sheboygan, WI

Stacey A. Maddox,
Dominican HS Whitefish Bay
Menomonee Falls WI

Kate Martin,
Westlake HS
Austin, TX

Holly Michels,
Gladstone HS
Gladstone, OR

Matt Misley,
Gladstone HS
Gladstone, OR

Jessica Ridenour,
Rockwood Summit HS
Fenton, MO

Katie Quinn,
Lake Forest HS
Lake Forest, IL

Ashlea Schaffers,
Stone Mountain HS
Stone Mountain, GA

Zak Schweiss,
Rockwood Summit HS
Fenton, MO

Jennifer Silvestri,
Penn HS
Mishawaka, IN

Lara Smith,
Eureka HS
Eureka, MO

Maricela Vega,
Burlingame HS
San Mateo, CA

Candace Walker,
Stone Mountain HS
Stone Mountain, GA

Jacob Winkler,
Columbia HS
Maplewood NJ

Nathan Winkler,
Columbia HS
Maplewood NJ

Carol Zombro,
Loy Norrix HSl
Kalamazoo, MI

Author and Title Index